WRITERS

DAN SLOTT, MATT FRACTION, DAN ABNETT, ANDY LANNING, JASON AARON, DANIEL WAY, JEFF PARKER, RICK REMENDER, ED BRUBAKER, BRIAN MICHAEL BENDIS, KIERON GILLEN & NICK SPENCER

ARTISTS

HUMBERTO RAMOS & CARLOS CUEVAS; SALVADOR LARROCA; MARK BROOKS; JEFTE PALO; BONG DAZO & JOE PIMENTAL; GABRIEL HARDMAN & TOM PALMER; RAFAEL ALBUQUERQUE; MITCH BREITWEISER; BRYAN HITCH & PAUL NEARY; CARLOS PACHECO & CAM SMITH with DAN GREEN & NORMAN LEE; and SCOT EATON & JAIME MENDOZA

COLORISTS

EDGAR DELGADO, FRANK D'ARMATA, SONIA OBACK, JOHN RAUCH, NATHAN FAIRBAIRN, ANDRES MOSSA, JIM CHARALAMPIDIS, DEAN WHITE, BETTIE BREITWEISER and PAUL MOUNTS

LETTERERS

VC'S JOE CARAMAGNA, VC'S JOE SABINO, VC'S CORY PETIT, ED DUKESHIRE & DAVE LANPHEAR

ASSISTANT EDITORS

ELLIE PYLE, CHARLIE BECKERMAN & JAKE THOMAS

ASSOCIATE EDITORS

LAUREN SANKOVITCH & DANIEL KETCHUM

EDITORS

ALEJANDRO ARBONA, JEANINE SCHAEFER, JODY LEHEUP & JORDAN D. WHITE

SENIOR EDITORS

STEPHEN WACKER, RALPH MACCHIO, NICK LOWE, MARK PANICCIA & TOM BREVOORT

COVER ART

PAULO SIQUEIRA, CARLOS CUEVAS & MORRY HOLLOWELL; SALVADOR LARROCA & FRANK D'ARMATA; ED McGUINNESS & LAURA MARTIN; PAOLO RIVERA; DAVE JOHNSON; RON GARNEY & JASON KEITH; SIMONE BIANCHI & SIMONE PERUZZI; DANIEL ACUÑA; BRYAN HITCH, PAUL NEARY & PAUL MOUNTS; CARLOS PACHECO, CAM SMITH & SOTOCOLOR; and MIKE DEODATO & RAIN BEREDO

COLLECTION EDITOR: JENNIFER GRÜNWALD
EDITORIAL ASSISTANTS: JAMES EMMETT & JOE HOCHSTEIN
ASSISTANT EDITORS: ALEX STARBUCK & NELSON RIBEIRO
EDITOR, SPECIAL PROJECTS: MARK D. BEAZLEY
SENIOR EDITOR, SPECIAL PROJECTS: JEFF YOUNGQUIST
SENIOR VICE PRESIDENT OF SALES: DAVID GABRIEL
SVP OF BRAND PLANNING & COMMUNICATIONS: MICHAEL PASCIULLO
BOOK DESIGN: JEFF POWELL

EDITOR IN CHIEF: AXEL ALONSO
CHIEF CREATIVE OFFICER: JOE QUESADA
PUBLISHER: DAN BUCKLEY
EXECUTIVE PRODUCER: ALAN FINE

JOE QUESADA TALKS ABOUT THE MARVEL POINT ONE INITIATIVE!

If there was ever such a thing as a First Commandment of Comics, it would have to be Stan Lee's old adage that "every comic is someone's first."

Over the course of our history, we've always taken that rule very seriously and now we've decided to emphasize the point with our new Marvel: Point One initiative.

Okay, okay, I know what you're thinking, "Gee, JQ, what the heck is Marvel: Point One?" I'm so glad you asked! Each of our top titles will be getting a special, low-priced Point One issue that offers a chance for both longtime Marvelites to catch up on a book they may have overlooked, and a perfect jumping on point for readers just getting interested in Marvel Comics and our mind-blowing universe. These entirely self-contained stories are must read road maps that'll be setting everyone from the Amazing Spider-Man to the Uncanny X-Force out on their next year's worth of adventures. And who better to tell these tales than some of the very best talents working in the world of comics today!

Now while it's almost impossible for me to imagine a world in which there are people who aren't familiar with the goings on in the Marvel Universe, each of these stories is one that any dedicated Marvel fan can hand to a friend, a relative, a colleague or even some stranger on the street, and all would enjoy the eye-popping action, explosive excitement and heartfelt tales of heroism with no need for explanations, footnotes or encyclopedic knowledge of the MU (that's Marvel Universe for you new kids — see, you already learned something). So whether you're a new fan to the fold, or a certified True Believer, there's never been a better chance to jump head first into the unexplored corners of the Marvel Universe — a place where, above all, anything is possible.

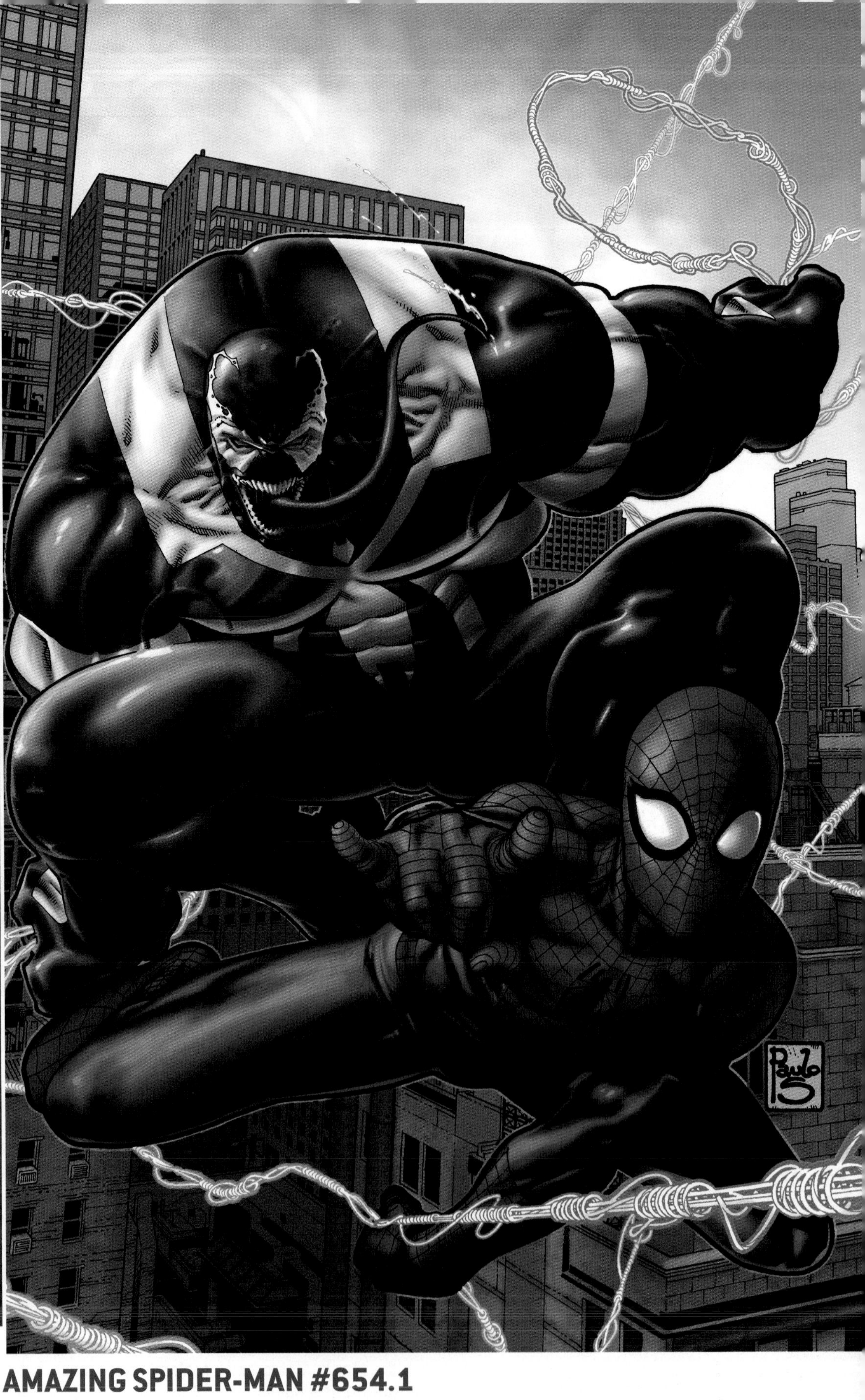

AMAZING SPIDER-MAN #654.1

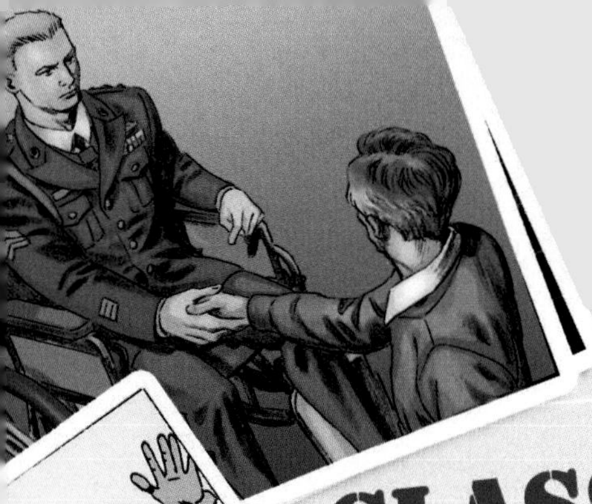

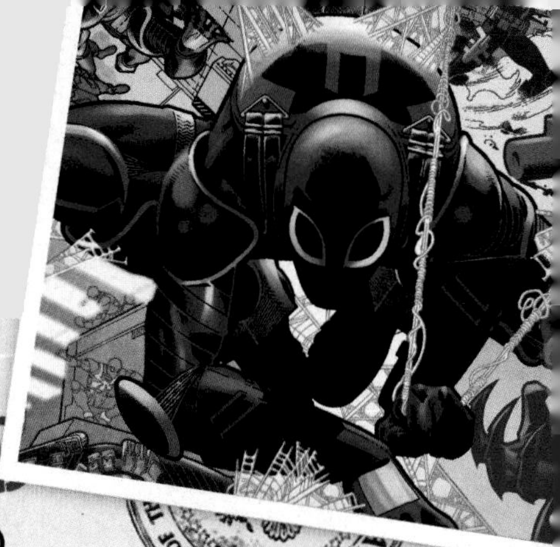

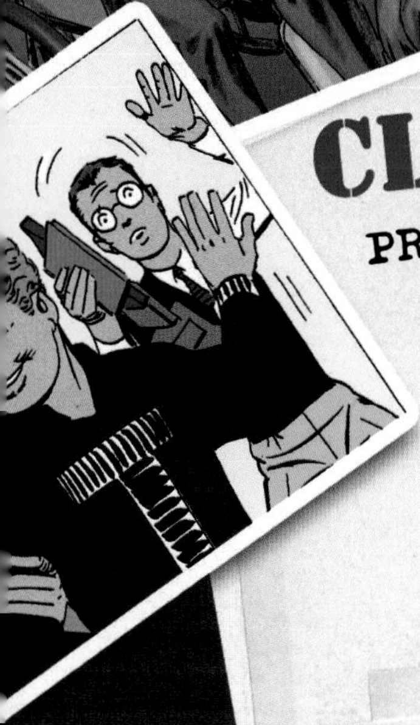

CLASSIFIED

PROJECT REBIRTH 2.0

Name: Eugene "Flash" Thompson

Rank: Corporal U.S. Army

SSN: 987 -08-1962

Notes: High school bully turned war hero, Flash Thompson has always been brave. As a teenager he even impersonated Spider-Man to try and save the hero's reputation. He lost his legs in the Middle East while saving his commanding officer. He said his heroism was "what Spider-Man would have done."

CLASSIFIED

Name: Venom

Organism: Symbiote

Origin: Extraterrestrial

Known Hosts: Spider-Man, Eddie Brock, Mac Gargan and others

Notes: The Venom Symbiote is a dangerous alien parasite that bonds with a human host, giving them extraordinary abilities including spider-like-powers and some shape-shifting abilities. It is known to cause madness in its hosts, as well as a taste for blood.

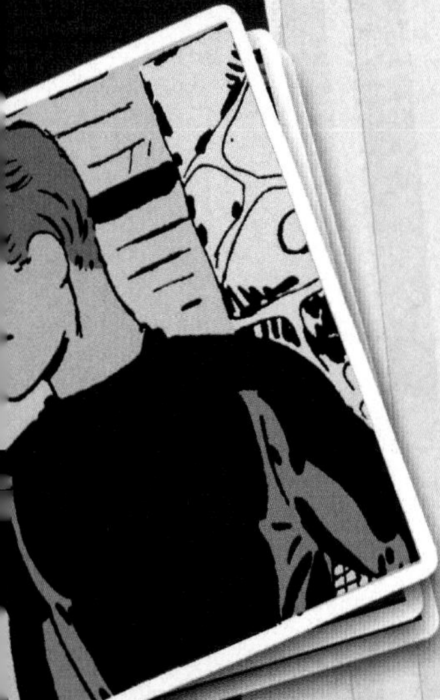

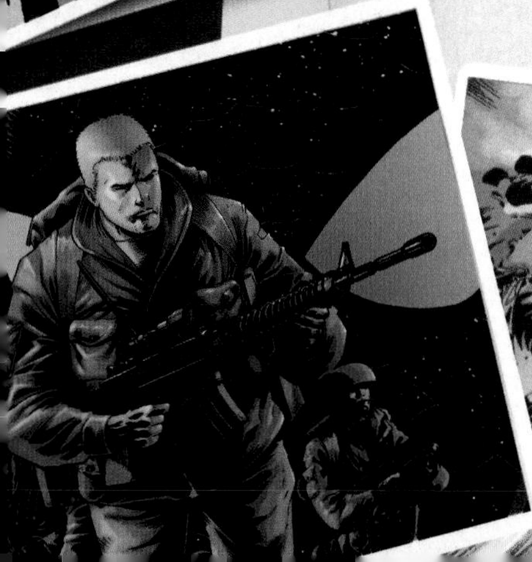

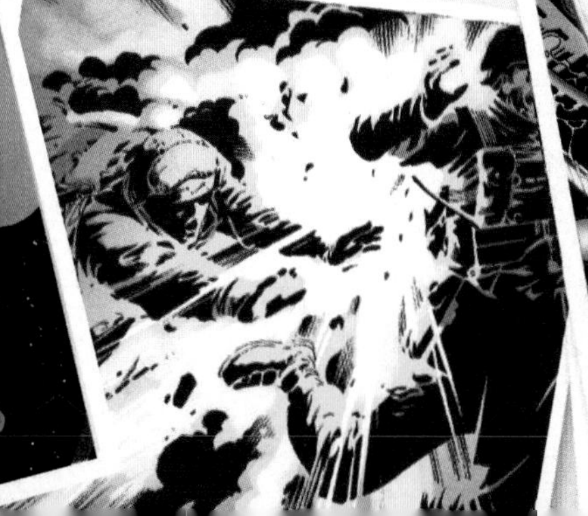

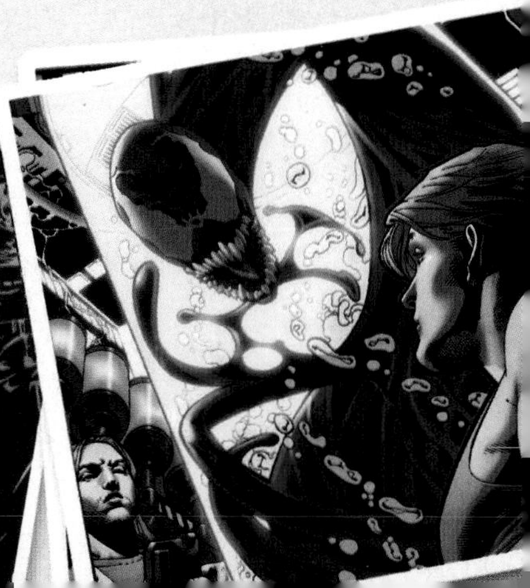

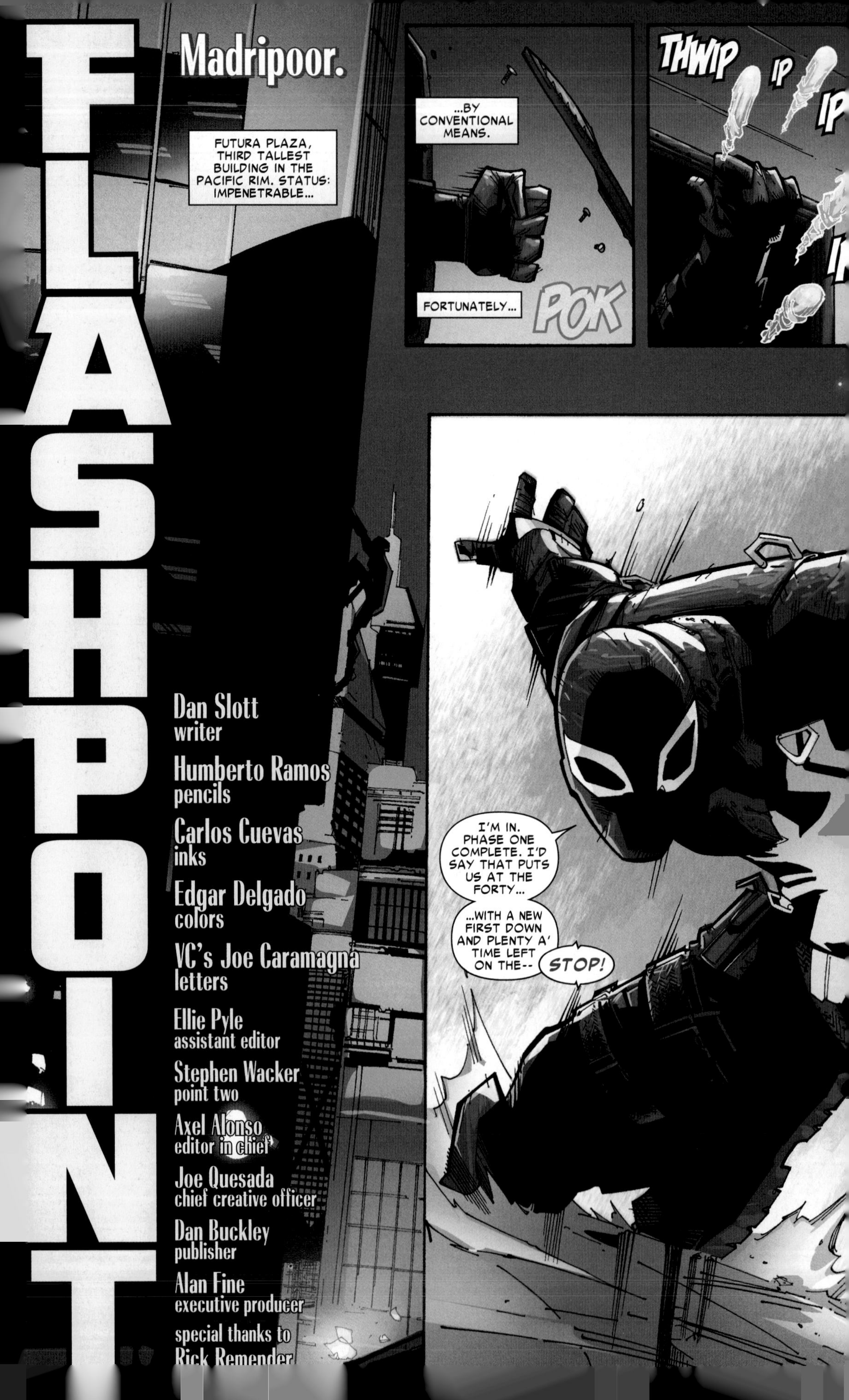

FLASHPOINT
Madripoor.
FUTURA PLAZA, THIRD TALLEST BUILDING IN THE PACIFIC RIM. STATUS: IMPENETRABLE...
...BY CONVENTIONAL MEANS.
FORTUNATELY...
POK
THWIP IP IP IP
I'M IN. PHASE ONE COMPLETE. I'D SAY THAT PUTS US AT THE FORTY...
...WITH A NEW FIRST DOWN AND PLENTY A' TIME LEFT ON THE--
STOP!
Dan Slott writer
Humberto Ramos pencils
Carlos Cuevas inks
Edgar Delgado colors
VC's Joe Caramagna letters
Ellie Pyle assistant editor
Stephen Wacker point two
Axel Alonso editor in chief
Joe Quesada chief creative officer
Dan Buckley publisher
Alan Fine executive producer
special thanks to Rick Remender

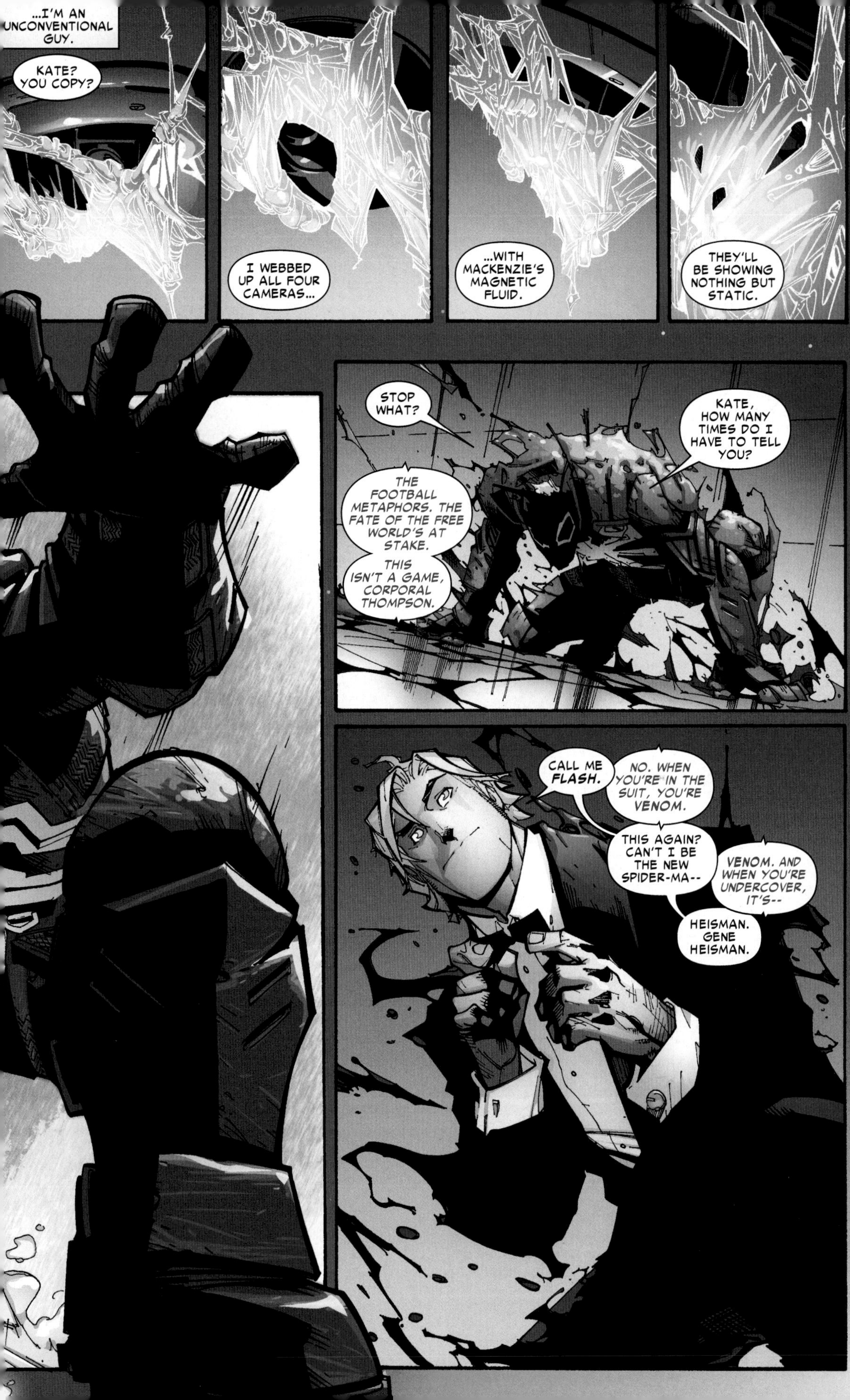

...I'M AN UNCONVENTIONAL GUY.
KATE? YOU COPY?
I WEBBED UP ALL FOUR CAMERAS...
...WITH MACKENZIE'S MAGNETIC FLUID.
THEY'LL BE SHOWING NOTHING BUT STATIC.
KATE, HOW MANY TIMES DO I HAVE TO TELL YOU?
STOP WHAT?
THE FOOTBALL METAPHORS. THE FATE OF THE FREE WORLD'S AT STAKE.
THIS ISN'T A GAME, CORPORAL THOMPSON.
CALL ME FLASH.
NO. WHEN YOU'RE IN THE SUIT, YOU'RE VENOM.
THIS AGAIN? CAN'T I BE THE NEW SPIDER-MA--
VENOM. AND WHEN YOU'RE UNDERCOVER, IT'S--
HEISMAN. GENE HEISMAN.

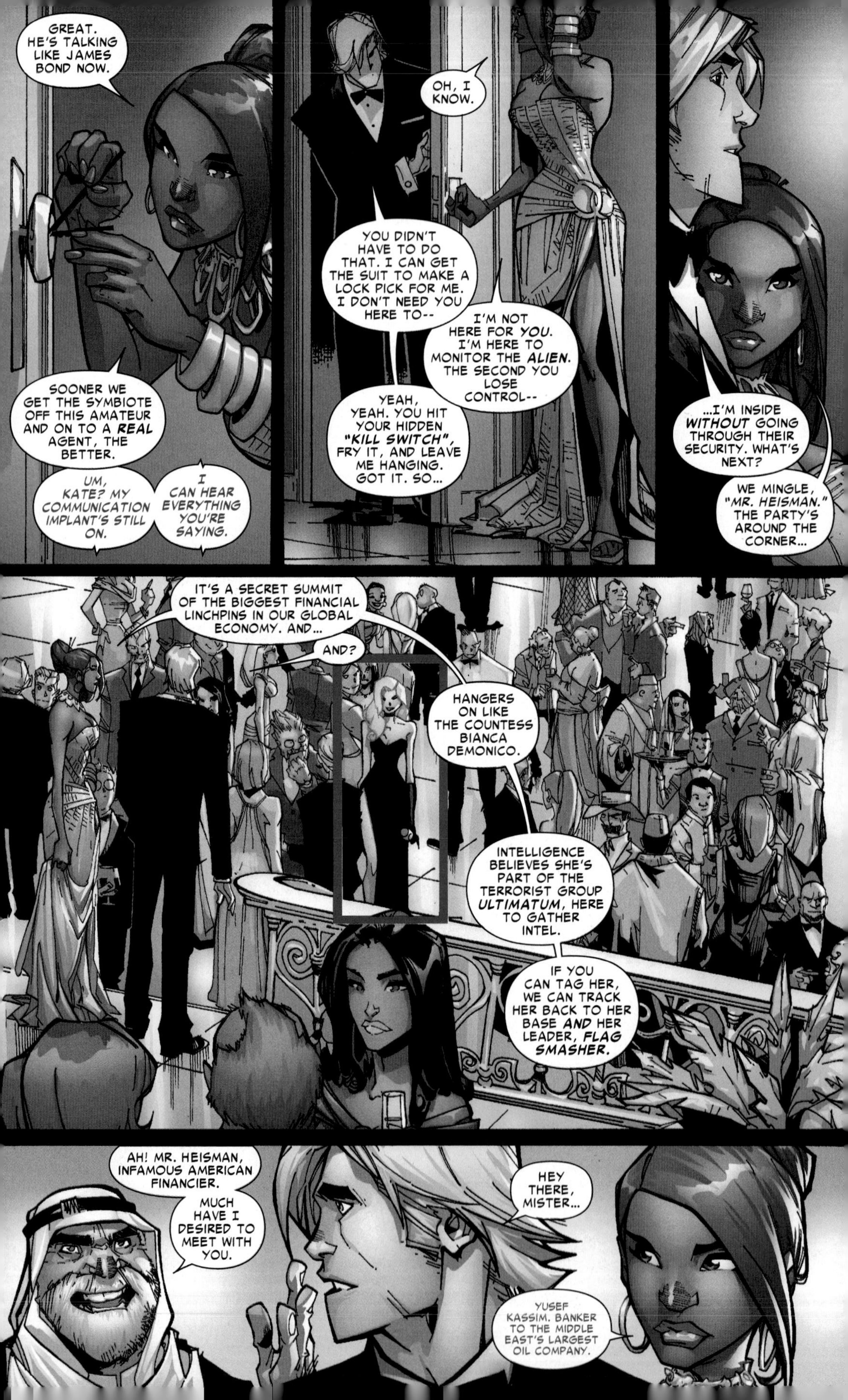

GREAT. HE'S TALKING LIKE JAMES BOND NOW.
SOONER WE GET THE SYMBIOTE OFF THIS AMATEUR AND ON TO A REAL AGENT, THE BETTER.
UM, KATE? MY COMMUNICATION IMPLANT'S STILL ON.
I CAN HEAR EVERYTHING YOU'RE SAYING.
OH, I KNOW.
YOU DIDN'T HAVE TO DO THAT. I CAN GET THE SUIT TO MAKE A LOCK PICK FOR ME. I DON'T NEED YOU HERE TO--
I'M NOT HERE FOR YOU. I'M HERE TO MONITOR THE ALIEN. THE SECOND YOU LOSE CONTROL--
YEAH, YEAH. YOU HIT YOUR HIDDEN "KILL SWITCH", FRY IT, AND LEAVE ME HANGING. GOT IT. SO...
...I'M INSIDE WITHOUT GOING THROUGH THEIR SECURITY. WHAT'S NEXT?
WE MINGLE, "MR. HEISMAN." THE PARTY'S AROUND THE CORNER...
IT'S A SECRET SUMMIT OF THE BIGGEST FINANCIAL LINCHPINS IN OUR GLOBAL ECONOMY. AND...
AND?
HANGERS ON LIKE THE COUNTESS BIANCA DEMONICO.
INTELLIGENCE BELIEVES SHE'S PART OF THE TERRORIST GROUP ULTIMATUM, HERE TO GATHER INTEL.
IF YOU CAN TAG HER, WE CAN TRACK HER BACK TO HER BASE AND HER LEADER, FLAG SMASHER.
AH! MR. HEISMAN, INFAMOUS AMERICAN FINANCIER.
MUCH HAVE I DESIRED TO MEET WITH YOU.
HEY THERE, MISTER...
YUSEF KASSIM. BANKER TO THE MIDDLE EAST'S LARGEST OIL COMPANY.

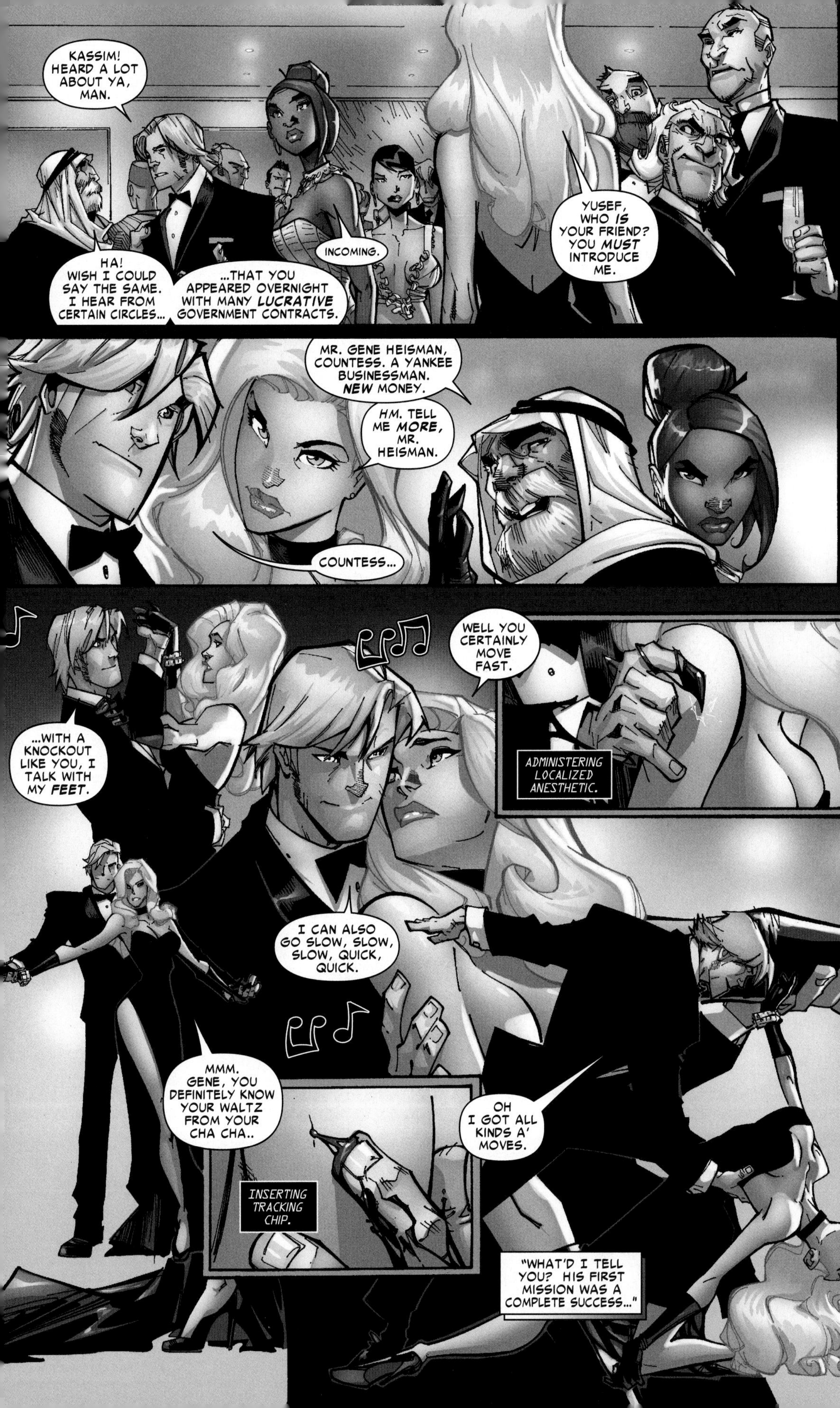
KASSIM! HEARD A LOT ABOUT YA, MAN.
HA! WISH I COULD SAY THE SAME. I HEAR FROM CERTAIN CIRCLES...
...THAT YOU APPEARED OVERNIGHT WITH MANY LUCRATIVE GOVERNMENT CONTRACTS.
INCOMING.
YUSEF, WHO IS YOUR FRIEND? YOU MUST INTRODUCE ME.
MR. GENE HEISMAN, COUNTESS. A YANKEE BUSINESSMAN. NEW MONEY.
HM. TELL ME MORE, MR. HEISMAN.
COUNTESS...
WELL YOU CERTAINLY MOVE FAST.
...WITH A KNOCKOUT LIKE YOU, I TALK WITH MY FEET.
ADMINISTERING LOCALIZED ANESTHETIC.
I CAN ALSO GO SLOW, SLOW, SLOW, QUICK, QUICK.
MMM. GENE, YOU DEFINITELY KNOW YOUR WALTZ FROM YOUR CHA CHA..
OH I GOT ALL KINDS A' MOVES.
INSERTING TRACKING CHIP.
"WHAT'D I TELL YOU? HIS FIRST MISSION WAS A COMPLETE SUCCESS..."

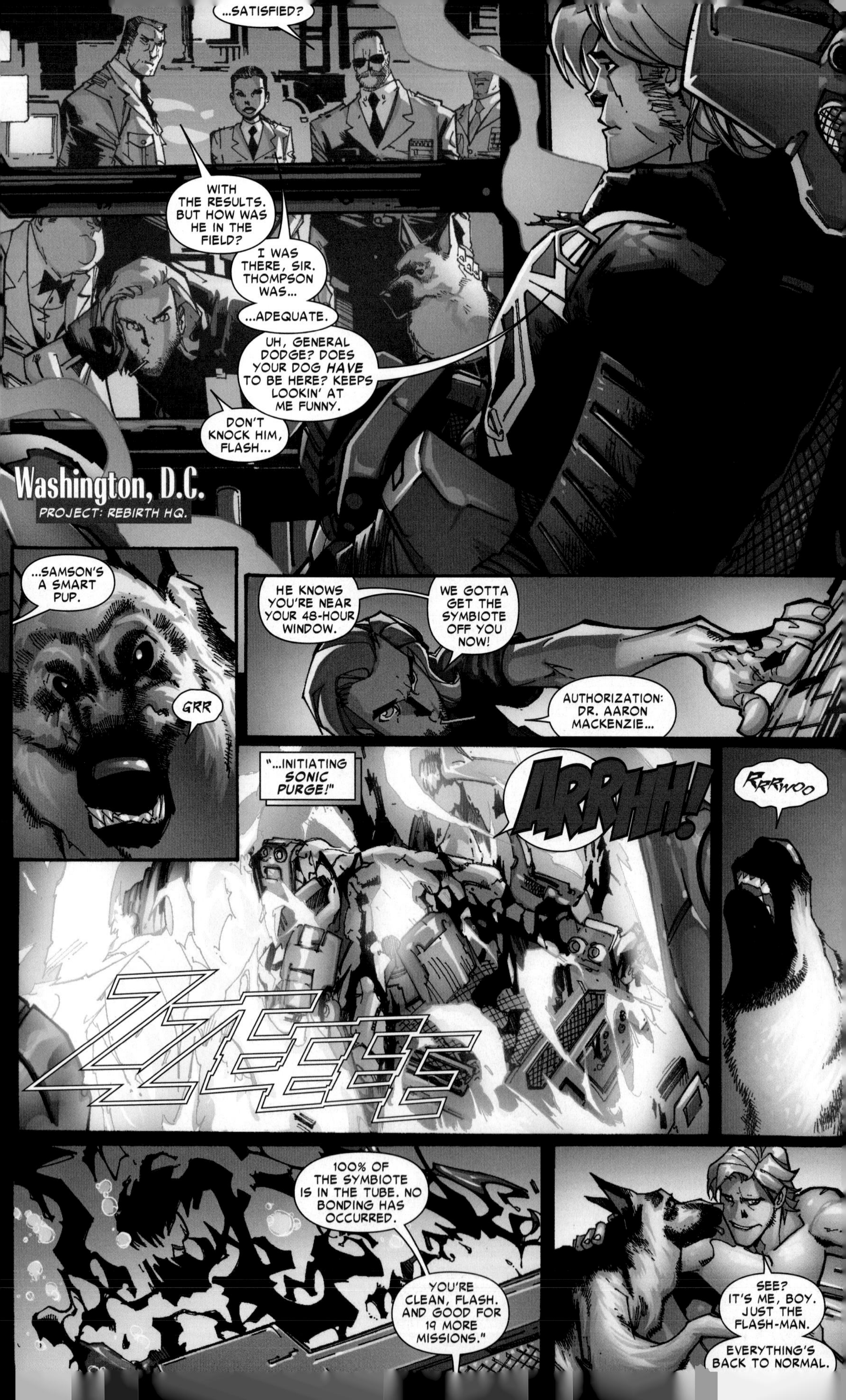
...SATISFIED?
WITH THE RESULTS. BUT HOW WAS HE IN THE FIELD?
I WAS THERE, SIR. THOMPSON WAS...
...ADEQUATE.
UH, GENERAL DODGE? DOES YOUR DOG HAVE TO BE HERE? KEEPS LOOKIN' AT ME FUNNY.
DON'T KNOCK HIM, FLASH...
Washington, D.C.
PROJECT: REBIRTH HQ.
...SAMSON'S A SMART PUP.
GRR
HE KNOWS YOU'RE NEAR YOUR 48-HOUR WINDOW.
WE GOTTA GET THE SYMBIOTE OFF YOU NOW!
AUTHORIZATION: DR. AARON MACKENZIE...
"...INITIATING SONIC PURGE!"
ARRHH!
RRRWOO
ZZEEEE
100% OF THE SYMBIOTE IS IN THE TUBE. NO BONDING HAS OCCURRED.
YOU'RE CLEAN, FLASH. AND GOOD FOR 19 MORE MISSIONS."
SEE? IT'S ME, BOY. JUST THE FLASH-MAN.
EVERYTHING'S BACK TO NORMAL.

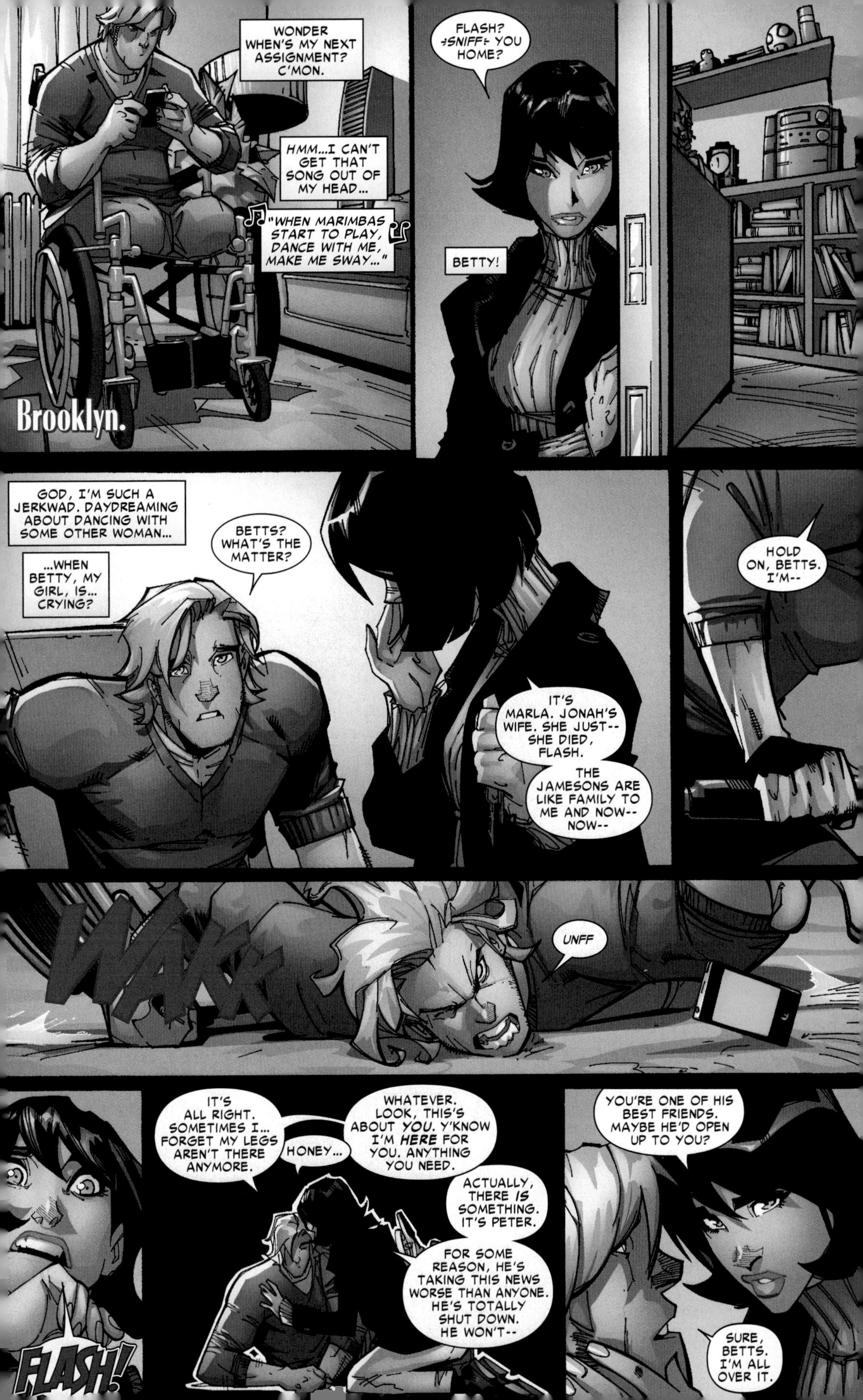
WONDER WHEN'S MY NEXT ASSIGNMENT? C'MON.
HMM...I CAN'T GET THAT SONG OUT OF MY HEAD...
"WHEN MARIMBAS START TO PLAY, DANCE WITH ME, MAKE ME SWAY..."
Brooklyn.
FLASH? *SNIFF* YOU HOME?
BETTY!
GOD, I'M SUCH A JERKWAD. DAYDREAMING ABOUT DANCING WITH SOME OTHER WOMAN...
...WHEN BETTY, MY GIRL, IS... CRYING?
BETTS? WHAT'S THE MATTER?
IT'S MARLA. JONAH'S WIFE. SHE JUST-- SHE DIED, FLASH.
THE JAMESONS ARE LIKE FAMILY TO ME AND NOW-- NOW--
HOLD ON, BETTS. I'M--
WAKK
UNFF
FLASH!
IT'S ALL RIGHT. SOMETIMES I... FORGET MY LEGS AREN'T THERE ANYMORE.
HONEY...
WHATEVER. LOOK, THIS'S ABOUT YOU. Y'KNOW I'M HERE FOR YOU. ANYTHING YOU NEED.
ACTUALLY, THERE IS SOMETHING. IT'S PETER.
FOR SOME REASON, HE'S TAKING THIS NEWS WORSE THAN ANYONE. HE'S TOTALLY SHUT DOWN. HE WON'T--
YOU'RE ONE OF HIS BEST FRIENDS. MAYBE HE'D OPEN UP TO YOU?
SURE, BETTS. I'M ALL OVER IT.

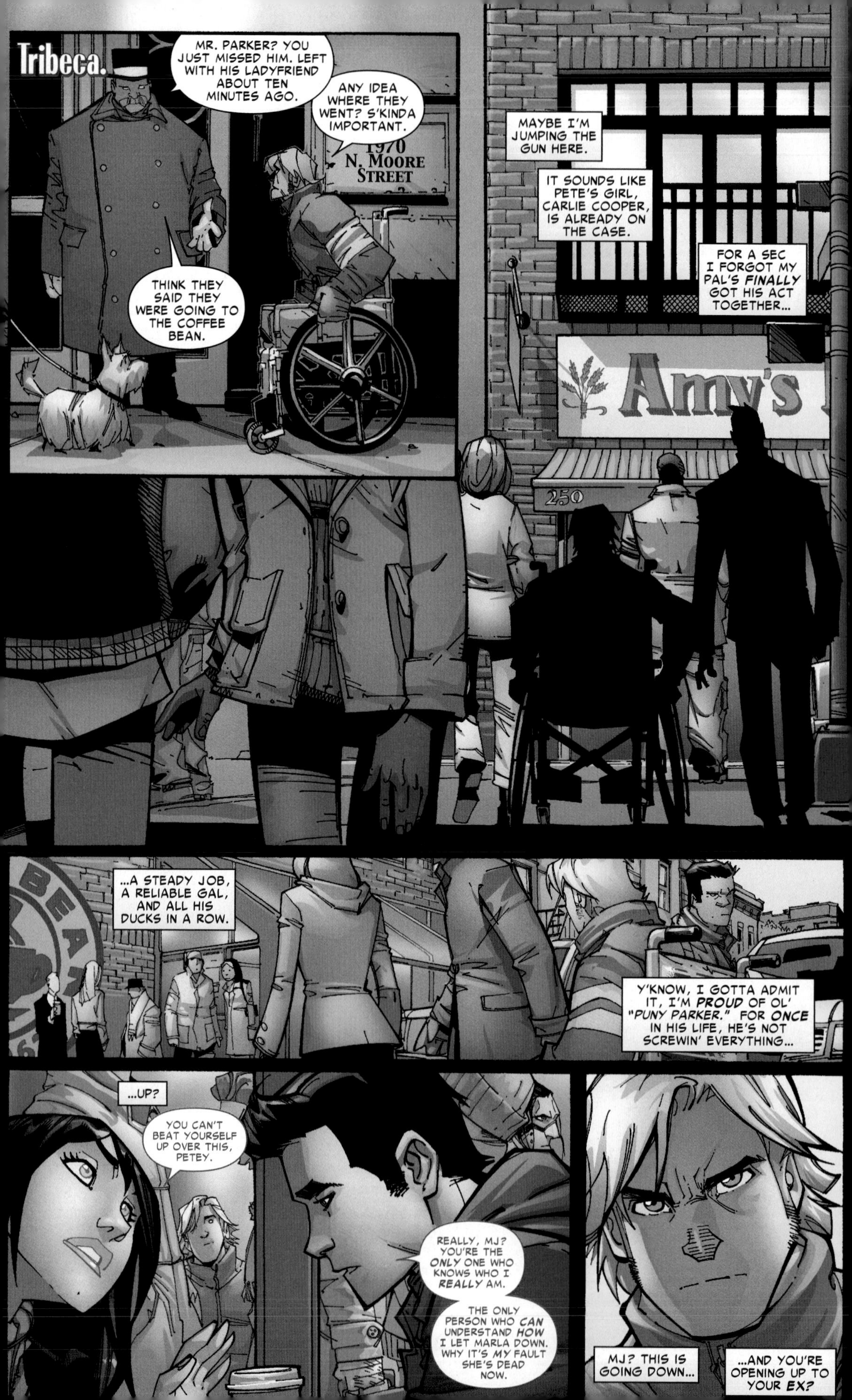
Tribeca.
MR. PARKER? YOU JUST MISSED HIM. LEFT WITH HIS LADYFRIEND ABOUT TEN MINUTES AGO.
ANY IDEA WHERE THEY WENT? S'KINDA IMPORTANT.
1970 N. MOORE STREET
THINK THEY SAID THEY WERE GOING TO THE COFFEE BEAN.
MAYBE I'M JUMPING THE GUN HERE.
IT SOUNDS LIKE PETE'S GIRL, CARLIE COOPER, IS ALREADY ON THE CASE.
FOR A SEC I FORGOT MY PAL'S FINALLY GOT HIS ACT TOGETHER...
Amy's
250
...A STEADY JOB, A RELIABLE GAL, AND ALL HIS DUCKS IN A ROW.
Y'KNOW, I GOTTA ADMIT IT, I'M PROUD OF OL' "PUNY PARKER." FOR ONCE IN HIS LIFE, HE'S NOT SCREWIN' EVERYTHING...
...UP?
YOU CAN'T BEAT YOURSELF UP OVER THIS, PETEY.
REALLY, MJ? YOU'RE THE ONLY ONE WHO KNOWS WHO I REALLY AM.
THE ONLY PERSON WHO CAN UNDERSTAND HOW I LET MARLA DOWN. WHY IT'S MY FAULT SHE'S DEAD NOW.
MJ? THIS IS GOING DOWN...
...AND YOU'RE OPENING UP TO YOUR EX?

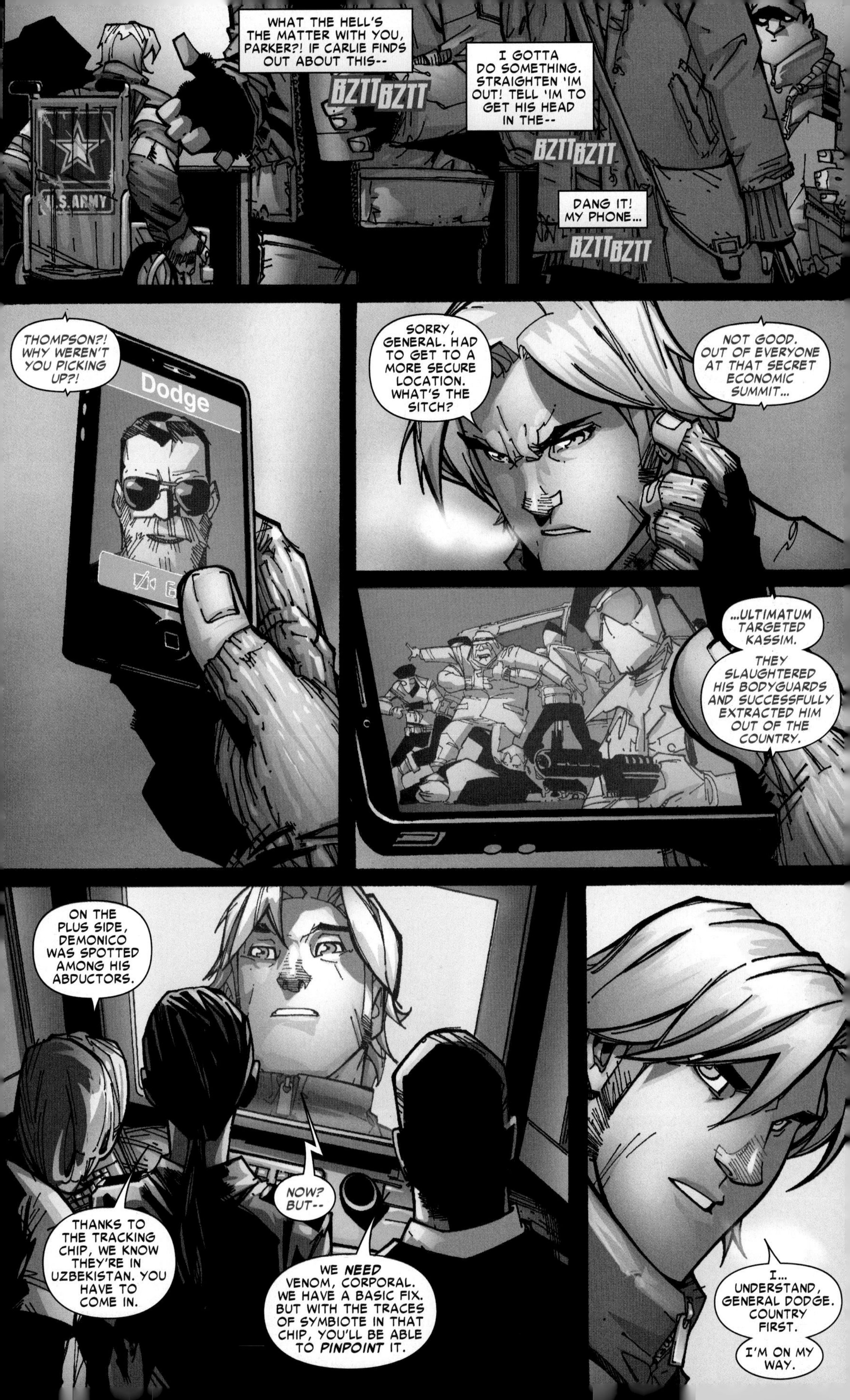
U.S. ARMY
WHAT THE HELL'S THE MATTER WITH YOU, PARKER?! IF CARLIE FINDS OUT ABOUT THIS--
BZTT BZTT
I GOTTA DO SOMETHING. STRAIGHTEN 'IM OUT! TELL 'IM TO GET HIS HEAD IN THE--
BZTT BZTT
DANG IT! MY PHONE...
BZTT BZTT
THOMPSON?! WHY WEREN'T YOU PICKING UP?!
Dodge
SORRY, GENERAL. HAD TO GET TO A MORE SECURE LOCATION. WHAT'S THE SITCH?
NOT GOOD. OUT OF EVERYONE AT THAT SECRET ECONOMIC SUMMIT...
...ULTIMATUM TARGETED KASSIM.
THEY SLAUGHTERED HIS BODYGUARDS AND SUCCESSFULLY EXTRACTED HIM OUT OF THE COUNTRY.
ON THE PLUS SIDE, DEMONICO WAS SPOTTED AMONG HIS ABDUCTORS.
THANKS TO THE TRACKING CHIP, WE KNOW THEY'RE IN UZBEKISTAN. YOU HAVE TO COME IN.
NOW? BUT--
WE NEED VENOM, CORPORAL. WE HAVE A BASIC FIX. BUT WITH THE TRACES OF SYMBIOTE IN THAT CHIP, YOU'LL BE ABLE TO PINPOINT IT.
I... UNDERSTAND, GENERAL DODGE. COUNTRY FIRST.
I'M ON MY WAY.

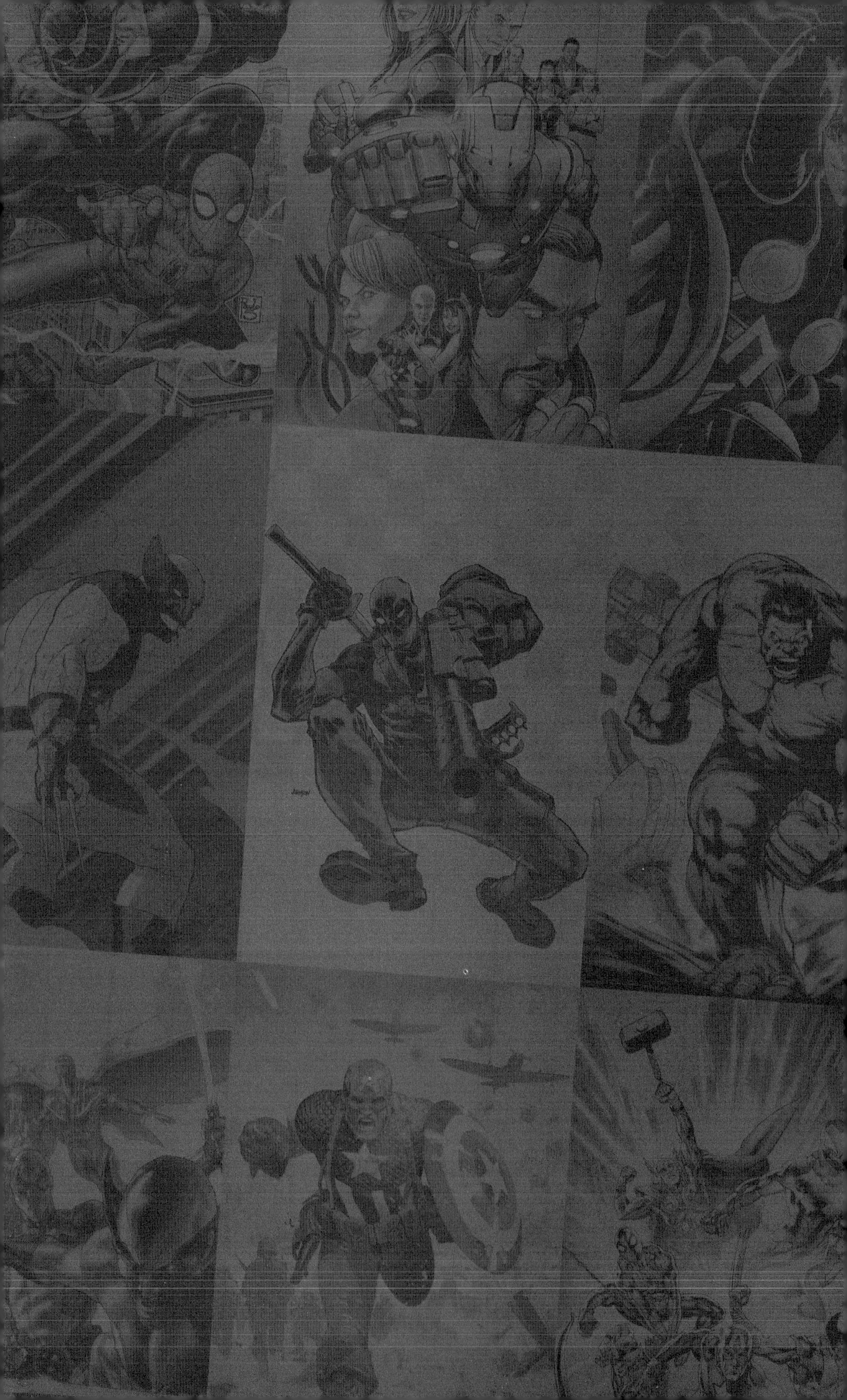

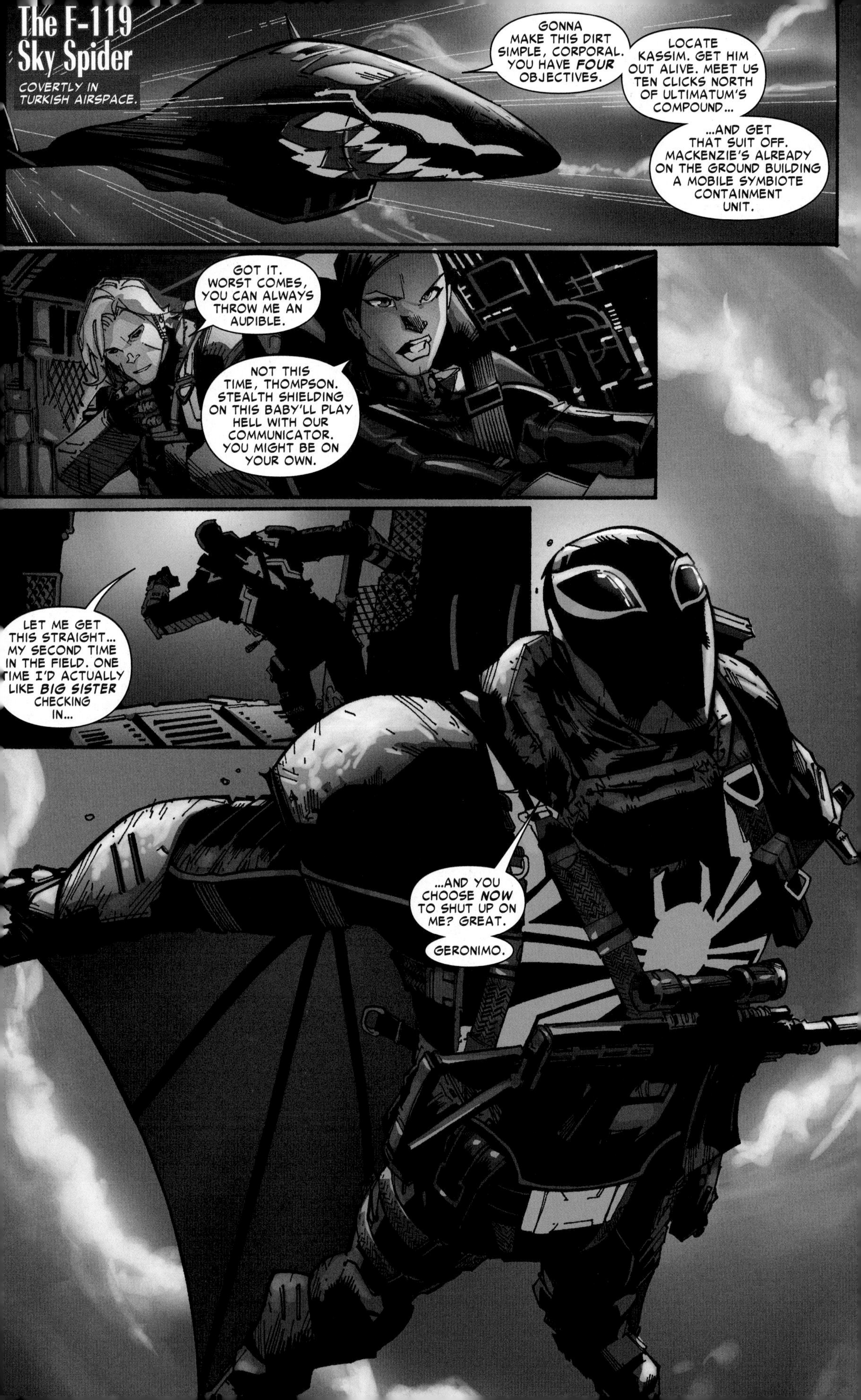
The F-119 Sky Spider
COVERTLY IN TURKISH AIRSPACE.
GONNA MAKE THIS DIRT SIMPLE, CORPORAL. YOU HAVE FOUR OBJECTIVES.
LOCATE KASSIM. GET HIM OUT ALIVE. MEET US TEN CLICKS NORTH OF ULTIMATUM'S COMPOUND...
...AND GET THAT SUIT OFF. MACKENZIE'S ALREADY ON THE GROUND BUILDING A MOBILE SYMBIOTE CONTAINMENT UNIT.
GOT IT. WORST COMES, YOU CAN ALWAYS THROW ME AN AUDIBLE.
NOT THIS TIME, THOMPSON. STEALTH SHIELDING ON THIS BABY'LL PLAY HELL WITH OUR COMMUNICATOR. YOU MIGHT BE ON YOUR OWN.
LET ME GET THIS STRAIGHT... MY SECOND TIME IN THE FIELD. ONE TIME I'D ACTUALLY LIKE BIG SISTER CHECKING IN...
...AND YOU CHOOSE NOW TO SHUT UP ON ME? GREAT.
GERONIMO.

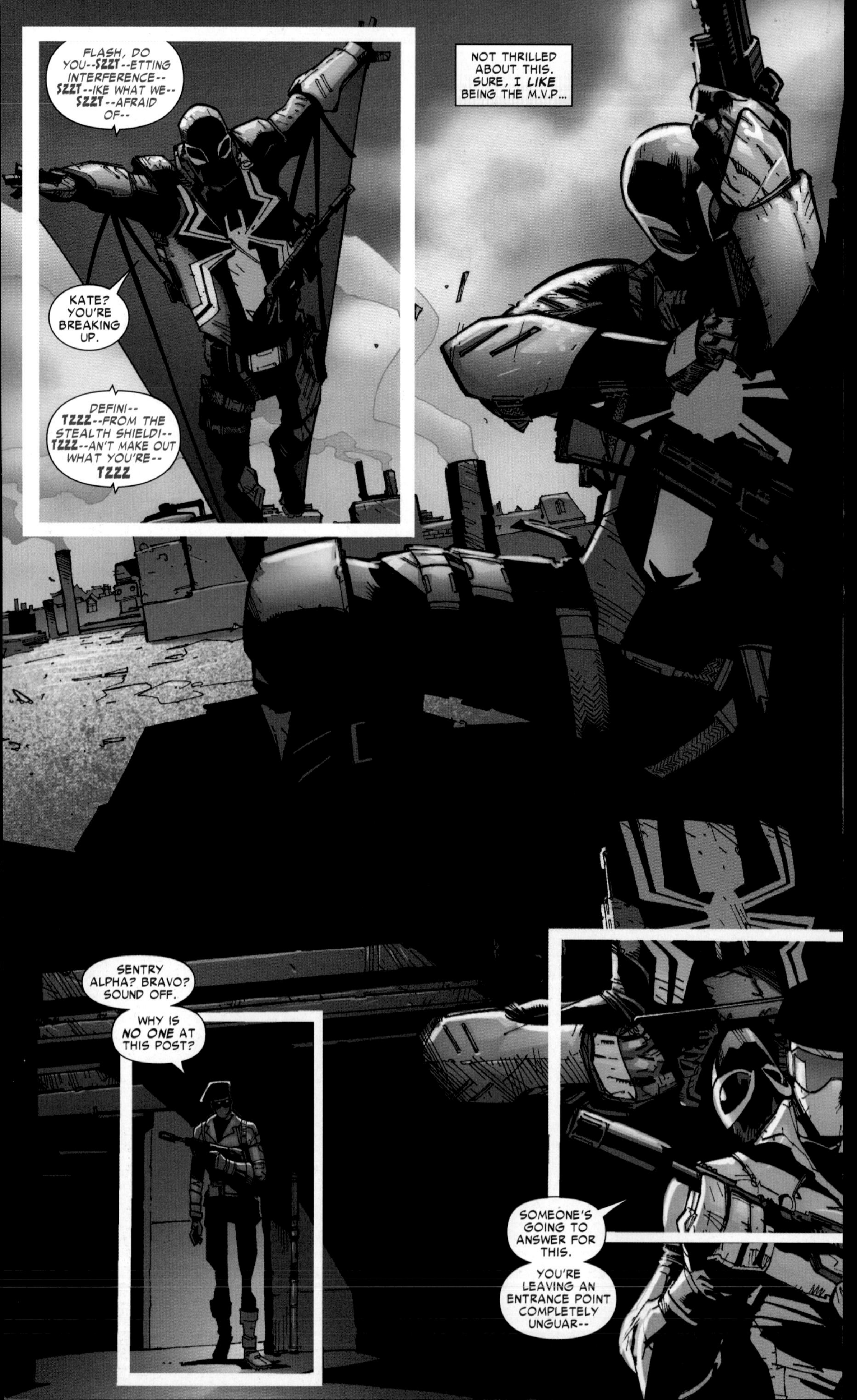
FLASH, DO YOU--SZZT--ETTING INTERFERENCE--SZZT--IKE WHAT WE--SZZT--AFRAID OF--
KATE? YOU'RE BREAKING UP.
DEFINI--TZZZ--FROM THE STEALTH SHIELD!--TZZZ--AN'T MAKE OUT WHAT YOU'RE--TZZZ
NOT THRILLED ABOUT THIS. SURE, I LIKE BEING THE M.V.P...
SENTRY ALPHA? BRAVO? SOUND OFF.
WHY IS NO ONE AT THIS POST?
SOMEONE'S GOING TO ANSWER FOR THIS.
YOU'RE LEAVING AN ENTRANCE POINT COMPLETELY UNGUAR--

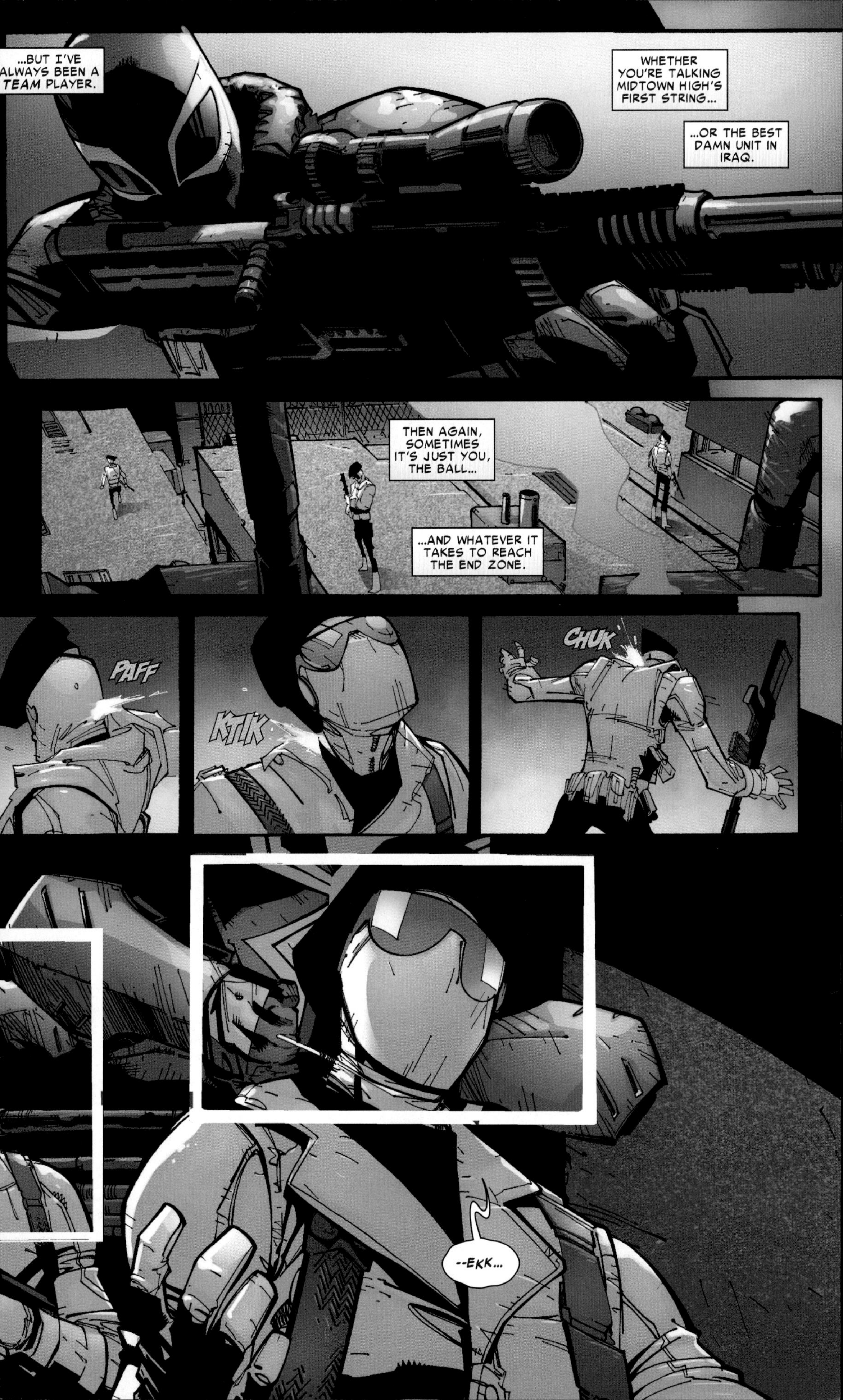

...BUT I'VE ALWAYS BEEN A *TEAM* PLAYER.
WHETHER YOU'RE TALKING MIDTOWN HIGH'S FIRST STRING...
...OR THE BEST DAMN UNIT IN IRAQ.
THEN AGAIN, SOMETIMES IT'S JUST YOU, THE BALL...
...AND WHATEVER IT TAKES TO REACH THE END ZONE.
PAFF
KTIK
CHUK
--EKK...

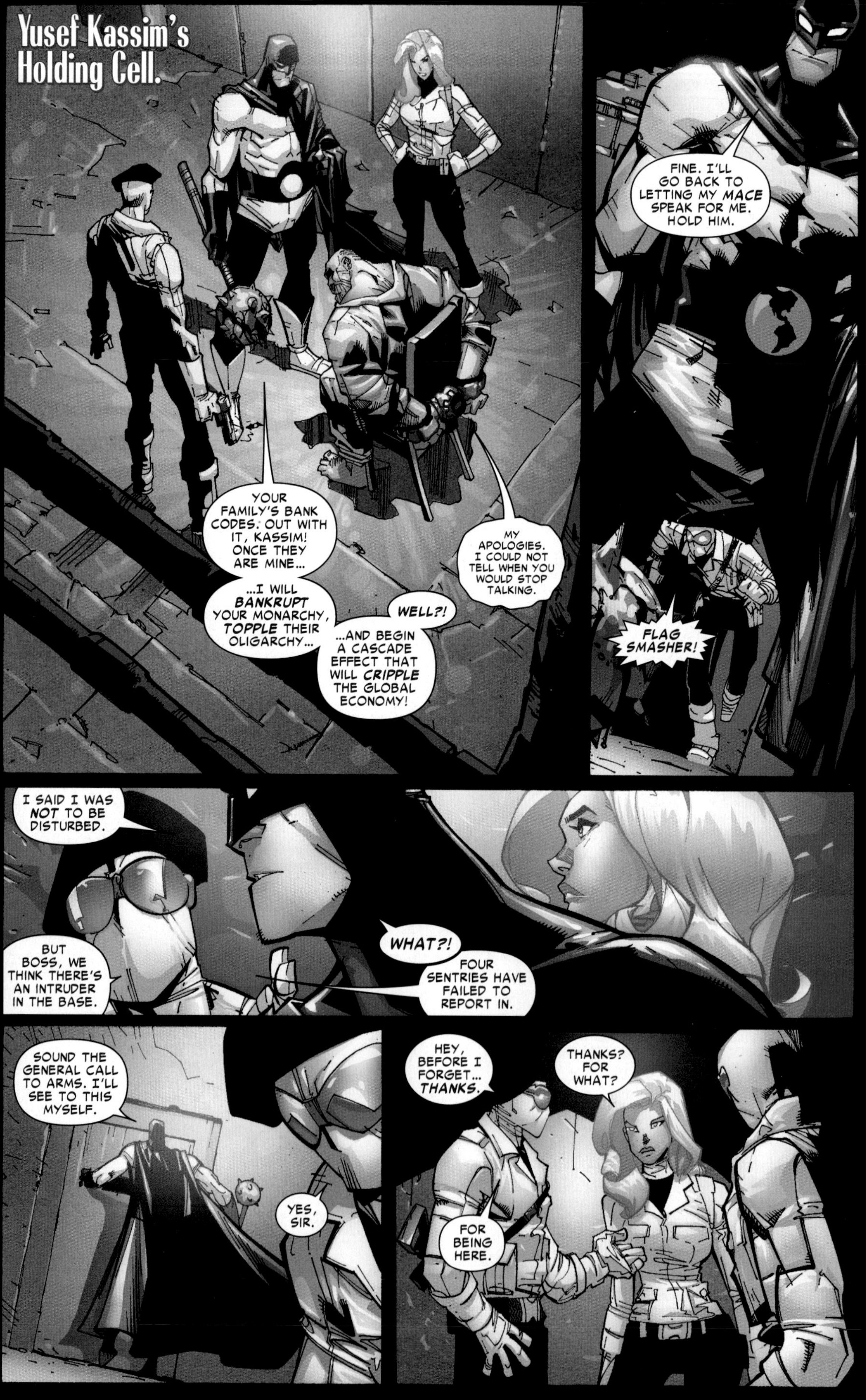
Yusef Kassim's Holding Cell.
YOUR FAMILY'S BANK CODES. OUT WITH IT, KASSIM! ONCE THEY ARE MINE...
...I WILL BANKRUPT YOUR MONARCHY, TOPPLE THEIR OLIGARCHY...
...AND BEGIN A CASCADE EFFECT THAT WILL CRIPPLE THE GLOBAL ECONOMY!
WELL?!
MY APOLOGIES. I COULD NOT TELL WHEN YOU WOULD STOP TALKING.
FINE. I'LL GO BACK TO LETTING MY MACE SPEAK FOR ME. HOLD HIM.
FLAG SMASHER!
I SAID I WAS NOT TO BE DISTURBED.
BUT BOSS, WE THINK THERE'S AN INTRUDER IN THE BASE.
WHAT?!
FOUR SENTRIES HAVE FAILED TO REPORT IN.
SOUND THE GENERAL CALL TO ARMS. I'LL SEE TO THIS MYSELF.
YES, SIR.
HEY, BEFORE I FORGET... THANKS.
THANKS? FOR WHAT?
FOR BEING HERE.

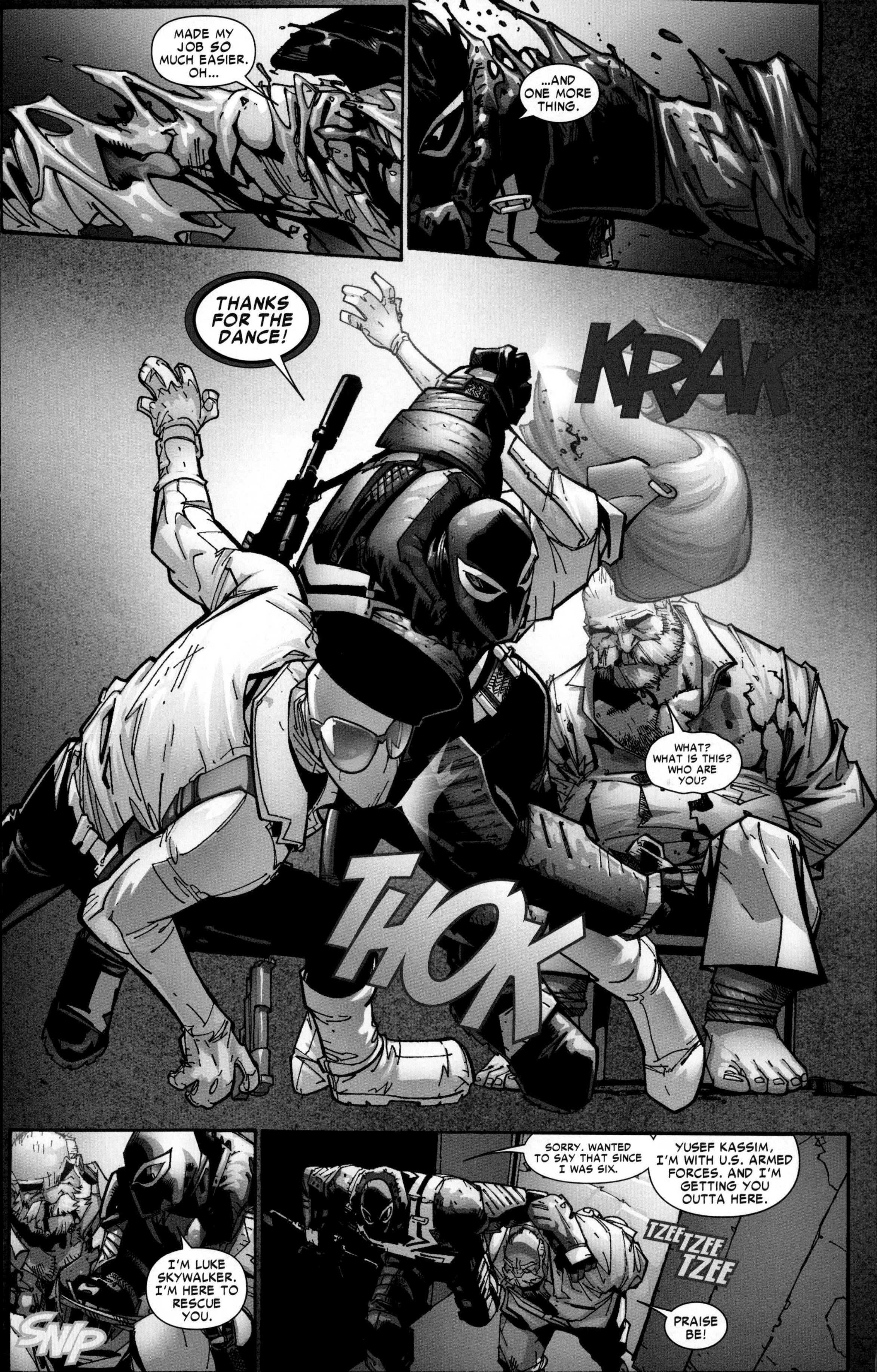
MADE MY JOB SO MUCH EASIER. OH...
...AND ONE MORE THING.
THANKS FOR THE DANCE!
KRAK
WHAT? WHAT IS THIS? WHO ARE YOU?
THOK
I'M LUKE SKYWALKER. I'M HERE TO RESCUE YOU.
SNIP
SORRY. WANTED TO SAY THAT SINCE I WAS SIX.
YUSEF KASSIM, I'M WITH U.S. ARMED FORCES. AND I'M GETTING YOU OUTTA HERE.
TZEE TZEE TZEE
PRAISE BE!

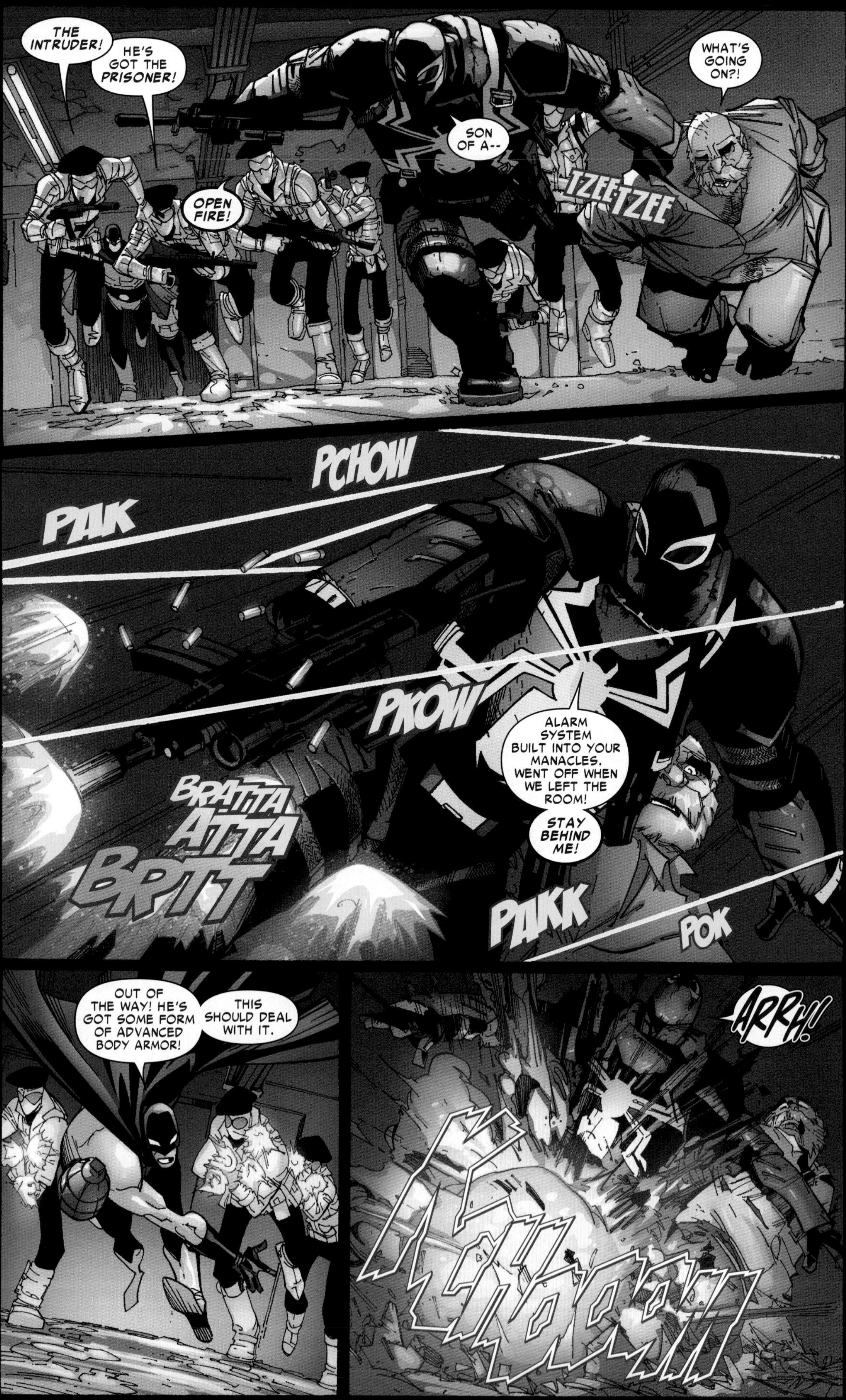
THE INTRUDER!
HE'S GOT THE PRISONER!
OPEN FIRE!
SON OF A--
WHAT'S GOING ON?!
TZEE TZEE
PCHOW
PAK
PKOW
BRATTA ATTA BRTT
ALARM SYSTEM BUILT INTO YOUR MANACLES. WENT OFF WHEN WE LEFT THE ROOM!
STAY BEHIND ME!
PAKK
POK
OUT OF THE WAY! HE'S GOT SOME FORM OF ADVANCED BODY ARMOR!
THIS SHOULD DEAL WITH IT.
ARRH!

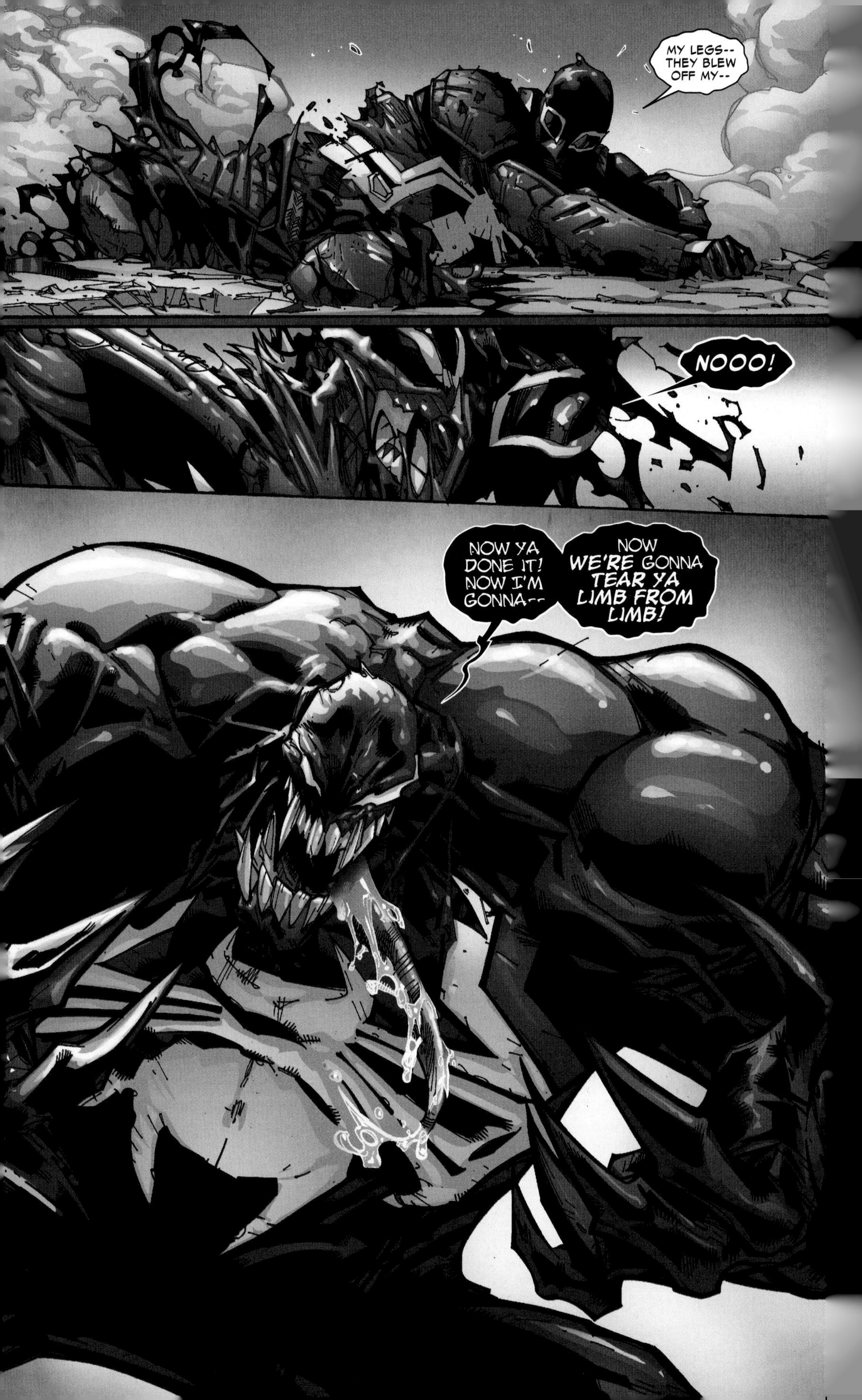
MY LEGS-- THEY BLEW OFF MY--
NOOO!
NOW YA DONE IT! NOW I'M GONNA--
NOW WE'RE GONNA TEAR YA LIMB FROM LIMB!

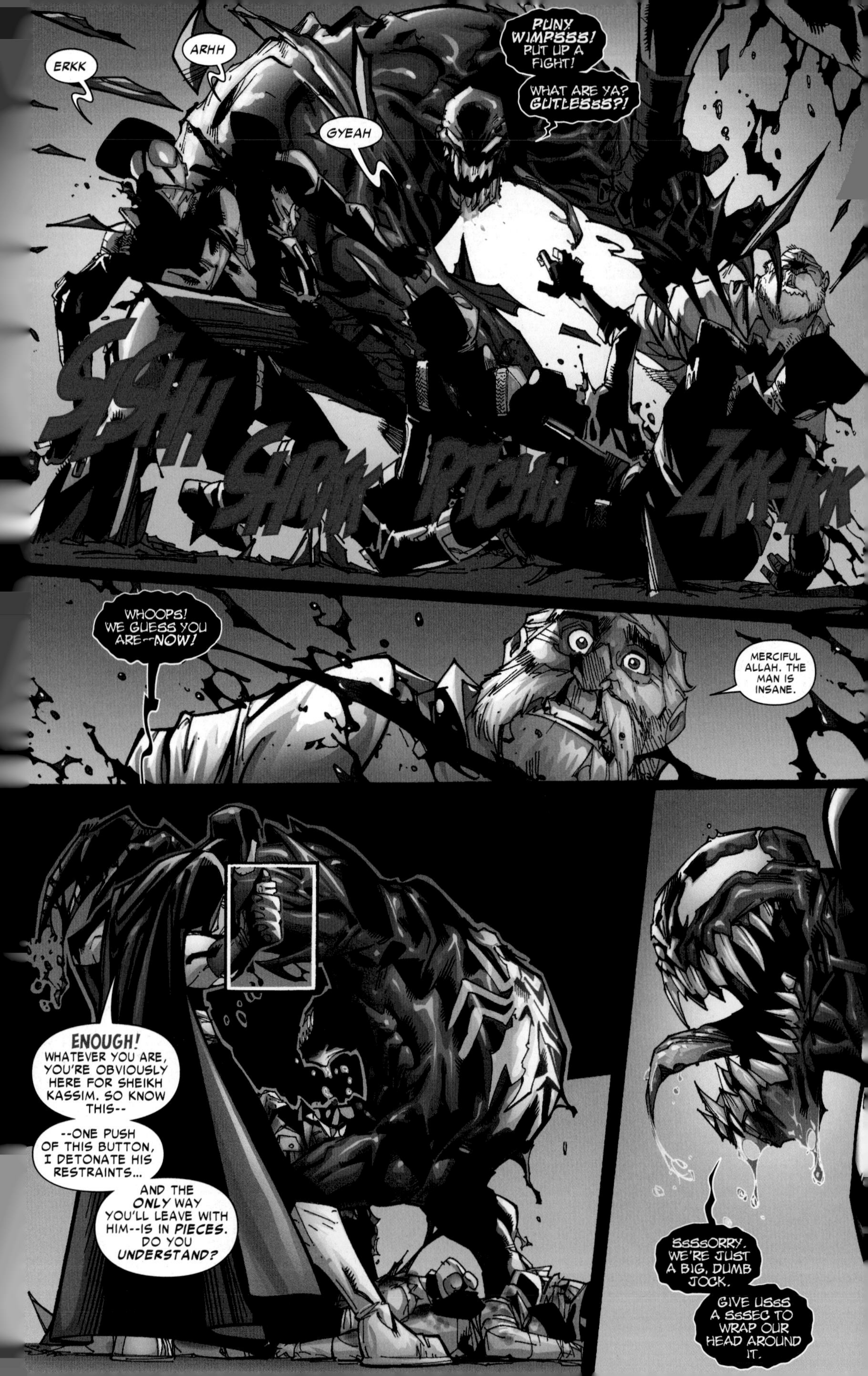
ERKK
ARHH
GYEAH
PUNY WIMPSSS! PUT UP A FIGHT!
WHAT ARE YA? GUTLESSS?!
WHOOPS! WE GUESS YOU ARE--NOW!
MERCIFUL ALLAH. THE MAN IS INSANE.
ENOUGH! WHATEVER YOU ARE, YOU'RE OBVIOUSLY HERE FOR SHEIKH KASSIM. SO KNOW THIS--
--ONE PUSH OF THIS BUTTON, I DETONATE HIS RESTRAINTS...
AND THE ONLY WAY YOU'LL LEAVE WITH HIM--IS IN PIECES. DO YOU UNDERSTAND?
SsssORRY. WE'RE JUST A BIG, DUMB JOCK.
GIVE USss A SssEC TO WRAP OUR HEAD AROUND IT.

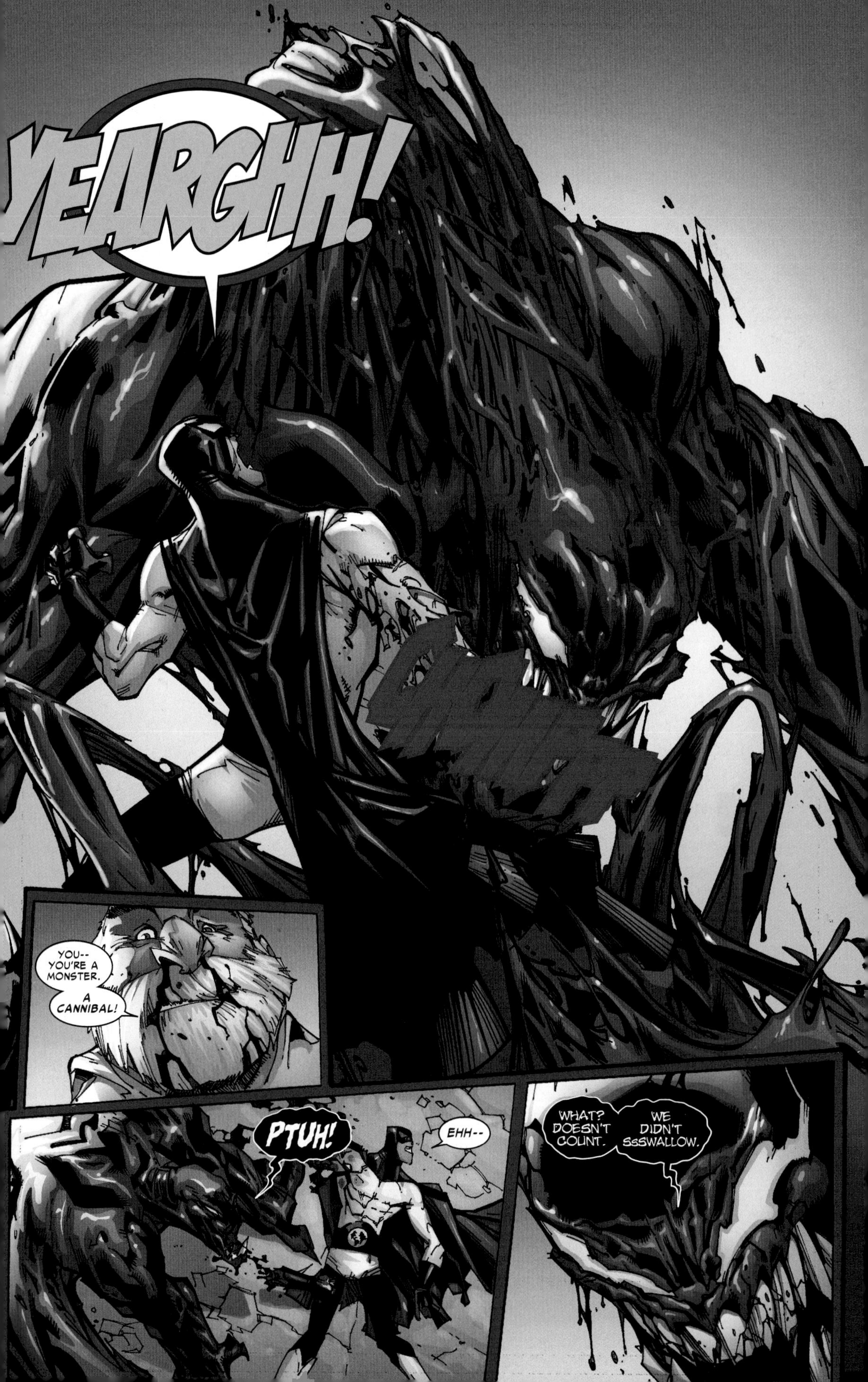
YEARGHH!
YOU-- YOU'RE A MONSTER.
A CANNIBAL!
PTUH!
EHH--
WHAT? DOESN'T COUNT.
WE DIDN'T SsSWALLOW.

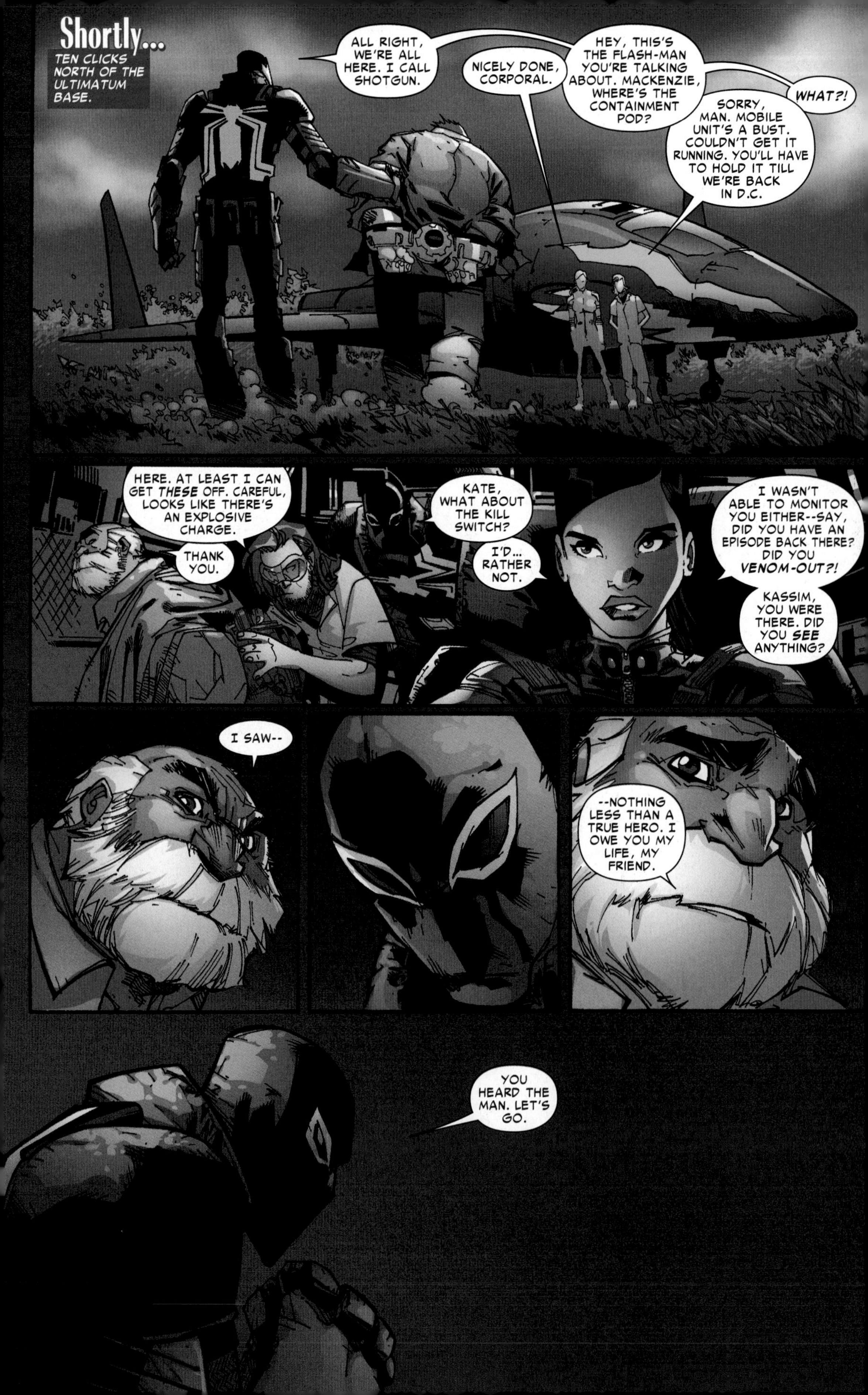
Shortly...
TEN CLICKS NORTH OF THE ULTIMATUM BASE.
ALL RIGHT, WE'RE ALL HERE. I CALL SHOTGUN.
NICELY DONE, CORPORAL.
HEY, THIS'S THE FLASH-MAN YOU'RE TALKING ABOUT. MACKENZIE, WHERE'S THE CONTAINMENT POD?
WHAT?!
SORRY, MAN. MOBILE UNIT'S A BUST. COULDN'T GET IT RUNNING. YOU'LL HAVE TO HOLD IT TILL WE'RE BACK IN D.C.
HERE. AT LEAST I CAN GET THESE OFF. CAREFUL, LOOKS LIKE THERE'S AN EXPLOSIVE CHARGE.
THANK YOU.
KATE, WHAT ABOUT THE KILL SWITCH?
I'D... RATHER NOT.
I WASN'T ABLE TO MONITOR YOU EITHER--SAY, DID YOU HAVE AN EPISODE BACK THERE? DID YOU VENOM-OUT?!
KASSIM, YOU WERE THERE. DID YOU SEE ANYTHING?
I SAW--
--NOTHING LESS THAN A TRUE HERO. I OWE YOU MY LIFE, MY FRIEND.
YOU HEARD THE MAN. LET'S GO.

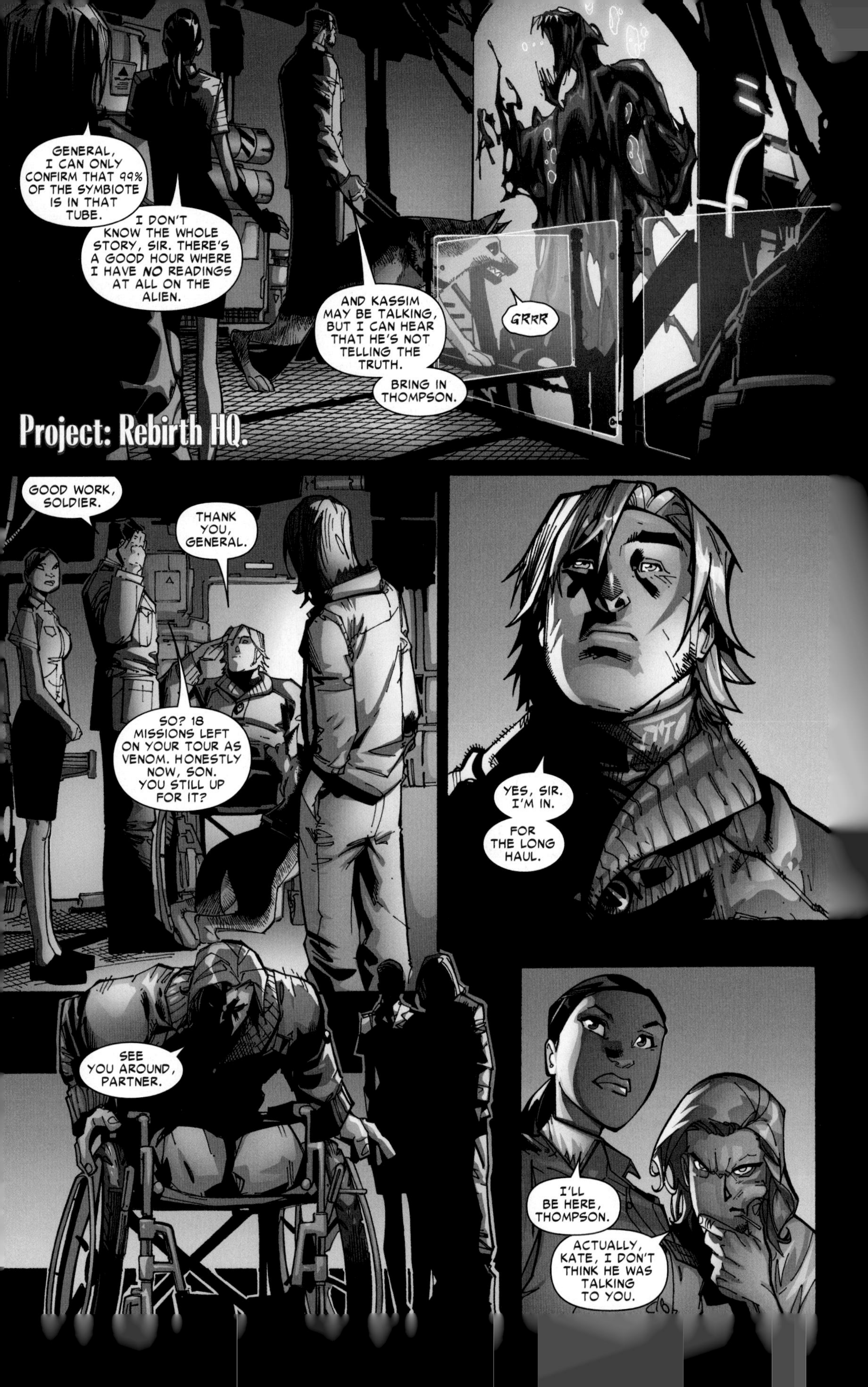
GENERAL, I CAN ONLY CONFIRM THAT 99% OF THE SYMBIOTE IS IN THAT TUBE.
I DON'T KNOW THE WHOLE STORY, SIR. THERE'S A GOOD HOUR WHERE I HAVE NO READINGS AT ALL ON THE ALIEN.
AND KASSIM MAY BE TALKING, BUT I CAN HEAR THAT HE'S NOT TELLING THE TRUTH.
GRRR
BRING IN THOMPSON.
Project: Rebirth HQ.
GOOD WORK, SOLDIER.
THANK YOU, GENERAL.
SO? 18 MISSIONS LEFT ON YOUR TOUR AS VENOM. HONESTLY NOW, SON. YOU STILL UP FOR IT?
YES, SIR. I'M IN.
FOR THE LONG HAUL.
SEE YOU AROUND, PARTNER.
I'LL BE HERE, THOMPSON.
ACTUALLY, KATE, I DON'T THINK HE WAS TALKING TO YOU.

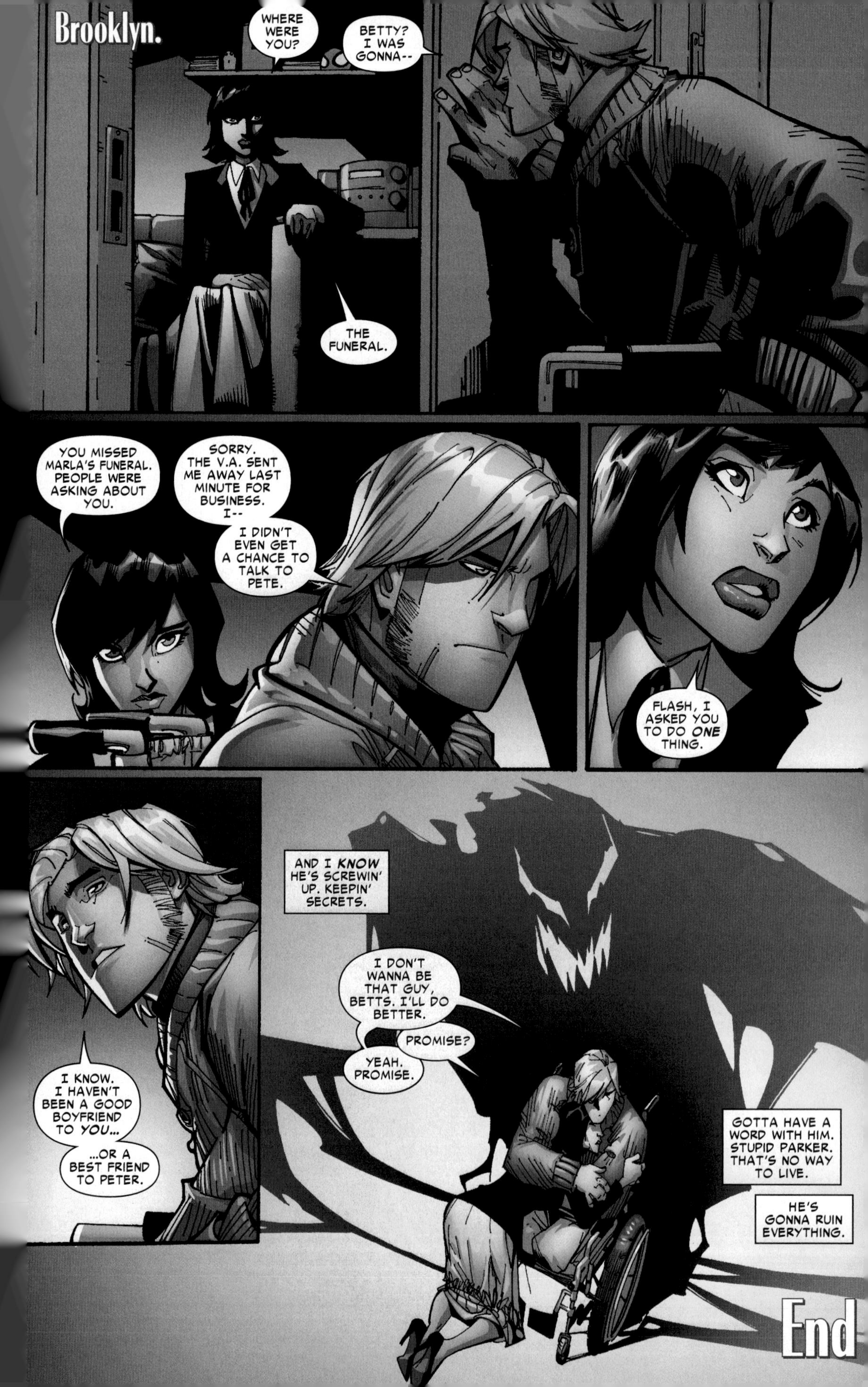
Brooklyn.
WHERE WERE YOU?
BETTY? I WAS GONNA--
THE FUNERAL.
YOU MISSED MARLA'S FUNERAL. PEOPLE WERE ASKING ABOUT YOU.
SORRY. THE V.A. SENT ME AWAY LAST MINUTE FOR BUSINESS. I--
I DIDN'T EVEN GET A CHANCE TO TALK TO PETE.
FLASH, I ASKED YOU TO DO ONE THING.
I KNOW. I HAVEN'T BEEN A GOOD BOYFRIEND TO YOU...
...OR A BEST FRIEND TO PETER.
AND I KNOW HE'S SCREWIN' UP. KEEPIN' SECRETS.
I DON'T WANNA BE THAT GUY, BETTS. I'LL DO BETTER.
PROMISE?
YEAH. PROMISE.
GOTTA HAVE A WORD WITH HIM. STUPID PARKER. THAT'S NO WAY TO LIVE.
HE'S GONNA RUIN EVERYTHING.
End

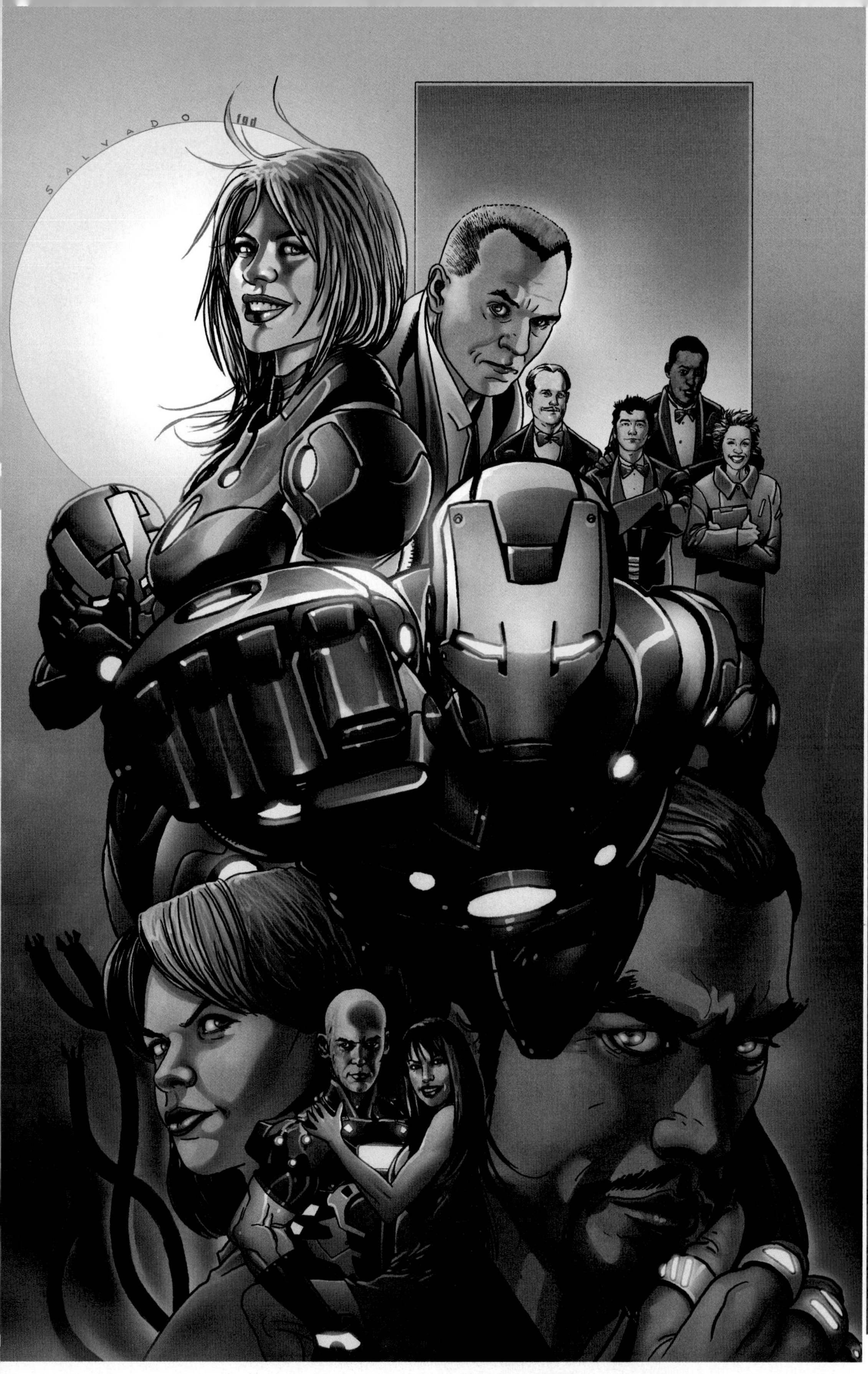
SALVADO

INVINCIBLE IRON MAN #500.1

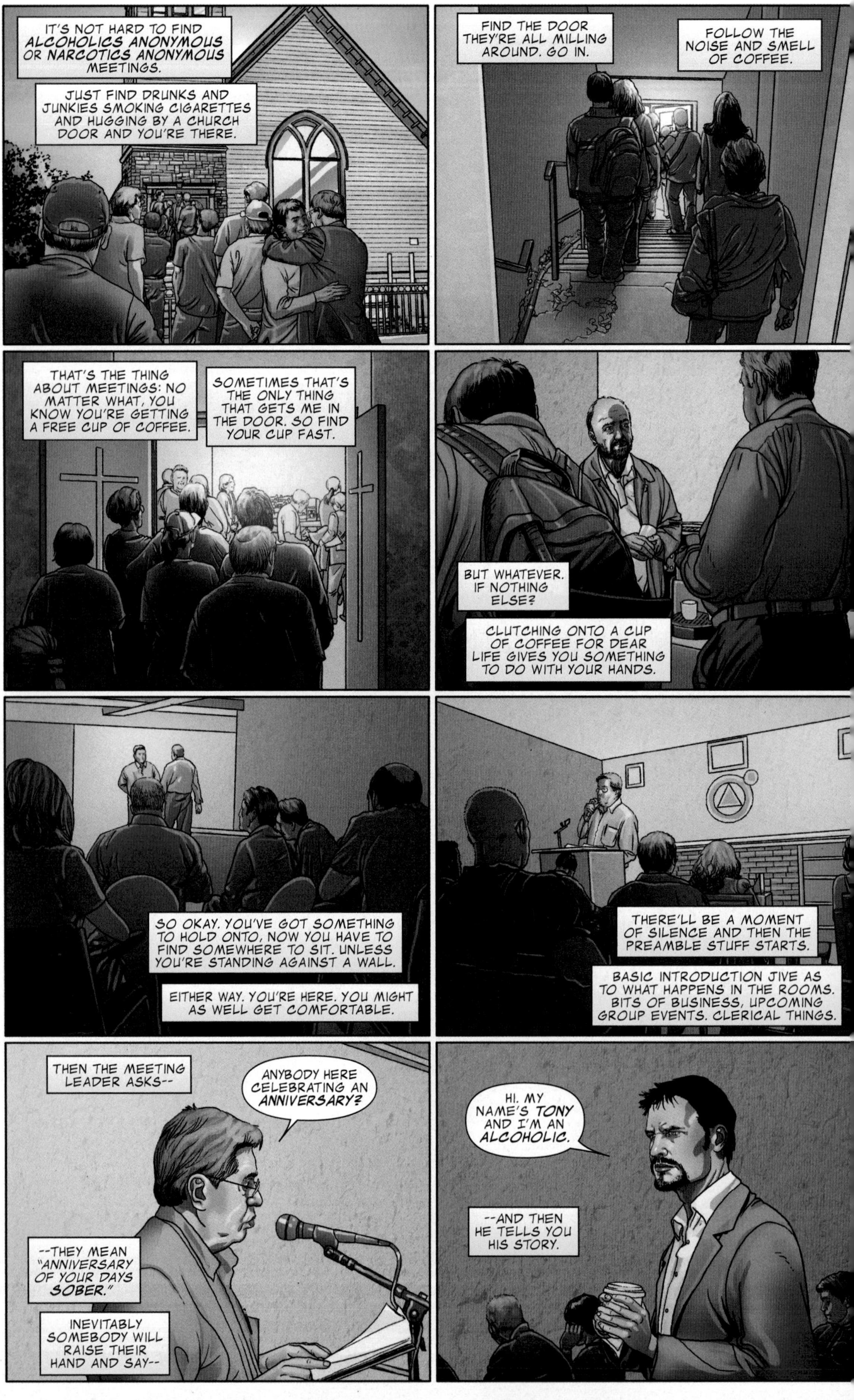
IT'S NOT HARD TO FIND ALCOHOLICS ANONYMOUS OR NARCOTICS ANONYMOUS MEETINGS.
JUST FIND DRUNKS AND JUNKIES SMOKING CIGARETTES AND HUGGING BY A CHURCH DOOR AND YOU'RE THERE.
FIND THE DOOR THEY'RE ALL MILLING AROUND. GO IN.
FOLLOW THE NOISE AND SMELL OF COFFEE.
THAT'S THE THING ABOUT MEETINGS: NO MATTER WHAT, YOU KNOW YOU'RE GETTING A FREE CUP OF COFFEE.
SOMETIMES THAT'S THE ONLY THING THAT GETS ME IN THE DOOR. SO FIND YOUR CUP FAST.
BUT WHATEVER. IF NOTHING ELSE?
CLUTCHING ONTO A CUP OF COFFEE FOR DEAR LIFE GIVES YOU SOMETHING TO DO WITH YOUR HANDS.
SO OKAY. YOU'VE GOT SOMETHING TO HOLD ONTO, NOW YOU HAVE TO FIND SOMEWHERE TO SIT. UNLESS YOU'RE STANDING AGAINST A WALL.
EITHER WAY. YOU'RE HERE. YOU MIGHT AS WELL GET COMFORTABLE.
THERE'LL BE A MOMENT OF SILENCE AND THEN THE PREAMBLE STUFF STARTS.
BASIC INTRODUCTION JIVE AS TO WHAT HAPPENS IN THE ROOMS. BITS OF BUSINESS, UPCOMING GROUP EVENTS. CLERICAL THINGS.
THEN THE MEETING LEADER ASKS--
ANYBODY HERE CELEBRATING AN ANNIVERSARY?
--THEY MEAN "ANNIVERSARY OF YOUR DAYS SOBER."
INEVITABLY SOMEBODY WILL RAISE THEIR HAND AND SAY--
HI. MY NAME'S TONY AND I'M AN ALCOHOLIC.
--AND THEN HE TELLS YOU HIS STORY.

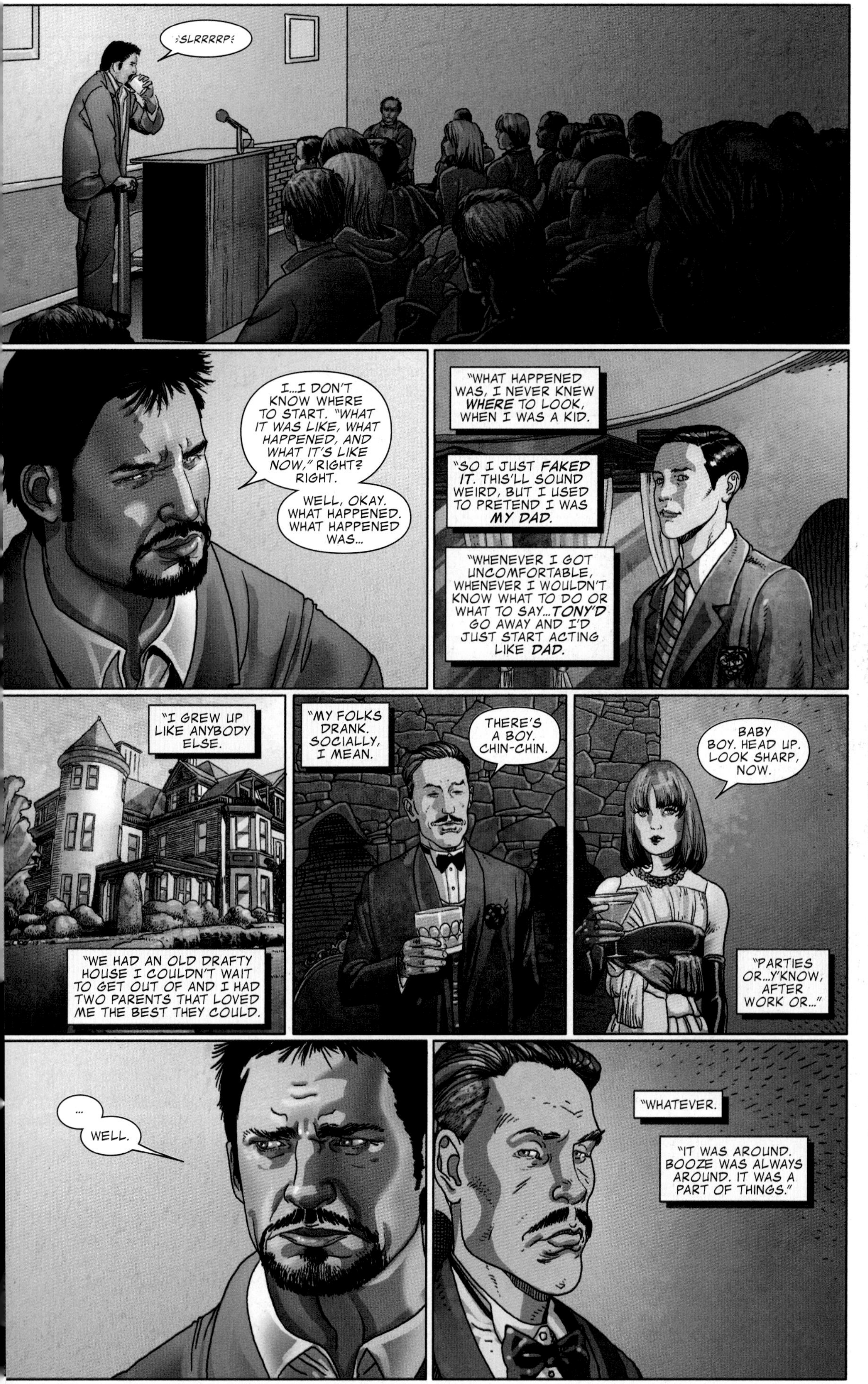

SLRRRRP
I...I DON'T KNOW WHERE TO START. "WHAT IT WAS LIKE, WHAT HAPPENED, AND WHAT IT'S LIKE NOW," RIGHT? RIGHT.
WELL, OKAY. WHAT HAPPENED. WHAT HAPPENED WAS...
"WHAT HAPPENED WAS, I NEVER KNEW WHERE TO LOOK, WHEN I WAS A KID.
"SO I JUST FAKED IT. THIS'LL SOUND WEIRD, BUT I USED TO PRETEND I WAS MY DAD.
"WHENEVER I GOT UNCOMFORTABLE, WHENEVER I WOULDN'T KNOW WHAT TO DO OR WHAT TO SAY...TONY'D GO AWAY AND I'D JUST START ACTING LIKE DAD.
"I GREW UP LIKE ANYBODY ELSE.
"WE HAD AN OLD DRAFTY HOUSE I COULDN'T WAIT TO GET OUT OF AND I HAD TWO PARENTS THAT LOVED ME THE BEST THEY COULD.
"MY FOLKS DRANK. SOCIALLY, I MEAN.
THERE'S A BOY. CHIN-CHIN.
BABY BOY. HEAD UP. LOOK SHARP, NOW.
"PARTIES OR...Y'KNOW, AFTER WORK OR..."
...
WELL.
"WHATEVER.
"IT WAS AROUND. BOOZE WAS ALWAYS AROUND. IT WAS A PART OF THINGS."

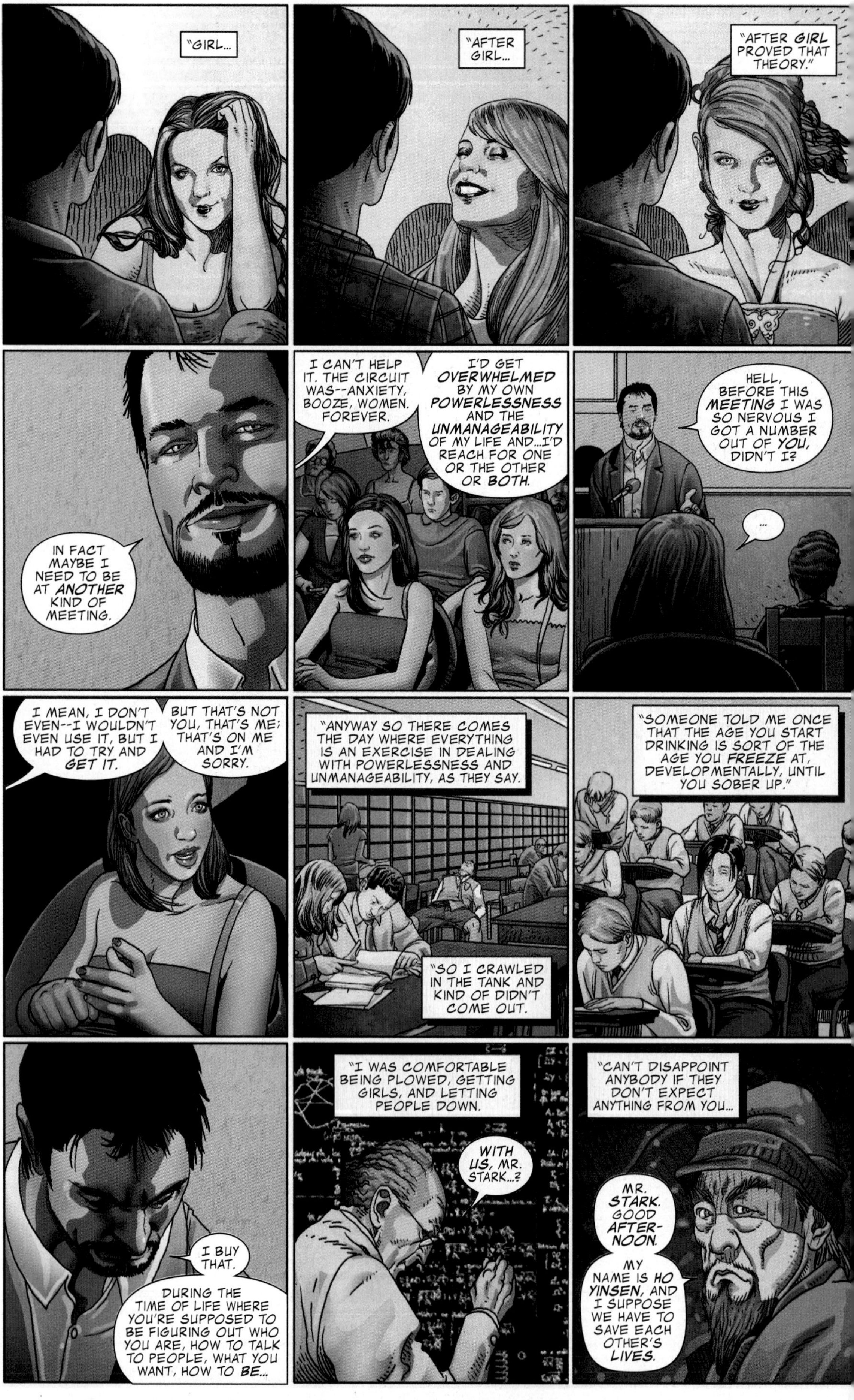
"GIRL...
"AFTER GIRL...
"AFTER GIRL PROVED THAT THEORY."
IN FACT MAYBE I NEED TO BE AT ANOTHER KIND OF MEETING.
I CAN'T HELP IT. THE CIRCUIT WAS--ANXIETY, BOOZE, WOMEN. FOREVER.
I'D GET OVERWHELMED BY MY OWN POWERLESSNESS AND THE UNMANAGEABILITY OF MY LIFE AND...I'D REACH FOR ONE OR THE OTHER OR BOTH.
HELL, BEFORE THIS MEETING I WAS SO NERVOUS I GOT A NUMBER OUT OF YOU, DIDN'T I?
...
I MEAN, I DON'T EVEN--I WOULDN'T EVEN USE IT, BUT I HAD TO TRY AND GET IT.
BUT THAT'S NOT YOU, THAT'S ME; THAT'S ON ME AND I'M SORRY.
"ANYWAY SO THERE COMES THE DAY WHERE EVERYTHING IS AN EXERCISE IN DEALING WITH POWERLESSNESS AND UNMANAGEABILITY, AS THEY SAY.
"SO I CRAWLED IN THE TANK AND KIND OF DIDN'T COME OUT.
"SOMEONE TOLD ME ONCE THAT THE AGE YOU START DRINKING IS SORT OF THE AGE YOU FREEZE AT, DEVELOPMENTALLY, UNTIL YOU SOBER UP."
I BUY THAT.
DURING THE TIME OF LIFE WHERE YOU'RE SUPPOSED TO BE FIGURING OUT WHO YOU ARE, HOW TO TALK TO PEOPLE, WHAT YOU WANT, HOW TO BE...
"I WAS COMFORTABLE BEING PLOWED, GETTING GIRLS, AND LETTING PEOPLE DOWN.
WITH US, MR. STARK...?
"CAN'T DISAPPOINT ANYBODY IF THEY DON'T EXPECT ANYTHING FROM YOU...
MR. STARK. GOOD AFTERNOON.
MY NAME IS HO YINSEN, AND I SUPPOSE WE HAVE TO SAVE EACH OTHER'S LIVES.

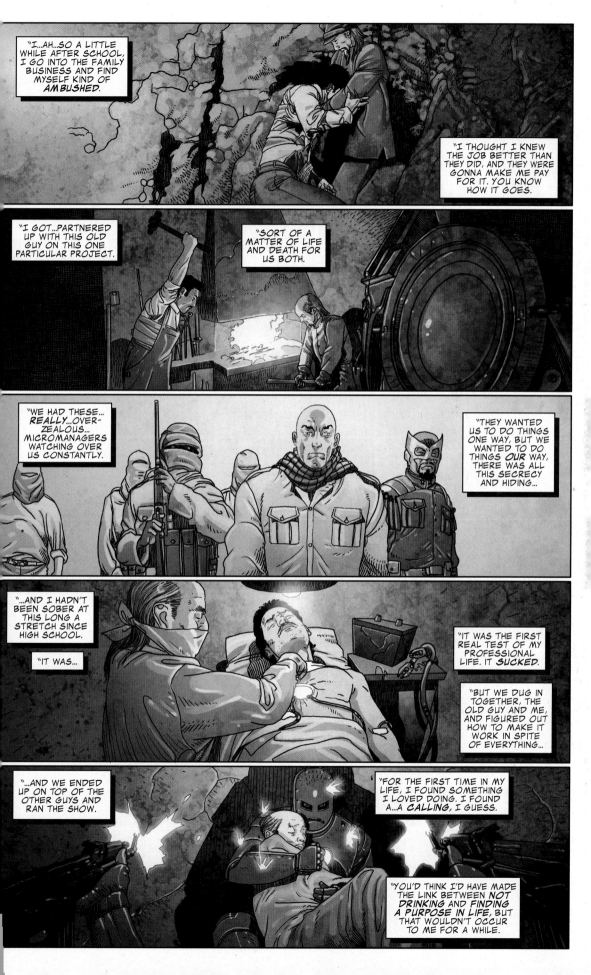

"I...AH...SO A LITTLE WHILE AFTER SCHOOL, I GO INTO THE FAMILY BUSINESS AND FIND MYSELF KIND OF *AMBUSHED.*

"I THOUGHT I KNEW THE JOB BETTER THAN THEY DID, AND THEY WERE GONNA MAKE ME PAY FOR IT. YOU KNOW HOW IT GOES.

"I GOT...PARTNERED UP WITH THIS OLD GUY ON THIS ONE PARTICULAR PROJECT.

"SORT OF A MATTER OF LIFE AND DEATH FOR US BOTH.

"WE HAD THESE... *REALLY*...OVER-ZEALOUS... MICROMANAGERS WATCHING OVER US CONSTANTLY.

"THEY WANTED US TO DO THINGS ONE WAY, BUT WE WANTED TO DO THINGS *OUR* WAY, THERE WAS ALL THIS SECRECY AND HIDING...

"...AND I HADN'T BEEN SOBER AT THIS LONG A STRETCH SINCE HIGH SCHOOL.

"IT WAS...

"IT WAS THE FIRST REAL TEST OF MY PROFESSIONAL LIFE. IT *SUCKED.*

"BUT WE DUG IN TOGETHER, THE OLD GUY AND ME, AND FIGURED OUT HOW TO MAKE IT WORK IN SPITE OF EVERYTHING...

"...AND WE ENDED UP ON TOP OF THE OTHER GUYS AND RAN THE SHOW.

"FOR THE FIRST TIME IN MY LIFE, I FOUND SOMETHING I LOVED DOING. I FOUND A...*CALLING*, I GUESS.

"YOU'D THINK I'D HAVE MADE THE LINK BETWEEN *NOT DRINKING* AND *FINDING A PURPOSE IN LIFE*, BUT THAT WOULDN'T OCCUR TO ME FOR A WHILE.

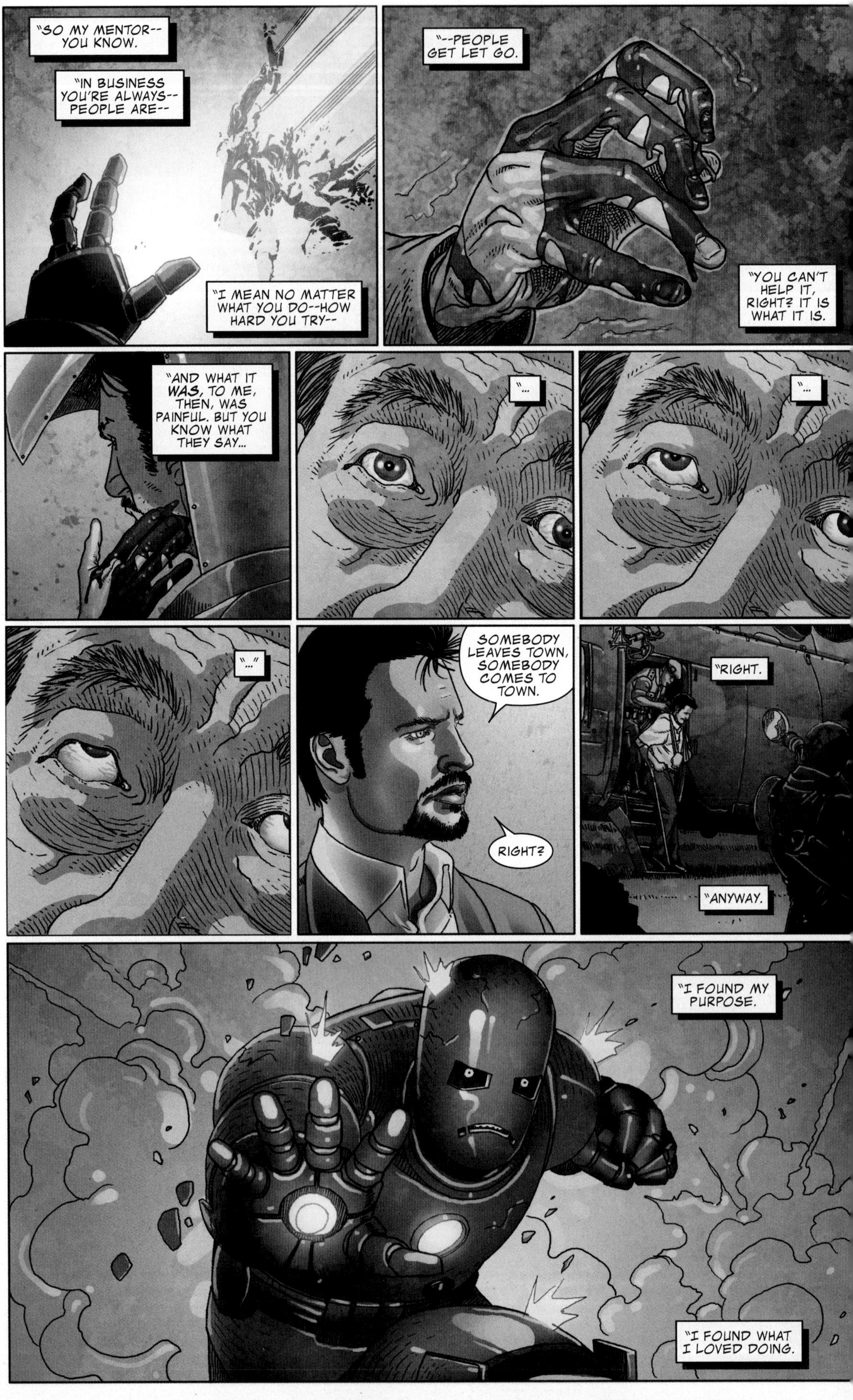

"SO MY MENTOR--
YOU KNOW.
"IN BUSINESS
YOU'RE ALWAYS--
PEOPLE ARE--
"I MEAN NO MATTER
WHAT YOU DO--HOW
HARD YOU TRY--
"--PEOPLE
GET LET GO.
"YOU CAN'T
HELP IT,
RIGHT? IT IS
WHAT IT IS.
"AND WHAT IT
WAS, TO ME,
THEN, WAS
PAINFUL. BUT YOU
KNOW WHAT
THEY SAY...
"...
"...
"..."
SOMEBODY
LEAVES TOWN,
SOMEBODY
COMES TO
TOWN.
RIGHT?
"RIGHT.
"ANYWAY.
"I FOUND MY
PURPOSE.
"I FOUND WHAT
I LOVED DOING.

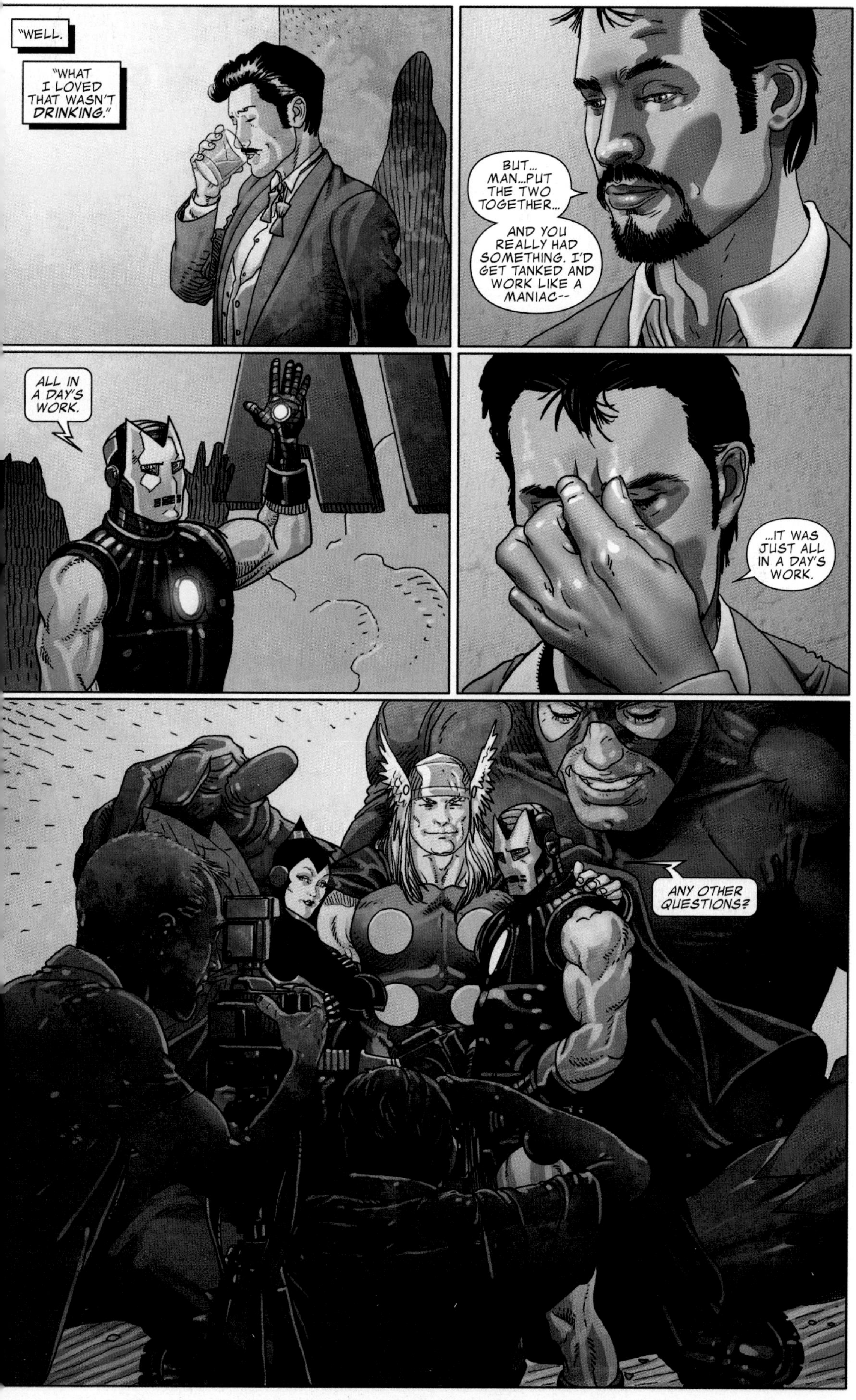
"WELL.
"WHAT I LOVED THAT WASN'T DRINKING."
BUT... MAN...PUT THE TWO TOGETHER...
AND YOU REALLY HAD SOMETHING. I'D GET TANKED AND WORK LIKE A MANIAC--
ALL IN A DAY'S WORK.
...IT WAS JUST ALL IN A DAY'S WORK.
ANY OTHER QUESTIONS?

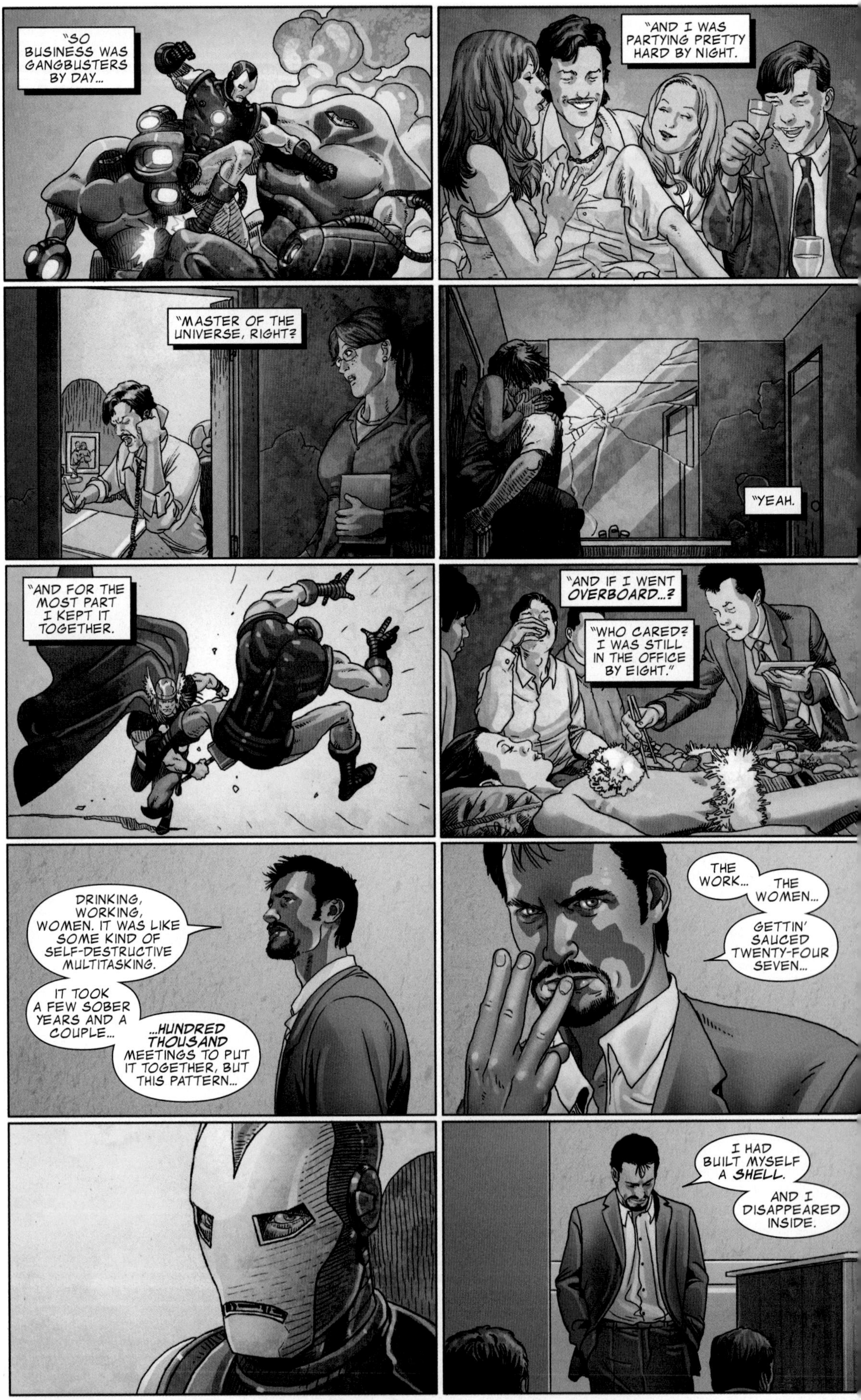
"SO BUSINESS WAS GANGBUSTERS BY DAY...
"AND I WAS PARTYING PRETTY HARD BY NIGHT.
"MASTER OF THE UNIVERSE, RIGHT?
"YEAH.
"AND FOR THE MOST PART I KEPT IT TOGETHER.
"AND IF I WENT OVERBOARD...?
"WHO CARED? I WAS STILL IN THE OFFICE BY EIGHT."
DRINKING, WORKING, WOMEN. IT WAS LIKE SOME KIND OF SELF-DESTRUCTIVE MULTITASKING.
IT TOOK A FEW SOBER YEARS AND A COUPLE...
...HUNDRED THOUSAND MEETINGS TO PUT IT TOGETHER, BUT THIS PATTERN...
THE WORK...
THE WOMEN...
GETTIN' SAUCED TWENTY-FOUR SEVEN...
I HAD BUILT MYSELF A SHELL.
AND I DISAPPEARED INSIDE.

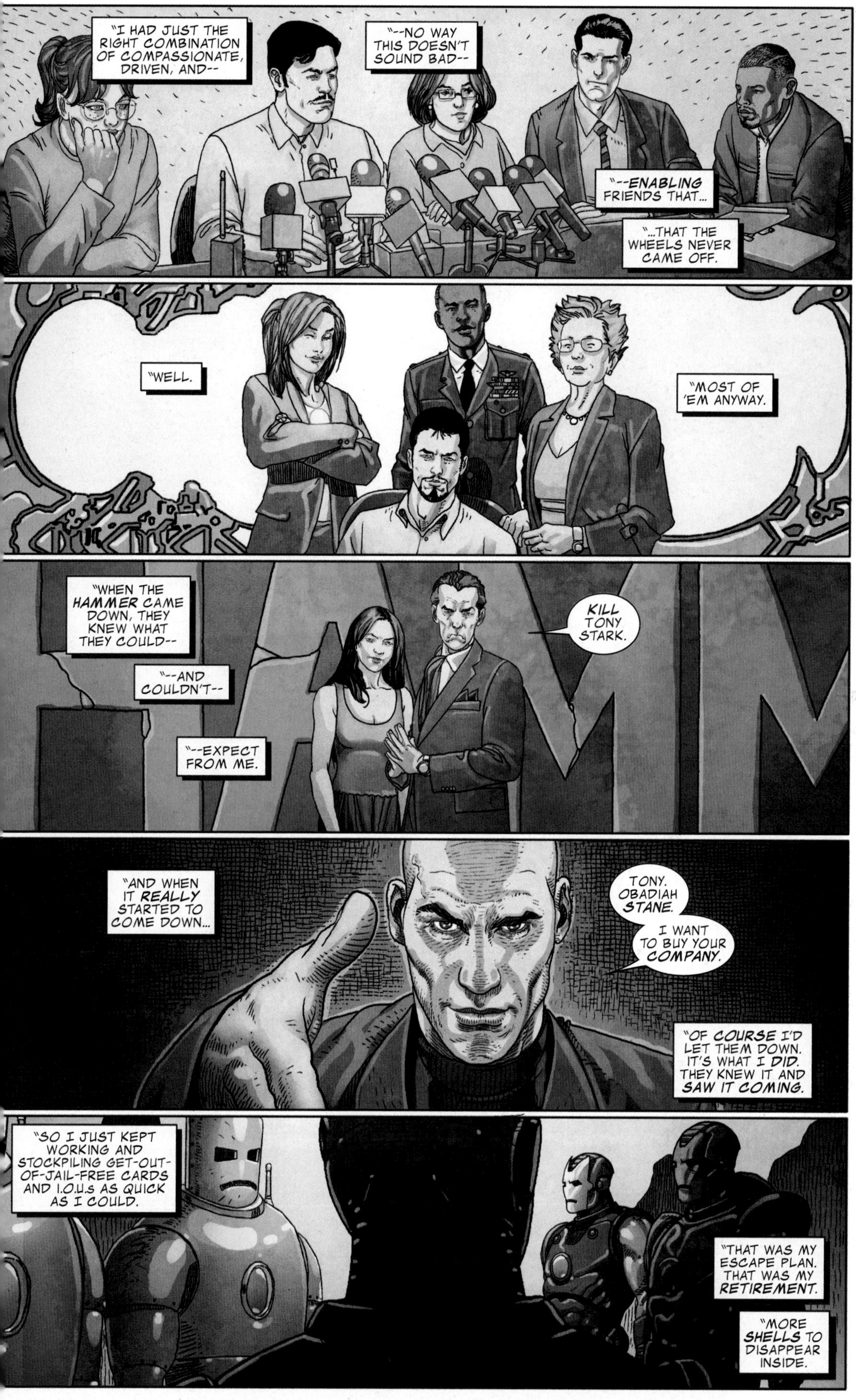
"I HAD JUST THE RIGHT COMBINATION OF COMPASSIONATE, DRIVEN, AND--
"--NO WAY THIS DOESN'T SOUND BAD--
"--ENABLING FRIENDS THAT...
"...THAT THE WHEELS NEVER CAME OFF.
"WELL.
"MOST OF 'EM ANYWAY.
"WHEN THE HAMMER CAME DOWN, THEY KNEW WHAT THEY COULD--
KILL TONY STARK.
"--AND COULDN'T--
"--EXPECT FROM ME.
"AND WHEN IT REALLY STARTED TO COME DOWN...
TONY. OBADIAH STANE.
I WANT TO BUY YOUR COMPANY.
"OF COURSE I'D LET THEM DOWN. IT'S WHAT I DID. THEY KNEW IT AND SAW IT COMING.
"SO I JUST KEPT WORKING AND STOCKPILING GET-OUT-OF-JAIL-FREE CARDS AND I.O.U.s AS QUICK AS I COULD.
"THAT WAS MY ESCAPE PLAN. THAT WAS MY RETIREMENT.
"MORE SHELLS TO DISAPPEAR INSIDE.

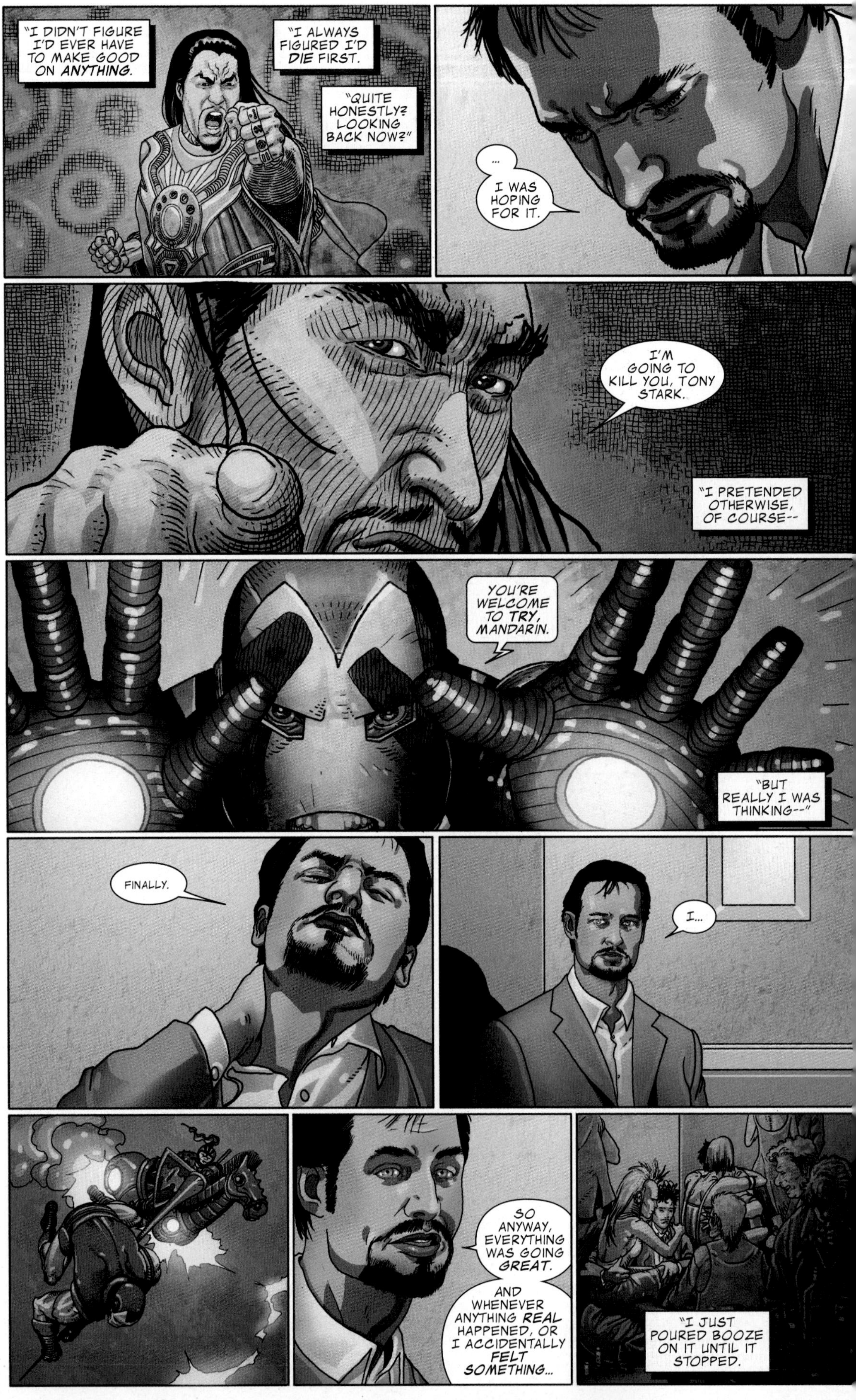
"I DIDN'T FIGURE I'D EVER HAVE TO MAKE GOOD ON ANYTHING.
"I ALWAYS FIGURED I'D DIE FIRST.
"QUITE HONESTLY? LOOKING BACK NOW?"
... I WAS HOPING FOR IT.
I'M GOING TO KILL YOU, TONY STARK.
"I PRETENDED OTHERWISE, OF COURSE--
YOU'RE WELCOME TO TRY, MANDARIN.
"BUT REALLY I WAS THINKING--"
FINALLY.
I...
SO ANYWAY, EVERYTHING WAS GOING GREAT.
AND WHENEVER ANYTHING REAL HAPPENED, OR I ACCIDENTALLY FELT SOMETHING...
"I JUST POURED BOOZE ON IT UNTIL IT STOPPED.

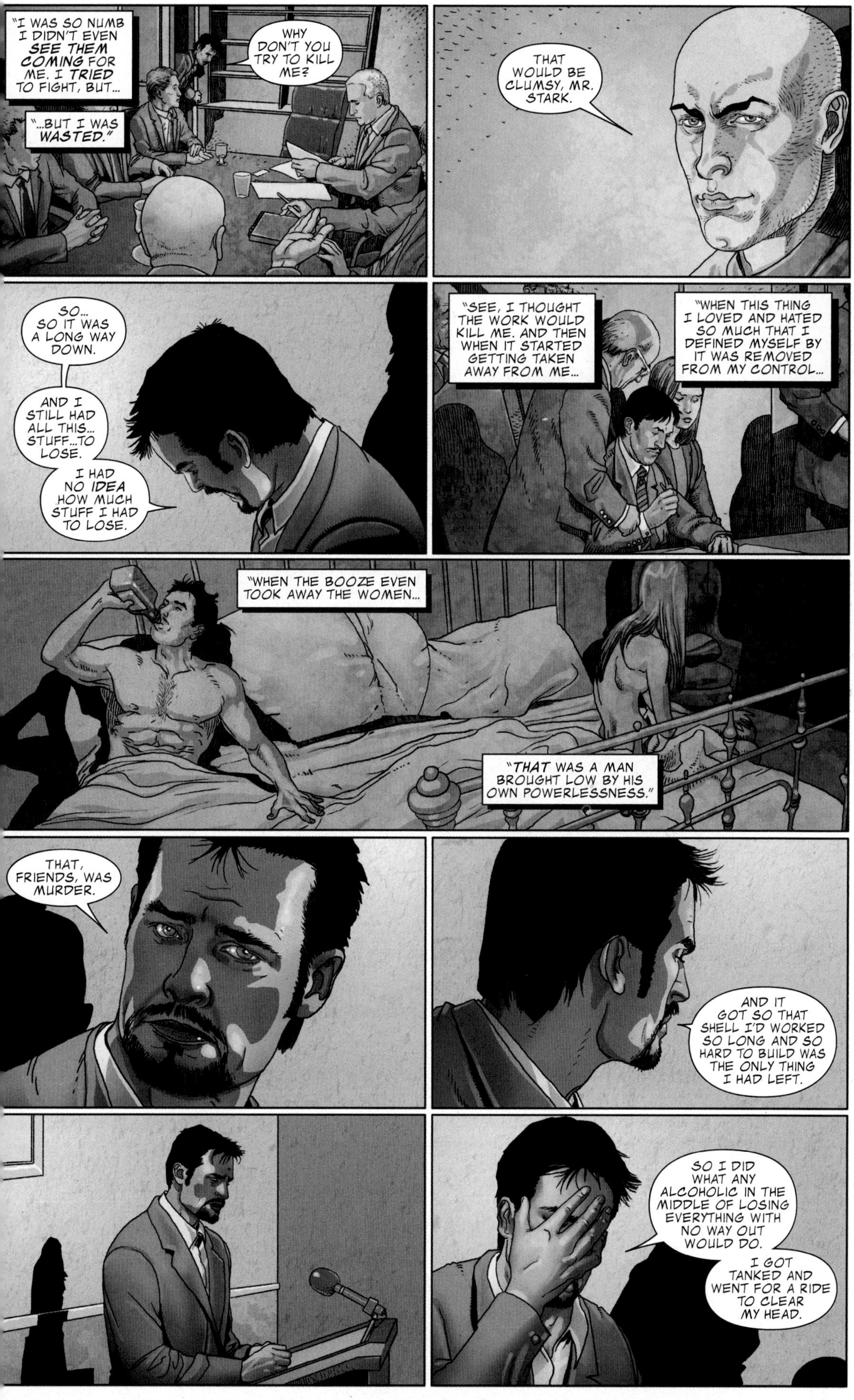
"I WAS SO NUMB I DIDN'T EVEN SEE THEM COMING FOR ME. I TRIED TO FIGHT, BUT...
"...BUT I WAS WASTED."
WHY DON'T YOU TRY TO KILL ME?
THAT WOULD BE CLUMSY, MR. STARK.
SO... SO IT WAS A LONG WAY DOWN.
AND I STILL HAD ALL THIS... STUFF...TO LOSE.
I HAD NO IDEA HOW MUCH STUFF I HAD TO LOSE.
"SEE, I THOUGHT THE WORK WOULD KILL ME. AND THEN WHEN IT STARTED GETTING TAKEN AWAY FROM ME...
"WHEN THIS THING I LOVED AND HATED SO MUCH THAT I DEFINED MYSELF BY IT WAS REMOVED FROM MY CONTROL...
"WHEN THE BOOZE EVEN TOOK AWAY THE WOMEN...
"THAT WAS A MAN BROUGHT LOW BY HIS OWN POWERLESSNESS."
THAT, FRIENDS, WAS MURDER.
AND IT GOT SO THAT SHELL I'D WORKED SO LONG AND SO HARD TO BUILD WAS THE ONLY THING I HAD LEFT.
SO I DID WHAT ANY ALCOHOLIC IN THE MIDDLE OF LOSING EVERYTHING WITH NO WAY OUT WOULD DO.
I GOT TANKED AND WENT FOR A RIDE TO CLEAR MY HEAD.

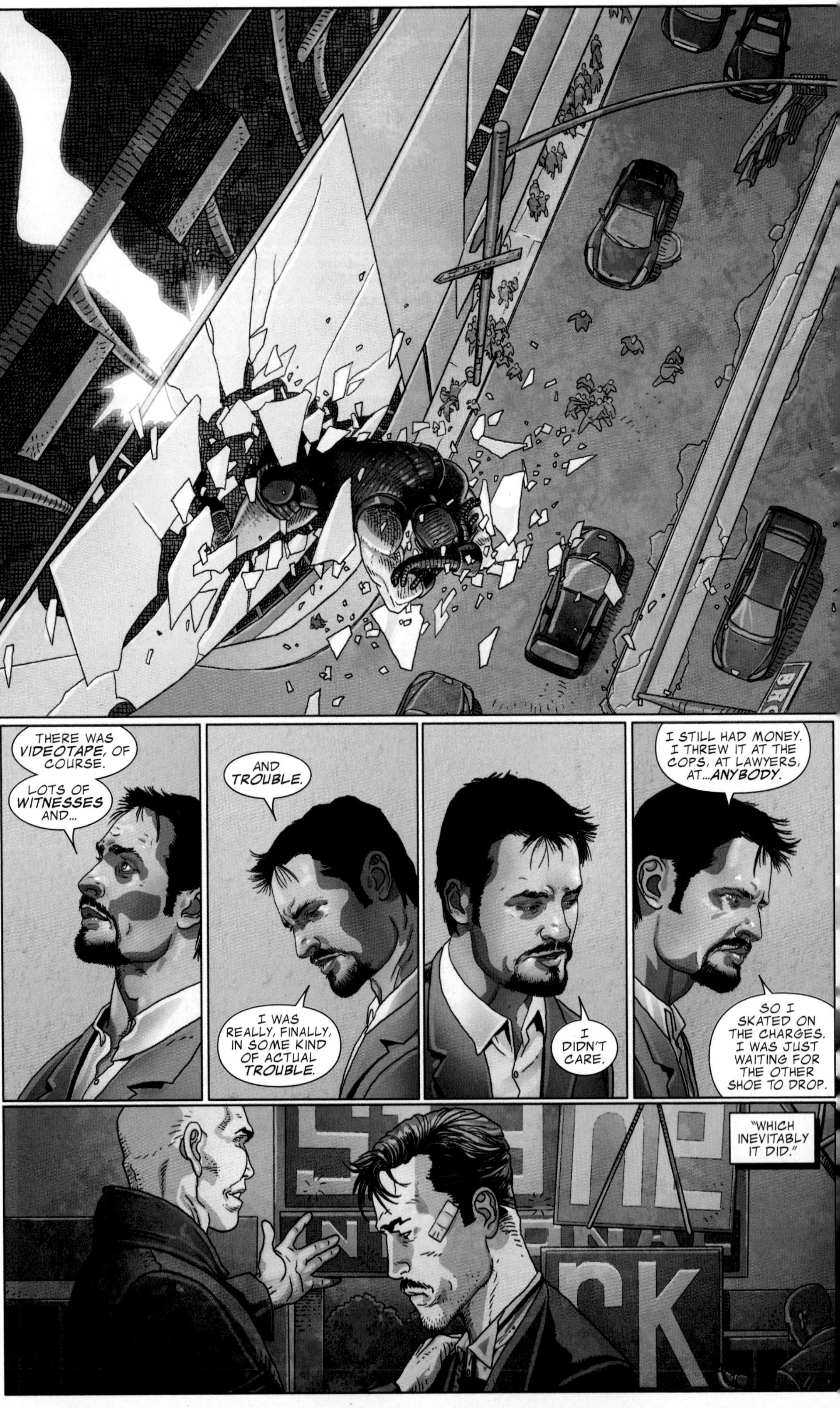
THERE WAS VIDEOTAPE, OF COURSE.
LOTS OF WITNESSES AND...
AND TROUBLE.
I WAS REALLY, FINALLY, IN SOME KIND OF ACTUAL TROUBLE.
I DIDN'T CARE.
I STILL HAD MONEY. I THREW IT AT THE COPS, AT LAWYERS, AT...ANYBODY.
SO I SKATED ON THE CHARGES. I WAS JUST WAITING FOR THE OTHER SHOE TO DROP.
"WHICH INEVITABLY IT DID."

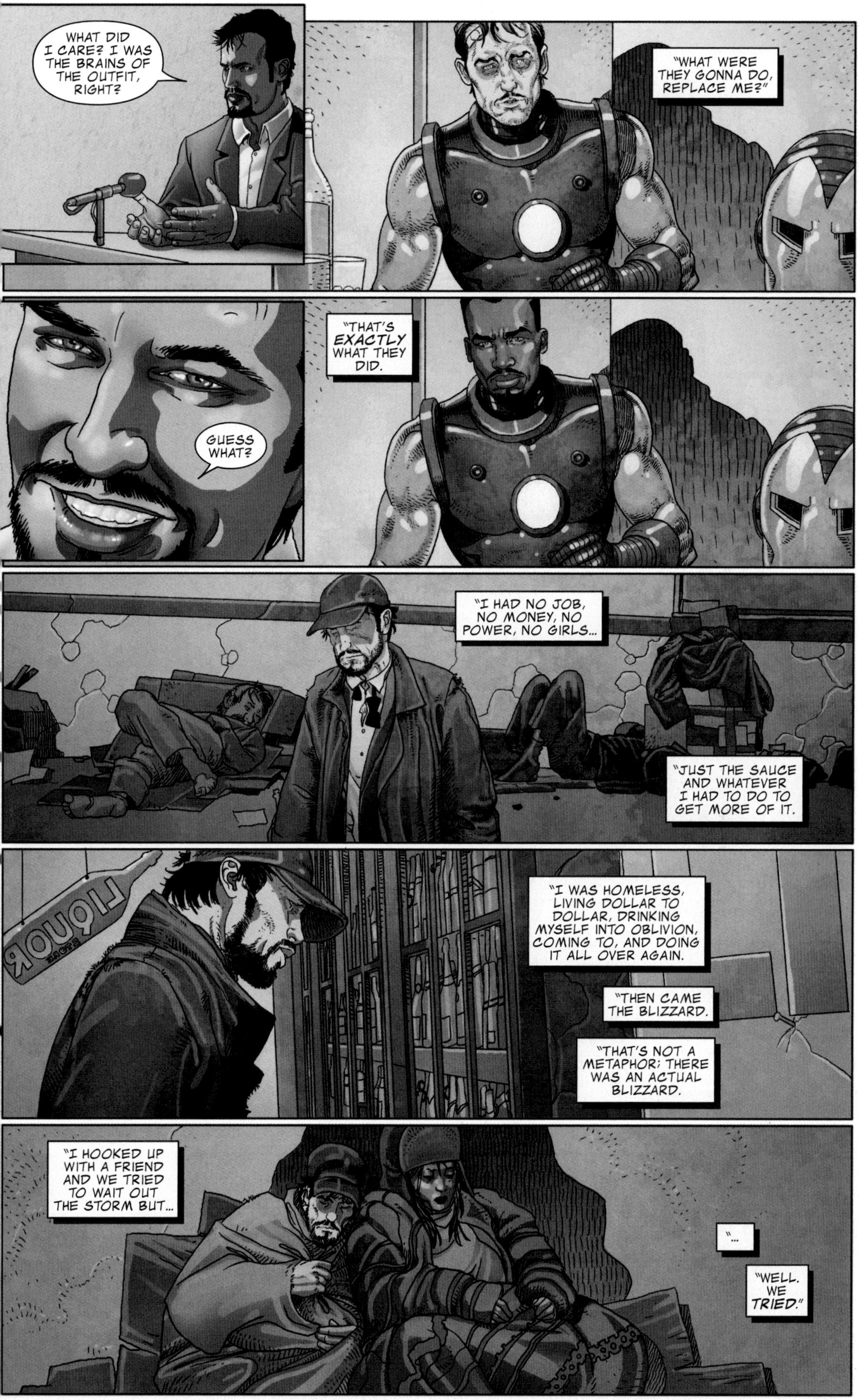
WHAT DID I CARE? I WAS THE BRAINS OF THE OUTFIT, RIGHT?
"WHAT WERE THEY GONNA DO, REPLACE ME?"
"THAT'S *EXACTLY* WHAT THEY DID.
GUESS WHAT?
"I HAD NO JOB, NO MONEY, NO POWER, NO GIRLS...
"JUST THE SAUCE AND WHATEVER I HAD TO DO TO GET MORE OF IT.
LIQUOR
"I WAS HOMELESS, LIVING DOLLAR TO DOLLAR, DRINKING MYSELF INTO OBLIVION, COMING TO, AND DOING IT ALL OVER AGAIN.
"THEN CAME THE BLIZZARD.
"THAT'S NOT A METAPHOR; THERE WAS AN ACTUAL BLIZZARD.
"I HOOKED UP WITH A FRIEND AND WE TRIED TO WAIT OUT THE STORM BUT...
"...
"WELL. WE *TRIED*."

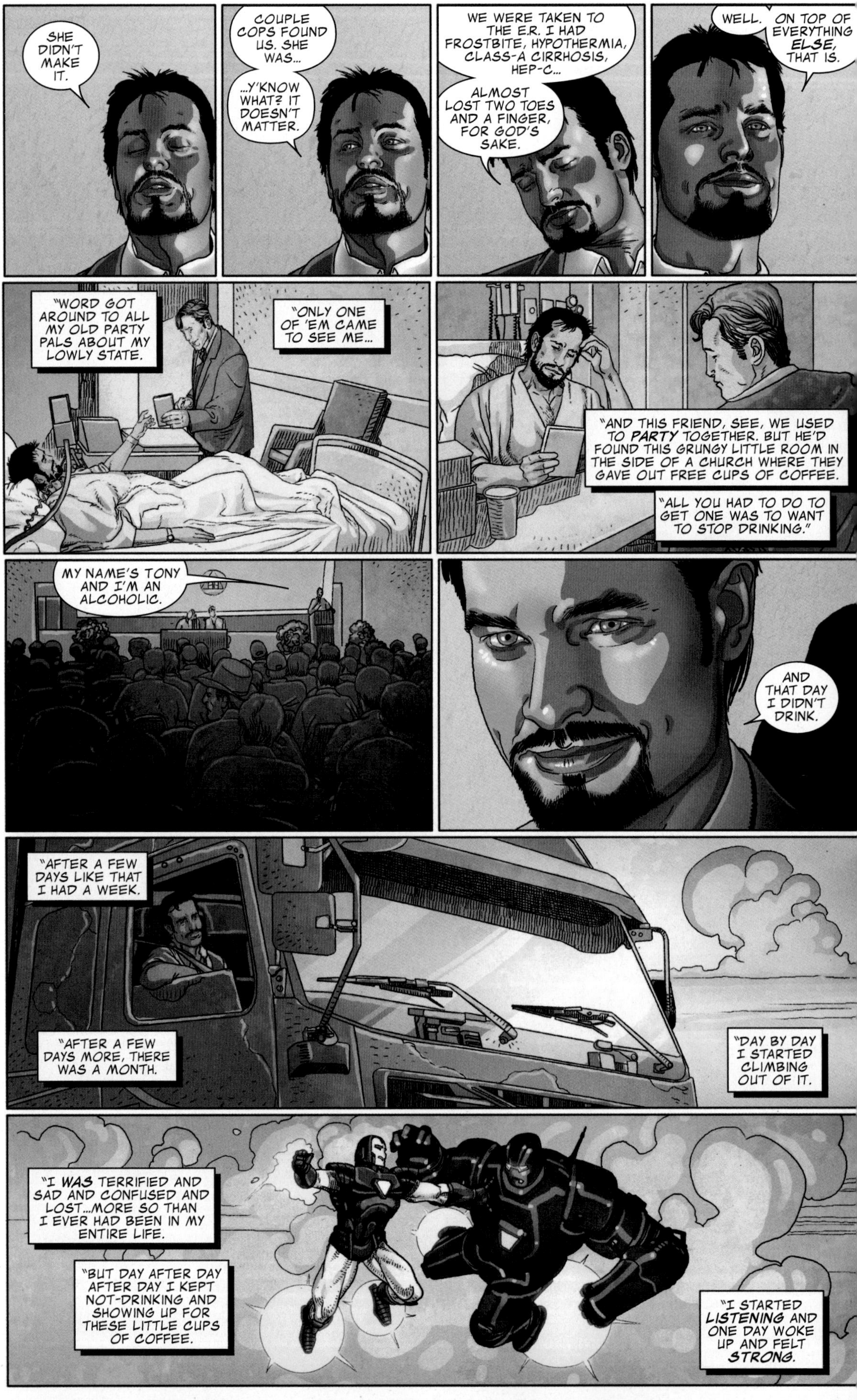

SHE DIDN'T MAKE IT.
COUPLE COPS FOUND US. SHE WAS...
...Y'KNOW WHAT? IT DOESN'T MATTER.
WE WERE TAKEN TO THE E.R. I HAD FROSTBITE, HYPOTHERMIA, CLASS-A CIRRHOSIS, HEP-C...
ALMOST LOST TWO TOES AND A FINGER, FOR GOD'S SAKE.
WELL.
ON TOP OF EVERYTHING ELSE, THAT IS.
"WORD GOT AROUND TO ALL MY OLD PARTY PALS ABOUT MY LOWLY STATE.
"ONLY ONE OF 'EM CAME TO SEE ME...
"AND THIS FRIEND, SEE, WE USED TO PARTY TOGETHER. BUT HE'D FOUND THIS GRUNGY LITTLE ROOM IN THE SIDE OF A CHURCH WHERE THEY GAVE OUT FREE CUPS OF COFFEE.
"ALL YOU HAD TO DO TO GET ONE WAS TO WANT TO STOP DRINKING."
MY NAME'S TONY AND I'M AN ALCOHOLIC.
AND THAT DAY I DIDN'T DRINK.
"AFTER A FEW DAYS LIKE THAT I HAD A WEEK.
"AFTER A FEW DAYS MORE, THERE WAS A MONTH.
"DAY BY DAY I STARTED CLIMBING OUT OF IT.
"I WAS TERRIFIED AND SAD AND CONFUSED AND LOST...MORE SO THAN I EVER HAD BEEN IN MY ENTIRE LIFE.
"BUT DAY AFTER DAY AFTER DAY I KEPT NOT-DRINKING AND SHOWING UP FOR THESE LITTLE CUPS OF COFFEE.
"I STARTED LISTENING AND ONE DAY WOKE UP AND FELT STRONG.

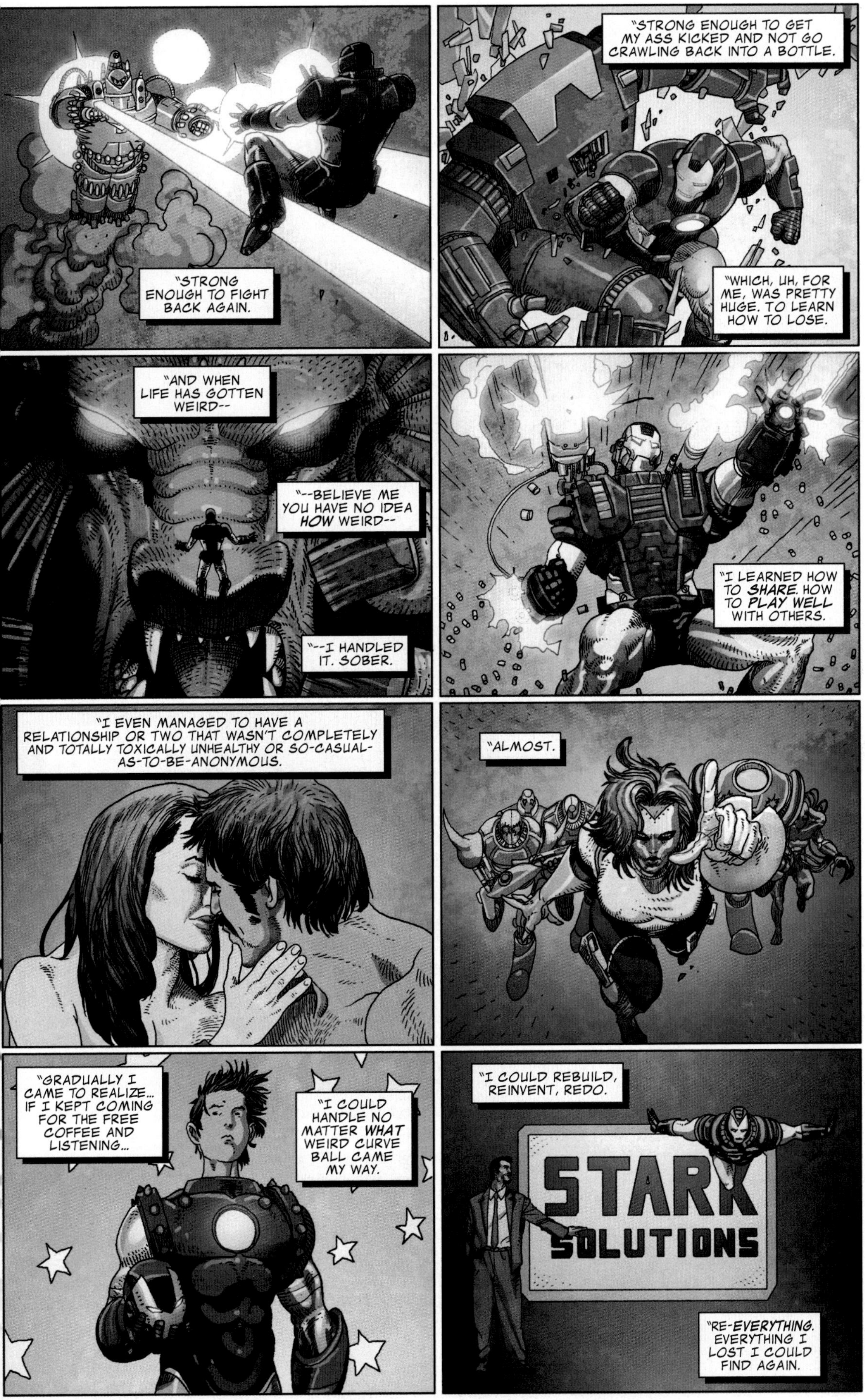
"STRONG ENOUGH TO FIGHT BACK AGAIN.
"STRONG ENOUGH TO GET MY ASS KICKED AND NOT GO CRAWLING BACK INTO A BOTTLE.
"WHICH, UH, FOR ME, WAS PRETTY HUGE. TO LEARN HOW TO LOSE.
"AND WHEN LIFE HAS GOTTEN WEIRD--
"--BELIEVE ME YOU HAVE NO IDEA *HOW* WEIRD--
"--I HANDLED IT. SOBER.
"I LEARNED HOW TO **SHARE**. HOW TO **PLAY WELL** WITH OTHERS.
"I EVEN MANAGED TO HAVE A RELATIONSHIP OR TWO THAT WASN'T COMPLETELY AND TOTALLY TOXICALLY UNHEALTHY OR SO-CASUAL-AS-TO-BE-ANONYMOUS.
"ALMOST.
"GRADUALLY I CAME TO REALIZE... IF I KEPT COMING FOR THE FREE COFFEE AND LISTENING...
"I COULD HANDLE NO MATTER *WHAT* WEIRD CURVE BALL CAME MY WAY.
"I COULD REBUILD, REINVENT, REDO.
STARK SOLUTIONS
"RE-*EVERYTHING*. EVERYTHING I LOST I COULD FIND AGAIN.

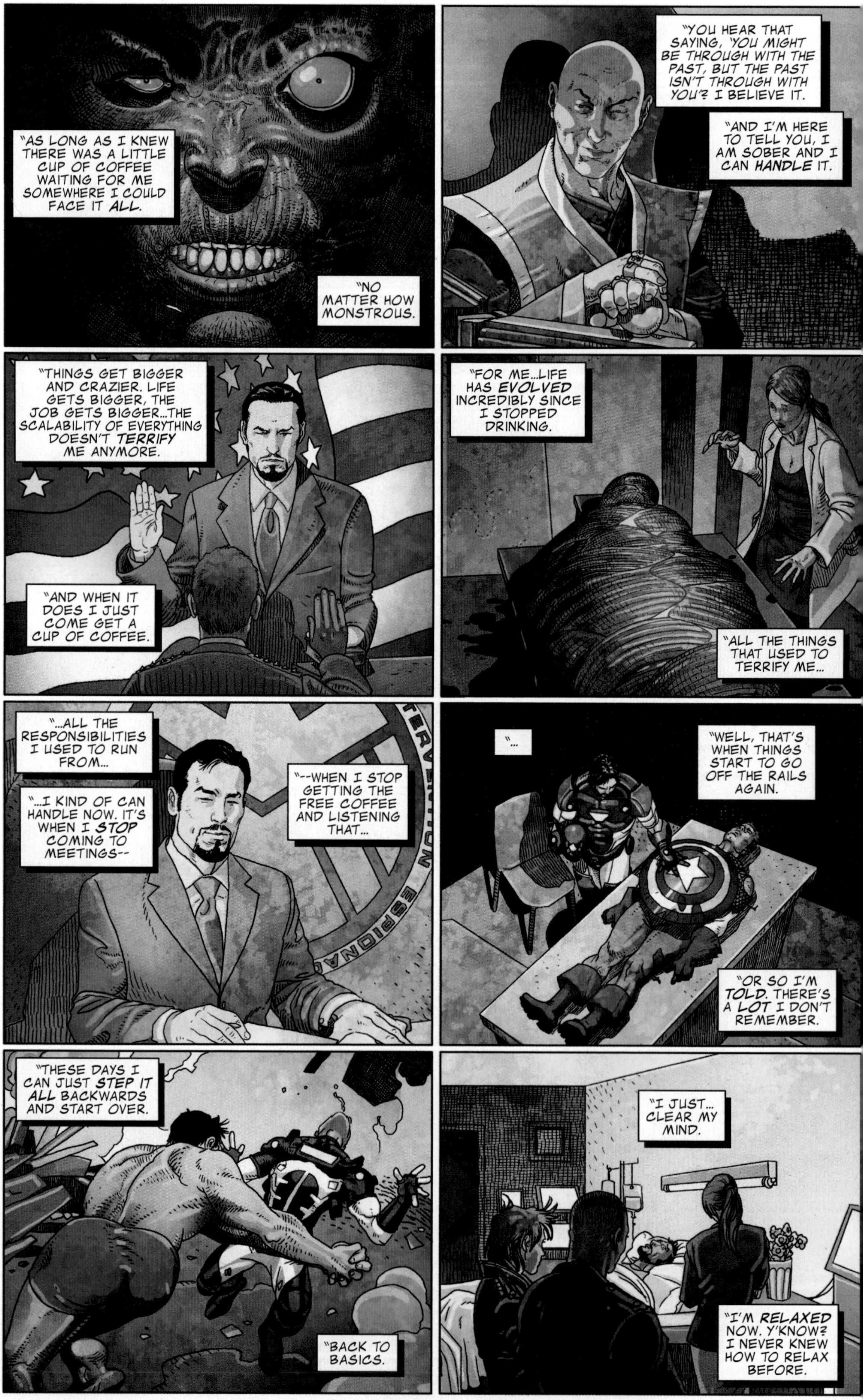
"AS LONG AS I KNEW THERE WAS A LITTLE CUP OF COFFEE WAITING FOR ME SOMEWHERE I COULD FACE IT ALL.
"NO MATTER HOW MONSTROUS.
"YOU HEAR THAT SAYING, 'YOU MIGHT BE THROUGH WITH THE PAST, BUT THE PAST ISN'T THROUGH WITH YOU'? I BELIEVE IT.
"AND I'M HERE TO TELL YOU, I AM SOBER AND I CAN HANDLE IT.
"THINGS GET BIGGER AND CRAZIER. LIFE GETS BIGGER, THE JOB GETS BIGGER...THE SCALABILITY OF EVERYTHING DOESN'T TERRIFY ME ANYMORE.
"AND WHEN IT DOES I JUST COME GET A CUP OF COFFEE.
"FOR ME...LIFE HAS EVOLVED INCREDIBLY SINCE I STOPPED DRINKING.
"ALL THE THINGS THAT USED TO TERRIFY ME...
"...ALL THE RESPONSIBILITIES I USED TO RUN FROM...
"...I KIND OF CAN HANDLE NOW. IT'S WHEN I STOP COMING TO MEETINGS--
"--WHEN I STOP GETTING THE FREE COFFEE AND LISTENING THAT...
"...
"WELL, THAT'S WHEN THINGS START TO GO OFF THE RAILS AGAIN.
"OR SO I'M TOLD. THERE'S A LOT I DON'T REMEMBER.
"THESE DAYS I CAN JUST STEP IT ALL BACKWARDS AND START OVER.
"BACK TO BASICS.
"I JUST... CLEAR MY MIND.
"I'M RELAXED NOW. Y'KNOW? I NEVER KNEW HOW TO RELAX BEFORE.

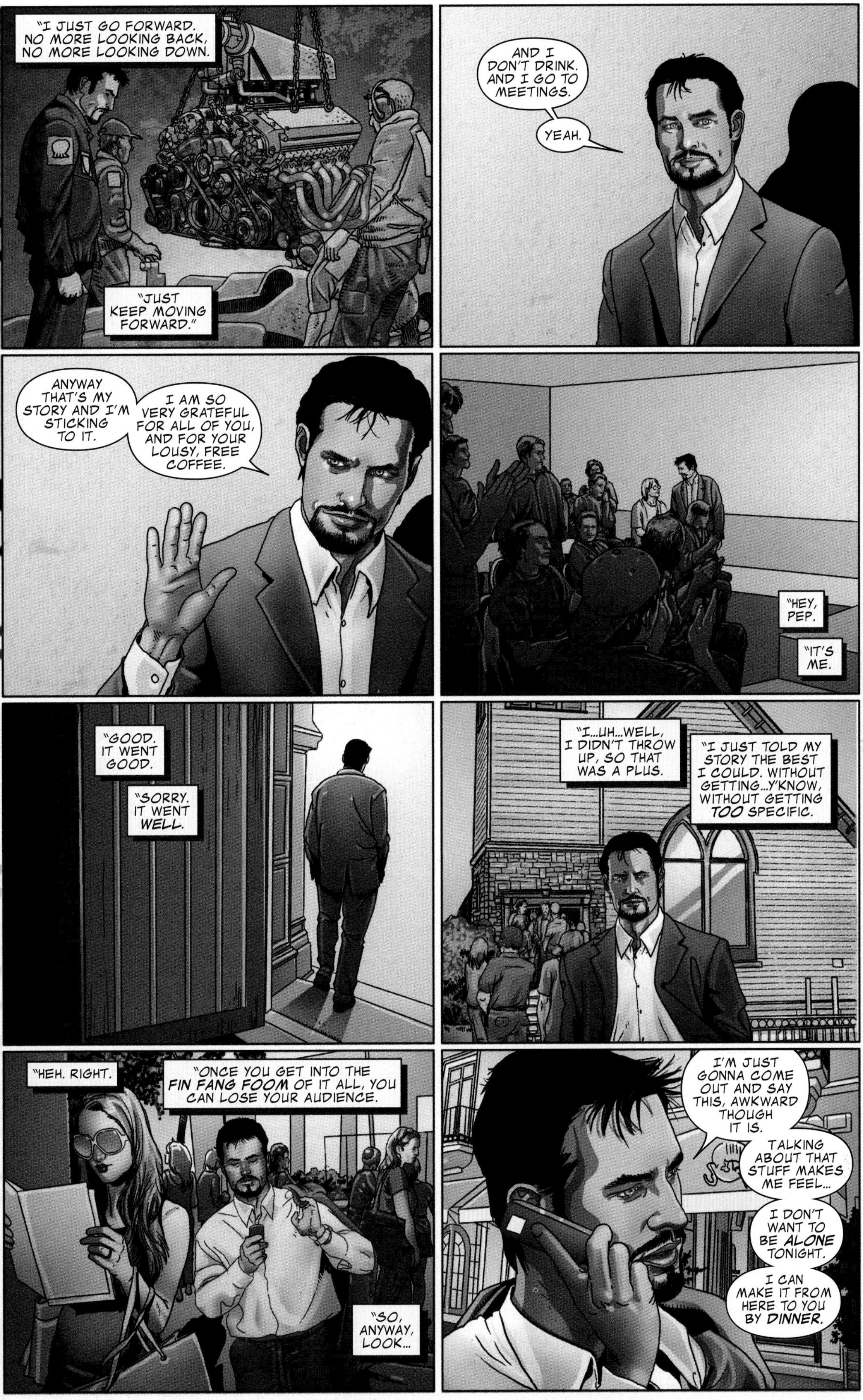
"I JUST GO FORWARD. NO MORE LOOKING BACK, NO MORE LOOKING DOWN.
"JUST KEEP MOVING FORWARD."
AND I DON'T DRINK. AND I GO TO MEETINGS.
YEAH.
ANYWAY THAT'S MY STORY AND I'M STICKING TO IT.
I AM SO VERY GRATEFUL FOR ALL OF YOU, AND FOR YOUR LOUSY, FREE COFFEE.
"HEY, PEP.
"IT'S ME.
"GOOD. IT WENT GOOD.
"SORRY. IT WENT WELL.
"I...UH...WELL, I DIDN'T THROW UP, SO THAT WAS A PLUS.
"I JUST TOLD MY STORY THE BEST I COULD. WITHOUT GETTING...Y'KNOW, WITHOUT GETTING TOO SPECIFIC.
"HEH. RIGHT.
"ONCE YOU GET INTO THE FIN FANG FOOM OF IT ALL, YOU CAN LOSE YOUR AUDIENCE.
"SO, ANYWAY, LOOK...
I'M JUST GONNA COME OUT AND SAY THIS, AWKWARD THOUGH IT IS.
TALKING ABOUT THAT STUFF MAKES ME FEEL...
I DON'T WANT TO BE ALONE TONIGHT.
I CAN MAKE IT FROM HERE TO YOU BY DINNER.

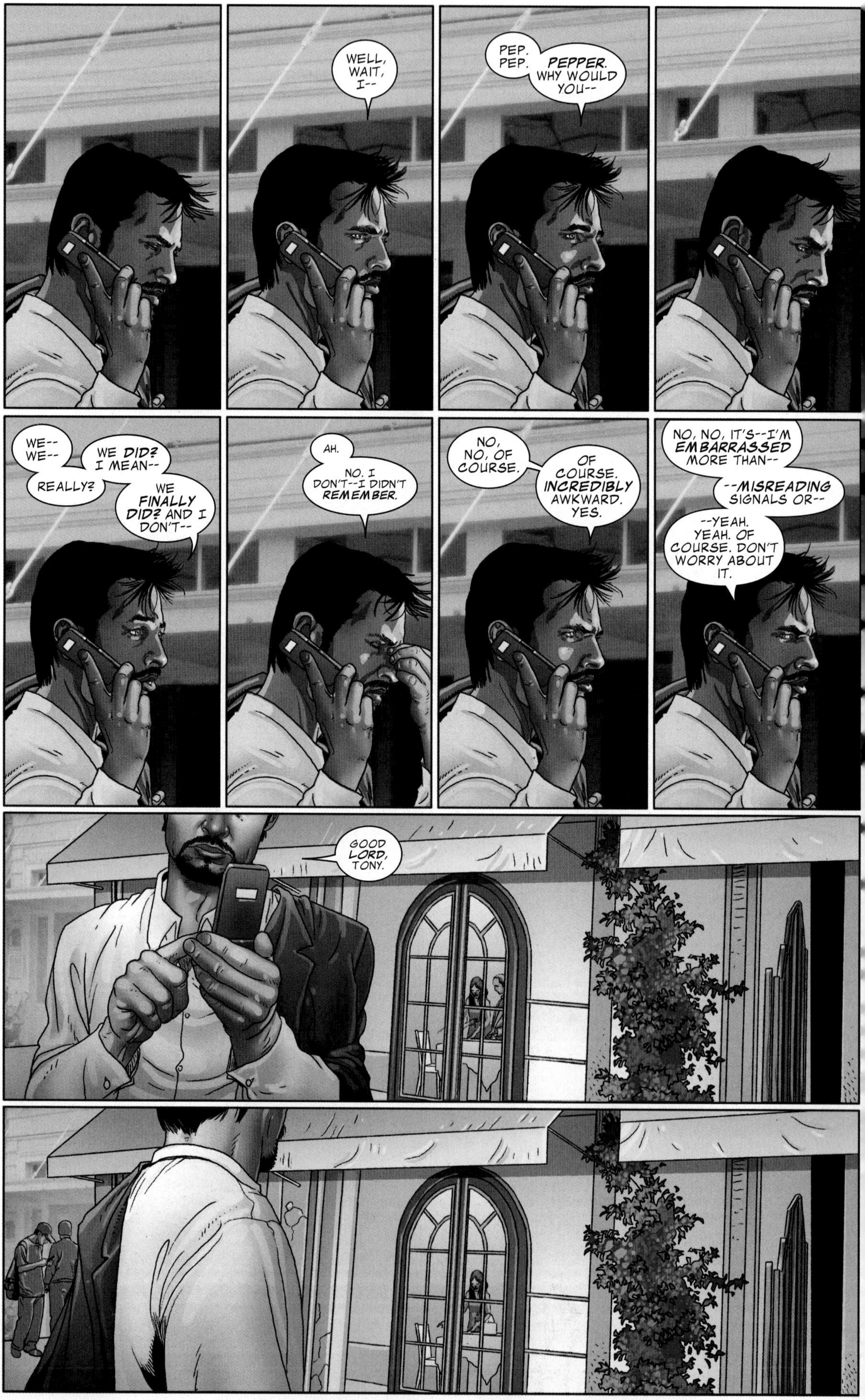
WELL, WAIT, I--
PEP. PEP.
PEPPER. WHY WOULD YOU--
WE-- WE--
WE DID? I MEAN--
REALLY?
WE FINALLY DID? AND I DON'T--
AH.
NO. I DON'T--I DIDN'T REMEMBER.
NO, NO, OF COURSE.
OF COURSE. INCREDIBLY AWKWARD. YES.
NO, NO, IT'S--I'M EMBARRASSED MORE THAN--
--MISREADING SIGNALS OR--
--YEAH. YEAH. OF COURSE. DON'T WORRY ABOUT IT.
GOOD LORD, TONY.

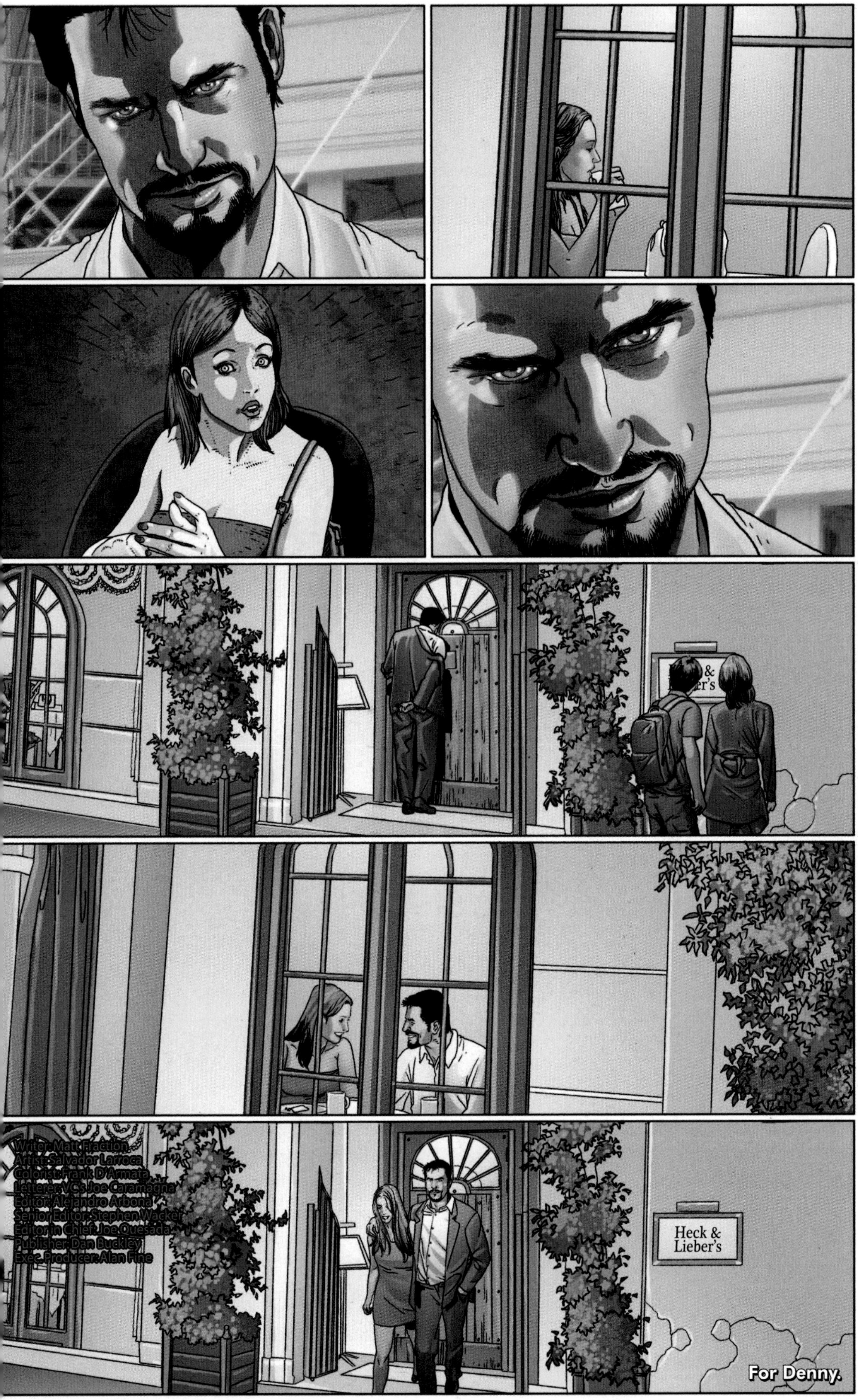
Heck &
Lieber's
Writer: Matt Fraction
Artist: Salvador Larroca
Colorist: Frank D'Armata
Letterer: VC's Joe Caramagna
Editor: Alejandro Arbona
Senior Editor: Stephen Wacker
Editor in Chief: Joe Quesada
Publisher: Dan Buckley
Exec. Producer: Alan Fine
Heck &
Lieber's
For Denny.

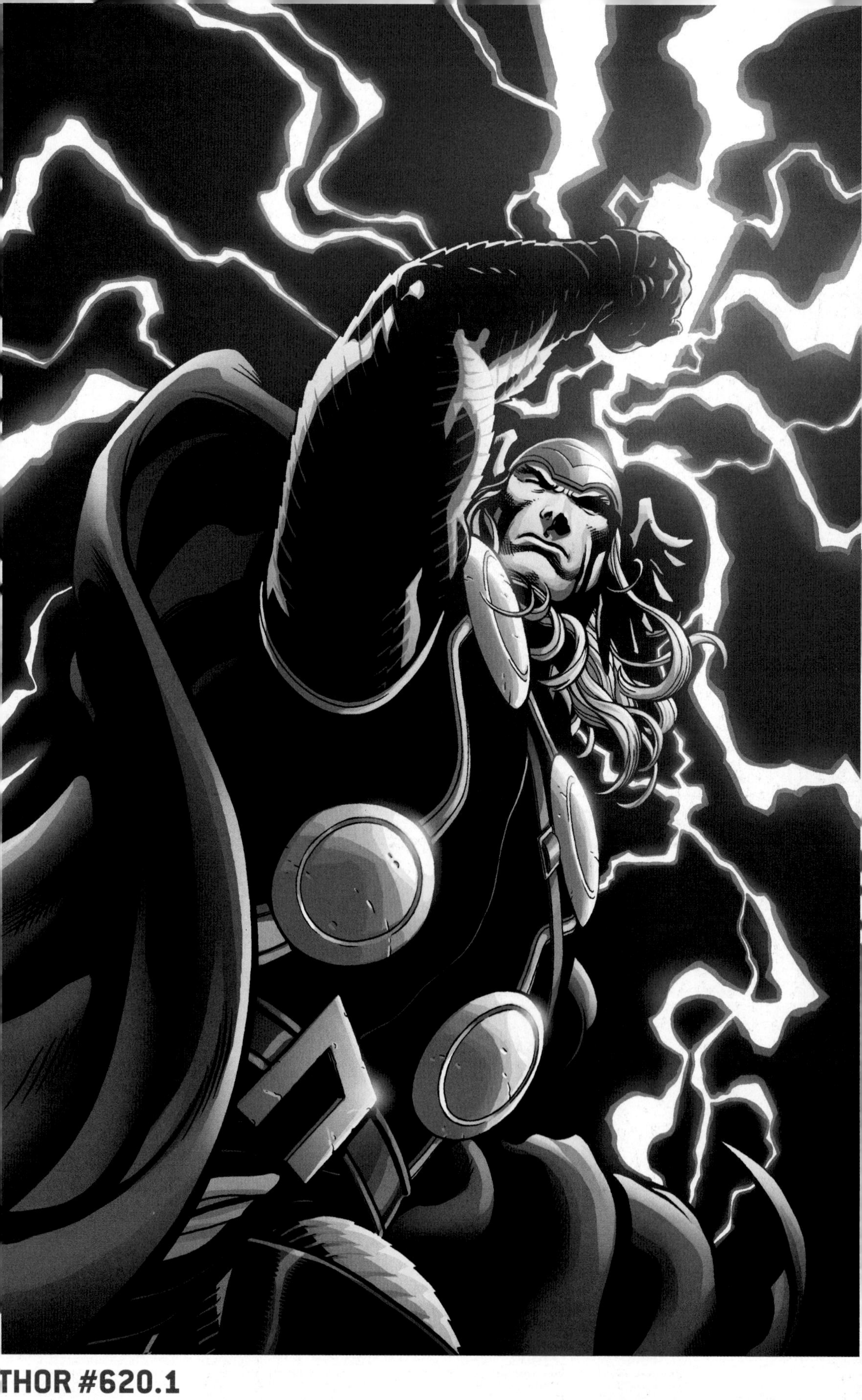

THOR #620.1

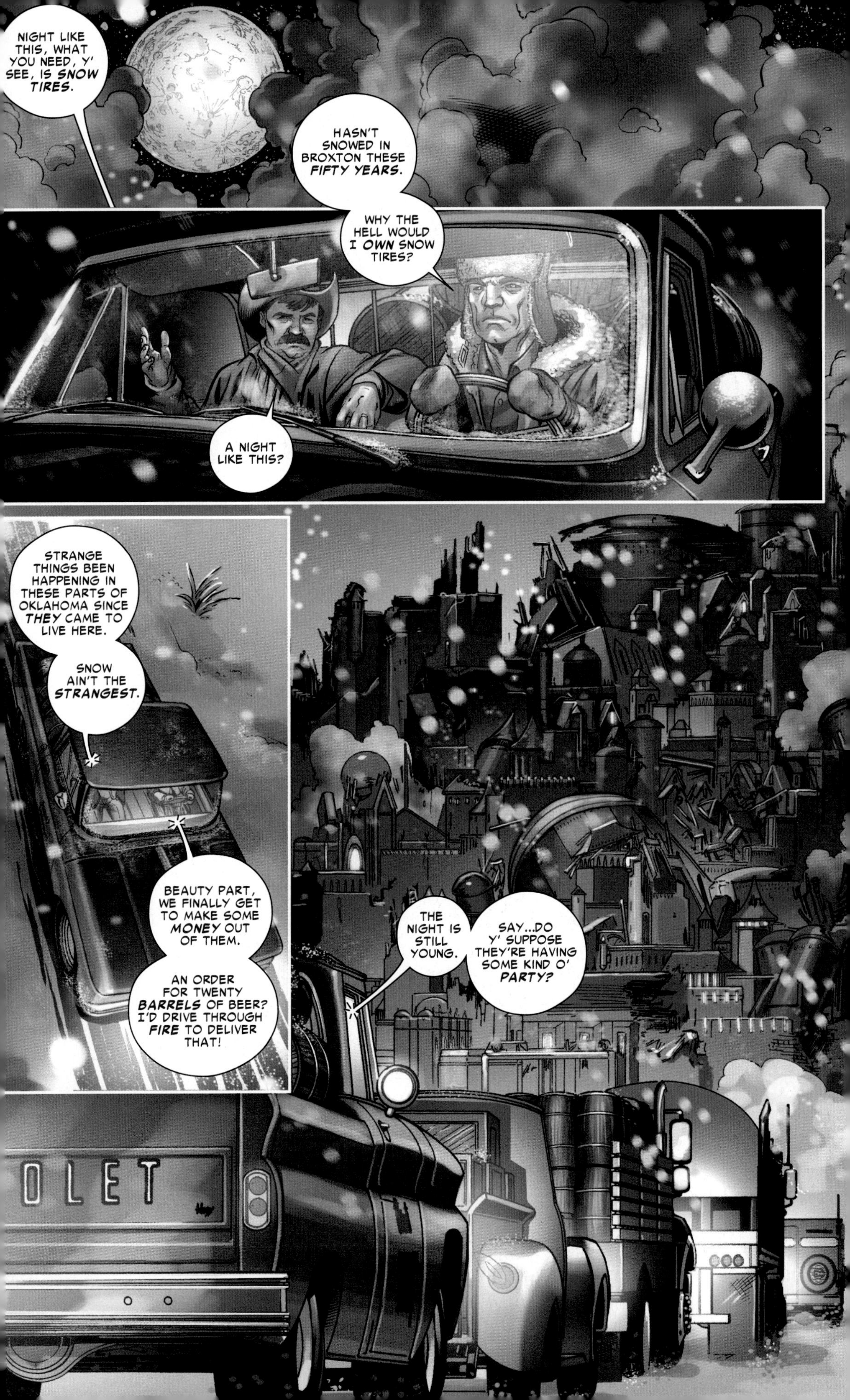
NIGHT LIKE THIS, WHAT YOU NEED, Y' SEE, IS SNOW TIRES.
HASN'T SNOWED IN BROXTON THESE FIFTY YEARS.
WHY THE HELL WOULD I OWN SNOW TIRES?
A NIGHT LIKE THIS?
STRANGE THINGS BEEN HAPPENING IN THESE PARTS OF OKLAHOMA SINCE THEY CAME TO LIVE HERE.
SNOW AIN'T THE STRANGEST.
BEAUTY PART, WE FINALLY GET TO MAKE SOME MONEY OUT OF THEM.
AN ORDER FOR TWENTY BARRELS OF BEER? I'D DRIVE THROUGH FIRE TO DELIVER THAT!
THE NIGHT IS STILL YOUNG.
SAY...DO Y' SUPPOSE THEY'RE HAVING SOME KIND O' PARTY?
OLET

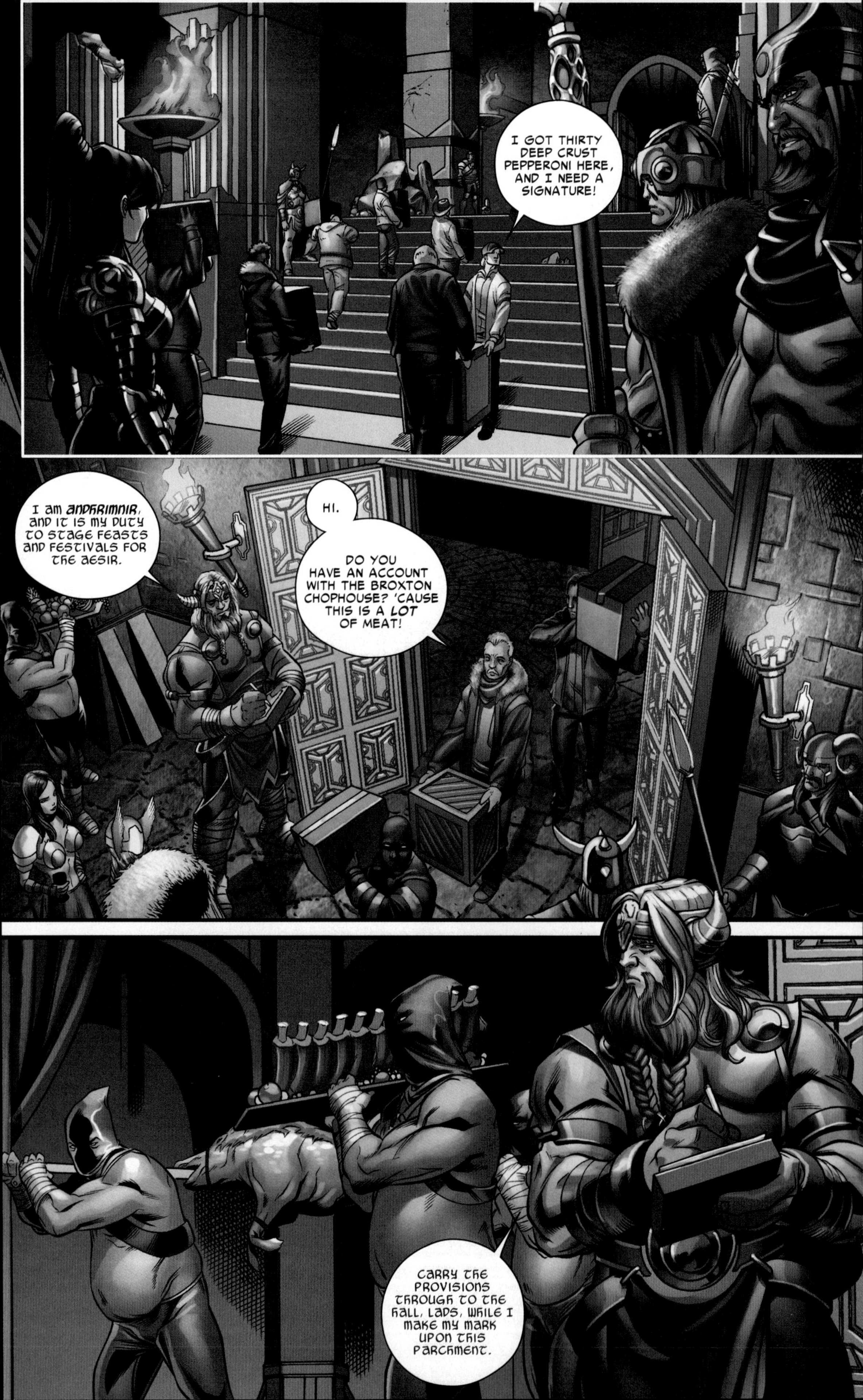
I GOT THIRTY DEEP CRUST PEPPERONI HERE, AND I NEED A SIGNATURE!
I AM ANDHRIMNIR, AND IT IS MY DUTY TO STAGE FEASTS AND FESTIVALS FOR THE AESIR.
HI.
DO YOU HAVE AN ACCOUNT WITH THE BROXTON CHOPHOUSE? 'CAUSE THIS IS A LOT OF MEAT!
CARRY THE PROVISIONS THROUGH TO THE HALL, LADS, WHILE I MAKE MY MARK UPON THIS PARCHMENT.

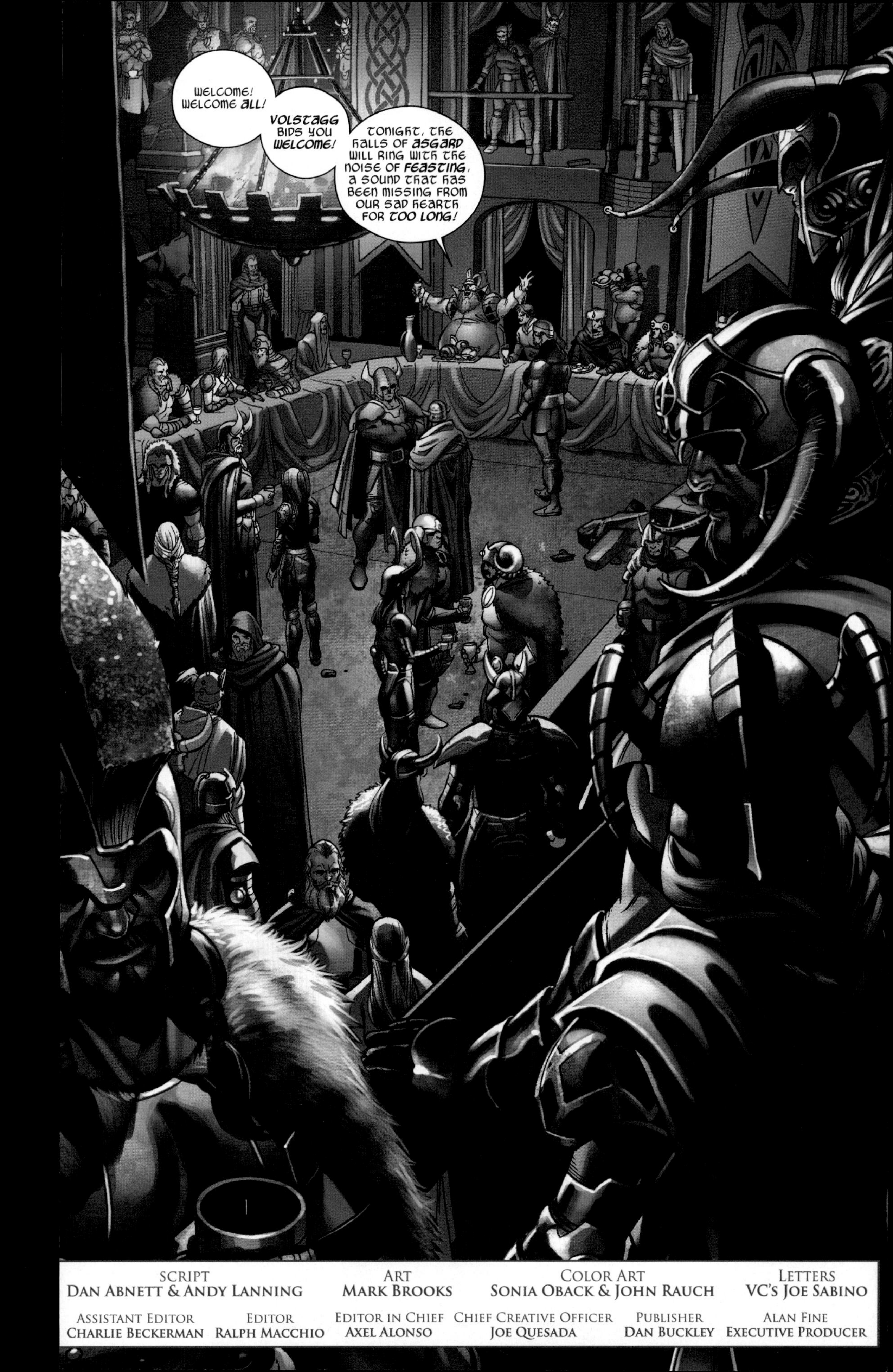
WELCOME! WELCOME ALL!
VOLSTAGG BIDS YOU WELCOME!
TONIGHT, THE HALLS OF ASGARD WILL RING WITH THE NOISE OF FEASTING, A SOUND THAT HAS BEEN MISSING FROM OUR SAD HEARTH FOR TOO LONG!

SCRIPT **DAN ABNETT & ANDY LANNING** ART **MARK BROOKS** COLOR ART **SONIA OBACK & JOHN RAUCH** LETTERS **VC's JOE SABINO**

ASSISTANT EDITOR **CHARLIE BECKERMAN** EDITOR **RALPH MACCHIO** EDITOR IN CHIEF **AXEL ALONSO** CHIEF CREATIVE OFFICER **JOE QUESADA** PUBLISHER **DAN BUCKLEY** ALAN FINE **EXECUTIVE PRODUCER**

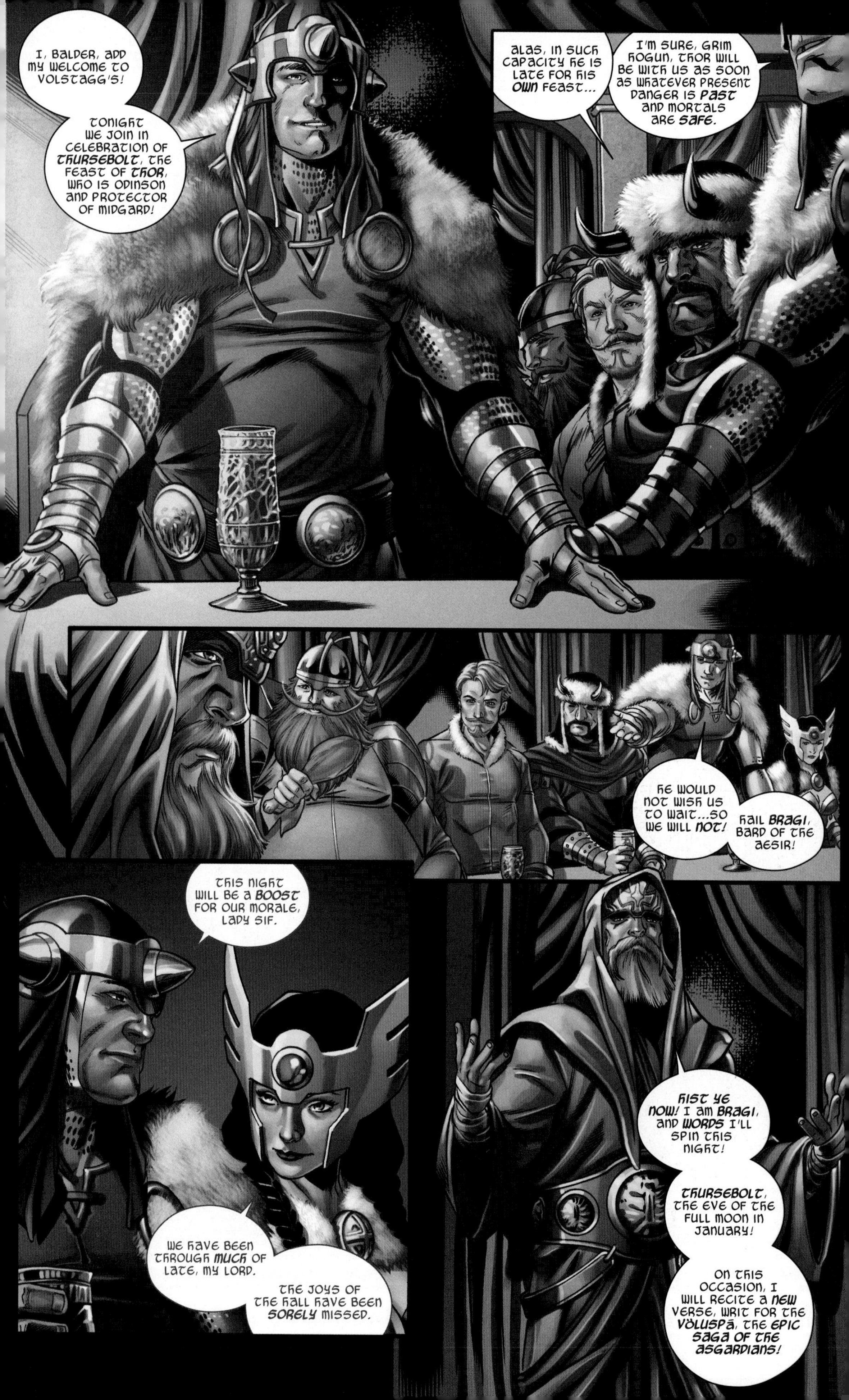
I, BALDER, ADD MY WELCOME TO VOLSTAGG'S!
TONIGHT WE JOIN IN CELEBRATION OF THURSEBOLT, THE FEAST OF THOR, WHO IS ODINSON AND PROTECTOR OF MIDGARD!
ALAS, IN SUCH CAPACITY HE IS LATE FOR HIS OWN FEAST...
I'M SURE, GRIM HOGUN, THOR WILL BE WITH US AS SOON AS WHATEVER PRESENT DANGER IS PAST AND MORTALS ARE SAFE.
HE WOULD NOT WISH US TO WAIT...SO WE WILL NOT!
HAIL BRAGI, BARD OF THE AESIR!
THIS NIGHT WILL BE A BOOST FOR OUR MORALE, LADY SIF.
WE HAVE BEEN THROUGH MUCH OF LATE, MY LORD.
THE JOYS OF THE HALL HAVE BEEN SORELY MISSED.
HIST YE NOW! I AM BRAGI, AND WORDS I'LL SPIN THIS NIGHT!
THURSEBOLT, THE EVE OF THE FULL MOON IN JANUARY!
ON THIS OCCASION, I WILL RECITE A NEW VERSE, WRIT FOR THE VÖLUSPÅ, THE EPIC SAGA OF THE ASGARDIANS!

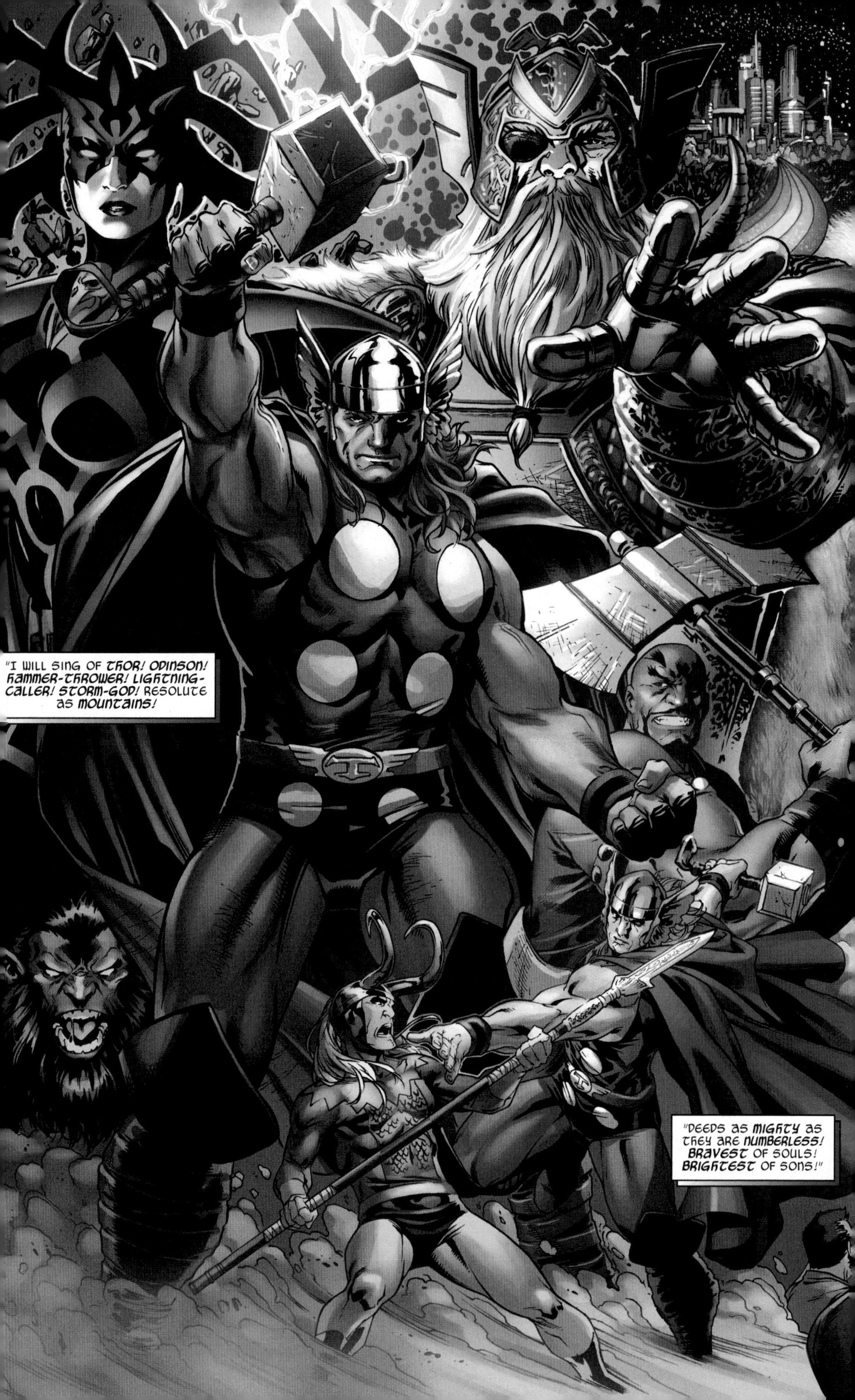
"I WILL SING OF THOR! ODINSON! HAMMER-THROWER! LIGHTNING-CALLER! STORM-GOD! RESOLUTE AS MOUNTAINS!
"DEEDS AS MIGHTY AS THEY ARE NUMBERLESS! BRAVEST OF SOULS! BRIGHTEST OF SONS!"

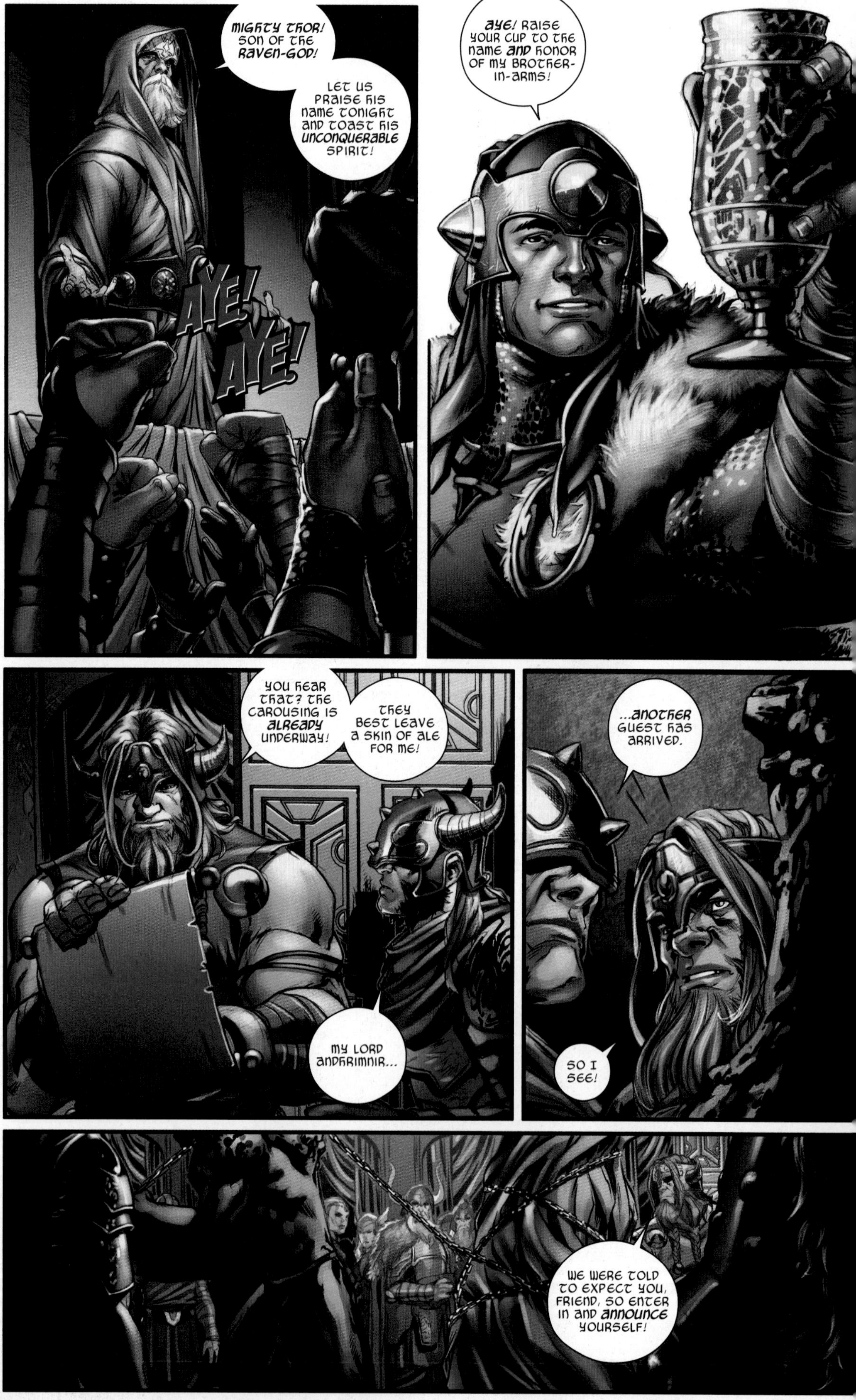
MIGHTY THOR! SON OF THE RAVEN-GOD!
LET US PRAISE HIS NAME TONIGHT AND TOAST HIS UNCONQUERABLE SPIRIT!
AYE! AYE!
AYE! RAISE YOUR CUP TO THE NAME AND HONOR OF MY BROTHER-IN-ARMS!
YOU HEAR THAT? THE CAROUSING IS ALREADY UNDERWAY!
THEY BEST LEAVE A SKIN OF ALE FOR ME!
MY LORD ANDHRIMNIR...
...ANOTHER GUEST HAS ARRIVED.
SO I SEE!
WE WERE TOLD TO EXPECT YOU, FRIEND, SO ENTER IN AND ANNOUNCE YOURSELF!

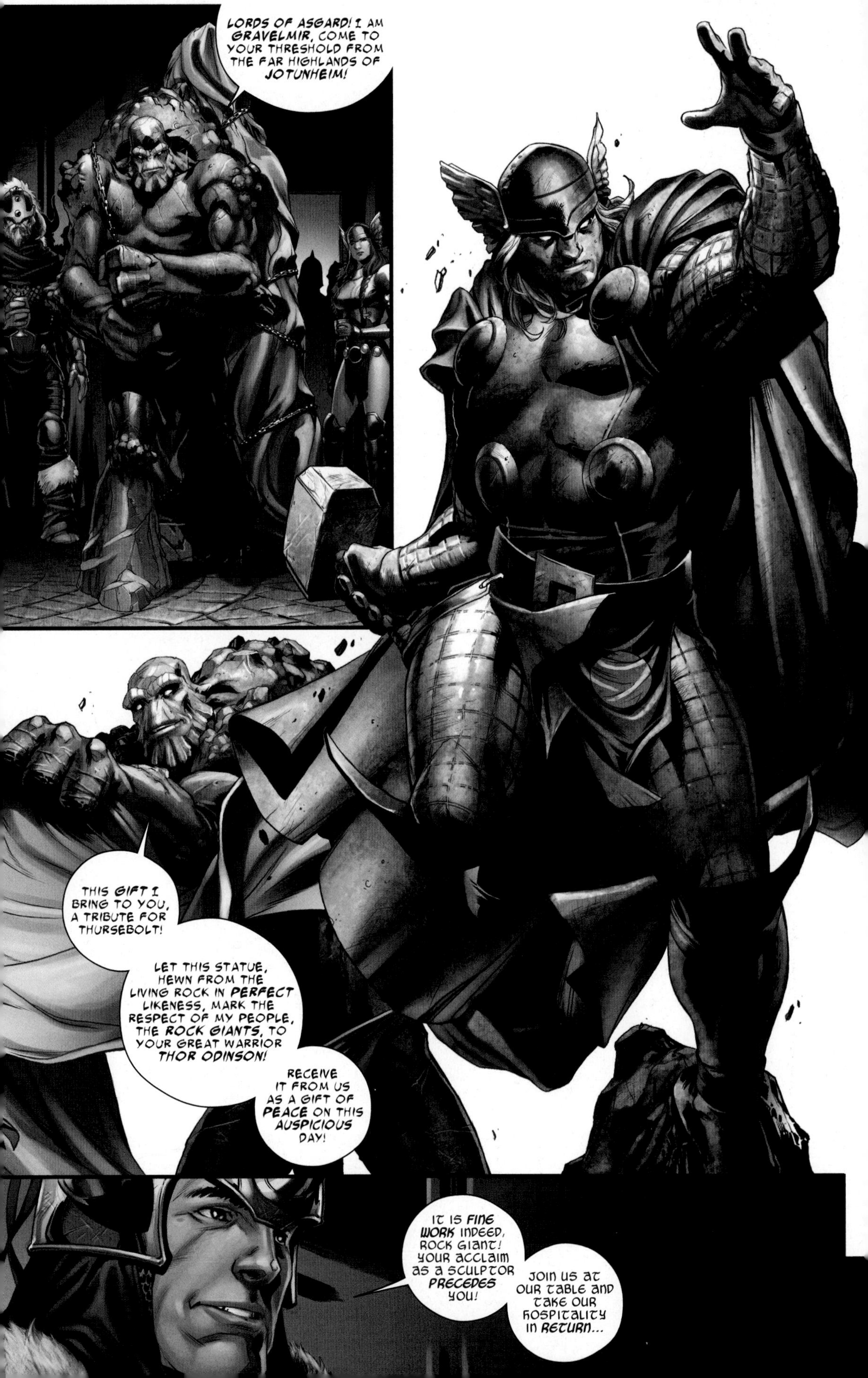
LORDS OF ASGARD! I AM GRAVELMIR, COME TO YOUR THRESHOLD FROM THE FAR HIGHLANDS OF JOTUNHEIM!
THIS GIFT I BRING TO YOU, A TRIBUTE FOR THURSEBOLT!
LET THIS STATUE, HEWN FROM THE LIVING ROCK IN PERFECT LIKENESS, MARK THE RESPECT OF MY PEOPLE, THE ROCK GIANTS, TO YOUR GREAT WARRIOR THOR ODINSON!
RECEIVE IT FROM US AS A GIFT OF PEACE ON THIS AUSPICIOUS DAY!
IT IS FINE WORK INDEED, ROCK GIANT! YOUR ACCLAIM AS A SCULPTOR PRECEDES YOU!
JOIN US AT OUR TABLE AND TAKE OUR HOSPITALITY IN RETURN...

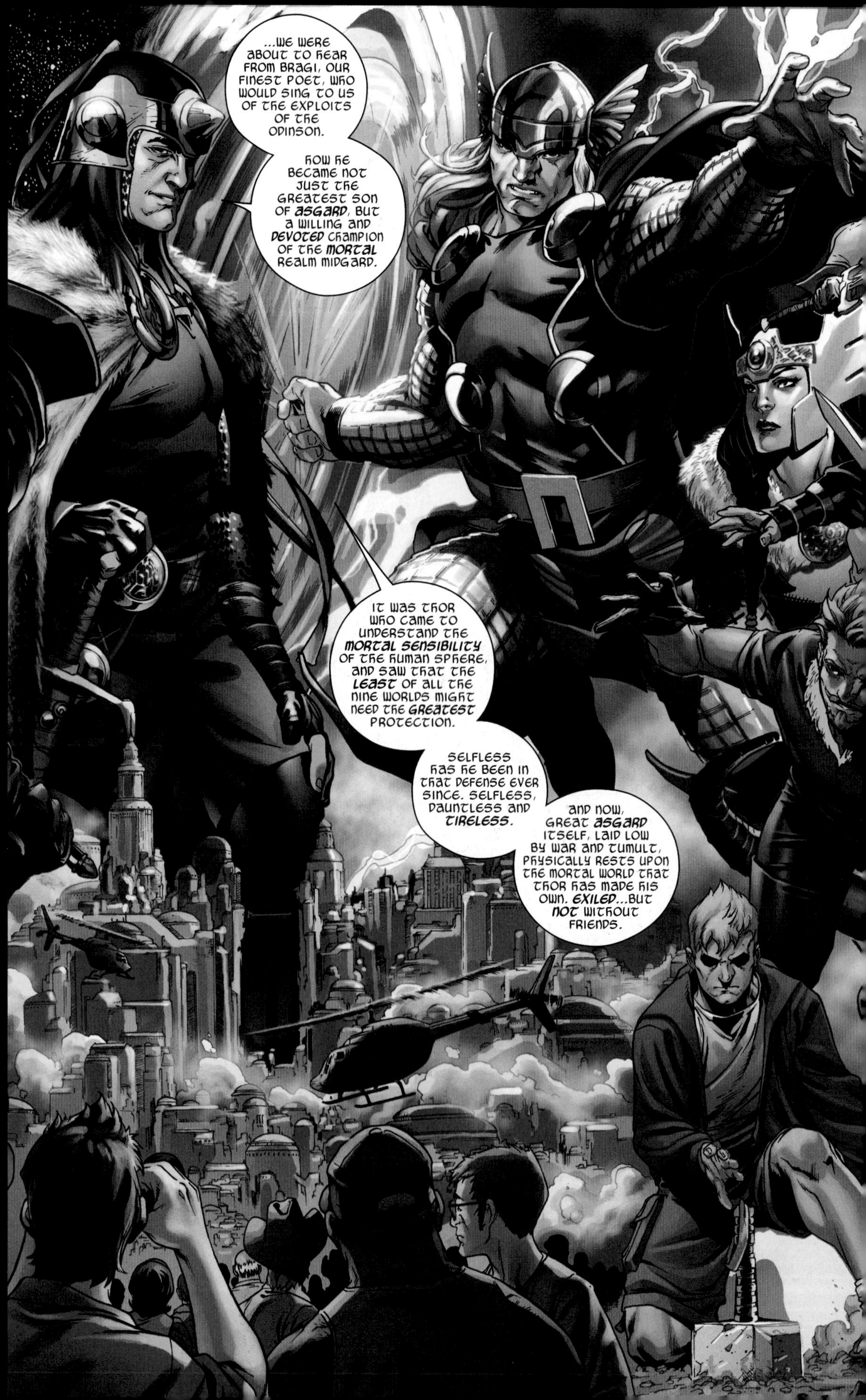
...WE WERE ABOUT TO HEAR FROM BRAGI, OUR FINEST POET, WHO WOULD SING TO US OF THE EXPLOITS OF THE ODINSON.
HOW HE BECAME NOT JUST THE GREATEST SON OF ASGARD, BUT A WILLING AND DEVOTED CHAMPION OF THE MORTAL REALM MIDGARD.
IT WAS THOR WHO CAME TO UNDERSTAND THE MORTAL SENSIBILITY OF THE HUMAN SPHERE, AND SAW THAT THE LEAST OF ALL THE NINE WORLDS MIGHT NEED THE GREATEST PROTECTION.
SELFLESS HAS HE BEEN IN THAT DEFENSE EVER SINCE. SELFLESS, DAUNTLESS AND TIRELESS.
AND NOW, GREAT ASGARD ITSELF, LAID LOW BY WAR AND TUMULT, PHYSICALLY RESTS UPON THE MORTAL WORLD THAT THOR HAS MADE HIS OWN. EXILED...BUT NOT WITHOUT FRIENDS.

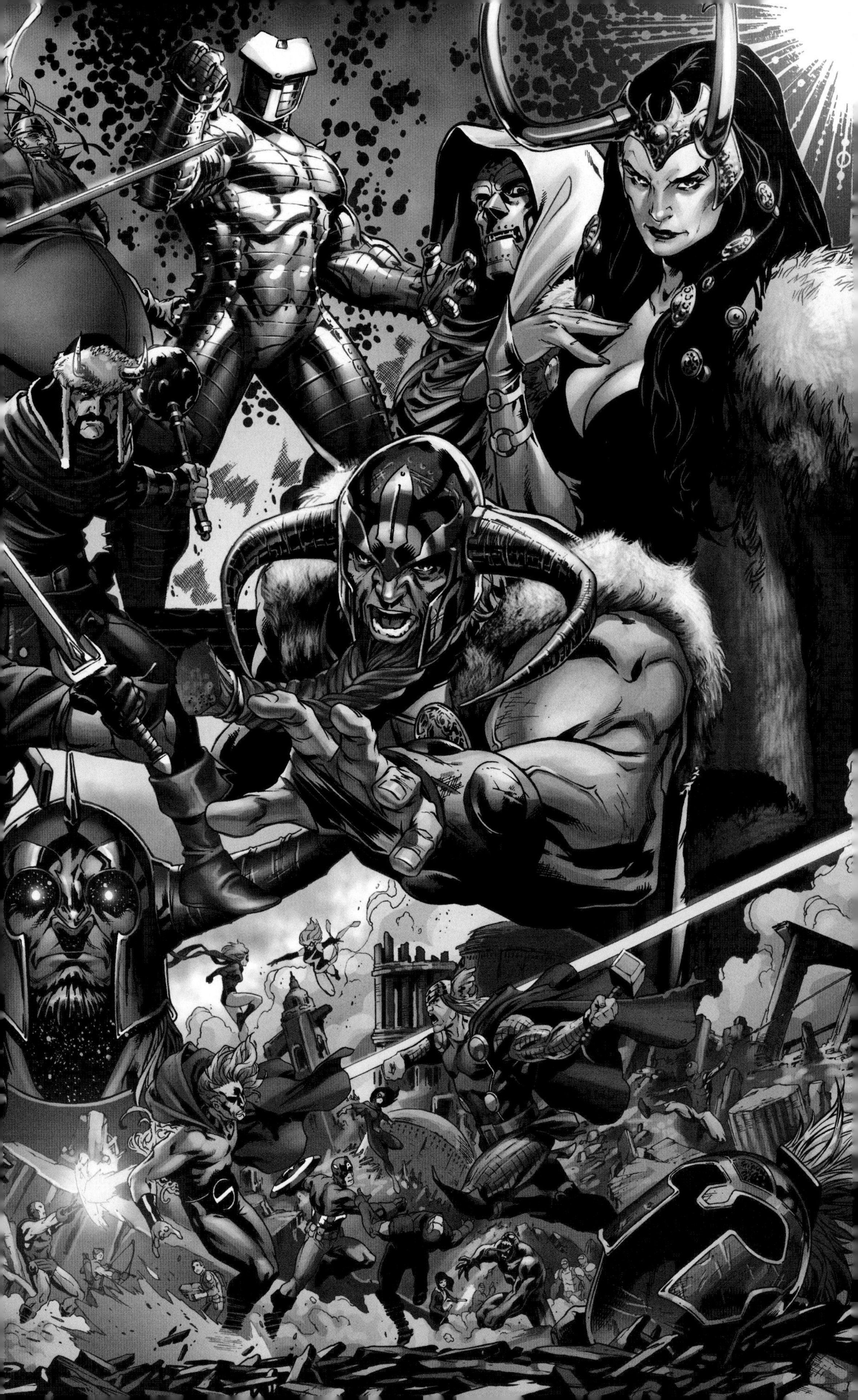

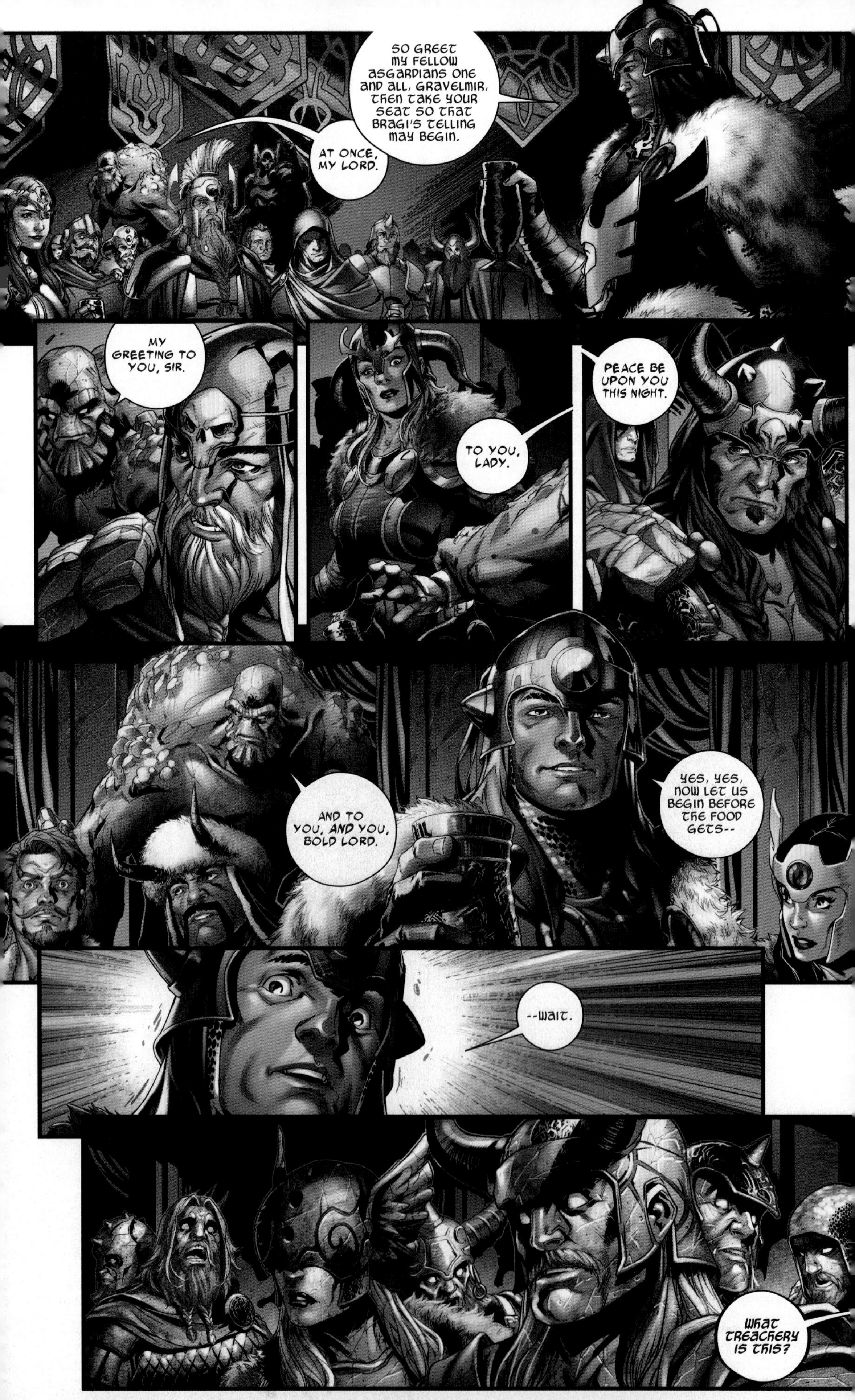
SO GREET MY FELLOW ASGARDIANS ONE AND ALL, GRAVELMIR, THEN TAKE YOUR SEAT SO THAT BRAGI'S TELLING MAY BEGIN.
AT ONCE, MY LORD.
MY GREETING TO YOU, SIR.
TO YOU, LADY.
PEACE BE UPON YOU THIS NIGHT.
AND TO YOU, AND YOU, BOLD LORD.
YES, YES, NOW LET US BEGIN BEFORE THE FOOD GETS--
--WAIT.
WHAT TREACHERY IS THIS?

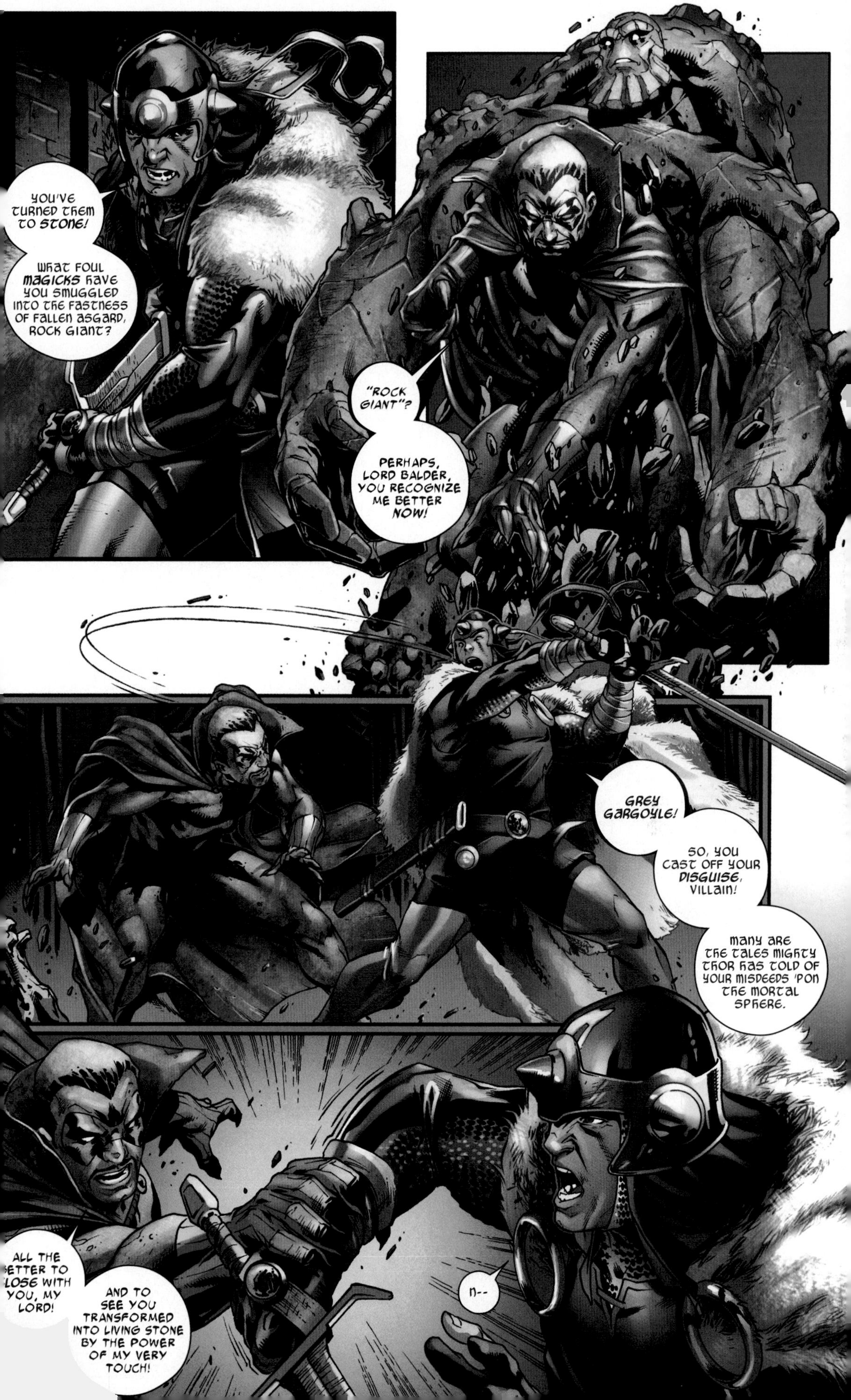
YOU'VE TURNED THEM TO STONE!
WHAT FOUL MAGICKS HAVE YOU SMUGGLED INTO THE FASTNESS OF FALLEN ASGARD, ROCK GIANT?
"ROCK GIANT"?
PERHAPS, LORD BALDER, YOU RECOGNIZE ME BETTER NOW!
GREY GARGOYLE!
SO, YOU CAST OFF YOUR DISGUISE, VILLAIN!
MANY ARE THE TALES MIGHTY THOR HAS TOLD OF YOUR MISDEEDS 'PON THE MORTAL SPHERE.
ALL THE BETTER TO CLOSE WITH YOU, MY LORD!
AND TO SEE YOU TRANSFORMED INTO LIVING STONE BY THE POWER OF MY VERY TOUCH!
N--

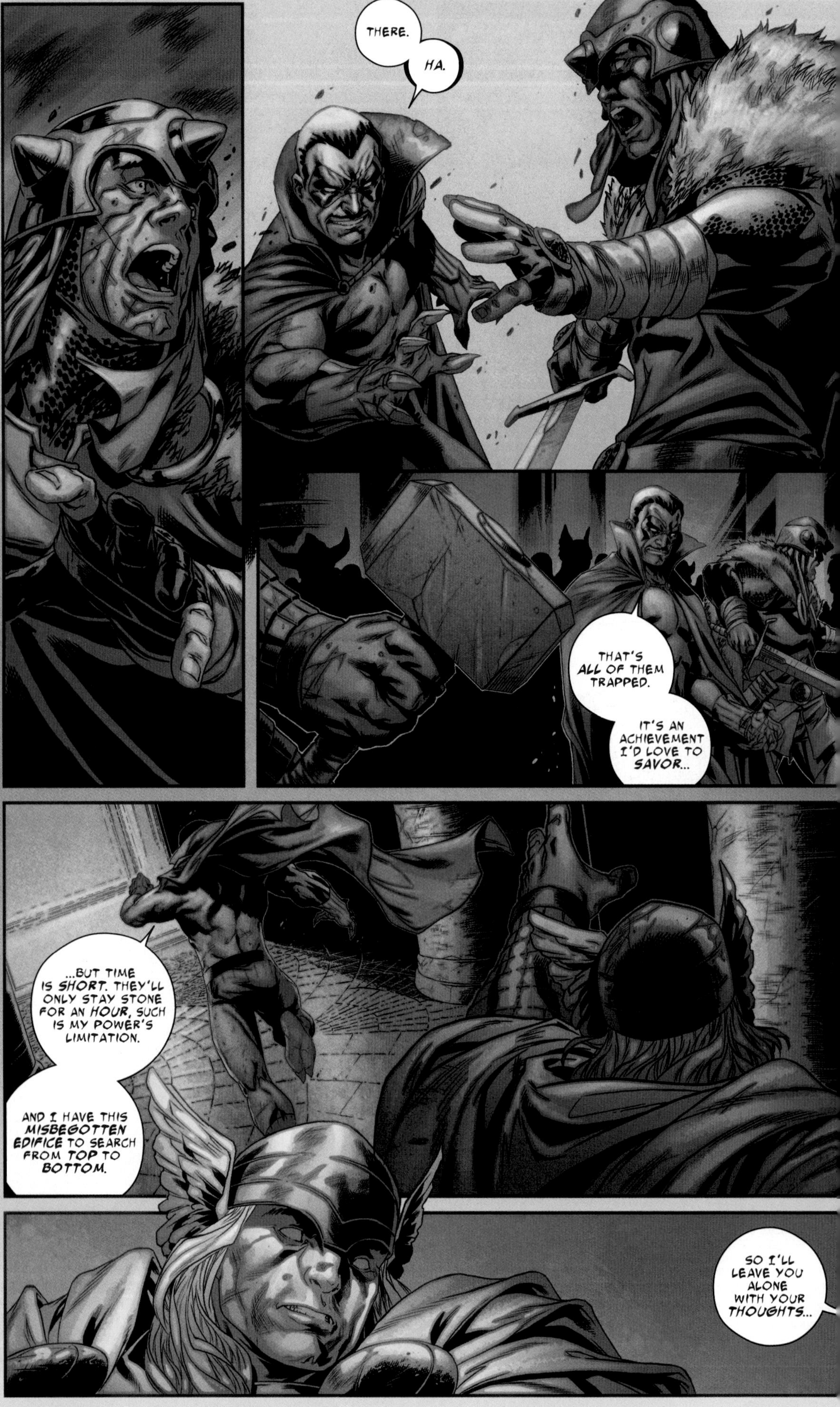
THERE.
HA.
THAT'S ALL OF THEM TRAPPED.
IT'S AN ACHIEVEMENT I'D LOVE TO SAVOR...
...BUT TIME IS SHORT. THEY'LL ONLY STAY STONE FOR AN HOUR, SUCH IS MY POWER'S LIMITATION.
AND I HAVE THIS MISBEGOTTEN EDIFICE TO SEARCH FROM TOP TO BOTTOM.
SO I'LL LEAVE YOU ALONE WITH YOUR THOUGHTS...

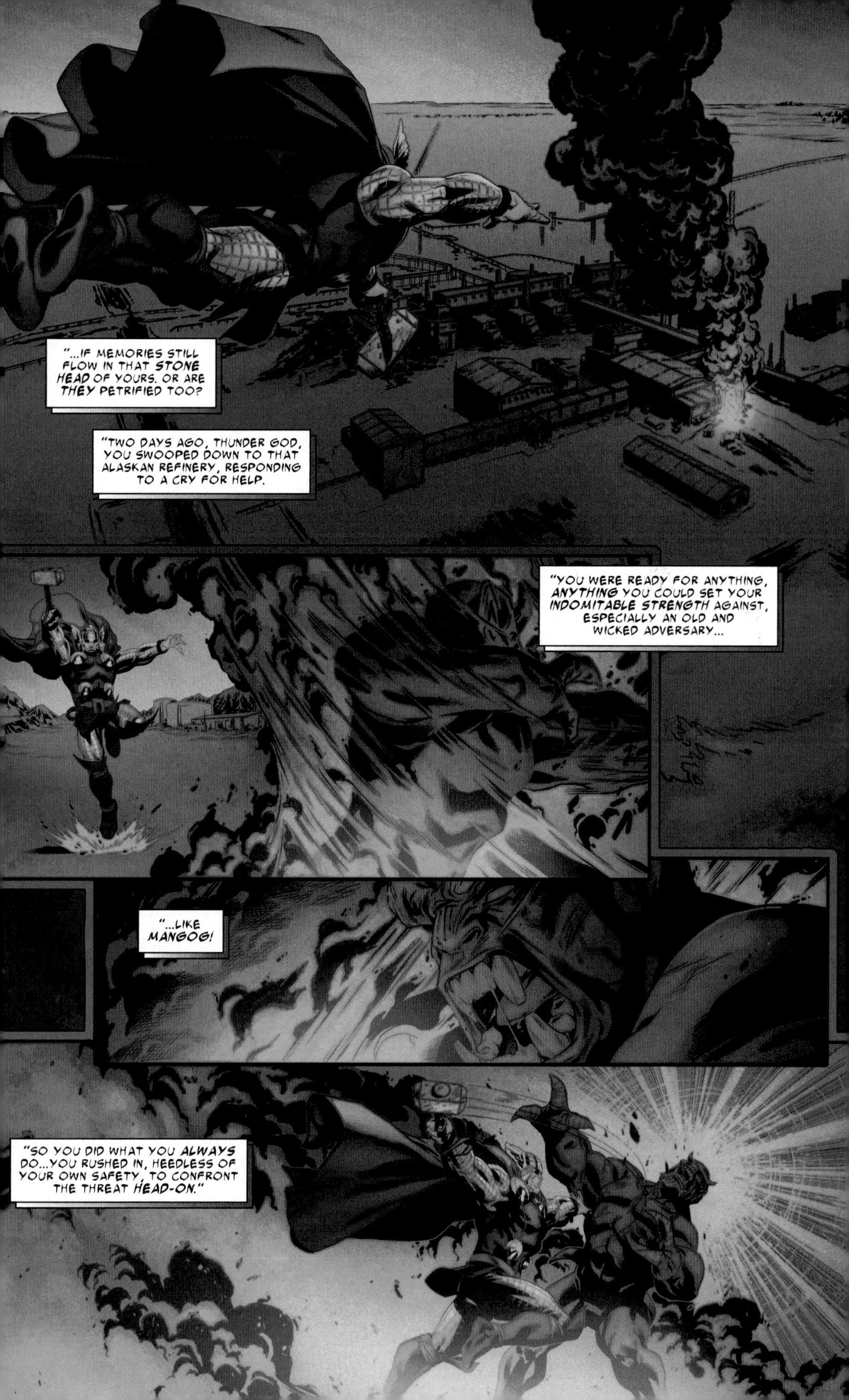
"...IF MEMORIES STILL FLOW IN THAT STONE HEAD OF YOURS, OR ARE THEY PETRIFIED TOO?
"TWO DAYS AGO, THUNDER GOD, YOU SWOOPED DOWN TO THAT ALASKAN REFINERY, RESPONDING TO A CRY FOR HELP.
"YOU WERE READY FOR ANYTHING, ANYTHING YOU COULD SET YOUR INDOMITABLE STRENGTH AGAINST, ESPECIALLY AN OLD AND WICKED ADVERSARY...
"...LIKE MANGOG!
"SO YOU DID WHAT YOU ALWAYS DO...YOU RUSHED IN, HEEDLESS OF YOUR OWN SAFETY, TO CONFRONT THE THREAT HEAD-ON."

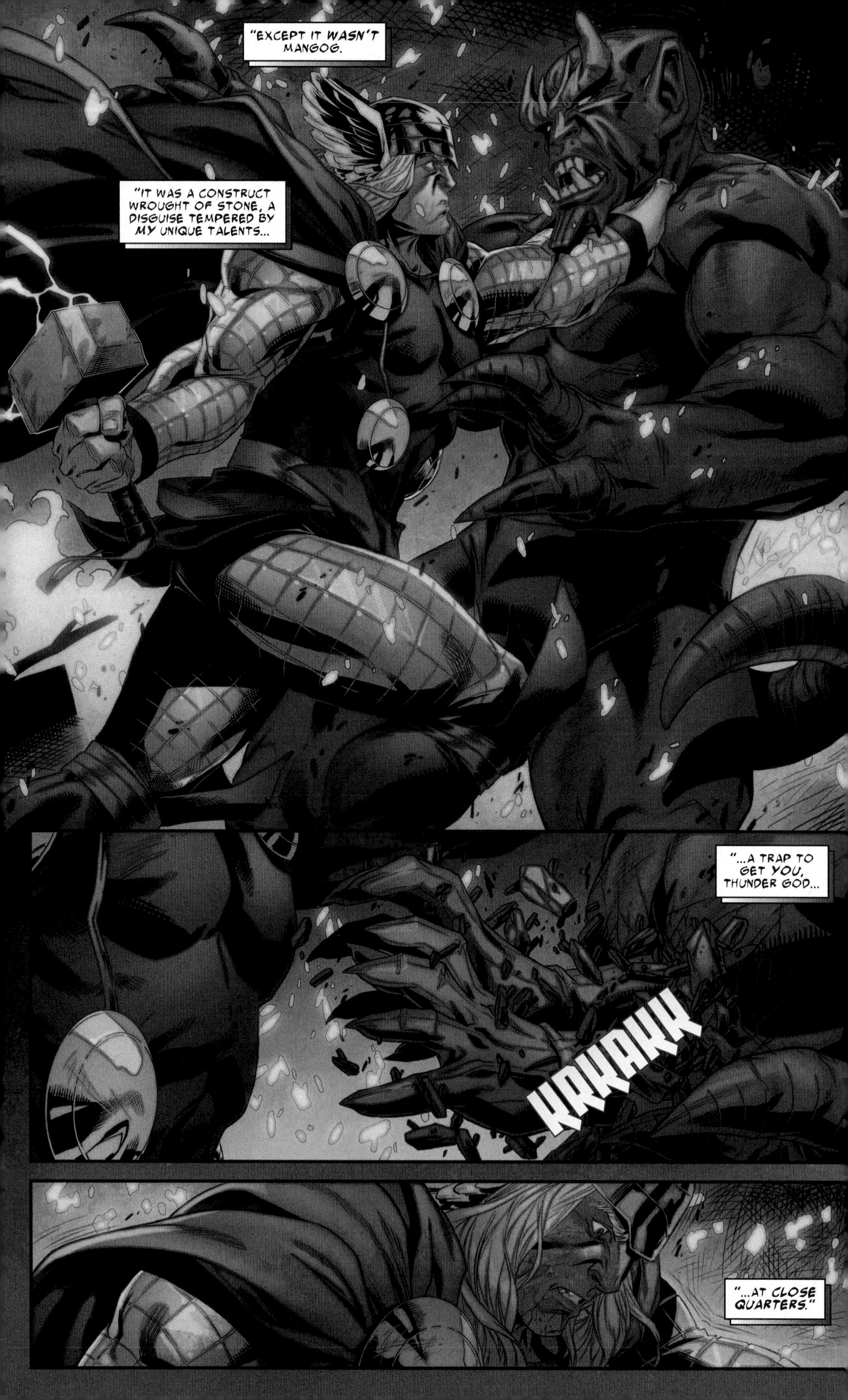
"EXCEPT IT WASN'T MANGOG.
"IT WAS A CONSTRUCT WROUGHT OF STONE, A DISGUISE TEMPERED BY MY UNIQUE TALENTS...
"...A TRAP TO GET YOU, THUNDER GOD...
KRKAKK
"...AT CLOSE QUARTERS."

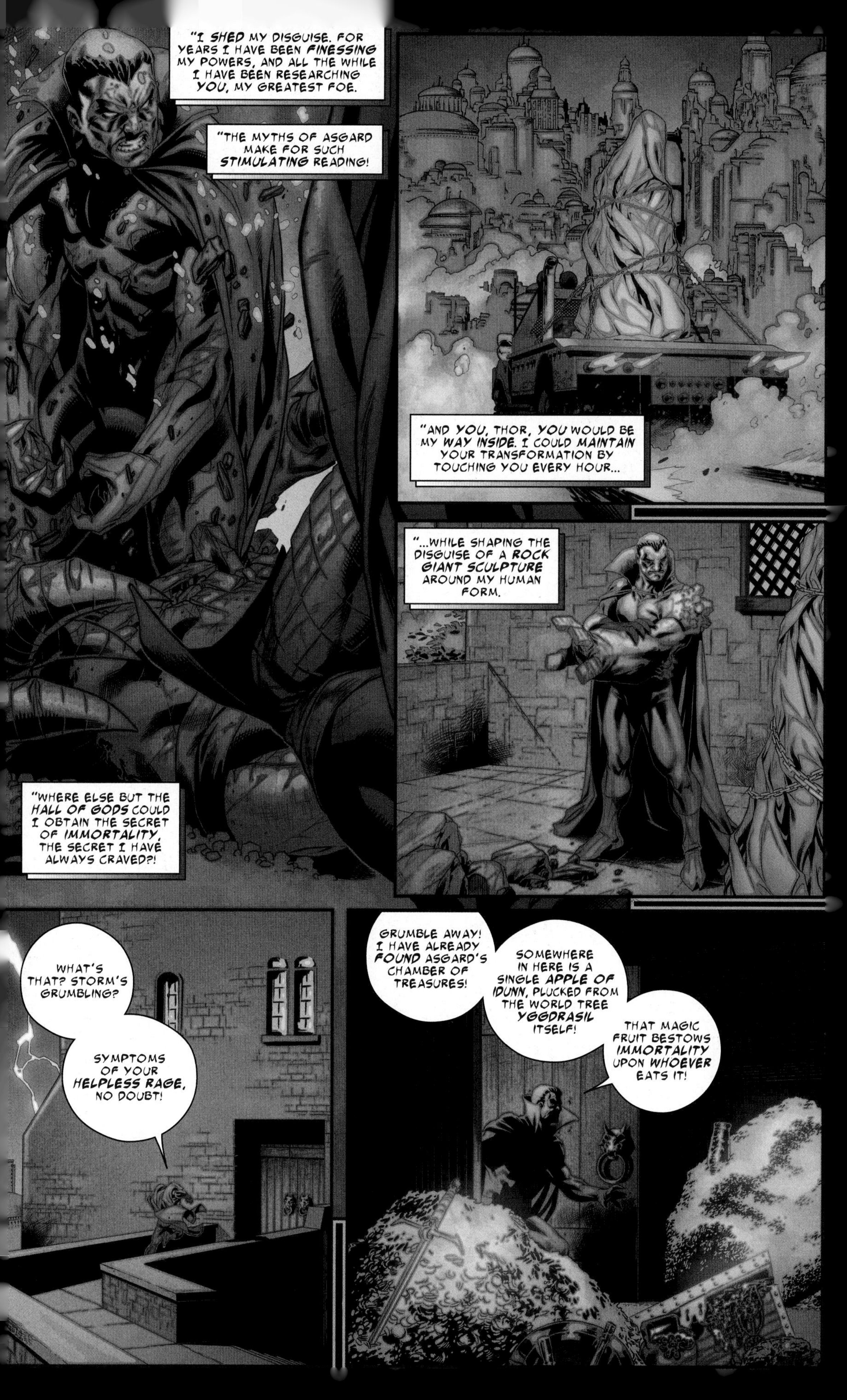
"I SHED MY DISGUISE. FOR YEARS I HAVE BEEN FINESSING MY POWERS, AND ALL THE WHILE I HAVE BEEN RESEARCHING YOU, MY GREATEST FOE.
"THE MYTHS OF ASGARD MAKE FOR SUCH STIMULATING READING!
"WHERE ELSE BUT THE HALL OF GODS COULD I OBTAIN THE SECRET OF IMMORTALITY, THE SECRET I HAVE ALWAYS CRAVED?!
"AND YOU, THOR, YOU WOULD BE MY WAY INSIDE. I COULD MAINTAIN YOUR TRANSFORMATION BY TOUCHING YOU EVERY HOUR...
"...WHILE SHAPING THE DISGUISE OF A ROCK GIANT SCULPTURE AROUND MY HUMAN FORM.
WHAT'S THAT? STORM'S GRUMBLING?
SYMPTOMS OF YOUR HELPLESS RAGE, NO DOUBT!
GRUMBLE AWAY! I HAVE ALREADY FOUND ASGARD'S CHAMBER OF TREASURES!
SOMEWHERE IN HERE IS A SINGLE APPLE OF IDUNN, PLUCKED FROM THE WORLD TREE YGGDRASIL ITSELF!
THAT MAGIC FRUIT BESTOWS IMMORTALITY UPON WHOEVER EATS IT!

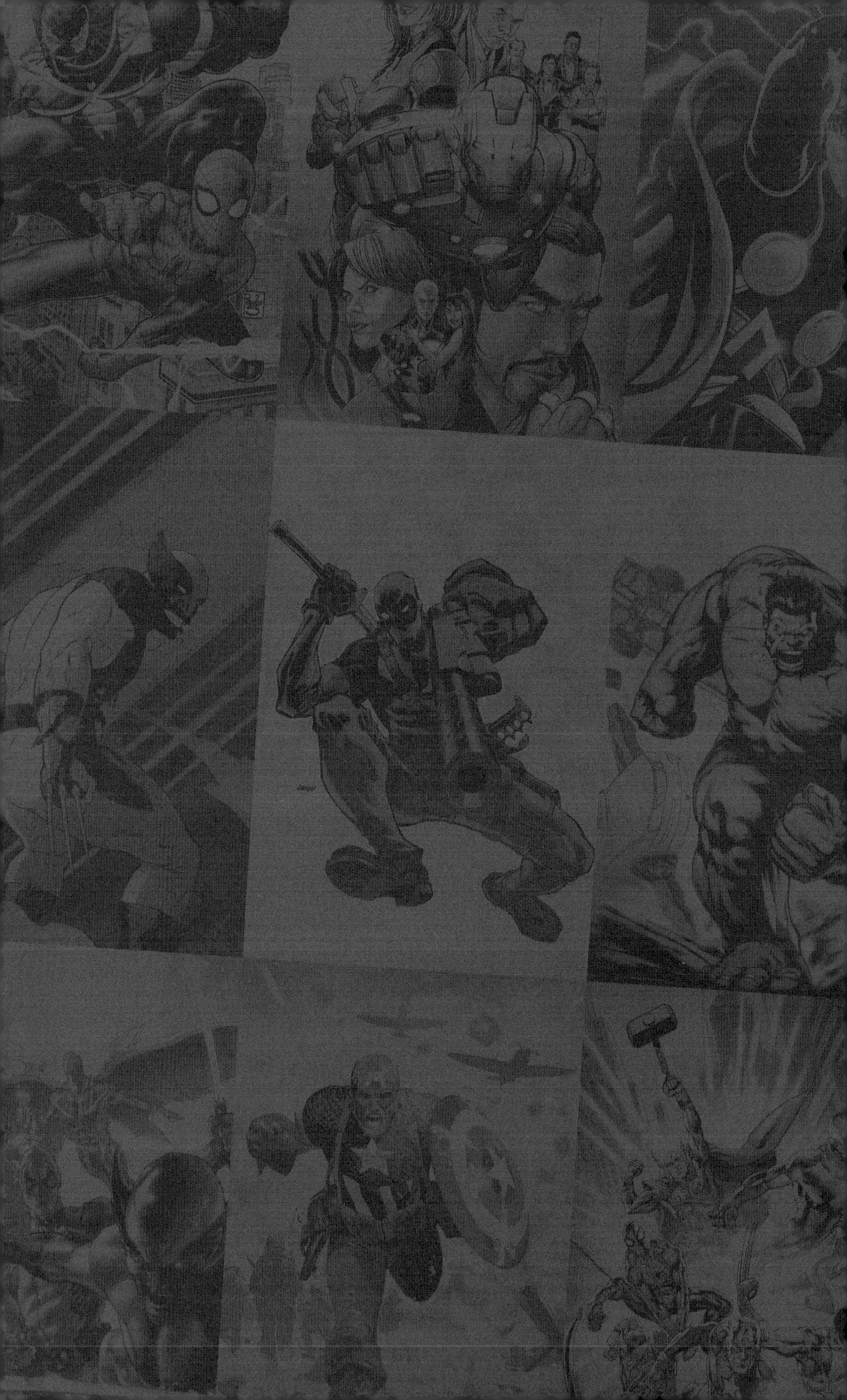

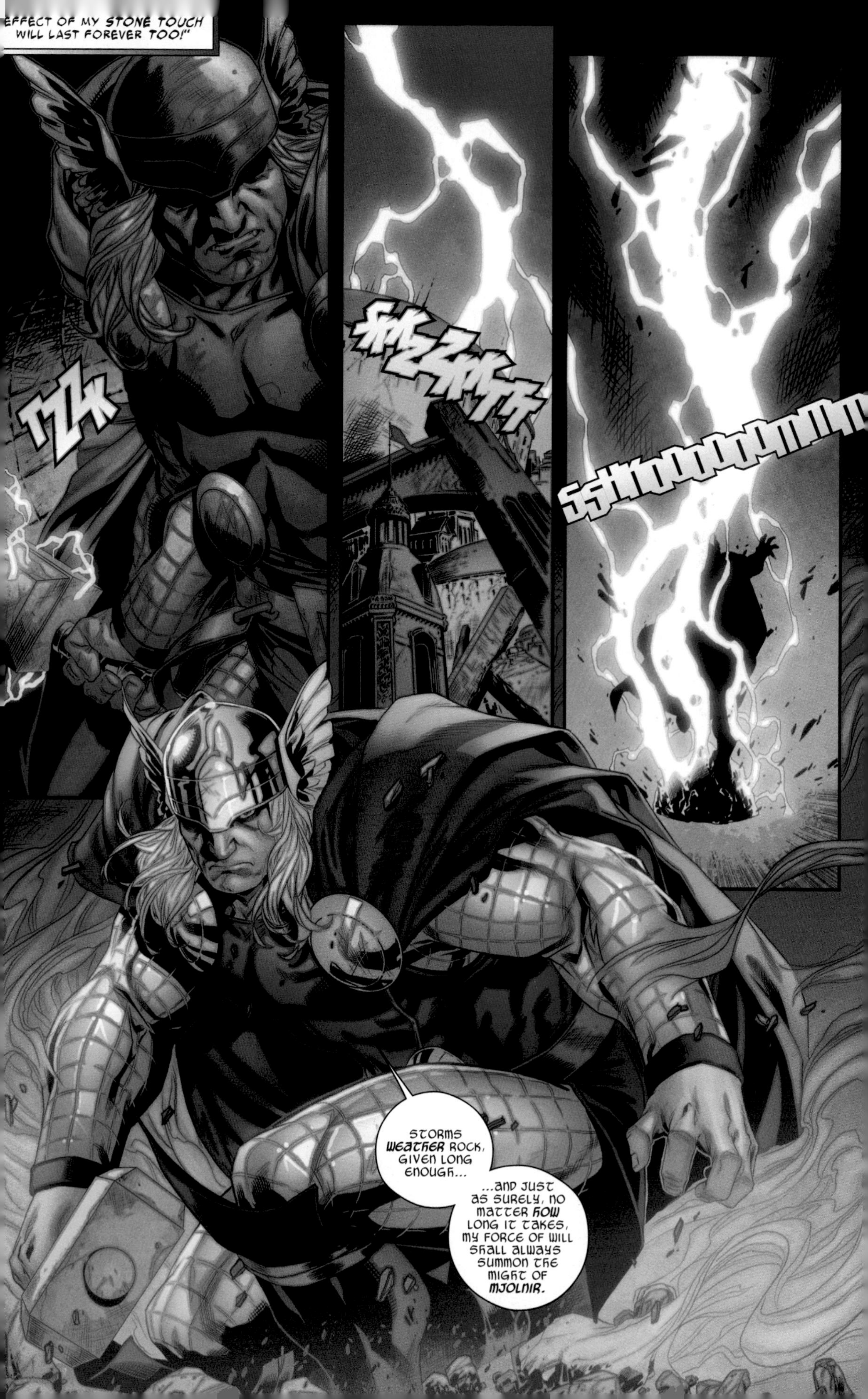

EFFECT OF MY STONE TOUCH WILL LAST FOREVER TOO!"
TZZK
SKZZZAKT
SSHKOOOOOOMMM
STORMS WEATHER ROCK, GIVEN LONG ENOUGH...
...AND JUST AS SURELY, NO MATTER HOW LONG IT TAKES, MY FORCE OF WILL SHALL ALWAYS SUMMON THE MIGHT OF MJOLNIR.

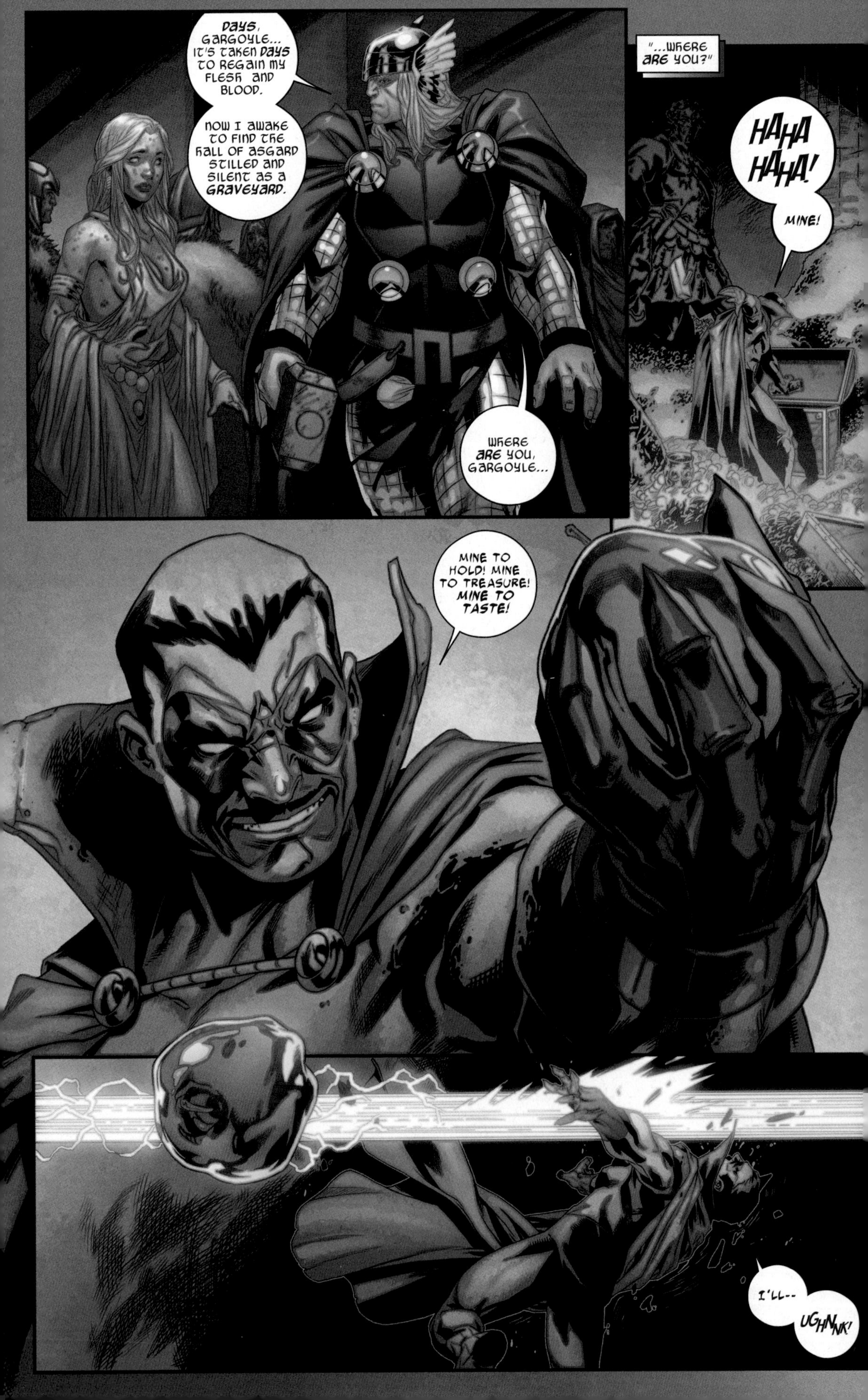
DAYS, GARGOYLE... IT'S TAKEN DAYS TO REGAIN MY FLESH AND BLOOD.
NOW I AWAKE TO FIND THE HALL OF ASGARD STILLED AND SILENT AS A GRAVEYARD.
WHERE ARE YOU, GARGOYLE...
"...WHERE ARE YOU?"
HAHA HAHA!
MINE!
MINE TO HOLD! MINE TO TREASURE! MINE TO TASTE!
I'LL--
UGHNNK!

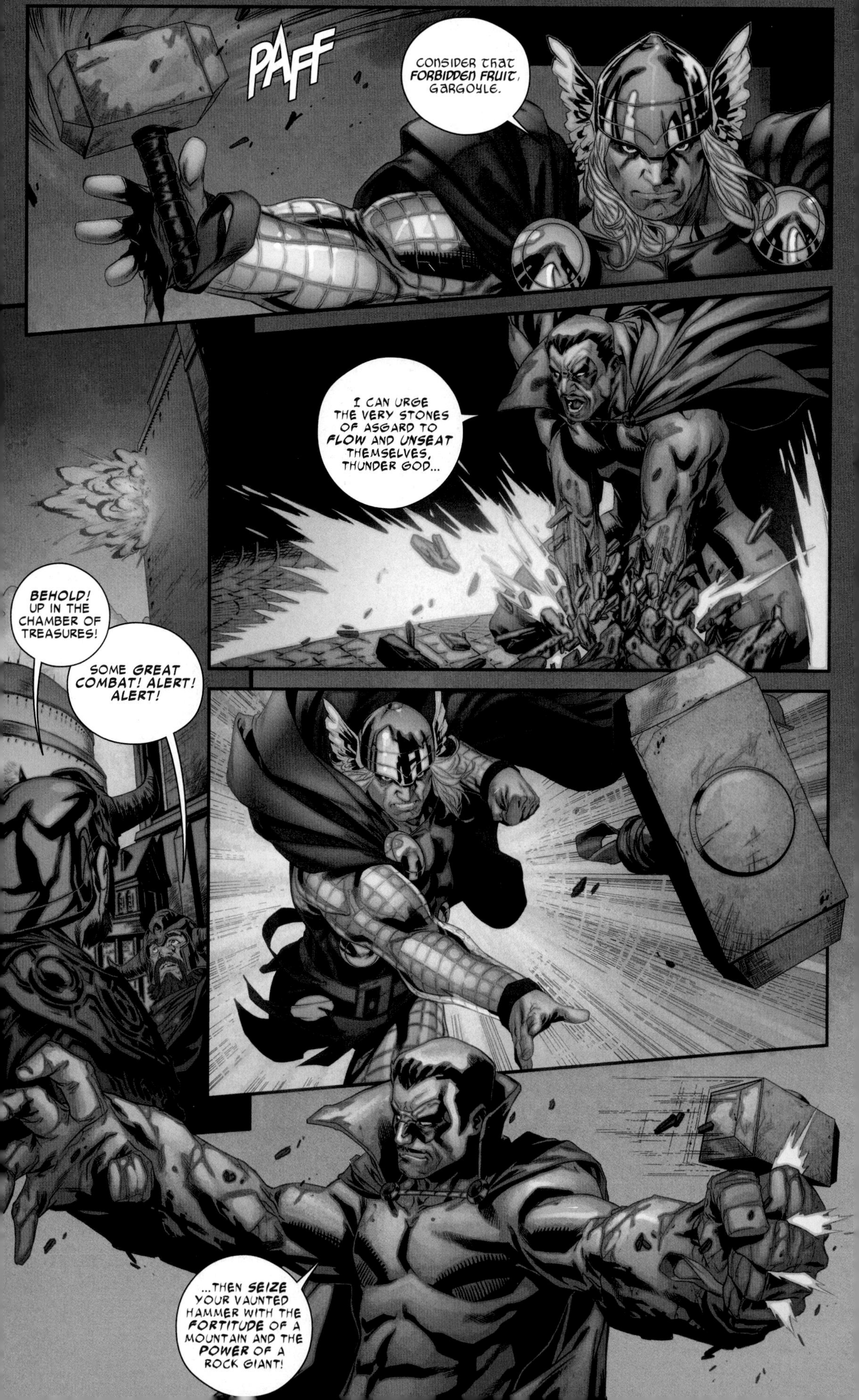
PAFF
CONSIDER THAT FORBIDDEN FRUIT, GARGOYLE.
I CAN URGE THE VERY STONES OF ASGARD TO FLOW AND UNSEAT THEMSELVES, THUNDER GOD...
BEHOLD! UP IN THE CHAMBER OF TREASURES!
SOME GREAT COMBAT! ALERT! ALERT!
...THEN SEIZE YOUR VAUNTED HAMMER WITH THE FORTITUDE OF A MOUNTAIN AND THE POWER OF A ROCK GIANT!

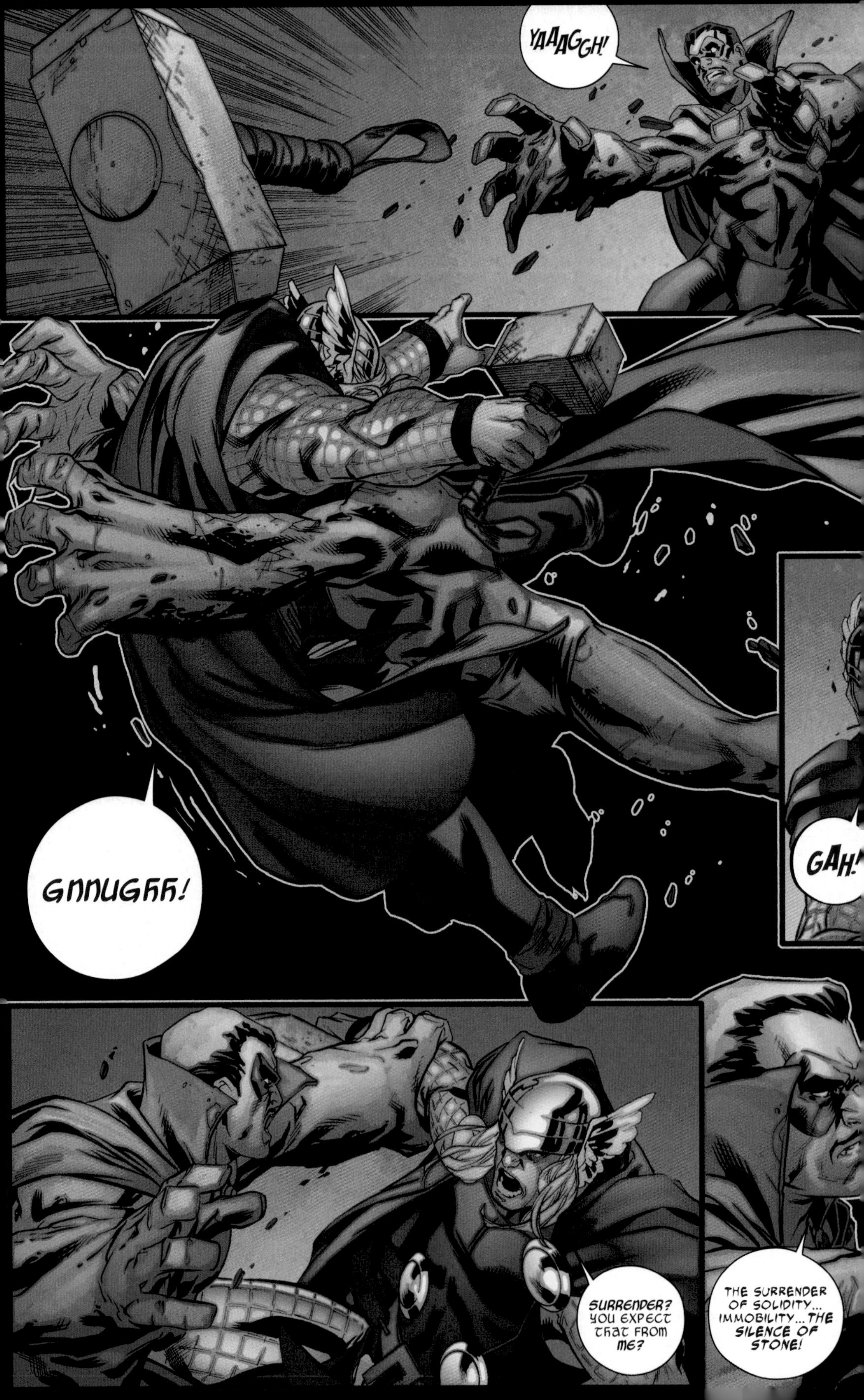
YAAAGGH!
GNNUGHH!
GAH!
SURRENDER? YOU EXPECT THAT FROM ME?
THE SURRENDER OF SOLIDITY... IMMOBILITY... THE SILENCE OF STONE!

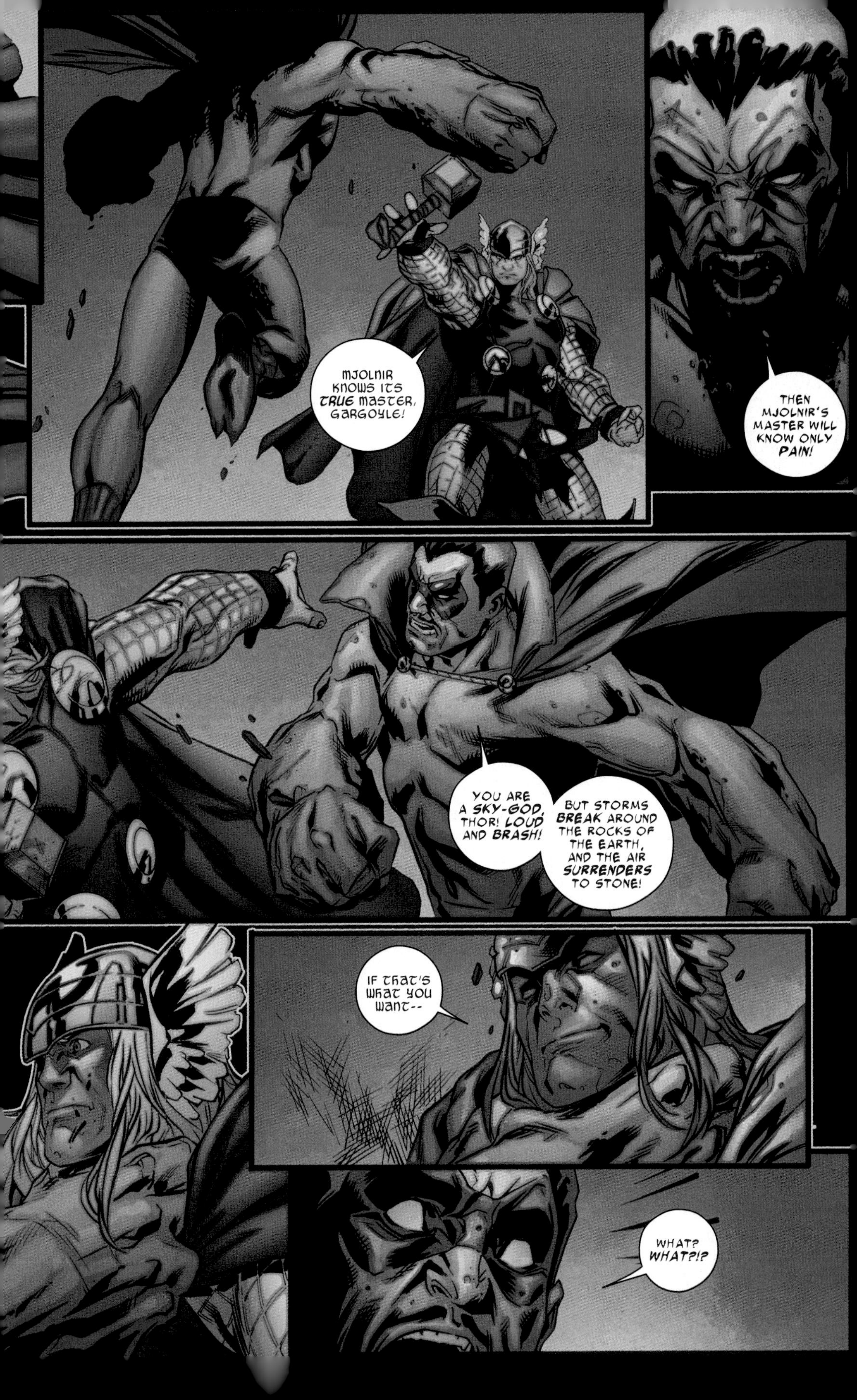
MJOLNIR KNOWS ITS TRUE MASTER, GARGOYLE!
THEN MJOLNIR'S MASTER WILL KNOW ONLY PAIN!
YOU ARE A SKY-GOD, THOR! LOUD AND BRASH!
BUT STORMS BREAK AROUND THE ROCKS OF THE EARTH, AND THE AIR SURRENDERS TO STONE!
IF THAT'S WHAT YOU WANT--
WHAT? WHAT?!?

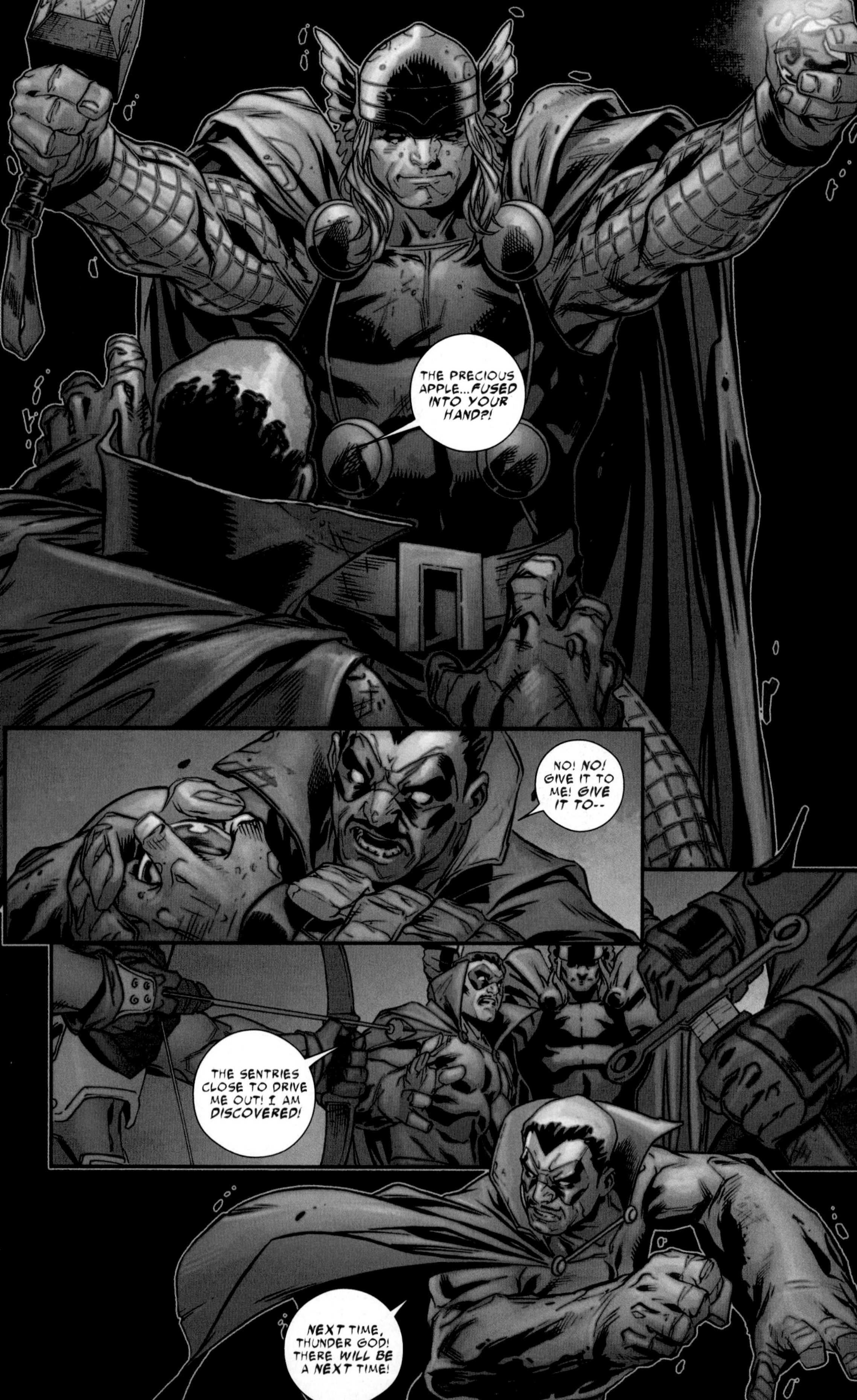
THE PRECIOUS APPLE... FUSED INTO YOUR HAND?!
NO! NO! GIVE IT TO ME! GIVE IT TO--
THE SENTRIES CLOSE TO DRIVE ME OUT! I AM DISCOVERED!
NEXT TIME, THUNDER GOD! THERE WILL BE A NEXT TIME!

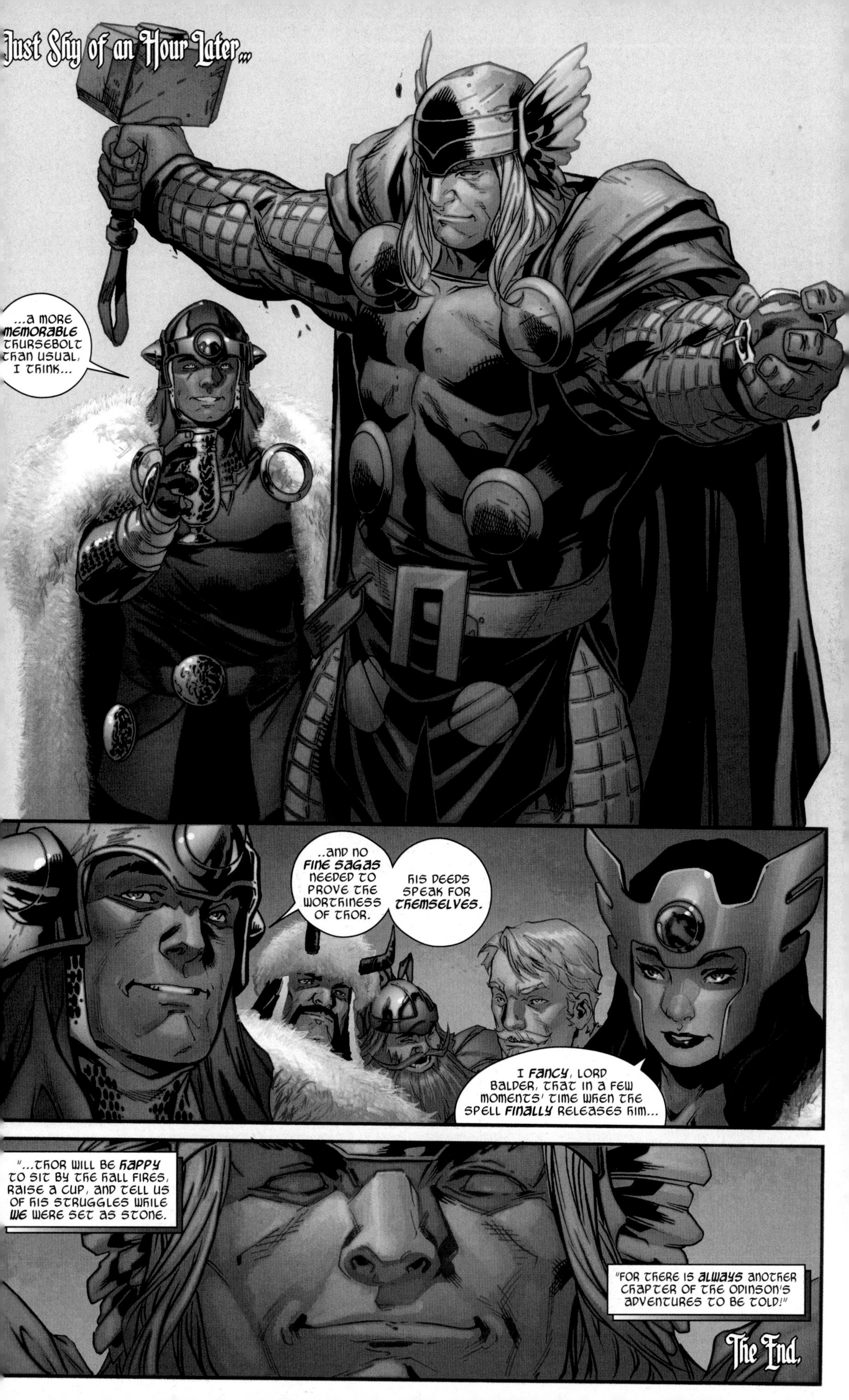
Just Shy of an Hour Later...
...A MORE MEMORABLE THURSEBOLT THAN USUAL, I THINK...
..AND NO FINE SAGAS NEEDED TO PROVE THE WORTHINESS OF THOR.
HIS DEEDS SPEAK FOR THEMSELVES.
I FANCY, LORD BALDER, THAT IN A FEW MOMENTS' TIME WHEN THE SPELL FINALLY RELEASES HIM...
"...THOR WILL BE HAPPY TO SIT BY THE HALL FIRES, RAISE A CUP, AND TELL US OF HIS STRUGGLES WHILE WE WERE SET AS STONE.
"FOR THERE IS ALWAYS ANOTHER CHAPTER OF THE ODINSON'S ADVENTURES TO BE TOLD!"
The End.

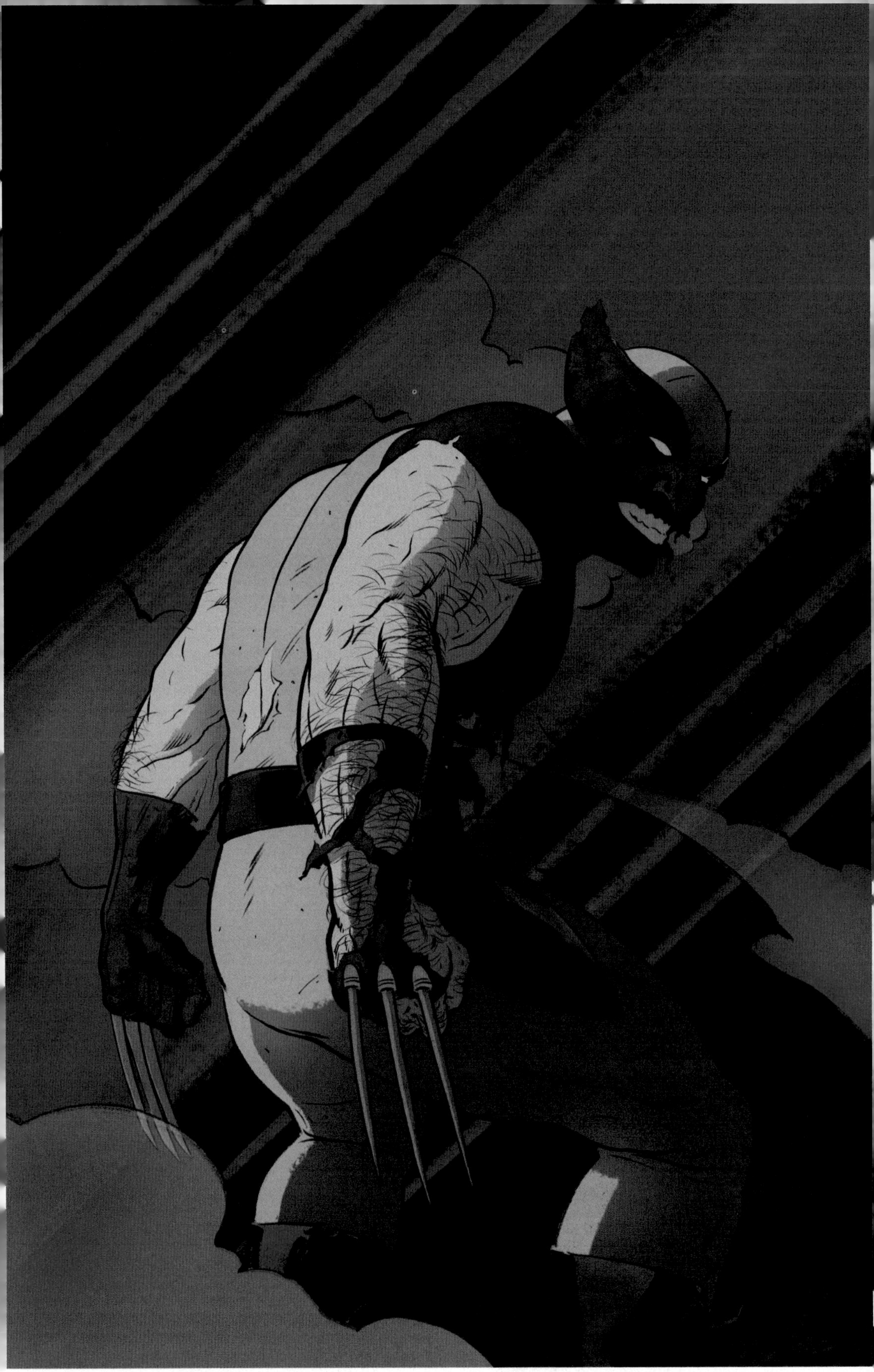

WOLVERINE #5.1

Many years ago, a secret government organization abducted the man called Logan, a mutant possessing razor-sharp bone claws and the ability to heal from any wound. In their attempt to create the perfect living weapon, the organization bonded the unbreakable metal Adamantium to his skeleton. The process was excruciating and by the end, there was little left of the man known as Logan. He had become...

WOLVERINE

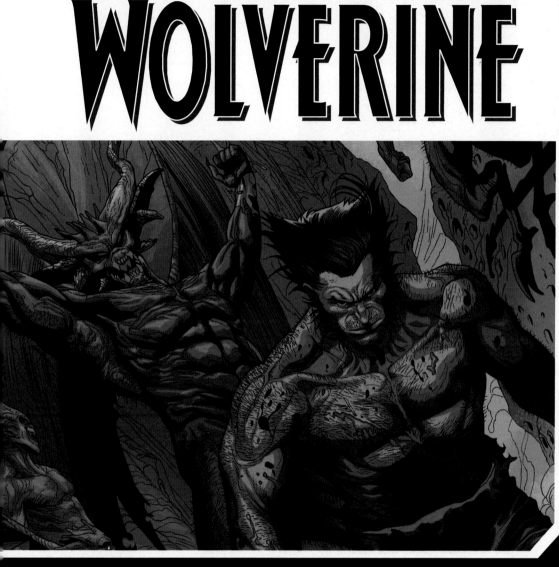

PREVIOUSLY...

A lot has changed in the years since Logan escaped from the organization that transformed him into a killing machine. He's become an invaluable member of the X-Men and their fight to save the mutant species from extinction. He's joined the super hero group known as the Avengers and saves the world on a regular basis with the likes of Captain America, Thor and Iron Man. He's battled his long lost son, Daken, and fought alongside his clone, the child soldier known as X-23. He's been witness to the deaths of countless friends, foes and lovers in his hundred plus years on this earth. He's been to hell and back. Literally. But there's one experience Logan's never had before...

WOLVERINE 5.1

JASON AARON WRITER   **JEFTE PALO** ART   **NATHAN FAIRBAIRN** COLOR ART
PAOLO RIVERA COVER ART   **VC'S CORY PETIT** LETTERER   **JARED K. FLETCHER** DESIGNER
JODY LEHEUP ASST. EDITOR   **JEANINE SCHAEFER** EDITOR
JOE QUESADA EDITOR IN CHIEF   **DAN BUCKLEY** PUBLISHER   **ALAN FINE** EXECUTIVE PRODUCER

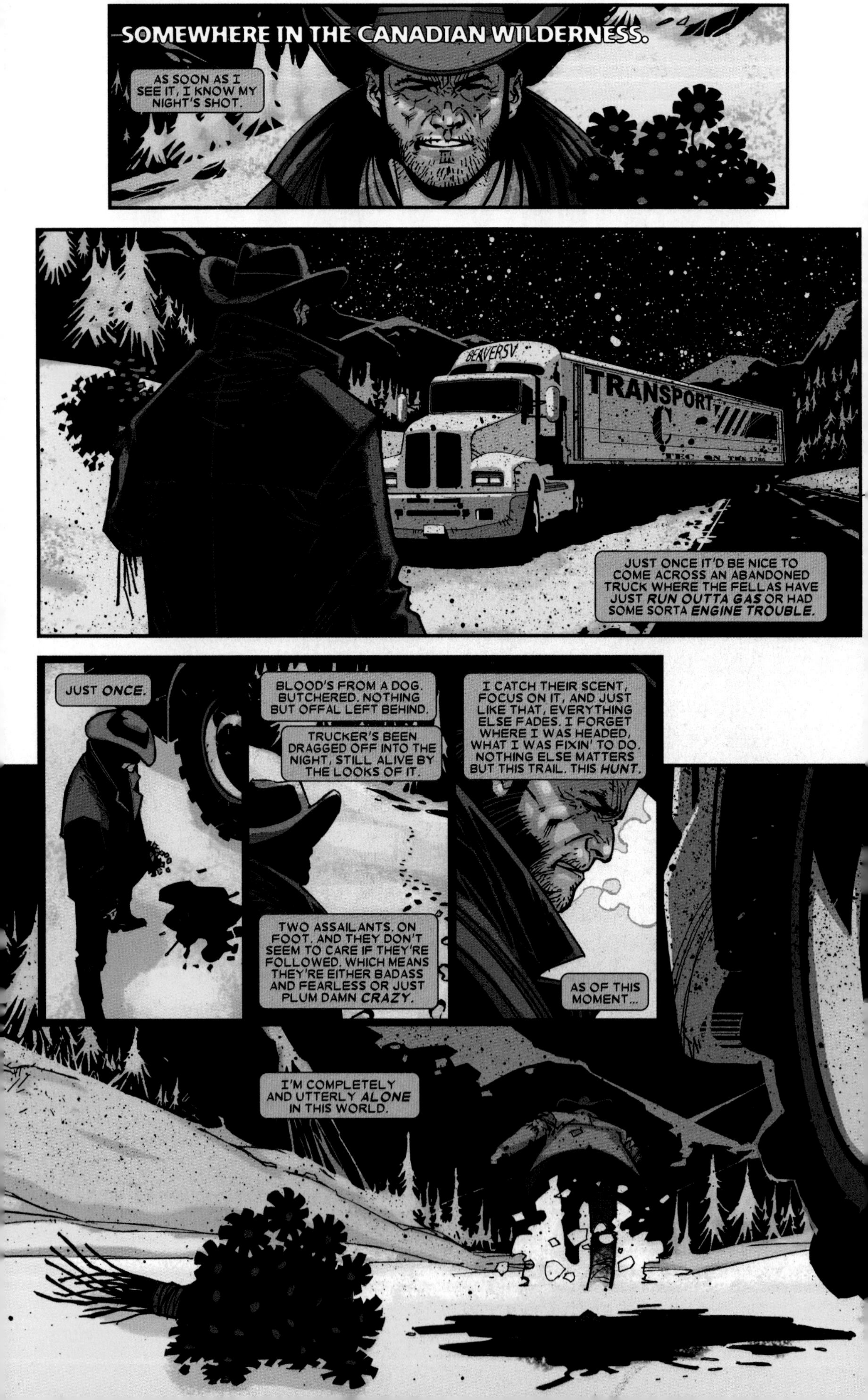
SOMEWHERE IN THE CANADIAN WILDERNESS.
AS SOON AS I SEE IT, I KNOW MY NIGHT'S SHOT.
BEAVERS V.
TRANSPORT
JUST ONCE IT'D BE NICE TO COME ACROSS AN ABANDONED TRUCK WHERE THE FELLAS HAVE JUST RUN OUTTA GAS OR HAD SOME SORTA ENGINE TROUBLE.
JUST ONCE.
BLOOD'S FROM A DOG. BUTCHERED. NOTHING BUT OFFAL LEFT BEHIND.
TRUCKER'S BEEN DRAGGED OFF INTO THE NIGHT, STILL ALIVE BY THE LOOKS OF IT.
TWO ASSAILANTS. ON FOOT. AND THEY DON'T SEEM TO CARE IF THEY'RE FOLLOWED. WHICH MEANS THEY'RE EITHER BADASS AND FEARLESS OR JUST PLUM DAMN CRAZY.
I CATCH THEIR SCENT, FOCUS ON IT, AND JUST LIKE THAT, EVERYTHING ELSE FADES. I FORGET WHERE I WAS HEADED, WHAT I WAS FIXIN' TO DO. NOTHING ELSE MATTERS BUT THIS TRAIL. THIS HUNT.
AS OF THIS MOMENT...
I'M COMPLETELY AND UTTERLY ALONE IN THIS WORLD.

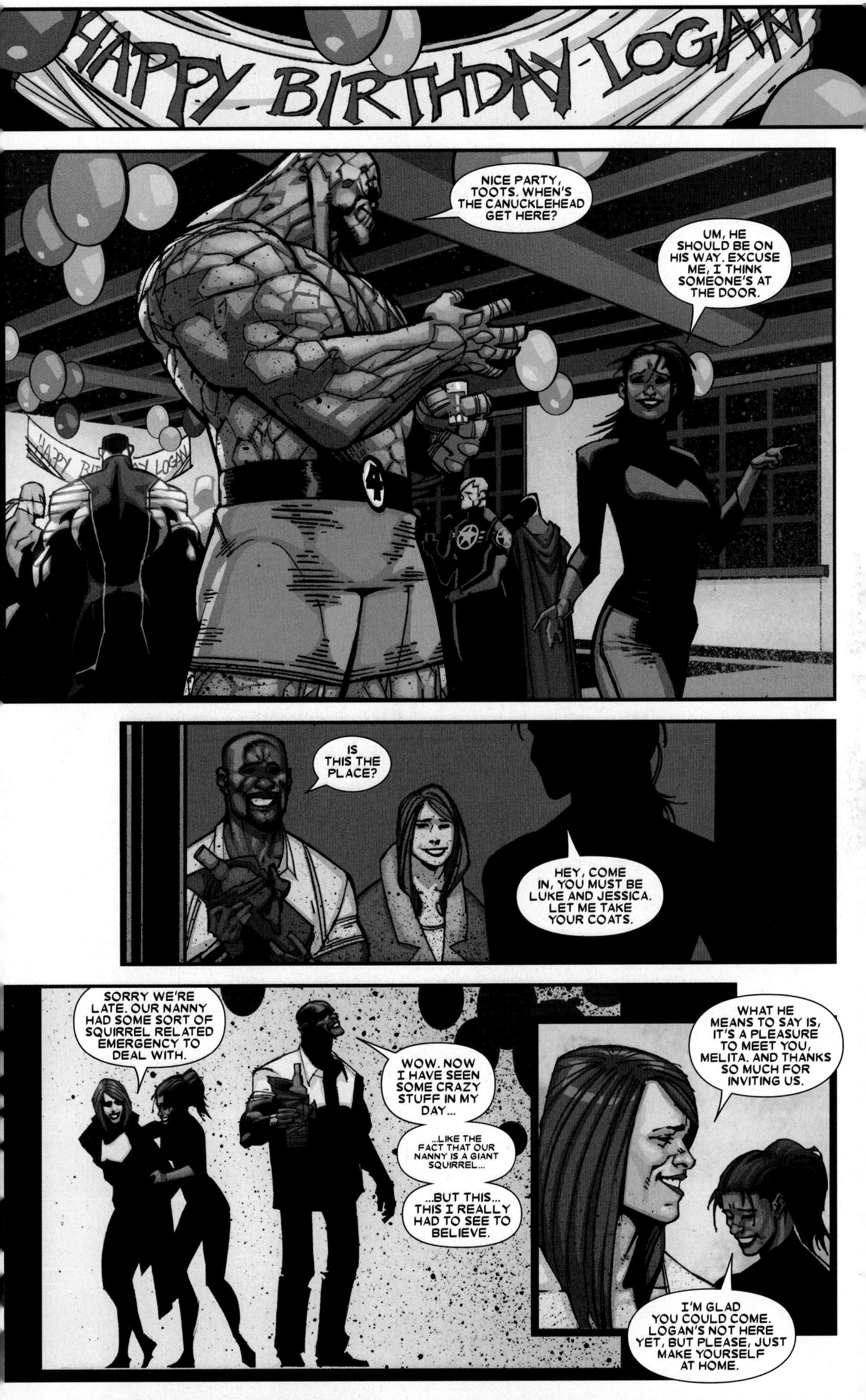
HAPPY BIRTHDAY LOGAN
NICE PARTY, TOOTS. WHEN'S THE CANUCKLEHEAD GET HERE?
UM, HE SHOULD BE ON HIS WAY. EXCUSE ME, I THINK SOMEONE'S AT THE DOOR.
IS THIS THE PLACE?
HEY, COME IN, YOU MUST BE LUKE AND JESSICA. LET ME TAKE YOUR COATS.
SORRY WE'RE LATE. OUR NANNY HAD SOME SORT OF SQUIRREL RELATED EMERGENCY TO DEAL WITH.
WOW. NOW I HAVE SEEN SOME CRAZY STUFF IN MY DAY...
...LIKE THE FACT THAT OUR NANNY IS A GIANT SQUIRREL...
...BUT THIS... THIS I REALLY HAD TO SEE TO BELIEVE.
WHAT HE MEANS TO SAY IS, IT'S A PLEASURE TO MEET YOU, MELITA. AND THANKS SO MUCH FOR INVITING US.
I'M GLAD YOU COULD COME. LOGAN'S NOT HERE YET, BUT PLEASE, JUST MAKE YOURSELF AT HOME.

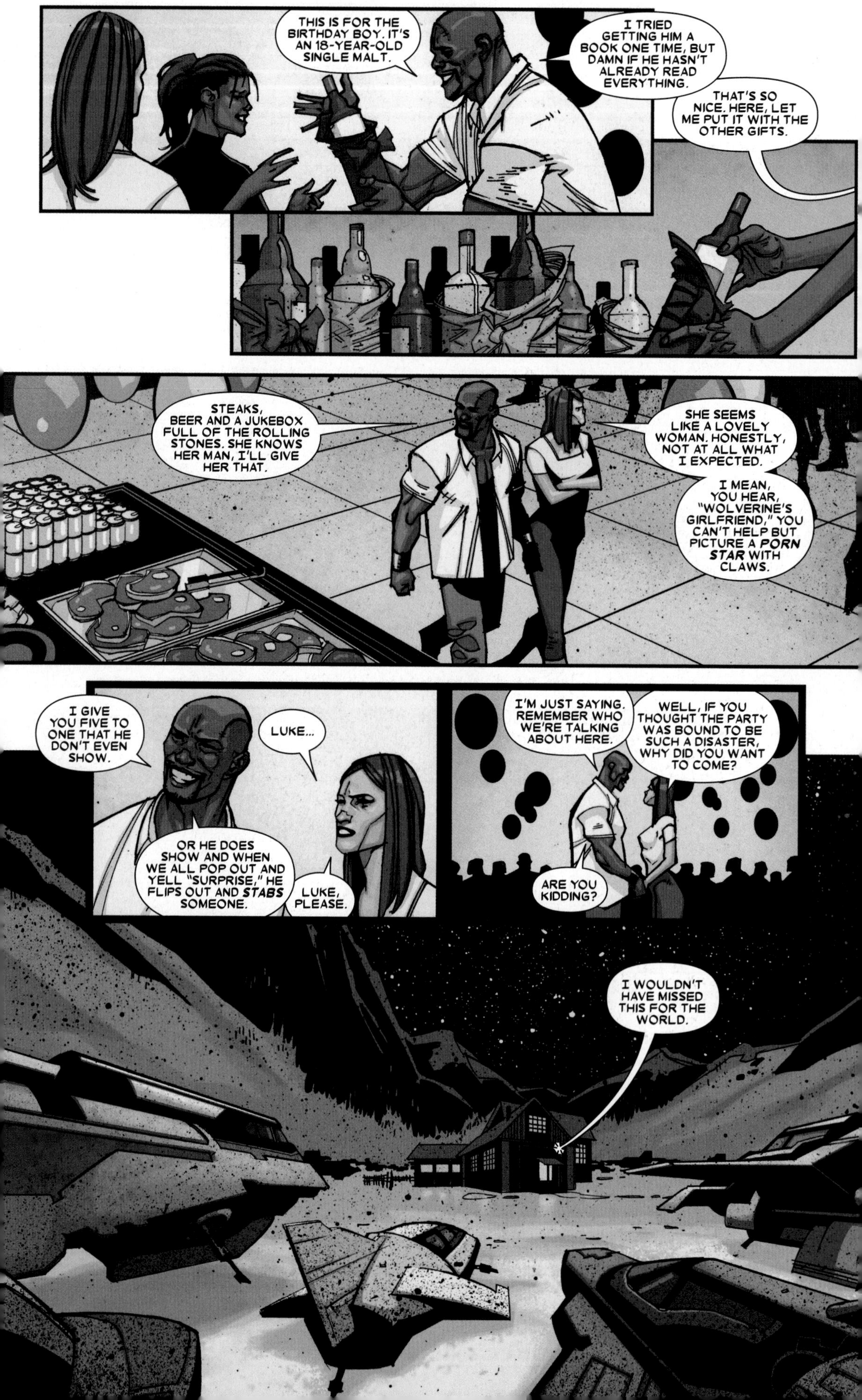
THIS IS FOR THE BIRTHDAY BOY. IT'S AN 18-YEAR-OLD SINGLE MALT.
I TRIED GETTING HIM A BOOK ONE TIME, BUT DAMN IF HE HASN'T ALREADY READ EVERYTHING.
THAT'S SO NICE. HERE, LET ME PUT IT WITH THE OTHER GIFTS.
STEAKS, BEER AND A JUKEBOX FULL OF THE ROLLING STONES. SHE KNOWS HER MAN, I'LL GIVE HER THAT.
SHE SEEMS LIKE A LOVELY WOMAN. HONESTLY, NOT AT ALL WHAT I EXPECTED.
I MEAN, YOU HEAR, "WOLVERINE'S GIRLFRIEND," YOU CAN'T HELP BUT PICTURE A PORN STAR WITH CLAWS.
I GIVE YOU FIVE TO ONE THAT HE DON'T EVEN SHOW.
LUKE...
OR HE DOES SHOW AND WHEN WE ALL POP OUT AND YELL "SURPRISE," HE FLIPS OUT AND STABS SOMEONE.
LUKE, PLEASE.
I'M JUST SAYING. REMEMBER WHO WE'RE TALKING ABOUT HERE.
WELL, IF YOU THOUGHT THE PARTY WAS BOUND TO BE SUCH A DISASTER, WHY DID YOU WANT TO COME?
ARE YOU KIDDING?
I WOULDN'T HAVE MISSED THIS FOR THE WORLD.

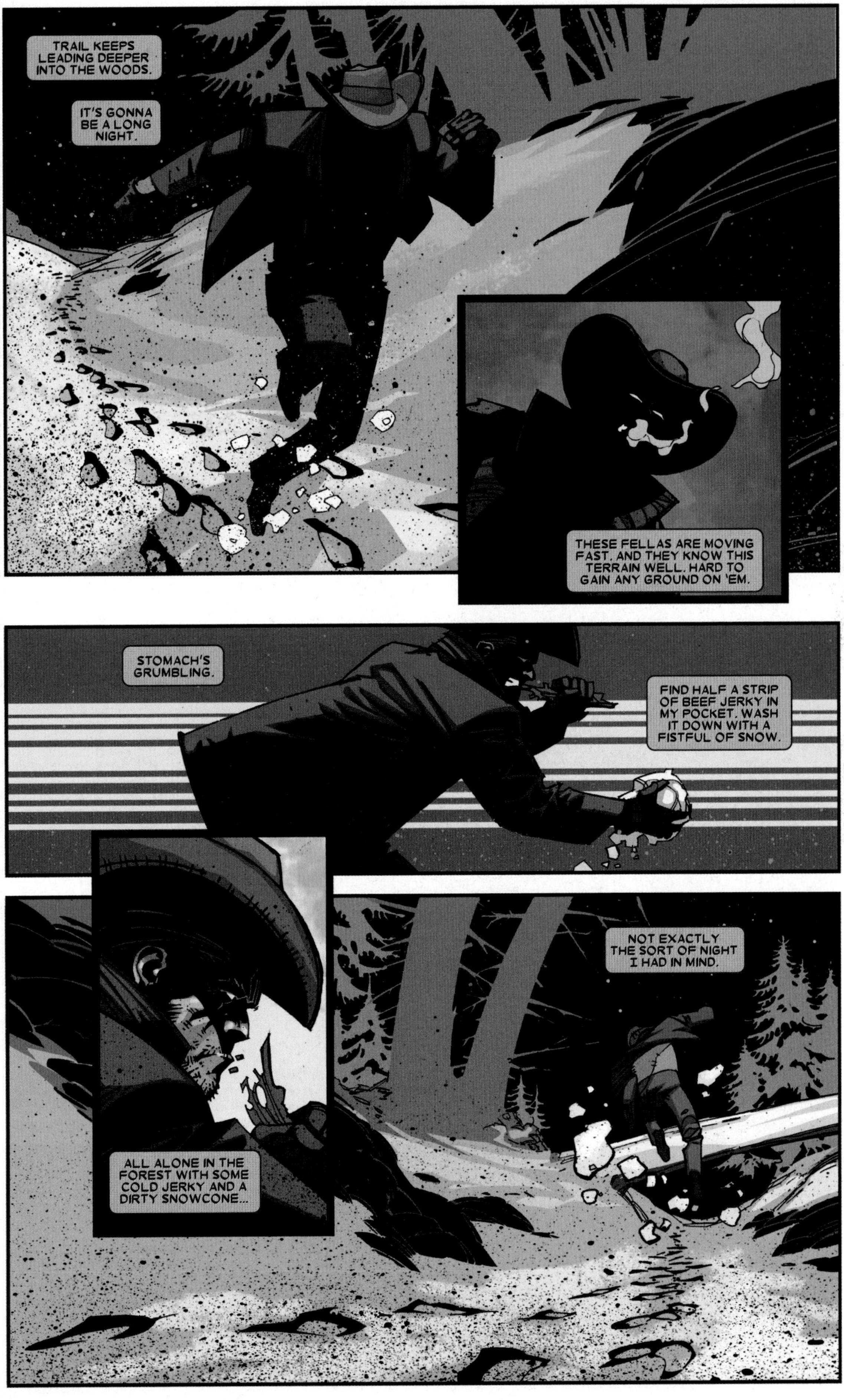
TRAIL KEEPS LEADING DEEPER INTO THE WOODS.
IT'S GONNA BE A LONG NIGHT.
THESE FELLAS ARE MOVING FAST, AND THEY KNOW THIS TERRAIN WELL. HARD TO GAIN ANY GROUND ON 'EM.
STOMACH'S GRUMBLING.
FIND HALF A STRIP OF BEEF JERKY IN MY POCKET. WASH IT DOWN WITH A FISTFUL OF SNOW.
ALL ALONE IN THE FOREST WITH SOME COLD JERKY AND A DIRTY SNOWCONE...
NOT EXACTLY THE SORT OF NIGHT I HAD IN MIND.

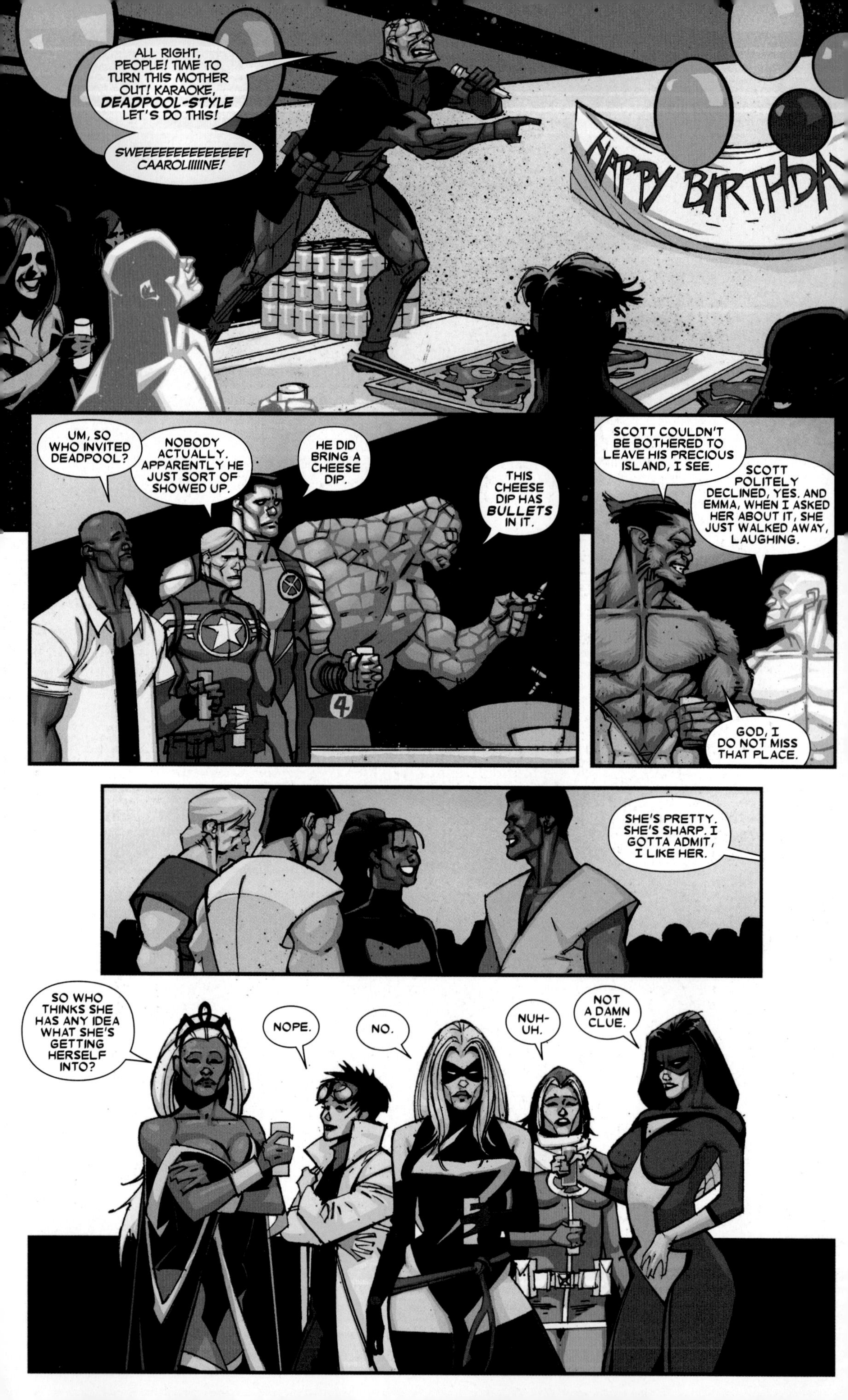

ALL RIGHT, PEOPLE! TIME TO TURN THIS MOTHER OUT! KARAOKE, DEADPOOL-STYLE LET'S DO THIS!
SWEEEEEEEEEEEEEET CAAROLIIIIINE!
HAPPY BIRTHDA
UM, SO WHO INVITED DEADPOOL?
NOBODY ACTUALLY. APPARENTLY HE JUST SORT OF SHOWED UP.
HE DID BRING A CHEESE DIP.
THIS CHEESE DIP HAS BULLETS IN IT.
SCOTT COULDN'T BE BOTHERED TO LEAVE HIS PRECIOUS ISLAND, I SEE.
SCOTT POLITELY DECLINED, YES. AND EMMA, WHEN I ASKED HER ABOUT IT, SHE JUST WALKED AWAY, LAUGHING.
GOD, I DO NOT MISS THAT PLACE.
SHE'S PRETTY. SHE'S SHARP. I GOTTA ADMIT, I LIKE HER.
SO WHO THINKS SHE HAS ANY IDEA WHAT SHE'S GETTING HERSELF INTO?
NOPE.
NO.
NUH-UH.
NOT A DAMN CLUE.

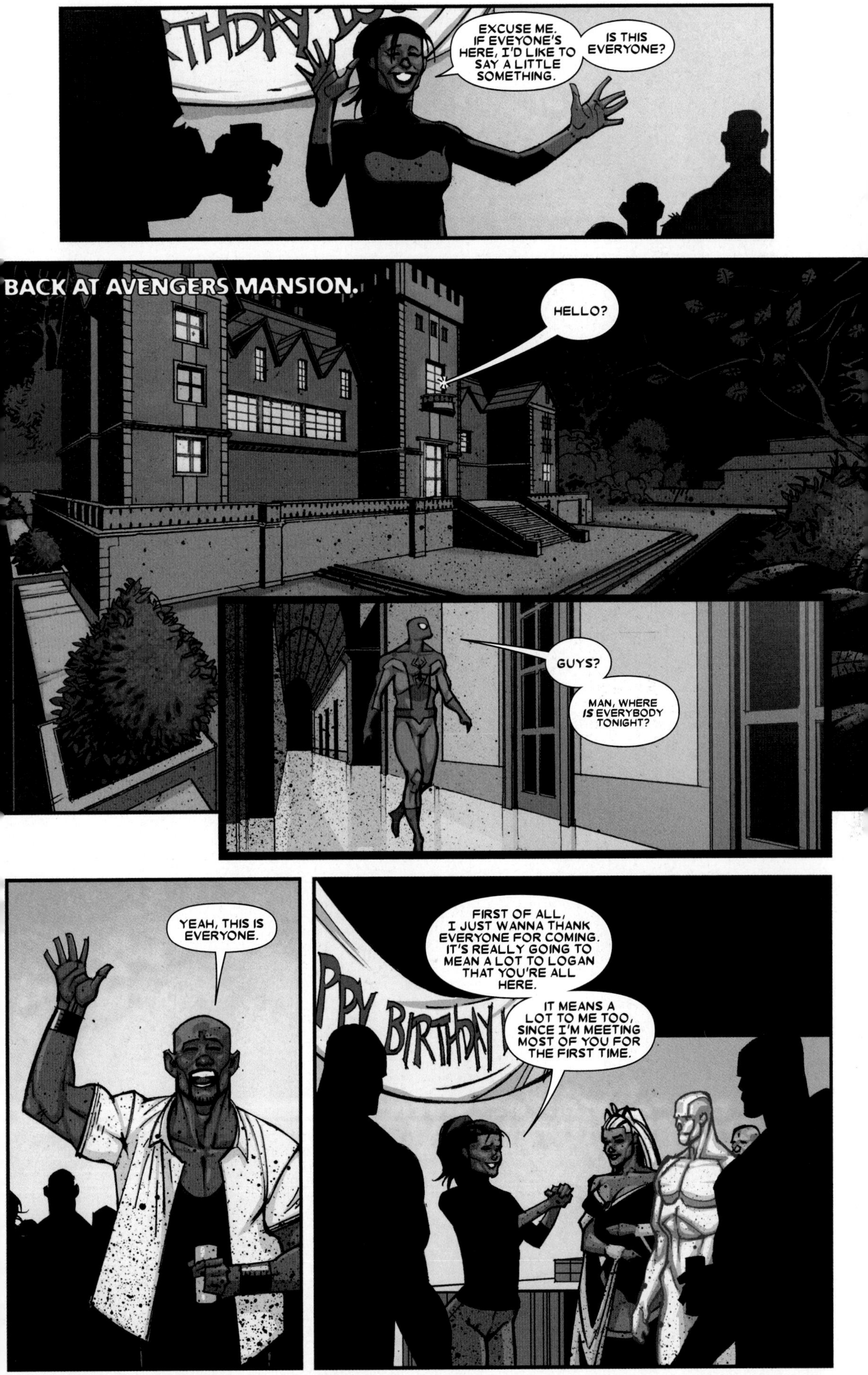

EXCUSE ME. IF EVEYONE'S HERE, I'D LIKE TO SAY A LITTLE SOMETHING.
IS THIS EVERYONE?
BACK AT AVENGERS MANSION.
HELLO?
GUYS?
MAN, WHERE IS EVERYBODY TONIGHT?
YEAH, THIS IS EVERYONE.
FIRST OF ALL, I JUST WANNA THANK EVERYONE FOR COMING. IT'S REALLY GOING TO MEAN A LOT TO LOGAN THAT YOU'RE ALL HERE.
IT MEANS A LOT TO ME TOO, SINCE I'M MEETING MOST OF YOU FOR THE FIRST TIME.

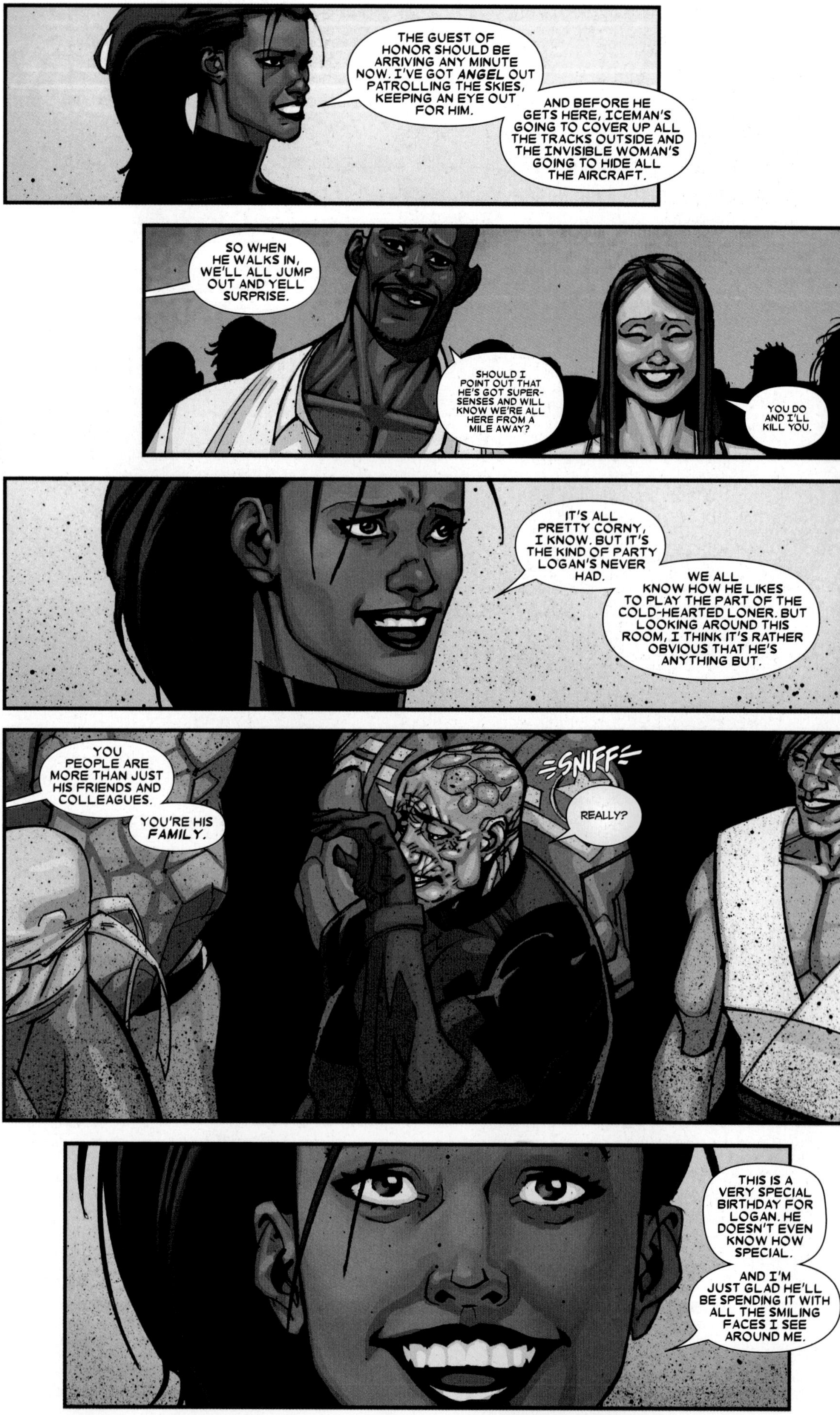
THE GUEST OF HONOR SHOULD BE ARRIVING ANY MINUTE NOW. I'VE GOT ANGEL OUT PATROLLING THE SKIES, KEEPING AN EYE OUT FOR HIM.
AND BEFORE HE GETS HERE, ICEMAN'S GOING TO COVER UP ALL THE TRACKS OUTSIDE AND THE INVISIBLE WOMAN'S GOING TO HIDE ALL THE AIRCRAFT.
SO WHEN HE WALKS IN, WE'LL ALL JUMP OUT AND YELL SURPRISE.
SHOULD I POINT OUT THAT HE'S GOT SUPER-SENSES AND WILL KNOW WE'RE ALL HERE FROM A MILE AWAY?
YOU DO AND I'LL KILL YOU.
IT'S ALL PRETTY CORNY, I KNOW. BUT IT'S THE KIND OF PARTY LOGAN'S NEVER HAD.
WE ALL KNOW HOW HE LIKES TO PLAY THE PART OF THE COLD-HEARTED LONER. BUT LOOKING AROUND THIS ROOM, I THINK IT'S RATHER OBVIOUS THAT HE'S ANYTHING BUT.
YOU PEOPLE ARE MORE THAN JUST HIS FRIENDS AND COLLEAGUES.
YOU'RE HIS FAMILY.
SNIFF
REALLY?
THIS IS A VERY SPECIAL BIRTHDAY FOR LOGAN. HE DOESN'T EVEN KNOW HOW SPECIAL.
AND I'M JUST GLAD HE'LL BE SPENDING IT WITH ALL THE SMILING FACES I SEE AROUND ME.

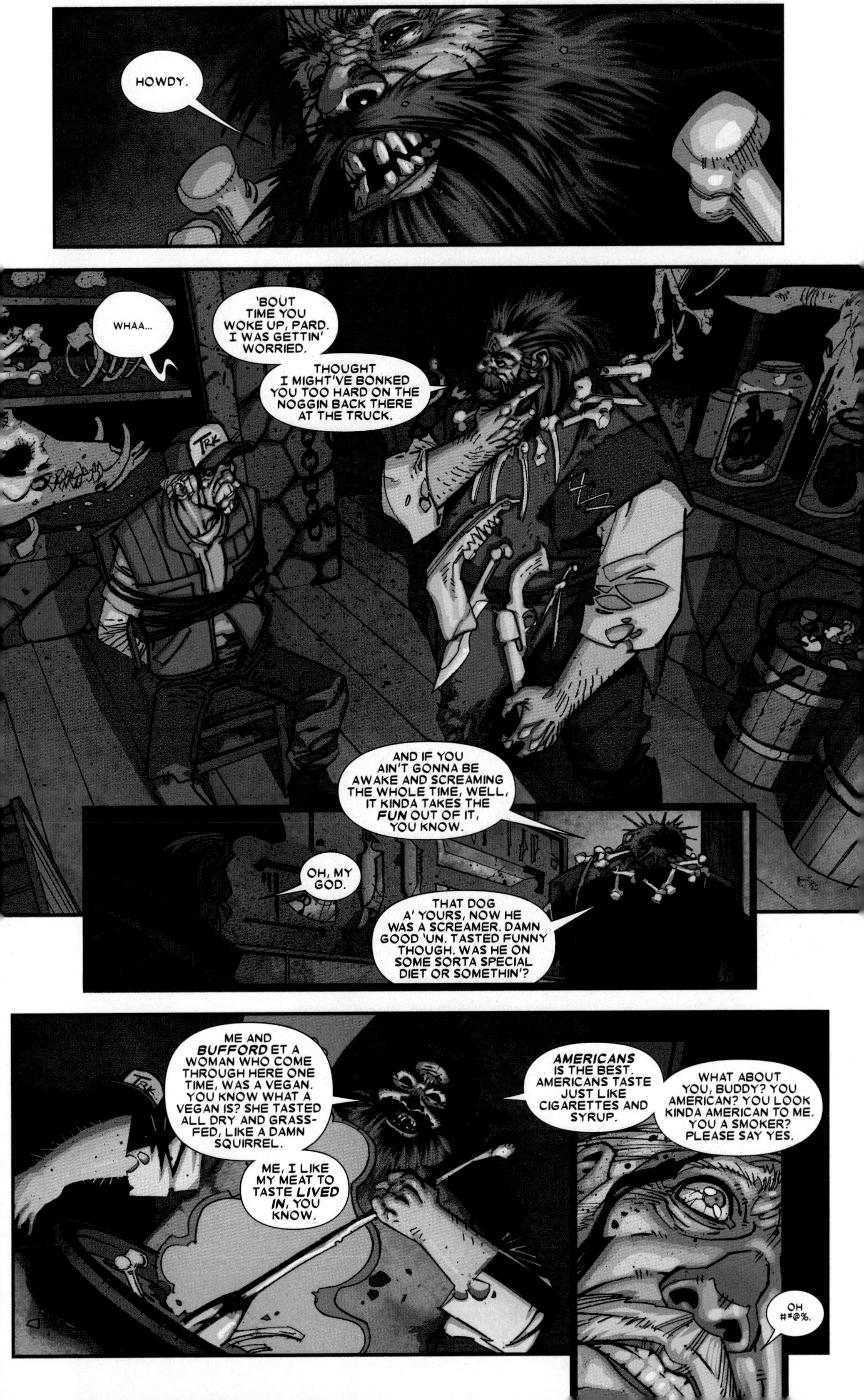
HOWDY.
WHAA...
'BOUT TIME YOU WOKE UP, PARD. I WAS GETTIN' WORRIED.
THOUGHT I MIGHT'VE BONKED YOU TOO HARD ON THE NOGGIN BACK THERE AT THE TRUCK.
AND IF YOU AIN'T GONNA BE AWAKE AND SCREAMING THE WHOLE TIME, WELL, IT KINDA TAKES THE FUN OUT OF IT, YOU KNOW.
OH, MY GOD.
THAT DOG A' YOURS, NOW HE WAS A SCREAMER. DAMN GOOD 'UN. TASTED FUNNY THOUGH. WAS HE ON SOME SORTA SPECIAL DIET OR SOMETHIN'?
ME AND BUFFORD ET A WOMAN WHO COME THROUGH HERE ONE TIME, WAS A VEGAN. YOU KNOW WHAT A VEGAN IS? SHE TASTED ALL DRY AND GRASS-FED, LIKE A DAMN SQUIRREL.
ME, I LIKE MY MEAT TO TASTE LIVED IN, YOU KNOW.
AMERICANS IS THE BEST. AMERICANS TASTE JUST LIKE CIGARETTES AND SYRUP.
WHAT ABOUT YOU, BUDDY? YOU AMERICAN? YOU LOOK KINDA AMERICAN TO ME. YOU A SMOKER? PLEASE SAY YES.
OH #*@%.

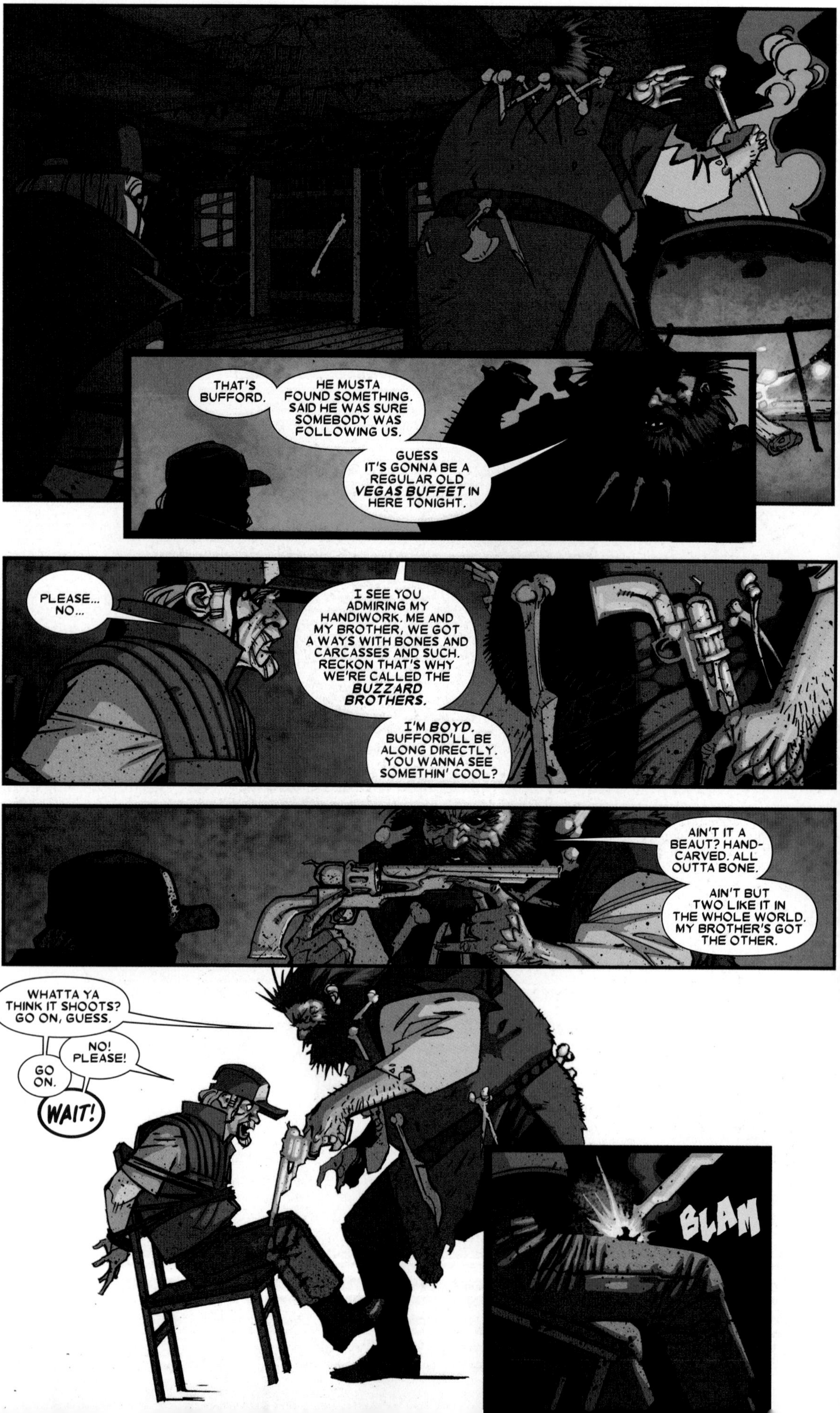

THAT'S BUFFORD.
HE MUSTA FOUND SOMETHING. SAID HE WAS SURE SOMEBODY WAS FOLLOWING US.
GUESS IT'S GONNA BE A REGULAR OLD *VEGAS BUFFET* IN HERE TONIGHT.
PLEASE... NO...
I SEE YOU ADMIRING MY HANDIWORK. ME AND MY BROTHER, WE GOT A WAYS WITH BONES AND CARCASSES AND SUCH. RECKON THAT'S WHY WE'RE CALLED THE *BUZZARD BROTHERS.*
I'M *BOYD.* BUFFORD'LL BE ALONG DIRECTLY. YOU WANNA SEE SOMETHIN' COOL?
AIN'T IT A BEAUT? HAND-CARVED. ALL OUTTA BONE.
AIN'T BUT TWO LIKE IT IN THE WHOLE WORLD. MY BROTHER'S GOT THE OTHER.
WHATTA YA THINK IT SHOOTS? GO ON, GUESS.
NO! PLEASE!
GO ON.
WAIT!
BLAM

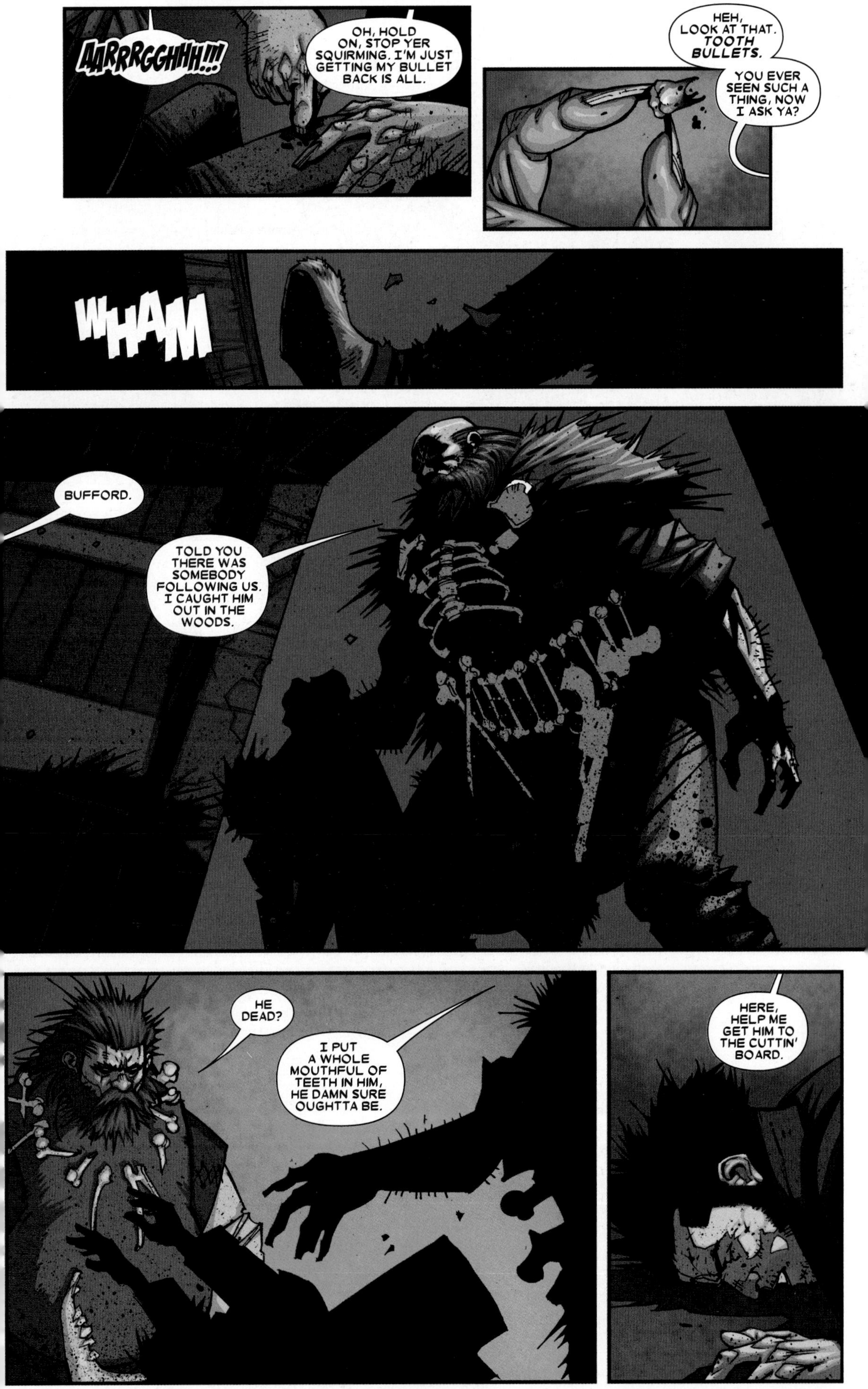
AARRRGGHHH!!!
OH, HOLD ON, STOP YER SQUIRMING. I'M JUST GETTING MY BULLET BACK IS ALL.
HEH, LOOK AT THAT. TOOTH BULLETS.
YOU EVER SEEN SUCH A THING, NOW I ASK YA?
WHAM
BUFFORD.
TOLD YOU THERE WAS SOMEBODY FOLLOWING US. I CAUGHT HIM OUT IN THE WOODS.
HE DEAD?
I PUT A WHOLE MOUTHFUL OF TEETH IN HIM, HE DAMN SURE OUGHTTA BE.
HERE, HELP ME GET HIM TO THE CUTTIN' BOARD.

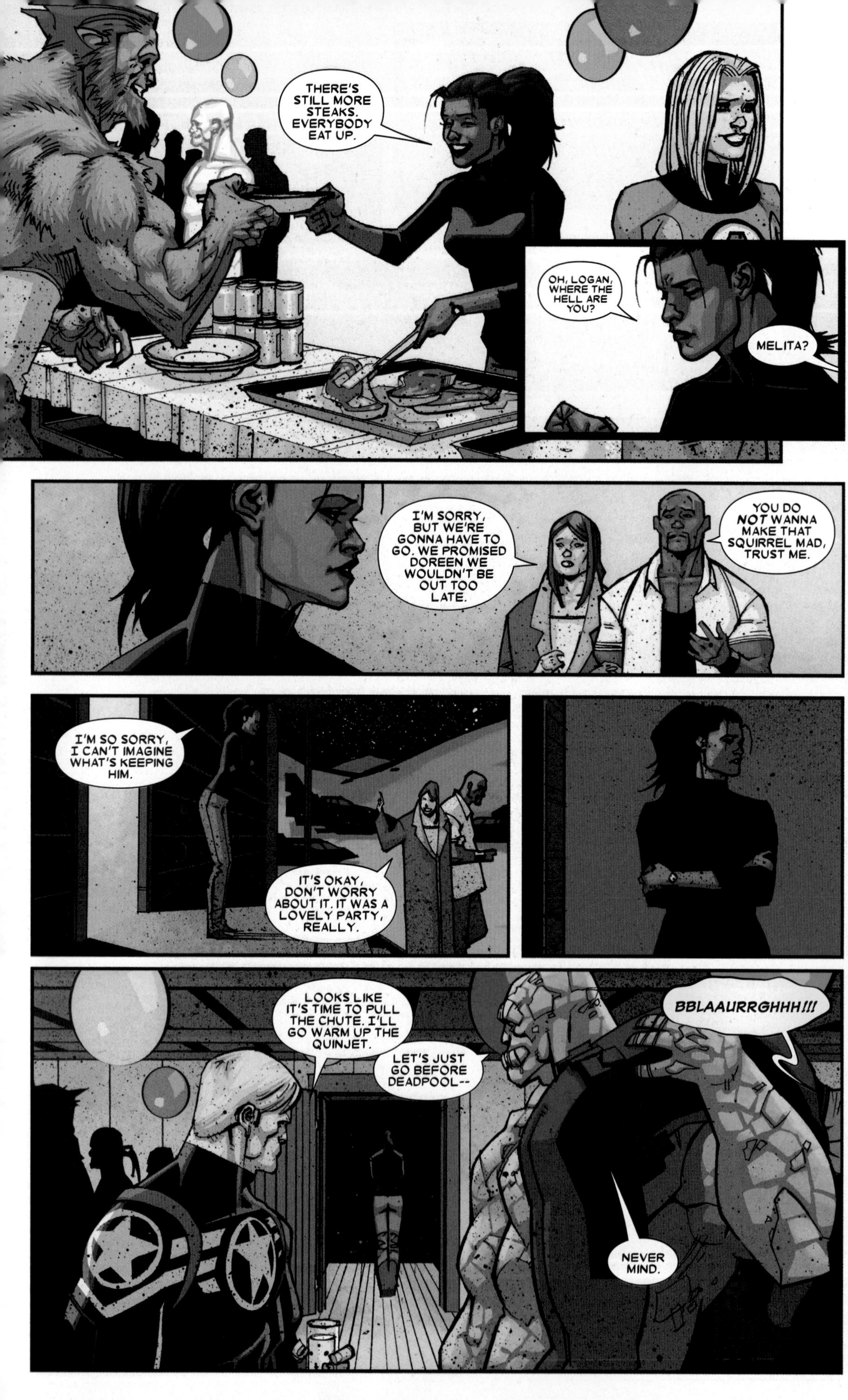
THERE'S STILL MORE STEAKS. EVERYBODY EAT UP.
OH, LOGAN, WHERE THE HELL ARE YOU?
MELITA?
I'M SORRY, BUT WE'RE GONNA HAVE TO GO. WE PROMISED DOREEN WE WOULDN'T BE OUT TOO LATE.
YOU DO NOT WANNA MAKE THAT SQUIRREL MAD, TRUST ME.
I'M SO SORRY, I CAN'T IMAGINE WHAT'S KEEPING HIM.
IT'S OKAY, DON'T WORRY ABOUT IT. IT WAS A LOVELY PARTY, REALLY.
LOOKS LIKE IT'S TIME TO PULL THE CHUTE. I'LL GO WARM UP THE QUINJET.
LET'S JUST GO BEFORE DEADPOOL--
BBLAAURRGHHH!!!
NEVER MIND.

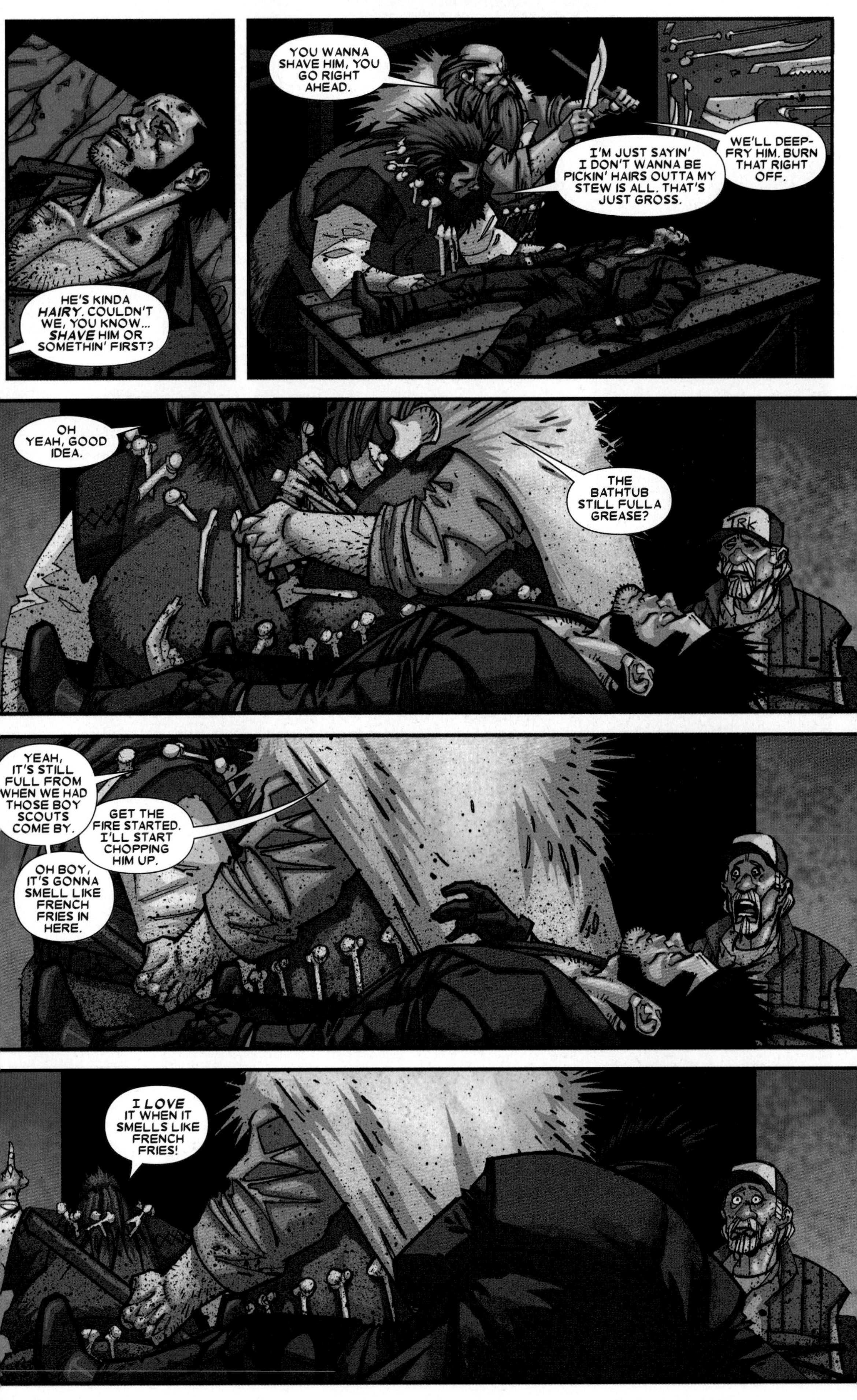
HE'S KINDA HAIRY. COULDN'T WE, YOU KNOW... SHAVE HIM OR SOMETHIN' FIRST?
YOU WANNA SHAVE HIM, YOU GO RIGHT AHEAD.
I'M JUST SAYIN' I DON'T WANNA BE PICKIN' HAIRS OUTTA MY STEW IS ALL. THAT'S JUST GROSS.
WE'LL DEEP-FRY HIM. BURN THAT RIGHT OFF.
OH YEAH, GOOD IDEA.
THE BATHTUB STILL FULLA GREASE?
YEAH, IT'S STILL FULL FROM WHEN WE HAD THOSE BOY SCOUTS COME BY.
GET THE FIRE STARTED. I'LL START CHOPPING HIM UP.
OH BOY, IT'S GONNA SMELL LIKE FRENCH FRIES IN HERE.
I LOVE IT WHEN IT SMELLS LIKE FRENCH FRIES!

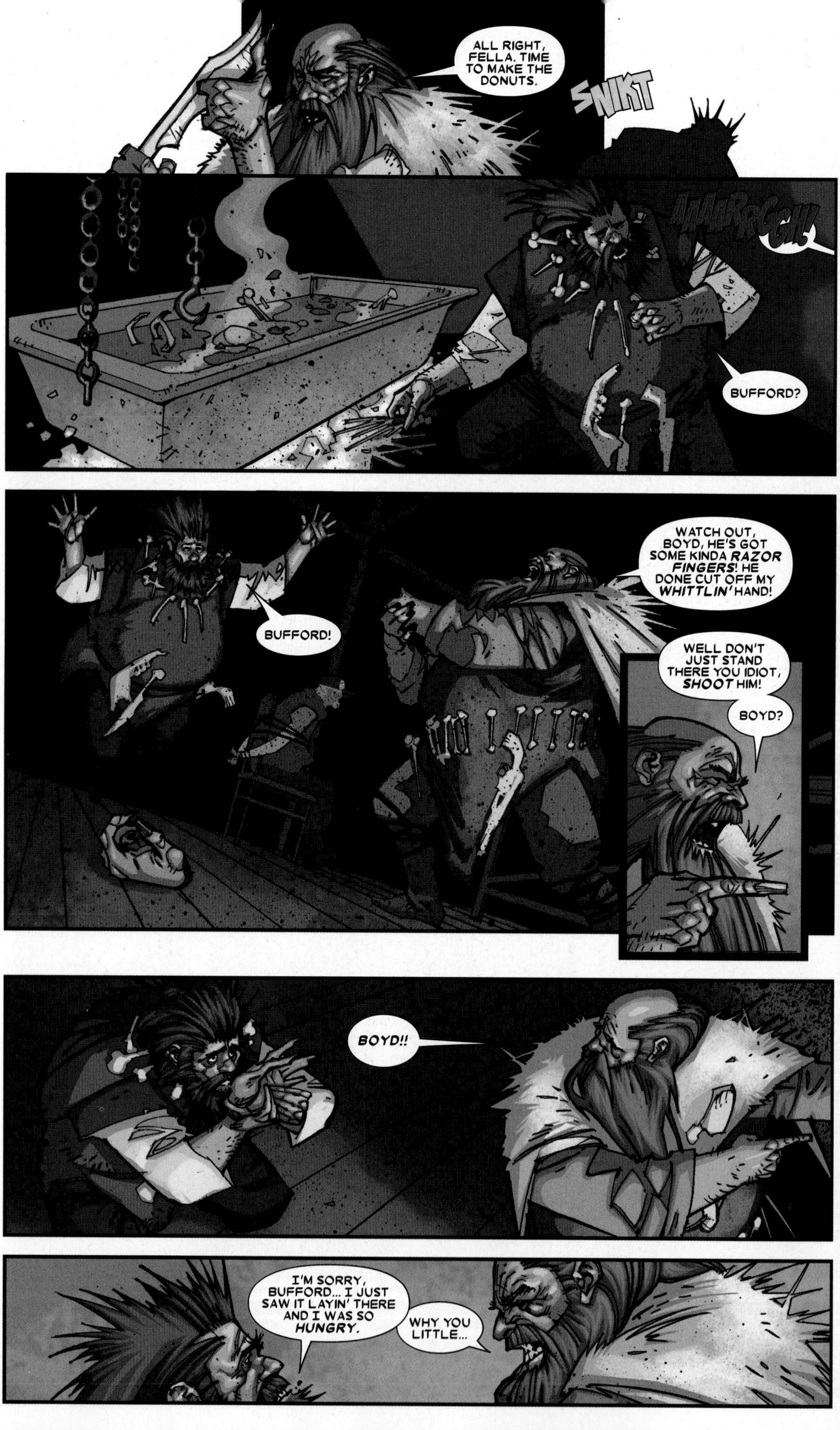

ALL RIGHT, FELLA. TIME TO MAKE THE DONUTS.
SNIKT
AAAARRGGH!
BUFFORD?
BUFFORD!
WATCH OUT, BOYD, HE'S GOT SOME KINDA RAZOR FINGERS! HE DONE CUT OFF MY WHITTLIN' HAND!
WELL DON'T JUST STAND THERE YOU IDIOT, SHOOT HIM!
BOYD?
BOYD!!
I'M SORRY, BUFFORD... I JUST SAW IT LAYIN' THERE AND I WAS SO HUNGRY.
WHY YOU LITTLE...

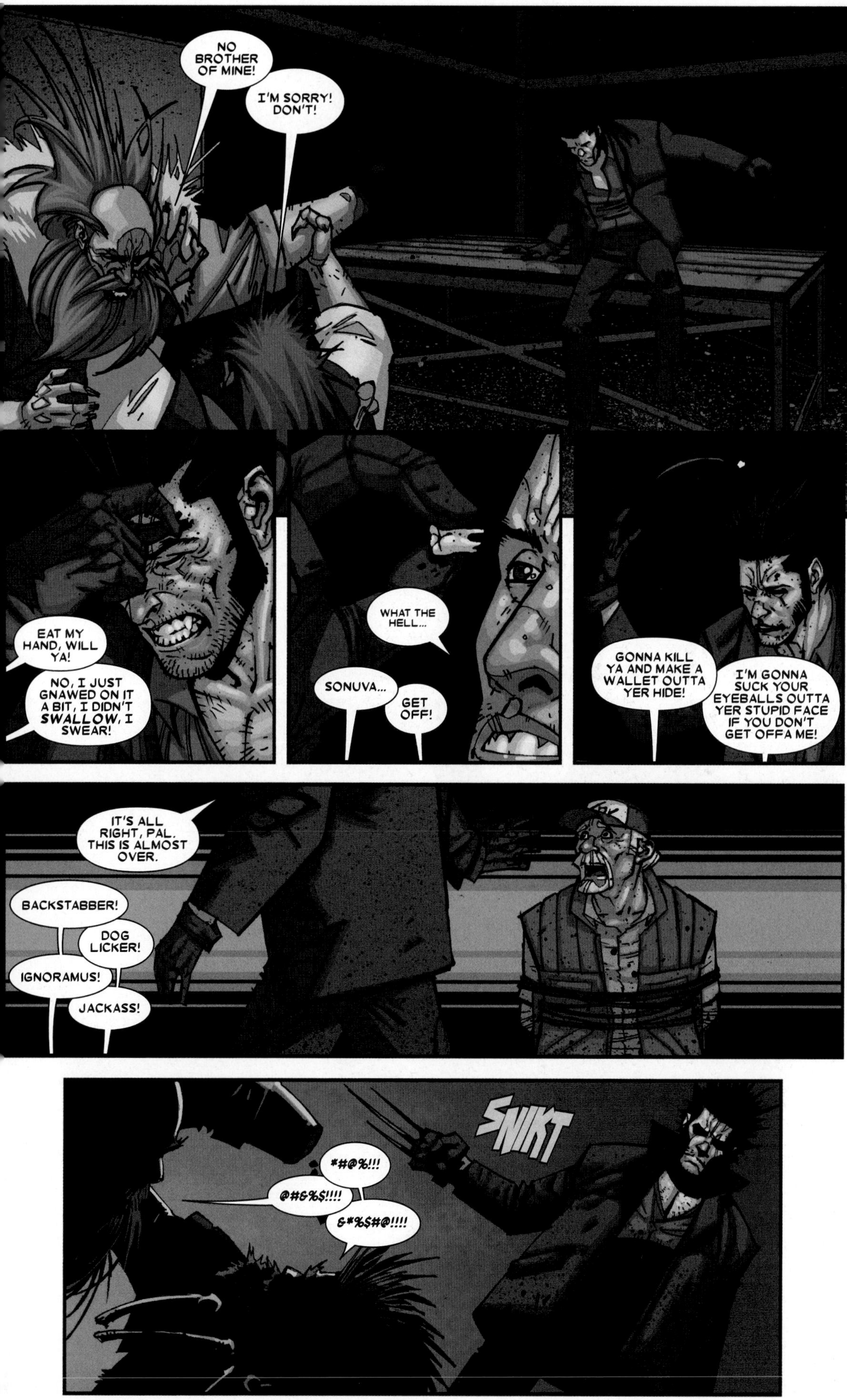
NO BROTHER OF MINE!
I'M SORRY! DON'T!
EAT MY HAND, WILL YA!
NO, I JUST GNAWED ON IT A BIT, I DIDN'T SWALLOW, I SWEAR!
WHAT THE HELL...
SONUVA...
GET OFF!
GONNA KILL YA AND MAKE A WALLET OUTTA YER HIDE!
I'M GONNA SUCK YOUR EYEBALLS OUTTA YER STUPID FACE IF YOU DON'T GET OFFA ME!
IT'S ALL RIGHT, PAL. THIS IS ALMOST OVER.
BACKSTABBER!
DOG LICKER!
IGNORAMUS!
JACKASS!
SNIKT
*#@%!!!
@#&%$!!!!
&*%$#@!!!!

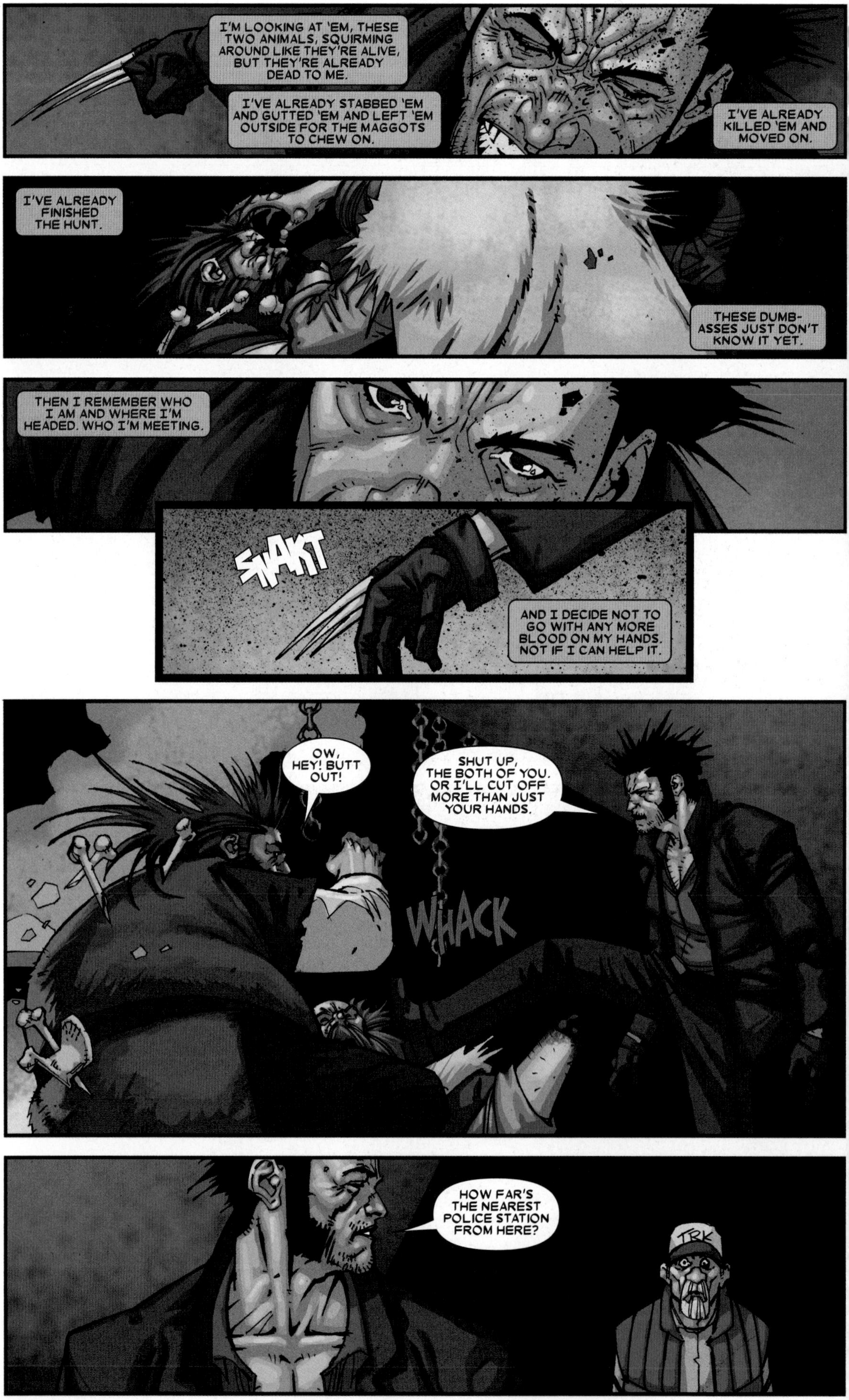
I'M LOOKING AT 'EM, THESE TWO ANIMALS, SQUIRMING AROUND LIKE THEY'RE ALIVE, BUT THEY'RE ALREADY DEAD TO ME.
I'VE ALREADY STABBED 'EM AND GUTTED 'EM AND LEFT 'EM OUTSIDE FOR THE MAGGOTS TO CHEW ON.
I'VE ALREADY KILLED 'EM AND MOVED ON.
I'VE ALREADY FINISHED THE HUNT.
THESE DUMB-ASSES JUST DON'T KNOW IT YET.
THEN I REMEMBER WHO I AM AND WHERE I'M HEADED. WHO I'M MEETING.
SNAKT
AND I DECIDE NOT TO GO WITH ANY MORE BLOOD ON MY HANDS. NOT IF I CAN HELP IT.
OW, HEY! BUTT OUT!
SHUT UP, THE BOTH OF YOU. OR I'LL CUT OFF MORE THAN JUST YOUR HANDS.
WHACK
HOW FAR'S THE NEAREST POLICE STATION FROM HERE?
TRK

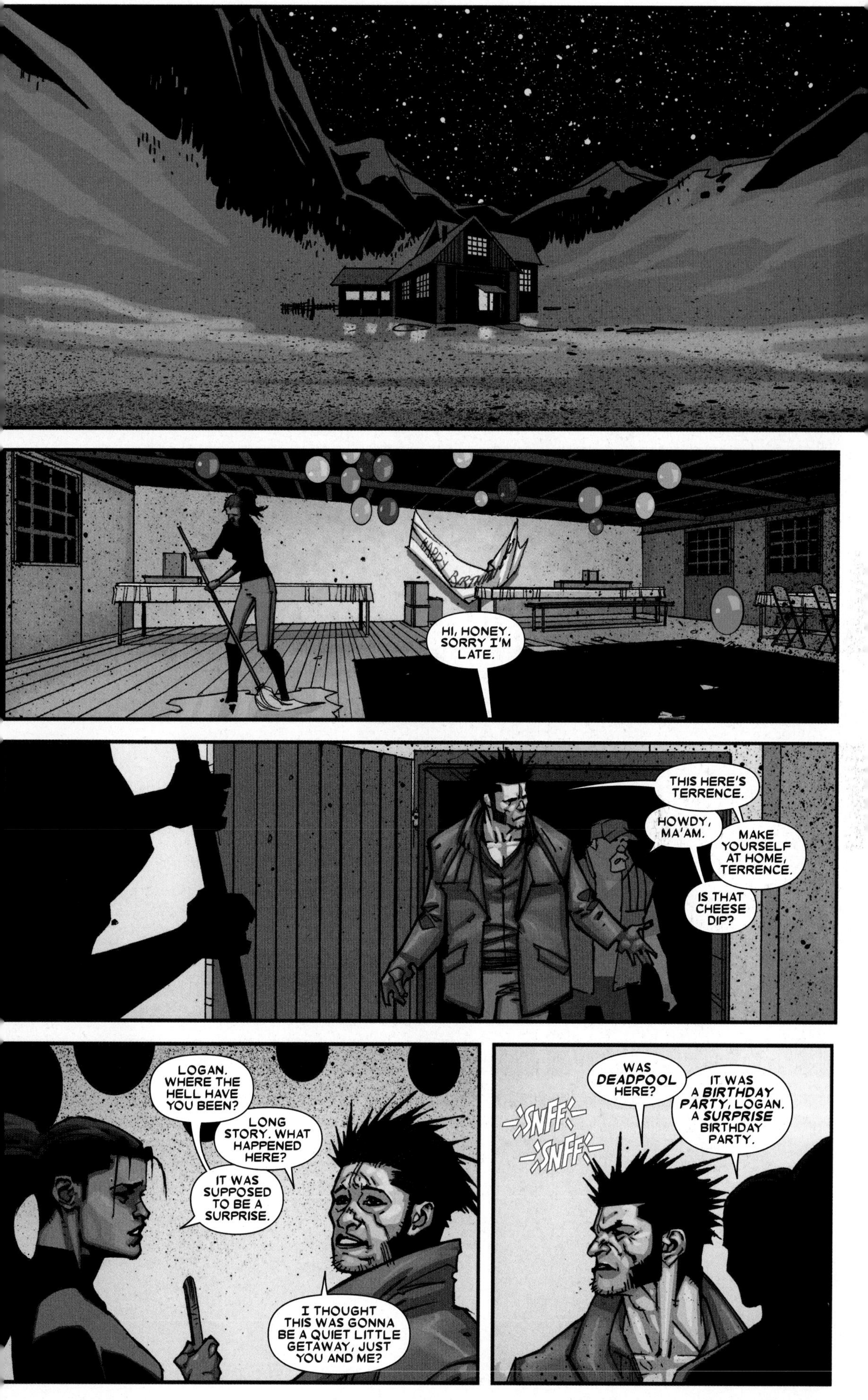

HAPPY BIRTHDAY
HI, HONEY. SORRY I'M LATE.
THIS HERE'S TERRENCE.
HOWDY, MA'AM.
MAKE YOURSELF AT HOME, TERRENCE.
IS THAT CHEESE DIP?
LOGAN. WHERE THE HELL HAVE YOU BEEN?
LONG STORY. WHAT HAPPENED HERE?
IT WAS SUPPOSED TO BE A SURPRISE.
I THOUGHT THIS WAS GONNA BE A QUIET LITTLE GETAWAY, JUST YOU AND ME?
SNFF
SNFF
WAS DEADPOOL HERE?
IT WAS A BIRTHDAY PARTY, LOGAN. A SURPRISE BIRTHDAY PARTY.

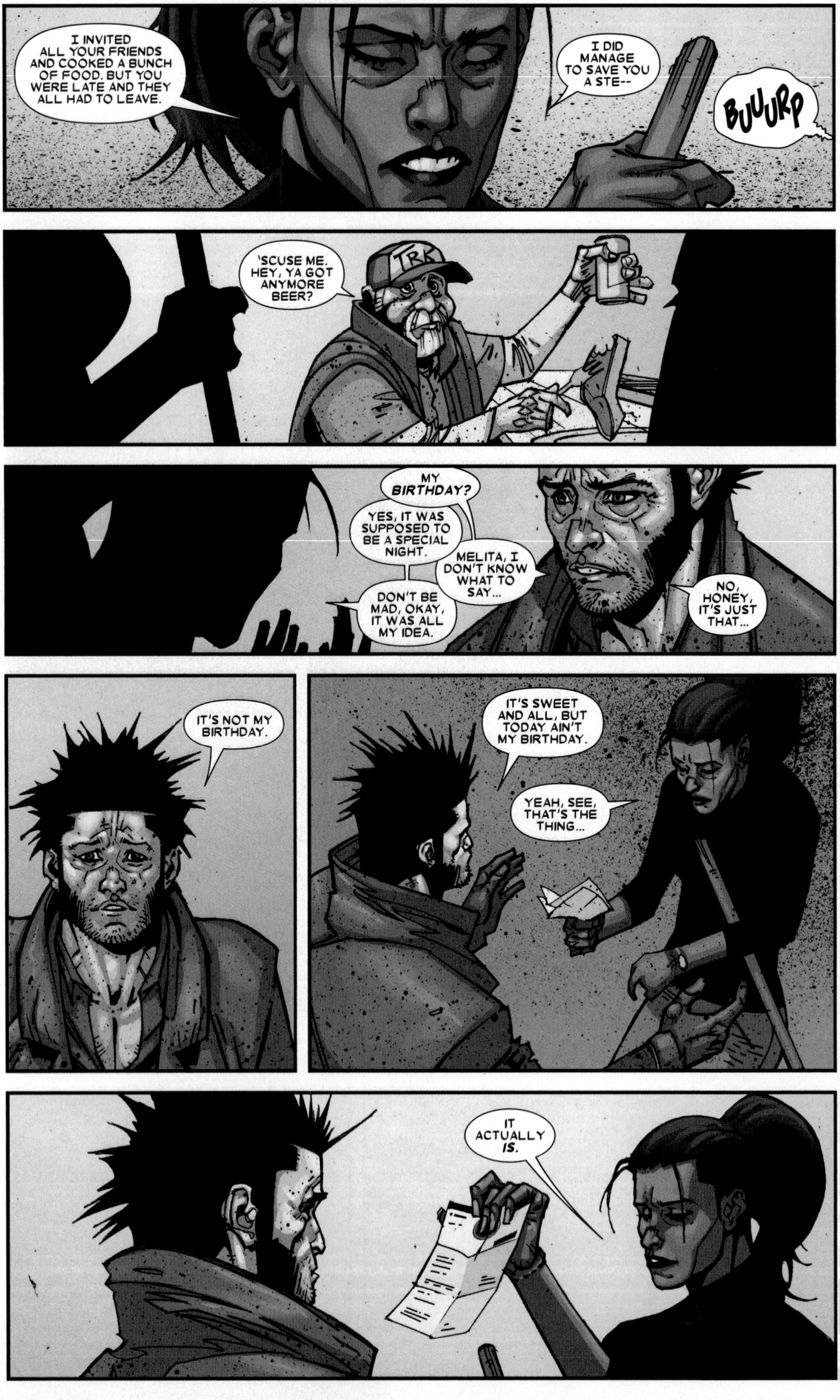
I INVITED ALL YOUR FRIENDS AND COOKED A BUNCH OF FOOD. BUT YOU WERE LATE AND THEY ALL HAD TO LEAVE.
I DID MANAGE TO SAVE YOU A STE--
BUUURP
'SCUSE ME. HEY, YA GOT ANYMORE BEER?
MY *BIRTHDAY?*
YES, IT WAS SUPPOSED TO BE A SPECIAL NIGHT.
MELITA, I DON'T KNOW WHAT TO SAY...
DON'T BE MAD, OKAY, IT WAS ALL MY IDEA.
NO, HONEY, IT'S JUST THAT...
IT'S NOT MY BIRTHDAY.
IT'S SWEET AND ALL, BUT TODAY AIN'T MY BIRTHDAY.
YEAH, SEE, THAT'S THE THING...
IT ACTUALLY *IS.*

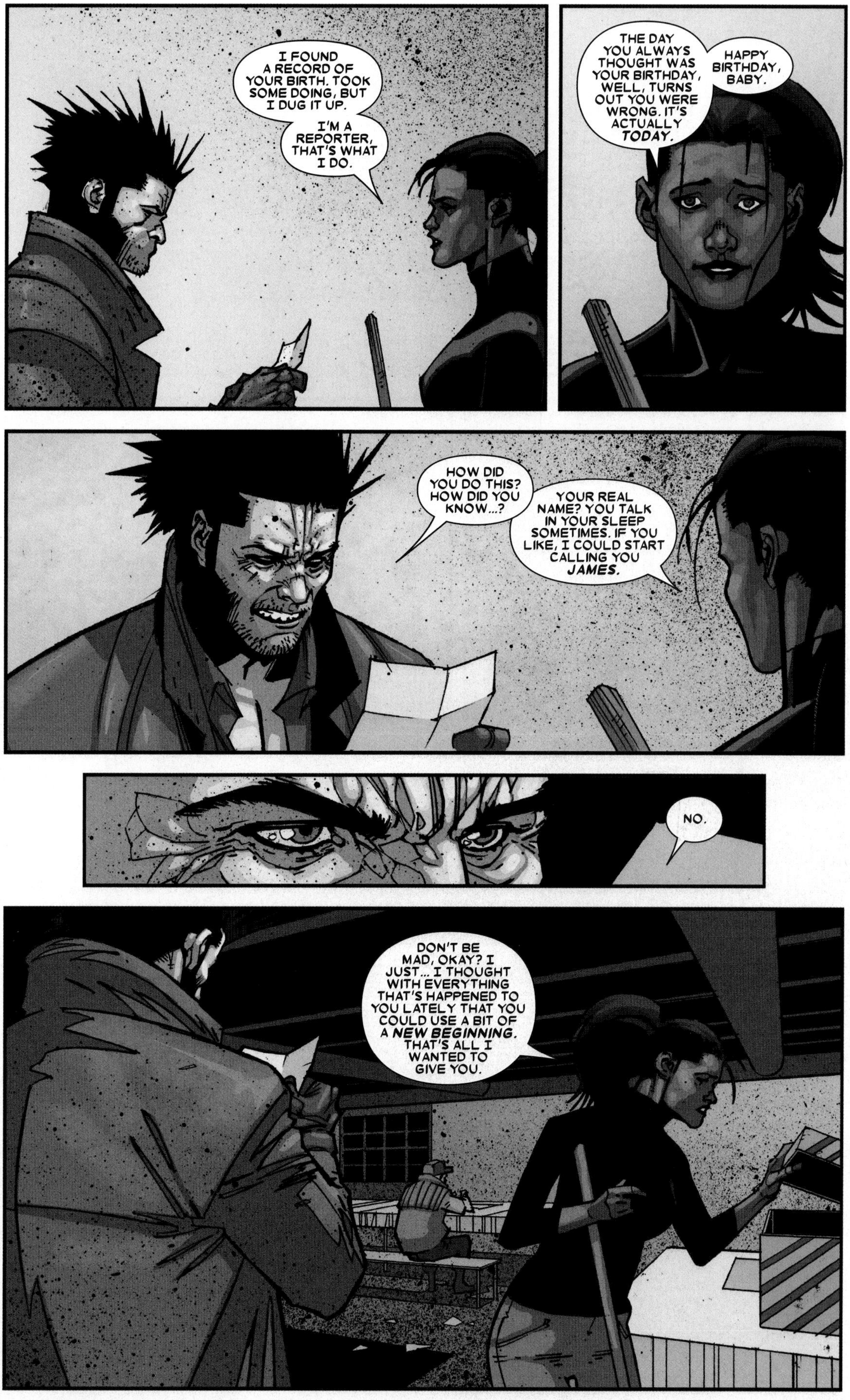
I FOUND A RECORD OF YOUR BIRTH. TOOK SOME DOING, BUT I DUG IT UP.
I'M A REPORTER, THAT'S WHAT I DO.
THE DAY YOU ALWAYS THOUGHT WAS YOUR BIRTHDAY, WELL, TURNS OUT YOU WERE WRONG. IT'S ACTUALLY *TODAY*.
HAPPY BIRTHDAY, BABY.
HOW DID YOU DO THIS? HOW DID YOU KNOW...?
YOUR REAL NAME? YOU TALK IN YOUR SLEEP SOMETIMES. IF YOU LIKE, I COULD START CALLING YOU ***JAMES.***
NO.
DON'T BE MAD, OKAY? I JUST... I THOUGHT WITH EVERYTHING THAT'S HAPPENED TO YOU LATELY THAT YOU COULD USE A BIT OF A ***NEW BEGINNING.*** THAT'S ALL I WANTED TO GIVE YOU.

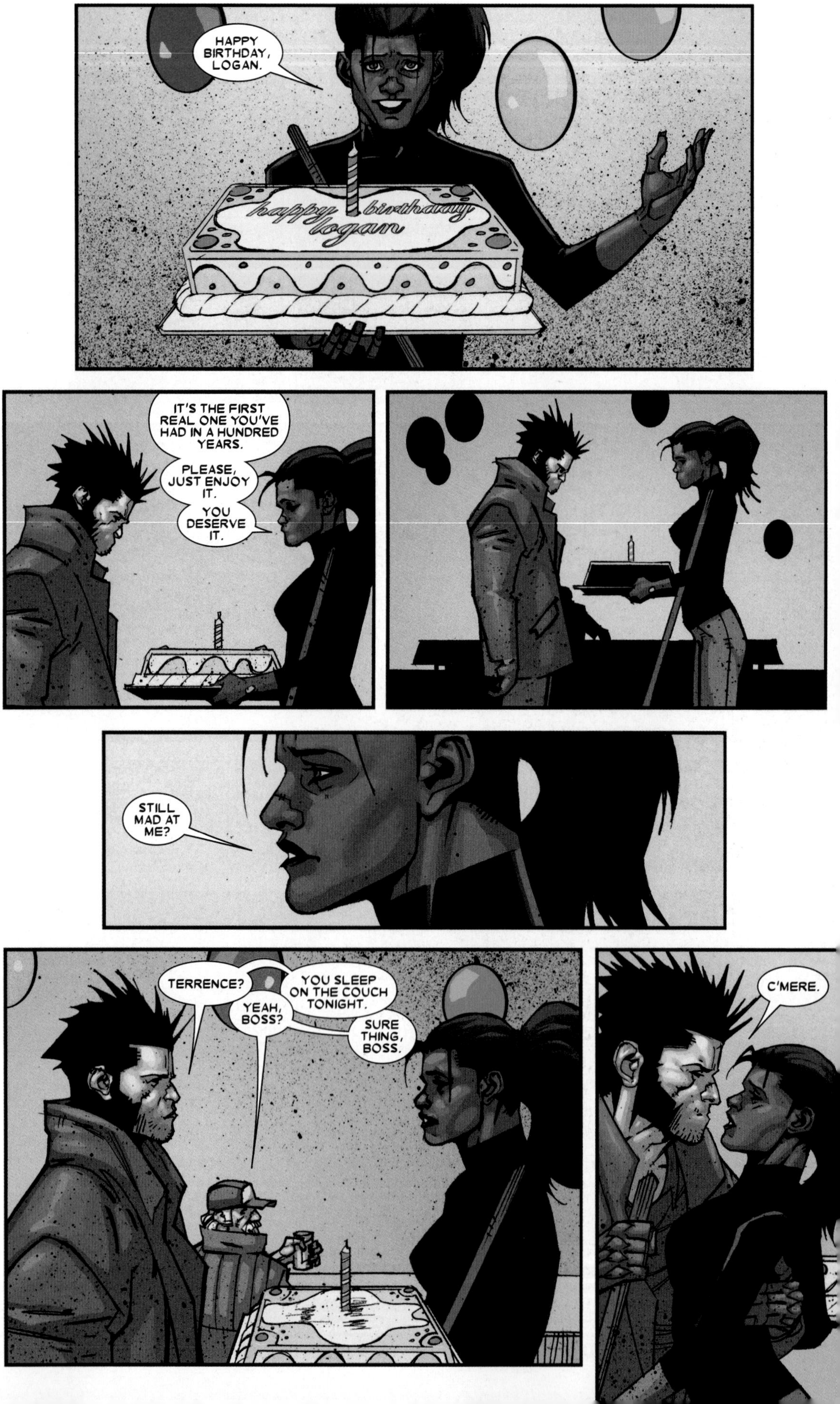
HAPPY BIRTHDAY, LOGAN.
happy birthday logan
IT'S THE FIRST REAL ONE YOU'VE HAD IN A HUNDRED YEARS.
PLEASE, JUST ENJOY IT.
YOU DESERVE IT.
STILL MAD AT ME?
TERRENCE?
YEAH, BOSS?
YOU SLEEP ON THE COUCH TONIGHT.
SURE THING, BOSS.
C'MERE.

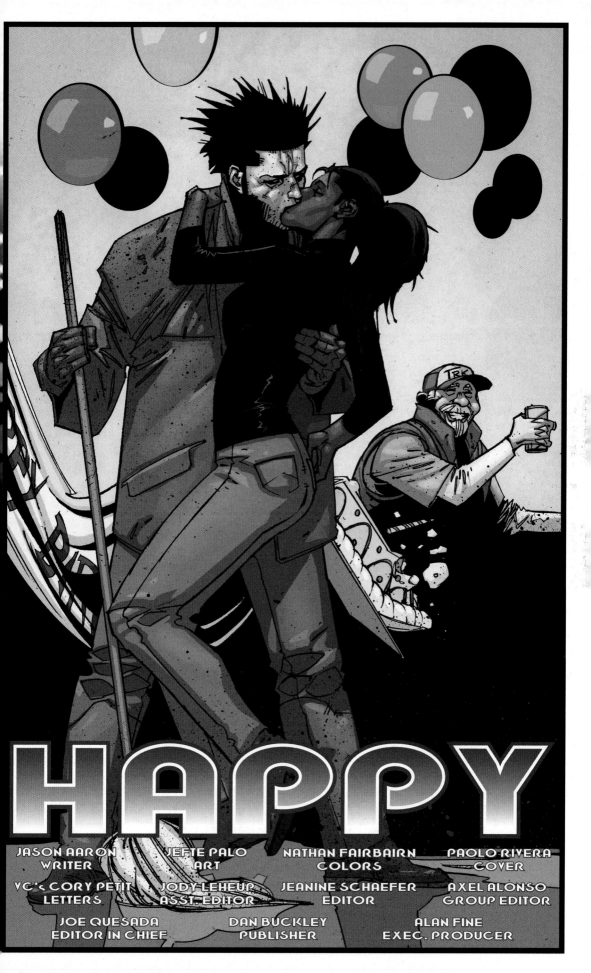

HAPPY

JASON AARON
WRITER

JEFTE PALO
ART

NATHAN FAIRBAIRN
COLORS

PAOLO RIVERA
COVER

VC's CORY PETIT
LETTERS

JODY LEHEUP
ASST. EDITOR

JEANINE SCHAEFER
EDITOR

AXEL ALONSO
GROUP EDITOR

JOE QUESADA
EDITOR IN CHIEF

DAN BUCKLEY
PUBLISHER

ALAN FINE
EXEC. PRODUCER

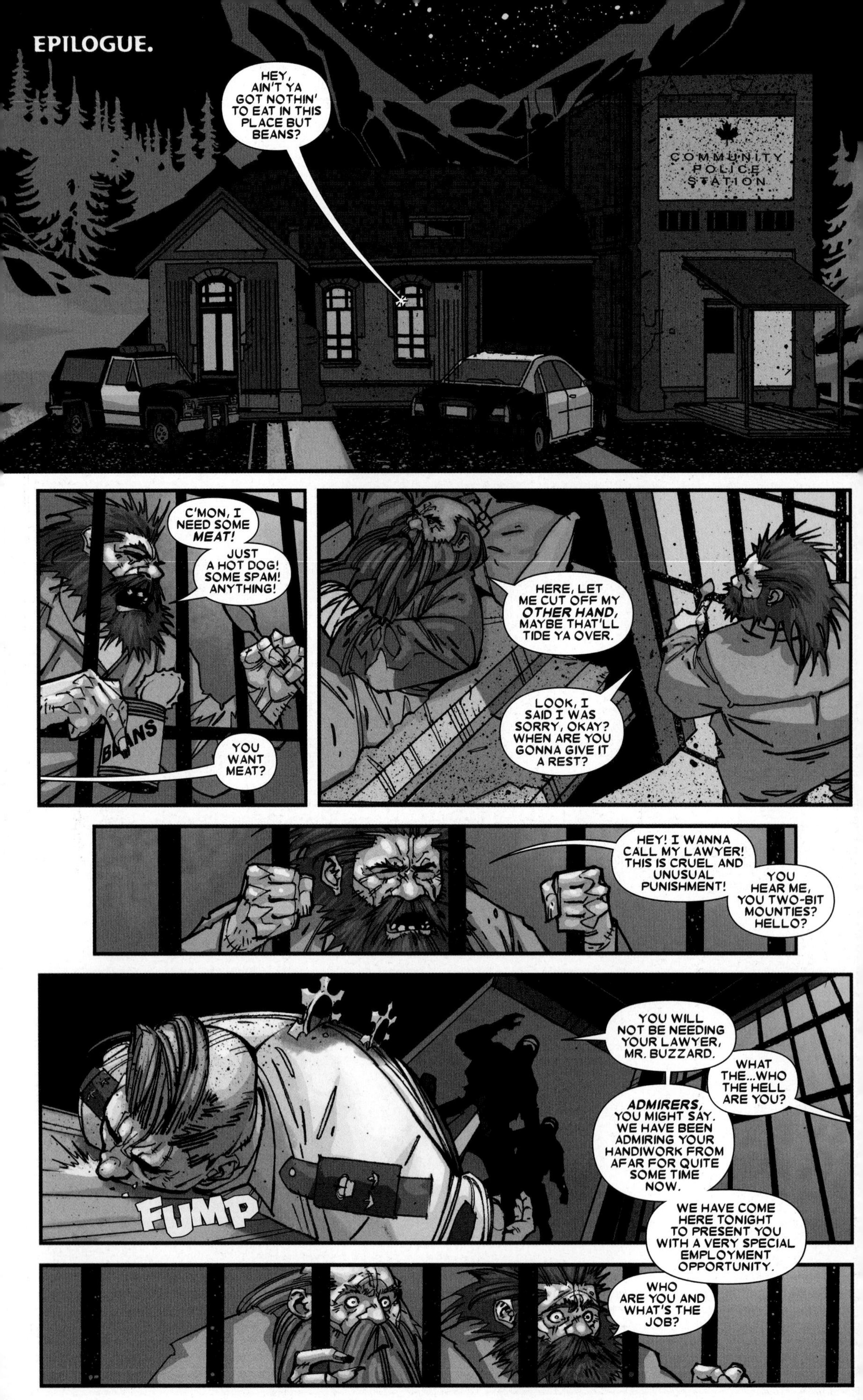
EPILOGUE.
HEY, AIN'T YA GOT NOTHIN' TO EAT IN THIS PLACE BUT BEANS?
COMMUNITY POLICE STATION
C'MON, I NEED SOME *MEAT!*
JUST A HOT DOG! SOME SPAM! ANYTHING!
BEANS
YOU WANT MEAT?
HERE, LET ME CUT OFF MY *OTHER HAND*, MAYBE THAT'LL TIDE YA OVER.
LOOK, I SAID I WAS SORRY, OKAY? WHEN ARE YOU GONNA GIVE IT A REST?
HEY! I WANNA CALL MY LAWYER! THIS IS CRUEL AND UNUSUAL PUNISHMENT!
YOU HEAR ME, YOU TWO-BIT MOUNTIES? HELLO?
FUMP
YOU WILL NOT BE NEEDING YOUR LAWYER, MR. BUZZARD.
WHAT THE...WHO THE HELL ARE YOU?
ADMIRERS, YOU MIGHT SAY. WE HAVE BEEN ADMIRING YOUR HANDIWORK FROM AFAR FOR QUITE SOME TIME NOW.
WE HAVE COME HERE TONIGHT TO PRESENT YOU WITH A VERY SPECIAL EMPLOYMENT OPPORTUNITY.
WHO ARE YOU AND WHAT'S THE JOB?

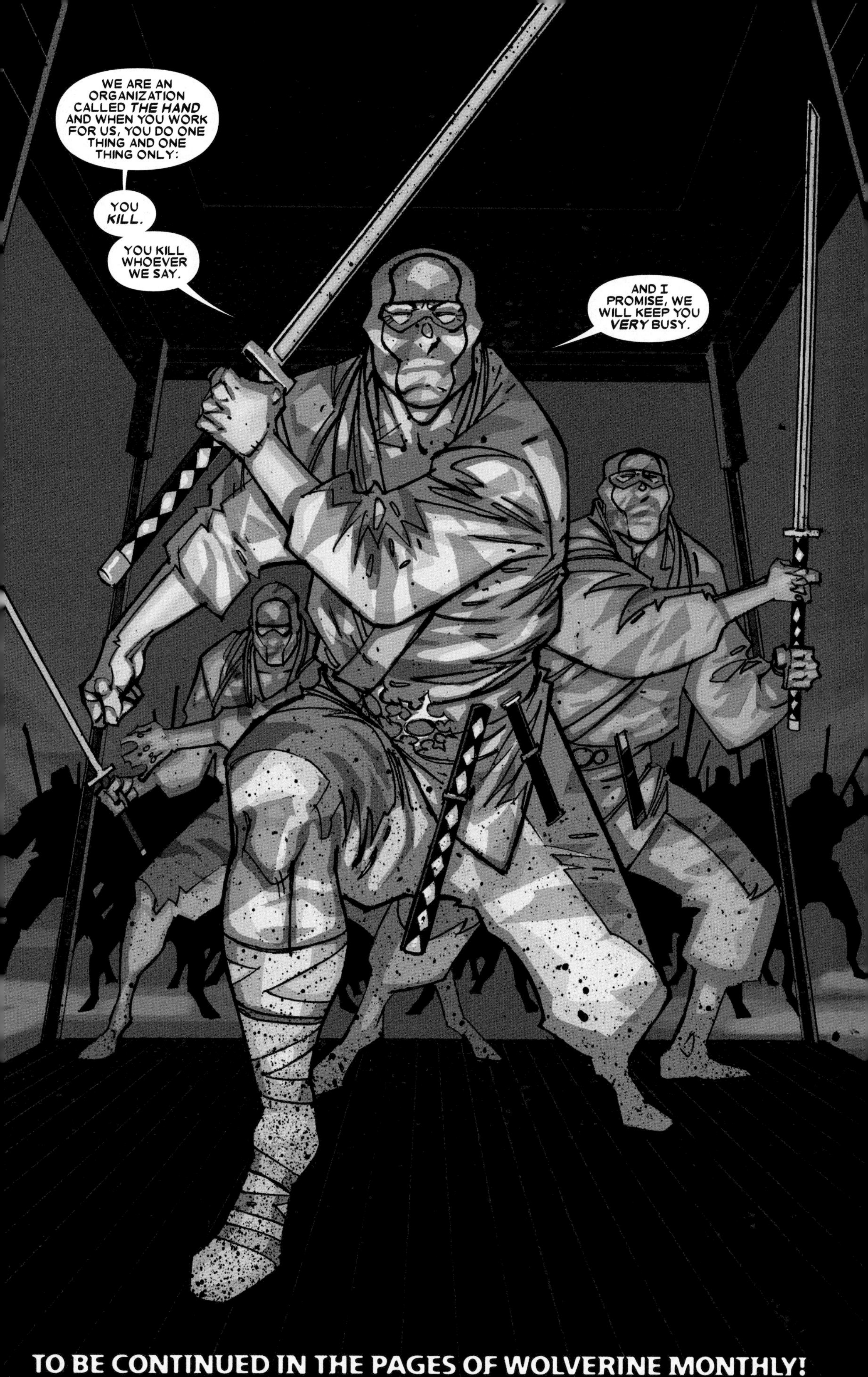
WE ARE AN ORGANIZATION CALLED *THE HAND* AND WHEN YOU WORK FOR US, YOU DO ONE THING AND ONE THING ONLY:
YOU *KILL.*
YOU KILL WHOEVER WE SAY.
AND I PROMISE, WE WILL KEEP YOU *VERY* BUSY.

TO BE CONTINUED IN THE PAGES OF WOLVERINE MONTHLY!

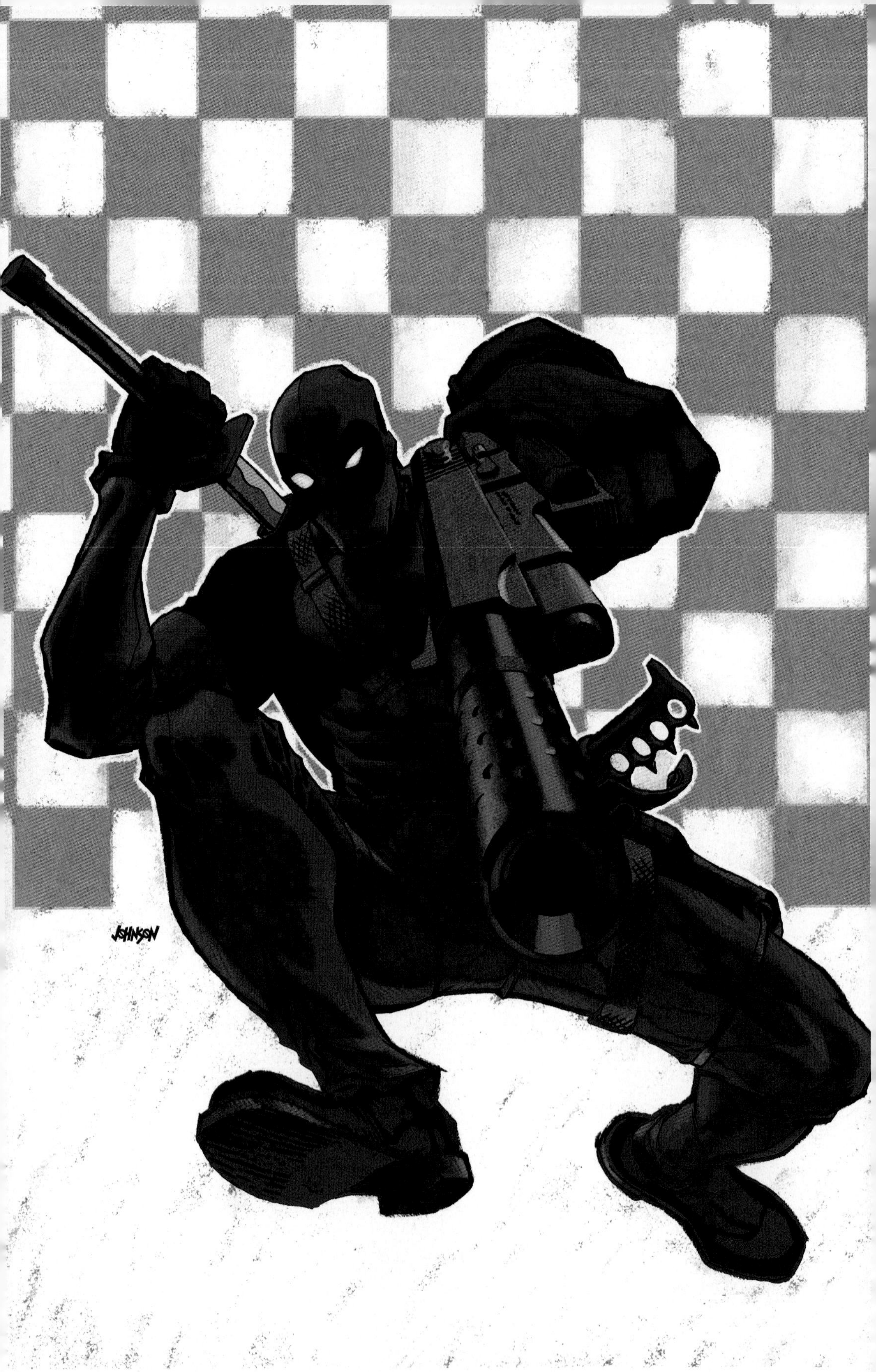
JOHNSON

DEADPOOL #33.1

HEY, KIDS!

MY NAME IS WADE WILSON, ALSO KNOWN AS THE MERC-WITH-A-MOUTH, DEADPOOL!

A MERCENARY WHO TALKS A LOT, GET IT?

Was there something to get?

THEY MIGHT HAVE THOUGHT IT MEANT OTHER MERCENARIES DON'T HAVE MOUTHS.

KEEP IT DOWN, GUYS, I'M DOING A RECAP PAGE.

ANYWAY, I'M A MERCENARY. AND, UH...I TALK A LOT.

I SAID THAT ALREADY.

Tell them about your incredible healing factor.

OH, RIGHT! I HAVE AN INCREDIBLE HEALING FACTOR--WAY BETTER THAN ANY WOLF OR BADGER BASED HERO'S WOULD BE.

Except that it can't heal your horribly scarred face.

ALL RIGHT, I AM READY FOR YOU TO SHUT UP NOW.

SO, BACK IN ISSUE 33, I WAS HEADING OUT INTO SPACE TO REAFFIRM MY STATUS AS EL MERCENARIADOR NUMERO ONE-O.

BUT FOR THIS SPECIAL "POINT ONE" ISSUE, I'M CATCHING A RIDE BACK TO EARTH REAL QUICK. WHEN I RETURN FOR NEXT ISSUE, I'LL BE OUT IN SPACE DOING THAT THANG. YOU'LL NEVER EVEN KNOW I WAS GONE.

SO KICK BACK AND ENJOY--DEADPOOL ISSUE THIRTY-THREE POINT ONE!

WAIT...WHY IS IT CALLED "POINT ONE"?

Who cares? At least this issue there *is* a point.

CRAB NEBULA 6 MIL LY
SIRIUS
ANDROMEDA 2 MIL LY
CIGNUS X-1 8 MIL LY
AURI 6 MIL LY
ALPHA
RIGEL 8 MIL LY
BABYLON 5 18

J. CALAFIORE '00
PETER PALMIOTTI
2/2000

DANIEL WAY — WRITER
BONG DAZO — PENCILS
JOE PIMENTAL — INKS
ANDRES MOSSA — COLORIST

VC'S JOE SABINO — LETTERER
DAVE JOHNSON — COVER
JODY LEHEUP & JORDAN D. WHITE — EDITORS

AXEL ALONSO — EDITOR IN CHIEF
JOE QUESADA — CHIEF CREATIVE OFFICER
DAN BUCKLEY — PUBLISHER
ALAN FINE — EXEC. PRODUCER

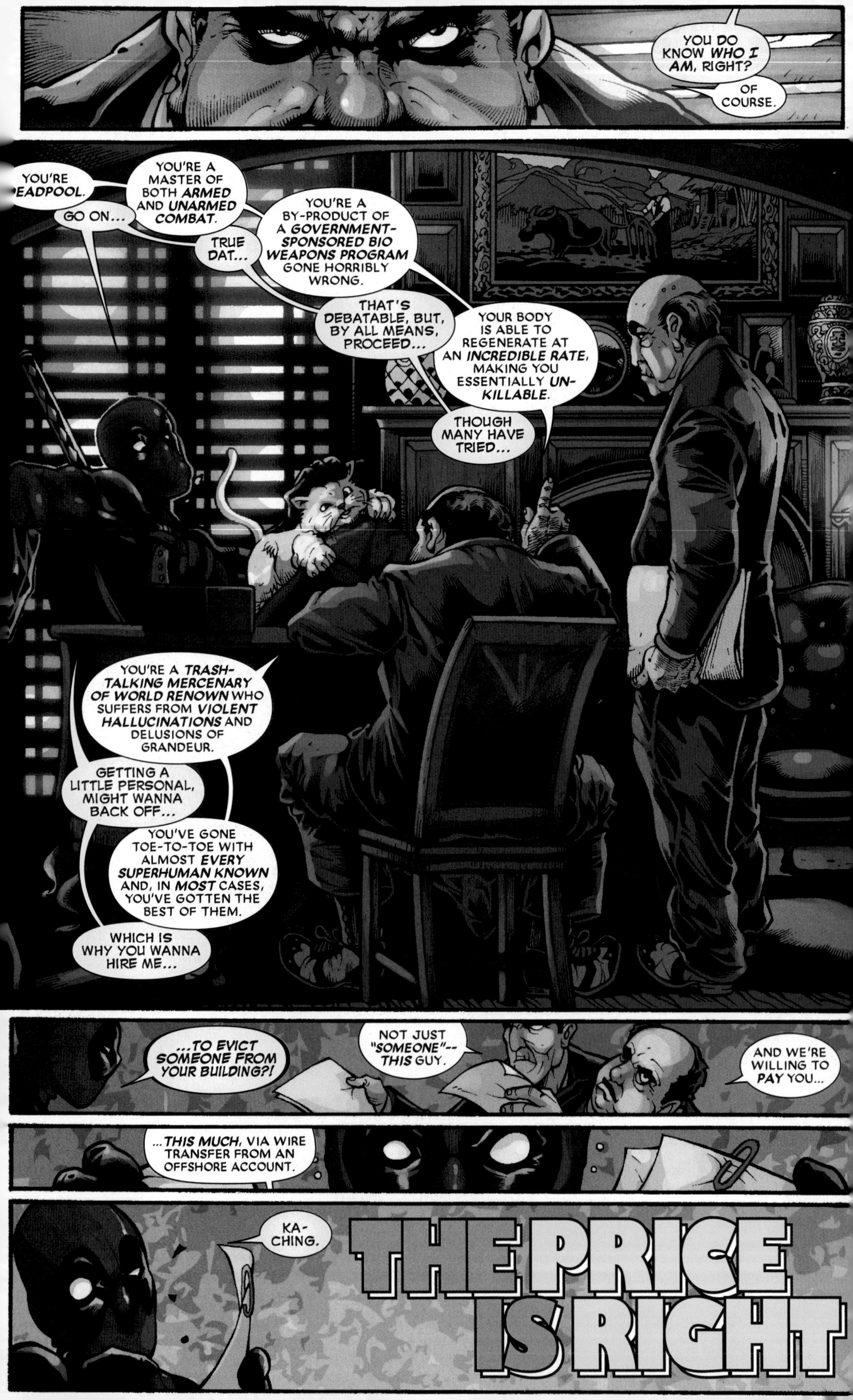
YOU DO KNOW WHO I AM, RIGHT?
OF COURSE.
YOU'RE DEADPOOL.
YOU'RE A MASTER OF BOTH ARMED AND UNARMED COMBAT.
GO ON...
TRUE DAT...
YOU'RE A BY-PRODUCT OF A GOVERNMENT-SPONSORED BIO WEAPONS PROGRAM GONE HORRIBLY WRONG.
THAT'S DEBATABLE, BUT, BY ALL MEANS, PROCEED...
YOUR BODY IS ABLE TO REGENERATE AT AN INCREDIBLE RATE, MAKING YOU ESSENTIALLY UN-KILLABLE.
THOUGH MANY HAVE TRIED...
YOU'RE A TRASH-TALKING MERCENARY OF WORLD RENOWN WHO SUFFERS FROM VIOLENT HALLUCINATIONS AND DELUSIONS OF GRANDEUR.
GETTING A LITTLE PERSONAL, MIGHT WANNA BACK OFF...
YOU'VE GONE TOE-TO-TOE WITH ALMOST EVERY SUPERHUMAN KNOWN AND, IN MOST CASES, YOU'VE GOTTEN THE BEST OF THEM.
WHICH IS WHY YOU WANNA HIRE ME...
...TO EVICT SOMEONE FROM YOUR BUILDING?!
NOT JUST "SOMEONE"-- THIS GUY.
AND WE'RE WILLING TO PAY YOU...
...THIS MUCH, VIA WIRE TRANSFER FROM AN OFFSHORE ACCOUNT.
KA-CHING.
THE PRICE IS RIGHT

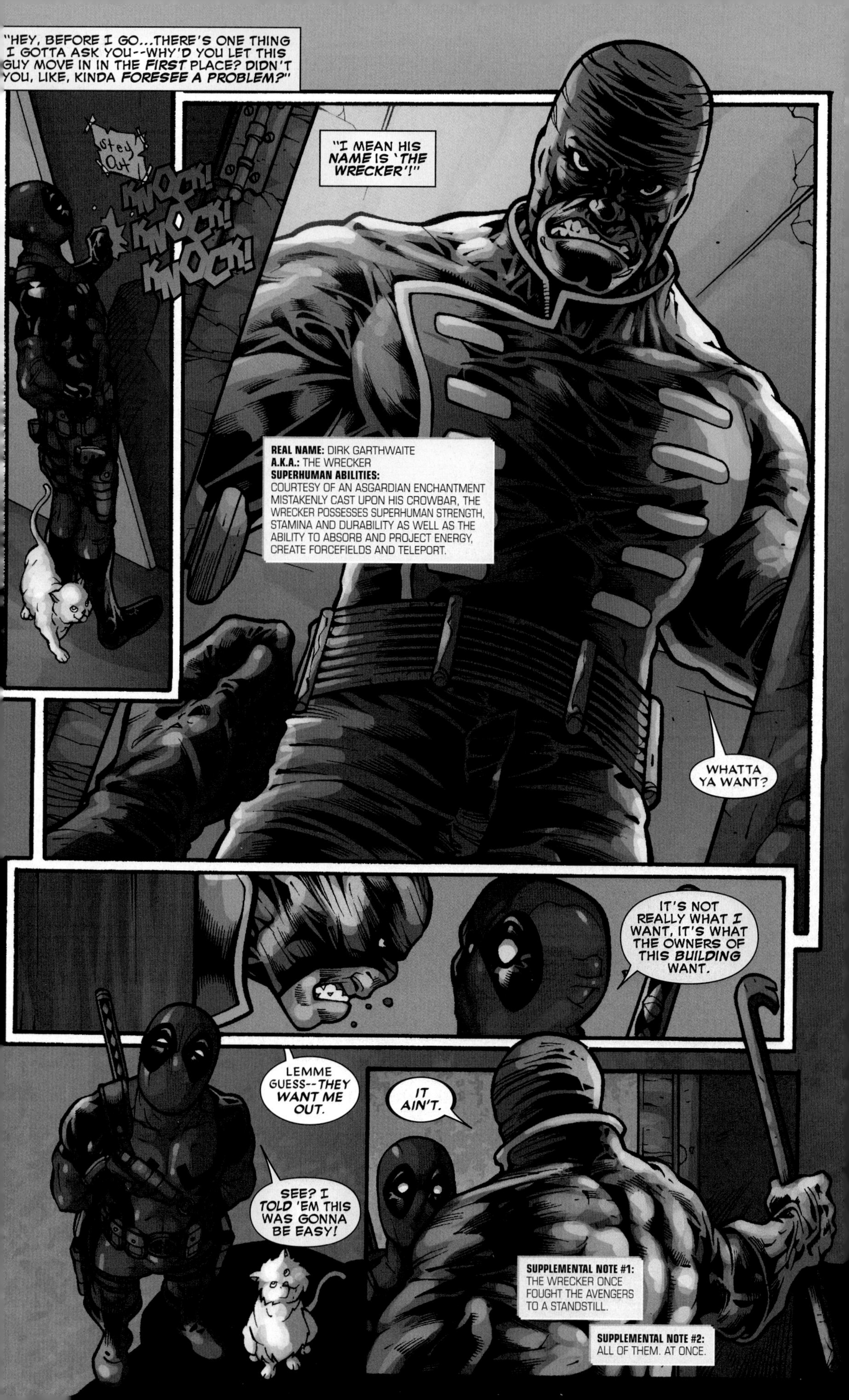
"HEY, BEFORE I GO...THERE'S ONE THING I GOTTA ASK YOU--WHY'D YOU LET THIS GUY MOVE IN IN THE FIRST PLACE? DIDN'T YOU, LIKE, KINDA FORESEE A PROBLEM?"
Stay Out
KNOCK! KNOCK! KNOCK!
"I MEAN HIS NAME IS 'THE WRECKER'!"
REAL NAME: DIRK GARTHWAITE
A.K.A.: THE WRECKER
SUPERHUMAN ABILITIES:
COURTESY OF AN ASGARDIAN ENCHANTMENT MISTAKENLY CAST UPON HIS CROWBAR, THE WRECKER POSSESSES SUPERHUMAN STRENGTH, STAMINA AND DURABILITY AS WELL AS THE ABILITY TO ABSORB AND PROJECT ENERGY, CREATE FORCEFIELDS AND TELEPORT.
WHATTA YA WANT?
IT'S NOT REALLY WHAT I WANT, IT'S WHAT THE OWNERS OF THIS BUILDING WANT.
LEMME GUESS--THEY WANT ME OUT.
IT AIN'T.
SEE? I TOLD 'EM THIS WAS GONNA BE EASY!
SUPPLEMENTAL NOTE #1:
THE WRECKER ONCE FOUGHT THE AVENGERS TO A STANDSTILL.
SUPPLEMENTAL NOTE #2:
ALL OF THEM. AT ONCE.

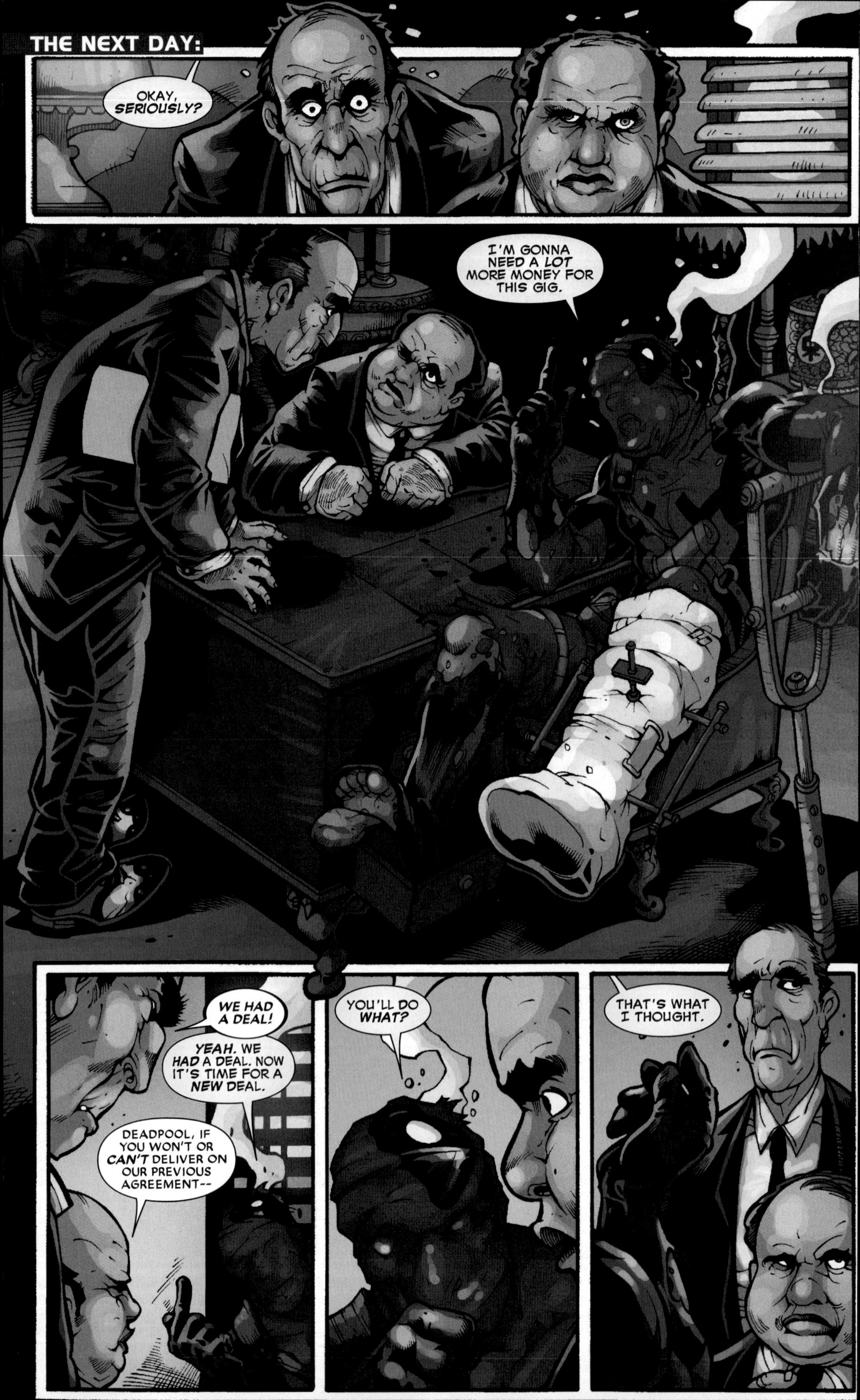
THE NEXT DAY:
OKAY, *SERIOUSLY?*
I'M GONNA NEED A *LOT* MORE MONEY FOR THIS GIG.
WE HAD A DEAL!
YEAH. WE *HAD* A DEAL. NOW IT'S TIME FOR A *NEW* DEAL.
DEADPOOL, IF YOU WON'T OR *CAN'T* DELIVER ON OUR PREVIOUS AGREEMENT--
YOU'LL DO *WHAT?*
THAT'S WHAT I THOUGHT.

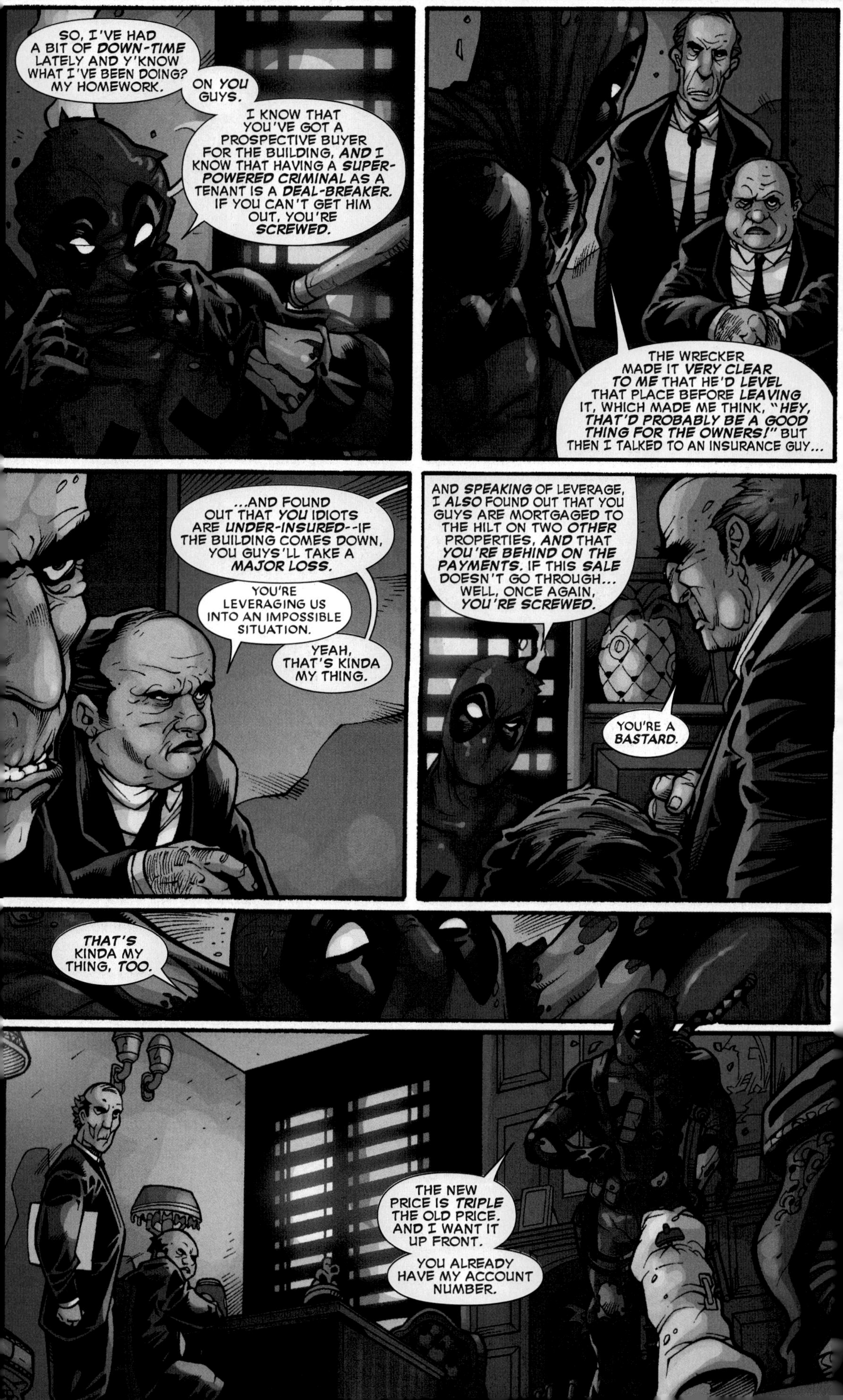
SO, I'VE HAD A BIT OF DOWN-TIME LATELY AND Y'KNOW WHAT I'VE BEEN DOING? MY HOMEWORK.
ON YOU GUYS.
I KNOW THAT YOU'VE GOT A PROSPECTIVE BUYER FOR THE BUILDING, AND I KNOW THAT HAVING A SUPER-POWERED CRIMINAL AS A TENANT IS A DEAL-BREAKER. IF YOU CAN'T GET HIM OUT, YOU'RE SCREWED.
THE WRECKER MADE IT VERY CLEAR TO ME THAT HE'D LEVEL THAT PLACE BEFORE LEAVING IT, WHICH MADE ME THINK, "HEY, THAT'D PROBABLY BE A GOOD THING FOR THE OWNERS!" BUT THEN I TALKED TO AN INSURANCE GUY...
...AND FOUND OUT THAT YOU IDIOTS ARE UNDER-INSURED--IF THE BUILDING COMES DOWN, YOU GUYS'LL TAKE A MAJOR LOSS.
YOU'RE LEVERAGING US INTO AN IMPOSSIBLE SITUATION.
YEAH, THAT'S KINDA MY THING.
AND SPEAKING OF LEVERAGE, I ALSO FOUND OUT THAT YOU GUYS ARE MORTGAGED TO THE HILT ON TWO OTHER PROPERTIES, AND THAT YOU'RE BEHIND ON THE PAYMENTS. IF THIS SALE DOESN'T GO THROUGH... WELL, ONCE AGAIN, YOU'RE SCREWED.
YOU'RE A BASTARD.
THAT'S KINDA MY THING, TOO.
THE NEW PRICE IS TRIPLE THE OLD PRICE. AND I WANT IT UP FRONT.
YOU ALREADY HAVE MY ACCOUNT NUMBER.

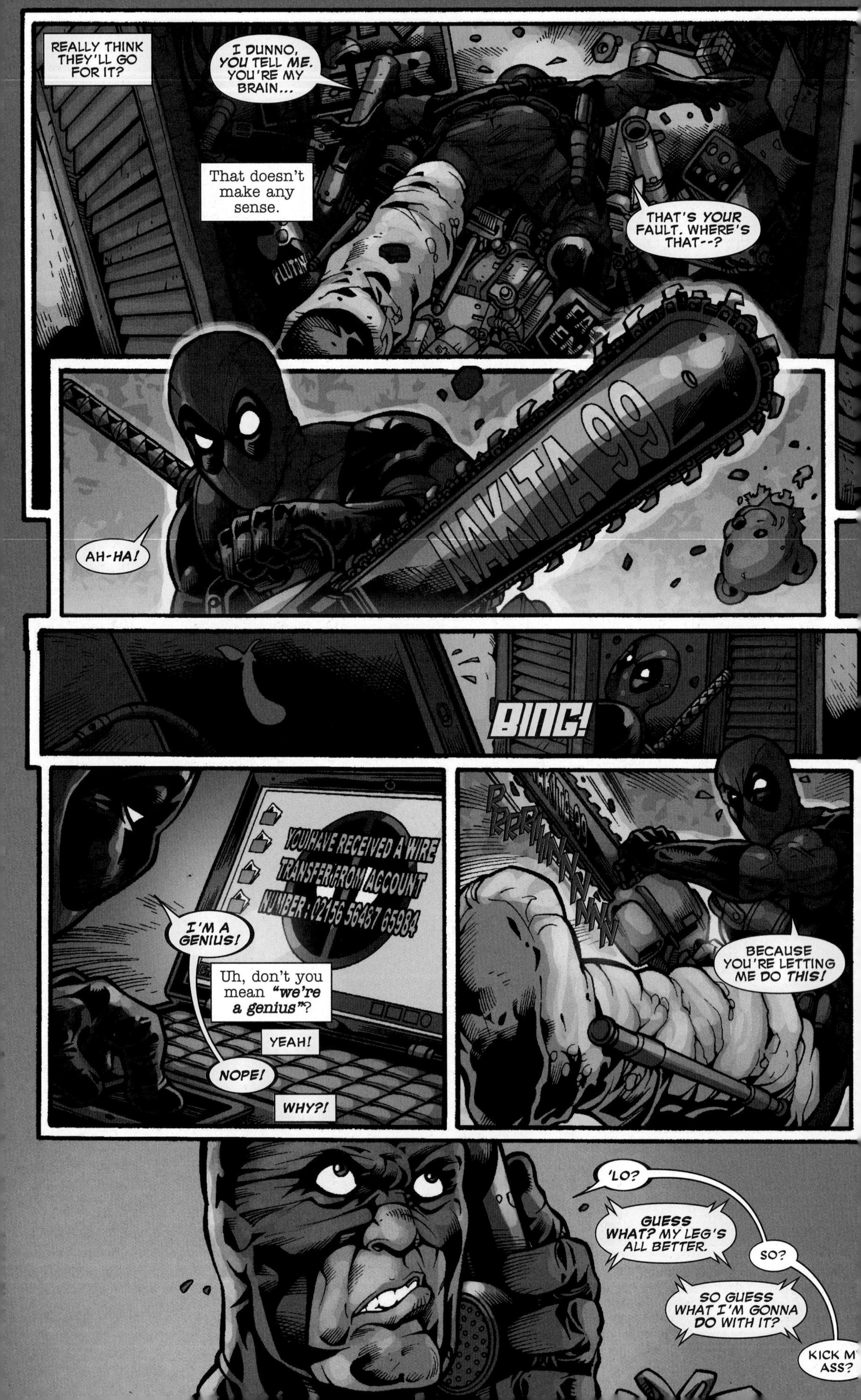
REALLY THINK THEY'LL GO FOR IT?
I DUNNO, YOU TELL ME. YOU'RE MY BRAIN...
That doesn't make any sense.
THAT'S YOUR FAULT. WHERE'S THAT--?
AH-HA!
NAKITA 99
BING!
YOU HAVE RECEIVED A WIRE TRANSFER FROM ACCOUNT NUMBER : 02156 56487 65984
I'M A GENIUS!
Uh, don't you mean "we're a genius"?
YEAH!
NOPE!
WHY?!
RRRRMMMNNNNNN
BECAUSE YOU'RE LETTING ME DO THIS!
'LO?
GUESS WHAT? MY LEG'S ALL BETTER.
SO?
SO GUESS WHAT I'M GONNA DO WITH IT?
KICK M ASS?

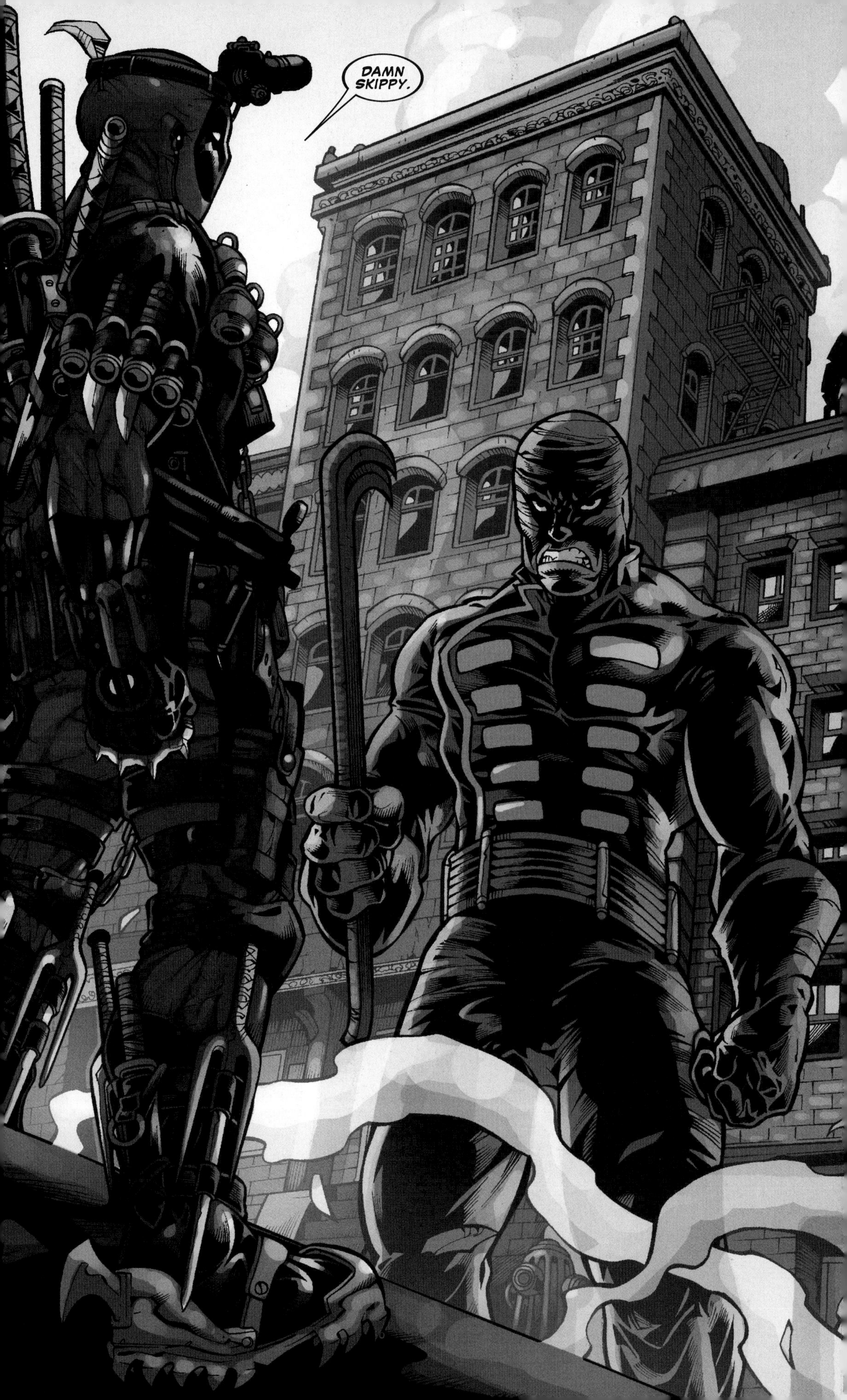
DAMN SKIPPY.

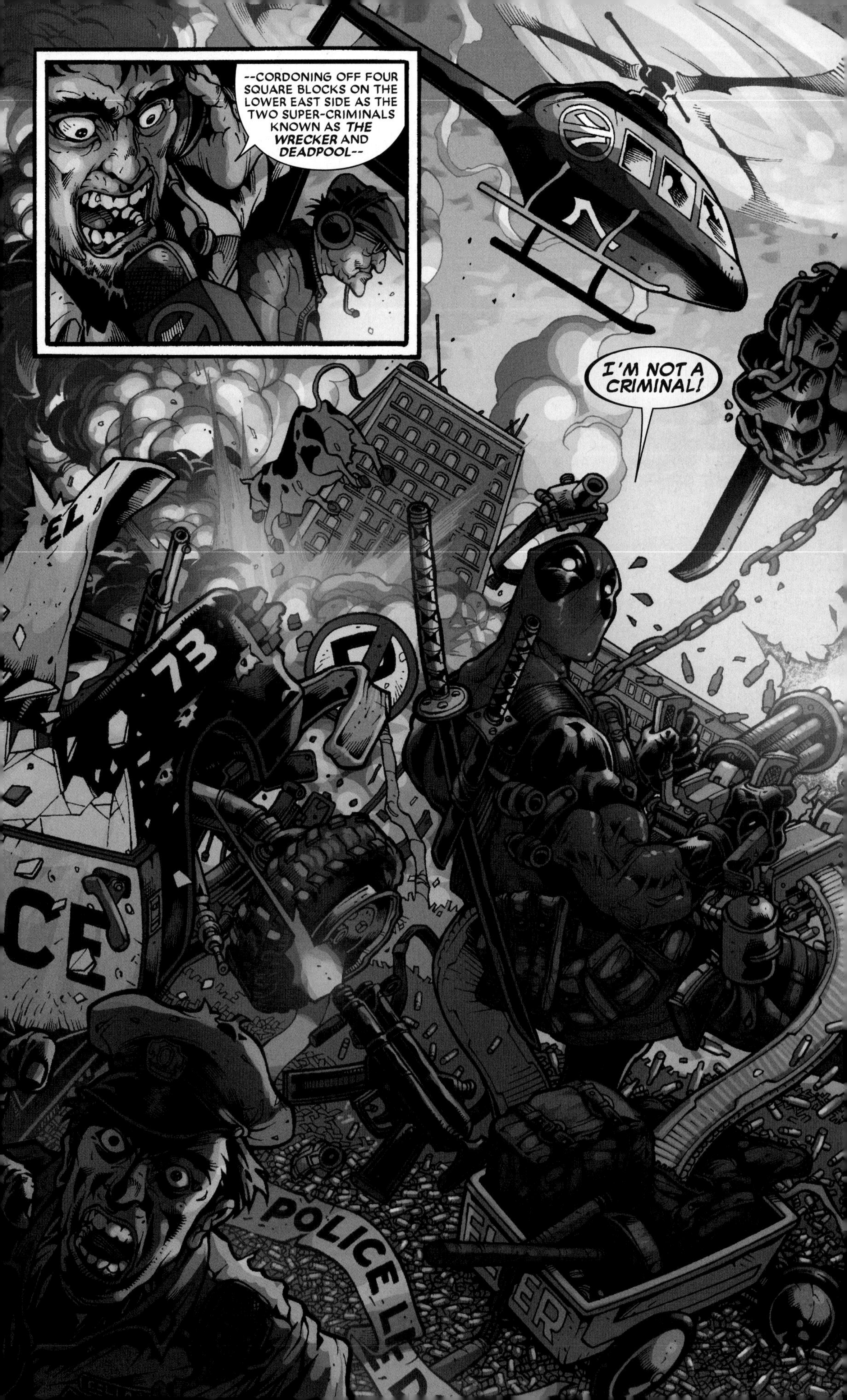
--CORDONING OFF FOUR SQUARE BLOCKS ON THE LOWER EAST SIDE AS THE TWO SUPER-CRIMINALS KNOWN AS THE WRECKER AND DEADPOOL--
I'M NOT A CRIMINAL!
73
POLICE

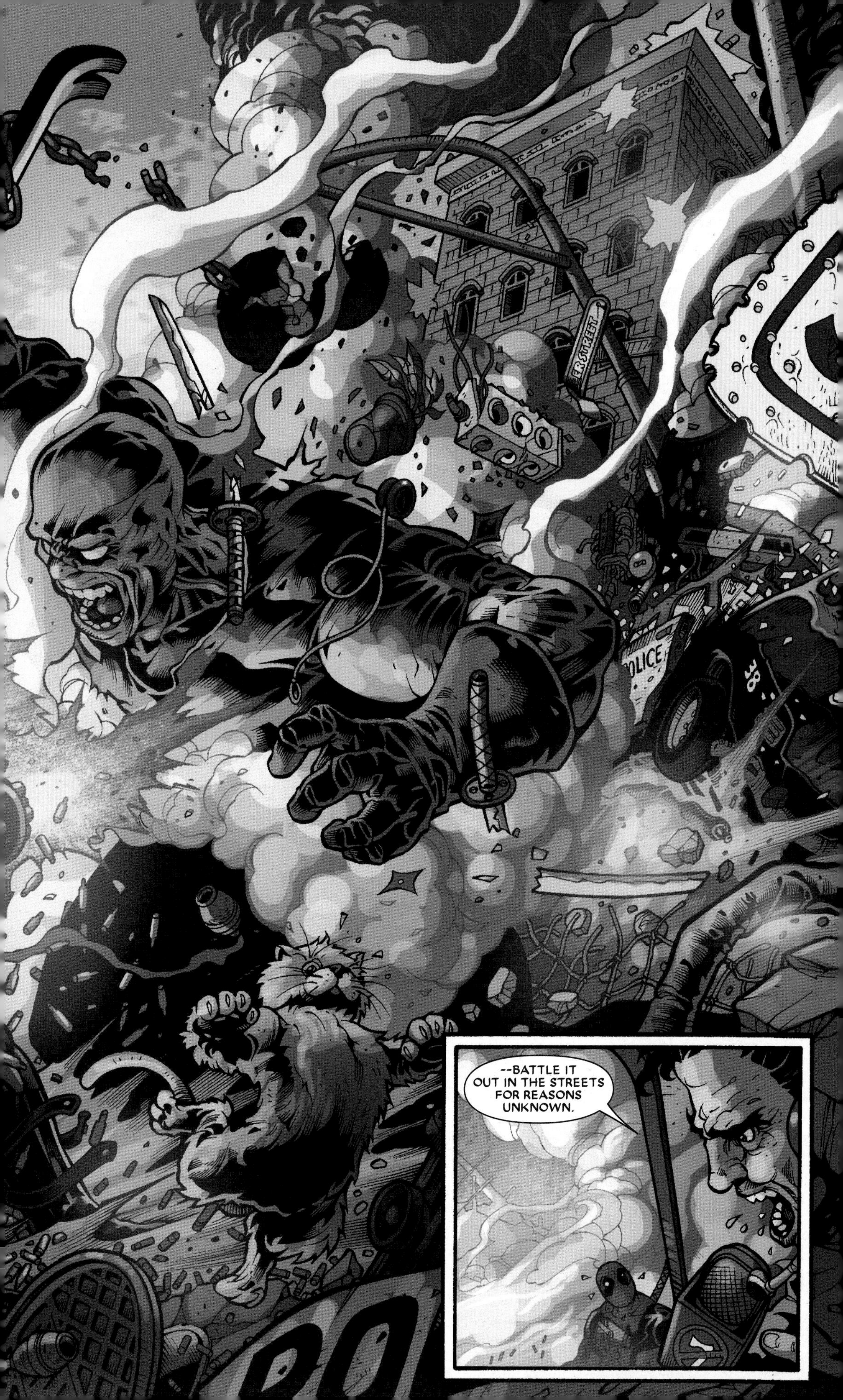
ERS STREET
POLICE
--BATTLE IT OUT IN THE STREETS FOR REASONS UNKNOWN.

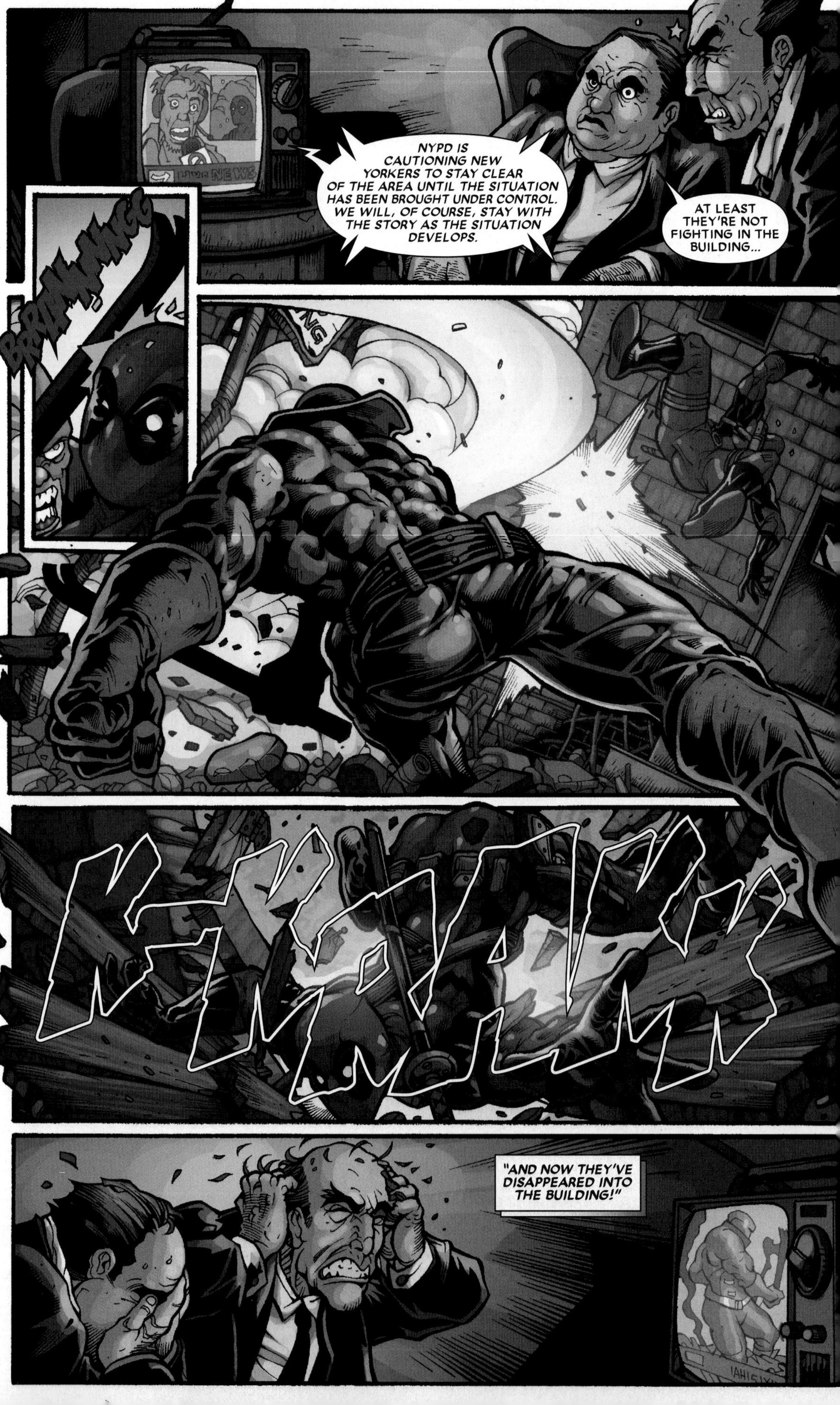
NYPD IS CAUTIONING NEW YORKERS TO STAY CLEAR OF THE AREA UNTIL THE SITUATION HAS BEEN BROUGHT UNDER CONTROL. WE WILL, OF COURSE, STAY WITH THE STORY AS THE SITUATION DEVELOPS.
AT LEAST THEY'RE NOT FIGHTING IN THE BUILDING...
KRAKK
"AND NOW THEY'VE DISAPPEARED INTO THE BUILDING!"

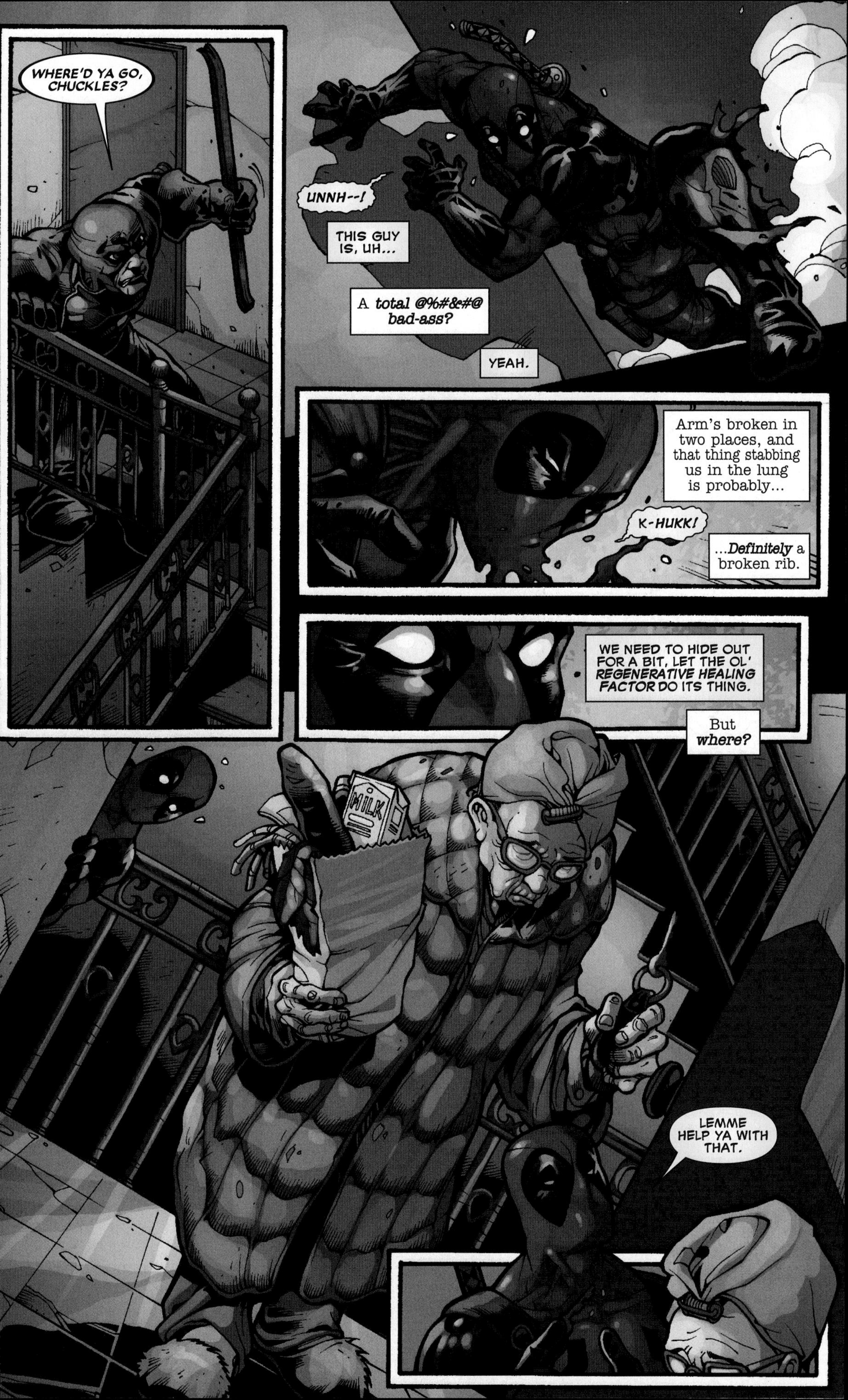
WHERE'D YA GO, CHUCKLES?
UNNH--!
THIS GUY IS, UH...
A total @%#&#@ bad-ass?
YEAH.
Arm's broken in two places, and that thing stabbing us in the lung is probably...
K-HUKK!
...Definitely a broken rib.
WE NEED TO HIDE OUT FOR A BIT, LET THE OL' REGENERATIVE HEALING FACTOR DO ITS THING.
But where?
MILK
LEMME HELP YA WITH THAT.

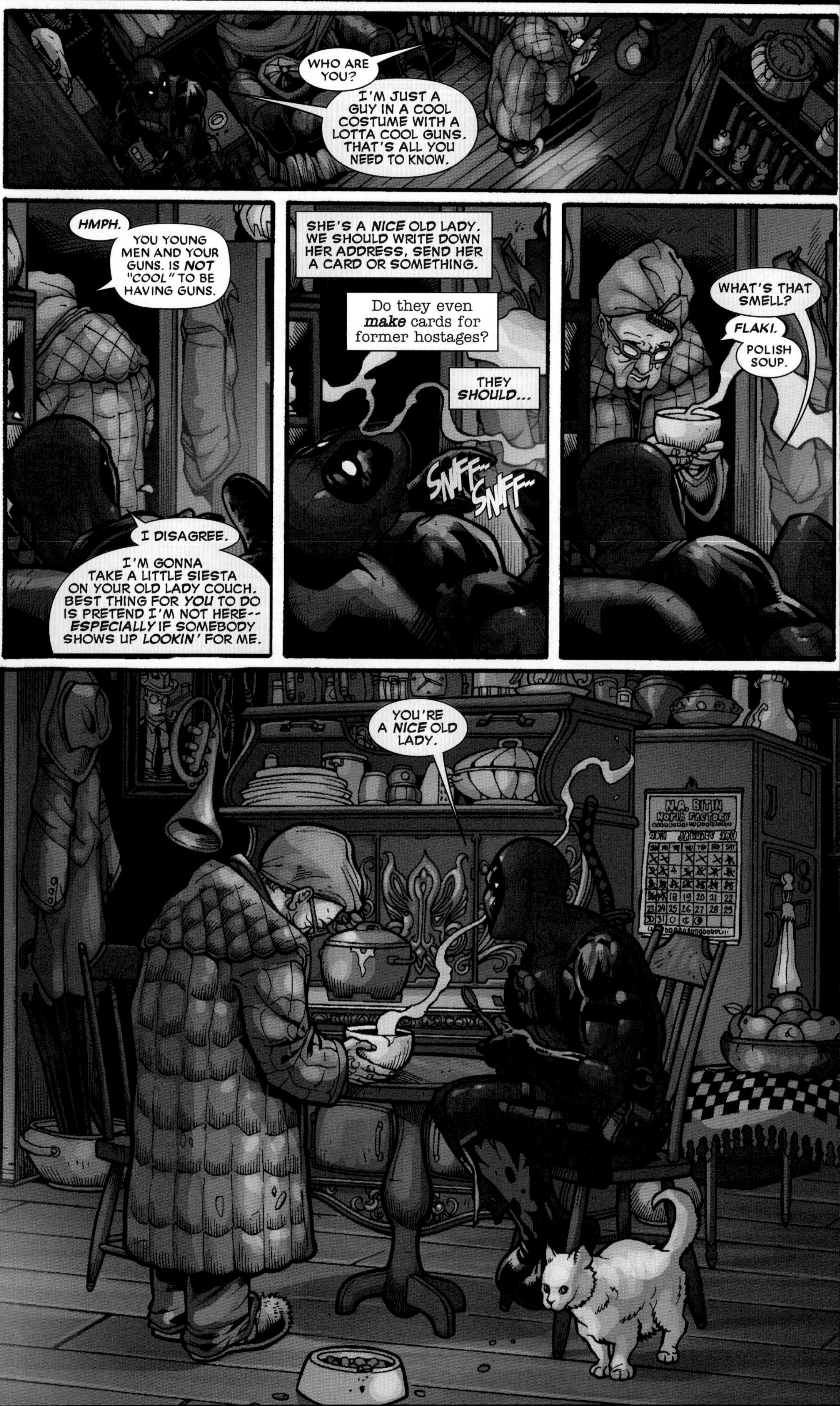
WHO ARE YOU?
I'M JUST A GUY IN A COOL COSTUME WITH A LOTTA COOL GUNS. THAT'S ALL YOU NEED TO KNOW.
HMPH.
YOU YOUNG MEN AND YOUR GUNS. IS NOT "COOL" TO BE HAVING GUNS.
I DISAGREE.
I'M GONNA TAKE A LITTLE SIESTA ON YOUR OLD LADY COUCH. BEST THING FOR YOU TO DO IS PRETEND I'M NOT HERE-- ESPECIALLY IF SOMEBODY SHOWS UP LOOKIN' FOR ME.
SHE'S A NICE OLD LADY. WE SHOULD WRITE DOWN HER ADDRESS, SEND HER A CARD OR SOMETHING.
Do they even make cards for former hostages?
THEY SHOULD...
SNIFF-- SNIFF--
WHAT'S THAT SMELL?
FLAKI.
POLISH SOUP.
YOU'RE A NICE OLD LADY.
N.A. BITIN

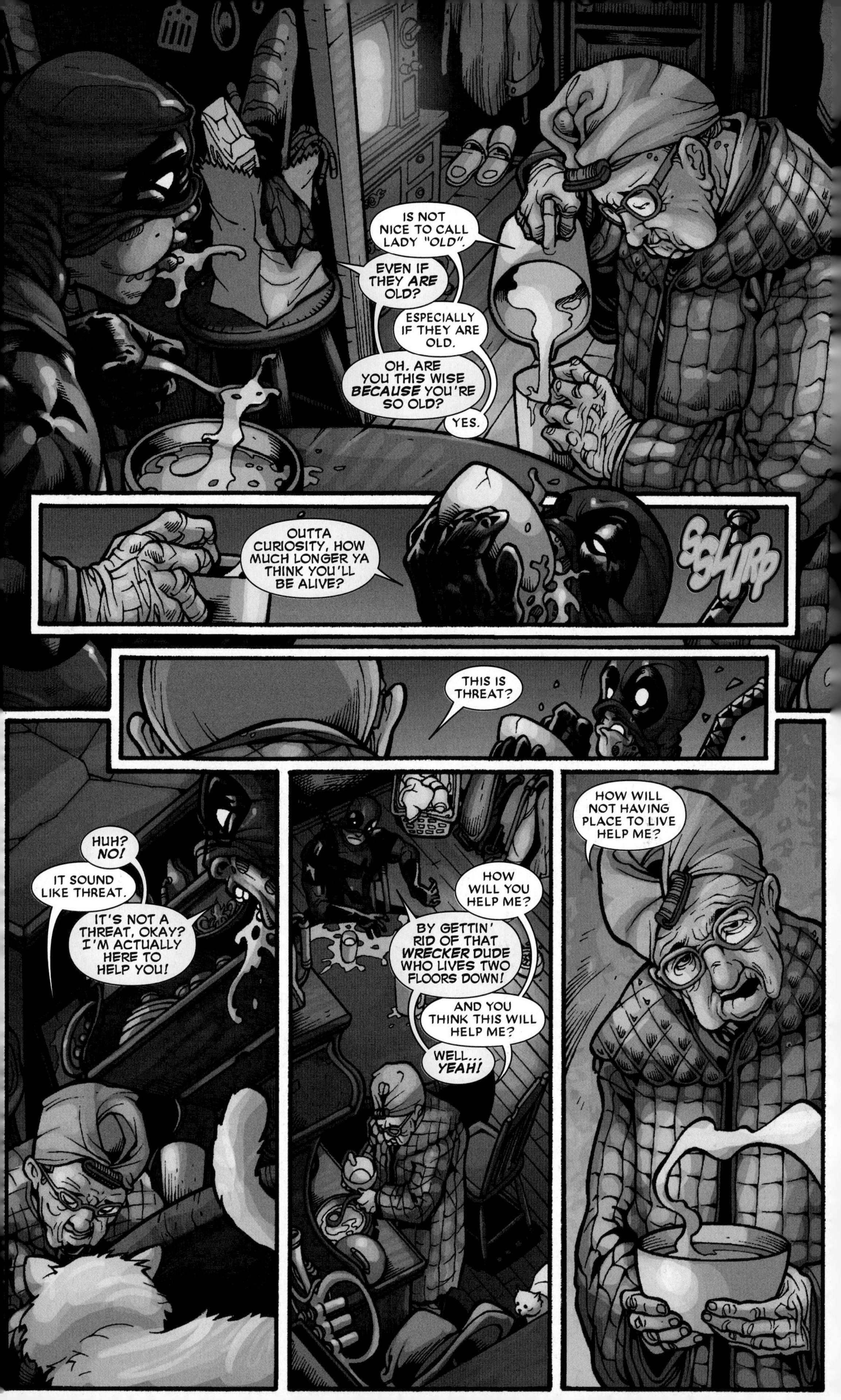

IS NOT NICE TO CALL LADY "OLD".
EVEN IF THEY ARE OLD?
ESPECIALLY IF THEY ARE OLD.
OH. ARE YOU THIS WISE BECAUSE YOU'RE SO OLD?
YES.
OUTTA CURIOSITY, HOW MUCH LONGER YA THINK YOU'LL BE ALIVE?
SSLURP
THIS IS THREAT?
HUH? NO!
IT SOUND LIKE THREAT.
IT'S NOT A THREAT, OKAY? I'M ACTUALLY HERE TO HELP YOU!
HOW WILL YOU HELP ME?
BY GETTIN' RID OF THAT WRECKER DUDE WHO LIVES TWO FLOORS DOWN!
AND YOU THINK THIS WILL HELP ME?
WELL... YEAH!
HOW WILL NOT HAVING PLACE TO LIVE HELP ME?

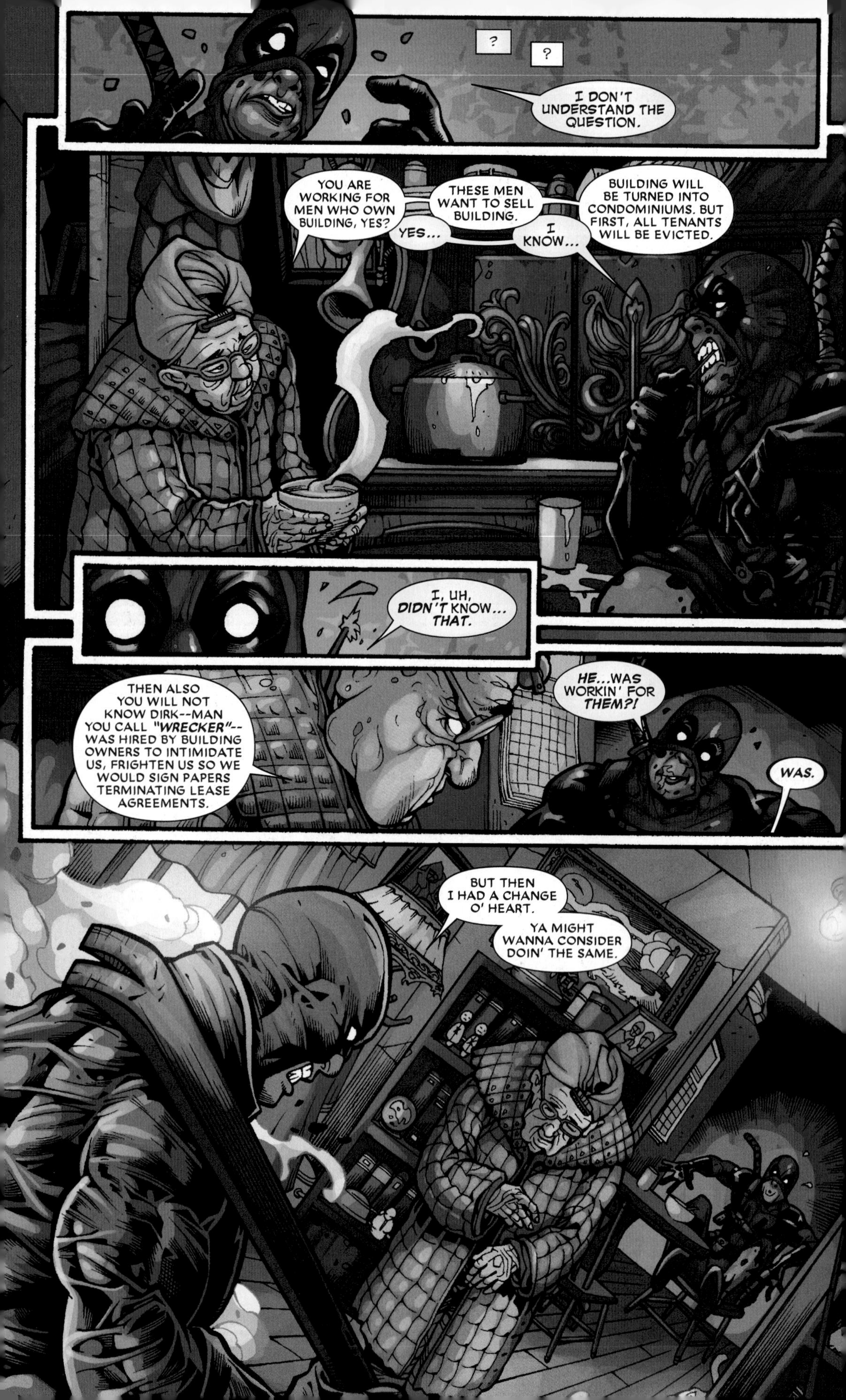
?
?
I DON'T UNDERSTAND THE QUESTION.
YOU ARE WORKING FOR MEN WHO OWN BUILDING, YES?
YES...
THESE MEN WANT TO SELL BUILDING.
I KNOW...
BUILDING WILL BE TURNED INTO CONDOMINIUMS. BUT FIRST, ALL TENANTS WILL BE EVICTED.
I, UH, DIDN'T KNOW... THAT.
THEN ALSO YOU WILL NOT KNOW DIRK--MAN YOU CALL "WRECKER"--WAS HIRED BY BUILDING OWNERS TO INTIMIDATE US, FRIGHTEN US SO WE WOULD SIGN PAPERS TERMINATING LEASE AGREEMENTS.
HE...WAS WORKIN' FOR THEM?!
WAS.
BUT THEN I HAD A CHANGE O' HEART.
YA MIGHT WANNA CONSIDER DOIN' THE SAME.

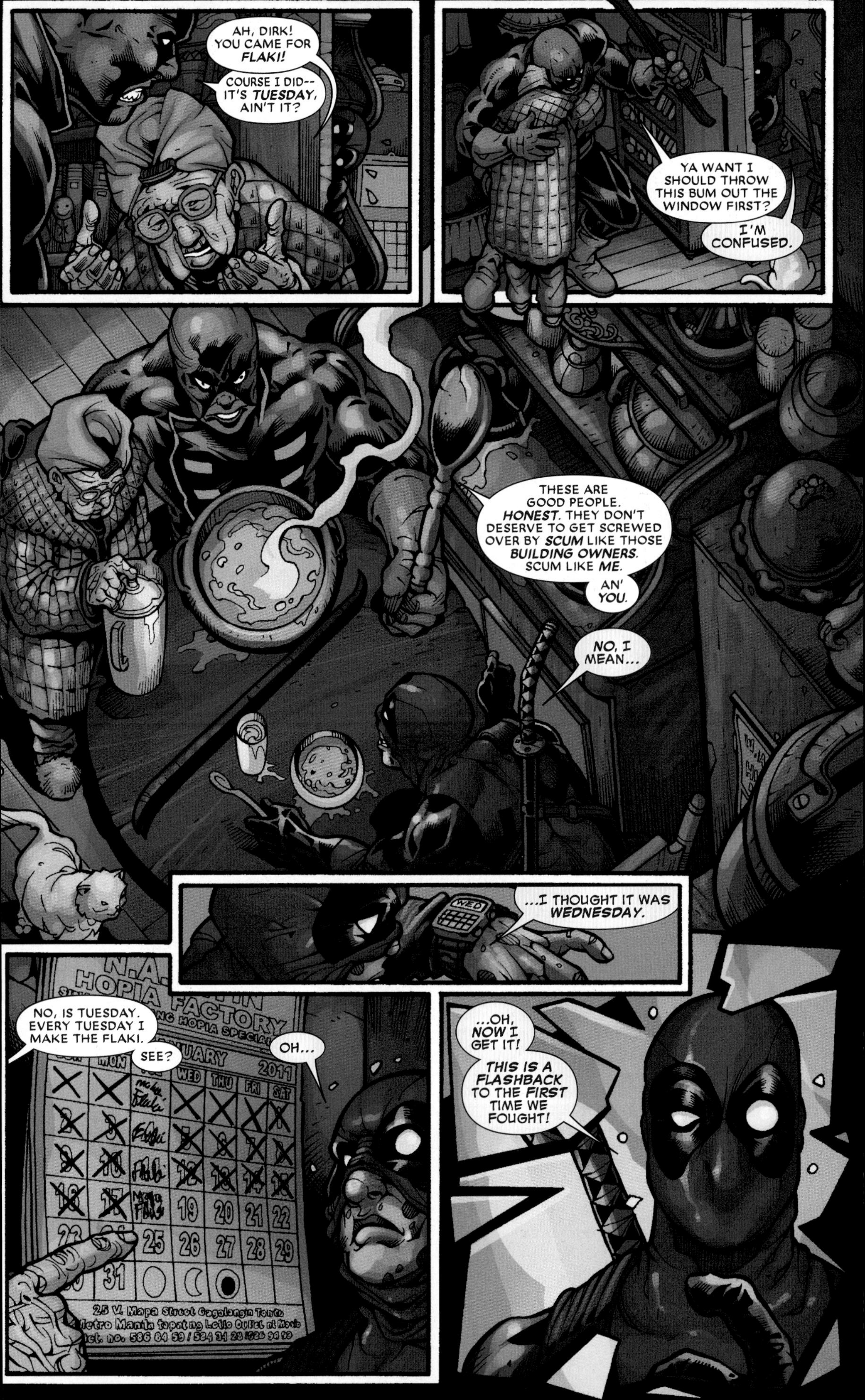
AH, DIRK! YOU CAME FOR *FLAKI!*
COURSE I DID-- IT'S *TUESDAY*, AIN'T IT?
YA WANT I SHOULD THROW THIS BUM OUT THE WINDOW FIRST?
I'M CONFUSED.
THESE ARE GOOD PEOPLE. *HONEST*. THEY DON'T DESERVE TO GET SCREWED OVER BY *SCUM* LIKE THOSE *BUILDING OWNERS*. SCUM LIKE *ME*.
AN' *YOU*.
NO, I MEAN...
WED
...I THOUGHT IT WAS *WEDNESDAY*.
N.A. HOPIA FACTORY
JANUARY 2011
WED THU FRI SAT
19 20 21 22
25 26 27 28 29
31
25 V. Mapa Street Sta. Mesa Manila
NO, IS TUESDAY. EVERY TUESDAY I MAKE THE FLAKI.
SEE?
OH...
...OH, *NOW* I GET IT!
THIS IS A FLASHBACK TO THE *FIRST* TIME WE FOUGHT!

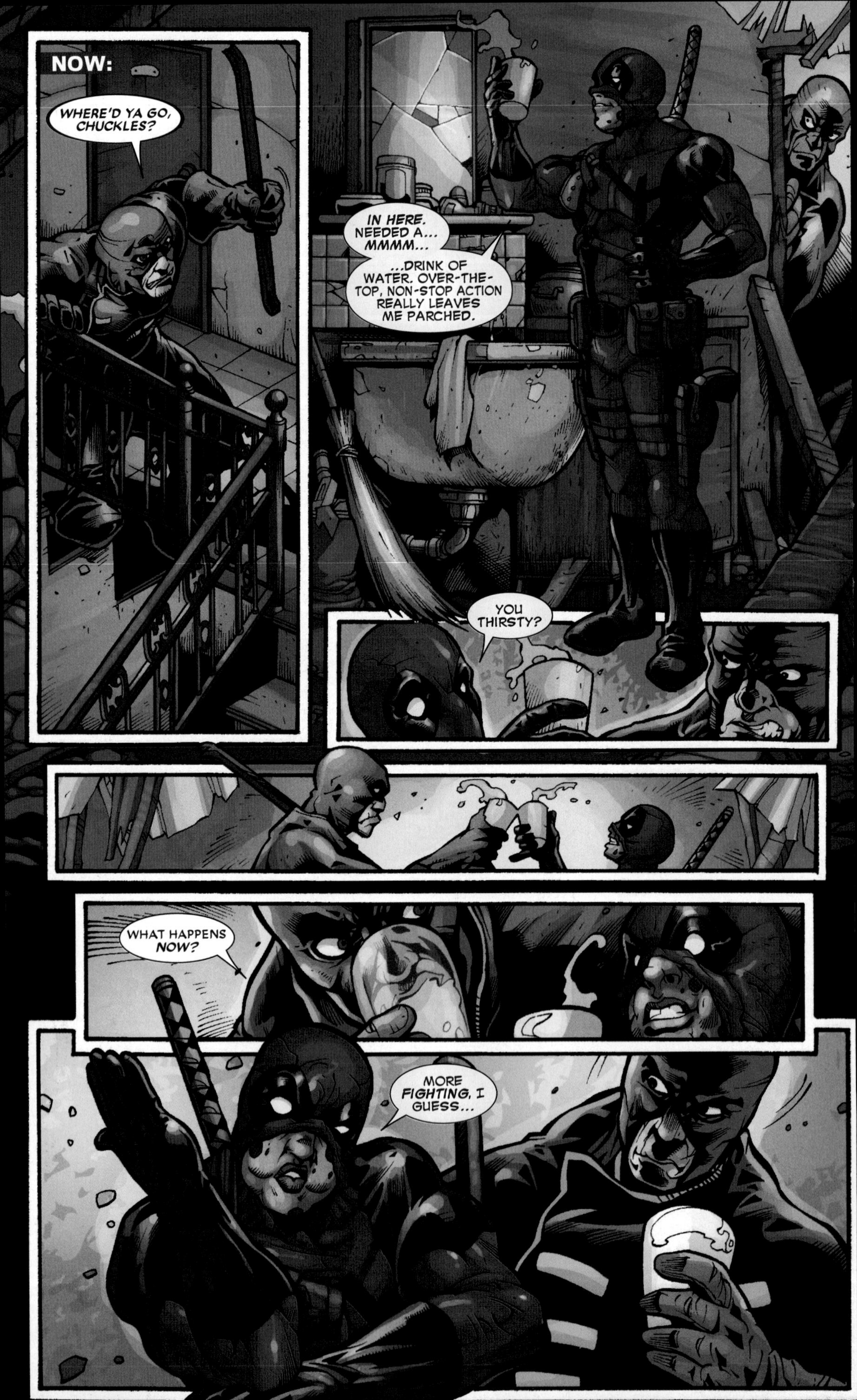
NOW:
WHERE'D YA GO, CHUCKLES?
IN HERE. NEEDED A... MMMM...
...DRINK OF WATER. OVER-THE-TOP, NON-STOP ACTION REALLY LEAVES ME PARCHED.
YOU THIRSTY?
WHAT HAPPENS NOW?
MORE FIGHTING, I GUESS...

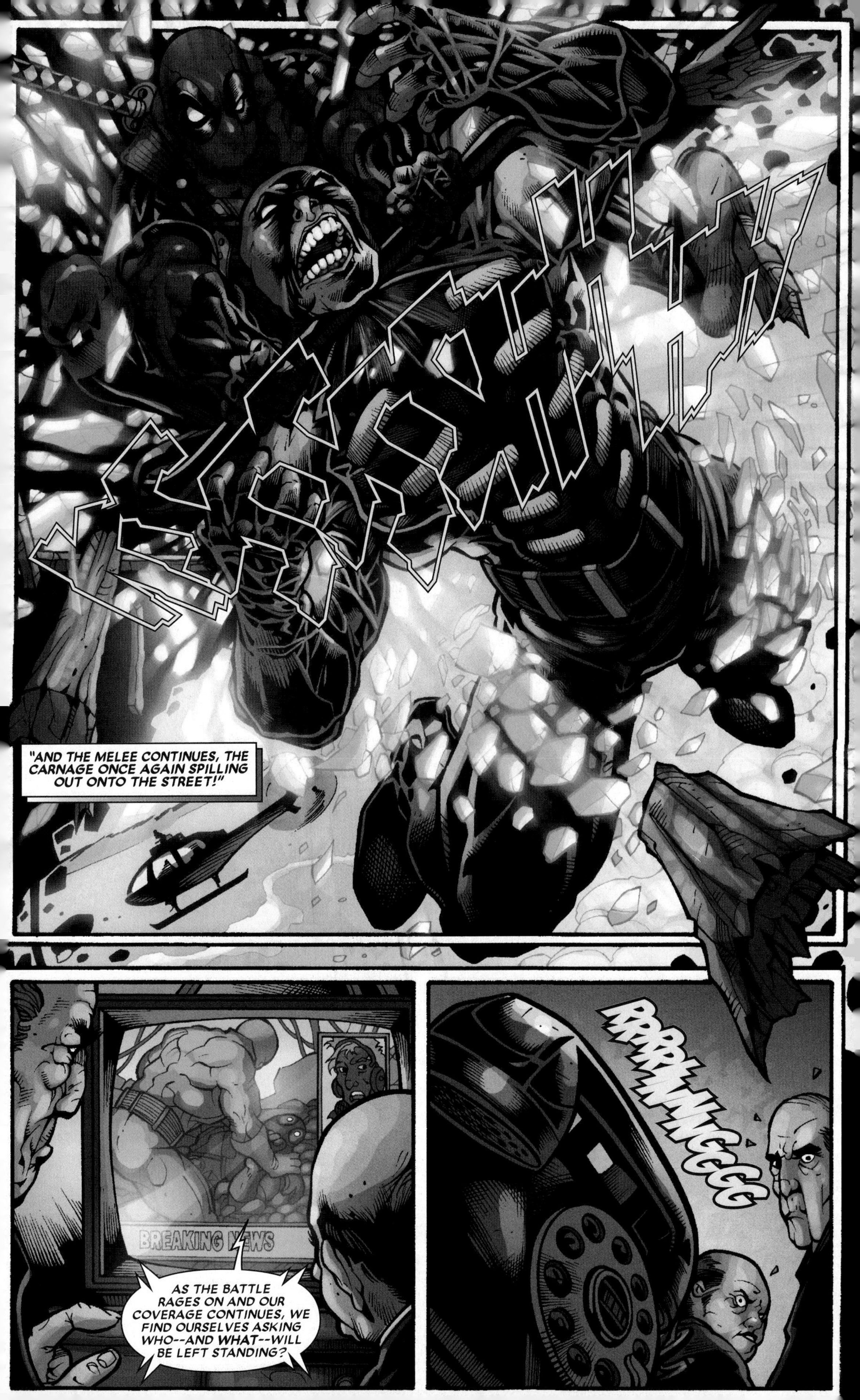
"AND THE MELEE CONTINUES, THE CARNAGE ONCE AGAIN SPILLING OUT ONTO THE STREET!"
AS THE BATTLE RAGES ON AND OUR COVERAGE CONTINUES, WE FIND OURSELVES ASKING WHO--AND WHAT--WILL BE LEFT STANDING?

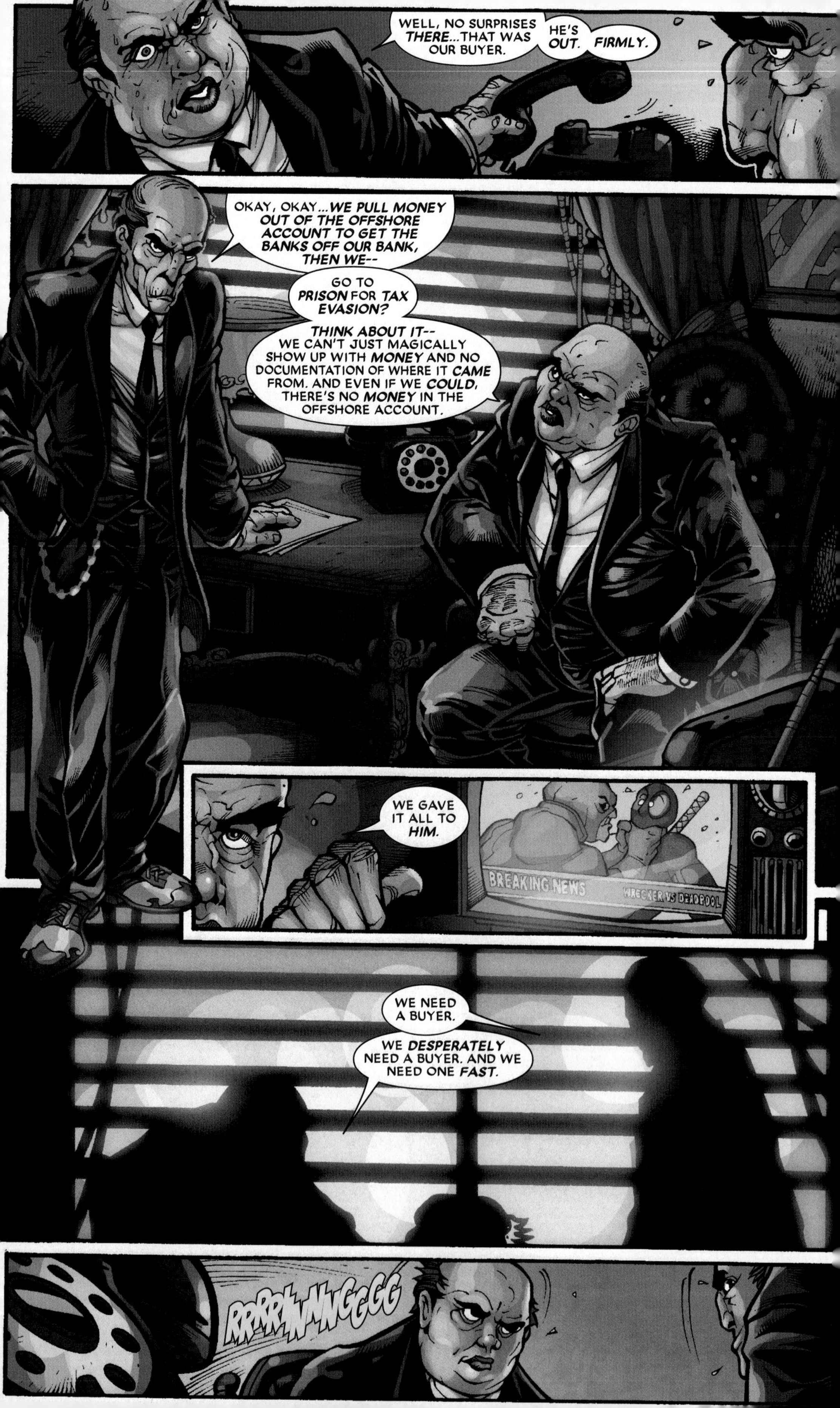
WELL, NO SURPRISES THERE...THAT WAS OUR BUYER.
HE'S OUT.
FIRMLY.
OKAY, OKAY...WE PULL MONEY OUT OF THE OFFSHORE ACCOUNT TO GET THE BANKS OFF OUR BANK, THEN WE--
GO TO PRISON FOR TAX EVASION?
THINK ABOUT IT-- WE CAN'T JUST MAGICALLY SHOW UP WITH MONEY AND NO DOCUMENTATION OF WHERE IT CAME FROM. AND EVEN IF WE COULD, THERE'S NO MONEY IN THE OFFSHORE ACCOUNT.
WE GAVE IT ALL TO HIM.
BREAKING NEWS
WRECKER VS DEADPOOL
WE NEED A BUYER.
WE DESPERATELY NEED A BUYER. AND WE NEED ONE FAST.
RRRRIINNNGGGG

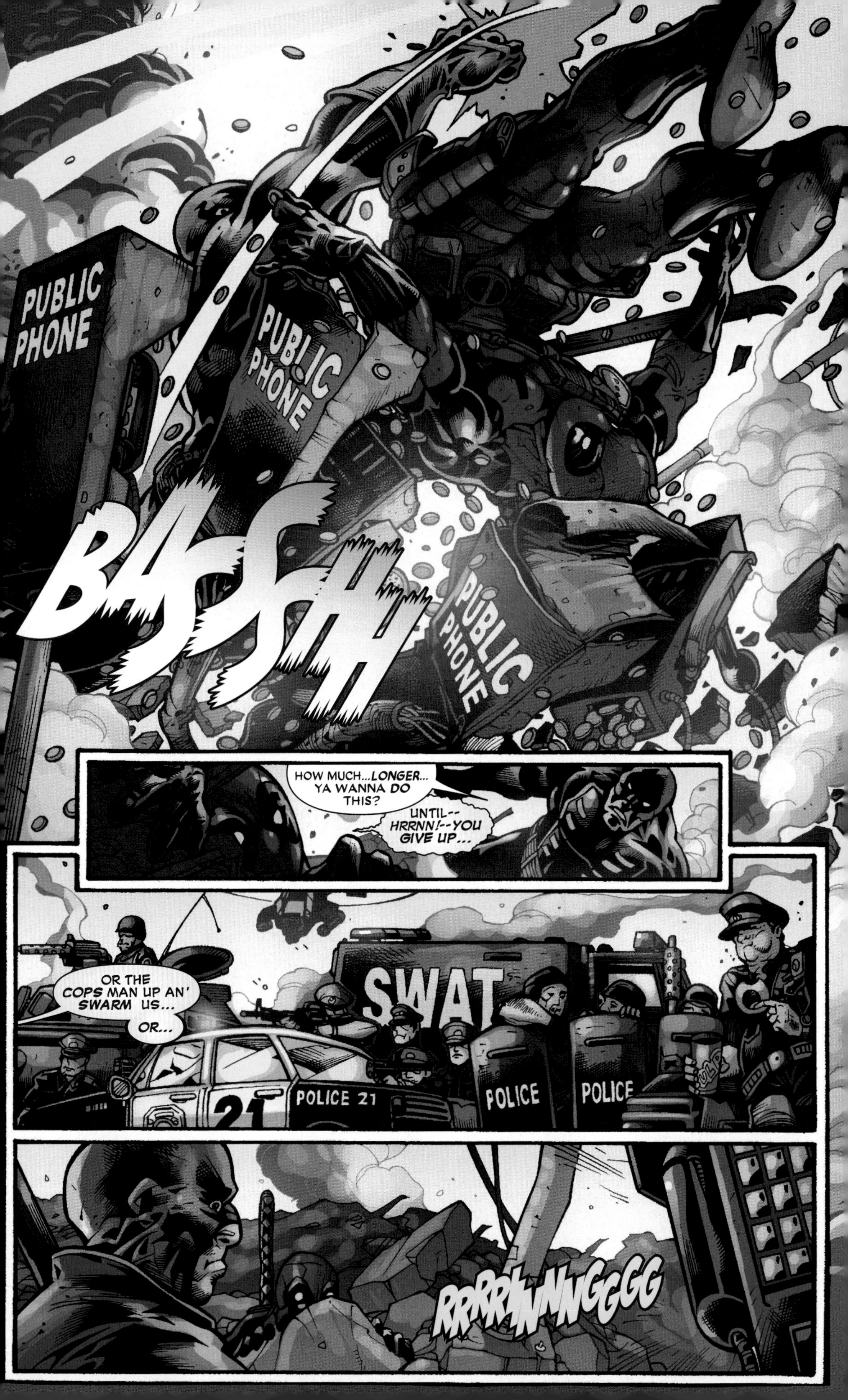
PUBLIC PHONE
PUBLIC PHONE
BASH
PUBLIC PHONE
HOW MUCH...LONGER... YA WANNA DO THIS?
UNTIL-- HRRNN!--YOU GIVE UP...
OR THE COPS MAN UP AN' SWARM US... OR...
SWAT
POLICE 21
21
POLICE
POLICE
RRRRINNNGGGG

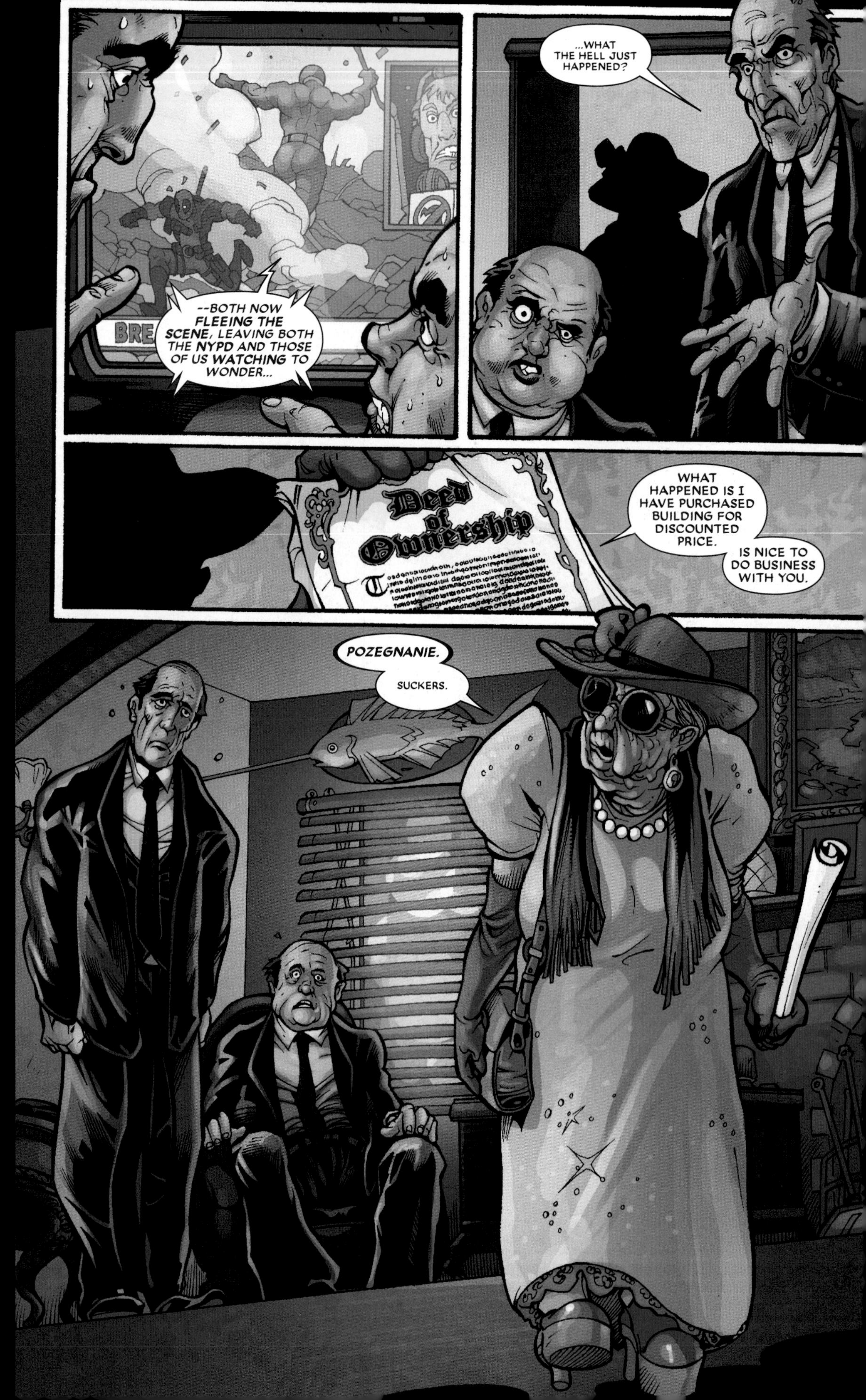
--BOTH NOW FLEEING THE SCENE, LEAVING BOTH THE NYPD AND THOSE OF US WATCHING TO WONDER...
...WHAT THE HELL JUST HAPPENED?
Deed of Ownership
WHAT HAPPENED IS I HAVE PURCHASED BUILDING FOR DISCOUNTED PRICE.
IS NICE TO DO BUSINESS WITH YOU.
POZEGNANIE.
SUCKERS.

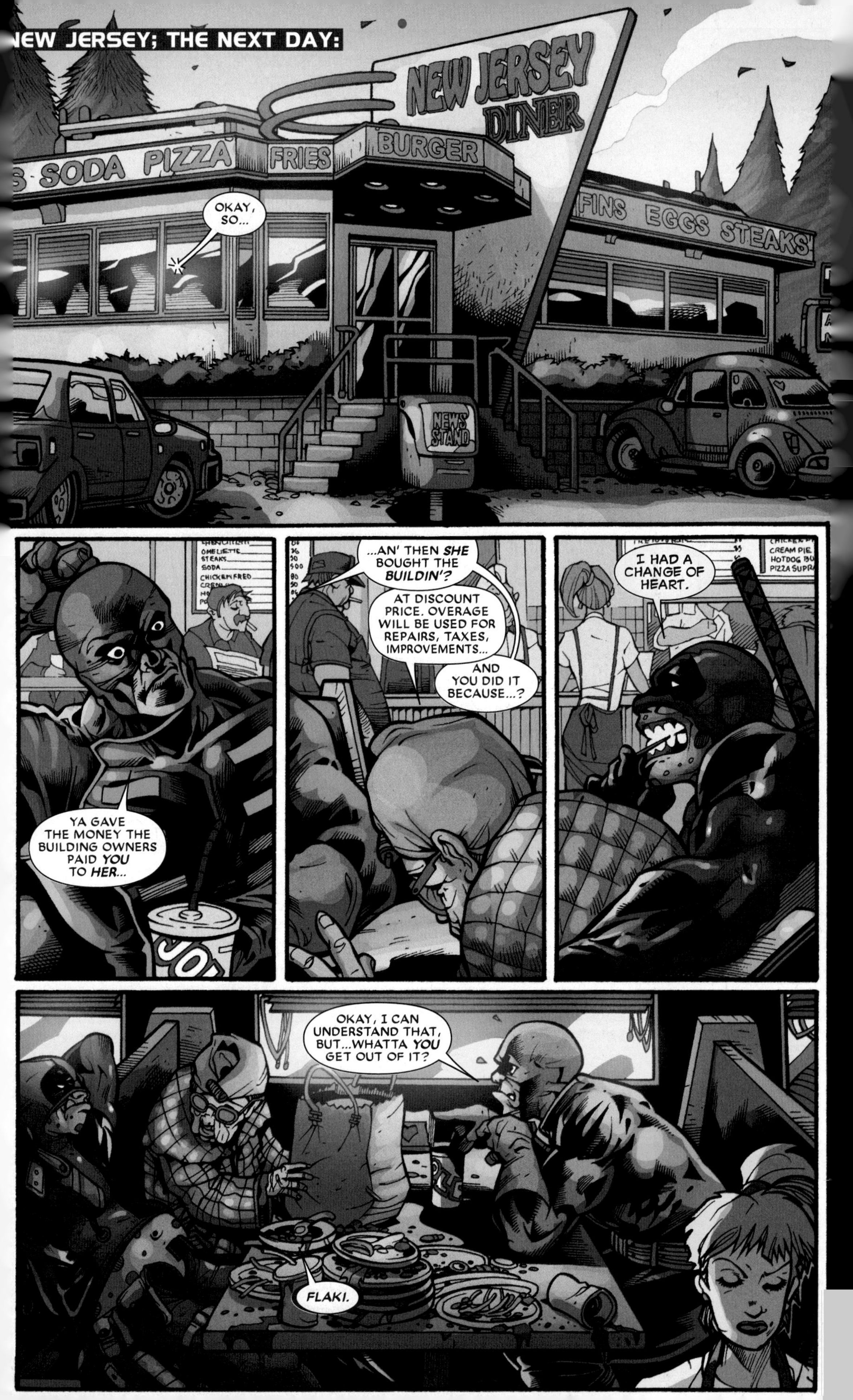
NEW JERSEY; THE NEXT DAY:
NEW JERSEY DINER
SODA PIZZA FRIES BURGER
FINS EGGS STEAKS
NEWS STAND
OKAY, SO...
YA GAVE THE MONEY THE BUILDING OWNERS PAID YOU TO HER...
...AN' THEN SHE BOUGHT THE BUILDIN'?
AT DISCOUNT PRICE. OVERAGE WILL BE USED FOR REPAIRS, TAXES, IMPROVEMENTS...
AND YOU DID IT BECAUSE...?
I HAD A CHANGE OF HEART.
OKAY, I CAN UNDERSTAND THAT, BUT...WHATTA YOU GET OUT OF IT?
FLAKI.

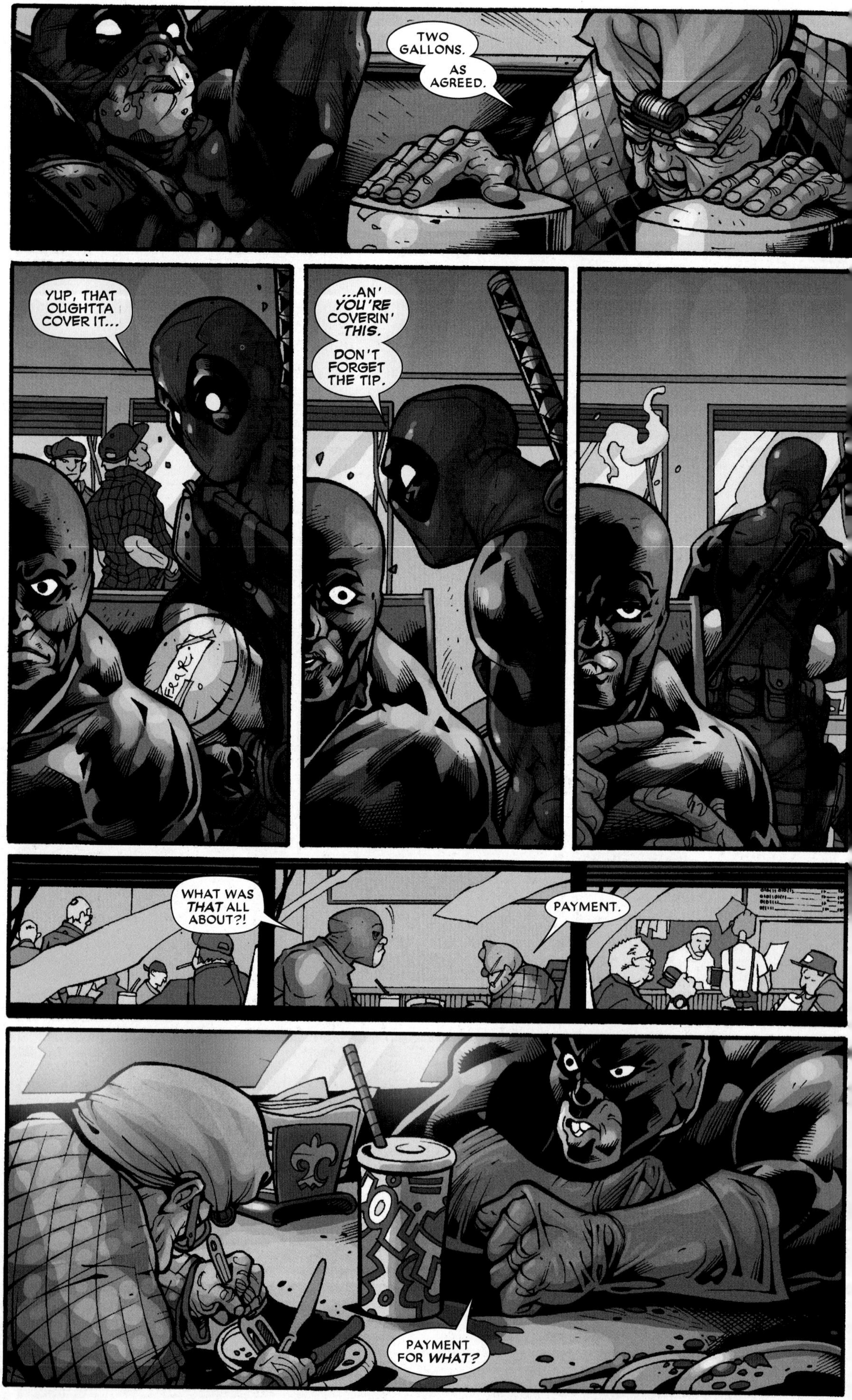
TWO GALLONS.
AS AGREED.
YUP, THAT OUGHTTA COVER IT...
...AN' YOU'RE COVERIN' THIS.
DON'T FORGET THE TIP.
WHAT WAS THAT ALL ABOUT?!
PAYMENT.
PAYMENT FOR WHAT?

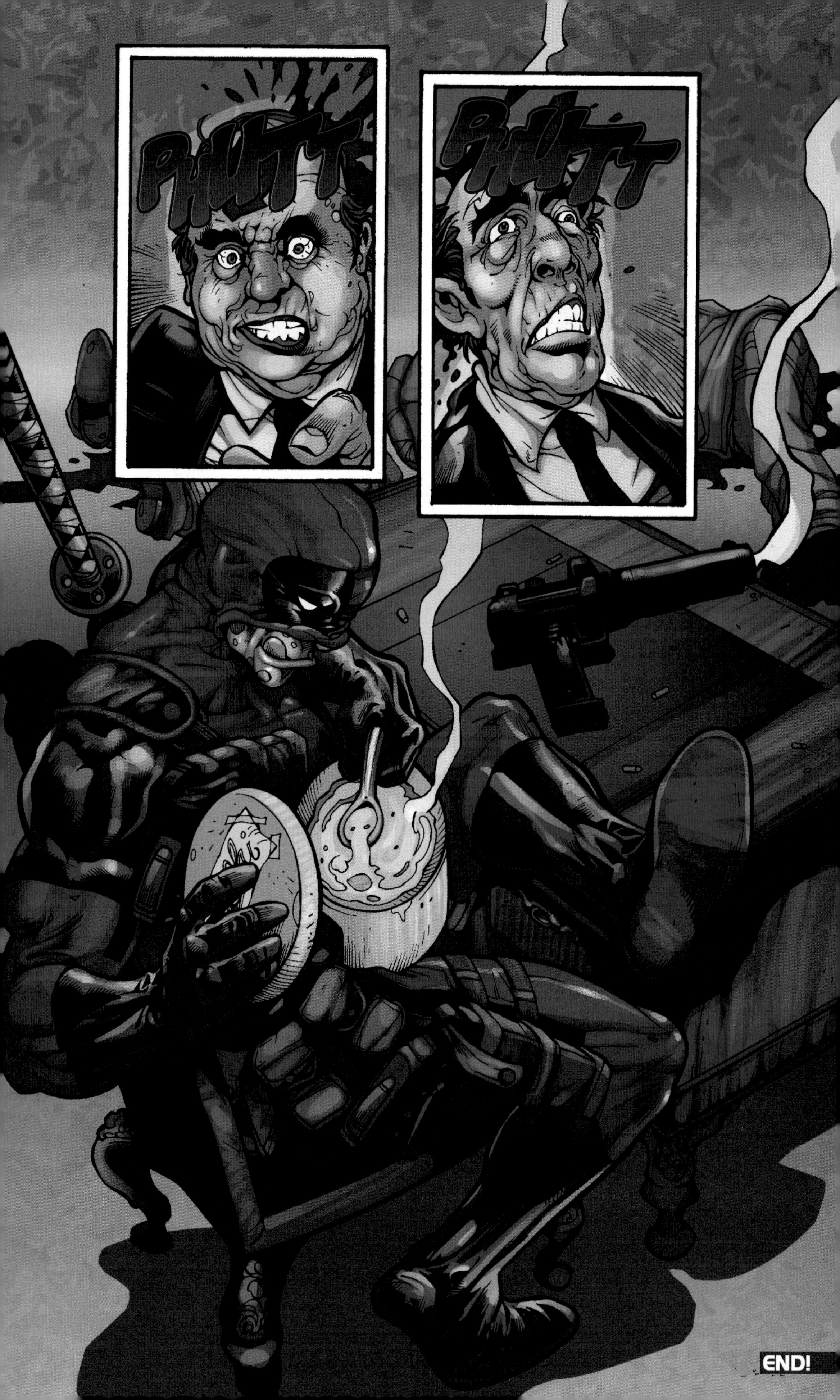
PHUTT
PHUTT
END!

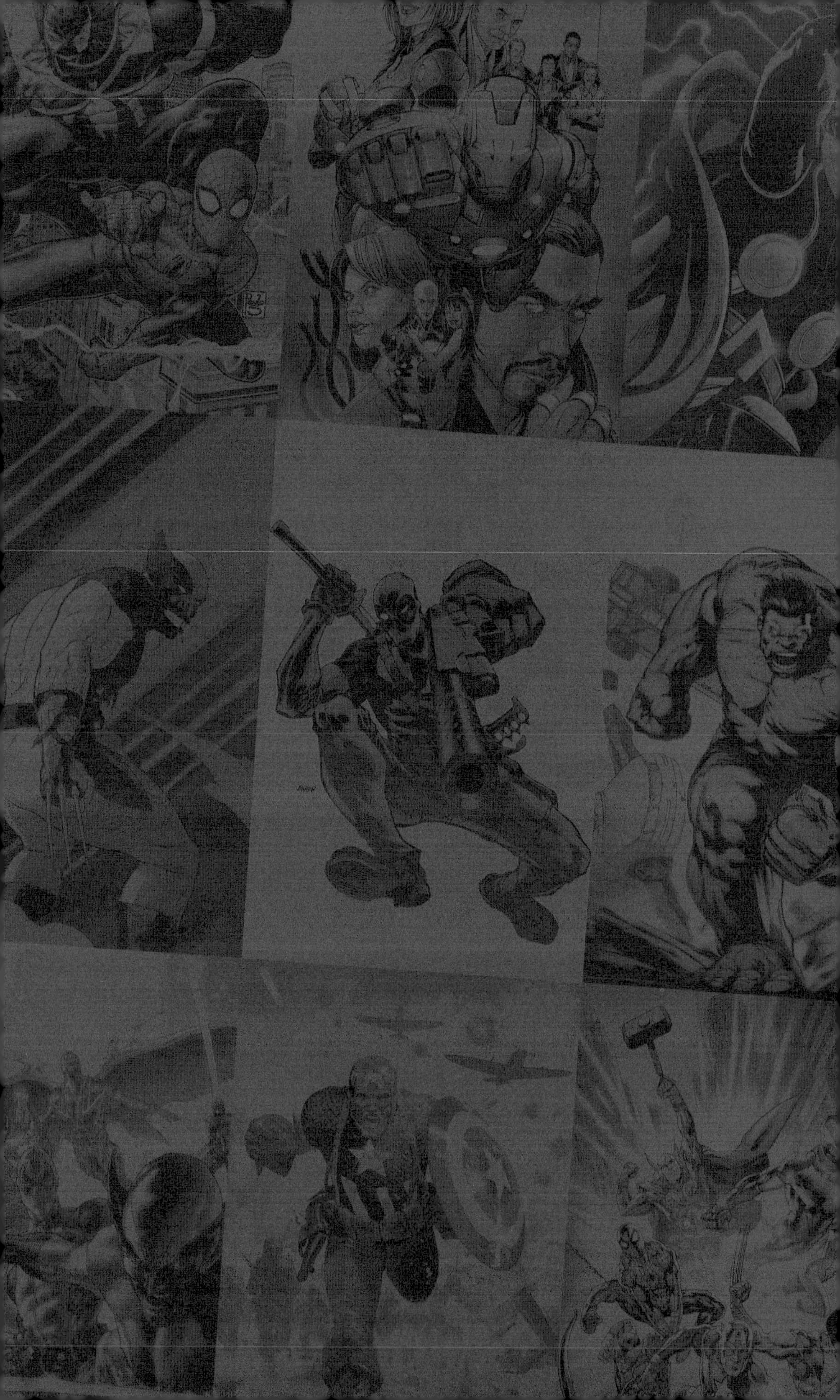

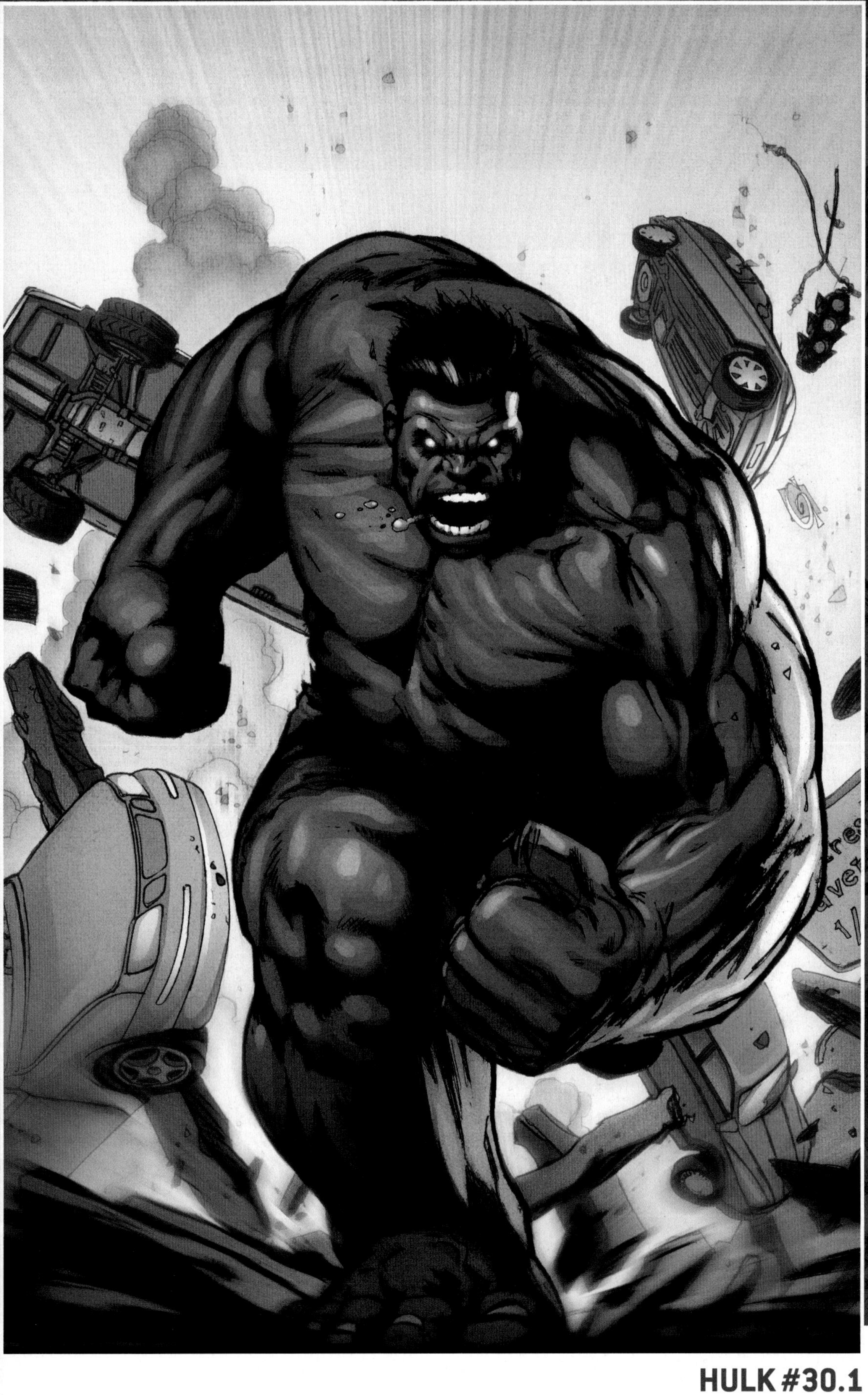

HULK #30.1

GENERAL "THUNDERBOLT" ROSS WAS DETERMINED TO RID THE WORLD OF THE HULK AT ANY COST. HIS RELENTLESS DRIVE TO DO SO ULTIMATELY LED HIM TO BECOME WHAT HE HATED MOST: A HULK. ROSS FAKED HIS OWN DEATH AND USED HIS RED HULK PERSONA TO EXECUTE AN INCREASINGLY MISGUIDED QUEST TO CORRECT A WORLD HE SAW AS SPINNING OUT OF CONTROL, WHICH CULMINATED IN HIS CAPTURE AS HE ATTACKED THE WHITE HOUSE.

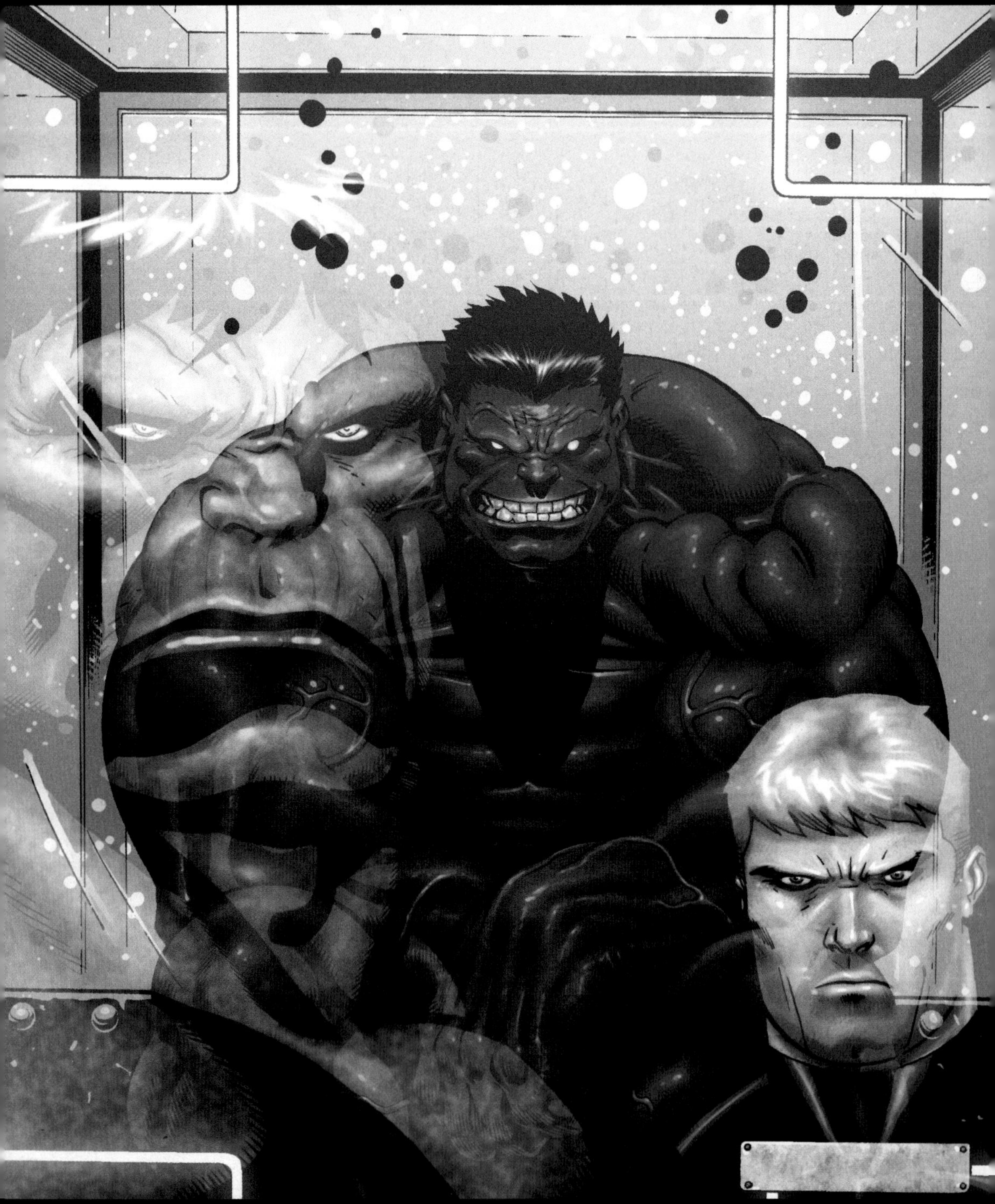

DESPITE THIS, THE RED HULK WAS ENLISTED BY STEVE ROGERS ON THE RECOMMENDATION OF BRUCE BANNER, THE MAN WHO ROSS ONCE HUNTED, TO OPERATE UNDER BANNER'S GUIDANCE AND UTILIZE HIS INCREDIBLE POWER FOR THE GOOD OF MANKIND... SO LONG AS THE FORMER GENERAL LEARNS HOW TO OBEY ORDERS.

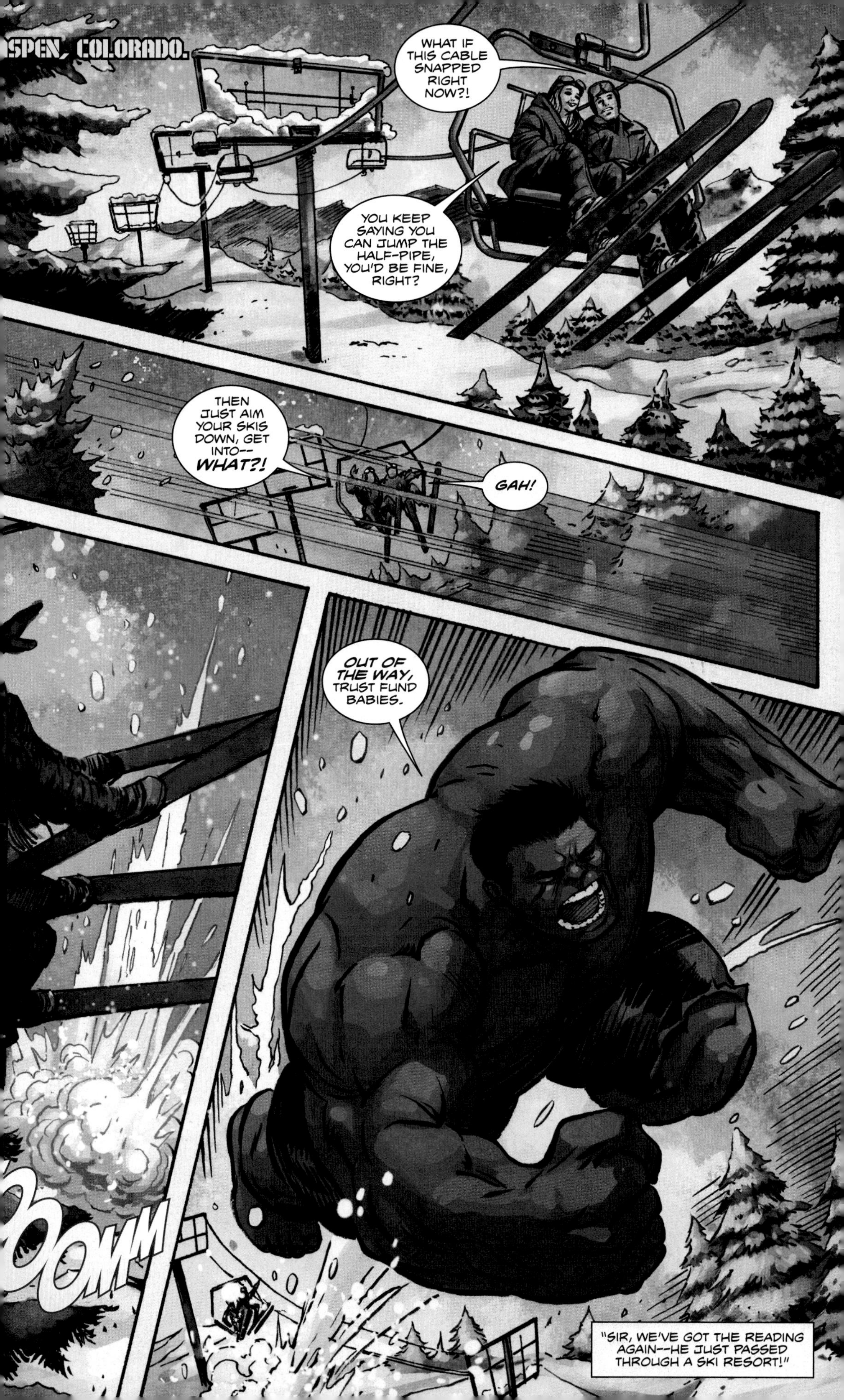
SPEN, COLORADO.
WHAT IF THIS CABLE SNAPPED RIGHT NOW?!
YOU KEEP SAYING YOU CAN JUMP THE HALF-PIPE, YOU'D BE FINE, RIGHT?
THEN JUST AIM YOUR SKIS DOWN, GET INTO-- WHAT?!
GAH!
OUT OF THE WAY, TRUST FUND BABIES.
"SIR, WE'VE GOT THE READING AGAIN--HE JUST PASSED THROUGH A SKI RESORT!"

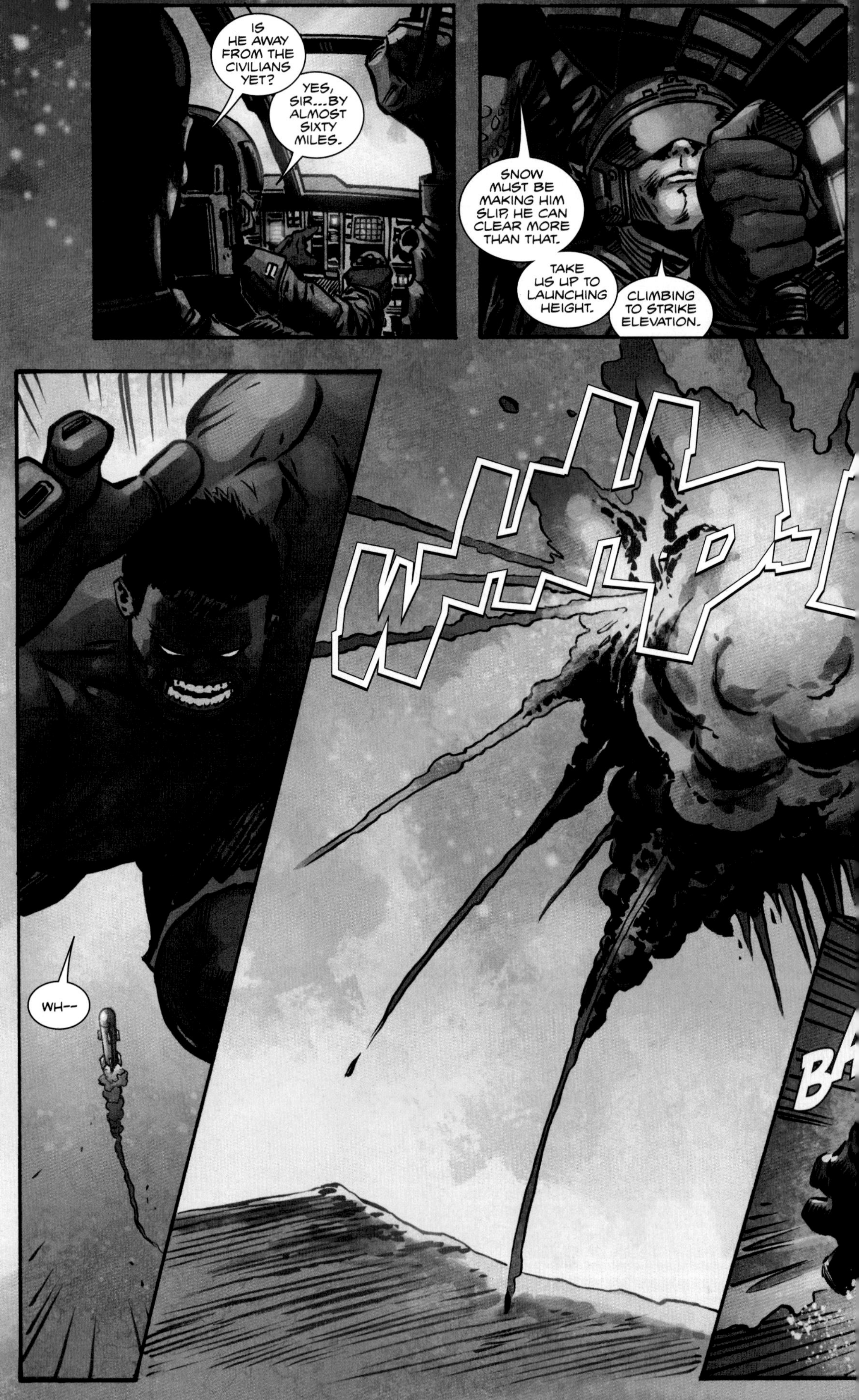
IS HE AWAY FROM THE CIVILIANS YET?
YES, SIR...BY ALMOST SIXTY MILES.
SNOW MUST BE MAKING HIM SLIP, HE CAN CLEAR MORE THAN THAT.
TAKE US UP TO LAUNCHING HEIGHT.
CLIMBING TO STRIKE ELEVATION.
WH--

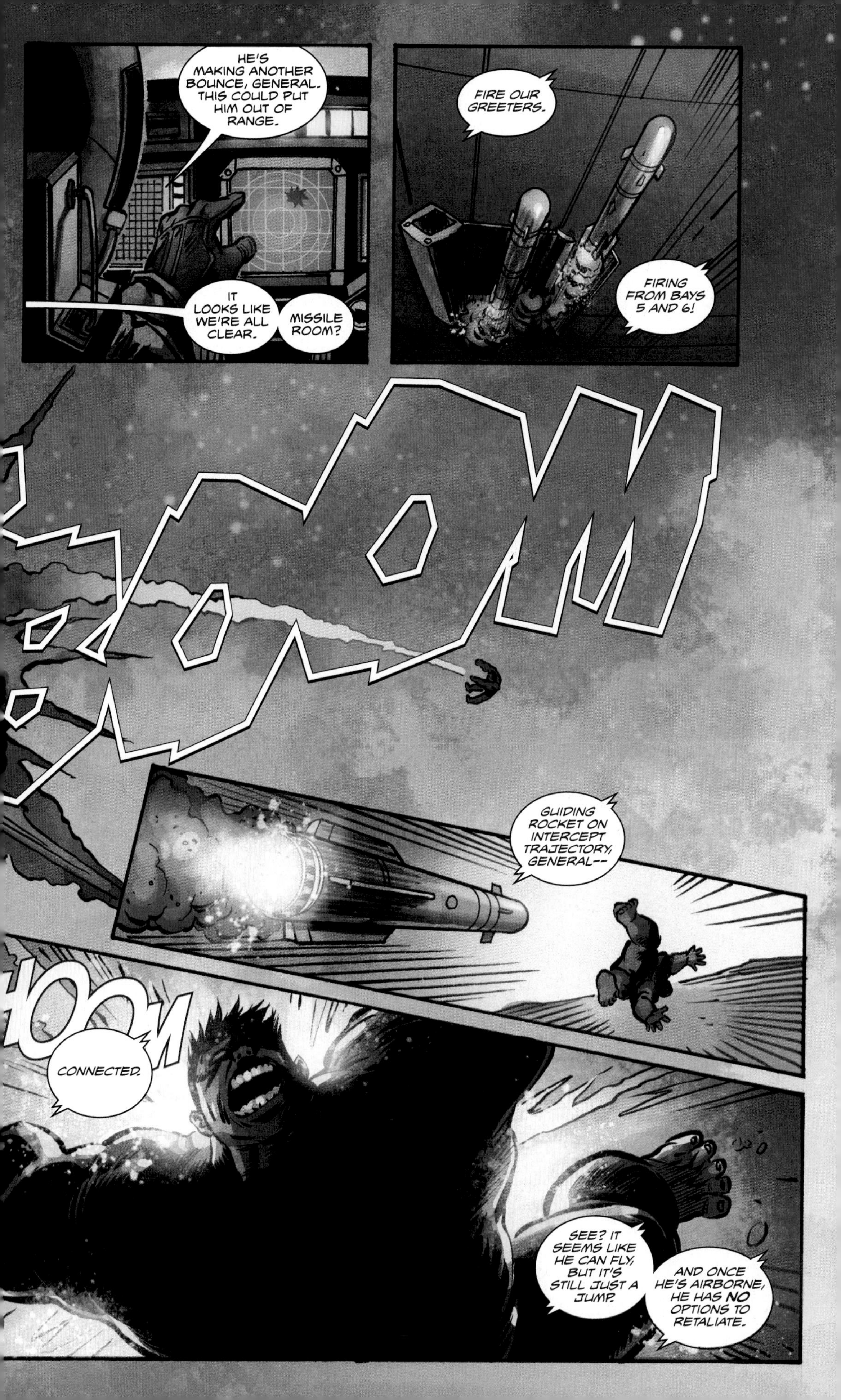

HE'S MAKING ANOTHER BOUNCE, GENERAL. THIS COULD PUT HIM OUT OF RANGE.
IT LOOKS LIKE WE'RE ALL CLEAR.
MISSILE ROOM?
FIRE OUR GREETERS.
FIRING FROM BAYS 5 AND 6!
GUIDING ROCKET ON INTERCEPT TRAJECTORY, GENERAL--
CONNECTED.
SEE? IT SEEMS LIKE HE CAN FLY, BUT IT'S STILL JUST A JUMP.
AND ONCE HE'S AIRBORNE, HE HAS NO OPTIONS TO RETALIATE.

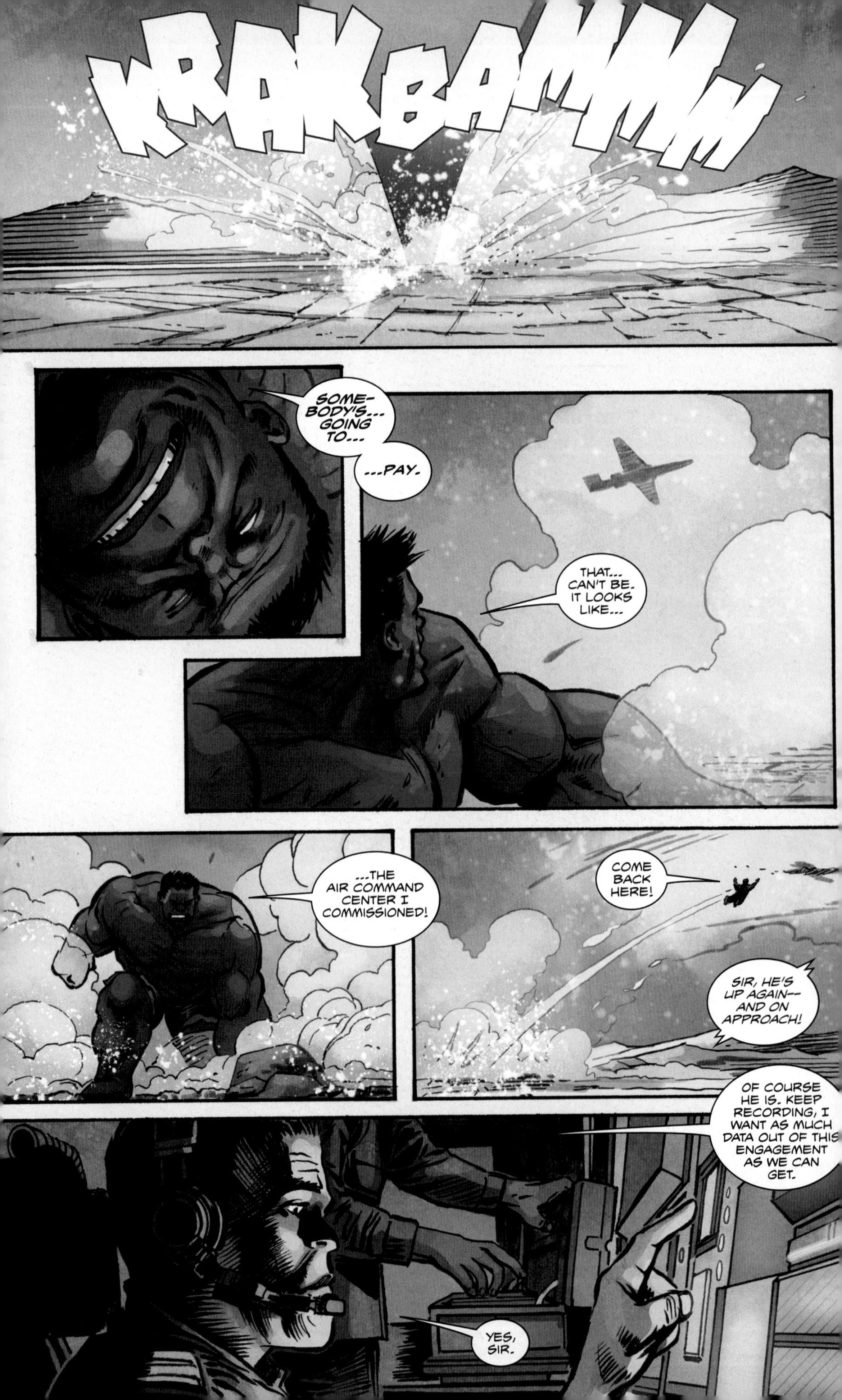
KRAKBAMMM
SOME-BODY'S... GOING TO...
...PAY.
THAT... CAN'T BE. IT LOOKS LIKE...
...THE AIR COMMAND CENTER I COMMISSIONED!
COME BACK HERE!
SIR, HE'S UP AGAIN-- AND ON APPROACH!
OF COURSE HE IS. KEEP RECORDING, I WANT AS MUCH DATA OUT OF THIS ENGAGEMENT AS WE CAN GET.
YES, SIR.

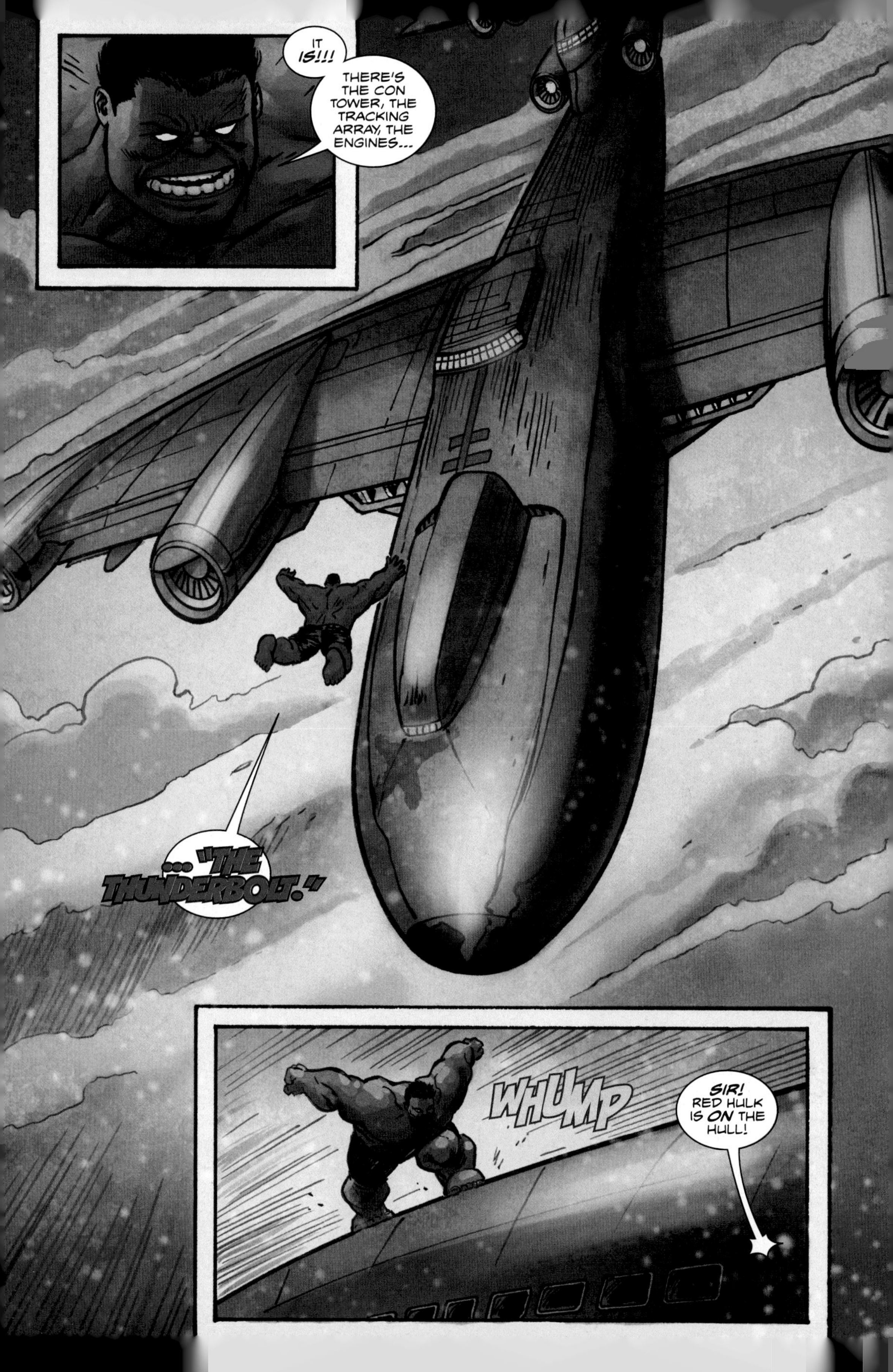
IT IS!!!
THERE'S THE CON TOWER, THE TRACKING ARRAY, THE ENGINES...
... "THE THUNDERBOLT."
WHUMP
SIR! RED HULK IS ON THE HULL!

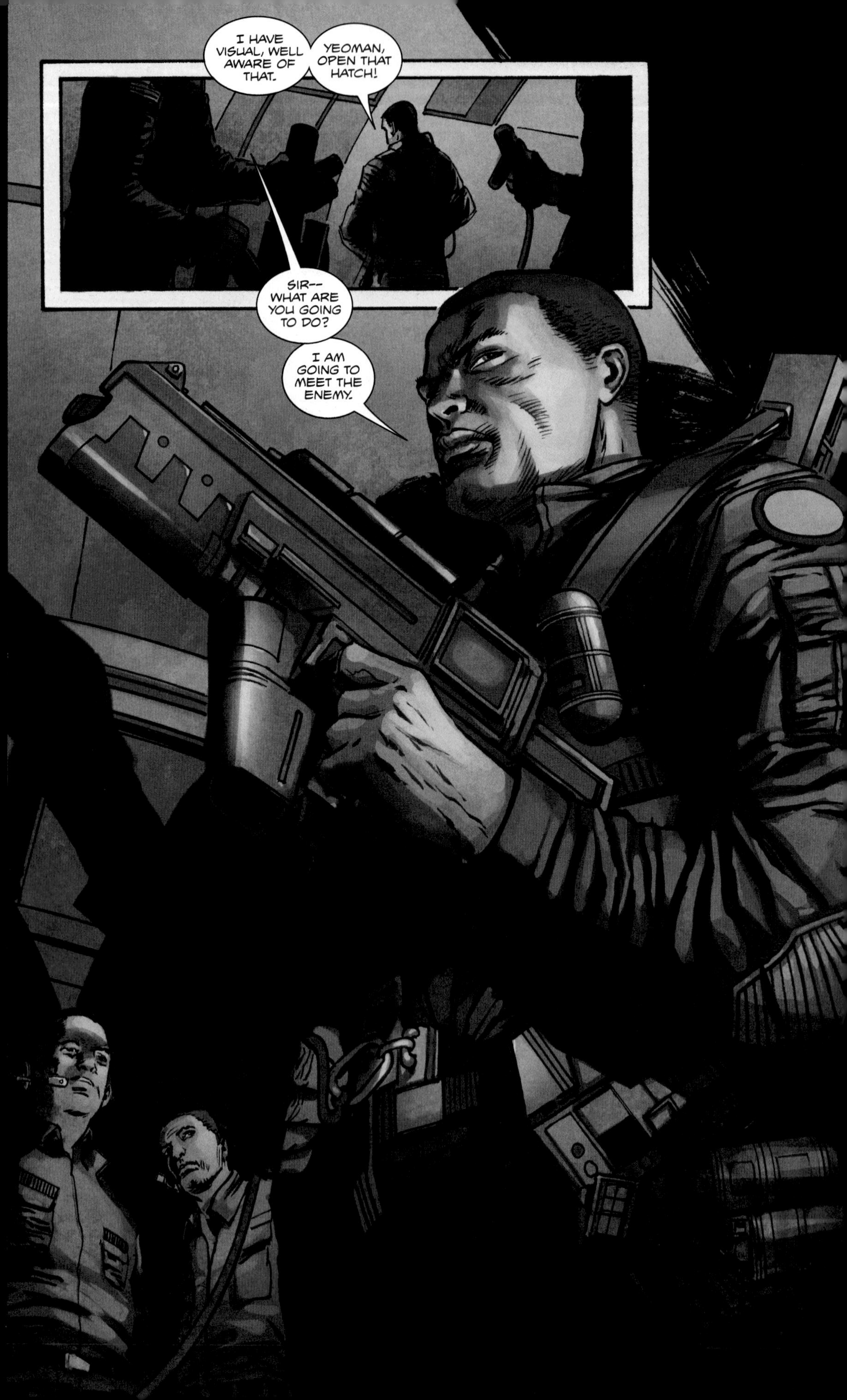

I HAVE VISUAL, WELL AWARE OF THAT.
YEOMAN, OPEN THAT HATCH!
SIR-- WHAT ARE YOU GOING TO DO?
I AM GOING TO MEET THE ENEMY.

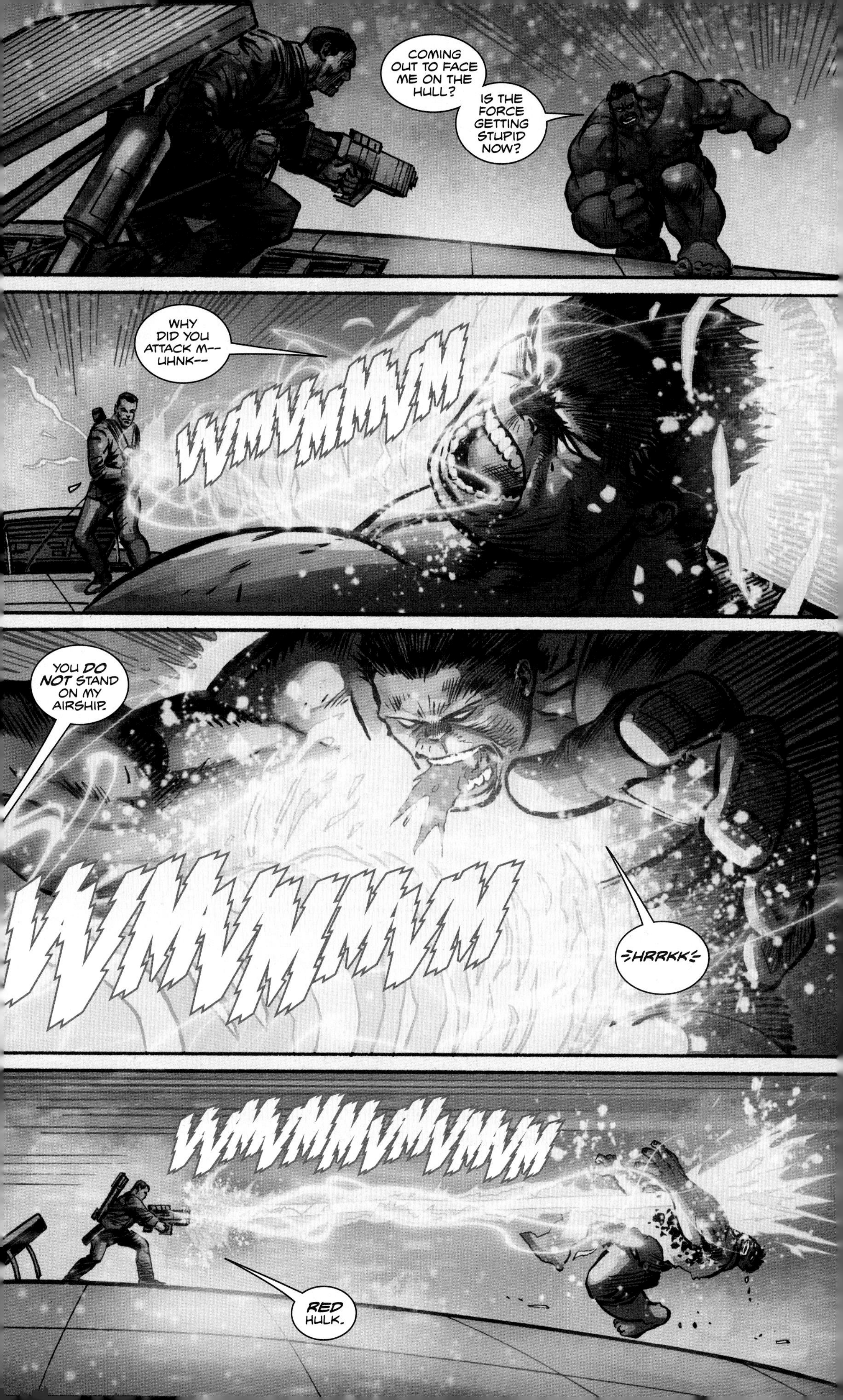
COMING OUT TO FACE ME ON THE HULL?
IS THE FORCE GETTING STUPID NOW?
WHY DID YOU ATTACK M-- UHNK--
WMVMMVM
YOU DO NOT STAND ON MY AIRSHIP.
WMVMMVM
HRRKK
VMMMMVMVMVM
RED HULK.

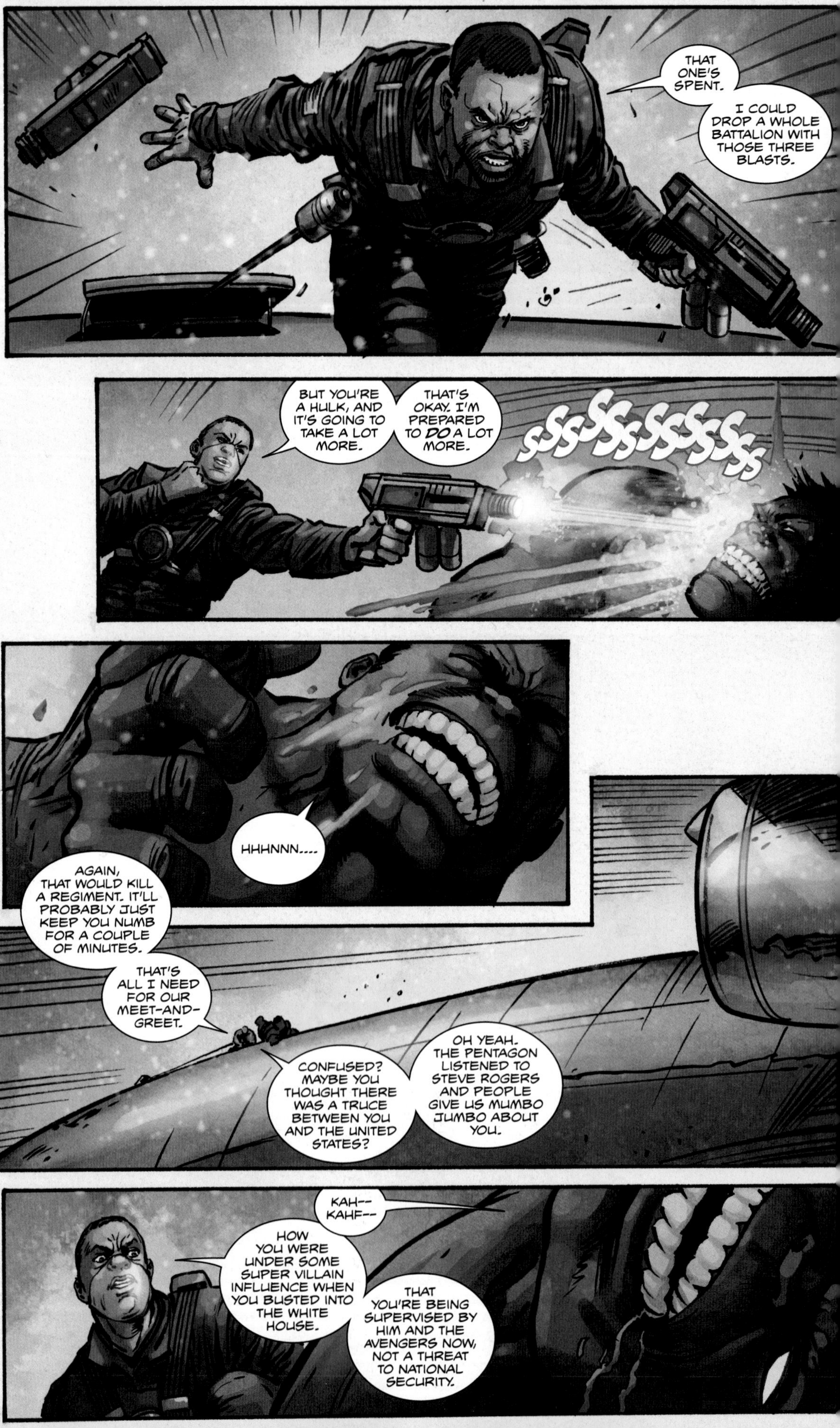
THAT ONE'S SPENT.
I COULD DROP A WHOLE BATTALION WITH THOSE THREE BLASTS.
BUT YOU'RE A HULK, AND IT'S GOING TO TAKE A LOT MORE.
THAT'S OKAY. I'M PREPARED TO DO A LOT MORE.
SSSSSSSSSSSSS
HHHNNN....
AGAIN, THAT WOULD KILL A REGIMENT. IT'LL PROBABLY JUST KEEP YOU NUMB FOR A COUPLE OF MINUTES.
THAT'S ALL I NEED FOR OUR MEET-AND-GREET.
CONFUSED? MAYBE YOU THOUGHT THERE WAS A TRUCE BETWEEN YOU AND THE UNITED STATES?
OH YEAH. THE PENTAGON LISTENED TO STEVE ROGERS AND PEOPLE GIVE US MUMBO JUMBO ABOUT YOU.
KAH-- KAHF--
HOW YOU WERE UNDER SOME SUPER VILLAIN INFLUENCE WHEN YOU BUSTED INTO THE WHITE HOUSE.
THAT YOU'RE BEING SUPERVISED BY HIM AND THE AVENGERS NOW, NOT A THREAT TO NATIONAL SECURITY.

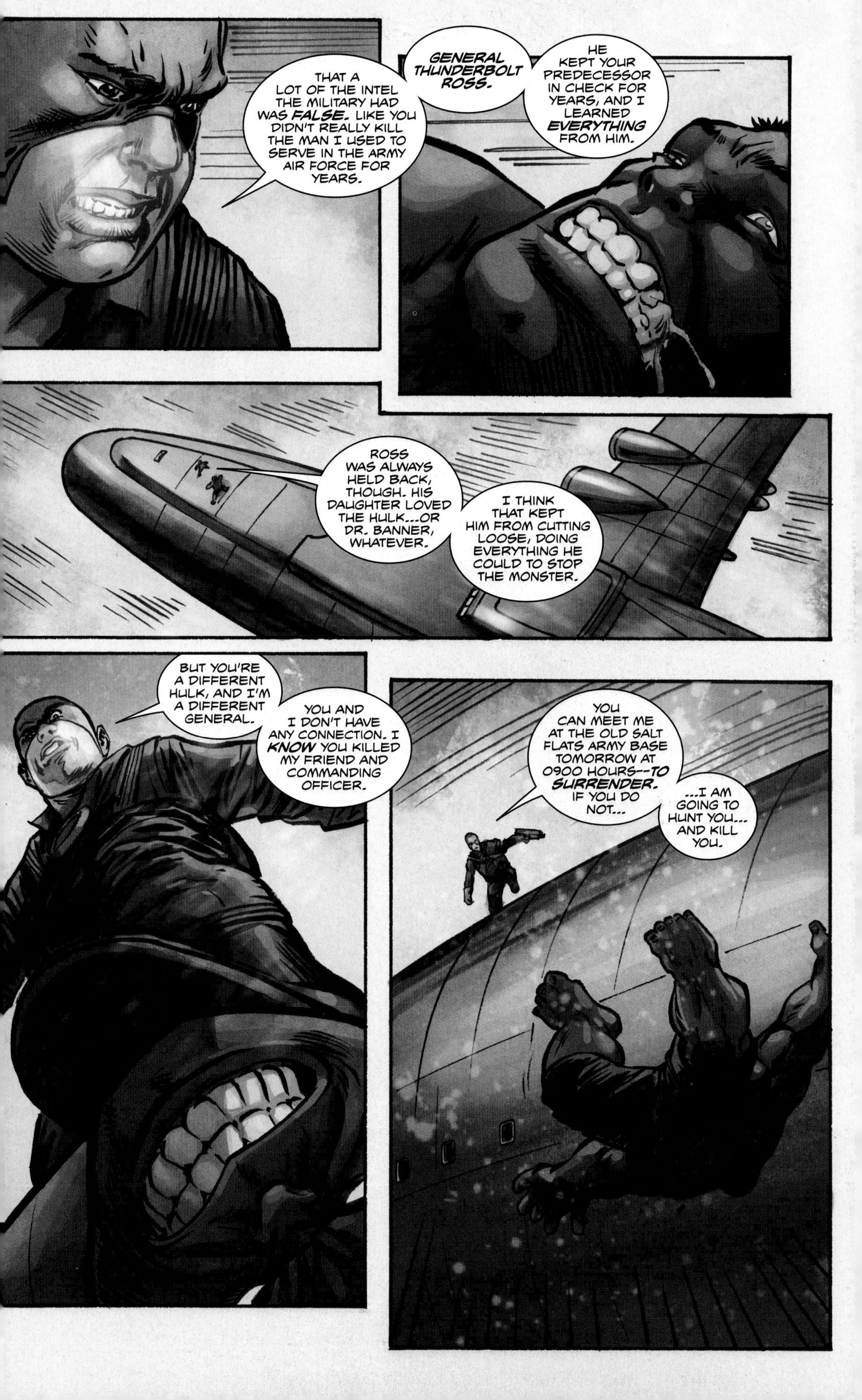
THAT A LOT OF THE INTEL THE MILITARY HAD WAS FALSE. LIKE YOU DIDN'T REALLY KILL THE MAN I USED TO SERVE IN THE ARMY AIR FORCE FOR YEARS.
GENERAL THUNDERBOLT ROSS.
HE KEPT YOUR PREDECESSOR IN CHECK FOR YEARS, AND I LEARNED EVERYTHING FROM HIM.
ROSS WAS ALWAYS HELD BACK, THOUGH. HIS DAUGHTER LOVED THE HULK...OR DR. BANNER, WHATEVER.
I THINK THAT KEPT HIM FROM CUTTING LOOSE, DOING EVERYTHING HE COULD TO STOP THE MONSTER.
BUT YOU'RE A DIFFERENT HULK, AND I'M A DIFFERENT GENERAL.
YOU AND I DON'T HAVE ANY CONNECTION. I KNOW YOU KILLED MY FRIEND AND COMMANDING OFFICER.
YOU CAN MEET ME AT THE OLD SALT FLATS ARMY BASE TOMORROW AT 0900 HOURS--TO SURRENDER. IF YOU DO NOT...
...I AM GOING TO HUNT YOU... AND KILL YOU.

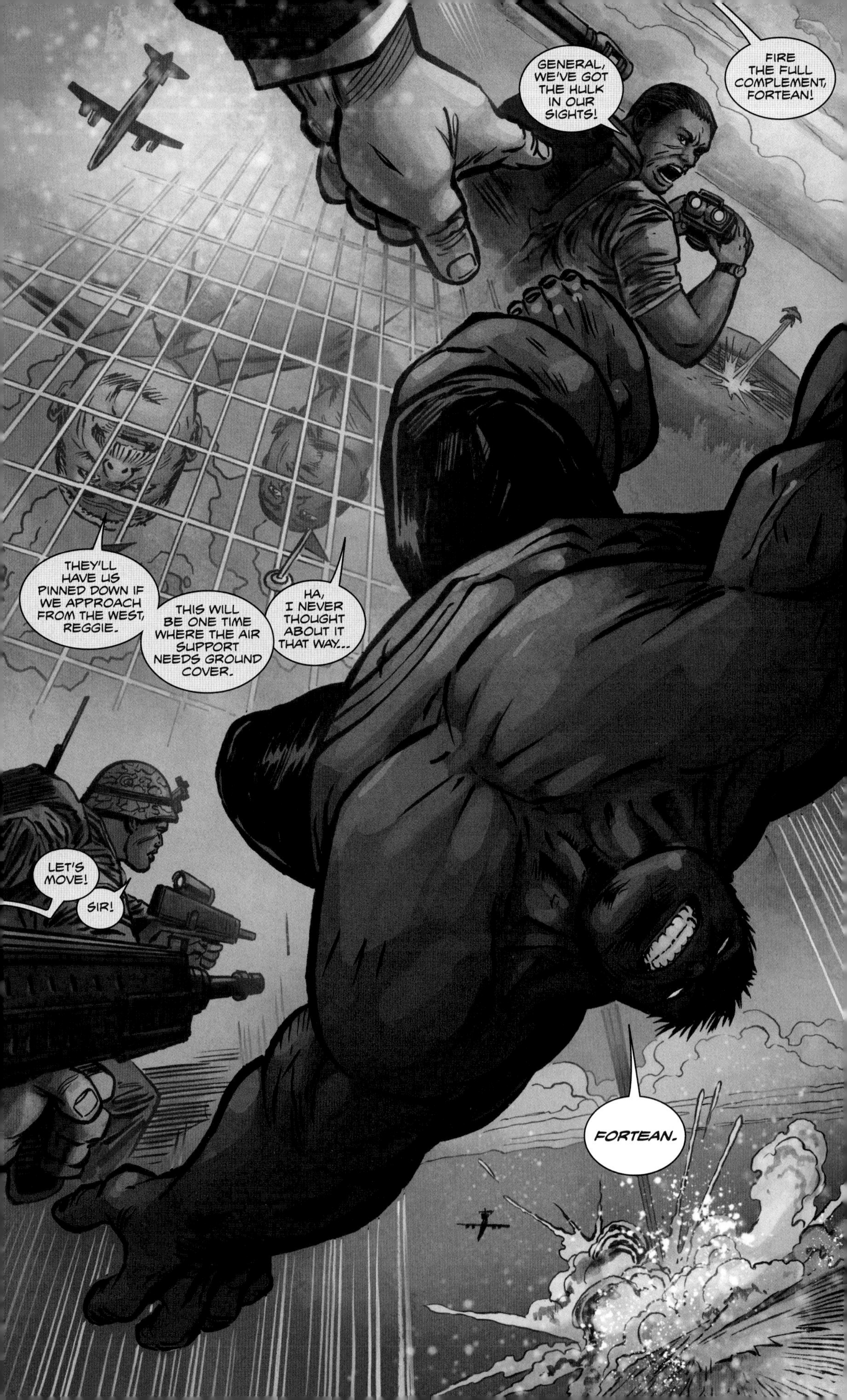
GENERAL, WE'VE GOT THE HULK IN OUR SIGHTS!
FIRE THE FULL COMPLEMENT, FORTEAN!
THEY'LL HAVE US PINNED DOWN IF WE APPROACH FROM THE WEST, REGGIE.
THIS WILL BE ONE TIME WHERE THE AIR SUPPORT NEEDS GROUND COVER.
HA, I NEVER THOUGHT ABOUT IT THAT WAY...
LET'S MOVE!
SIR!
FORTEAN.

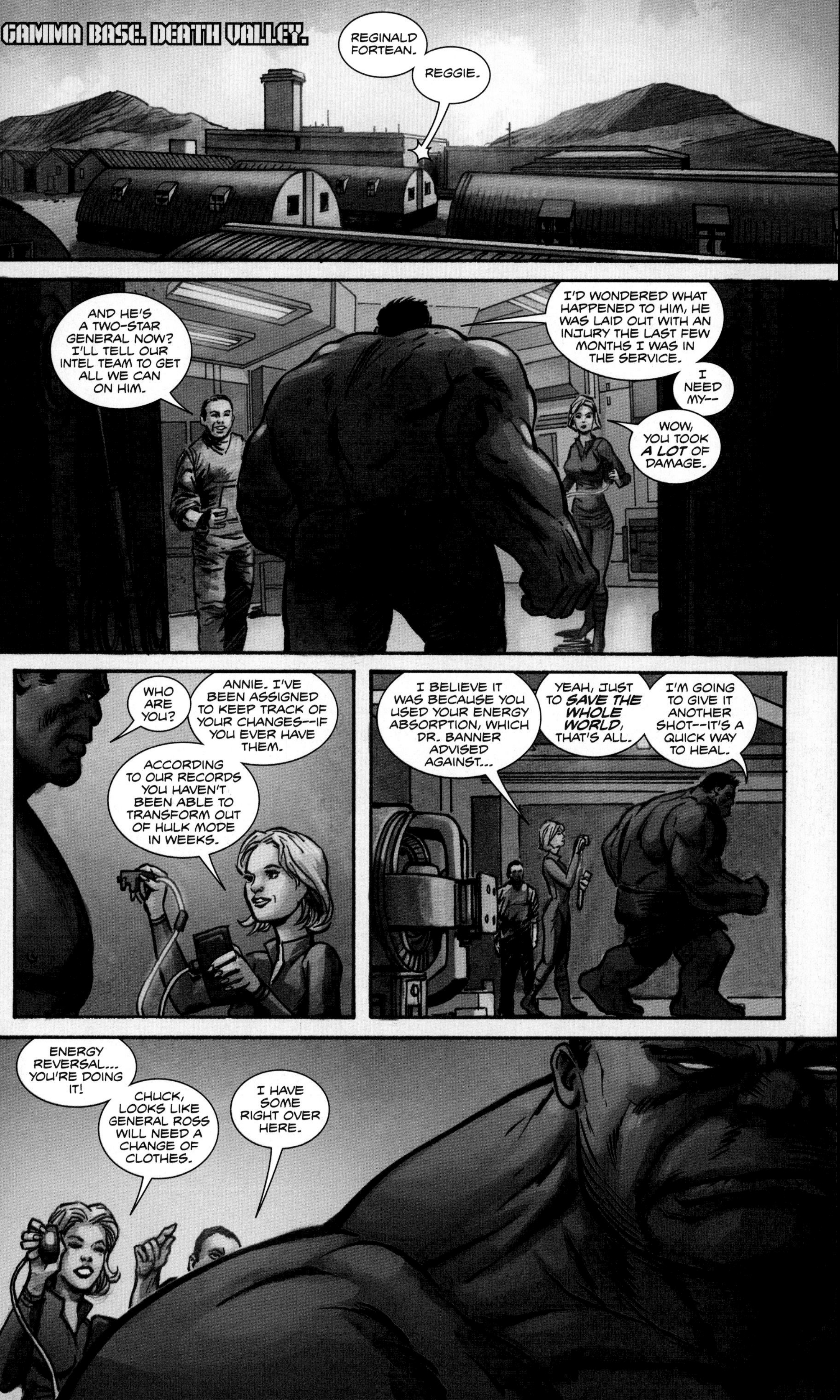

GAMMA BASE. DEATH VALLEY.
REGINALD FORTEAN.
REGGIE.
AND HE'S A TWO-STAR GENERAL NOW? I'LL TELL OUR INTEL TEAM TO GET ALL WE CAN ON HIM.
I'D WONDERED WHAT HAPPENED TO HIM, HE WAS LAID OUT WITH AN INJURY THE LAST FEW MONTHS I WAS IN THE SERVICE.
I NEED MY--
WOW, YOU TOOK *A LOT* OF DAMAGE.
WHO ARE YOU?
ANNIE. I'VE BEEN ASSIGNED TO KEEP TRACK OF YOUR CHANGES--IF YOU EVER HAVE THEM.
ACCORDING TO OUR RECORDS YOU HAVEN'T BEEN ABLE TO TRANSFORM OUT OF HULK MODE IN WEEKS.
I BELIEVE IT WAS BECAUSE YOU USED YOUR ENERGY ABSORPTION, WHICH DR. BANNER ADVISED AGAINST...
YEAH, JUST TO *SAVE THE WHOLE WORLD*, THAT'S ALL.
I'M GOING TO GIVE IT ANOTHER SHOT--IT'S A QUICK WAY TO HEAL.
ENERGY REVERSAL... YOU'RE DOING IT!
CHUCK, LOOKS LIKE GENERAL ROSS WILL NEED A CHANGE OF CLOTHES.
I HAVE SOME RIGHT OVER HERE.

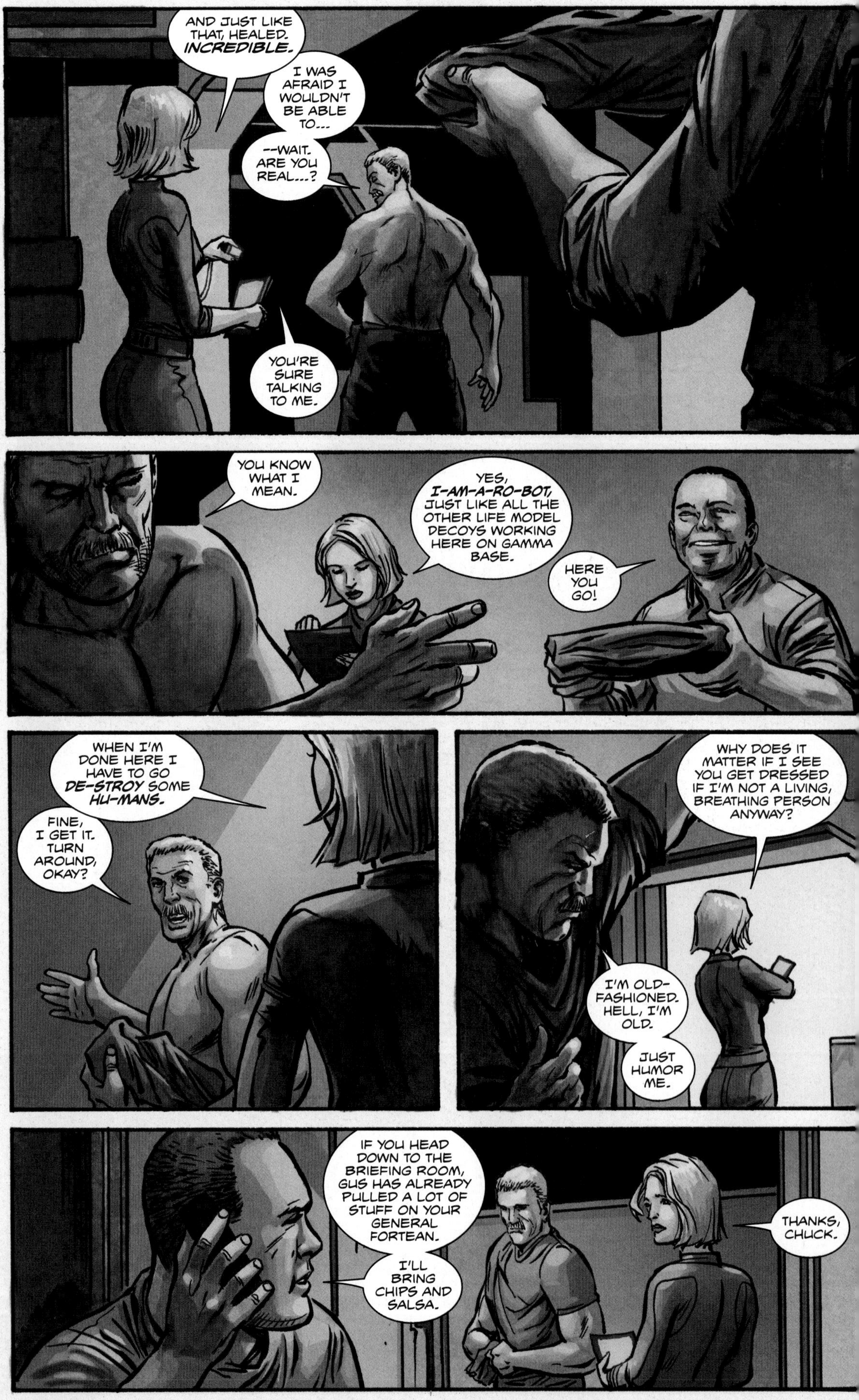
AND JUST LIKE THAT, HEALED. INCREDIBLE.
I WAS AFRAID I WOULDN'T BE ABLE TO...
--WAIT. ARE YOU REAL...?
YOU'RE SURE TALKING TO ME.
YOU KNOW WHAT I MEAN.
YES, I-AM-A-RO-BOT, JUST LIKE ALL THE OTHER LIFE MODEL DECOYS WORKING HERE ON GAMMA BASE.
HERE YOU GO!
WHEN I'M DONE HERE I HAVE TO GO DE-STROY SOME HU-MANS.
FINE, I GET IT. TURN AROUND, OKAY?
WHY DOES IT MATTER IF I SEE YOU GET DRESSED IF I'M NOT A LIVING, BREATHING PERSON ANYWAY?
I'M OLD-FASHIONED. HELL, I'M OLD.
JUST HUMOR ME.
IF YOU HEAD DOWN TO THE BRIEFING ROOM, GUS HAS ALREADY PULLED A LOT OF STUFF ON YOUR GENERAL FORTEAN.
I'LL BRING CHIPS AND SALSA.
THANKS, CHUCK.

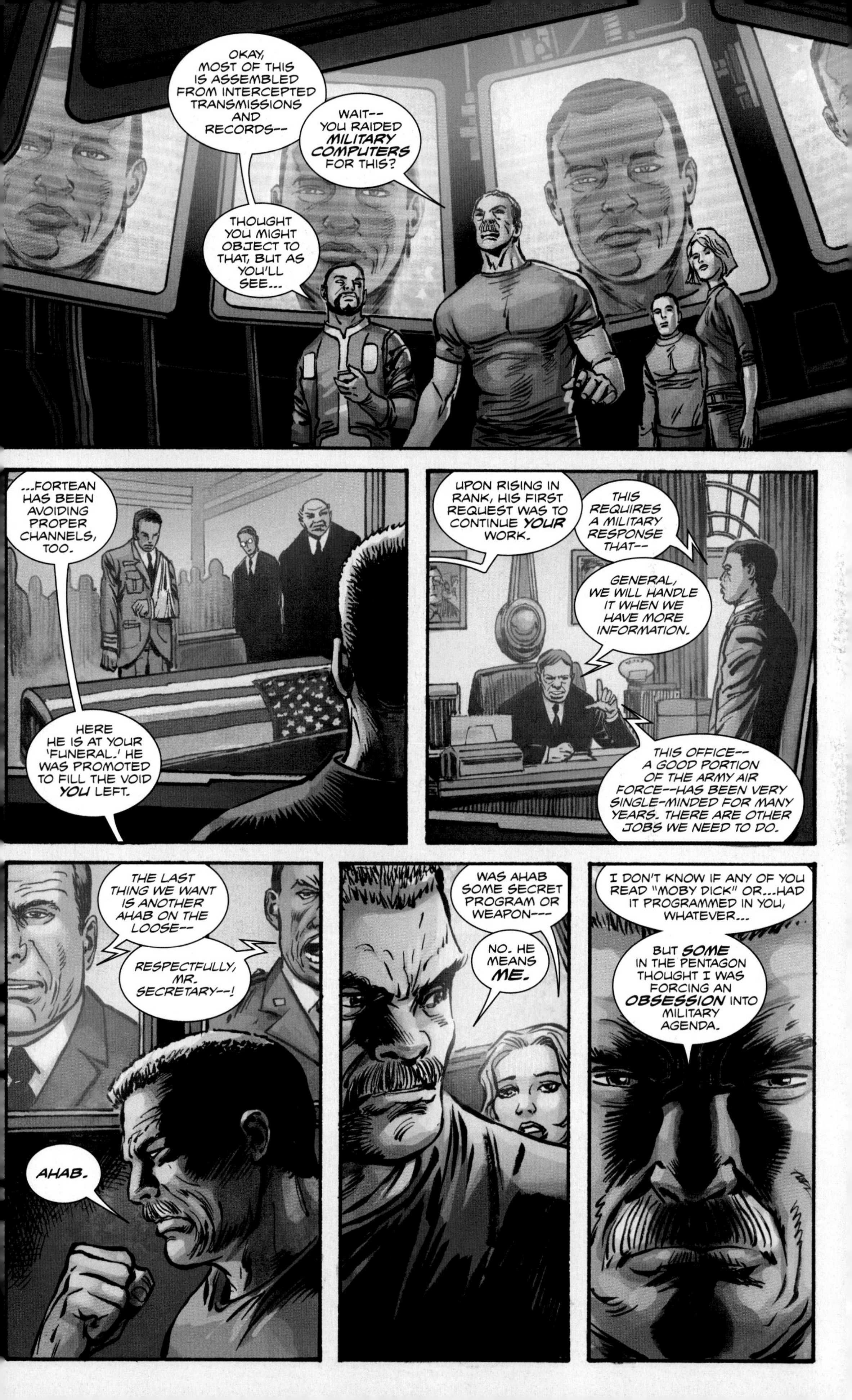

OKAY, MOST OF THIS IS ASSEMBLED FROM INTERCEPTED TRANSMISSIONS AND RECORDS--
WAIT-- YOU RAIDED MILITARY COMPUTERS FOR THIS?
THOUGHT YOU MIGHT OBJECT TO THAT, BUT AS YOU'LL SEE...
...FORTEAN HAS BEEN AVOIDING PROPER CHANNELS, TOO.
HERE HE IS AT YOUR 'FUNERAL.' HE WAS PROMOTED TO FILL THE VOID YOU LEFT.
UPON RISING IN RANK, HIS FIRST REQUEST WAS TO CONTINUE YOUR WORK.
THIS REQUIRES A MILITARY RESPONSE THAT--
GENERAL, WE WILL HANDLE IT WHEN WE HAVE MORE INFORMATION.
THIS OFFICE-- A GOOD PORTION OF THE ARMY AIR FORCE--HAS BEEN VERY SINGLE-MINDED FOR MANY YEARS. THERE ARE OTHER JOBS WE NEED TO DO.
THE LAST THING WE WANT IS ANOTHER AHAB ON THE LOOSE--
RESPECTFULLY, MR. SECRETARY--!
AHAB.
WAS AHAB SOME SECRET PROGRAM OR WEAPON---
NO. HE MEANS ME.
I DON'T KNOW IF ANY OF YOU READ "MOBY DICK" OR...HAD IT PROGRAMMED IN YOU, WHATEVER...
BUT SOME IN THE PENTAGON THOUGHT I WAS FORCING AN OBSESSION INTO MILITARY AGENDA.

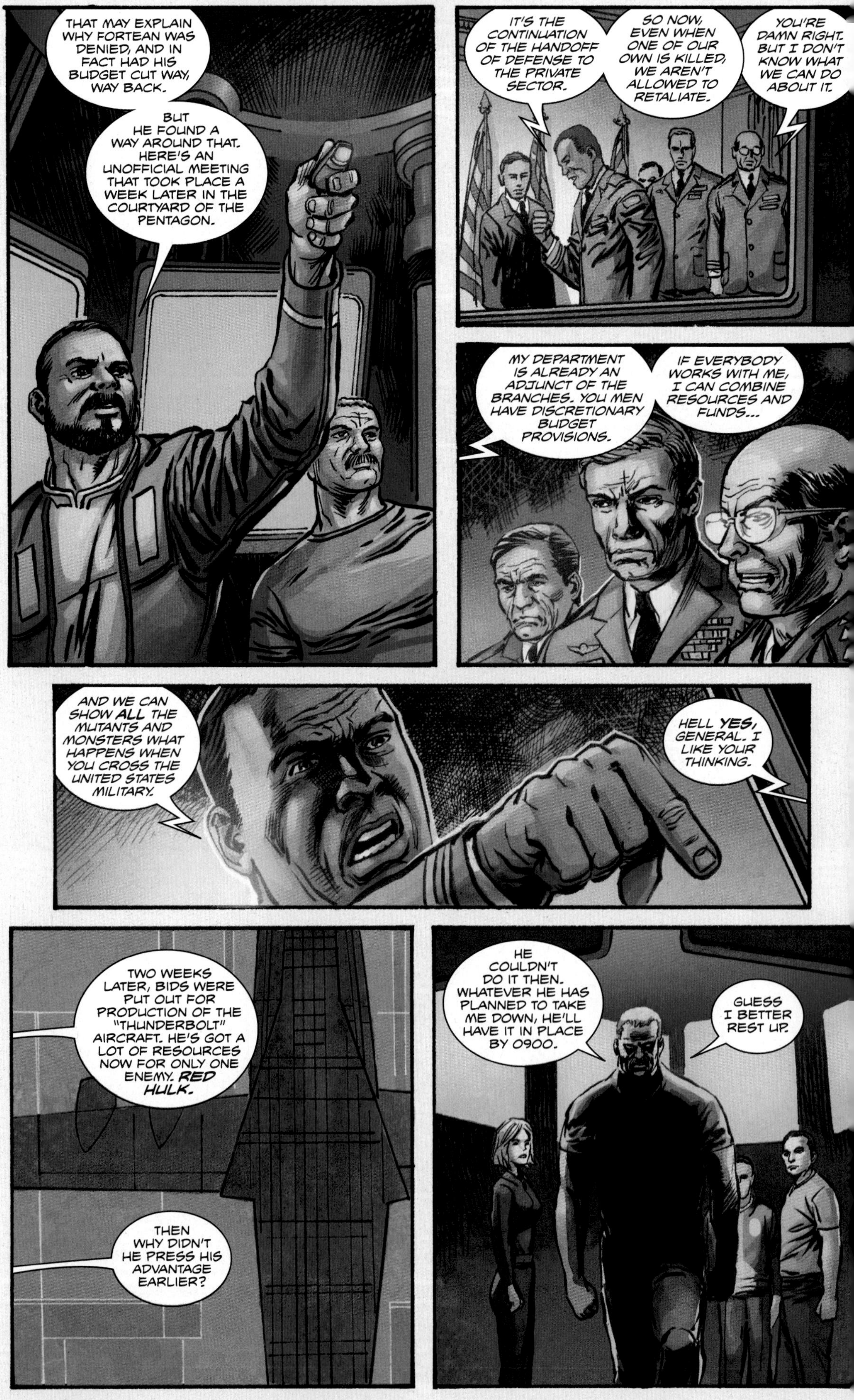
THAT MAY EXPLAIN WHY FORTEAN WAS DENIED, AND IN FACT HAD HIS BUDGET CUT WAY, WAY BACK.
BUT HE FOUND A WAY AROUND THAT. HERE'S AN UNOFFICIAL MEETING THAT TOOK PLACE A WEEK LATER IN THE COURTYARD OF THE PENTAGON.
IT'S THE CONTINUATION OF THE HANDOFF OF DEFENSE TO THE PRIVATE SECTOR.
SO NOW, EVEN WHEN ONE OF OUR OWN IS KILLED, WE AREN'T ALLOWED TO RETALIATE.
YOU'RE DAMN RIGHT. BUT I DON'T KNOW WHAT WE CAN DO ABOUT IT.
MY DEPARTMENT IS ALREADY AN ADJUNCT OF THE BRANCHES. YOU MEN HAVE DISCRETIONARY BUDGET PROVISIONS.
IF EVERYBODY WORKS WITH ME, I CAN COMBINE RESOURCES AND FUNDS...
AND WE CAN SHOW ALL THE MUTANTS AND MONSTERS WHAT HAPPENS WHEN YOU CROSS THE UNITED STATES MILITARY.
HELL YES, GENERAL. I LIKE YOUR THINKING.
TWO WEEKS LATER, BIDS WERE PUT OUT FOR PRODUCTION OF THE "THUNDERBOLT" AIRCRAFT. HE'S GOT A LOT OF RESOURCES NOW FOR ONLY ONE ENEMY. RED HULK.
THEN WHY DIDN'T HE PRESS HIS ADVANTAGE EARLIER?
HE COULDN'T DO IT THEN. WHATEVER HE HAS PLANNED TO TAKE ME DOWN, HE'LL HAVE IT IN PLACE BY 0900.
GUESS I BETTER REST UP.

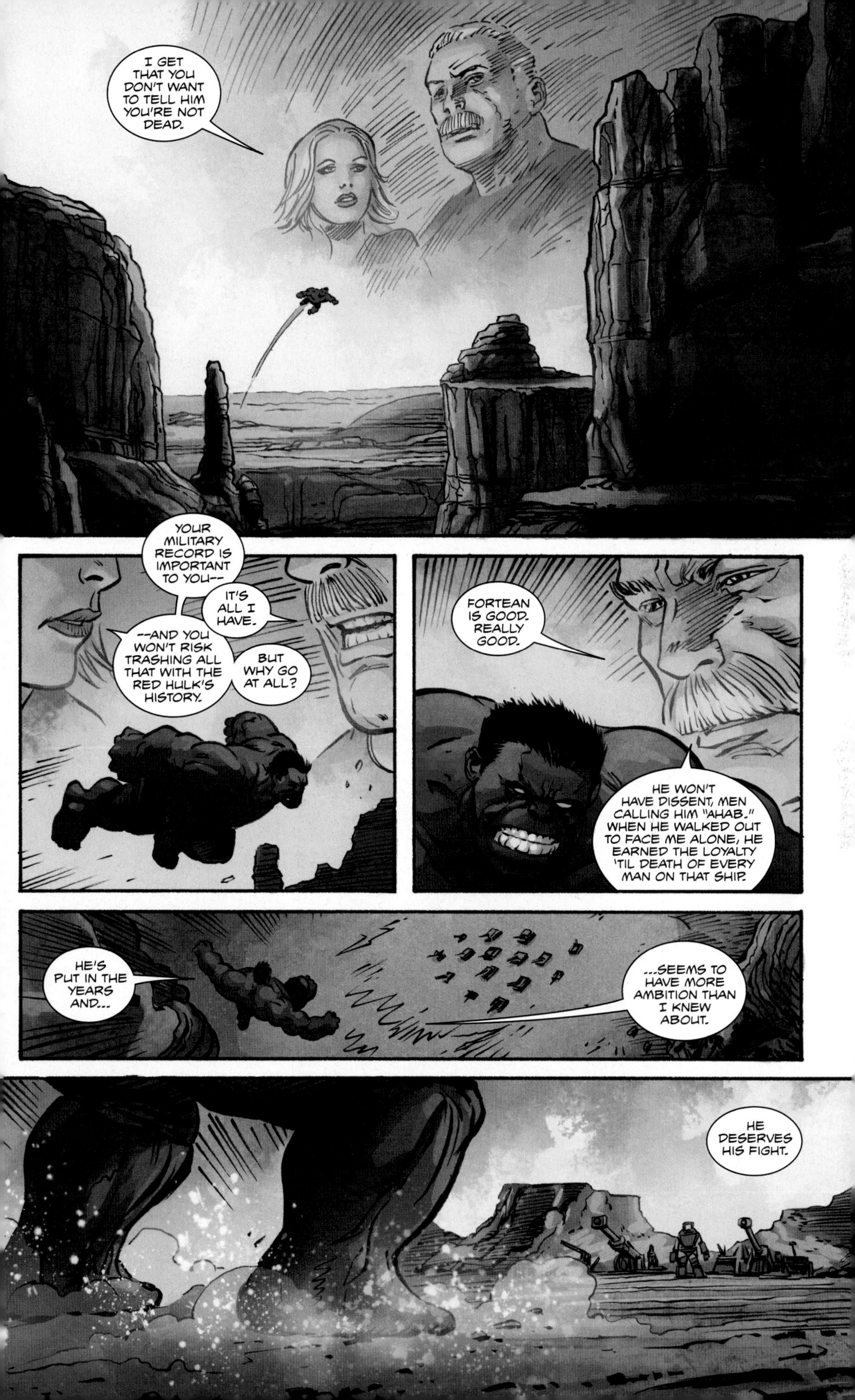
I GET THAT YOU DON'T WANT TO TELL HIM YOU'RE NOT DEAD.
YOUR MILITARY RECORD IS IMPORTANT TO YOU--
IT'S ALL I HAVE.
--AND YOU WON'T RISK TRASHING ALL THAT WITH THE RED HULK'S HISTORY.
BUT WHY GO AT ALL?
FORTEAN IS GOOD. REALLY GOOD.
HE WON'T HAVE DISSENT, MEN CALLING HIM "AHAB." WHEN HE WALKED OUT TO FACE ME ALONE, HE EARNED THE LOYALTY 'TIL DEATH OF EVERY MAN ON THAT SHIP.
HE'S PUT IN THE YEARS AND...
...SEEMS TO HAVE MORE AMBITION THAN I KNEW ABOUT.
HE DESERVES HIS FIGHT.

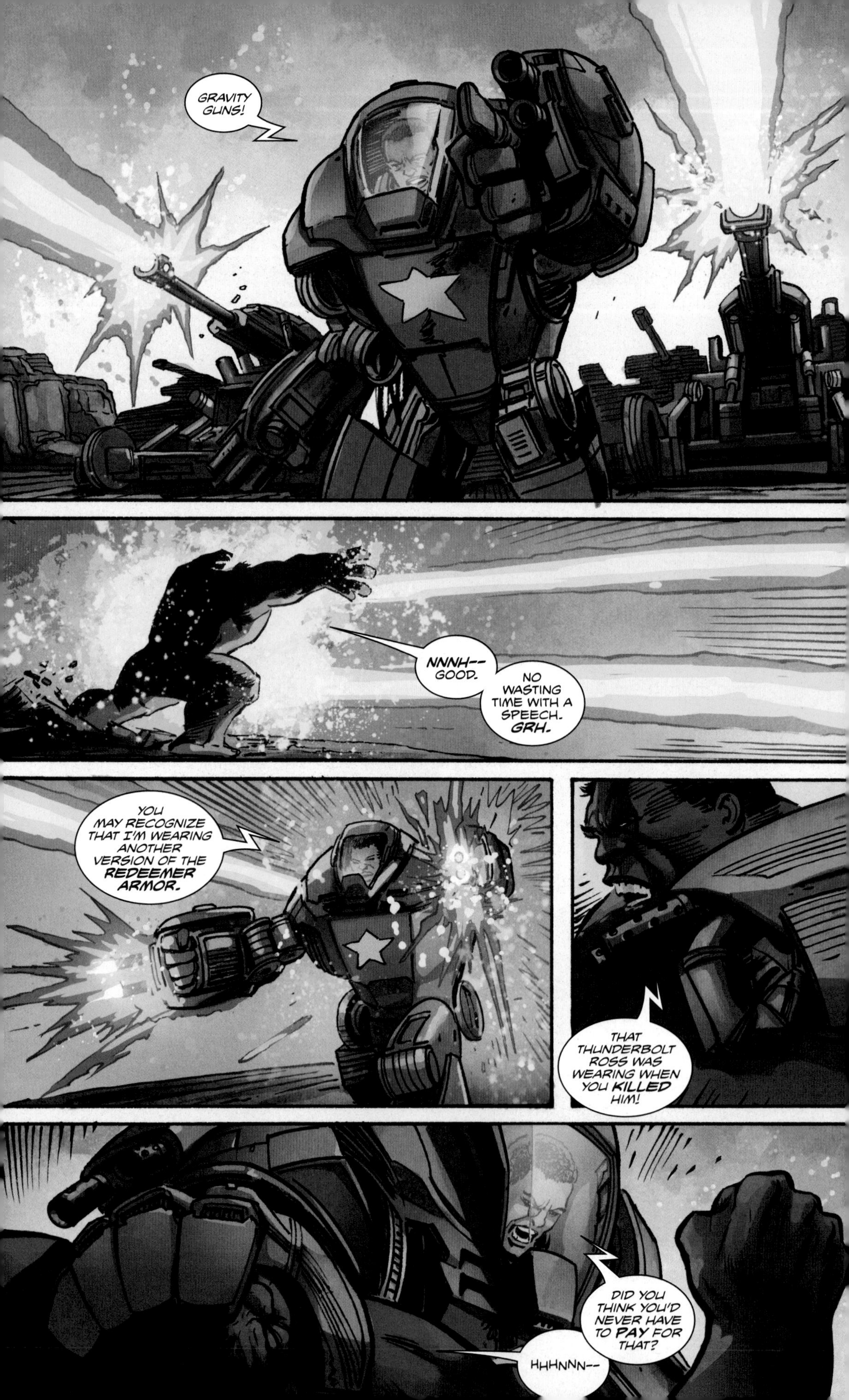
GRAVITY GUNS!
NNNH-- GOOD.
NO WASTING TIME WITH A SPEECH. GRH.
YOU MAY RECOGNIZE THAT I'M WEARING ANOTHER VERSION OF THE REDEEMER ARMOR.
THAT THUNDERBOLT ROSS WAS WEARING WHEN YOU KILLED HIM!
DID YOU THINK YOU'D NEVER HAVE TO PAY FOR THAT?
HHHNNN--

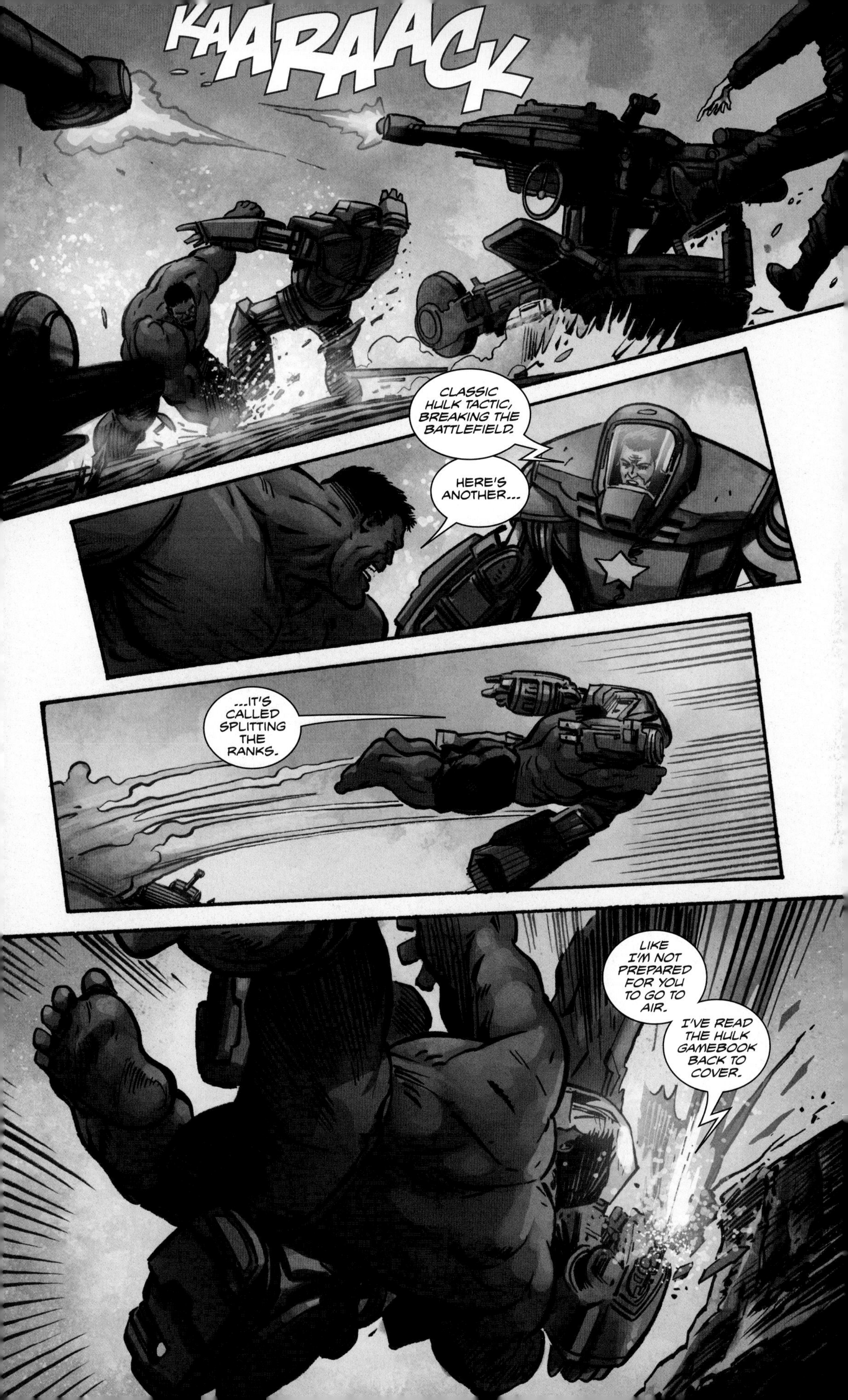
KAARAACK
CLASSIC HULK TACTIC, BREAKING THE BATTLEFIELD.
HERE'S ANOTHER...
...IT'S CALLED SPLITTING THE RANKS.
LIKE I'M NOT PREPARED FOR YOU TO GO TO AIR.
I'VE READ THE HULK GAMEBOOK BACK TO COVER.

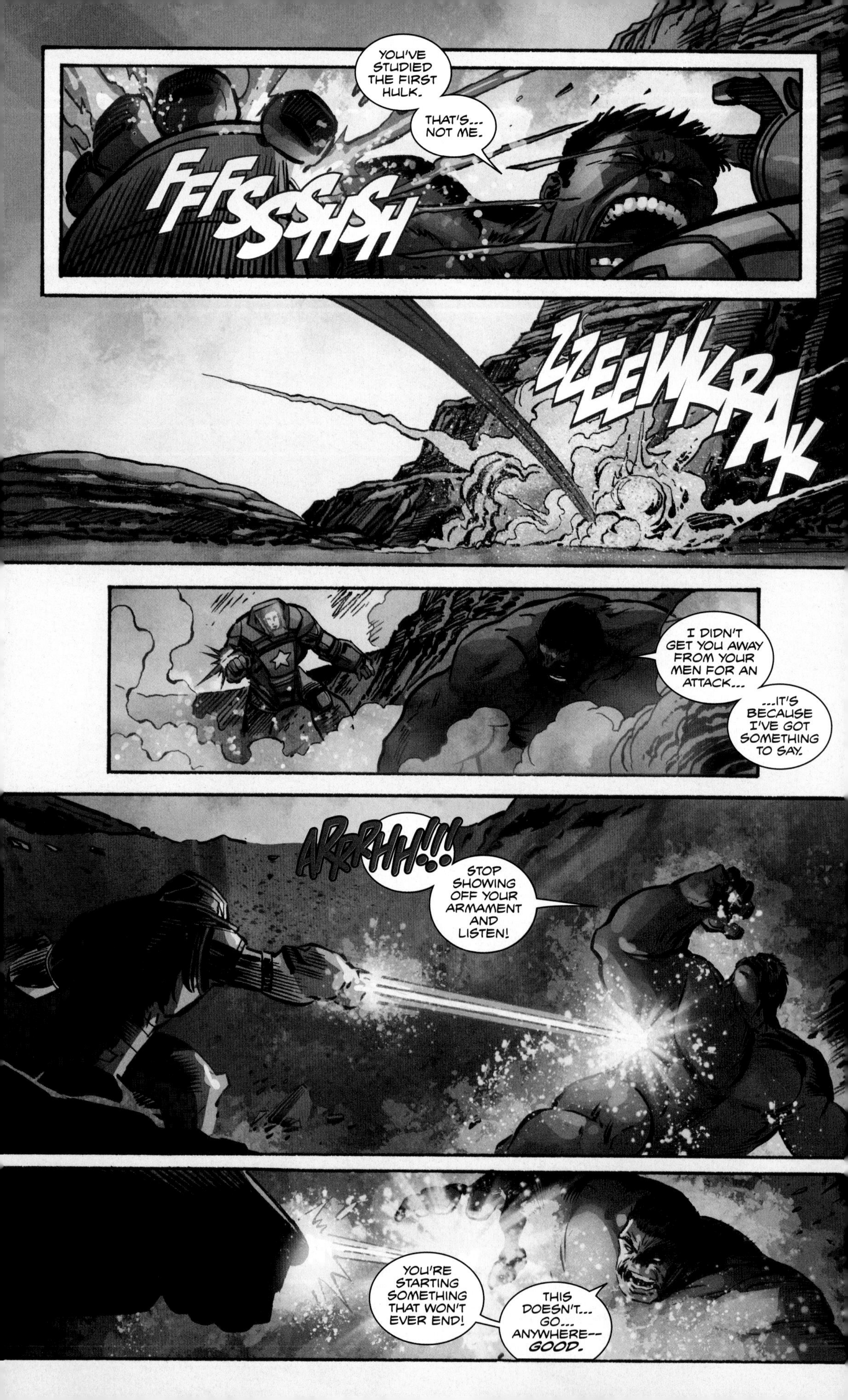

YOU'VE STUDIED THE FIRST HULK.
THAT'S... NOT ME.
FFFSSSHSH
ZZZEEWKRAK
I DIDN'T GET YOU AWAY FROM YOUR MEN FOR AN ATTACK...
...IT'S BECAUSE I'VE GOT SOMETHING TO SAY.
ARRRHH!!!
STOP SHOWING OFF YOUR ARMAMENT AND LISTEN!
YOU'RE STARTING SOMETHING THAT WON'T EVER END!
THIS DOESN'T... GO... ANYWHERE-- GOOD.

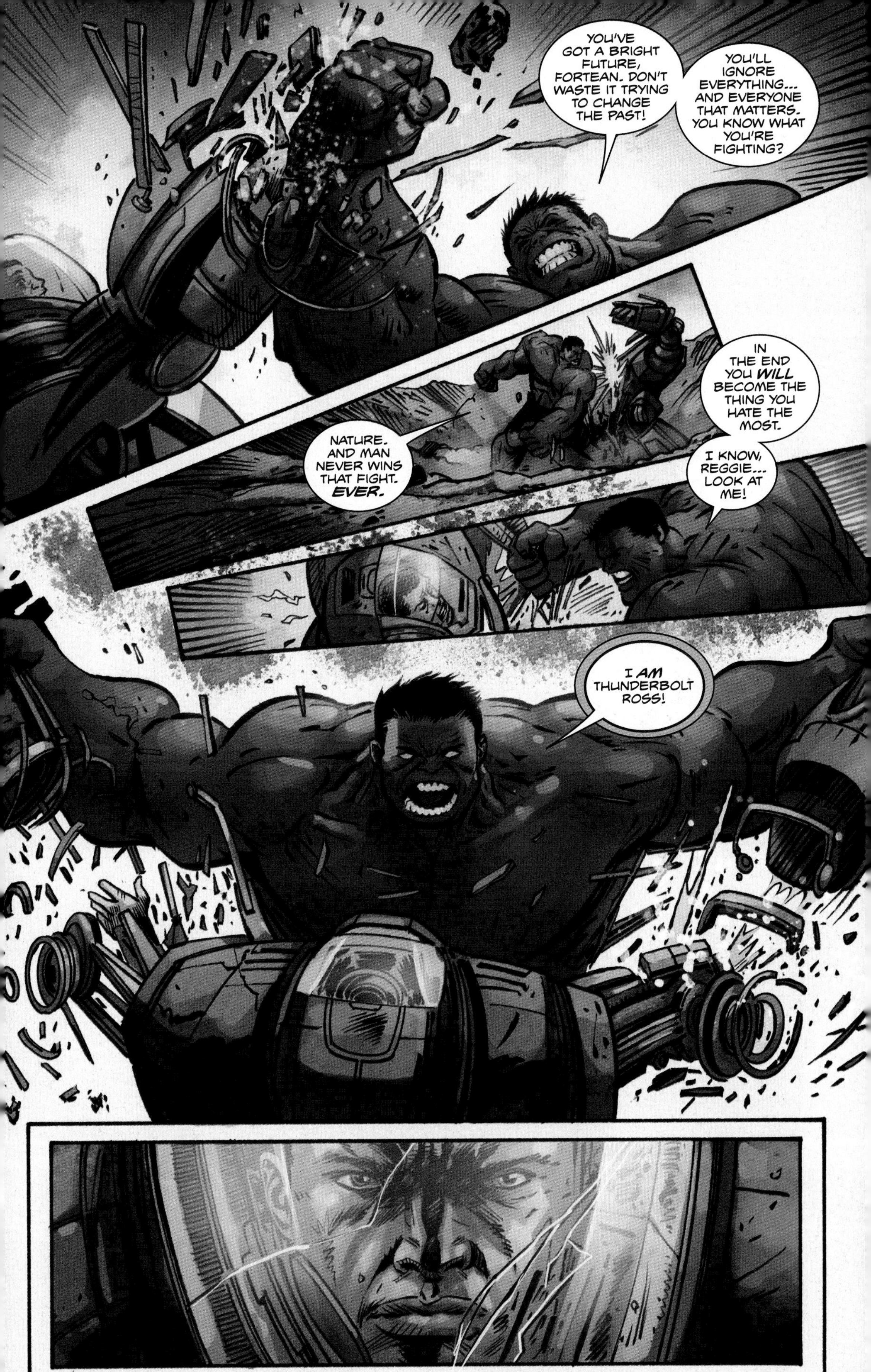

YOU'VE GOT A BRIGHT FUTURE, FORTEAN. DON'T WASTE IT TRYING TO CHANGE THE PAST!
YOU'LL IGNORE EVERYTHING... AND EVERYONE THAT MATTERS. YOU KNOW WHAT YOU'RE FIGHTING?
NATURE. AND MAN NEVER WINS THAT FIGHT. EVER.
IN THE END YOU WILL BECOME THE THING YOU HATE THE MOST.
I KNOW, REGGIE... LOOK AT ME!
I AM THUNDERBOLT ROSS!

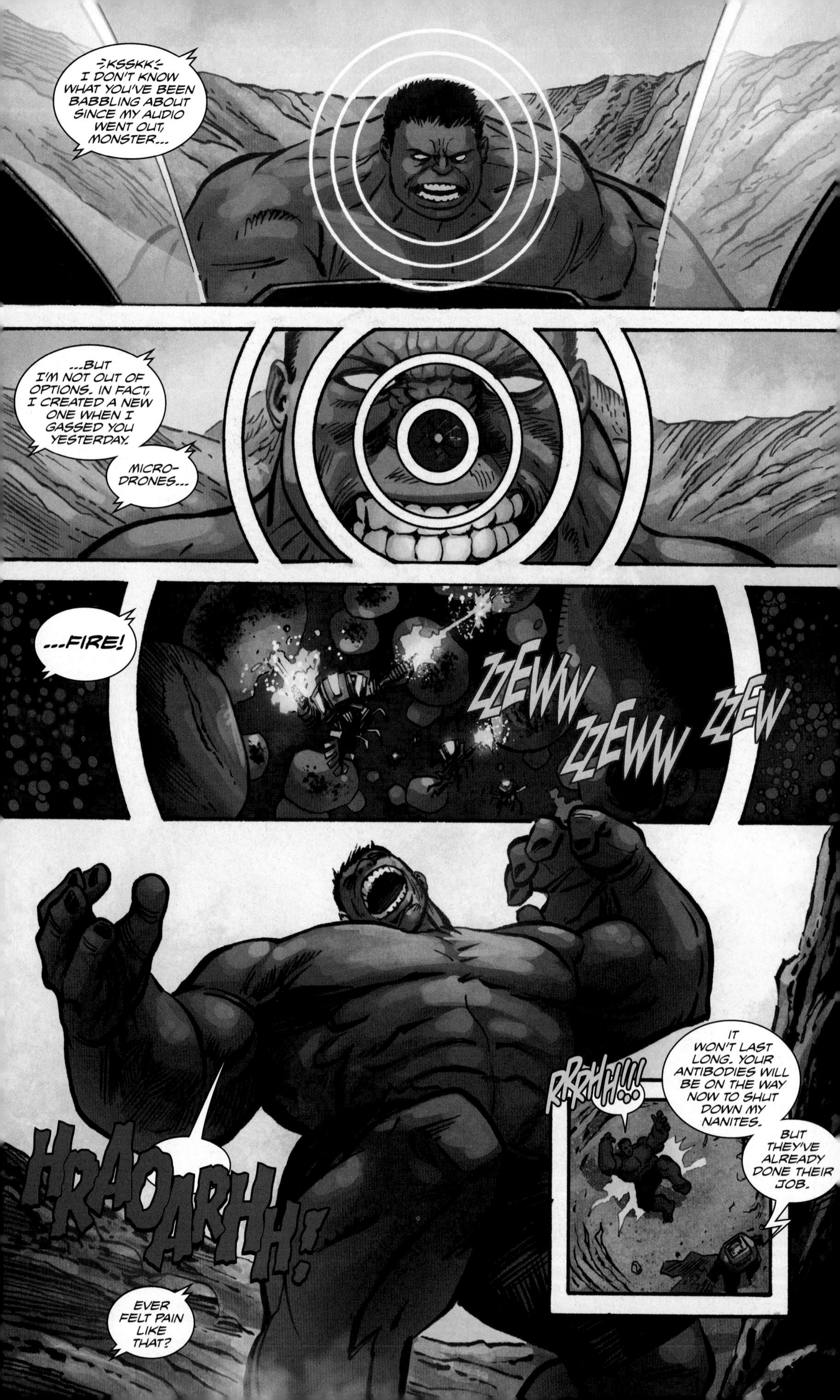

=KSSKK= I DON'T KNOW WHAT YOU'VE BEEN BABBLING ABOUT SINCE MY AUDIO WENT OUT, MONSTER...
...BUT I'M NOT OUT OF OPTIONS. IN FACT, I CREATED A NEW ONE WHEN I GASSED YOU YESTERDAY.
MICRO-DRONES...
...FIRE!
ZZEWW
ZZEWW
ZZEW
HRAOARHH!
EVER FELT PAIN LIKE THAT?
RRRHH!!!..
IT WON'T LAST LONG. YOUR ANTIBODIES WILL BE ON THE WAY NOW TO SHUT DOWN MY NANITES.
BUT THEY'VE ALREADY DONE THEIR JOB.

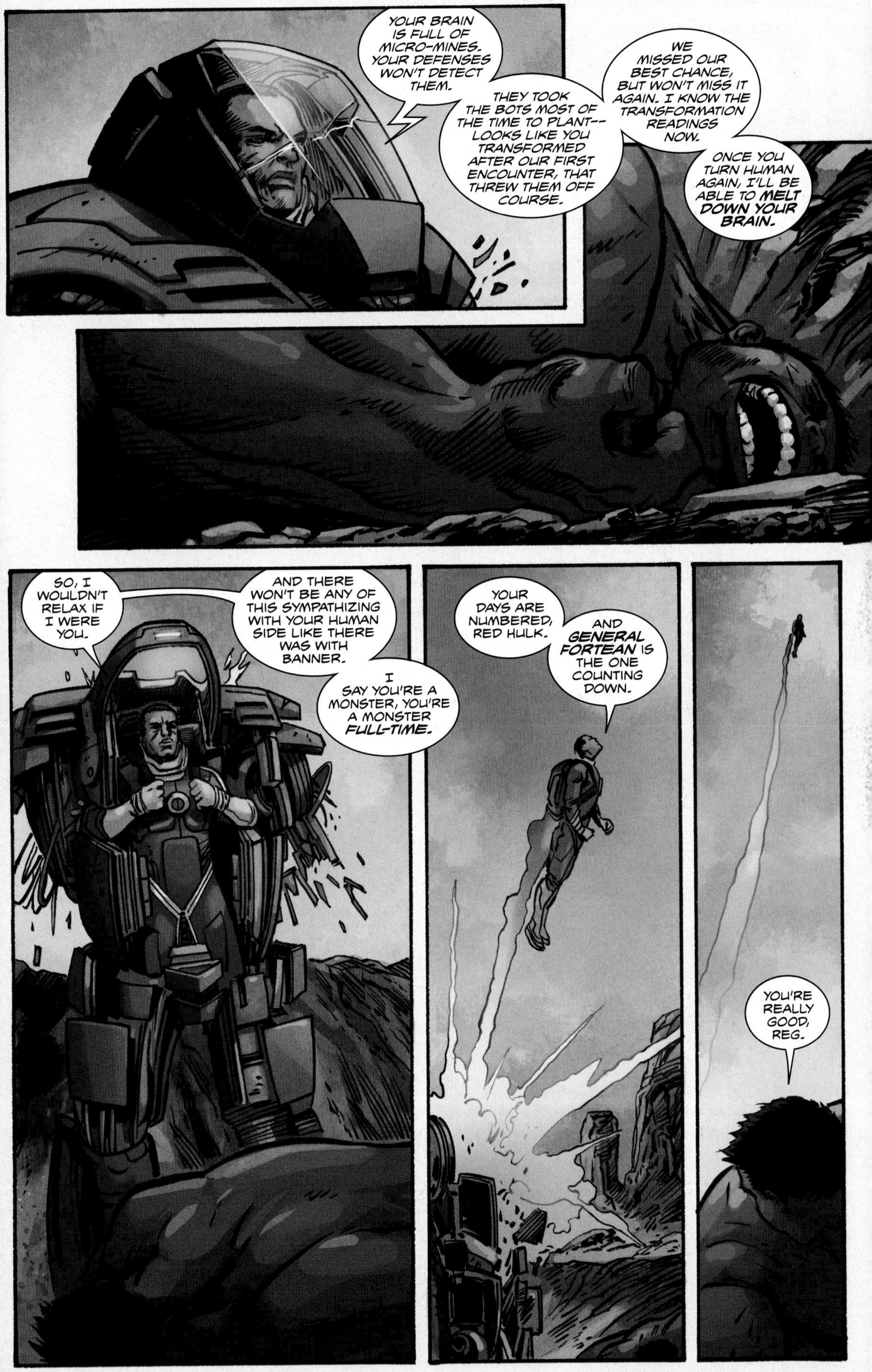
YOUR BRAIN IS FULL OF MICRO-MINES. YOUR DEFENSES WON'T DETECT THEM.
THEY TOOK THE BOTS MOST OF THE TIME TO PLANT-- LOOKS LIKE YOU TRANSFORMED AFTER OUR FIRST ENCOUNTER, THAT THREW THEM OFF COURSE.
WE MISSED OUR BEST CHANCE, BUT WON'T MISS IT AGAIN. I KNOW THE TRANSFORMATION READINGS NOW.
ONCE YOU TURN HUMAN AGAIN, I'LL BE ABLE TO MELT DOWN YOUR BRAIN.
SO, I WOULDN'T RELAX IF I WERE YOU.
AND THERE WON'T BE ANY OF THIS SYMPATHIZING WITH YOUR HUMAN SIDE LIKE THERE WAS WITH BANNER.
I SAY YOU'RE A MONSTER, YOU'RE A MONSTER FULL-TIME.
YOUR DAYS ARE NUMBERED, RED HULK.
AND GENERAL FORTEAN IS THE ONE COUNTING DOWN.
YOU'RE REALLY GOOD, REG.

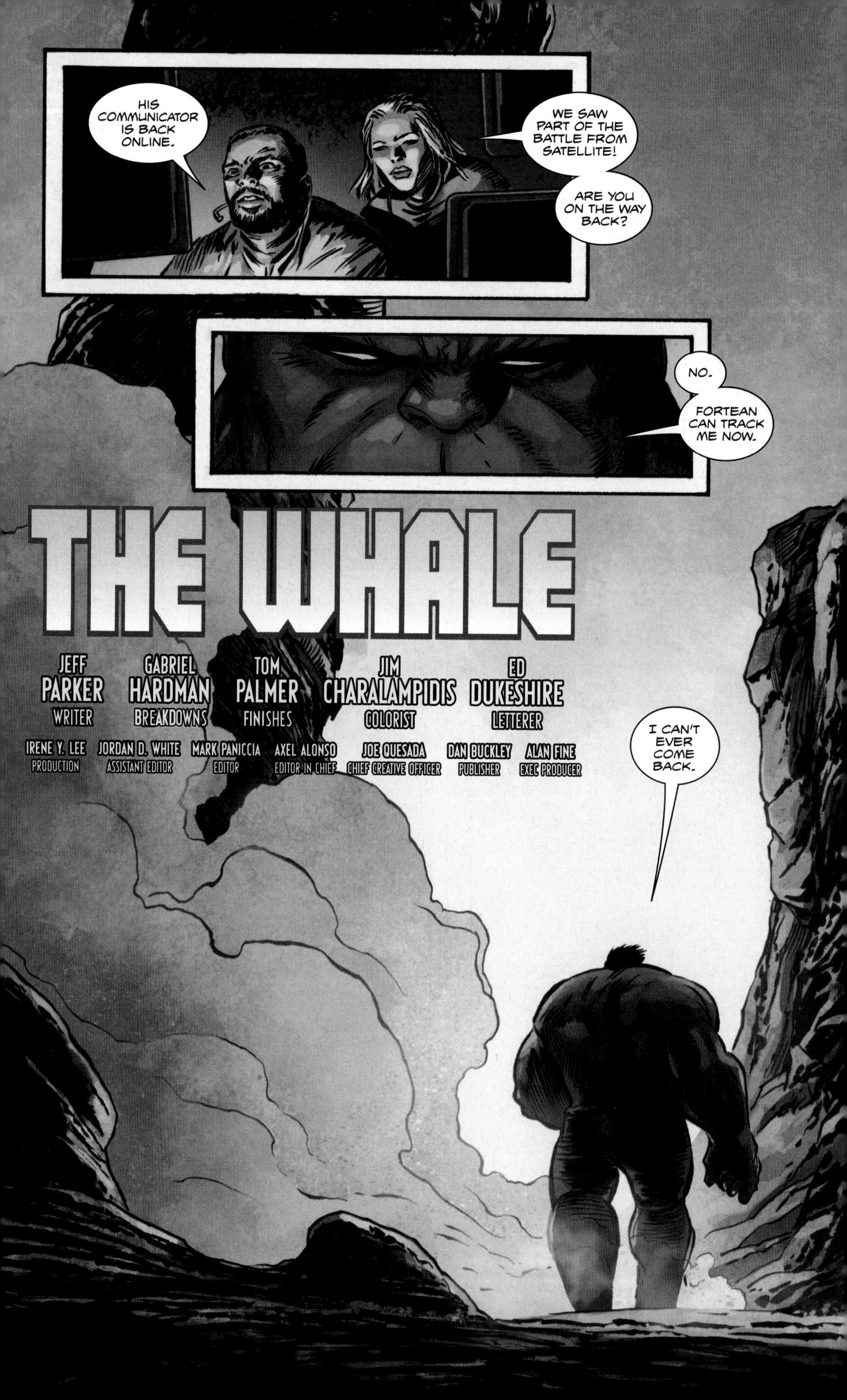
HIS COMMUNICATOR IS BACK ONLINE.
WE SAW PART OF THE BATTLE FROM SATELLITE!
ARE YOU ON THE WAY BACK?
NO.
FORTEAN CAN TRACK ME NOW.
THE WHALE
JEFF PARKER WRITER
GABRIEL HARDMAN BREAKDOWNS
TOM PALMER FINISHES
JIM CHARALAMPIDIS COLORIST
ED DUKESHIRE LETTERER
IRENE Y. LEE PRODUCTION
JORDAN D. WHITE ASSISTANT EDITOR
MARK PANICCIA EDITOR
AXEL ALONSO EDITOR IN CHIEF
JOE QUESADA CHIEF CREATIVE OFFICER
DAN BUCKLEY PUBLISHER
ALAN FINE EXEC PRODUCER
I CAN'T EVER COME BACK.

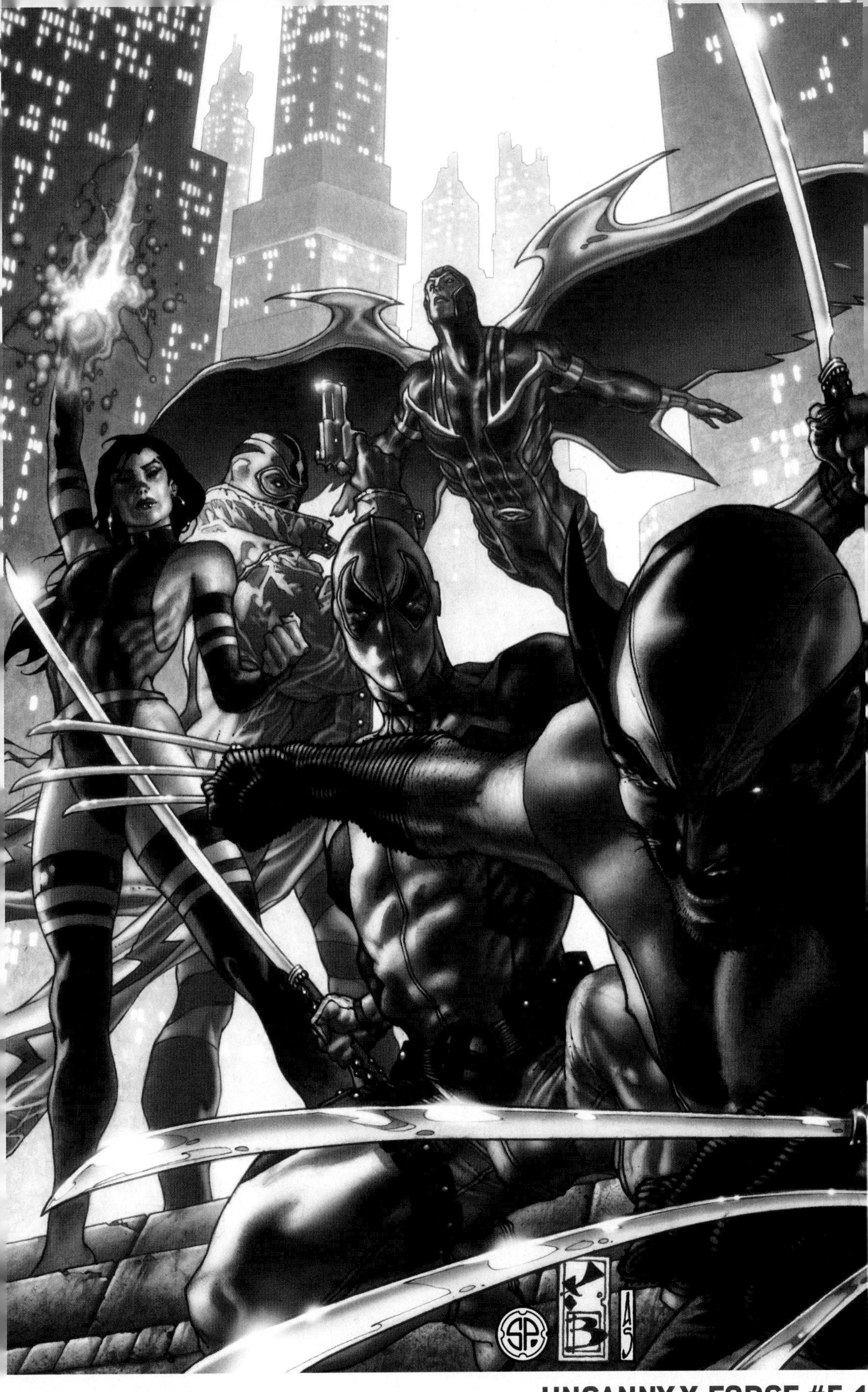

UNCANNY X-FORCE #5.1

Some evil won't stop. Some evil no prisons can hold, no force can contain, no plea can soften. Sometimes to truly save lives the only option is to take them. The burden of that truth falls on a secret, covert team of mutants assigned to those jobs too dirty, too dangerous for the X-Men. That team is the...

UNCANNY X-FORCE

ARCHANGEL

WOLVERINE

PSYLOCKE

FANTOMEX

DEADPOOL

After the X-Men's leader Cyclops disbanded the original X-Force team, Wolverine and Archangel secretly formed a new band of mutant assassins and tasked them with eliminating threats to the mutant species. Their first mission was to destroy the newly returned incarnation of one of the X-Men's most fearsome enemies: the man responsible for the countless deaths of mutants and humans alike as well as the excruciating transformation of Warren into Archangel—Apocalypse!

The team finally reached their target after fighting tooth and nail only to discover that Apocalypse's followers, the Clan Akkaba, had resurrected their leader in the form of an innocent boy, one the Clan had begun to indoctrinate. The X-Force members then became divided on their next course of action. Could the boy be saved? Or had destiny, genetics and brainwashing already taken hold? Was the boy's fate a foregone conclusion? Wolverine, Psylocke and Archangel all ultimately agreed that they couldn't kill the child. That they must at least try to save him. But the argument was abruptly rendered moot when Fantomex shot the child in the head...

FIVE POINT ONE

writer RICK REMENDER
art RAFAEL ALBUQUERQUE
color art DEAN WHITE
cover art SIMONE BIANCHI
with SIMONE PERUZZI
letters VC's CORY PETIT
design JARED K. FLETCHER
editor JODY LEHEUP
group editor NICK LOWE
editor in chief AXEL ALONSO
chief creative officer JOE QUESADA
publisher DAN BUCKLEY
executive producer ALAN FINE

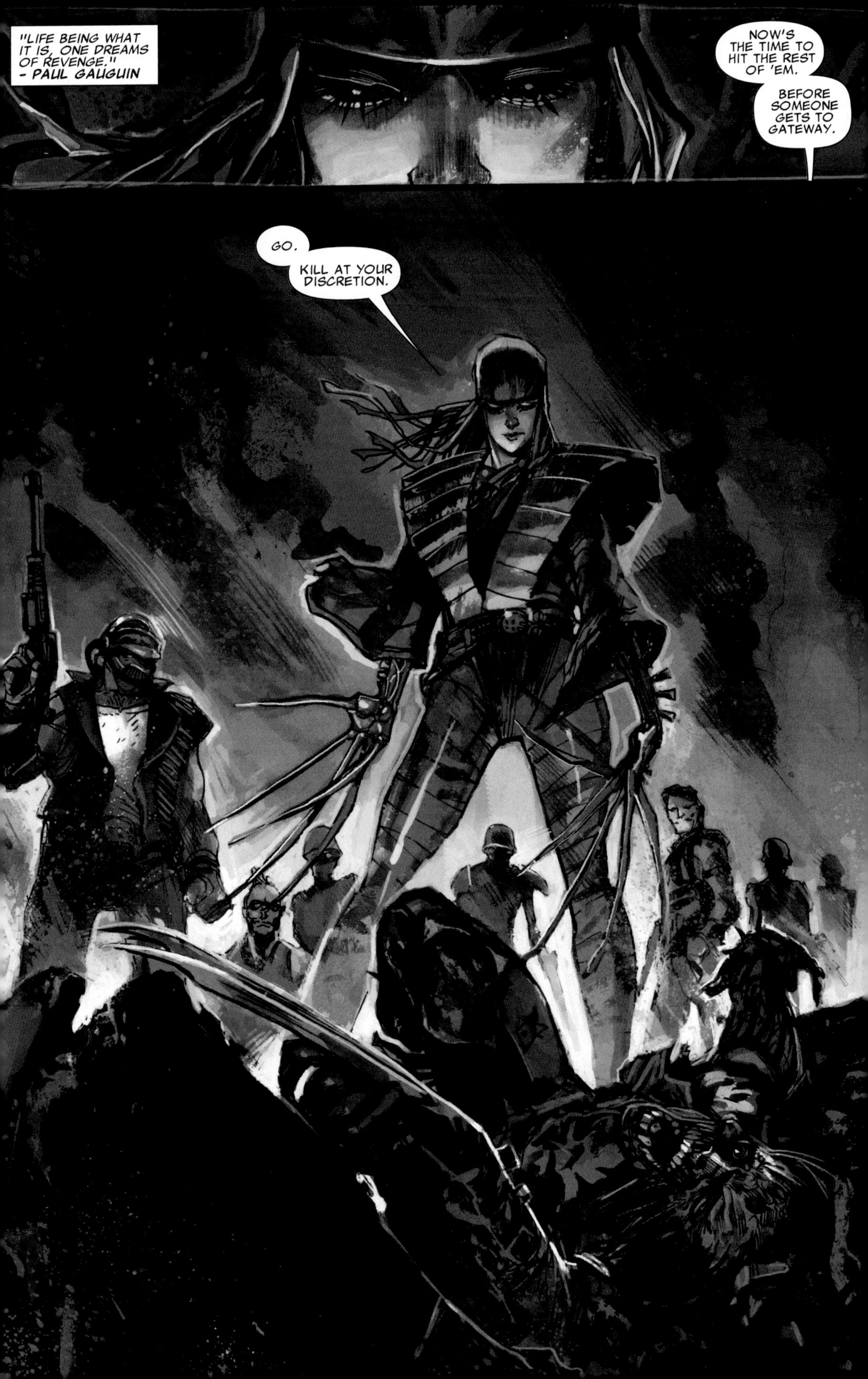
"LIFE BEING WHAT IT IS, ONE DREAMS OF REVENGE."
- PAUL GAUGUIN
NOW'S THE TIME TO HIT THE REST OF 'EM.
BEFORE SOMEONE GETS TO GATEWAY.
GO.
KILL AT YOUR DISCRETION.

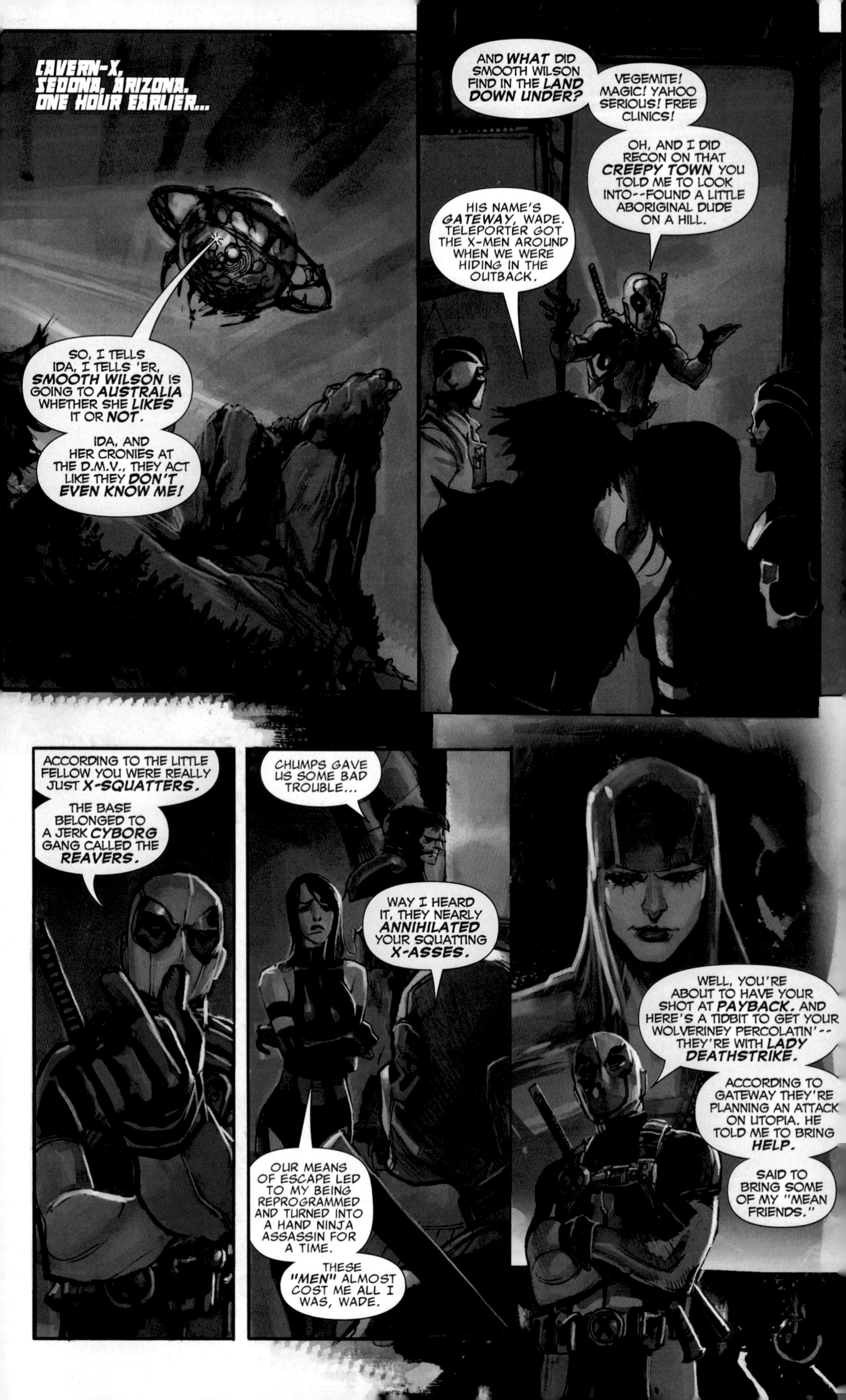
CAVERN-X, SEDONA, ARIZONA. ONE HOUR EARLIER...
SO, I TELLS IDA, I TELLS 'ER, SMOOTH WILSON IS GOING TO AUSTRALIA WHETHER SHE LIKES IT OR NOT.
IDA, AND HER CRONIES AT THE D.M.V., THEY ACT LIKE THEY DON'T EVEN KNOW ME!
AND WHAT DID SMOOTH WILSON FIND IN THE LAND DOWN UNDER?
VEGEMITE! MAGIC! YAHOO SERIOUS! FREE CLINICS!
OH, AND I DID RECON ON THAT CREEPY TOWN YOU TOLD ME TO LOOK INTO--FOUND A LITTLE ABORIGINAL DUDE ON A HILL.
HIS NAME'S GATEWAY, WADE. TELEPORTER GOT THE X-MEN AROUND WHEN WE WERE HIDING IN THE OUTBACK.
ACCORDING TO THE LITTLE FELLOW YOU WERE REALLY JUST X-SQUATTERS.
THE BASE BELONGED TO A JERK CYBORG GANG CALLED THE REAVERS.
CHUMPS GAVE US SOME BAD TROUBLE...
WAY I HEARD IT, THEY NEARLY ANNIHILATED YOUR SQUATTING X-ASSES.
OUR MEANS OF ESCAPE LED TO MY BEING REPROGRAMMED AND TURNED INTO A HAND NINJA ASSASSIN FOR A TIME.
THESE "MEN" ALMOST COST ME ALL I WAS, WADE.
WELL, YOU'RE ABOUT TO HAVE YOUR SHOT AT PAYBACK. AND HERE'S A TIDBIT TO GET YOUR WOLVERINEY PERCOLATIN'--THEY'RE WITH LADY DEATHSTRIKE.
ACCORDING TO GATEWAY THEY'RE PLANNING AN ATTACK ON UTOPIA. HE TOLD ME TO BRING HELP.
SAID TO BRING SOME OF MY "MEAN FRIENDS."

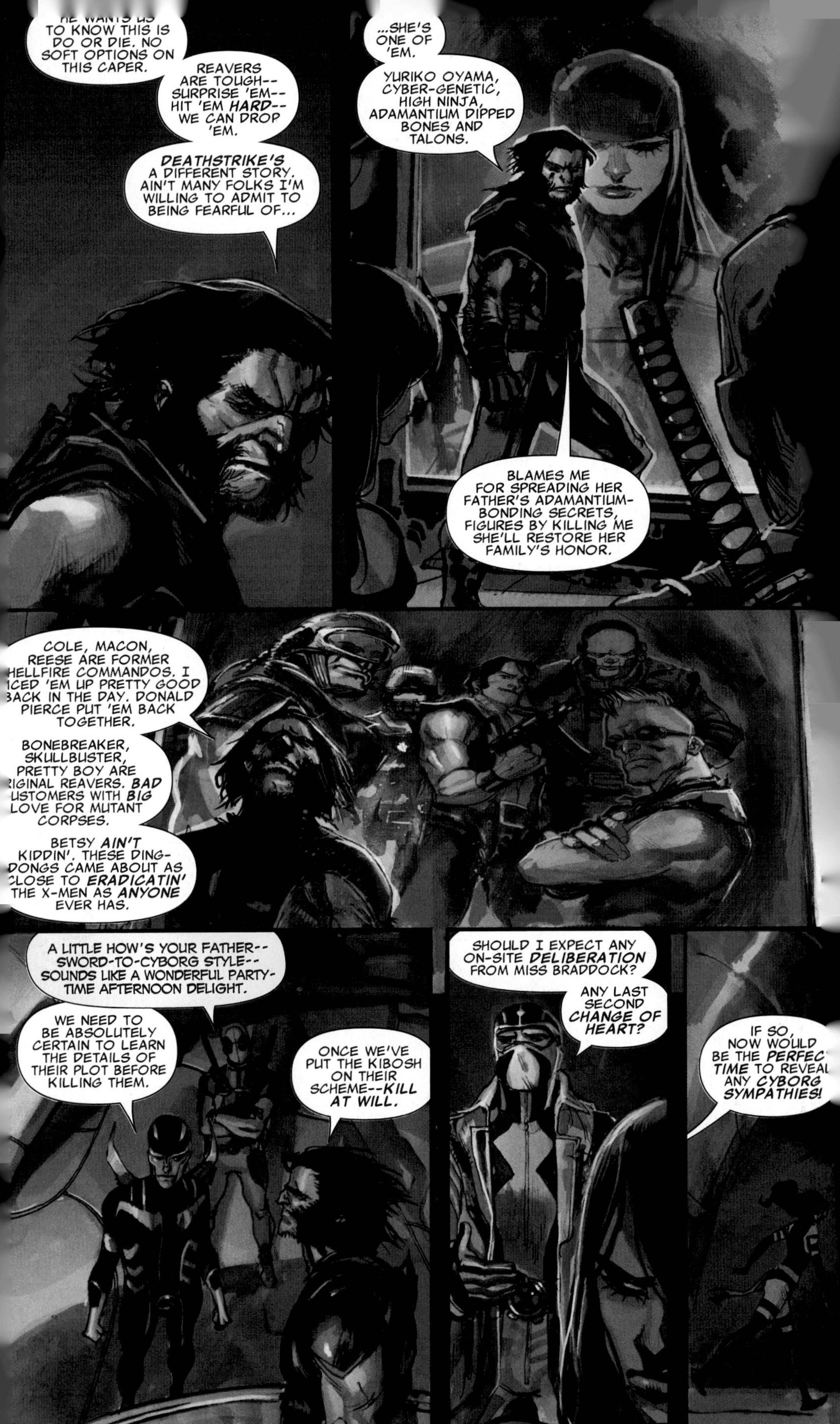

HE WANTS US TO KNOW THIS IS DO OR DIE. NO SOFT OPTIONS ON THIS CAPER.
REAVERS ARE TOUGH-- SURPRISE 'EM-- HIT 'EM HARD-- WE CAN DROP 'EM.
DEATHSTRIKE'S A DIFFERENT STORY. AIN'T MANY FOLKS I'M WILLING TO ADMIT TO BEING FEARFUL OF...
...SHE'S ONE OF 'EM.
YURIKO OYAMA, CYBER-GENETIC, HIGH NINJA, ADAMANTIUM DIPPED BONES AND TALONS.
BLAMES ME FOR SPREADING HER FATHER'S ADAMANTIUM-BONDING SECRETS, FIGURES BY KILLING ME SHE'LL RESTORE HER FAMILY'S HONOR.
COLE, MACON, REESE ARE FORMER HELLFIRE COMMANDOS. I ICED 'EM UP PRETTY GOOD BACK IN THE DAY. DONALD PIERCE PUT 'EM BACK TOGETHER.
BONEBREAKER, SKULLBUSTER, PRETTY BOY ARE ORIGINAL REAVERS. BAD CUSTOMERS WITH BIG LOVE FOR MUTANT CORPSES.
BETSY AIN'T KIDDIN'. THESE DING-DONGS CAME ABOUT AS CLOSE TO ERADICATIN' THE X-MEN AS ANYONE EVER HAS.
A LITTLE HOW'S YOUR FATHER-- SWORD-TO-CYBORG STYLE-- SOUNDS LIKE A WONDERFUL PARTY-TIME AFTERNOON DELIGHT.
WE NEED TO BE ABSOLUTELY CERTAIN TO LEARN THE DETAILS OF THEIR PLOT BEFORE KILLING THEM.
ONCE WE'VE PUT THE KIBOSH ON THEIR SCHEME--KILL AT WILL.
SHOULD I EXPECT ANY ON-SITE DELIBERATION FROM MISS BRADDOCK?
ANY LAST SECOND CHANGE OF HEART?
IF SO, NOW WOULD BE THE PERFECT TIME TO REVEAL ANY CYBORG SYMPATHIES!

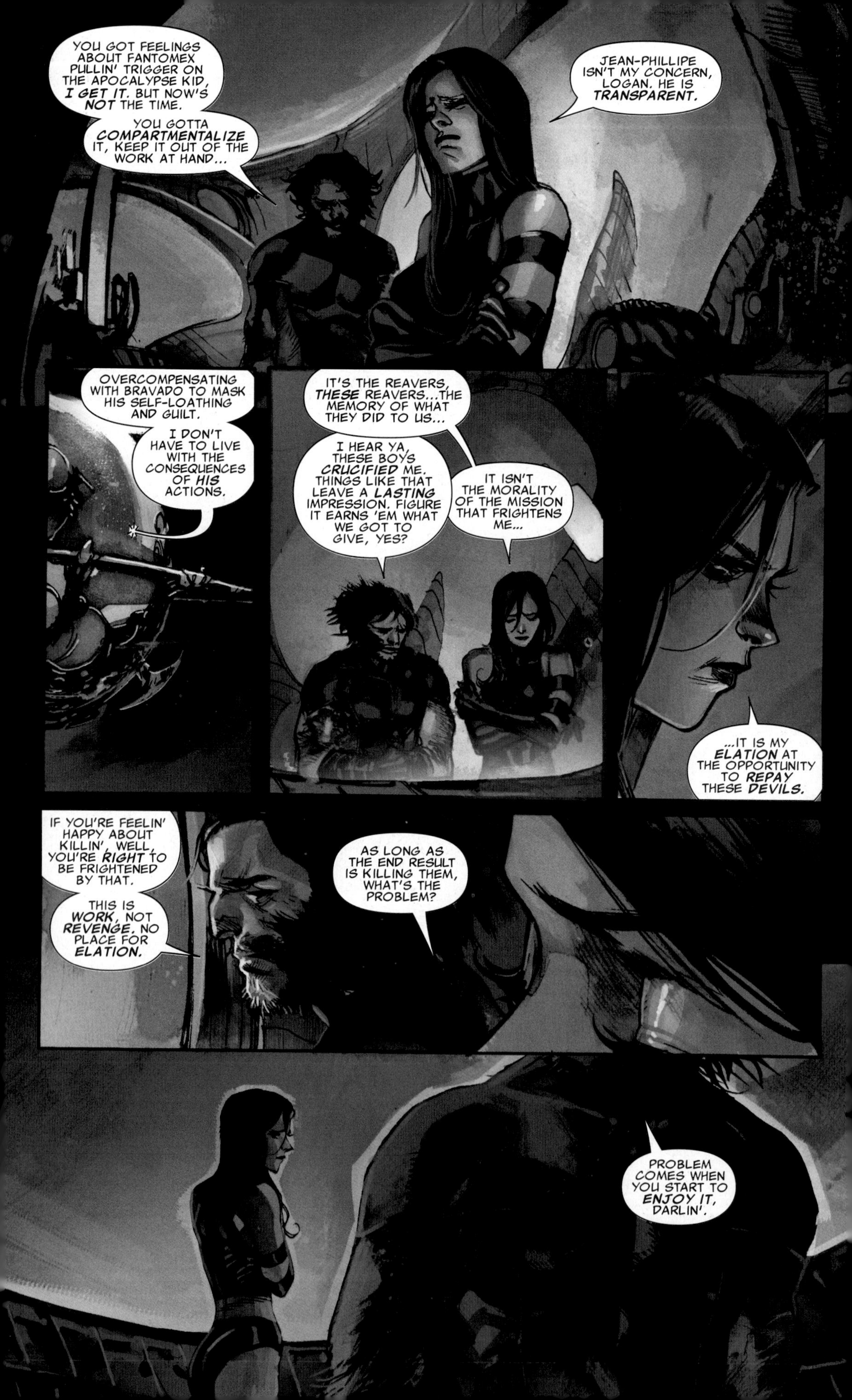
YOU GOT FEELINGS ABOUT FANTOMEX PULLIN' TRIGGER ON THE APOCALYPSE KID, I GET IT. BUT NOW'S NOT THE TIME.
YOU GOTTA COMPARTMENTALIZE IT, KEEP IT OUT OF THE WORK AT HAND...
JEAN-PHILLIPE ISN'T MY CONCERN, LOGAN. HE IS TRANSPARENT.
OVERCOMPENSATING WITH BRAVADO TO MASK HIS SELF-LOATHING AND GUILT.
I DON'T HAVE TO LIVE WITH THE CONSEQUENCES OF HIS ACTIONS.
IT'S THE REAVERS, THESE REAVERS...THE MEMORY OF WHAT THEY DID TO US...
I HEAR YA, THESE BOYS CRUCIFIED ME. THINGS LIKE THAT LEAVE A LASTING IMPRESSION. FIGURE IT EARNS 'EM WHAT WE GOT TO GIVE, YES?
IT ISN'T THE MORALITY OF THE MISSION THAT FRIGHTENS ME...
...IT IS MY ELATION AT THE OPPORTUNITY TO REPAY THESE DEVILS.
IF YOU'RE FEELIN' HAPPY ABOUT KILLIN', WELL, YOU'RE RIGHT TO BE FRIGHTENED BY THAT.
THIS IS WORK, NOT REVENGE. NO PLACE FOR ELATION.
AS LONG AS THE END RESULT IS KILLING THEM, WHAT'S THE PROBLEM?
PROBLEM COMES WHEN YOU START TO ENJOY IT, DARLIN'.

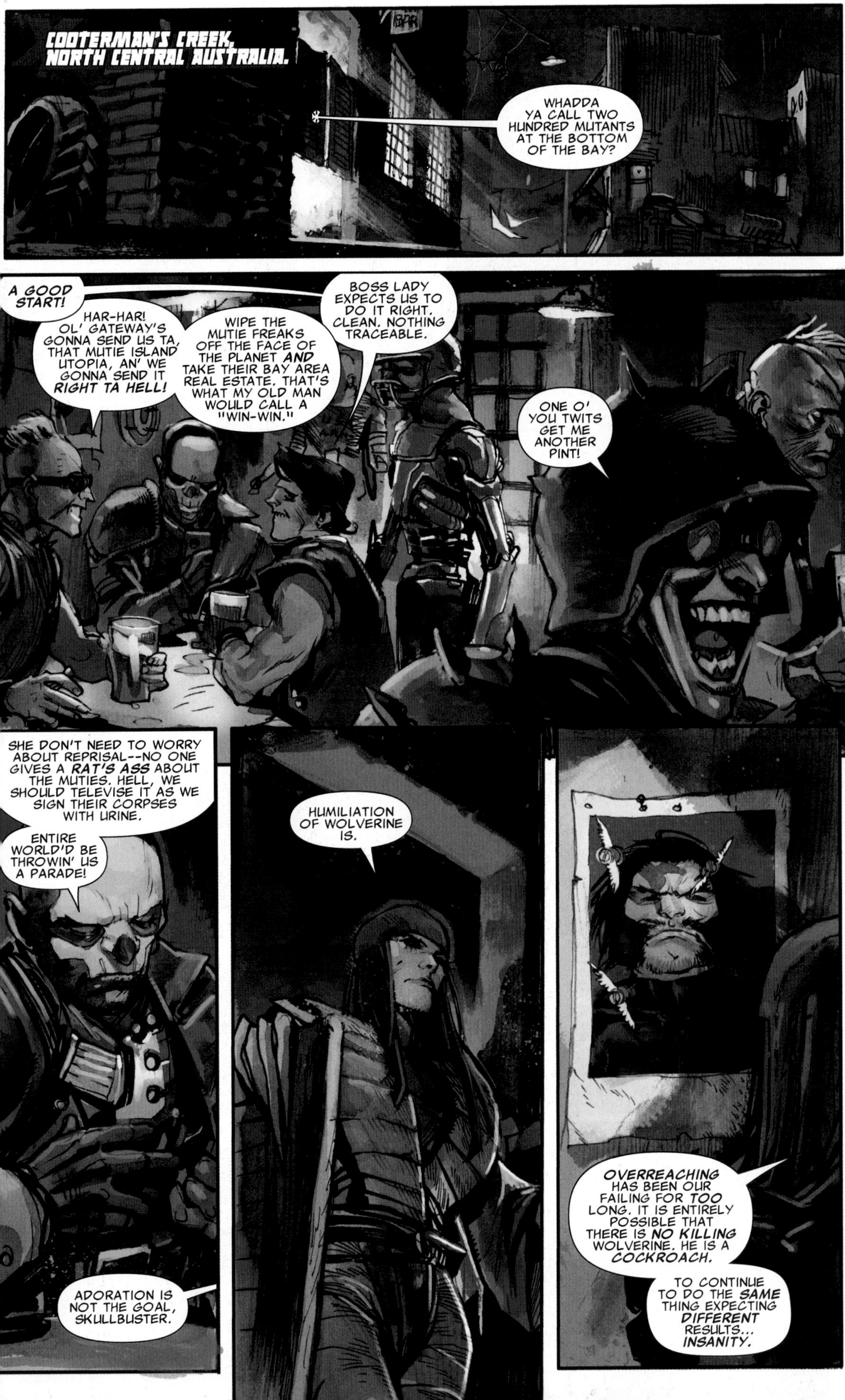
COOTERMAN'S CREEK, NORTH CENTRAL AUSTRALIA.
WHADDA YA CALL TWO HUNDRED MUTANTS AT THE BOTTOM OF THE BAY?
A GOOD START!
HAR-HAR! OL' GATEWAY'S GONNA SEND US TA, THAT MUTIE ISLAND UTOPIA, AN' WE GONNA SEND IT RIGHT TA HELL!
WIPE THE MUTIE FREAKS OFF THE FACE OF THE PLANET AND TAKE THEIR BAY AREA REAL ESTATE. THAT'S WHAT MY OLD MAN WOULD CALL A "WIN-WIN."
BOSS LADY EXPECTS US TO DO IT RIGHT. CLEAN. NOTHING TRACEABLE.
ONE O' YOU TWITS GET ME ANOTHER PINT!
SHE DON'T NEED TO WORRY ABOUT REPRISAL--NO ONE GIVES A RAT'S ASS ABOUT THE MUTIES. HELL, WE SHOULD TELEVISE IT AS WE SIGN THEIR CORPSES WITH URINE.
ENTIRE WORLD'D BE THROWIN' US A PARADE!
ADORATION IS NOT THE GOAL, SKULLBUSTER.
HUMILIATION OF WOLVERINE IS.
OVERREACHING HAS BEEN OUR FAILING FOR TOO LONG. IT IS ENTIRELY POSSIBLE THAT THERE IS NO KILLING WOLVERINE. HE IS A COCKROACH.
TO CONTINUE TO DO THE SAME THING EXPECTING DIFFERENT RESULTS... INSANITY.

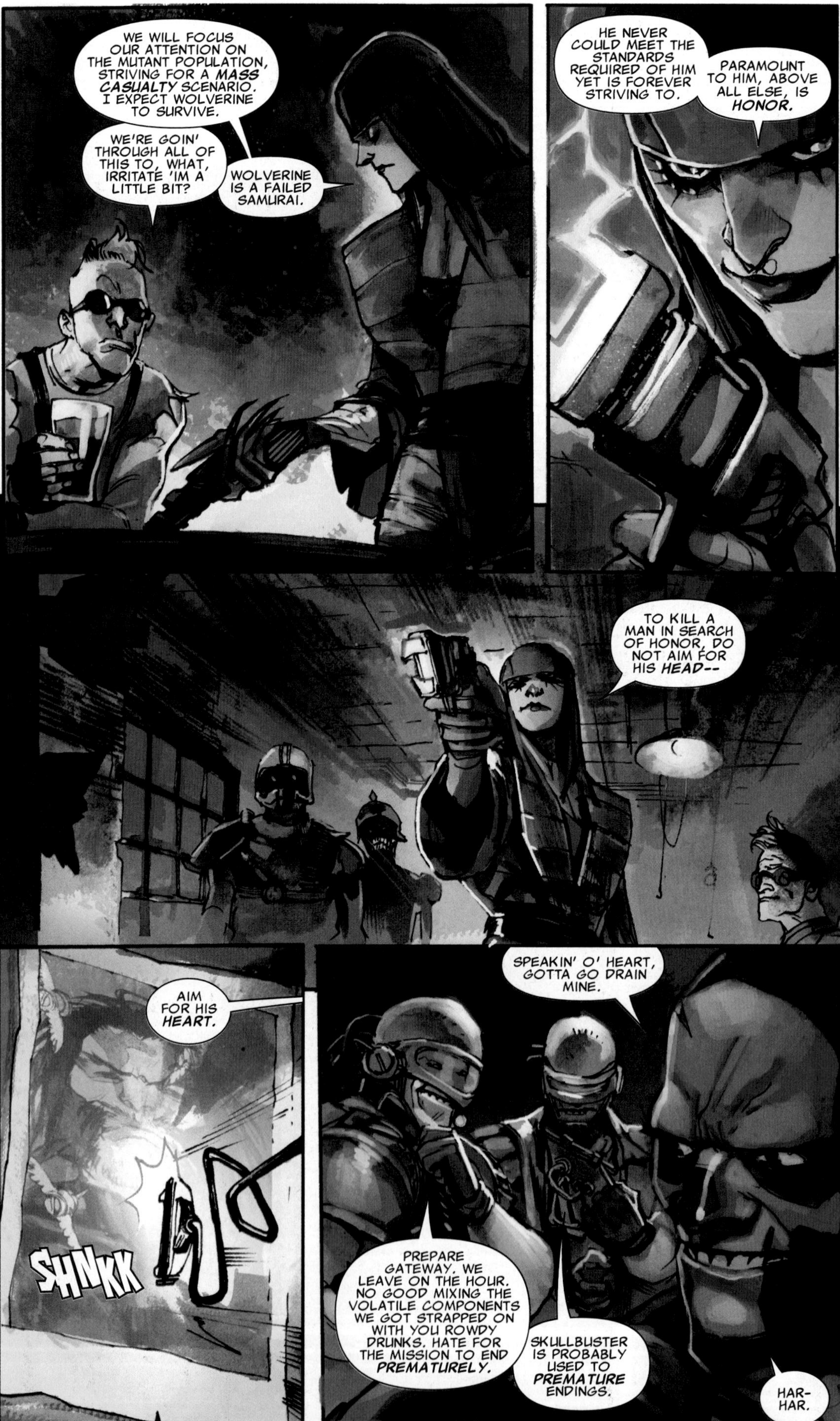

WE WILL FOCUS OUR ATTENTION ON THE MUTANT POPULATION, STRIVING FOR A MASS CASUALTY SCENARIO. I EXPECT WOLVERINE TO SURVIVE.
WE'RE GOIN' THROUGH ALL OF THIS TO, WHAT, IRRITATE 'IM A LITTLE BIT?
WOLVERINE IS A FAILED SAMURAI.
HE NEVER COULD MEET THE STANDARDS REQUIRED OF HIM YET IS FOREVER STRIVING TO.
PARAMOUNT TO HIM, ABOVE ALL ELSE, IS HONOR.
TO KILL A MAN IN SEARCH OF HONOR, DO NOT AIM FOR HIS HEAD--
AIM FOR HIS HEART.
SHNKK
SPEAKIN' O' HEART, GOTTA GO DRAIN MINE.
PREPARE GATEWAY. WE LEAVE ON THE HOUR. NO GOOD MIXING THE VOLATILE COMPONENTS WE GOT STRAPPED ON WITH YOU ROWDY DRUNKS. HATE FOR THE MISSION TO END PREMATURELY.
SKULLBUSTER IS PROBABLY USED TO PREMATURE ENDINGS.
HAR-HAR.

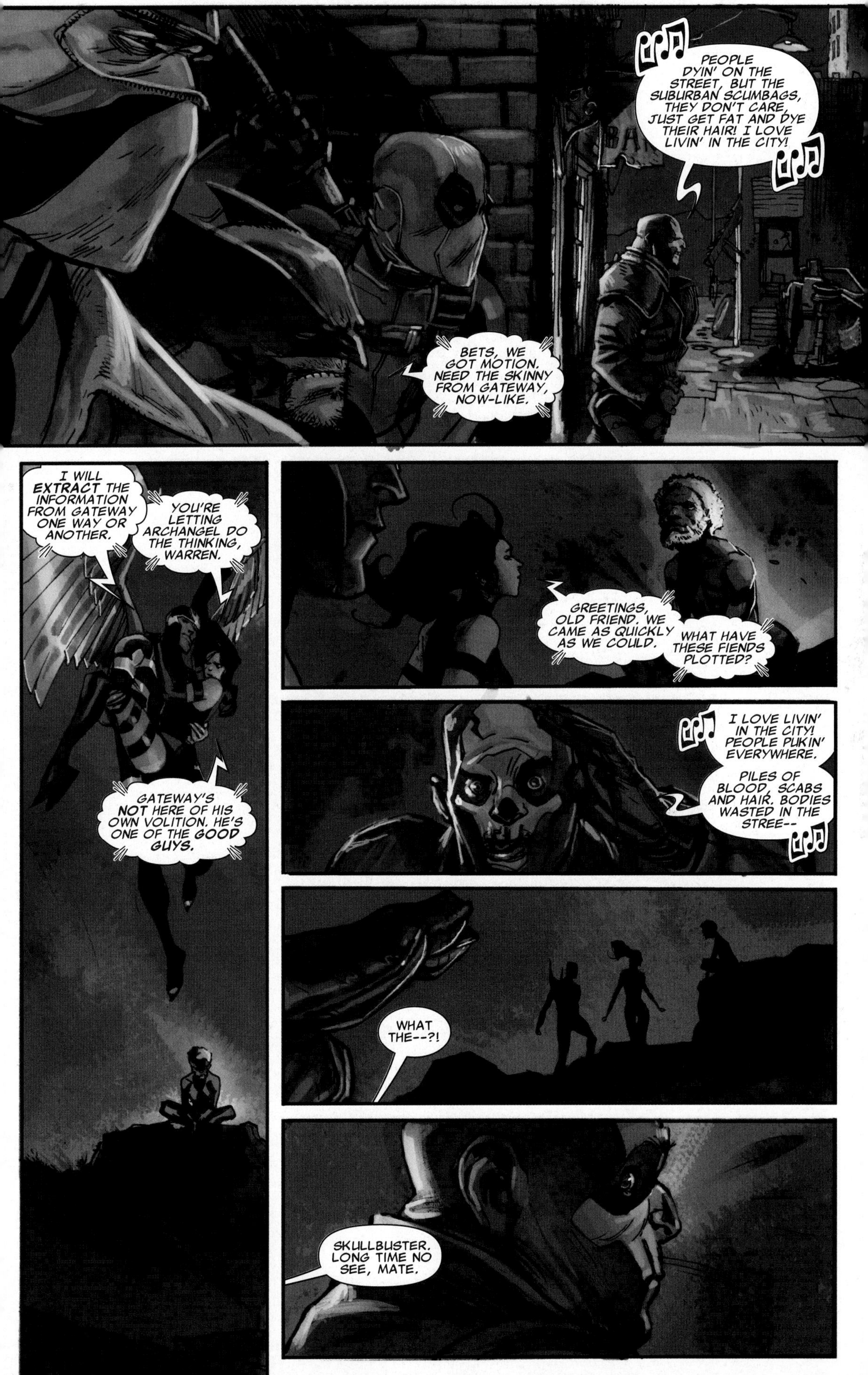
PEOPLE DYIN' ON THE STREET, BUT THE SUBURBAN SCUMBAGS, THEY DON'T CARE, JUST GET FAT AND DYE THEIR HAIR! I LOVE LIVIN' IN THE CITY!
BETS, WE GOT MOTION. NEED THE SKINNY FROM GATEWAY, NOW-LIKE.
I WILL EXTRACT THE INFORMATION FROM GATEWAY ONE WAY OR ANOTHER.
YOU'RE LETTING ARCHANGEL DO THE THINKING, WARREN.
GATEWAY'S NOT HERE OF HIS OWN VOLITION. HE'S ONE OF THE GOOD GUYS.
GREETINGS, OLD FRIEND. WE CAME AS QUICKLY AS WE COULD.
WHAT HAVE THESE FIENDS PLOTTED?
I LOVE LIVIN' IN THE CITY! PEOPLE PUKIN' EVERYWHERE.
PILES OF BLOOD, SCABS AND HAIR. BODIES WASTED IN THE STREE--
WHAT THE--?!
SKULLBUSTER. LONG TIME NO SEE, MATE.

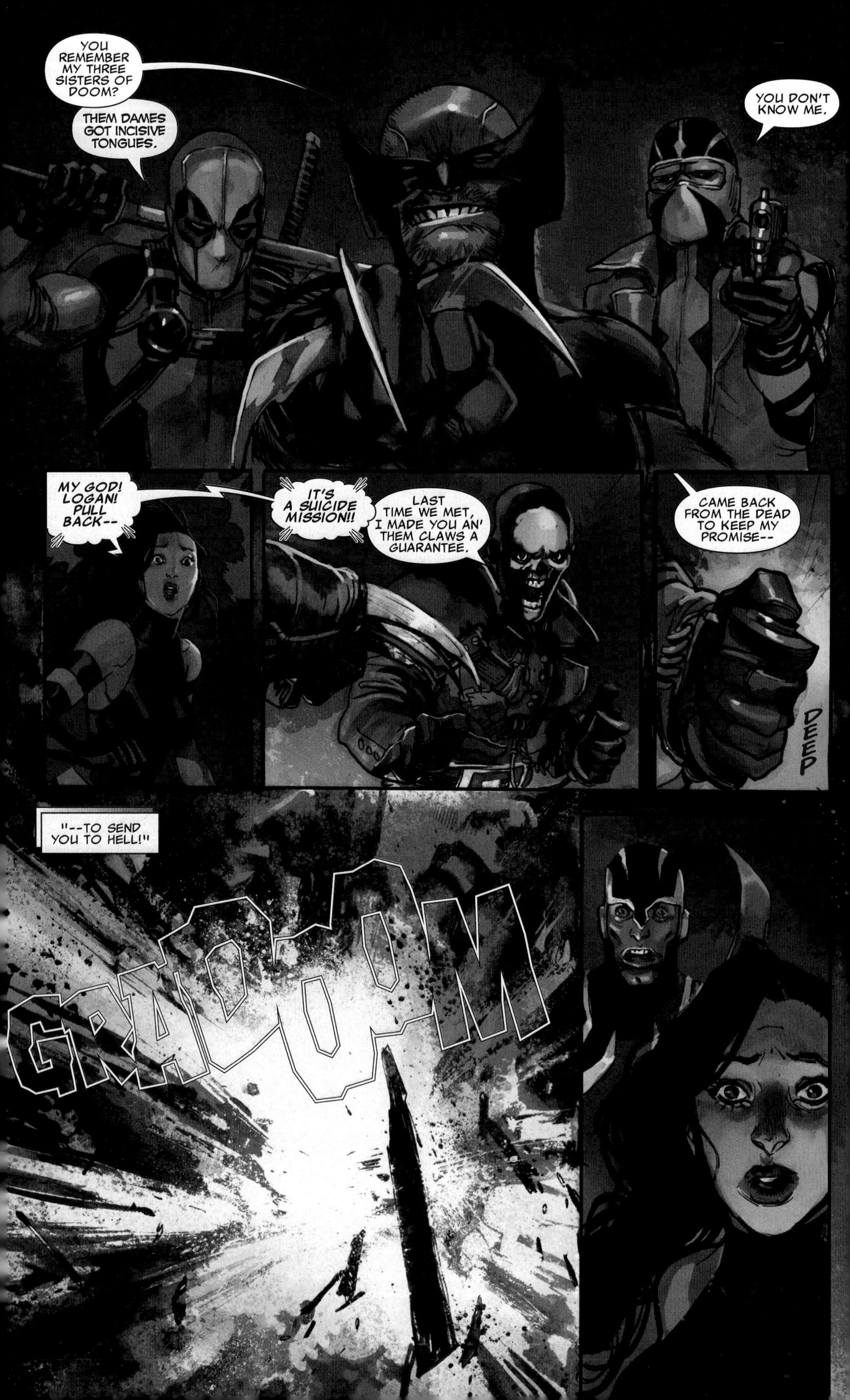
YOU REMEMBER MY THREE SISTERS OF DOOM?
THEM DAMES GOT INCISIVE TONGUES.
YOU DON'T KNOW ME.
MY GOD! LOGAN! PULL BACK--
IT'S A SUICIDE MISSION!!
LAST TIME WE MET, I MADE YOU AN' THEM CLAWS A GUARANTEE.
CAME BACK FROM THE DEAD TO KEEP MY PROMISE--
DEEP
"--TO SEND YOU TO HELL!"
GRADOOOM

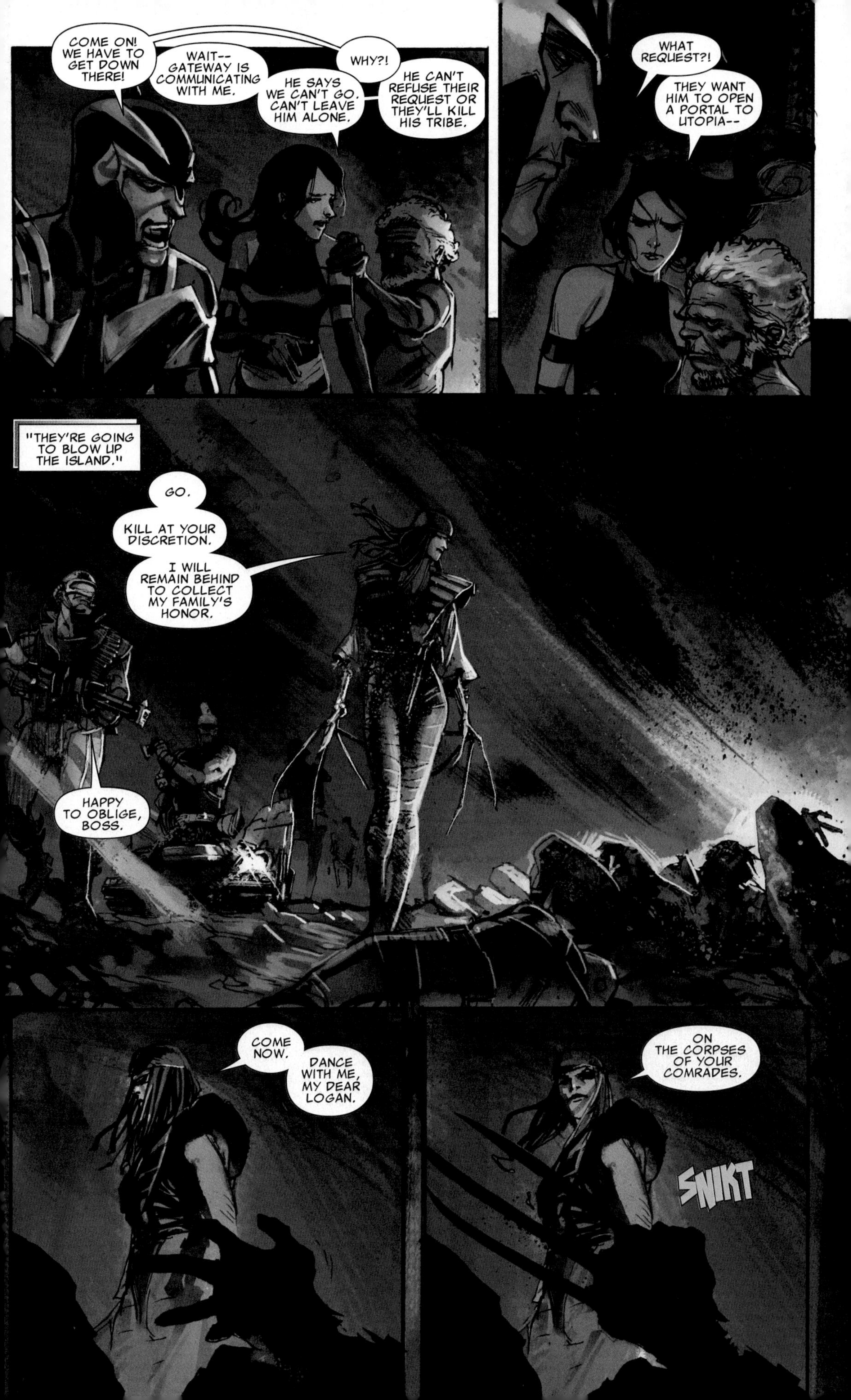
COME ON! WE HAVE TO GET DOWN THERE!
WAIT-- GATEWAY IS COMMUNICATING WITH ME.
WHY?!
HE SAYS WE CAN'T GO. CAN'T LEAVE HIM ALONE.
HE CAN'T REFUSE THEIR REQUEST OR THEY'LL KILL HIS TRIBE.
WHAT REQUEST?!
THEY WANT HIM TO OPEN A PORTAL TO UTOPIA--
"THEY'RE GOING TO BLOW UP THE ISLAND."
GO.
KILL AT YOUR DISCRETION.
I WILL REMAIN BEHIND TO COLLECT MY FAMILY'S HONOR.
HAPPY TO OBLIGE, BOSS.
COME NOW.
DANCE WITH ME, MY DEAR LOGAN.
ON THE CORPSES OF YOUR COMRADES.
SNIKT

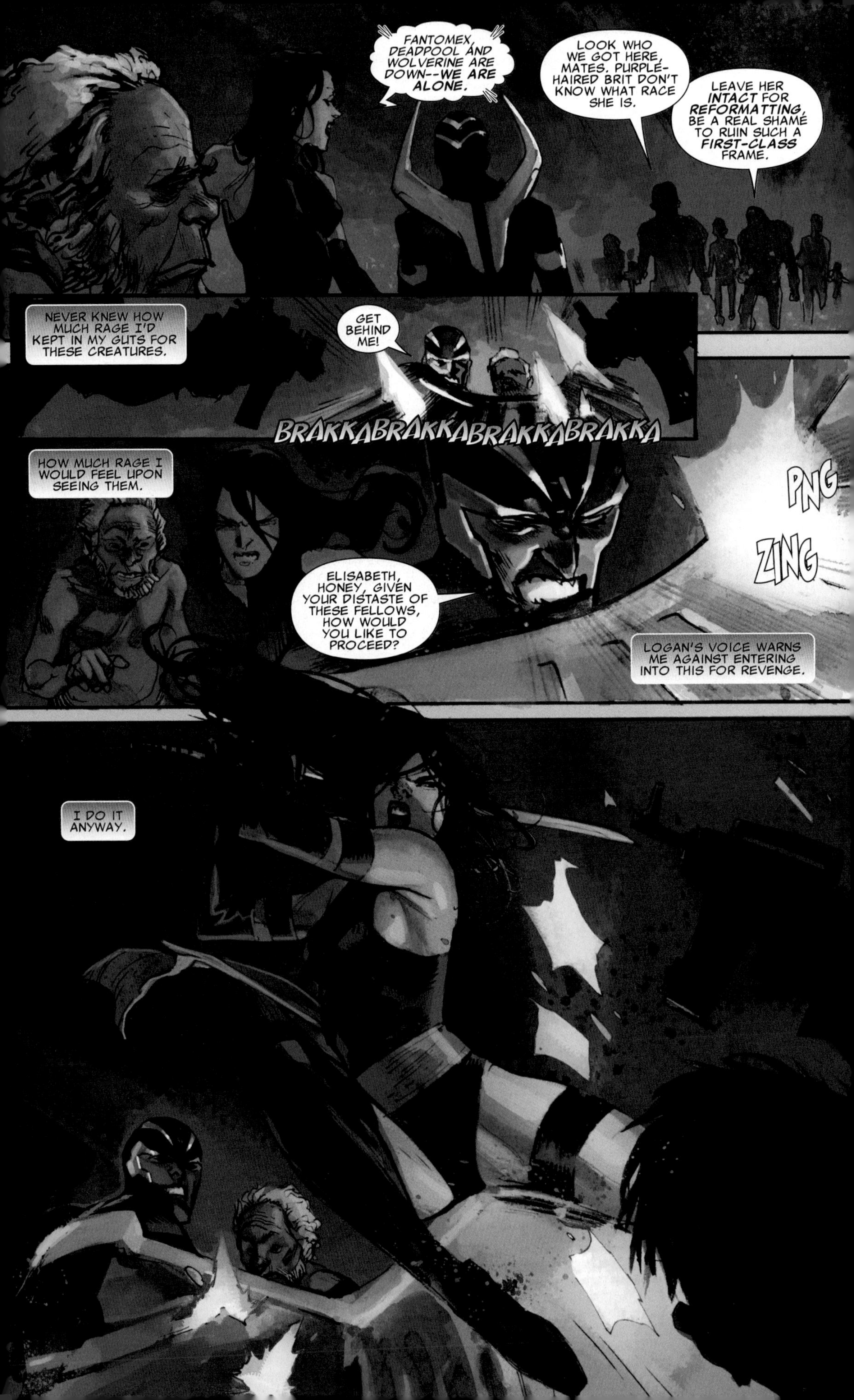
FANTOMEX, DEADPOOL AND WOLVERINE ARE DOWN--WE ARE ALONE.
LOOK WHO WE GOT HERE, MATES. PURPLE-HAIRED BRIT DON'T KNOW WHAT RACE SHE IS.
LEAVE HER INTACT FOR REFORMATTING, BE A REAL SHAME TO RUIN SUCH A FIRST-CLASS FRAME.
NEVER KNEW HOW MUCH RAGE I'D KEPT IN MY GUTS FOR THESE CREATURES.
GET BEHIND ME!
BRAKKABRAKKABRAKKABRAKKA
HOW MUCH RAGE I WOULD FEEL UPON SEEING THEM.
PNG
ZING
ELISABETH, HONEY, GIVEN YOUR DISTASTE OF THESE FELLOWS, HOW WOULD YOU LIKE TO PROCEED?
LOGAN'S VOICE WARNS ME AGAINST ENTERING INTO THIS FOR REVENGE.
I DO IT ANYWAY.

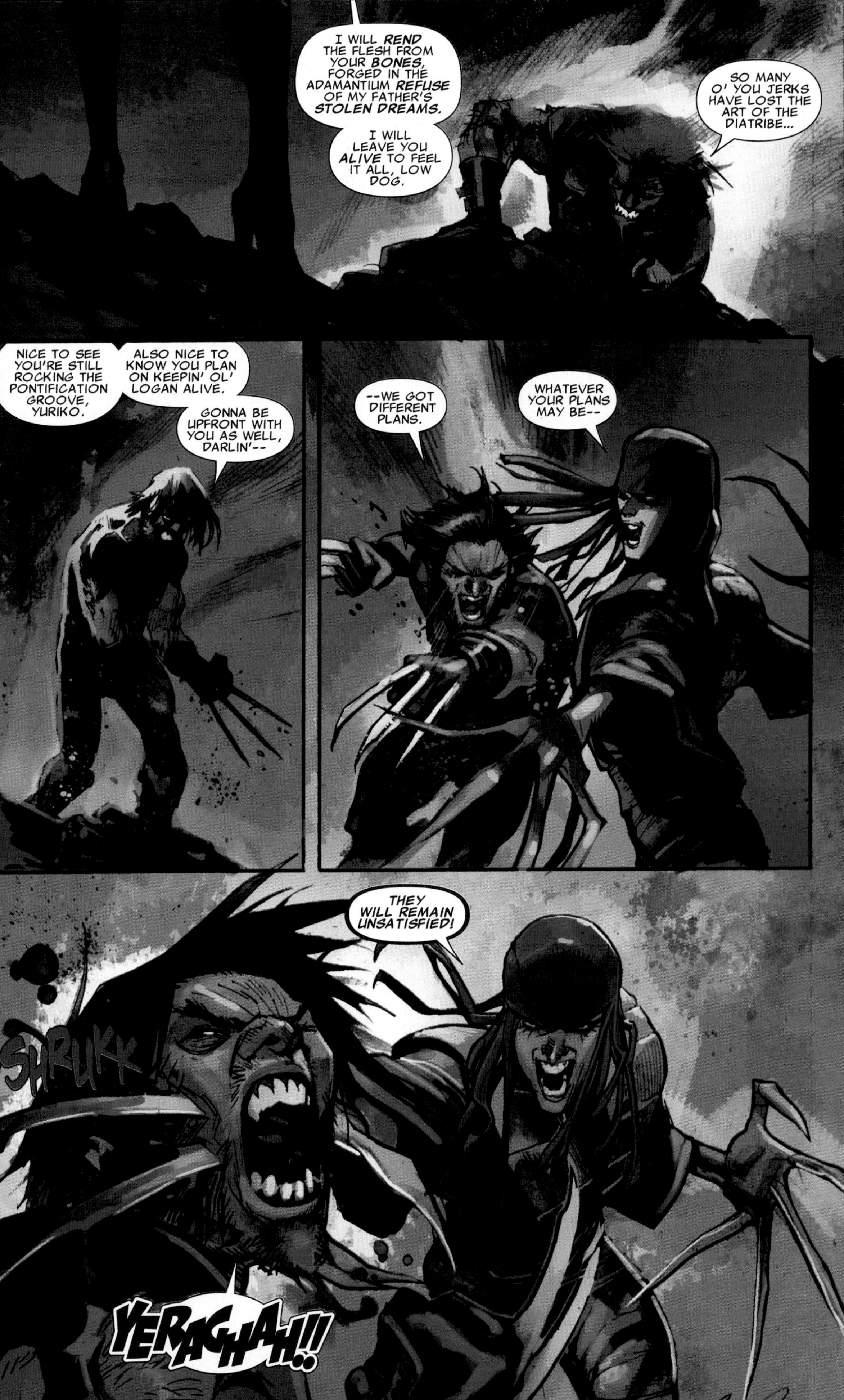
I WILL REND THE FLESH FROM YOUR BONES, FORGED IN THE ADAMANTIUM REFUSE OF MY FATHER'S STOLEN DREAMS.
I WILL LEAVE YOU ALIVE TO FEEL IT ALL, LOW DOG.
SO MANY O' YOU JERKS HAVE LOST THE ART OF THE DIATRIBE...
NICE TO SEE YOU'RE STILL ROCKING THE PONTIFICATION GROOVE, YURIKO.
ALSO NICE TO KNOW YOU PLAN ON KEEPIN' OL' LOGAN ALIVE.
GONNA BE UPFRONT WITH YOU AS WELL, DARLIN'--
WHATEVER YOUR PLANS MAY BE--
--WE GOT DIFFERENT PLANS.
THEY WILL REMAIN UNSATISFIED!
SHRUKK
YERAGHAH!!

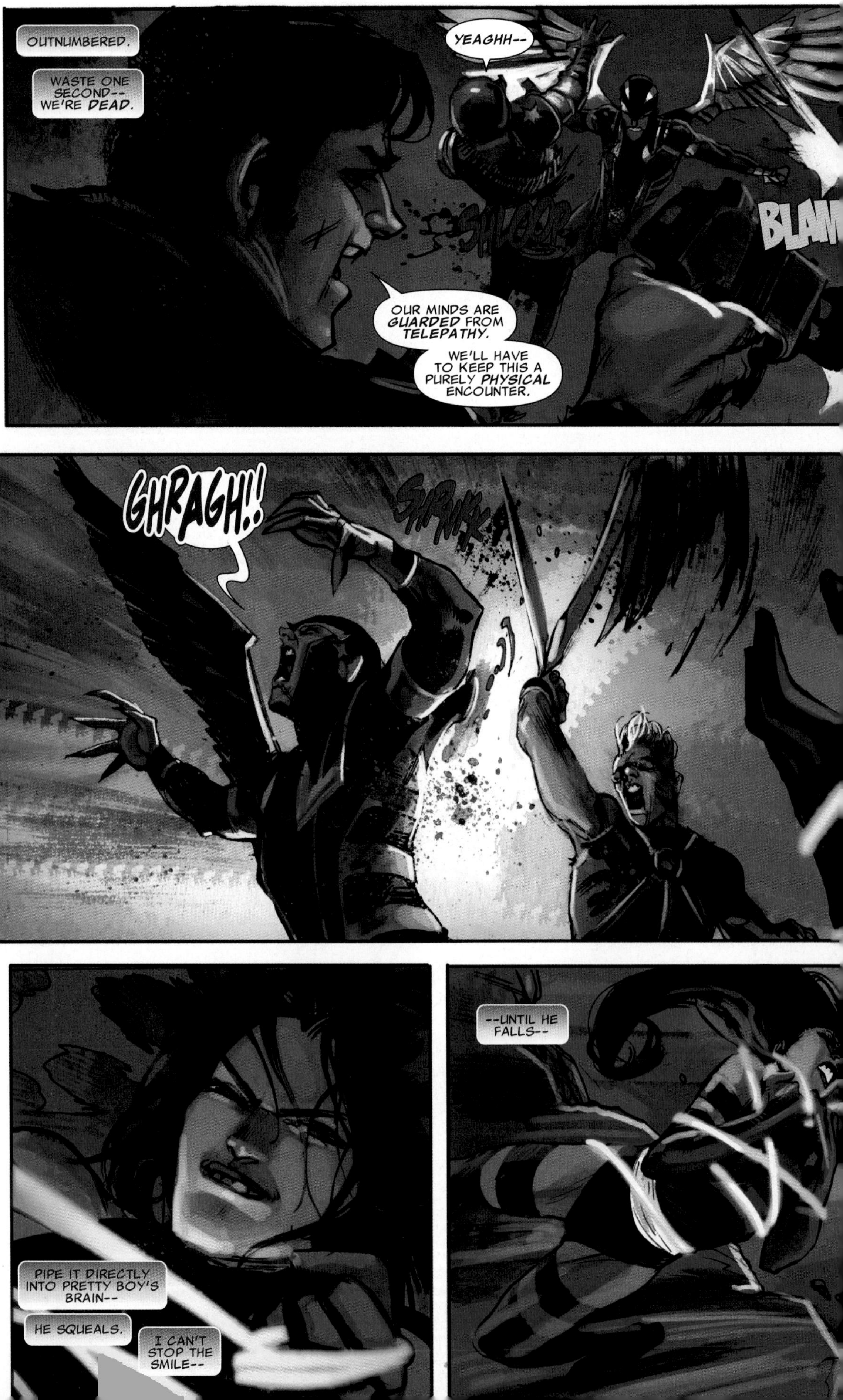
OUTNUMBERED.
WASTE ONE SECOND-- WE'RE DEAD.
YEAGHH--
SHLOOR
BLAM
OUR MINDS ARE GUARDED FROM TELEPATHY.
WE'LL HAVE TO KEEP THIS A PURELY PHYSICAL ENCOUNTER.
GHRAGH!!
--UNTIL HE FALLS--
PIPE IT DIRECTLY INTO PRETTY BOY'S BRAIN--
HE SQUEALS.
I CAN'T STOP THE SMILE--

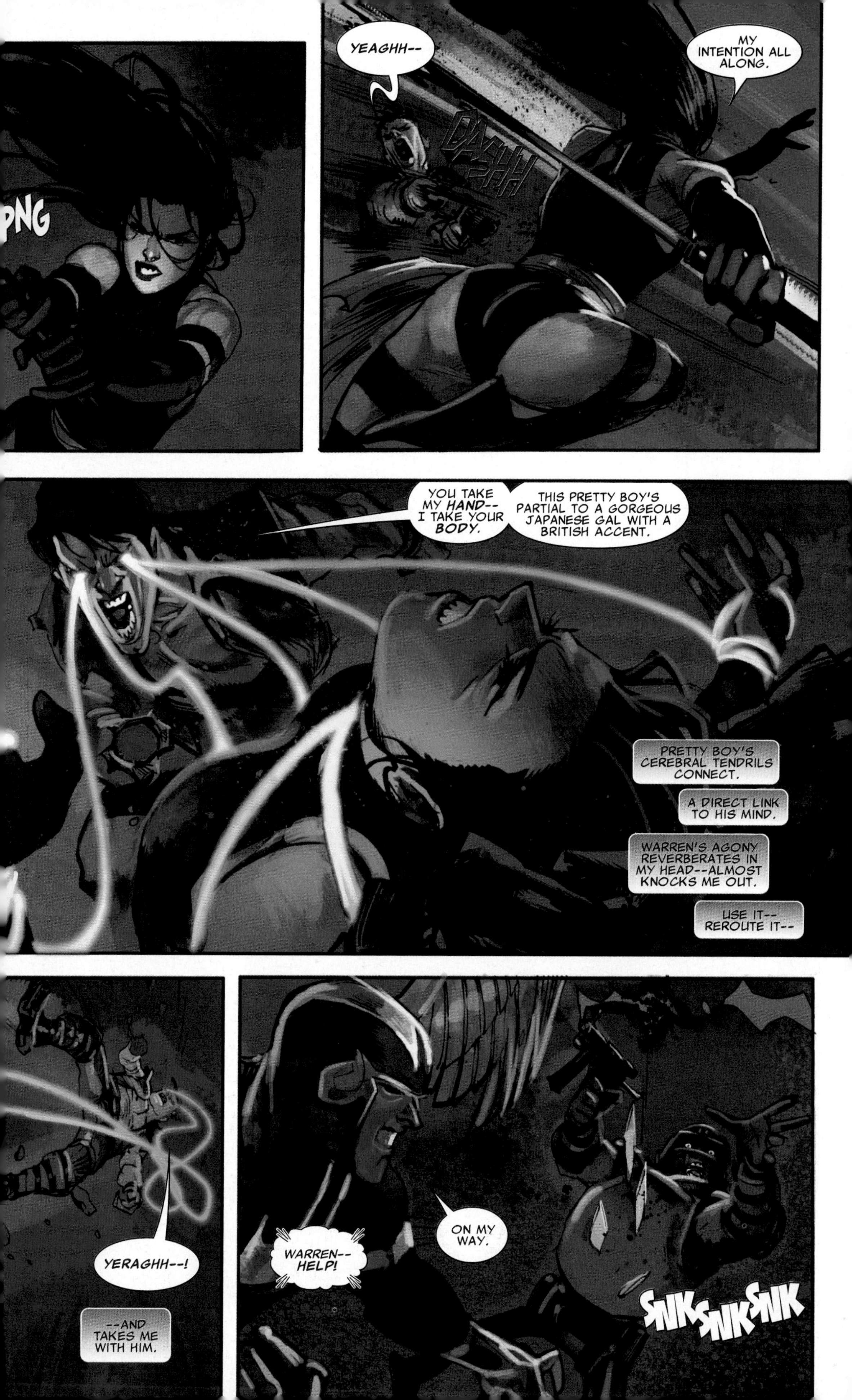
PNG
YEAGHH--
MY INTENTION ALL ALONG.
YOU TAKE MY HAND-- I TAKE YOUR BODY.
THIS PRETTY BOY'S PARTIAL TO A GORGEOUS JAPANESE GAL WITH A BRITISH ACCENT.
PRETTY BOY'S CEREBRAL TENDRILS CONNECT.
A DIRECT LINK TO HIS MIND.
WARREN'S AGONY REVERBERATES IN MY HEAD--ALMOST KNOCKS ME OUT.
USE IT-- REROUTE IT--
YERAGHH--!
--AND TAKES ME WITH HIM.
WARREN-- HELP!
ON MY WAY.
SNIKSNIKSNIK

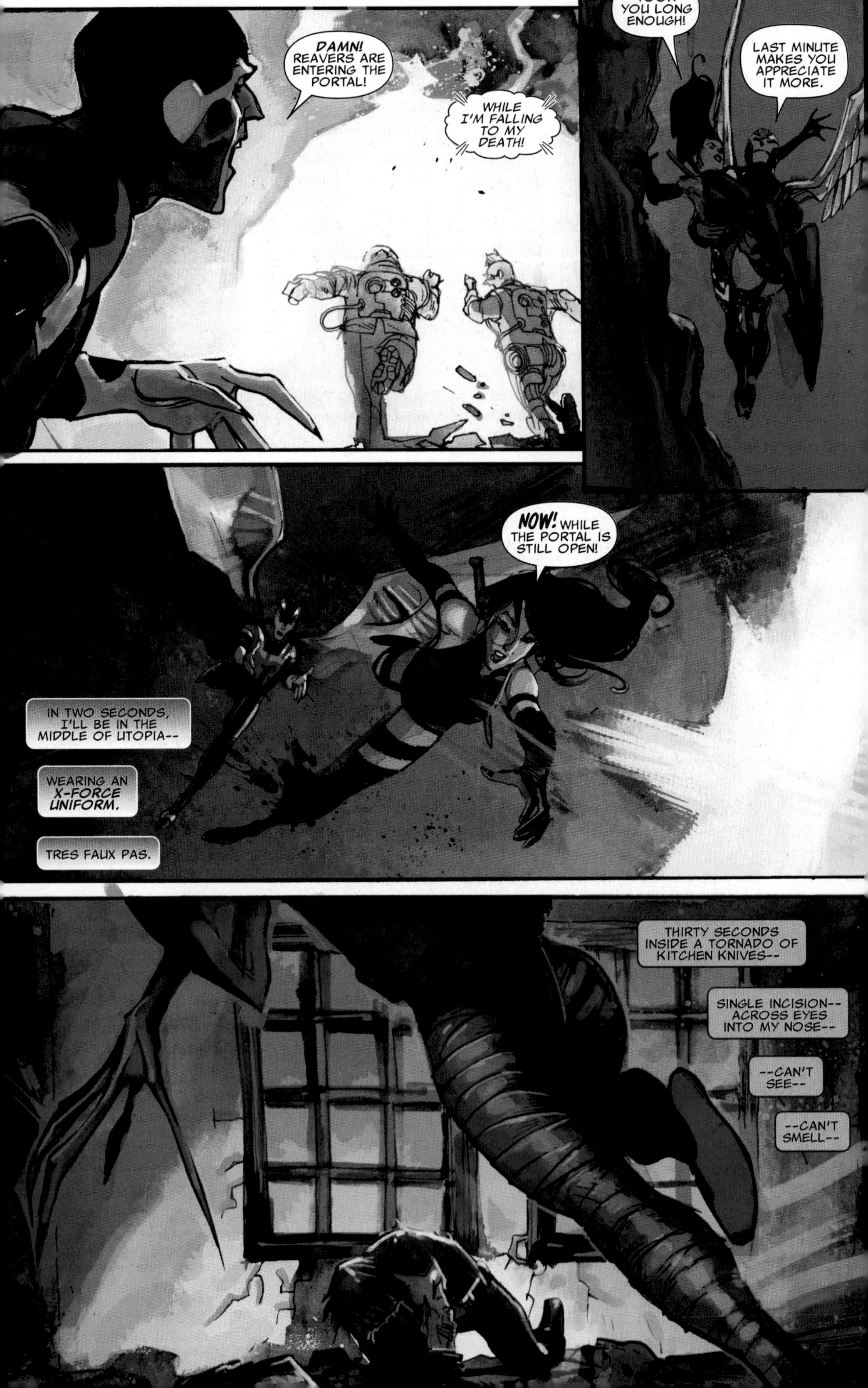
DAMN! REAVERS ARE ENTERING THE PORTAL!
WHILE I'M FALLING TO MY DEATH!
TOOK YOU LONG ENOUGH!
LAST MINUTE MAKES YOU APPRECIATE IT MORE.
NOW! WHILE THE PORTAL IS STILL OPEN!
IN TWO SECONDS, I'LL BE IN THE MIDDLE OF UTOPIA--
WEARING AN X-FORCE UNIFORM.
TRES FAUX PAS.
THIRTY SECONDS INSIDE A TORNADO OF KITCHEN KNIVES--
SINGLE INCISION-- ACROSS EYES INTO MY NOSE--
--CAN'T SEE--
--CAN'T SMELL--

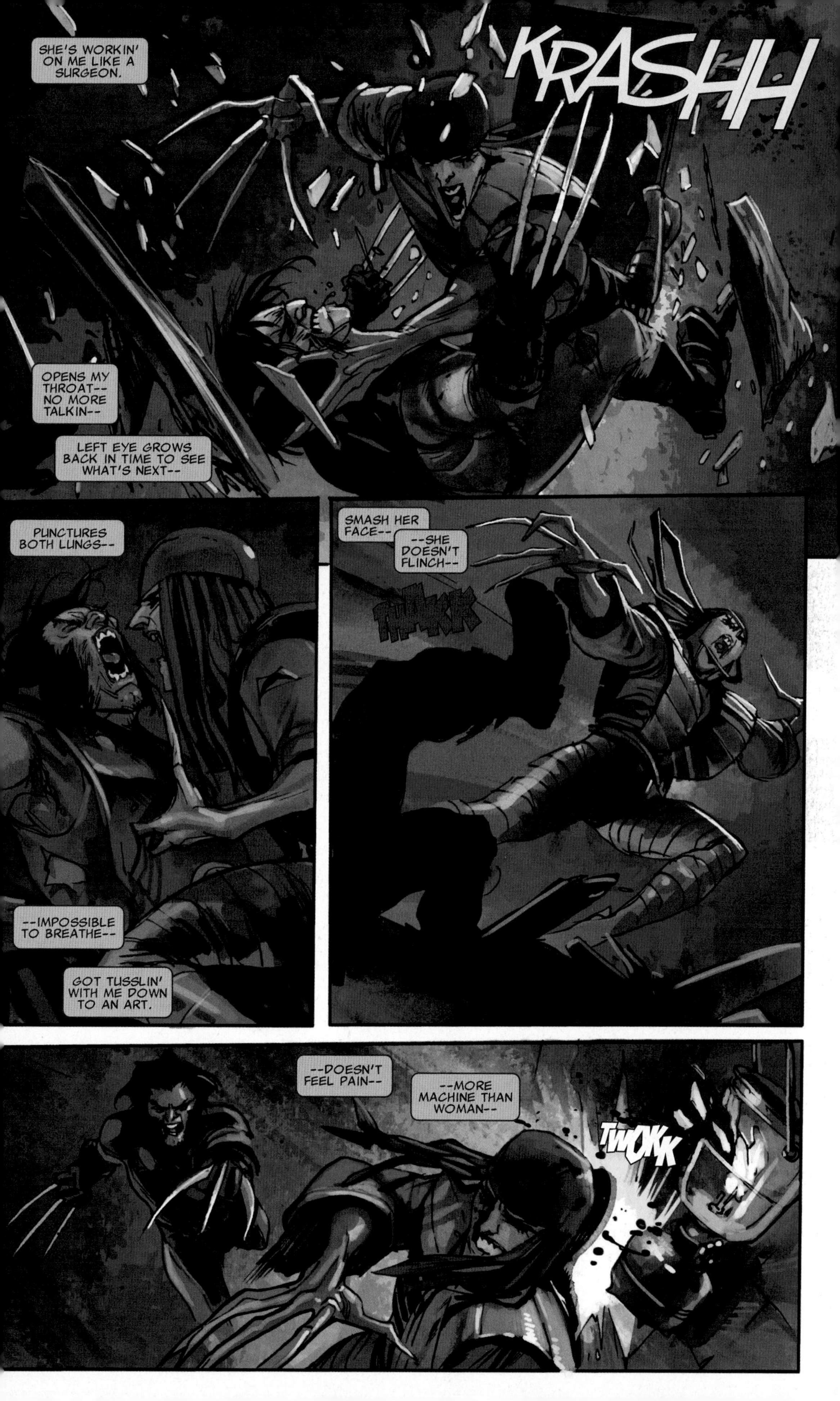
SHE'S WORKIN' ON ME LIKE A SURGEON.
KRASHH
OPENS MY THROAT-- NO MORE TALKIN--
LEFT EYE GROWS BACK IN TIME TO SEE WHAT'S NEXT--
PUNCTURES BOTH LUNGS--
--IMPOSSIBLE TO BREATHE--
GOT TUSSLIN' WITH ME DOWN TO AN ART.
SMASH HER FACE--
--SHE DOESN'T FLINCH--
THWKK
--DOESN'T FEEL PAIN--
--MORE MACHINE THAN WOMAN--
TWOKK

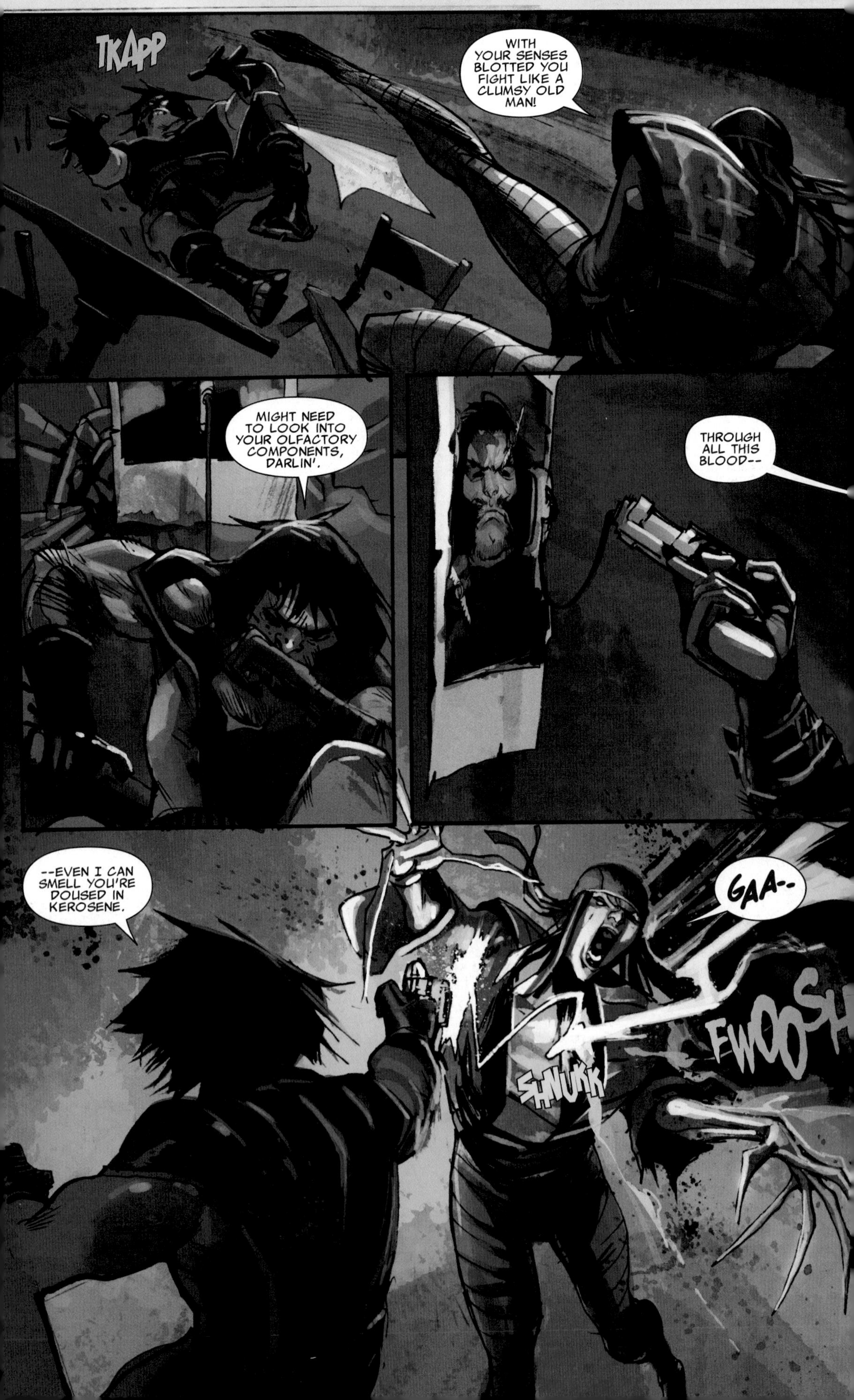
TKAPP
WITH YOUR SENSES BLOTTED YOU FIGHT LIKE A CLUMSY OLD MAN!
MIGHT NEED TO LOOK INTO YOUR OLFACTORY COMPONENTS, DARLIN'.
THROUGH ALL THIS BLOOD--
--EVEN I CAN SMELL YOU'RE DOUSED IN KEROSENE.
GAA--
SHNUKK
FWOOSH

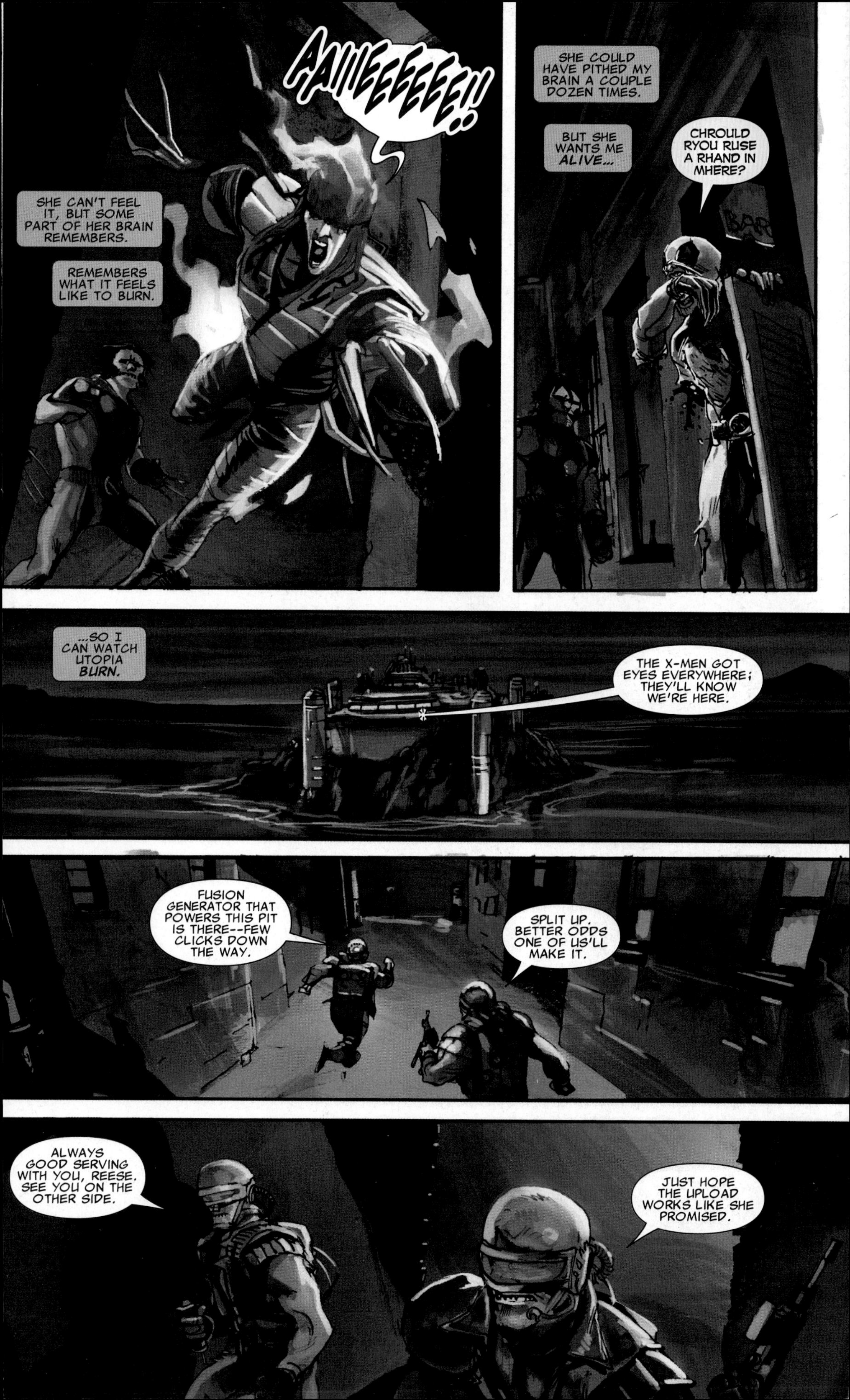
AAIIEEEEEE!!
SHE CAN'T FEEL IT, BUT SOME PART OF HER BRAIN REMEMBERS.
REMEMBERS WHAT IT FEELS LIKE TO BURN.
SHE COULD HAVE PITHED MY BRAIN A COUPLE DOZEN TIMES.
BUT SHE WANTS ME ALIVE...
CHROULD RYOU RUSE A RHAND IN MHERE?
...SO I CAN WATCH UTOPIA BURN.
THE X-MEN GOT EYES EVERYWHERE; THEY'LL KNOW WE'RE HERE.
FUSION GENERATOR THAT POWERS THIS PIT IS THERE--FEW CLICKS DOWN THE WAY.
SPLIT UP. BETTER ODDS ONE OF US'LL MAKE IT.
ALWAYS GOOD SERVING WITH YOU, REESE. SEE YOU ON THE OTHER SIDE.
JUST HOPE THE UPLOAD WORKS LIKE SHE PROMISED.

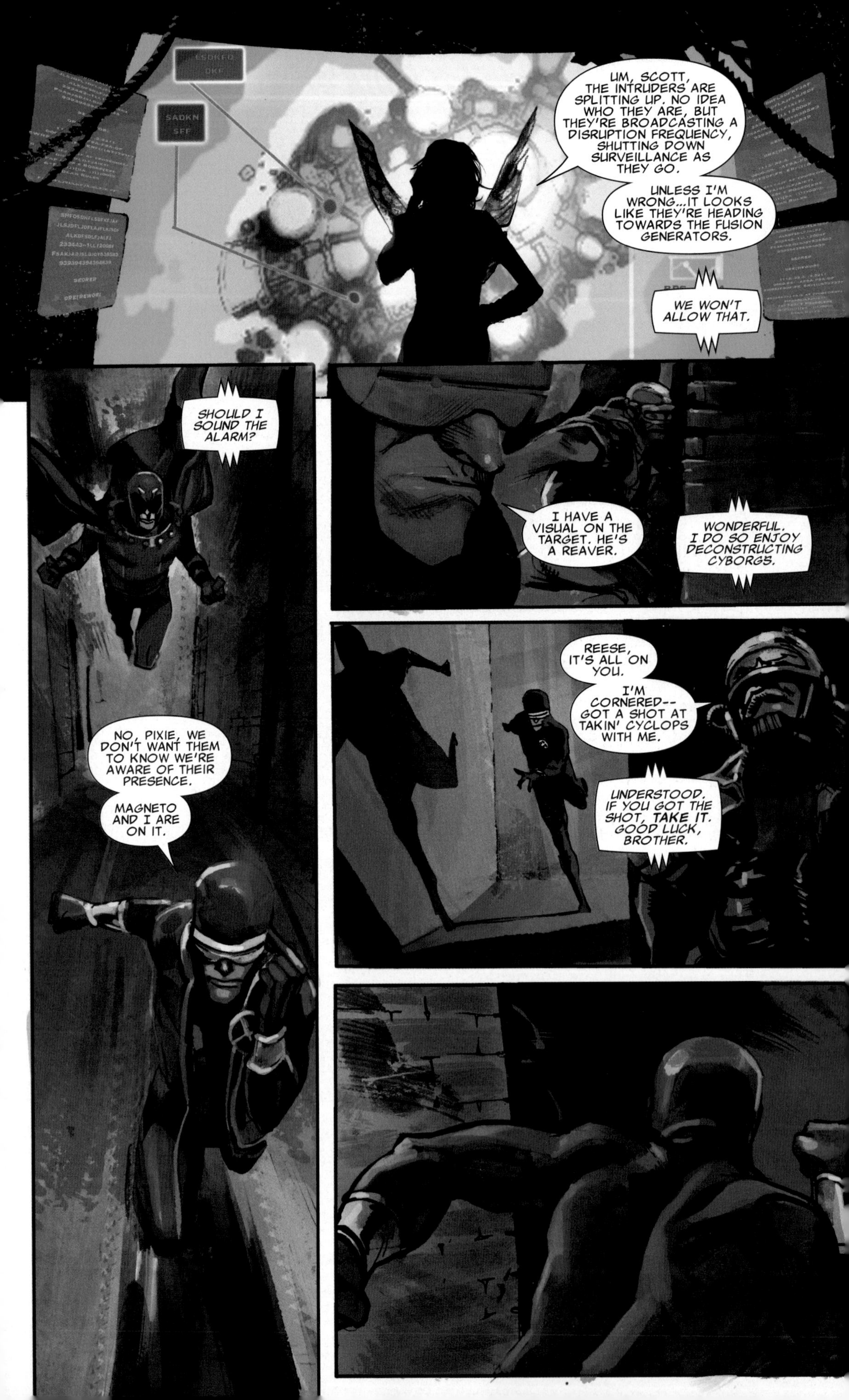
UM, SCOTT, THE INTRUDERS ARE SPLITTING UP. NO IDEA WHO THEY ARE, BUT THEY'RE BROADCASTING A DISRUPTION FREQUENCY, SHUTTING DOWN SURVEILLANCE AS THEY GO.
UNLESS I'M WRONG...IT LOOKS LIKE THEY'RE HEADING TOWARDS THE FUSION GENERATORS.
WE WON'T ALLOW THAT.
SHOULD I SOUND THE ALARM?
NO, PIXIE, WE DON'T WANT THEM TO KNOW WE'RE AWARE OF THEIR PRESENCE.
MAGNETO AND I ARE ON IT.
I HAVE A VISUAL ON THE TARGET. HE'S A REAVER.
WONDERFUL. I DO SO ENJOY DECONSTRUCTING CYBORGS.
REESE, IT'S ALL ON YOU.
I'M CORNERED-- GOT A SHOT AT TAKIN' CYCLOPS WITH ME.
UNDERSTOOD. IF YOU GOT THE SHOT, TAKE IT. GOOD LUCK, BROTHER.

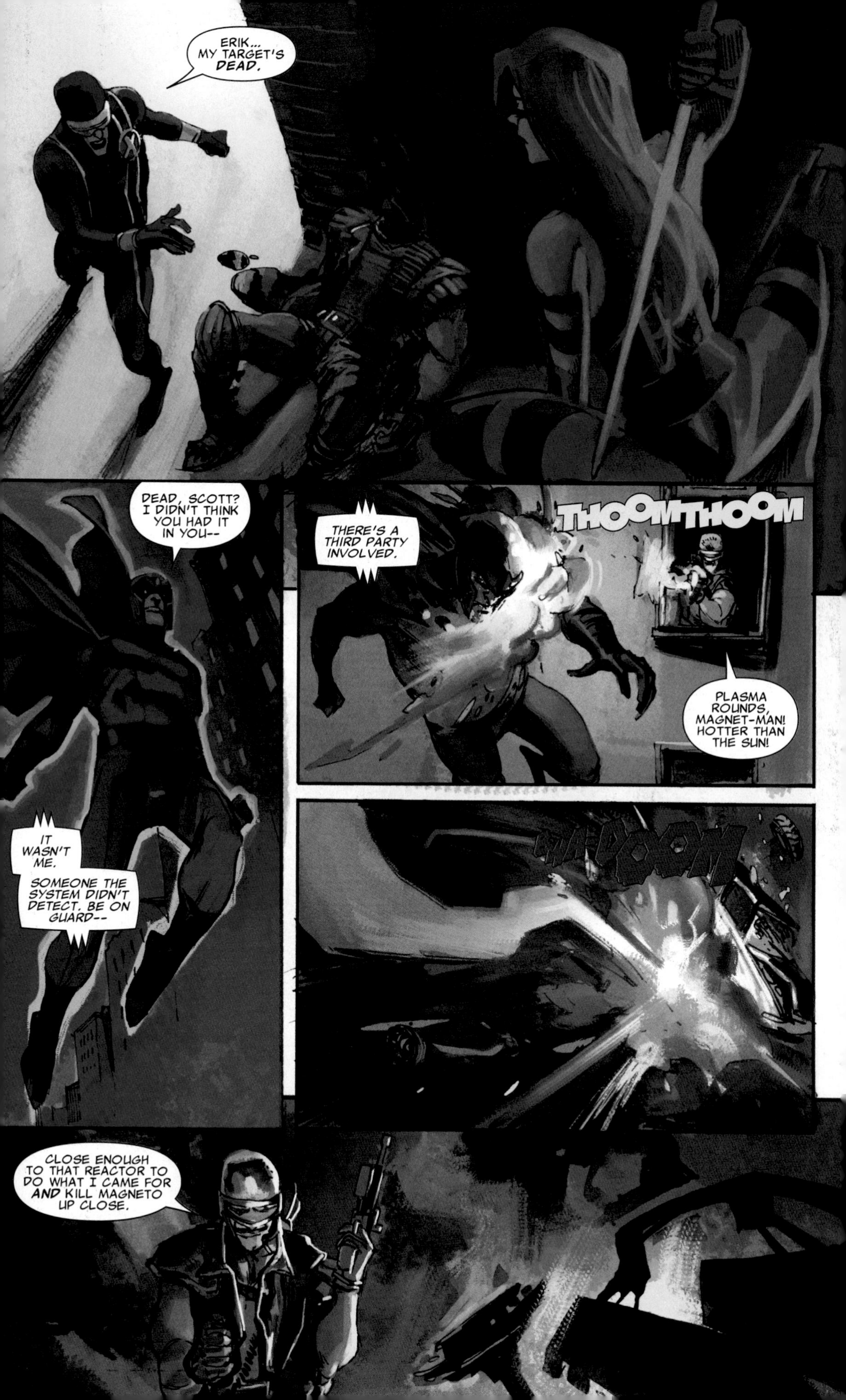
ERIK... MY TARGET'S DEAD.
DEAD, SCOTT? I DIDN'T THINK YOU HAD IT IN YOU--
THERE'S A THIRD PARTY INVOLVED.
THOOMTHOOM
PLASMA ROUNDS, MAGNET-MAN! HOTTER THAN THE SUN!
IT WASN'T ME.
SOMEONE THE SYSTEM DIDN'T DETECT. BE ON GUARD--
CLOSE ENOUGH TO THAT REACTOR TO DO WHAT I CAME FOR AND KILL MAGNETO UP CLOSE.

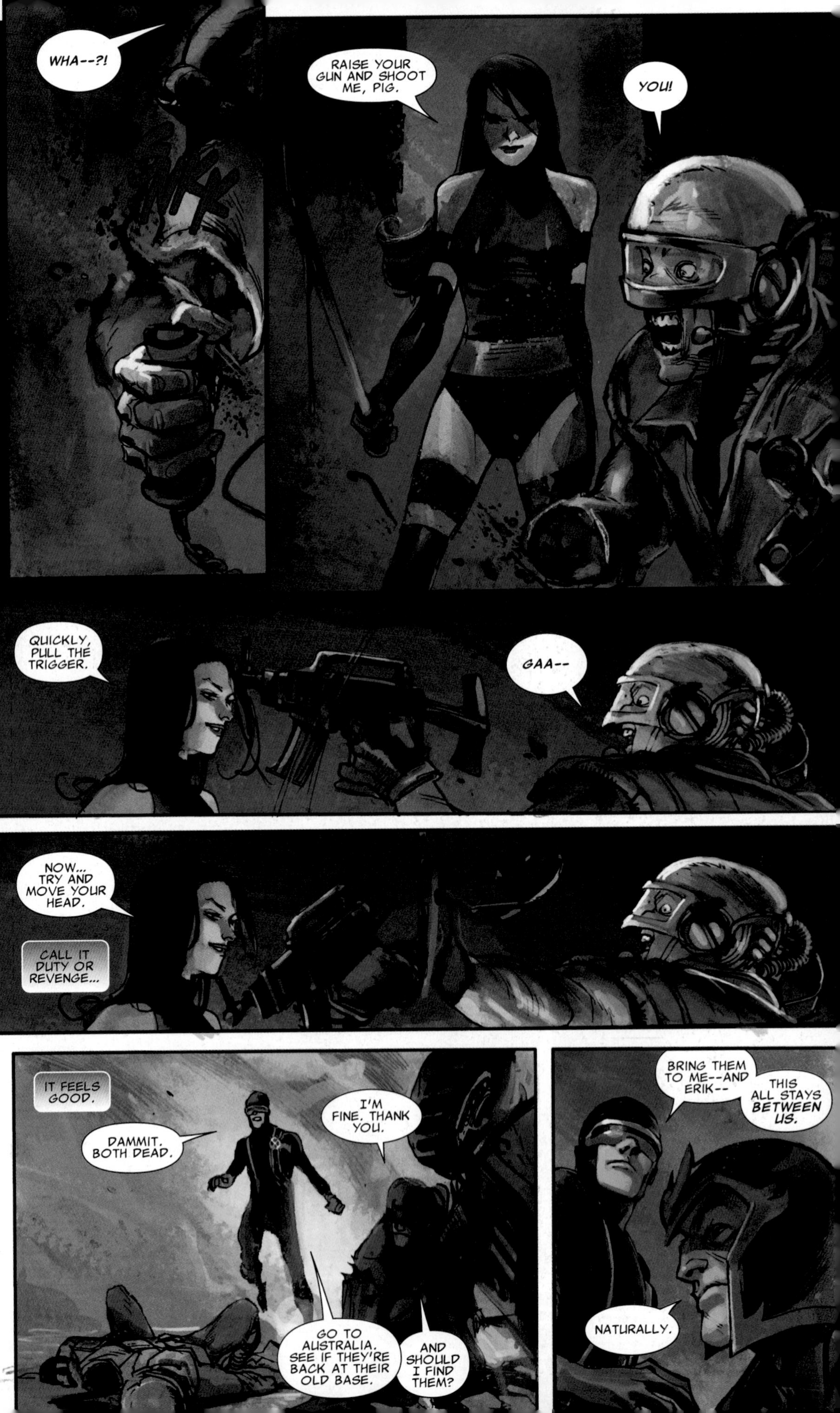
WHA--?!
RAISE YOUR GUN AND SHOOT ME, PIG.
YOU!
QUICKLY, PULL THE TRIGGER.
GAA--
NOW... TRY AND MOVE YOUR HEAD.
CALL IT DUTY OR REVENGE...
IT FEELS GOOD.
DAMMIT. BOTH DEAD.
I'M FINE. THANK YOU.
GO TO AUSTRALIA. SEE IF THEY'RE BACK AT THEIR OLD BASE.
AND SHOULD I FIND THEM?
BRING THEM TO ME--AND ERIK--
THIS ALL STAYS BETWEEN US.
NATURALLY.

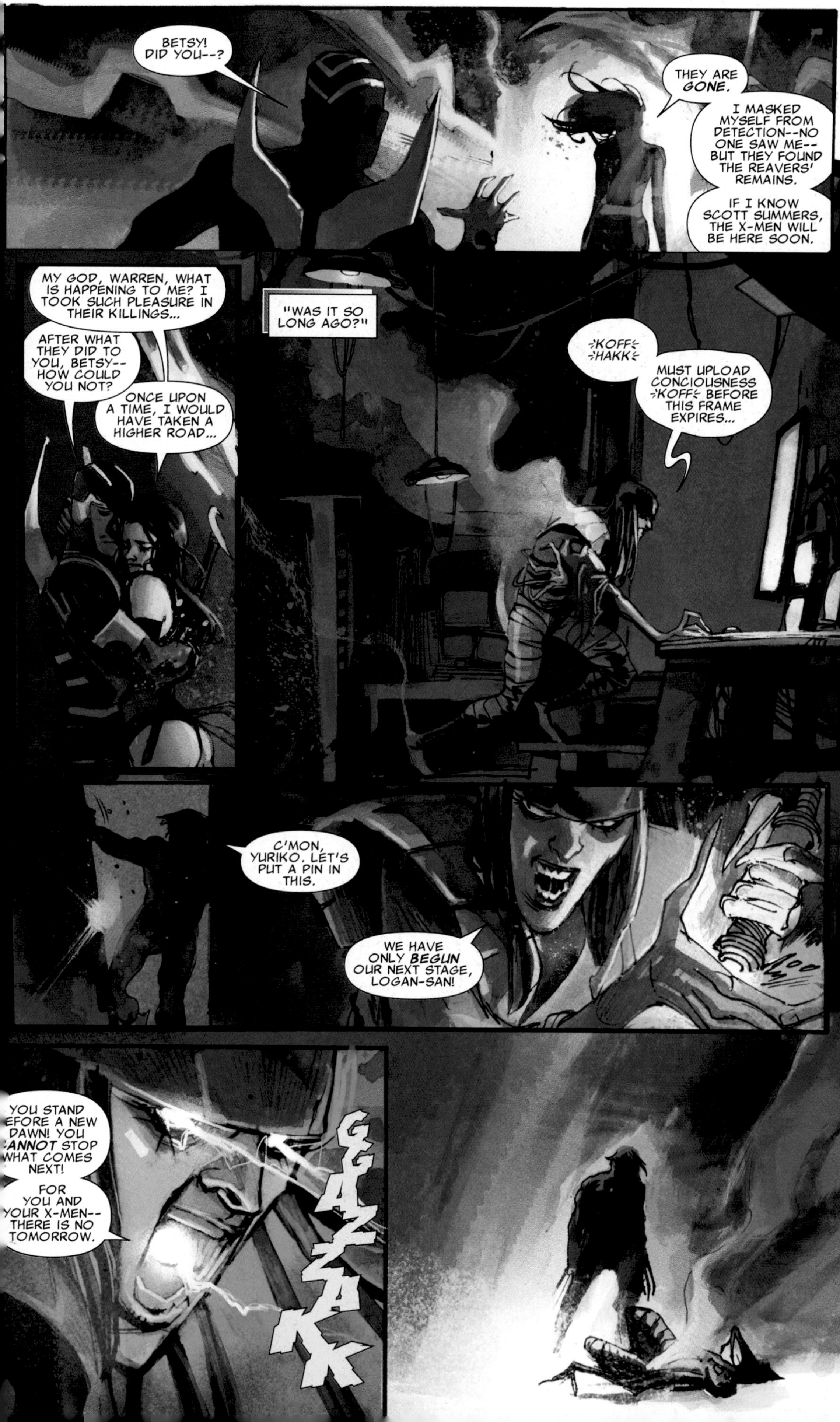
BETSY! DID YOU--?
THEY ARE GONE.
I MASKED MYSELF FROM DETECTION--NO ONE SAW ME--BUT THEY FOUND THE REAVERS' REMAINS.
IF I KNOW SCOTT SUMMERS, THE X-MEN WILL BE HERE SOON.
MY GOD, WARREN, WHAT IS HAPPENING TO ME? I TOOK SUCH PLEASURE IN THEIR KILLINGS...
AFTER WHAT THEY DID TO YOU, BETSY--HOW COULD YOU NOT?
ONCE UPON A TIME, I WOULD HAVE TAKEN A HIGHER ROAD...
"WAS IT SO LONG AGO?"
KOFF HAKK
MUST UPLOAD CONCIOUSNESS KOFF BEFORE THIS FRAME EXPIRES...
C'MON, YURIKO. LET'S PUT A PIN IN THIS.
WE HAVE ONLY BEGUN OUR NEXT STAGE, LOGAN-SAN!
YOU STAND BEFORE A NEW DAWN! YOU CANNOT STOP WHAT COMES NEXT!
FOR YOU AND YOUR X-MEN--THERE IS NO TOMORROW.
GGAZZAKK

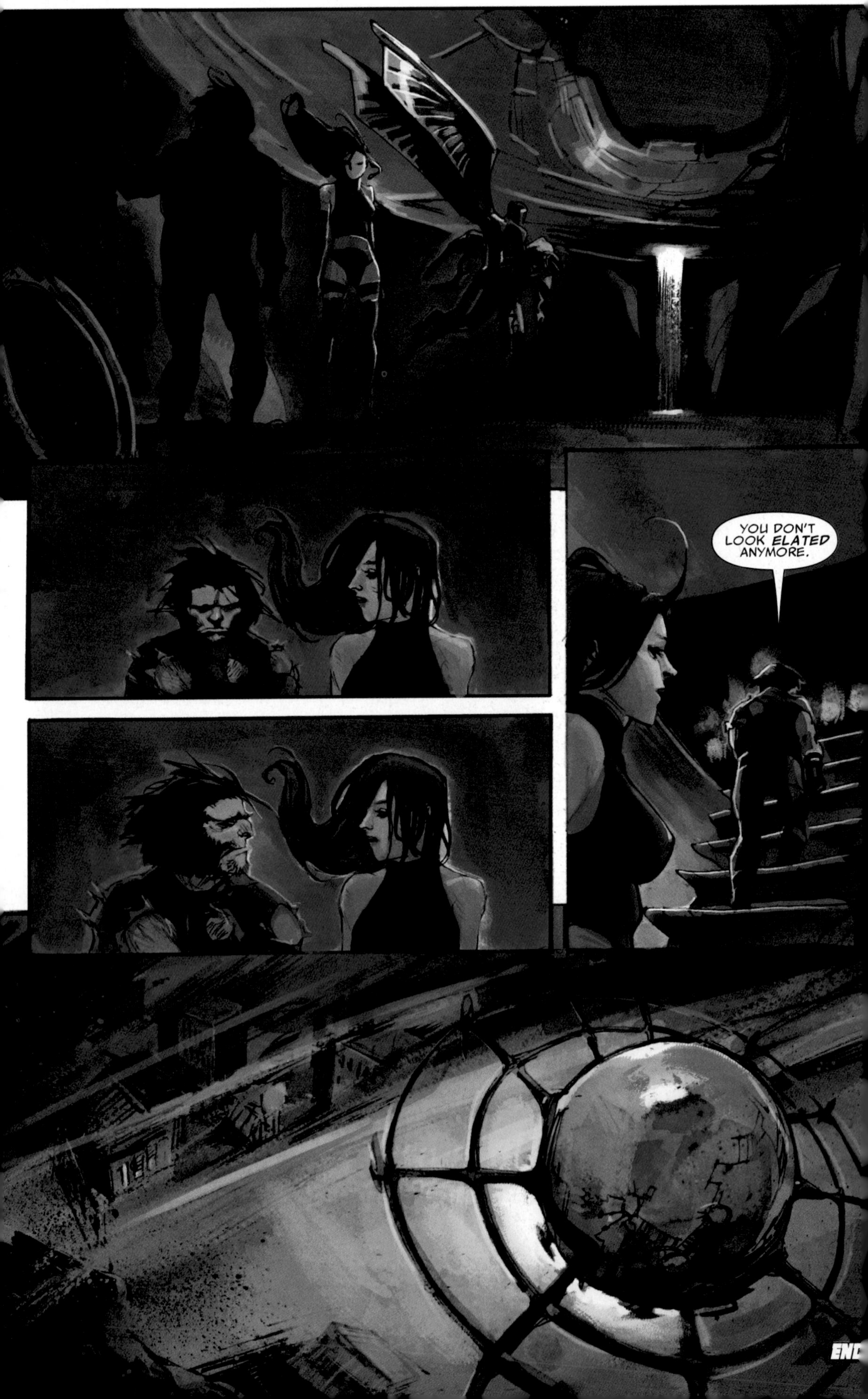
YOU DON'T LOOK ELATED ANYMORE.
END

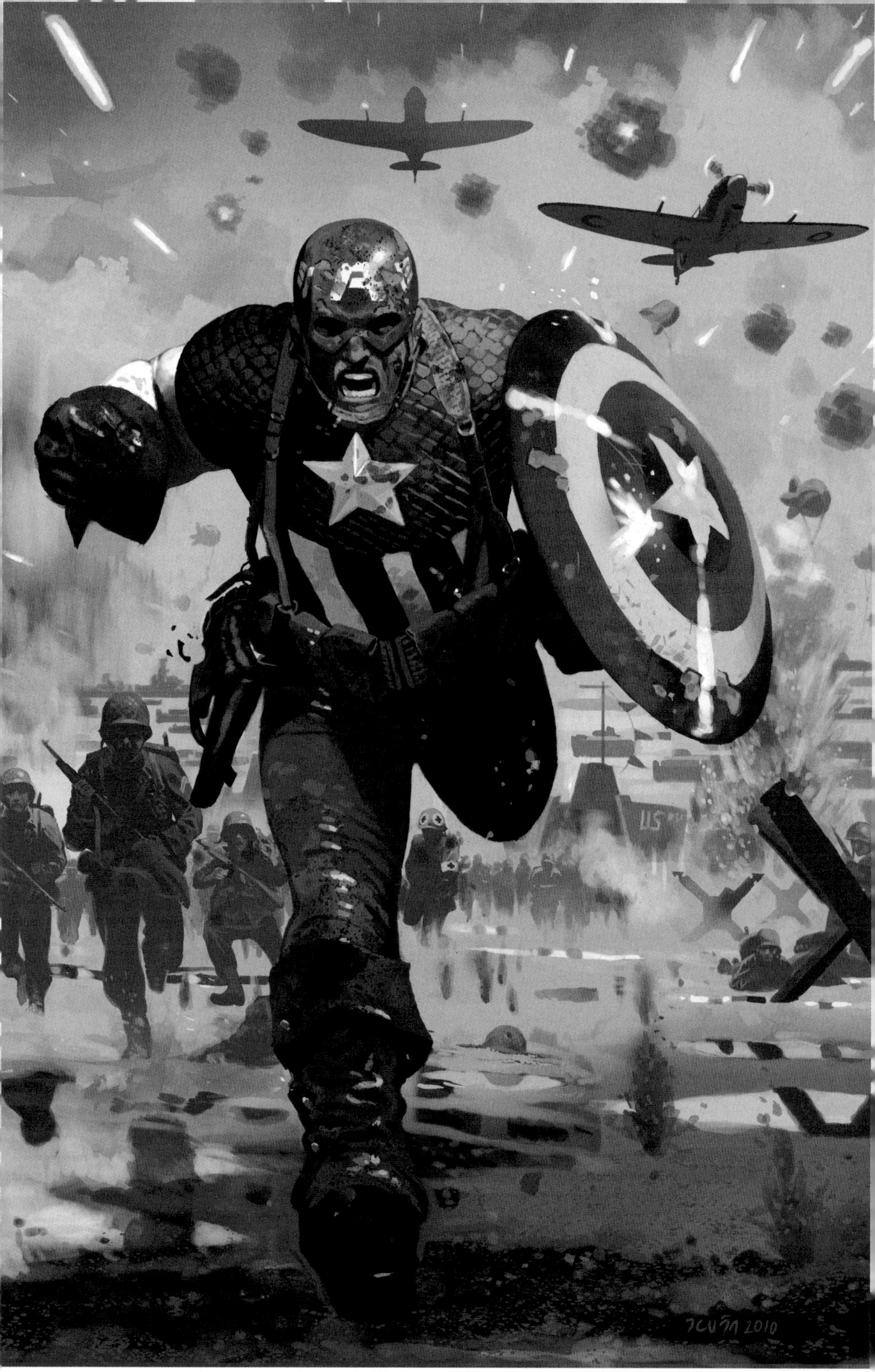

CAPTAIN AMERICA #615.1

AS WORLD WAR II RAGED ON, A YOUNG, SCRAWNY **STEVE ROGERS,** WAS SELECTED TO PARTICIPATE IN **OPERATION: REBIRTH,** WHERE HE WAS INJECTED WITH THE SUPER-SOLDIER FORMULA DEVELOPED BY PROFESSOR ERSKINE. AS SOON AS STEVE ABSORBED THE SERUM, A NAZI SPY SHOT ERSKINE, KILLING THE ONLY SOURCE FOR THE FORMULA. STEVE WENT ON TO FIGHT FOR HIS COUNTRY AS

CAPTAIN AMERICA

IN THE PRESENT, ROGERS CARRIES ON THE BATTLE FOR FREEDOM AND DEMOCRACY AS AMERICA'S TOP LAW-ENFORCEMENT OPERATIVE AND COMMANDER OF THE MIGHTY AVENGERS.

WRITER: ED BRUBAKER

ARTIST: MITCH BREITWEISER

COLOR ARTIST: BETTIE BREITWEISER

LETTERER & PRODUCTION:
VC'S JOE CARAMAGNA

COVER ART: DANIEL ACUÑA

ASSOCIATE EDITOR:
LAUREN SANKOVITCH

EDITOR: TOM BREVOORT

EDITOR IN CHIEF: AXEL ALONSO

CHIEF CREATIVE OFFICER: JOE QUESADA

PUBLISHER: DAN BUCKLEY

EXECUTIVE PRODUCER: ALAN FINE

CAPTAIN AMERICA CREATED BY **JOE SIMON** AND **JACK KIRBY**

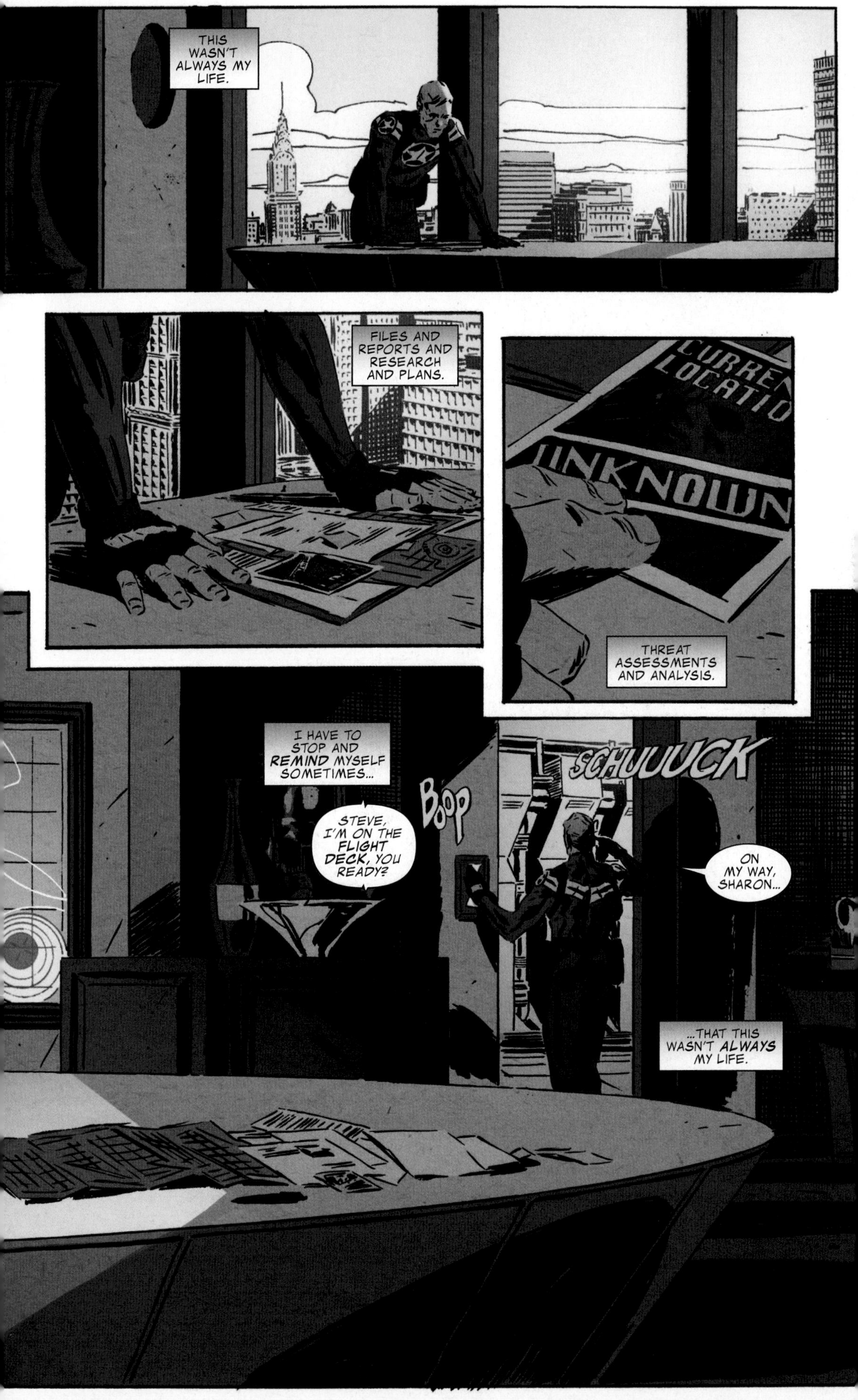
THIS WASN'T ALWAYS MY LIFE.
FILES AND REPORTS AND RESEARCH AND PLANS.
CURRE LOCATIO
UNKNOWN
THREAT ASSESSMENTS AND ANALYSIS.
I HAVE TO STOP AND REMIND MYSELF SOMETIMES...
BOOP
STEVE, I'M ON THE FLIGHT DECK, YOU READY?
SCHUUUCK
ON MY WAY, SHARON...
...THAT THIS WASN'T ALWAYS MY LIFE.

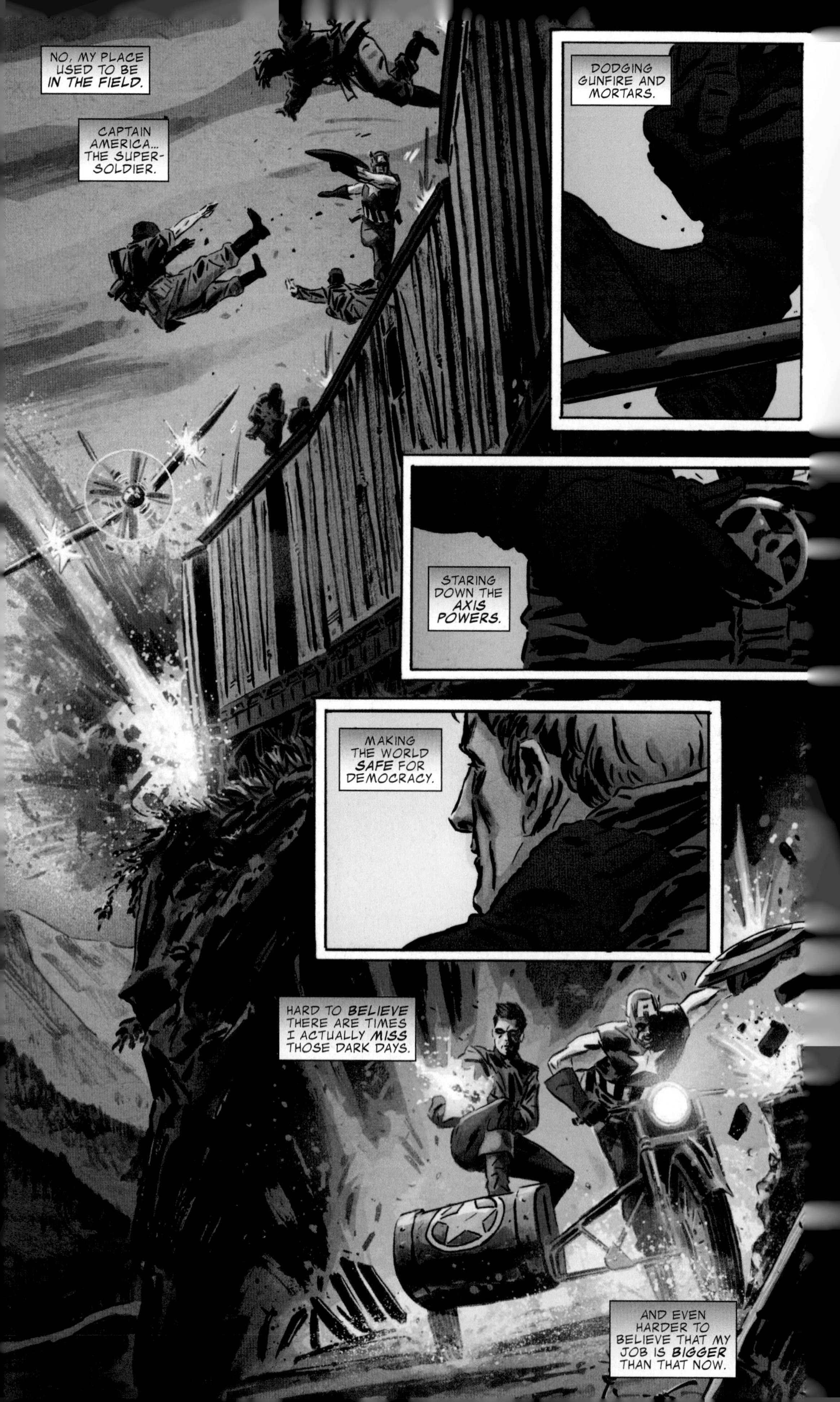
NO, MY PLACE USED TO BE IN THE FIELD.
CAPTAIN AMERICA... THE SUPER-SOLDIER.
DODGING GUNFIRE AND MORTARS.
STARING DOWN THE AXIS POWERS.
MAKING THE WORLD SAFE FOR DEMOCRACY.
HARD TO BELIEVE THERE ARE TIMES I ACTUALLY MISS THOSE DARK DAYS.
AND EVEN HARDER TO BELIEVE THAT MY JOB IS BIGGER THAN THAT NOW.

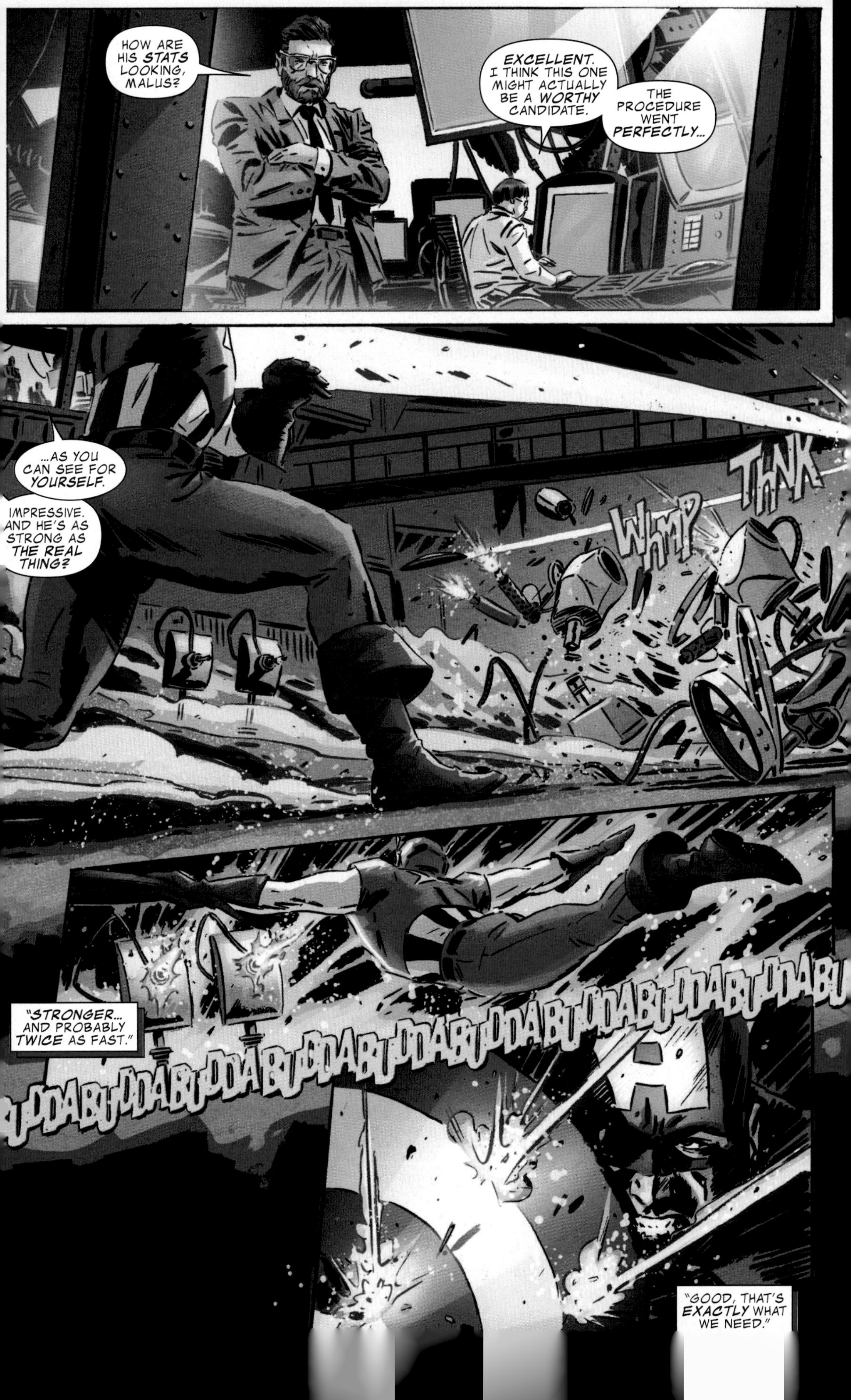

HOW ARE HIS STATS LOOKING, MALUS?
EXCELLENT. I THINK THIS ONE MIGHT ACTUALLY BE A WORTHY CANDIDATE.
THE PROCEDURE WENT PERFECTLY...
...AS YOU CAN SEE FOR YOURSELF.
IMPRESSIVE. AND HE'S AS STRONG AS THE REAL THING?
THNK
WHMP
"STRONGER... AND PROBABLY TWICE AS FAST."
UDDABUDDABUDDABUDDABUDDABUDDABUDDABUDDABUDDABUDDABU
"GOOD, THAT'S EXACTLY WHAT WE NEED."

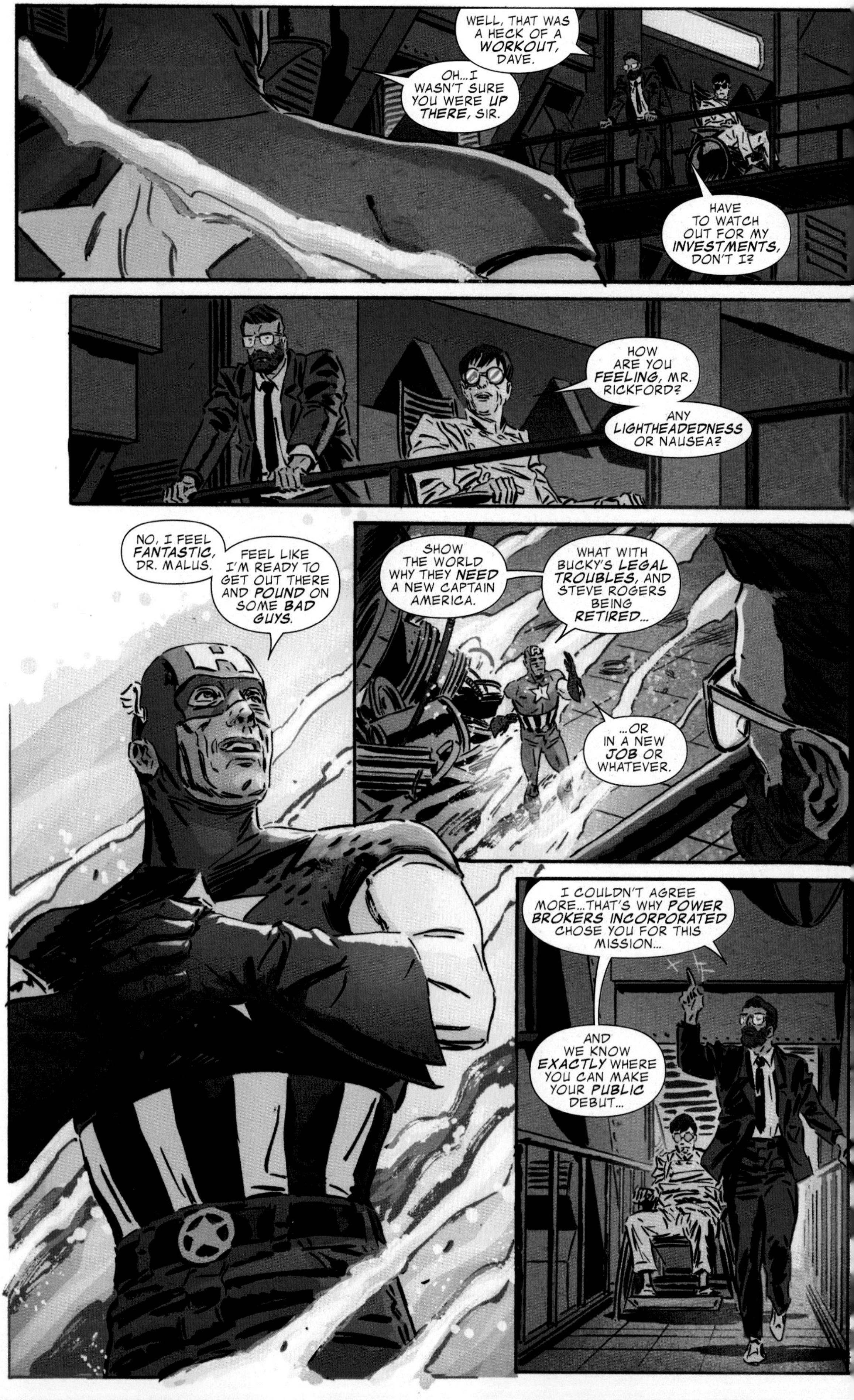
WELL, THAT WAS A HECK OF A WORKOUT, DAVE.
OH...I WASN'T SURE YOU WERE UP THERE, SIR.
HAVE TO WATCH OUT FOR MY INVESTMENTS, DON'T I?
HOW ARE YOU FEELING, MR. RICKFORD?
ANY LIGHTHEADEDNESS OR NAUSEA?
NO, I FEEL FANTASTIC, DR. MALUS.
FEEL LIKE I'M READY TO GET OUT THERE AND POUND ON SOME BAD GUYS.
SHOW THE WORLD WHY THEY NEED A NEW CAPTAIN AMERICA.
WHAT WITH BUCKY'S LEGAL TROUBLES, AND STEVE ROGERS BEING RETIRED...
...OR IN A NEW JOB OR WHATEVER.
I COULDN'T AGREE MORE...THAT'S WHY POWER BROKERS INCORPORATED CHOSE YOU FOR THIS MISSION...
AND WE KNOW EXACTLY WHERE YOU CAN MAKE YOUR PUBLIC DEBUT...

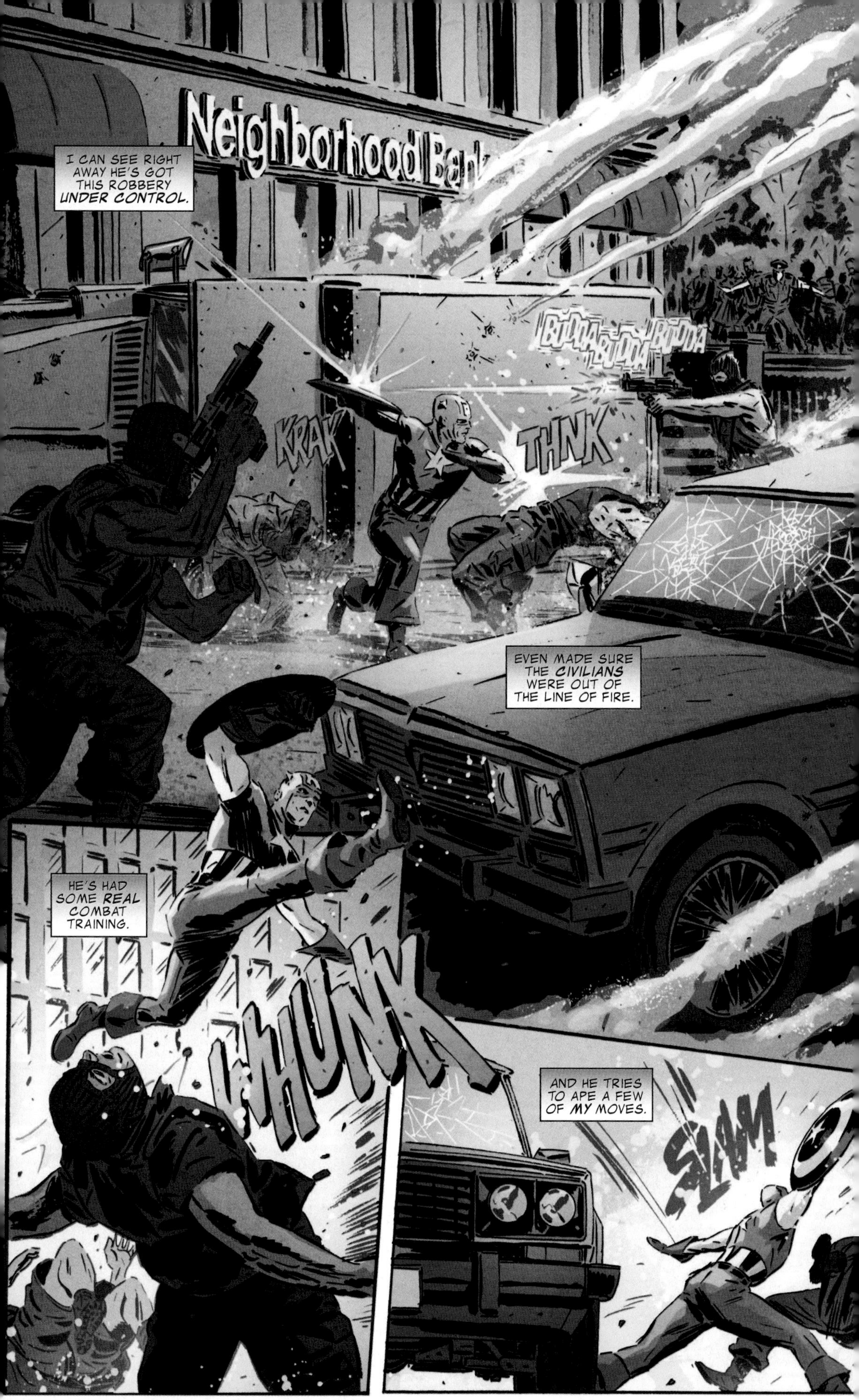
Neighborhood Bank
I CAN SEE RIGHT AWAY HE'S GOT THIS ROBBERY UNDER CONTROL.
BUDDA BUDDA BUDDA
KRAK
THNK
EVEN MADE SURE THE CIVILIANS WERE OUT OF THE LINE OF FIRE.
HE'S HAD SOME REAL COMBAT TRAINING.
WHUNK
AND HE TRIES TO APE A FEW OF MY MOVES.
SLAM

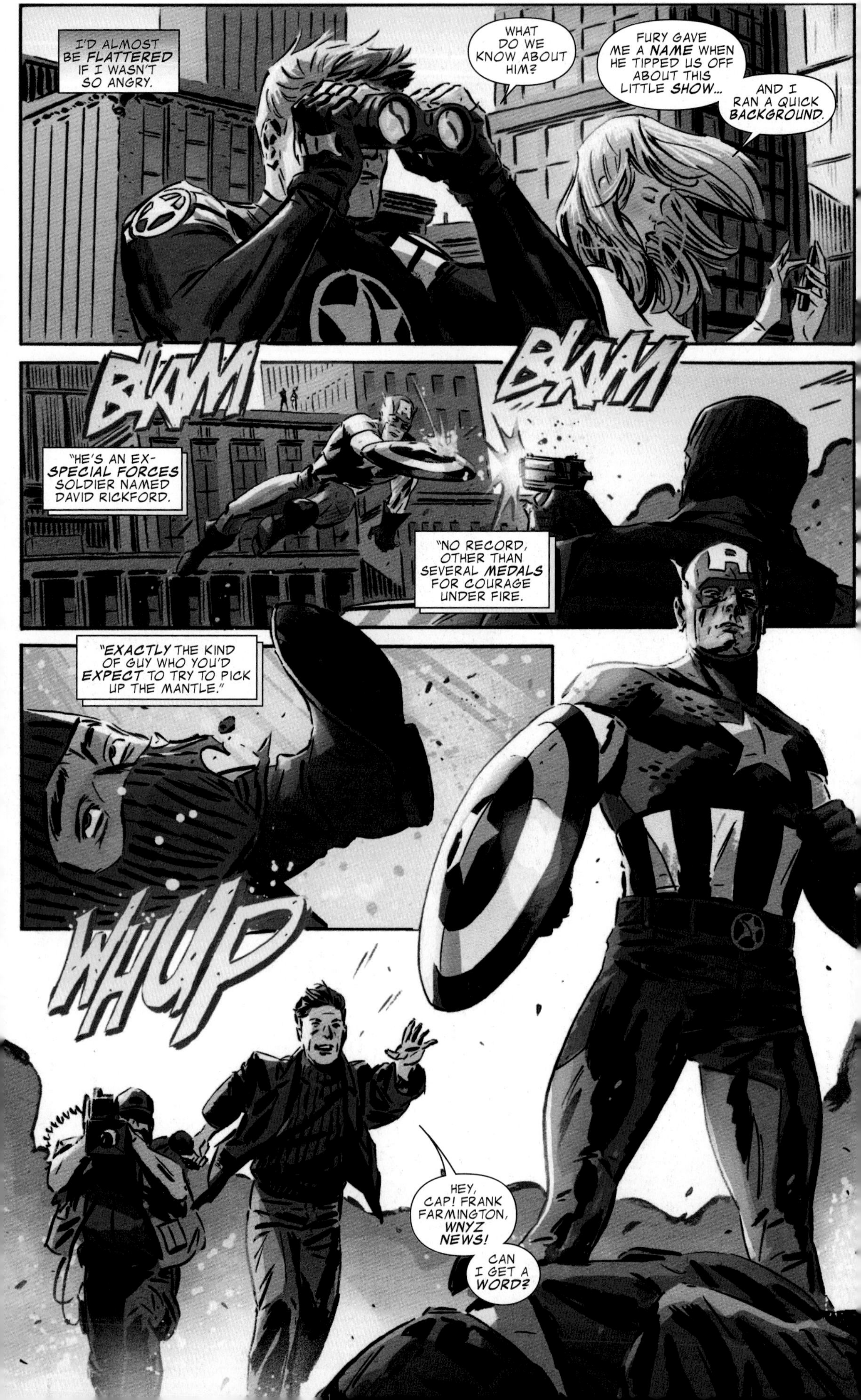
I'D ALMOST BE FLATTERED IF I WASN'T SO ANGRY.
WHAT DO WE KNOW ABOUT HIM?
FURY GAVE ME A NAME WHEN HE TIPPED US OFF ABOUT THIS LITTLE SHOW...
AND I RAN A QUICK BACKGROUND.
BLAM
BLAM
"HE'S AN EX-SPECIAL FORCES SOLDIER NAMED DAVID RICKFORD.
"NO RECORD, OTHER THAN SEVERAL MEDALS FOR COURAGE UNDER FIRE.
"EXACTLY THE KIND OF GUY WHO YOU'D EXPECT TO TRY TO PICK UP THE MANTLE."
WHUP
HEY, CAP! FRANK FARMINGTON, WNYZ NEWS!
CAN I GET A WORD?

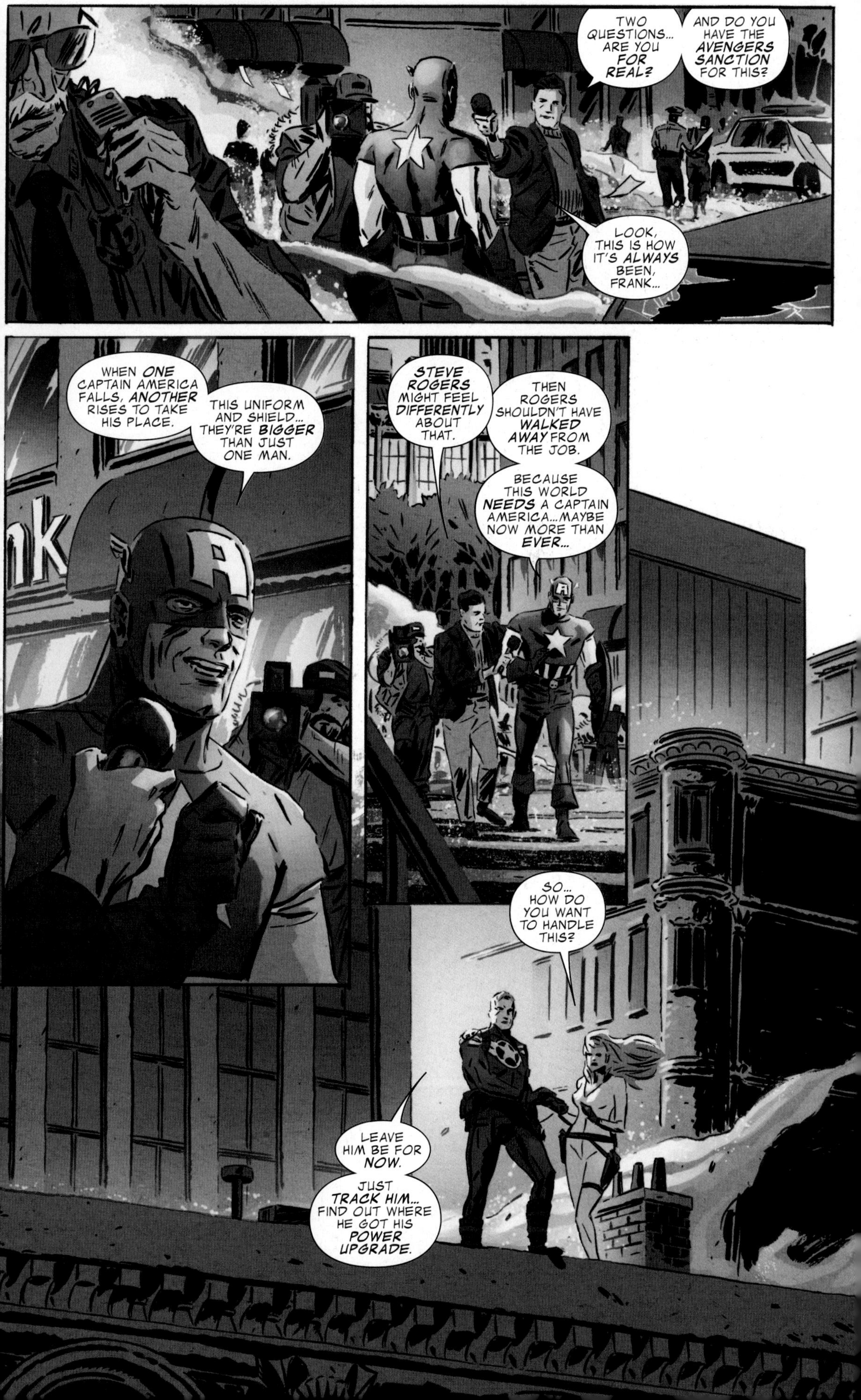
TWO QUESTIONS... ARE YOU FOR REAL?
AND DO YOU HAVE THE AVENGERS SANCTION FOR THIS?
LOOK, THIS IS HOW IT'S ALWAYS BEEN, FRANK...
WHEN ONE CAPTAIN AMERICA FALLS, ANOTHER RISES TO TAKE HIS PLACE.
THIS UNIFORM AND SHIELD... THEY'RE BIGGER THAN JUST ONE MAN.
STEVE ROGERS MIGHT FEEL DIFFERENTLY ABOUT THAT.
THEN ROGERS SHOULDN'T HAVE WALKED AWAY FROM THE JOB.
BECAUSE THIS WORLD NEEDS A CAPTAIN AMERICA...MAYBE NOW MORE THAN EVER...
SO... HOW DO YOU WANT TO HANDLE THIS?
LEAVE HIM BE FOR NOW.
JUST TRACK HIM... FIND OUT WHERE HE GOT HIS POWER UPGRADE.

OF COURSE, THE NEW GUY IS RIGHT. THERE HAVE BEEN OTHERS WHO WORE MY UNIFORM...

WILLIAM NASLUND, THE SPIRIT OF '76, WAS THE FIRST...

...AND WHEN HE WAS KILLED, *JEFF MACE*, THE PATRIOT, COMPLETED HIS MISSION.

BUT NOT MANY CAN CARRY THE *BURDEN*...

DAILY BUGLE

HAS CAR GONE CRAZY

March 13rd, 1954

OBIT

ROSCOE SIMONS

...NO MATTER HOW HARD THEY TRAIN OR HOW MUCH THEY WANT IT.

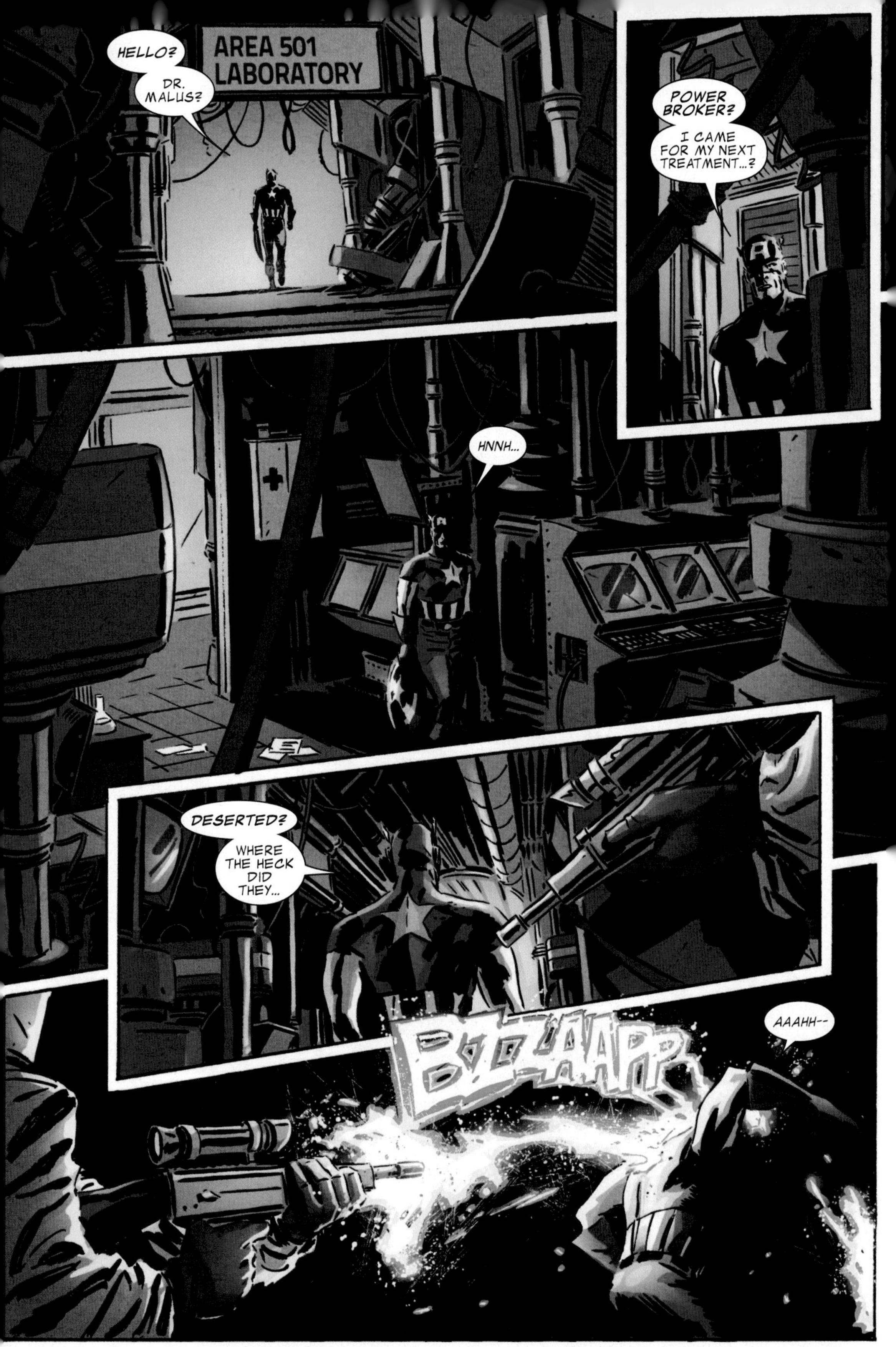
AREA 501 LABORATORY
HELLO?
DR. MALUS?
POWER BROKER?
I CAME FOR MY NEXT TREATMENT...?
HNNH...
DESERTED?
WHERE THE HECK DID THEY...
BZZAAPP
AAAHH--

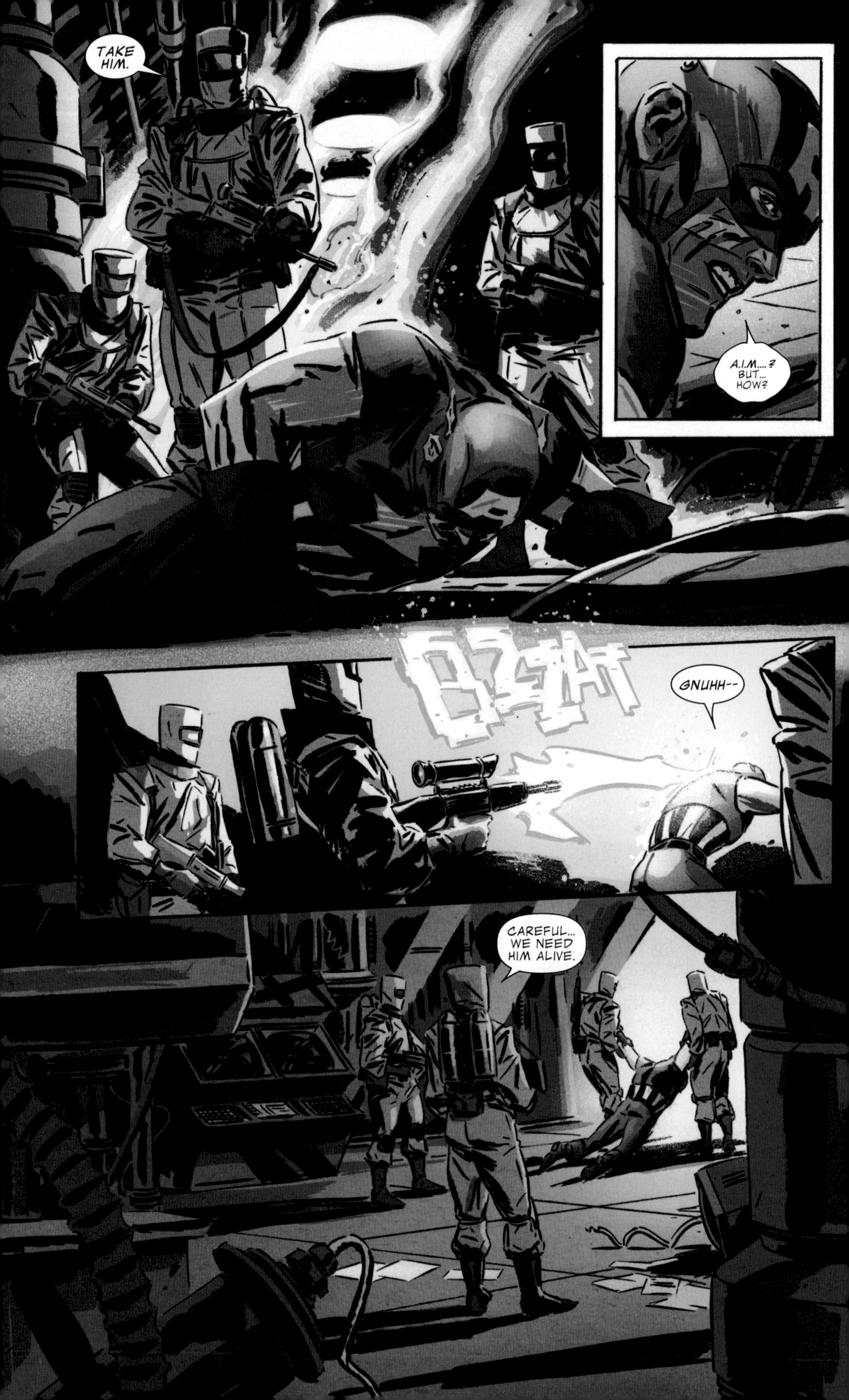
TAKE HIM.
A.I.M....? BUT... HOW?
BZZAT
GNUHH--
CAREFUL... WE NEED HIM ALIVE.

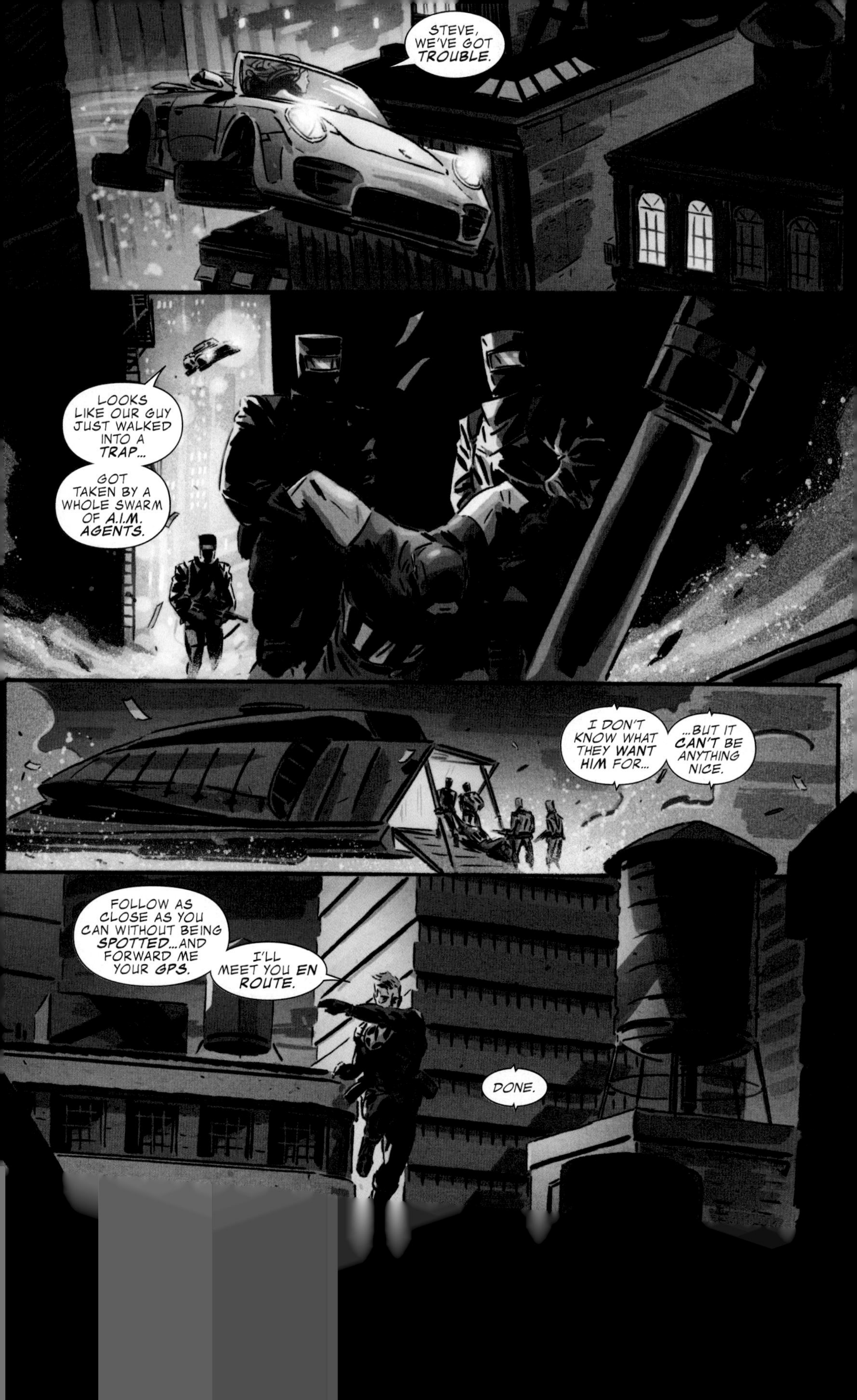
STEVE, WE'VE GOT TROUBLE.
LOOKS LIKE OUR GUY JUST WALKED INTO A TRAP...
GOT TAKEN BY A WHOLE SWARM OF A.I.M. AGENTS.
I DON'T KNOW WHAT THEY WANT HIM FOR...
...BUT IT CAN'T BE ANYTHING NICE.
FOLLOW AS CLOSE AS YOU CAN WITHOUT BEING SPOTTED...AND FORWARD ME YOUR GPS.
I'LL MEET YOU EN ROUTE.
DONE.

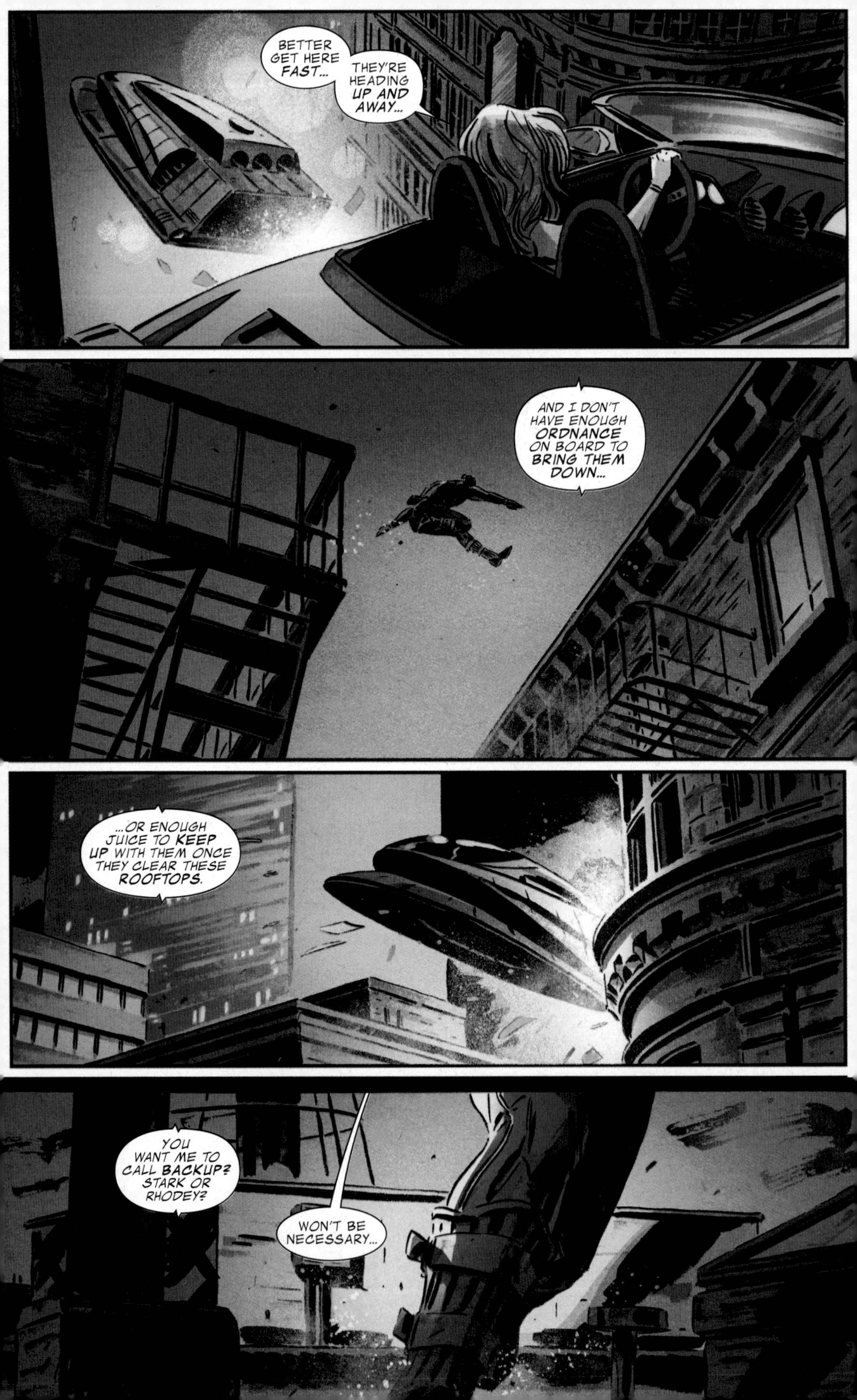
BETTER GET HERE FAST...
THEY'RE HEADING UP AND AWAY...
AND I DON'T HAVE ENOUGH ORDNANCE ON BOARD TO BRING THEM DOWN...
...OR ENOUGH JUICE TO KEEP UP WITH THEM ONCE THEY CLEAR THESE ROOFTOPS.
YOU WANT ME TO CALL BACKUP? STARK OR RHODEY?
WON'T BE NECESSARY...

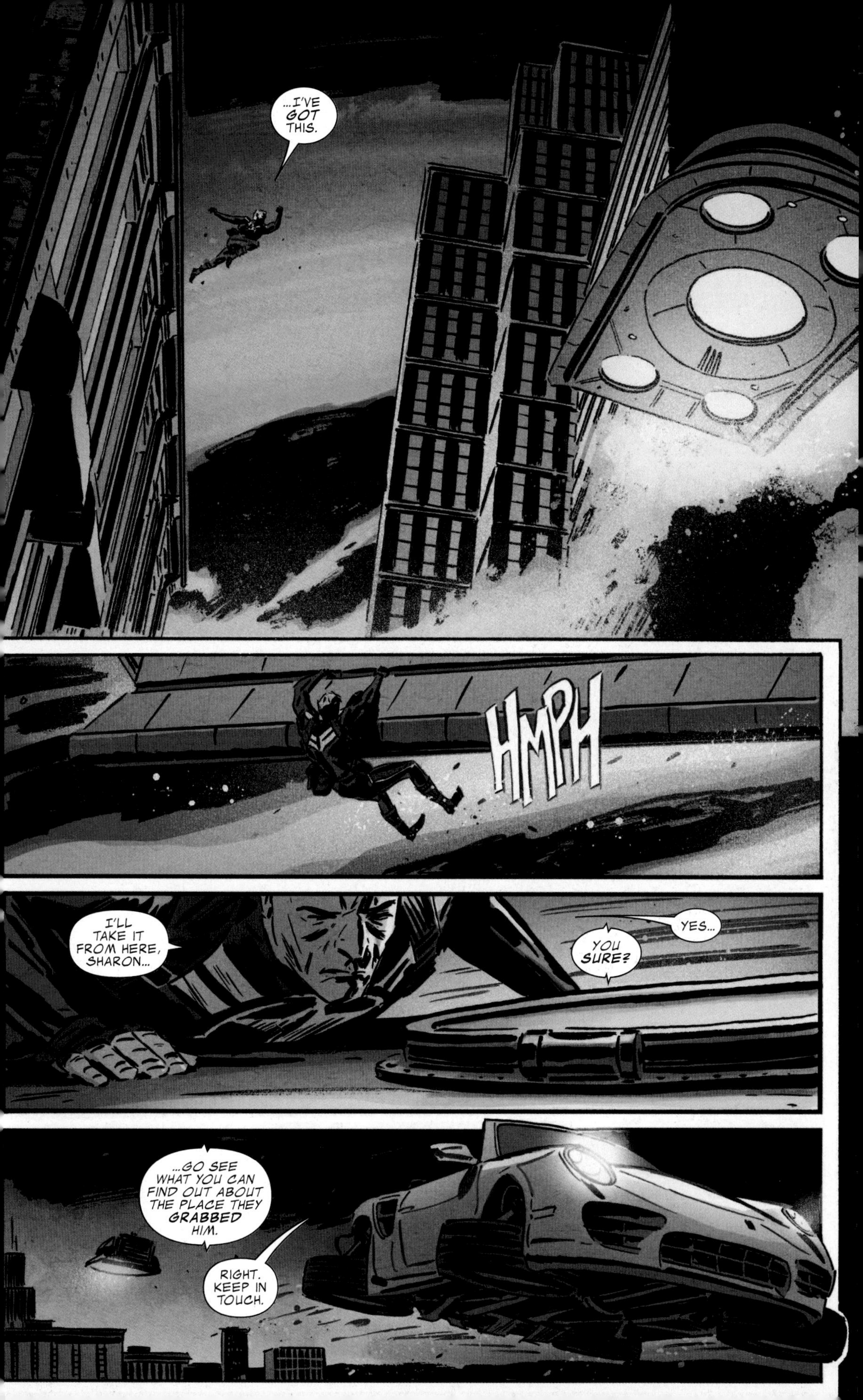
...I'VE GOT THIS.
HMPH
I'LL TAKE IT FROM HERE, SHARON...
YOU SURE?
YES...
...GO SEE WHAT YOU CAN FIND OUT ABOUT THE PLACE THEY GRABBED HIM.
RIGHT. KEEP IN TOUCH.

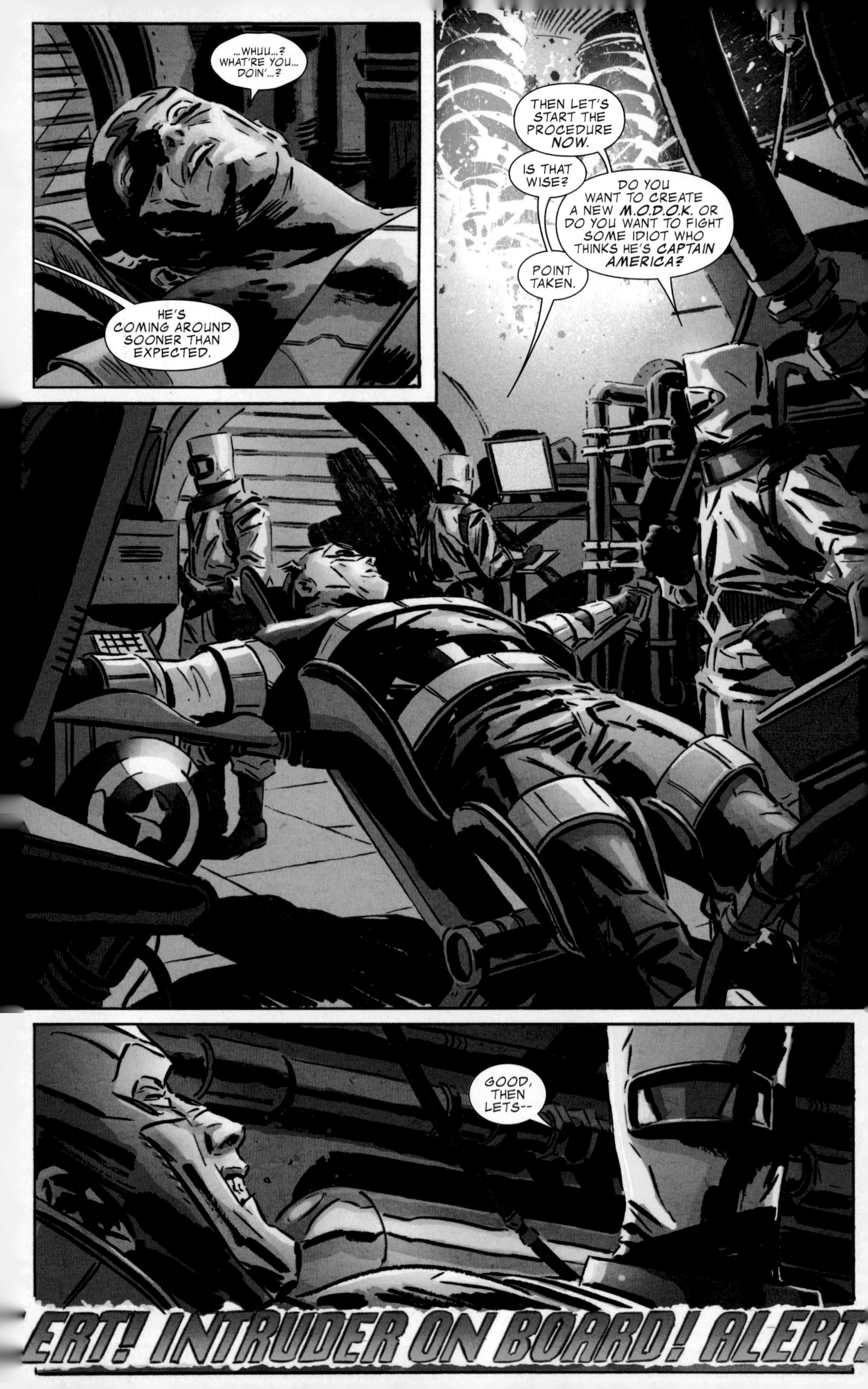
...WHUU...?
WHAT'RE YOU...
DOIN'...?
HE'S COMING AROUND SOONER THAN EXPECTED.
THEN LET'S START THE PROCEDURE NOW.
IS THAT WISE?
DO YOU WANT TO CREATE A NEW M.O.D.O.K. OR DO YOU WANT TO FIGHT SOME IDIOT WHO THINKS HE'S CAPTAIN AMERICA?
POINT TAKEN.
GOOD, THEN LETS--
ERT! INTRUDER ON BOARD! ALERT!

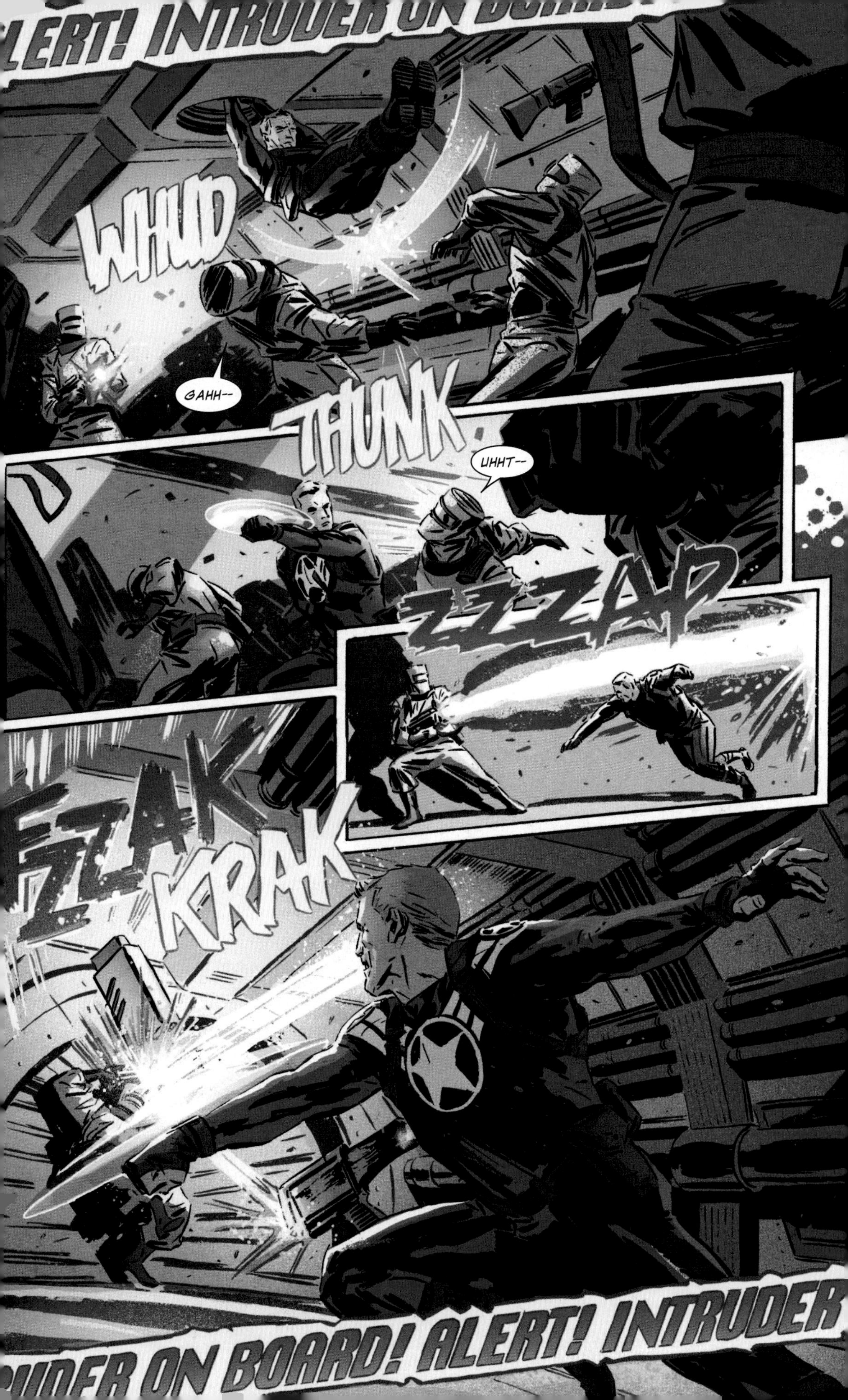
ALERT! INTRUDER ON BOARD!
WHUD
GAHH--
THUNK
UHHT--
ZZZAP
ZZAK
KRAK
UDER ON BOARD! ALERT! INTRUDER

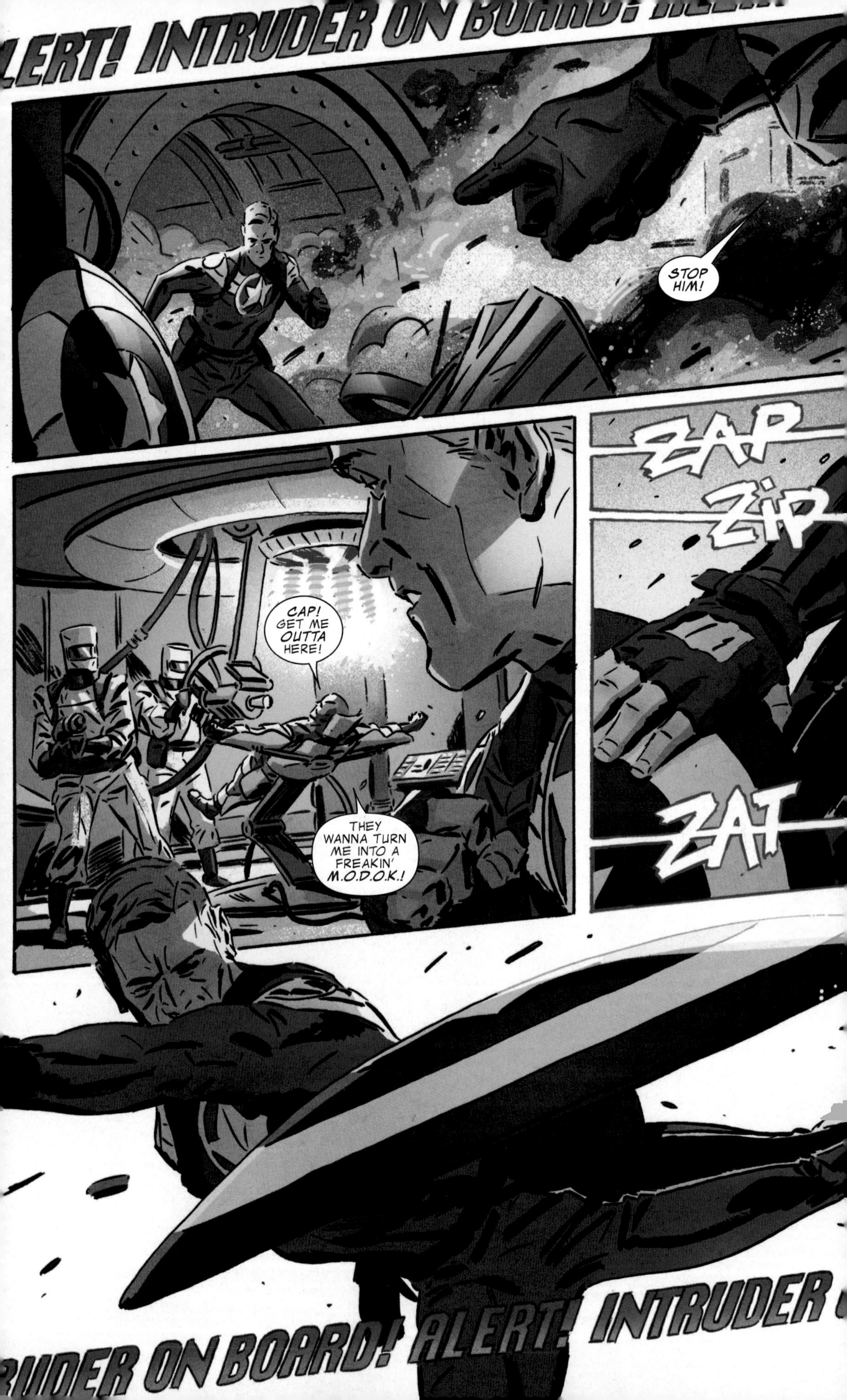
LERT! INTRUDER ON
STOP HIM!
CAP! GET ME OUTTA HERE!
THEY WANNA TURN ME INTO A FREAKIN' M.O.D.O.K.!
ZAP
ZIP
ZAT
RUDER ON BOARD! ALERT! INTRUDER

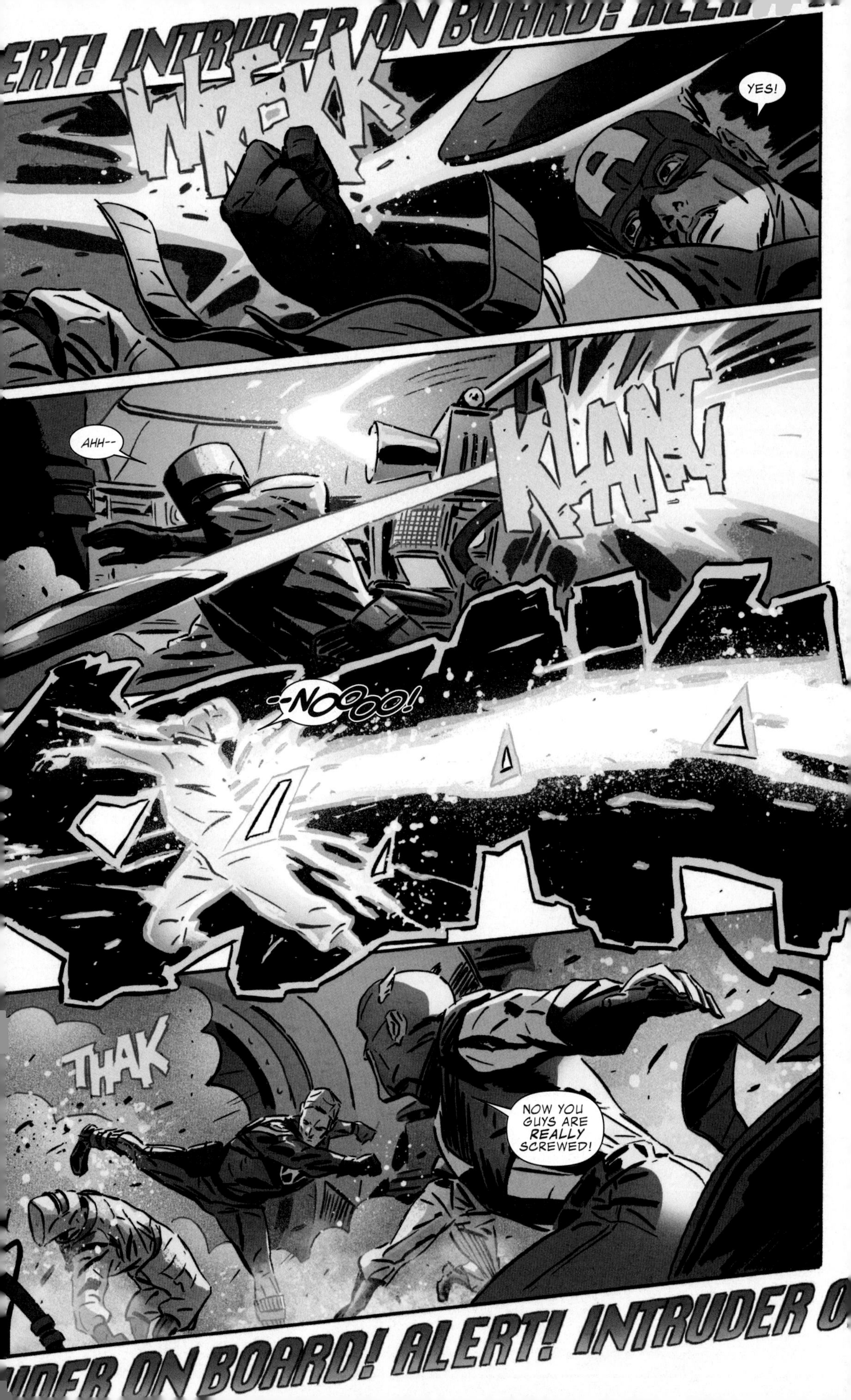
ERT! INTRUDER ON BOARD!
WHAKK
YES!
AHH--
KLANG
-NOOOOO!
THAK
NOW YOU GUYS ARE *REALLY* SCREWED!
UDER ON BOARD! ALERT! INTRUDER O

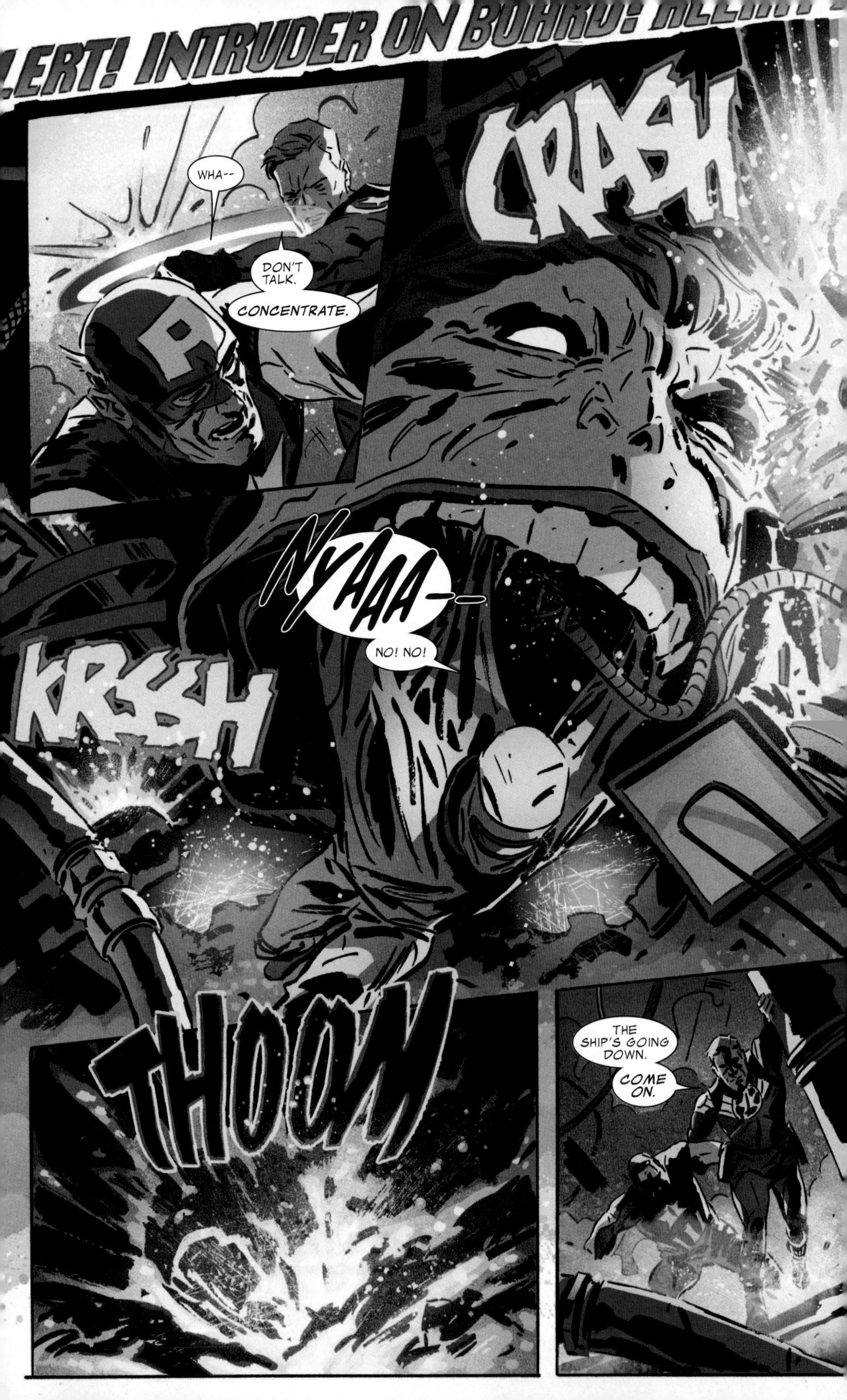

LERT! INTRUDER ON BOARD!
WHA--
DON'T TALK.
CONCENTRATE.
CRASH
NYAAA--
NO! NO!
KRSH
THOOM
THE SHIP'S GOING DOWN.
COME ON.

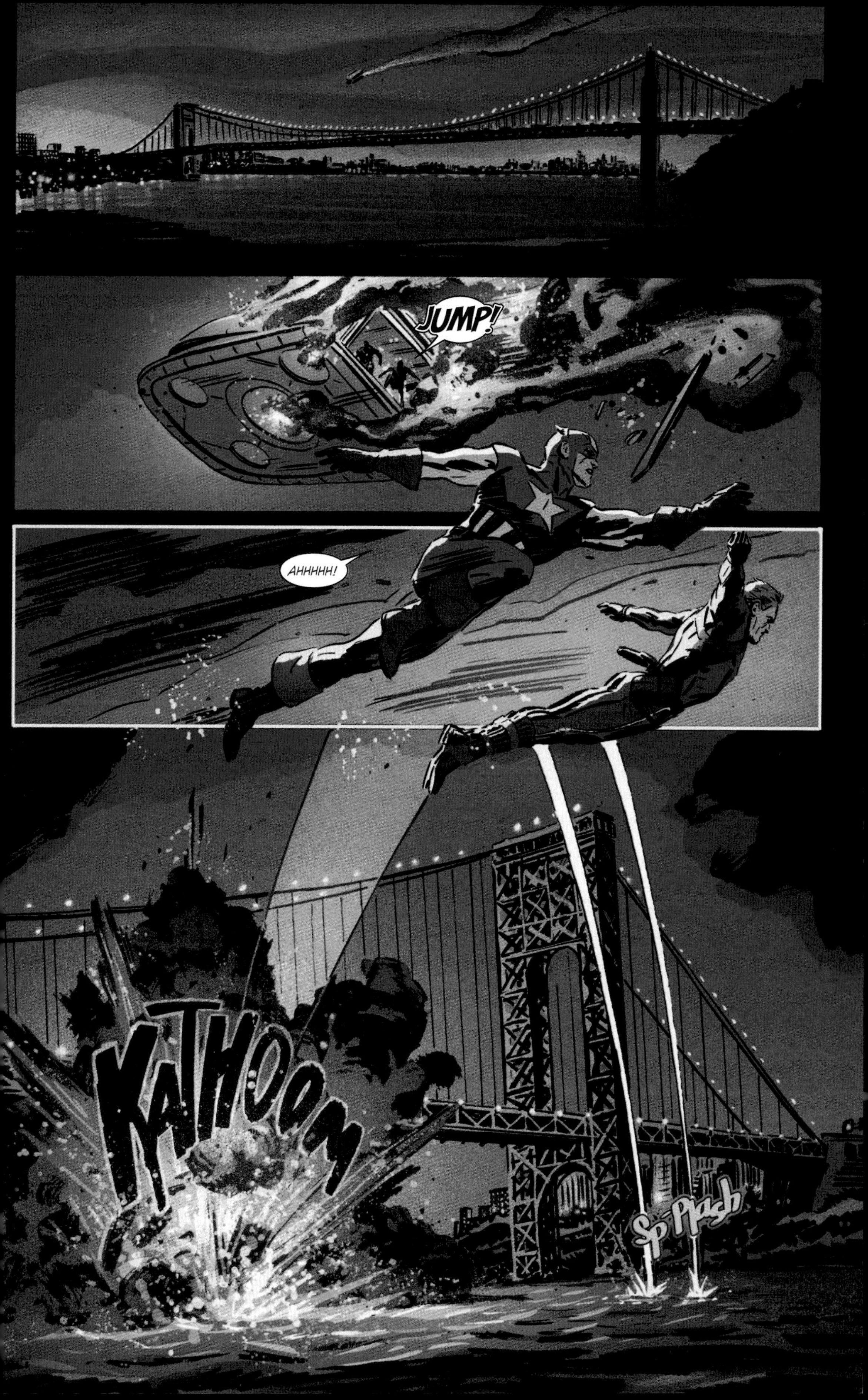

JUMP!
AHHHHH!
KATHOOM
Sp-Plash

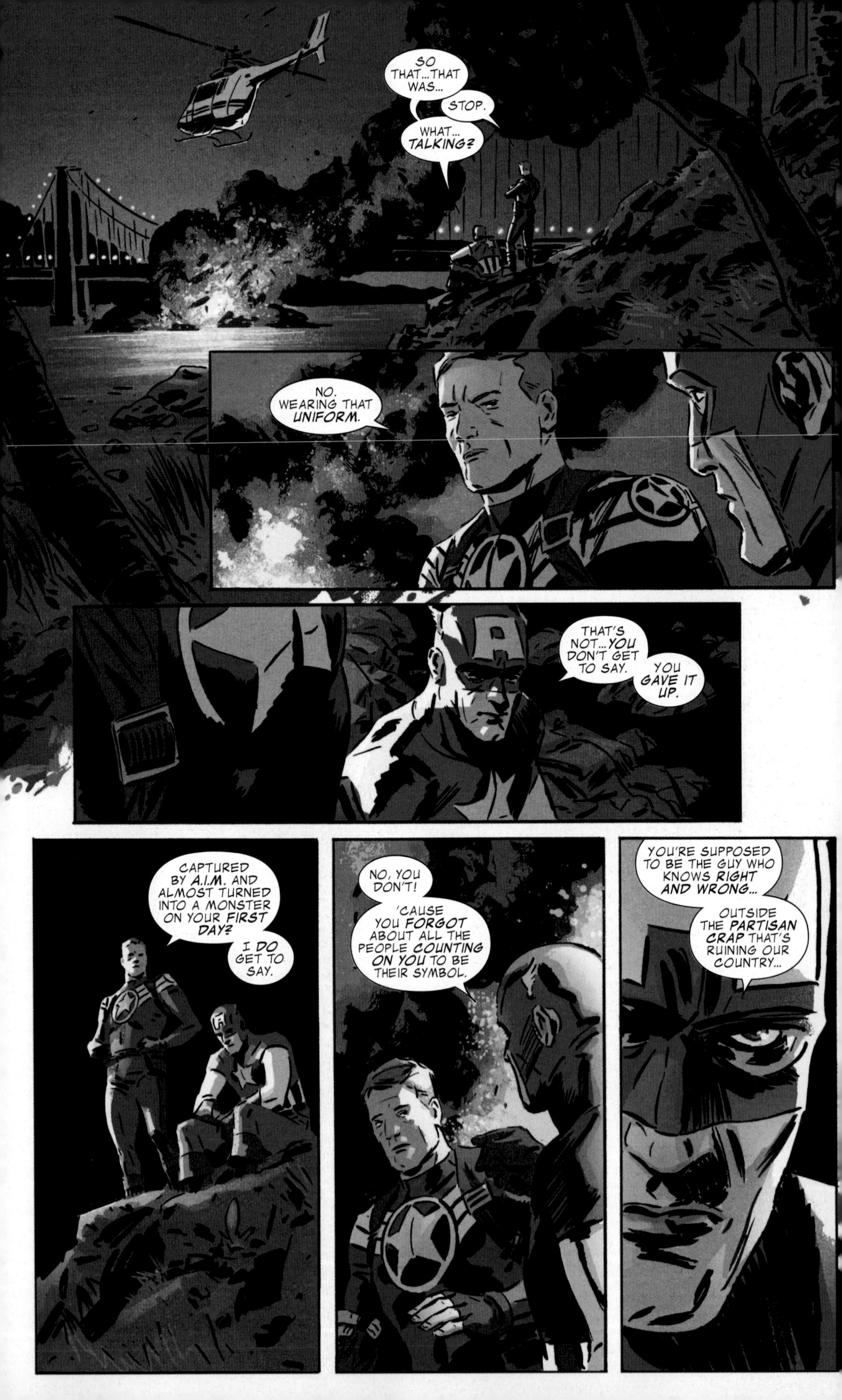

SO THAT...THAT WAS...
STOP.
WHAT... TALKING?
NO. WEARING THAT UNIFORM.
THAT'S NOT...YOU DON'T GET TO SAY.
YOU GAVE IT UP.
CAPTURED BY A.I.M. AND ALMOST TURNED INTO A MONSTER ON YOUR FIRST DAY?
I DO GET TO SAY.
NO, YOU DON'T!
'CAUSE YOU FORGOT ABOUT ALL THE PEOPLE COUNTING ON YOU TO BE THEIR SYMBOL.
YOU'RE SUPPOSED TO BE THE GUY WHO KNOWS RIGHT AND WRONG...
OUTSIDE THE PARTISAN CRAP THAT'S RUINING OUR COUNTRY...

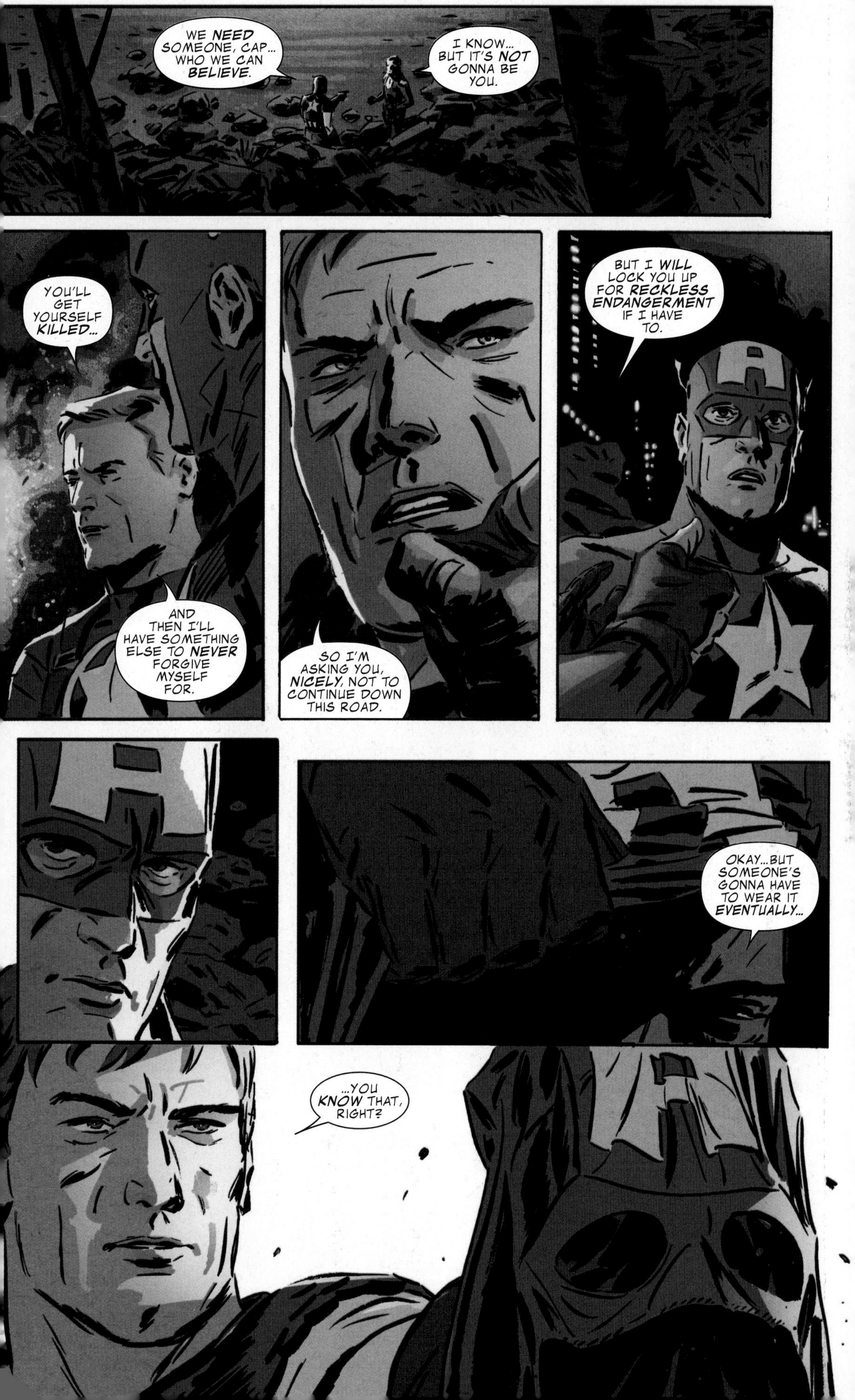
WE NEED SOMEONE, CAP... WHO WE CAN BELIEVE.
I KNOW... BUT IT'S NOT GONNA BE YOU.
YOU'LL GET YOURSELF KILLED...
AND THEN I'LL HAVE SOMETHING ELSE TO NEVER FORGIVE MYSELF FOR.
SO I'M ASKING YOU, NICELY, NOT TO CONTINUE DOWN THIS ROAD.
BUT I WILL LOCK YOU UP FOR RECKLESS ENDANGERMENT IF I HAVE TO.
OKAY...BUT SOMEONE'S GONNA HAVE TO WEAR IT EVENTUALLY...
...YOU KNOW THAT, RIGHT?

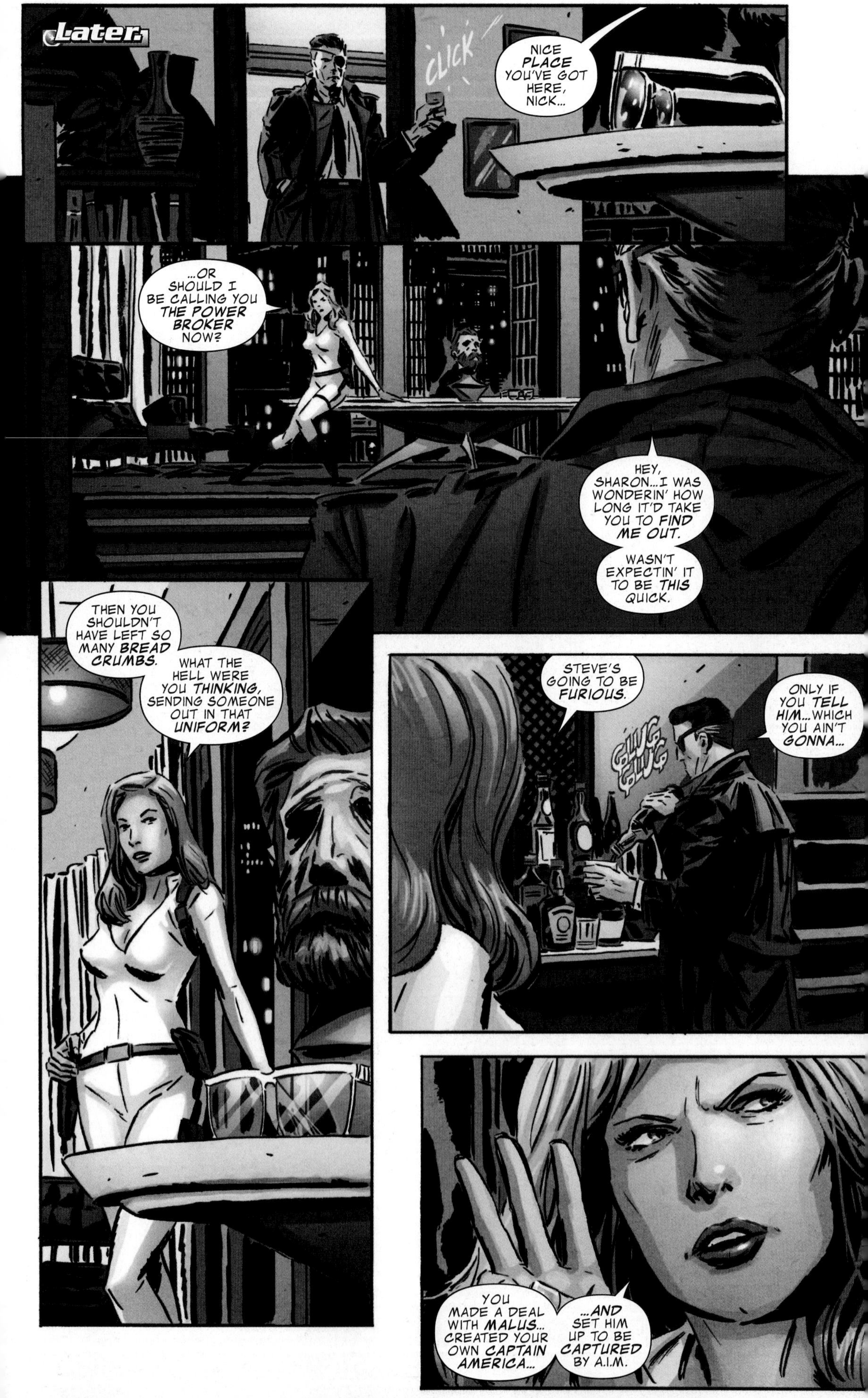
Later.
CLICK
NICE PLACE YOU'VE GOT HERE, NICK...
...OR SHOULD I BE CALLING YOU THE POWER BROKER NOW?
HEY, SHARON...I WAS WONDERIN' HOW LONG IT'D TAKE YOU TO FIND ME OUT.
WASN'T EXPECTIN' IT TO BE THIS QUICK.
THEN YOU SHOULDN'T HAVE LEFT SO MANY BREAD CRUMBS.
WHAT THE HELL WERE YOU THINKING, SENDING SOMEONE OUT IN THAT UNIFORM?
STEVE'S GOING TO BE FURIOUS.
GLUG GLUG
ONLY IF YOU TELL HIM...WHICH YOU AIN'T GONNA...
YOU MADE A DEAL WITH MALUS... CREATED YOUR OWN CAPTAIN AMERICA...
...AND SET HIM UP TO BE CAPTURED BY A.I.M.

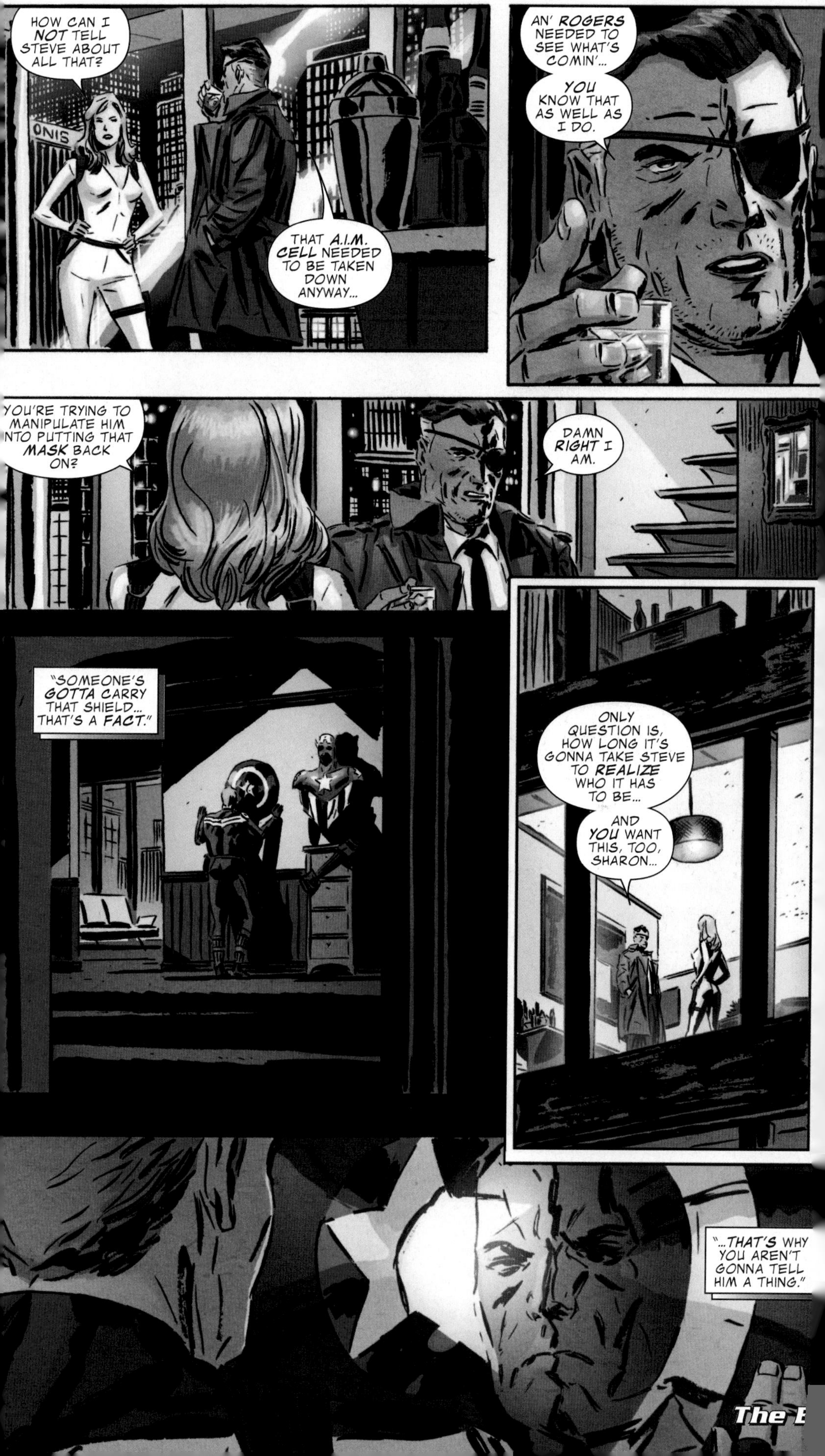

HOW CAN I NOT TELL STEVE ABOUT ALL THAT?
ONIS
THAT A.I.M. CELL NEEDED TO BE TAKEN DOWN ANYWAY...
AN' ROGERS NEEDED TO SEE WHAT'S COMIN'...
YOU KNOW THAT AS WELL AS I DO.
YOU'RE TRYING TO MANIPULATE HIM NTO PUTTING THAT MASK BACK ON?
DAMN RIGHT I AM.
"SOMEONE'S GOTTA CARRY THAT SHIELD... THAT'S A FACT."
ONLY QUESTION IS, HOW LONG IT'S GONNA TAKE STEVE TO REALIZE WHO IT HAS TO BE...
AND YOU WANT THIS, TOO, SHARON...
"...THAT'S WHY YOU AREN'T GONNA TELL HIM A THING."
The E

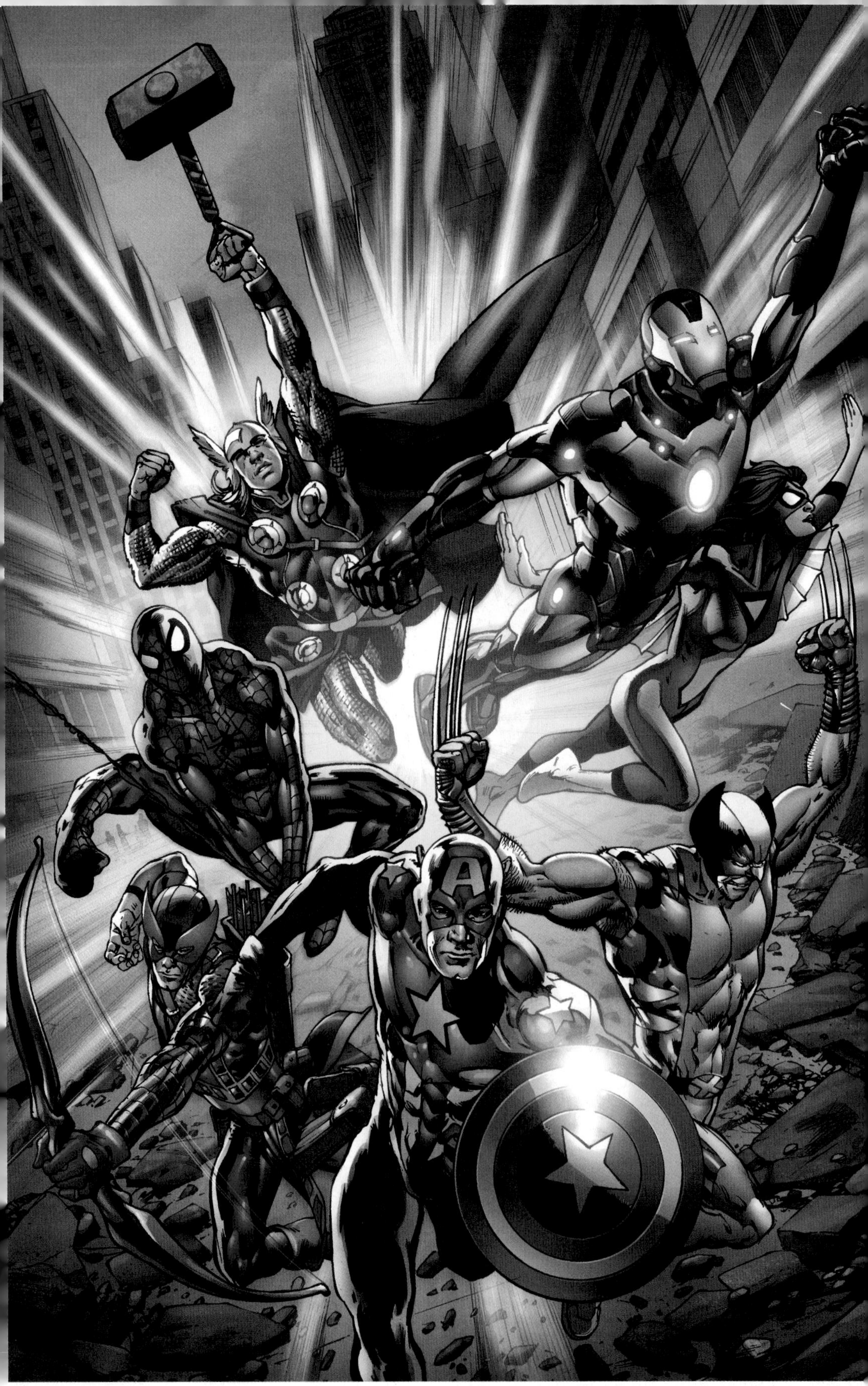

AVENGERS #12.1

EARTH'S MIGHTIEST HEROES, UNITED AGAINST A COMMON THREAT! ON THAT DAY THE AVENGERS WERE BORN, TO FIGHT FOES THAT NO SINGLE HERO COULD WITHSTAND!

THE AVENGERS

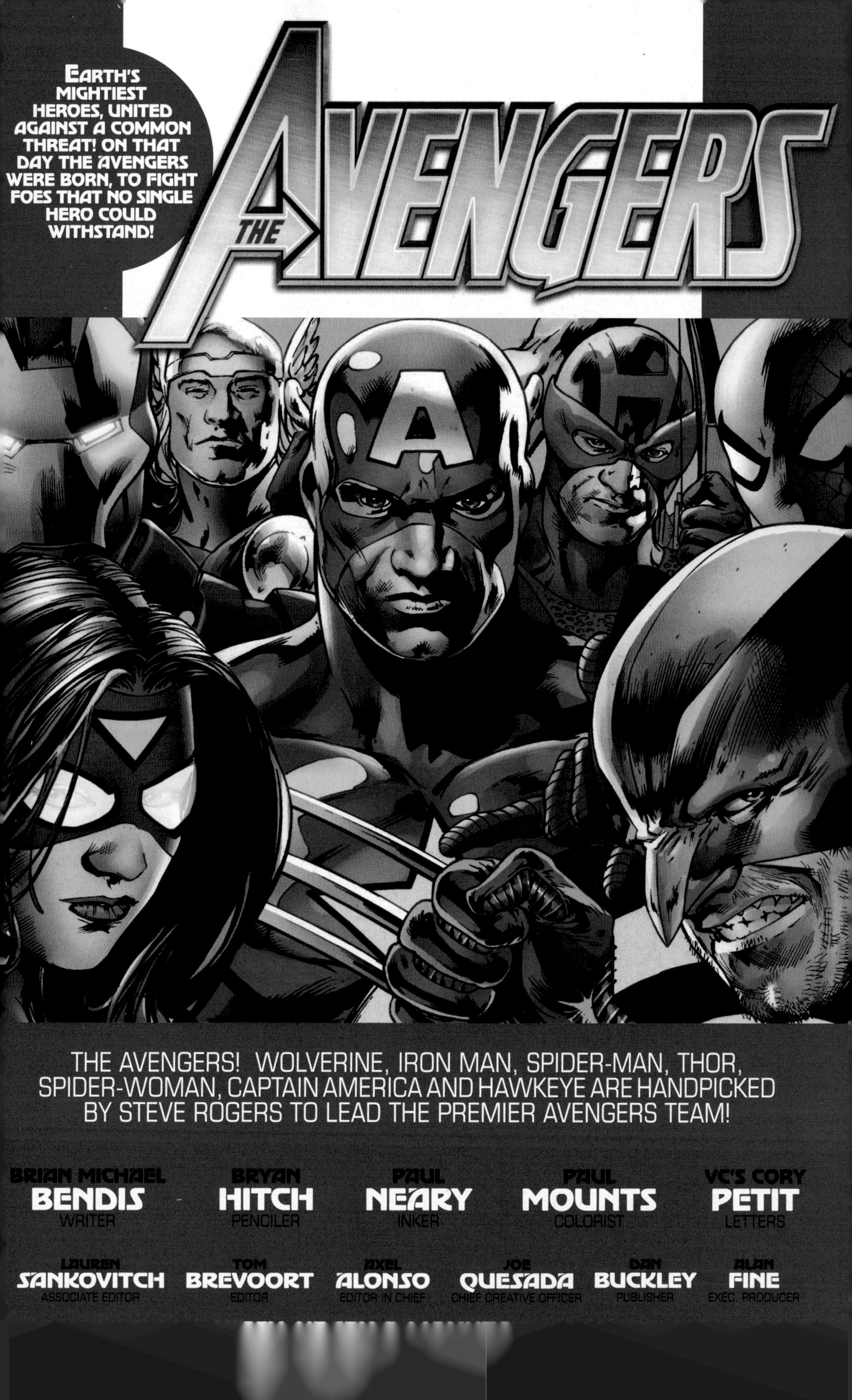

THE AVENGERS! WOLVERINE, IRON MAN, SPIDER-MAN, THOR, SPIDER-WOMAN, CAPTAIN AMERICA AND HAWKEYE ARE HANDPICKED BY STEVE ROGERS TO LEAD THE PREMIER AVENGERS TEAM!

BRIAN MICHAEL **BENDIS** WRITER

BRYAN **HITCH** PENCILER

PAUL **NEARY** INKER

PAUL **MOUNTS** COLORIST

VC'S CORY **PETIT** LETTERS

LAUREN **SANKOVITCH** ASSOCIATE EDITOR

TOM **BREVOORT** EDITOR

AXEL **ALONSO** EDITOR IN CHIEF

JOE **QUESADA** CHIEF CREATIVE OFFICER

DAN **BUCKLEY** PUBLISHER

ALAN **FINE** EXEC. PRODUCER

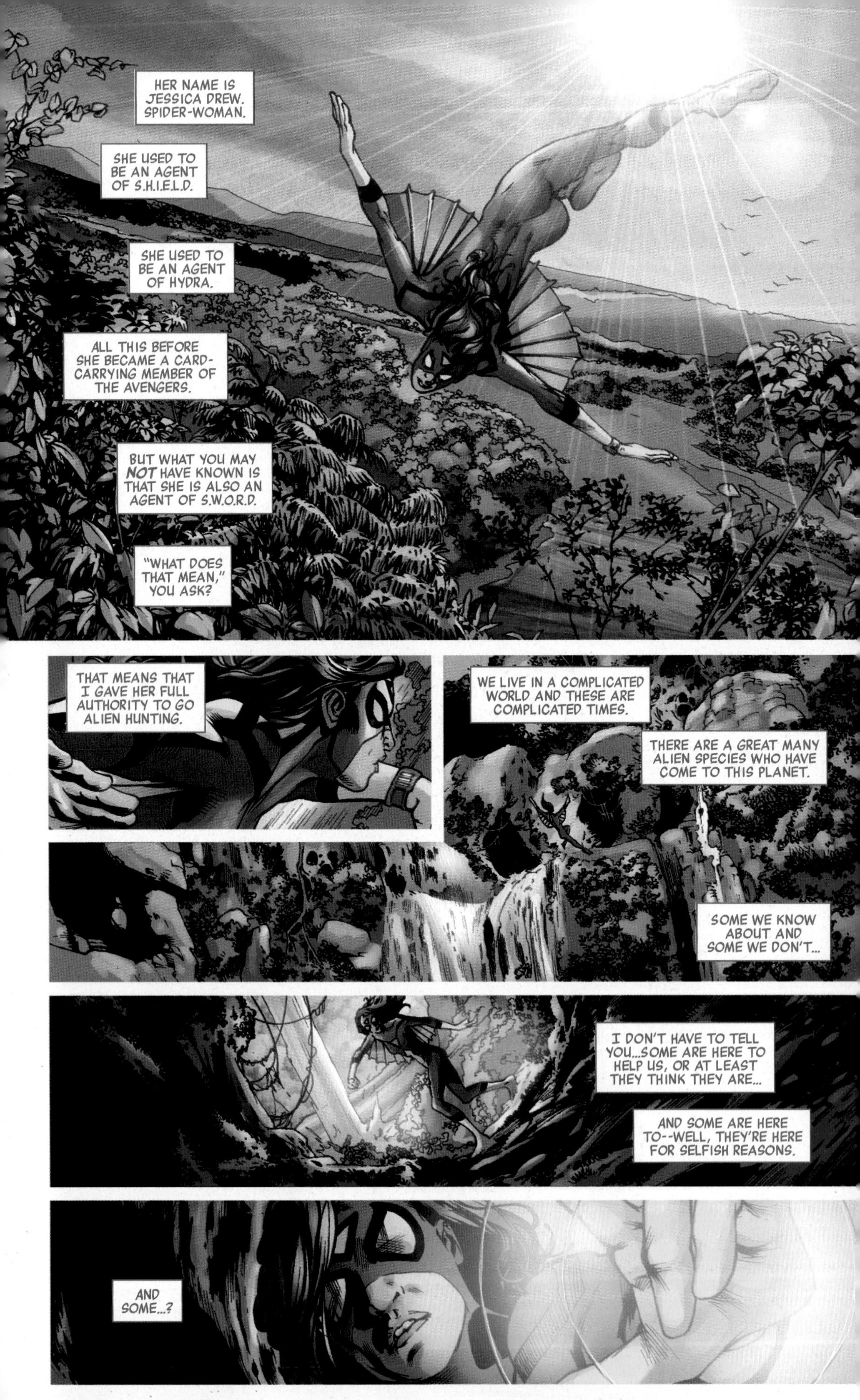
HER NAME IS JESSICA DREW. SPIDER-WOMAN.
SHE USED TO BE AN AGENT OF S.H.I.E.L.D.
SHE USED TO BE AN AGENT OF HYDRA.
ALL THIS BEFORE SHE BECAME A CARD-CARRYING MEMBER OF THE AVENGERS.
BUT WHAT YOU MAY ***NOT*** HAVE KNOWN IS THAT SHE IS ALSO AN AGENT OF S.W.O.R.D.
"WHAT DOES THAT MEAN," YOU ASK?
THAT MEANS THAT I GAVE HER FULL AUTHORITY TO GO ALIEN HUNTING.
WE LIVE IN A COMPLICATED WORLD AND THESE ARE COMPLICATED TIMES.
THERE ARE A GREAT MANY ALIEN SPECIES WHO HAVE COME TO THIS PLANET.
SOME WE KNOW ABOUT AND SOME WE DON'T...
I DON'T HAVE TO TELL YOU...SOME ARE HERE TO HELP US, OR AT LEAST THEY THINK THEY ARE...
AND SOME ARE HERE TO--WELL, THEY'RE HERE FOR SELFISH REASONS.
AND SOME...?

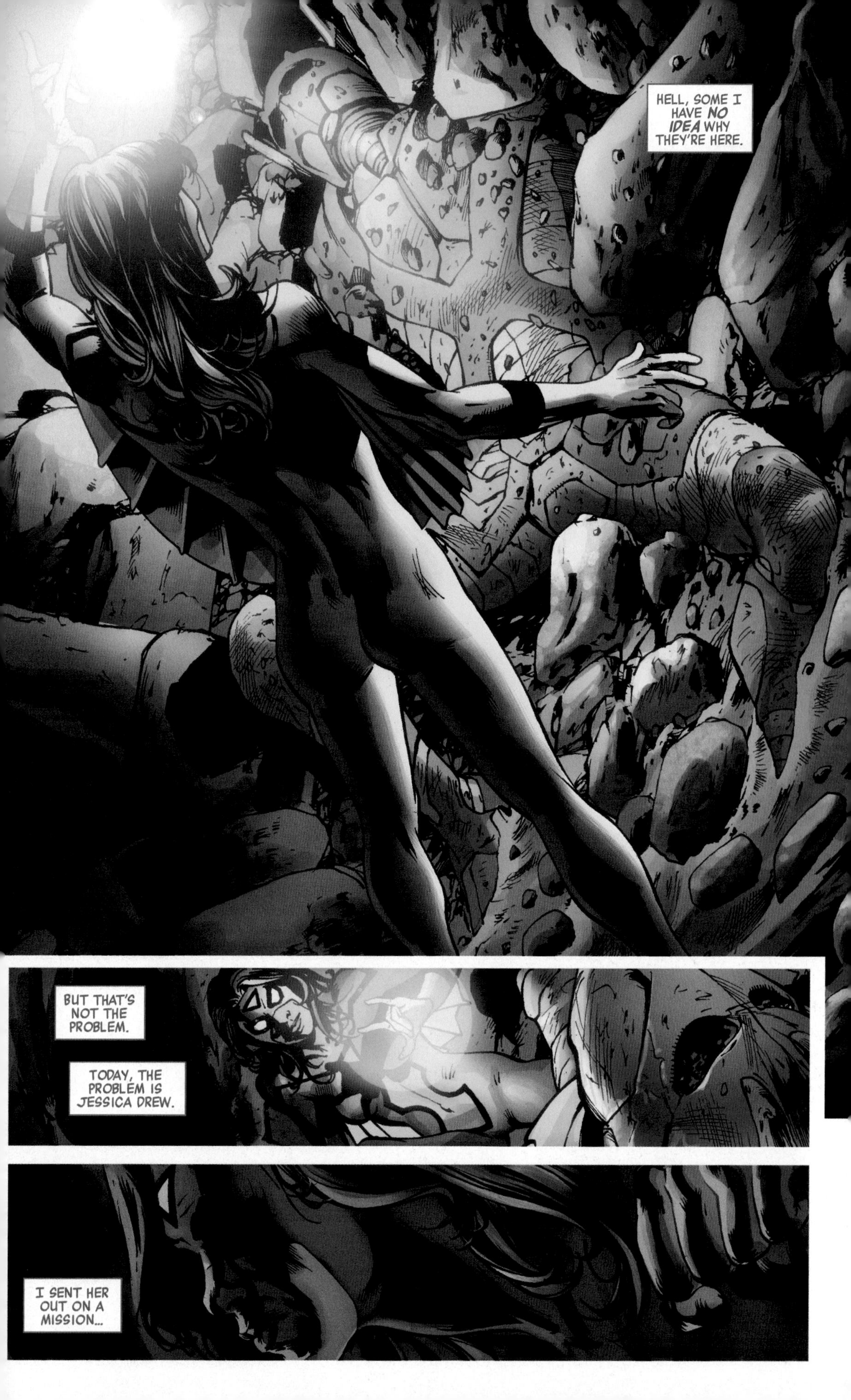
HELL, SOME I HAVE NO IDEA WHY THEY'RE HERE.
BUT THAT'S NOT THE PROBLEM.
TODAY, THE PROBLEM IS JESSICA DREW.
I SENT HER OUT ON A MISSION...

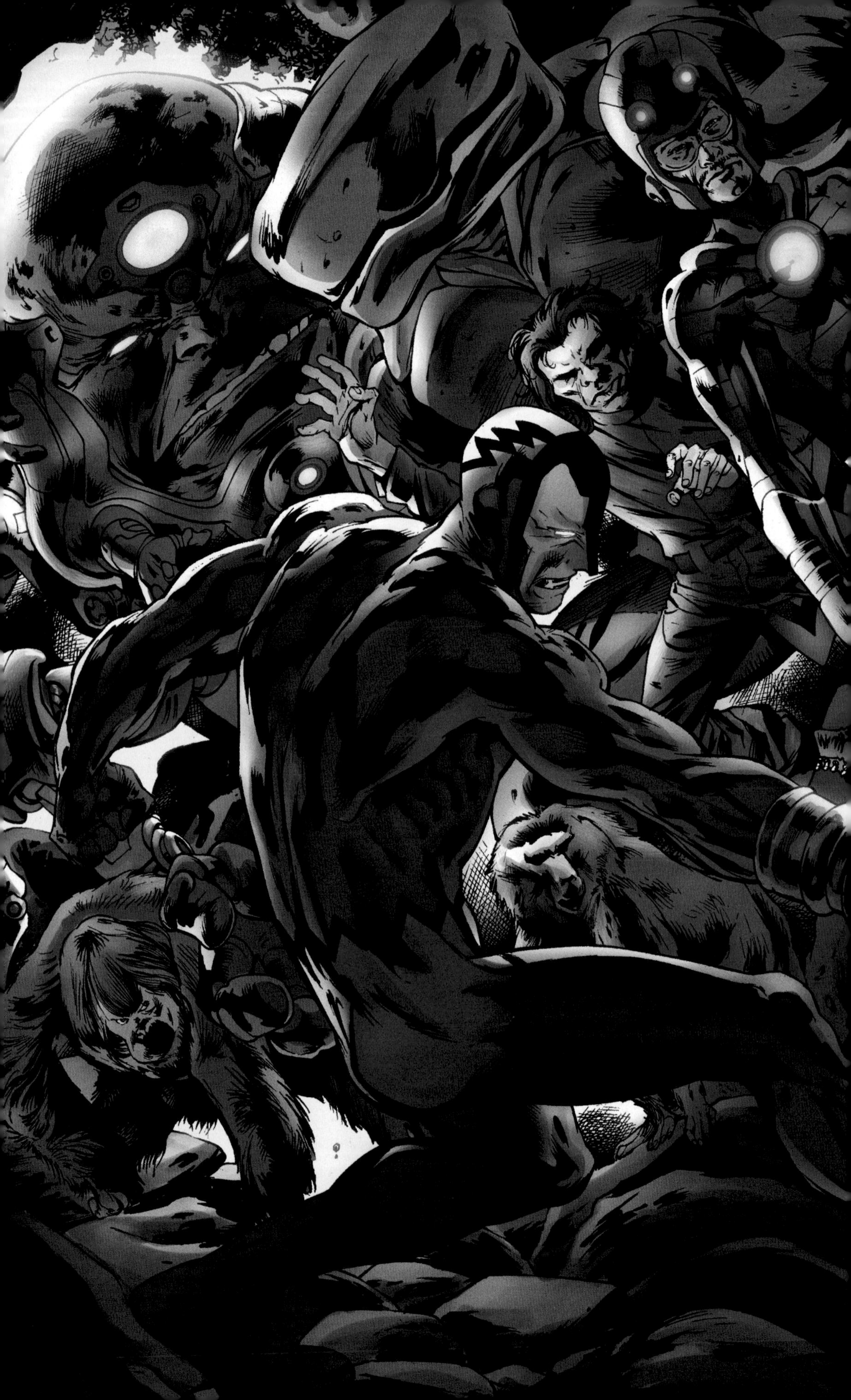

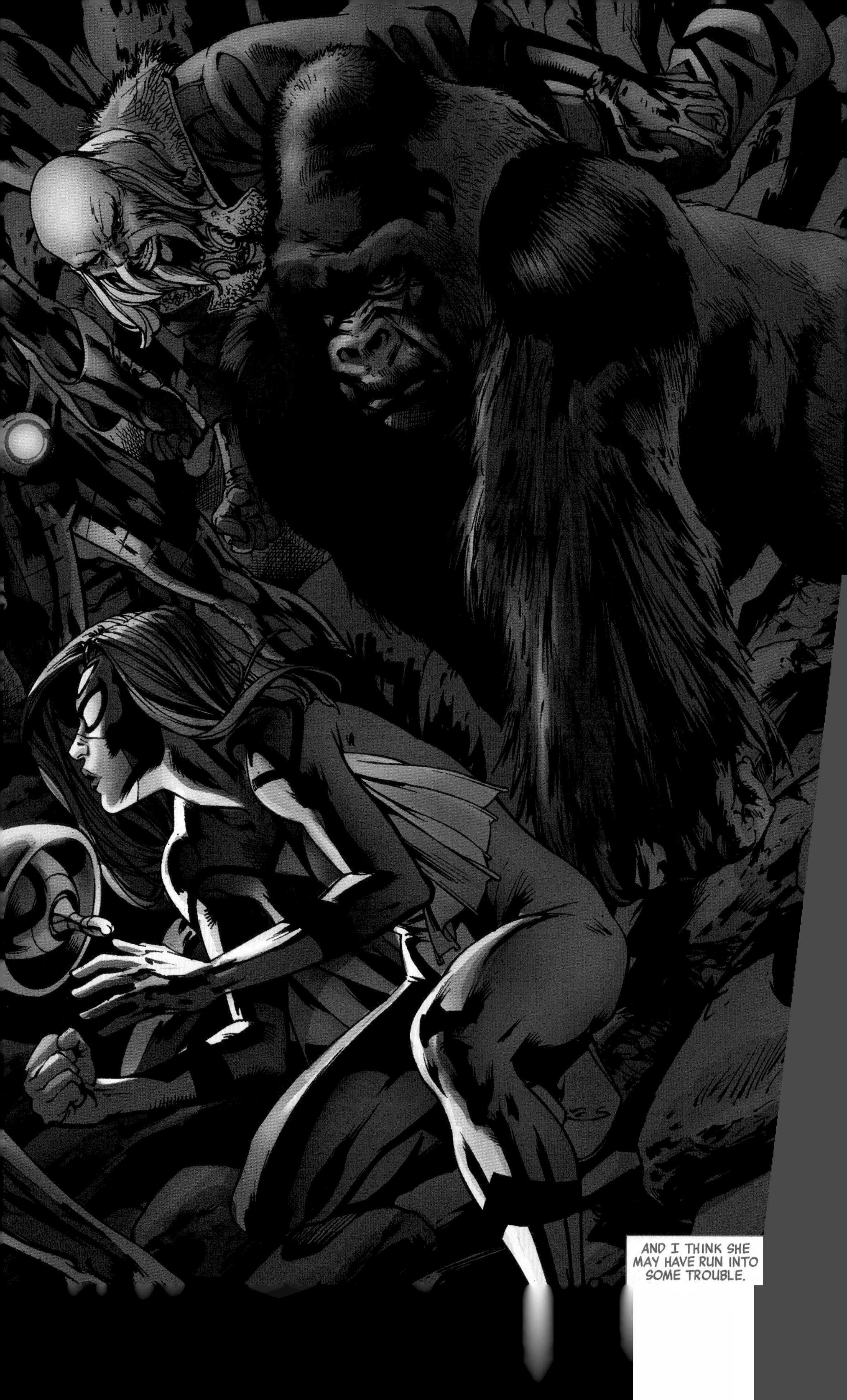
AND I THINK SHE MAY HAVE RUN INTO SOME TROUBLE.

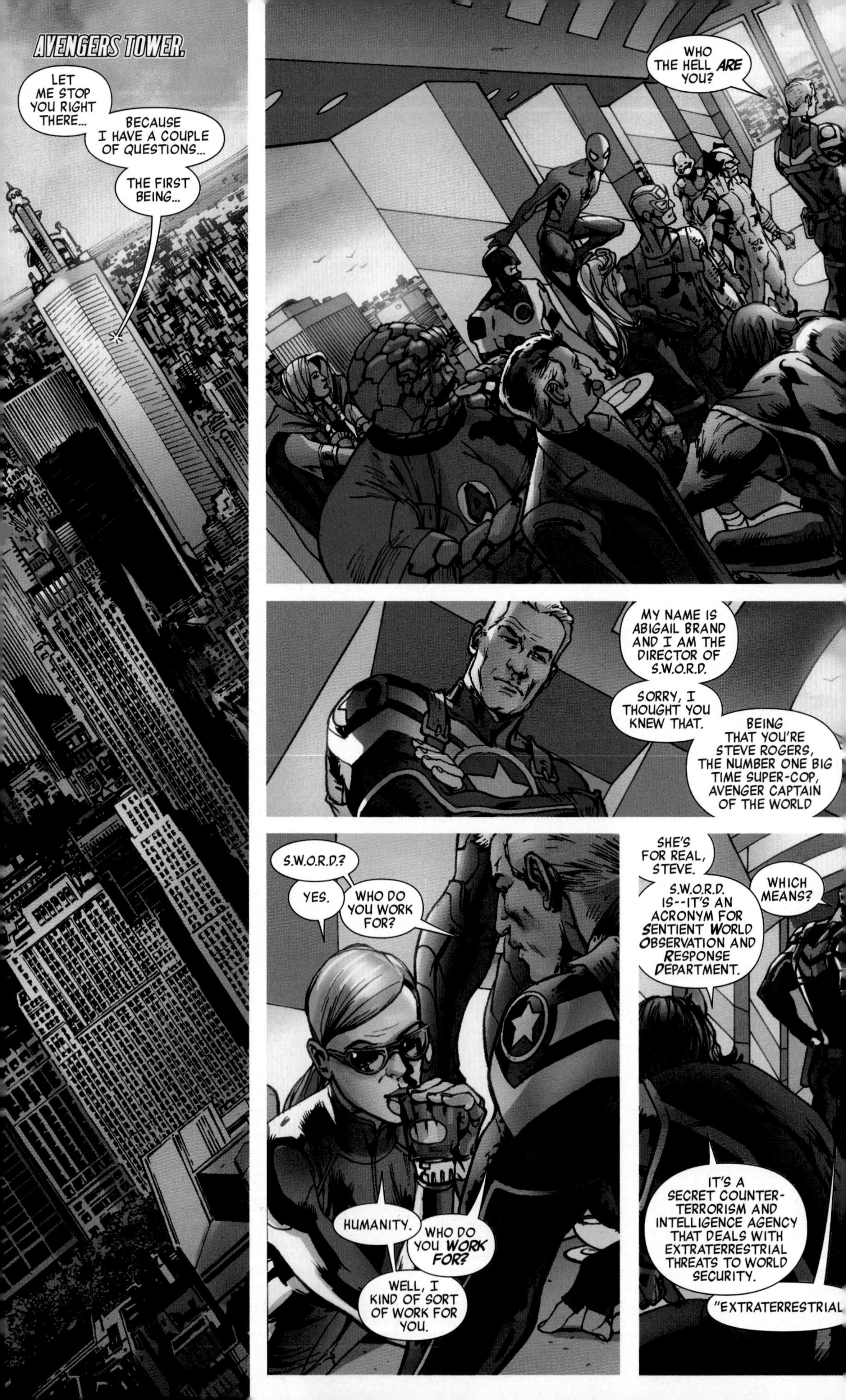
AVENGERS TOWER.
LET ME STOP YOU RIGHT THERE...
BECAUSE I HAVE A COUPLE OF QUESTIONS...
THE FIRST BEING...
WHO THE HELL ARE YOU?
MY NAME IS ABIGAIL BRAND AND I AM THE DIRECTOR OF S.W.O.R.D.
SORRY, I THOUGHT YOU KNEW THAT.
BEING THAT YOU'RE STEVE ROGERS, THE NUMBER ONE BIG TIME SUPER-COP, AVENGER CAPTAIN OF THE WORLD
S.W.O.R.D.?
YES.
WHO DO YOU WORK FOR?
HUMANITY.
WHO DO YOU WORK FOR?
WELL, I KIND OF SORT OF WORK FOR YOU.
SHE'S FOR REAL, STEVE.
S.W.O.R.D. IS--IT'S AN ACRONYM FOR SENTIENT WORLD OBSERVATION AND RESPONSE DEPARTMENT.
WHICH MEANS?
IT'S A SECRET COUNTER-TERRORISM AND INTELLIGENCE AGENCY THAT DEALS WITH EXTRATERRESTRIAL THREATS TO WORLD SECURITY.
"EXTRATERRESTRIAL

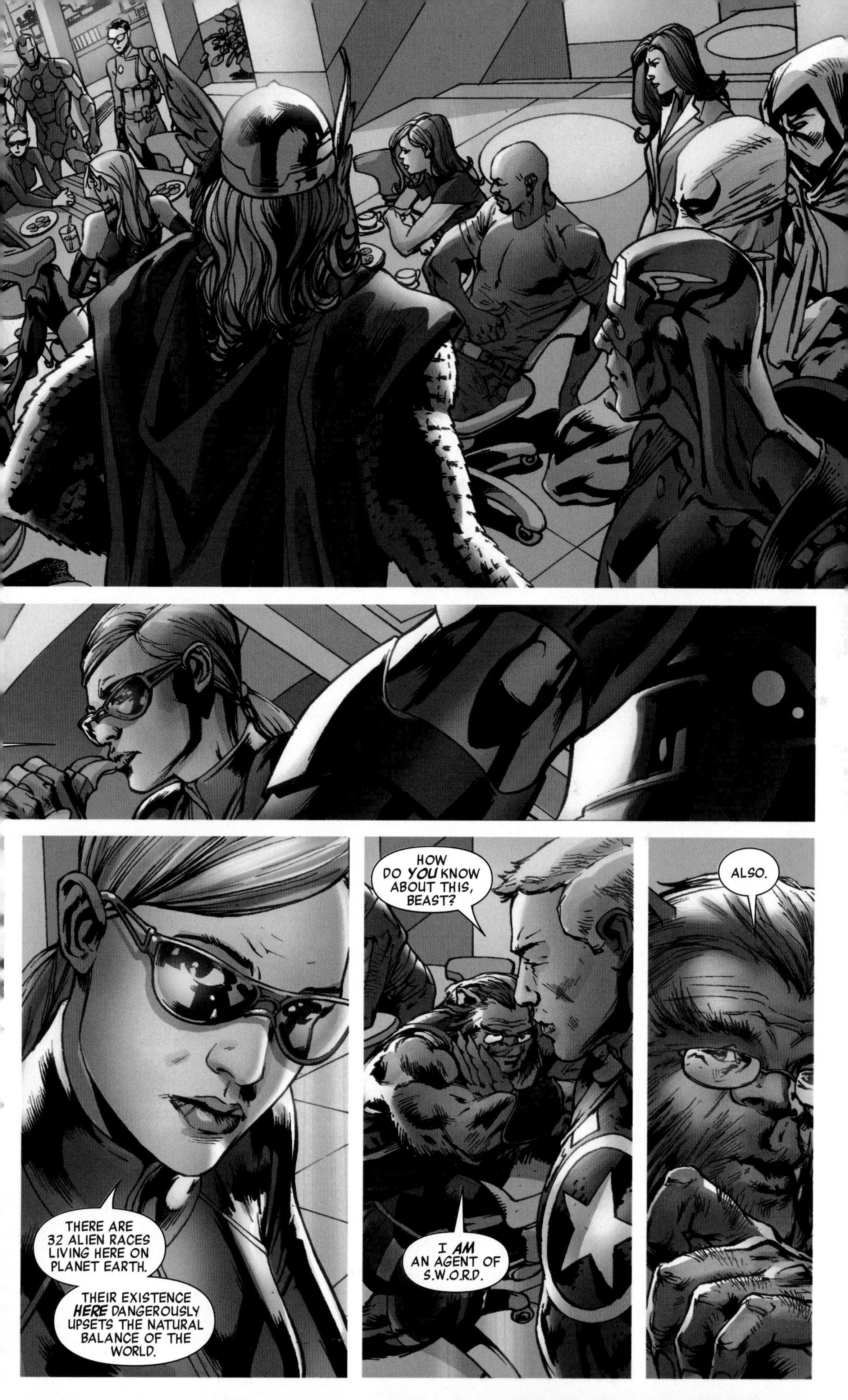
THERE ARE 32 ALIEN RACES LIVING HERE ON PLANET EARTH.
THEIR EXISTENCE HERE DANGEROUSLY UPSETS THE NATURAL BALANCE OF THE WORLD.
HOW DO YOU KNOW ABOUT THIS, BEAST?
I AM AN AGENT OF S.W.O.R.D.
ALSO.

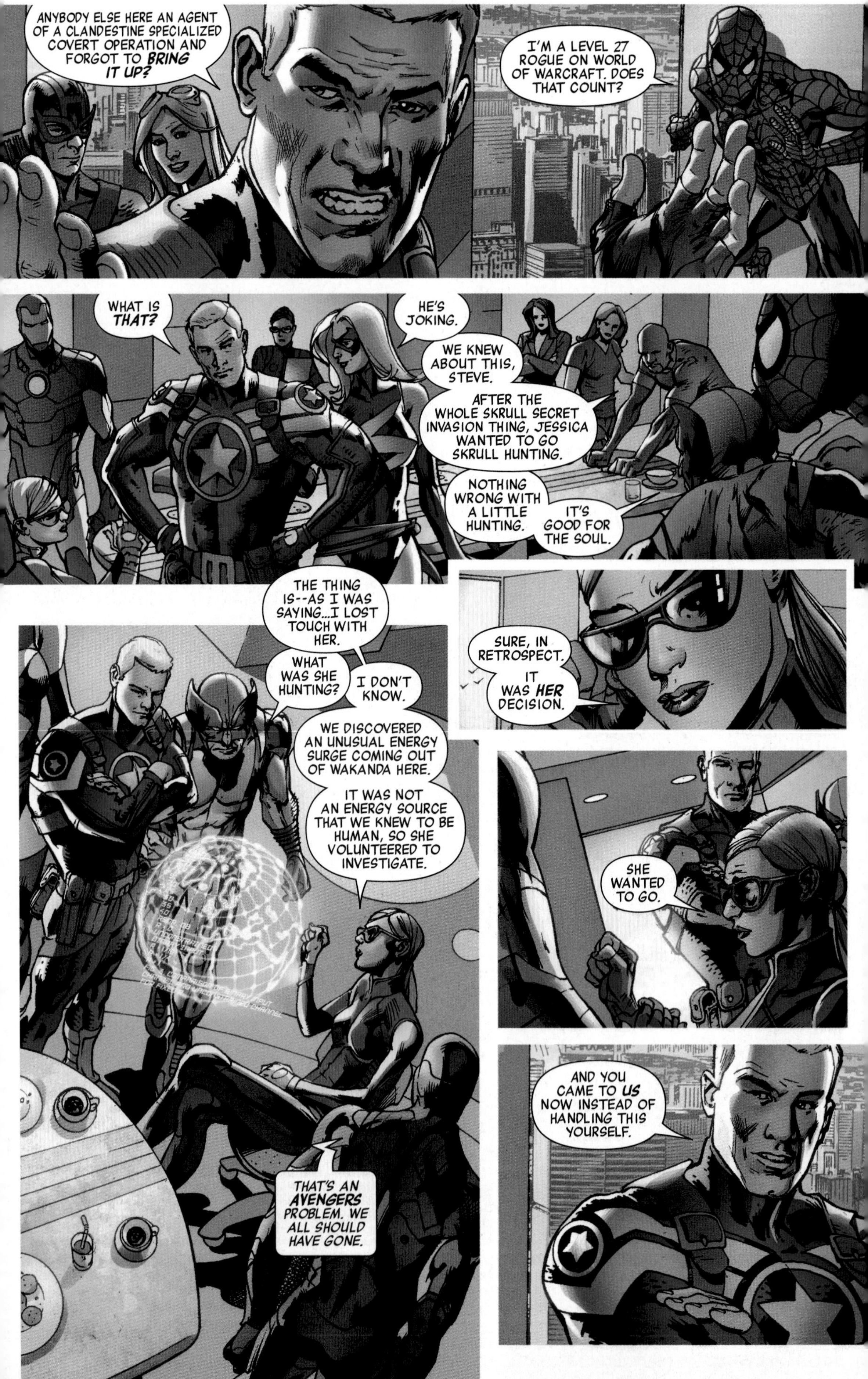

ANYBODY ELSE HERE AN AGENT OF A CLANDESTINE SPECIALIZED COVERT OPERATION AND FORGOT TO BRING IT UP?
I'M A LEVEL 27 ROGUE ON WORLD OF WARCRAFT. DOES THAT COUNT?
WHAT IS THAT?
HE'S JOKING.
WE KNEW ABOUT THIS, STEVE.
AFTER THE WHOLE SKRULL SECRET INVASION THING, JESSICA WANTED TO GO SKRULL HUNTING.
NOTHING WRONG WITH A LITTLE HUNTING.
IT'S GOOD FOR THE SOUL.
THE THING IS--AS I WAS SAYING...I LOST TOUCH WITH HER.
WHAT WAS SHE HUNTING?
I DON'T KNOW.
WE DISCOVERED AN UNUSUAL ENERGY SURGE COMING OUT OF WAKANDA HERE.
IT WAS NOT AN ENERGY SOURCE THAT WE KNEW TO BE HUMAN, SO SHE VOLUNTEERED TO INVESTIGATE.
THAT'S AN AVENGERS PROBLEM. WE ALL SHOULD HAVE GONE.
SURE, IN RETROSPECT.
IT WAS HER DECISION.
SHE WANTED TO GO.
AND YOU CAME TO US NOW INSTEAD OF HANDLING THIS YOURSELF.

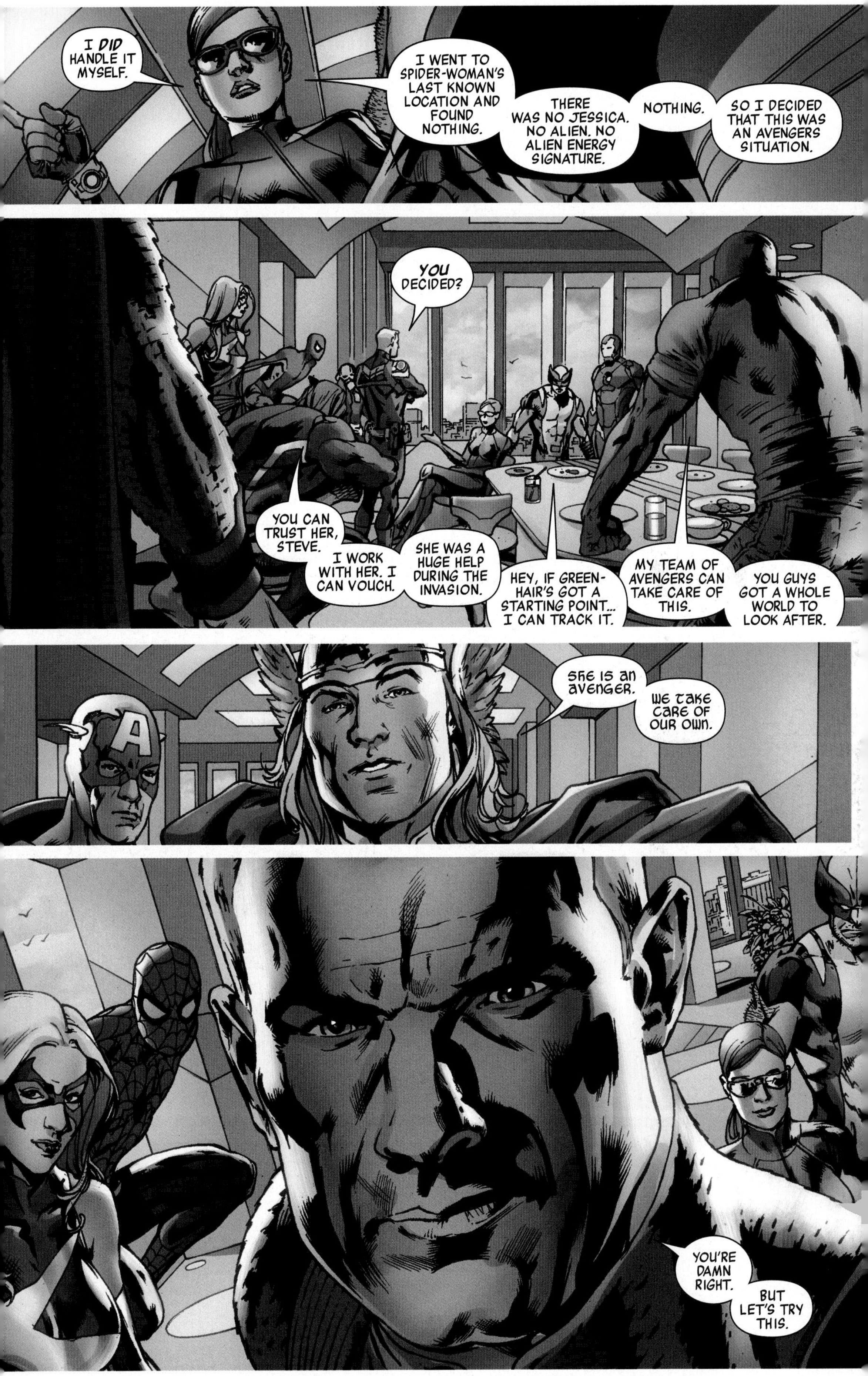
I DID HANDLE IT MYSELF.
I WENT TO SPIDER-WOMAN'S LAST KNOWN LOCATION AND FOUND NOTHING.
THERE WAS NO JESSICA. NO ALIEN. NO ALIEN ENERGY SIGNATURE.
NOTHING.
SO I DECIDED THAT THIS WAS AN AVENGERS SITUATION.
YOU DECIDED?
YOU CAN TRUST HER, STEVE.
I WORK WITH HER. I CAN VOUCH.
SHE WAS A HUGE HELP DURING THE INVASION.
HEY, IF GREEN-HAIR'S GOT A STARTING POINT... I CAN TRACK IT.
MY TEAM OF AVENGERS CAN TAKE CARE OF THIS.
YOU GUYS GOT A WHOLE WORLD TO LOOK AFTER.
SHE IS AN AVENGER.
WE TAKE CARE OF OUR OWN.
YOU'RE DAMN RIGHT.
BUT LET'S TRY THIS.

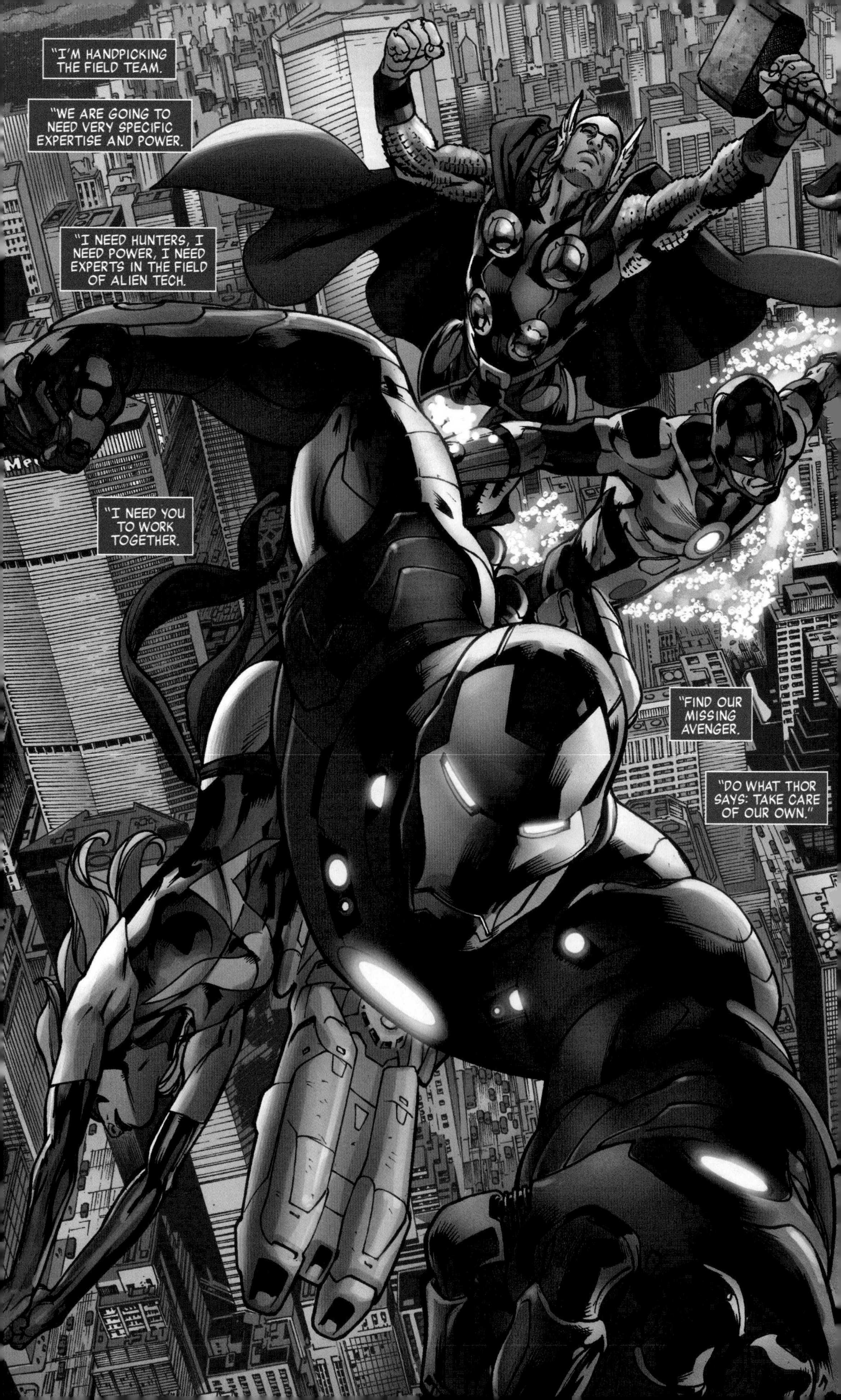

"I'M HANDPICKING THE FIELD TEAM.
"WE ARE GOING TO NEED VERY SPECIFIC EXPERTISE AND POWER.
"I NEED HUNTERS, I NEED POWER, I NEED EXPERTS IN THE FIELD OF ALIEN TECH.
"I NEED YOU TO WORK TOGETHER.
"FIND OUR MISSING AVENGER.
"DO WHAT THOR SAYS: TAKE CARE OF OUR OWN."

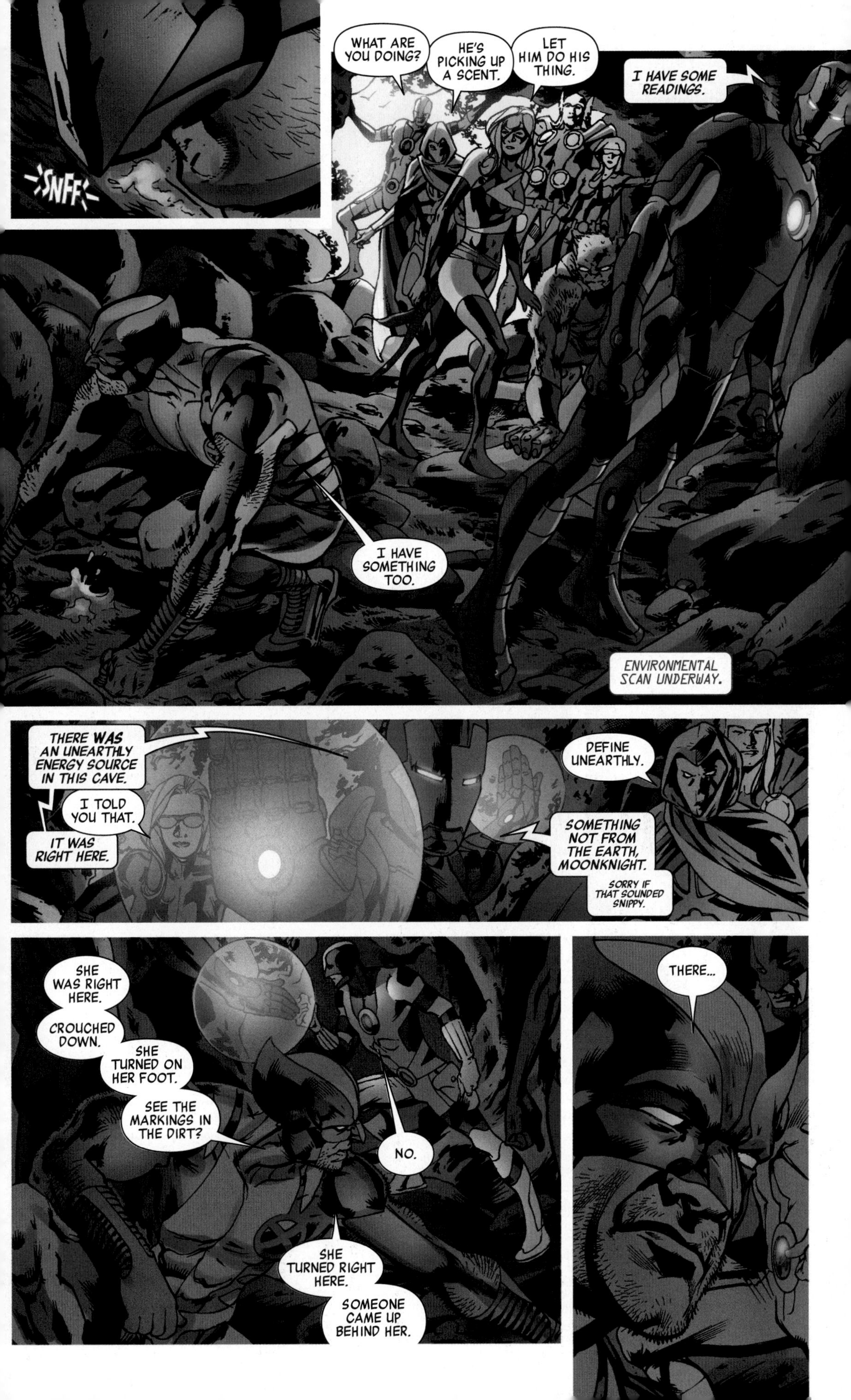
SNFF
WHAT ARE YOU DOING?
HE'S PICKING UP A SCENT.
LET HIM DO HIS THING.
I HAVE SOME READINGS.
I HAVE SOMETHING TOO.
ENVIRONMENTAL SCAN UNDERWAY.
THERE WAS AN UNEARTHLY ENERGY SOURCE IN THIS CAVE.
I TOLD YOU THAT.
IT WAS RIGHT HERE.
DEFINE UNEARTHLY.
SOMETHING NOT FROM THE EARTH, MOONKNIGHT.
SORRY IF THAT SOUNDED SNIPPY.
SHE WAS RIGHT HERE.
CROUCHED DOWN.
SHE TURNED ON HER FOOT.
SEE THE MARKINGS IN THE DIRT?
NO.
SHE TURNED RIGHT HERE.
SOMEONE CAME UP BEHIND HER.
THERE...

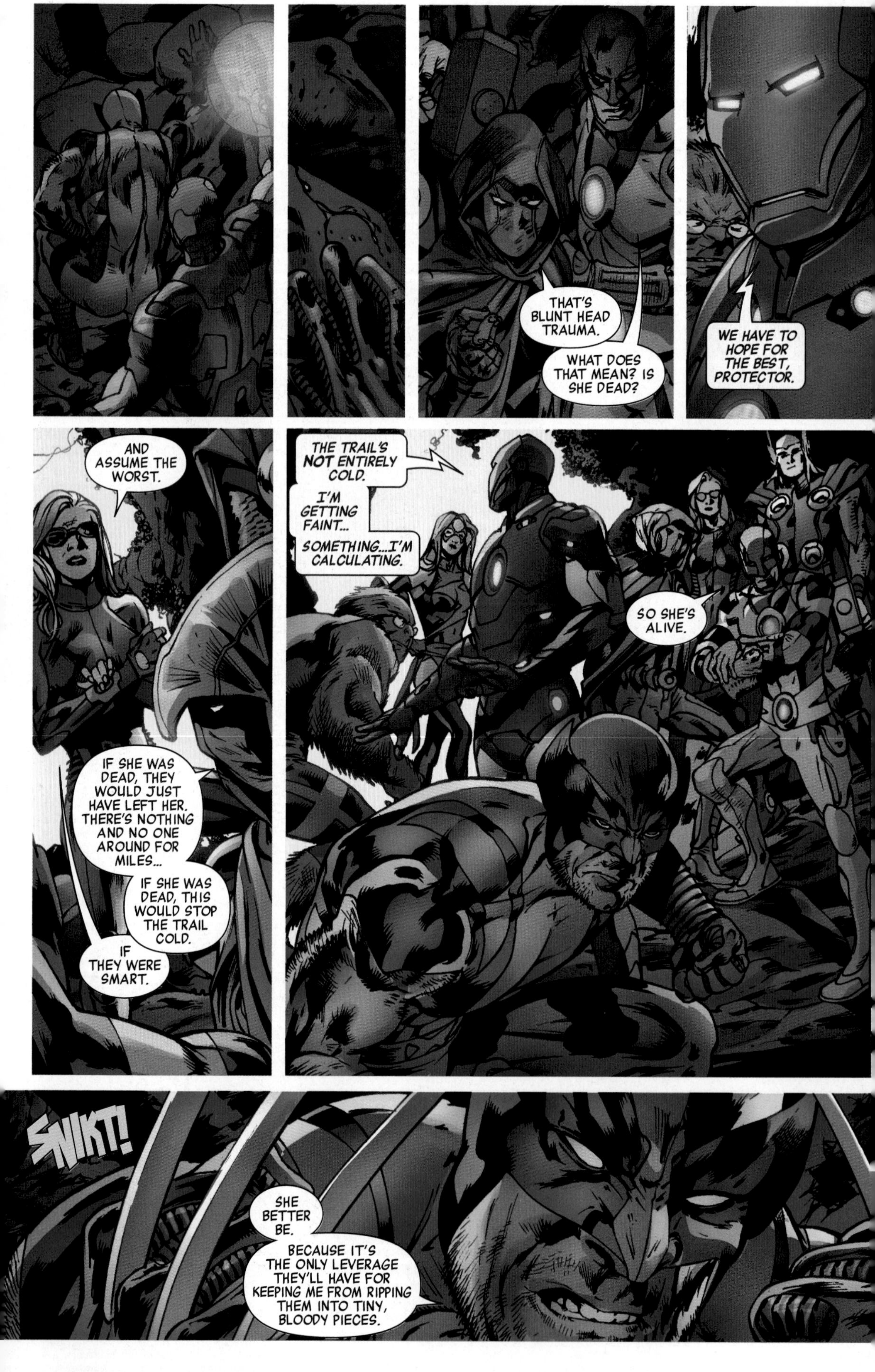
THAT'S BLUNT HEAD TRAUMA.
WHAT DOES THAT MEAN? IS SHE DEAD?
WE HAVE TO HOPE FOR THE BEST, PROTECTOR.
AND ASSUME THE WORST.
THE TRAIL'S NOT ENTIRELY COLD.
I'M GETTING FAINT...
SOMETHING...I'M CALCULATING.
SO SHE'S ALIVE.
IF SHE WAS DEAD, THEY WOULD JUST HAVE LEFT HER. THERE'S NOTHING AND NO ONE AROUND FOR MILES...
IF SHE WAS DEAD, THIS WOULD STOP THE TRAIL COLD.
IF THEY WERE SMART.
SNIKT!
SHE BETTER BE.
BECAUSE IT'S THE ONLY LEVERAGE THEY'LL HAVE FOR KEEPING ME FROM RIPPING THEM INTO TINY, BLOODY PIECES.

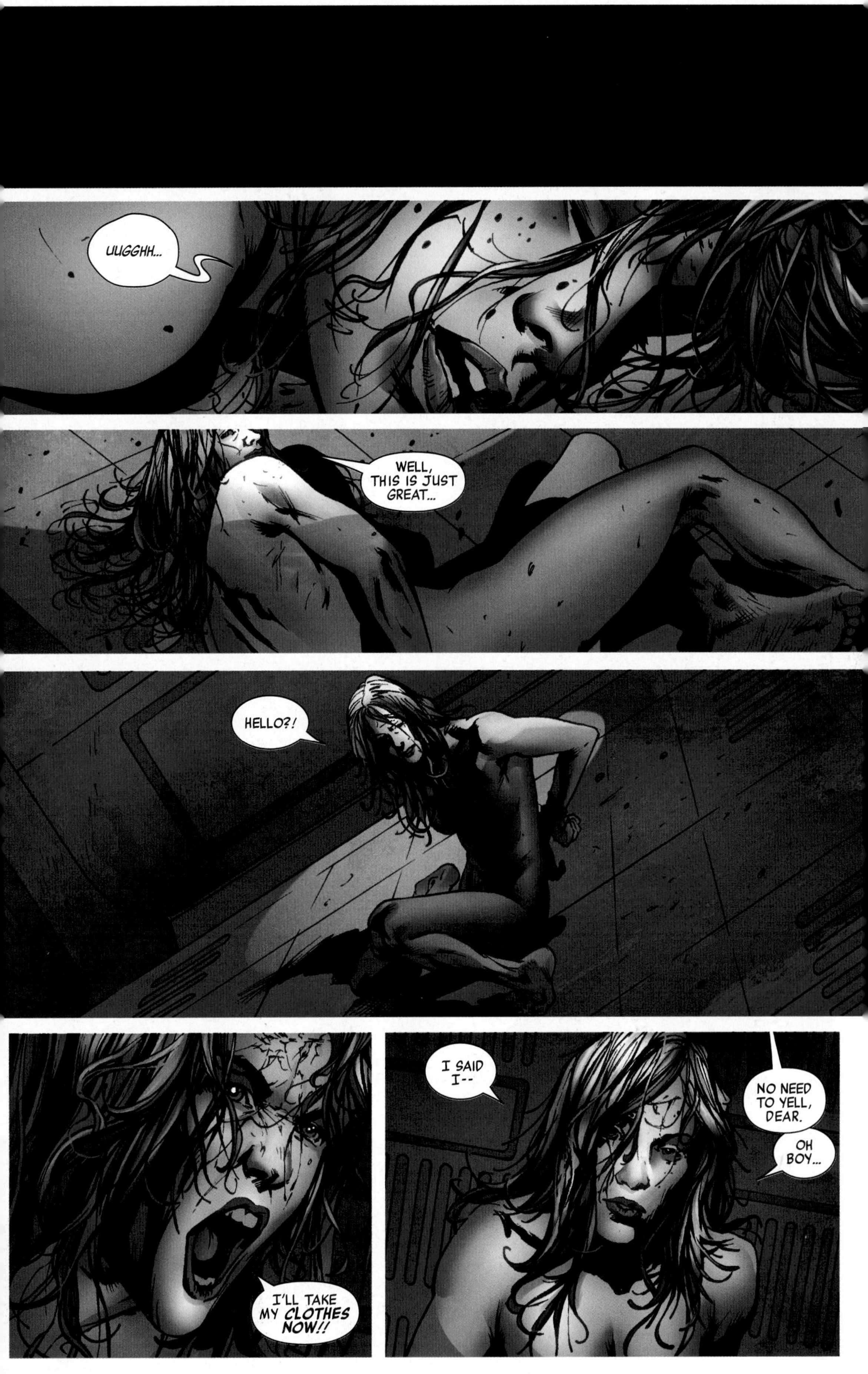
UUGGHH...
WELL, THIS IS JUST GREAT...
HELLO?!
I'LL TAKE MY CLOTHES NOW!!
I SAID I--
NO NEED TO YELL, DEAR.
OH BOY...

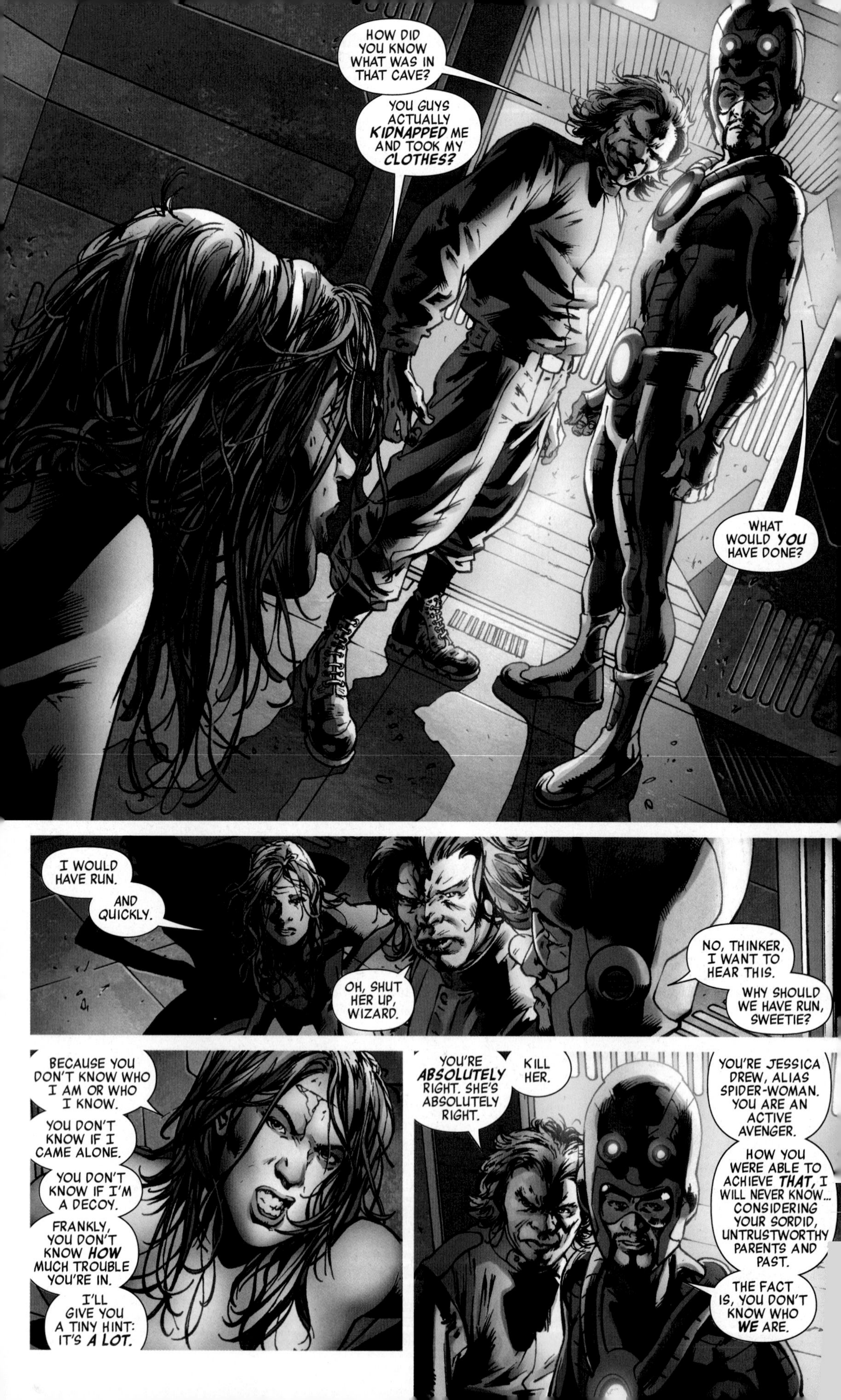

HOW DID YOU KNOW WHAT WAS IN THAT CAVE?
YOU GUYS ACTUALLY KIDNAPPED ME AND TOOK MY CLOTHES?
WHAT WOULD YOU HAVE DONE?
I WOULD HAVE RUN.
AND QUICKLY.
OH, SHUT HER UP, WIZARD.
NO, THINKER, I WANT TO HEAR THIS.
WHY SHOULD WE HAVE RUN, SWEETIE?
BECAUSE YOU DON'T KNOW WHO I AM OR WHO I KNOW.
YOU DON'T KNOW IF I CAME ALONE.
YOU DON'T KNOW IF I'M A DECOY.
FRANKLY, YOU DON'T KNOW HOW MUCH TROUBLE YOU'RE IN.
I'LL GIVE YOU A TINY HINT: IT'S A LOT.
YOU'RE ABSOLUTELY RIGHT. SHE'S ABSOLUTELY RIGHT.
KILL HER.
YOU'RE JESSICA DREW, ALIAS SPIDER-WOMAN. YOU ARE AN ACTIVE AVENGER.
HOW YOU WERE ABLE TO ACHIEVE THAT, I WILL NEVER KNOW... CONSIDERING YOUR SORDID, UNTRUSTWORTHY PARENTS AND PAST.
THE FACT IS, YOU DON'T KNOW WHO WE ARE.

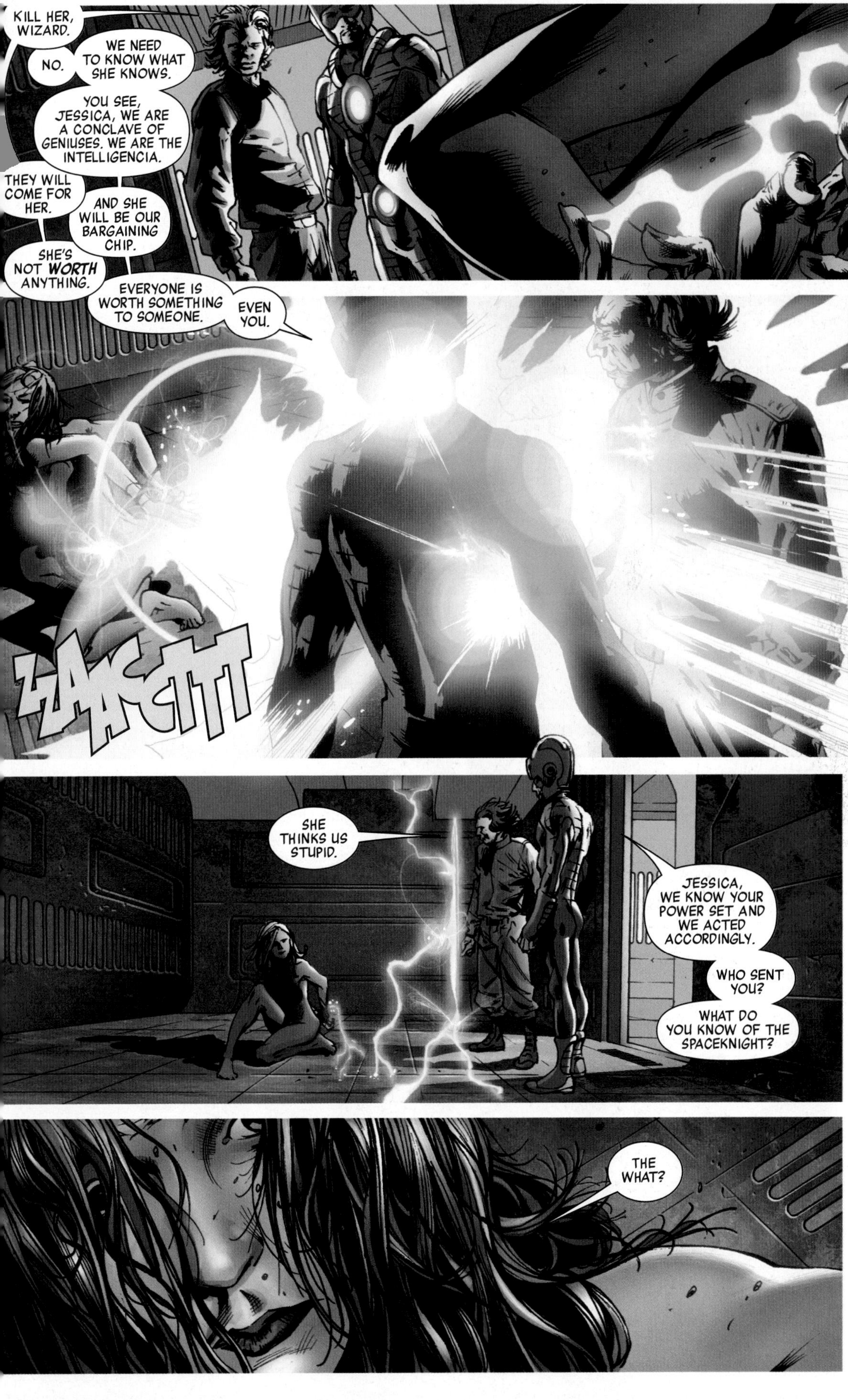
KILL HER, WIZARD.
NO.
WE NEED TO KNOW WHAT SHE KNOWS.
YOU SEE, JESSICA, WE ARE A CONCLAVE OF GENIUSES. WE ARE THE INTELLIGENCIA.
THEY WILL COME FOR HER.
AND SHE WILL BE OUR BARGAINING CHIP.
SHE'S NOT **WORTH** ANYTHING.
EVERYONE IS WORTH SOMETHING TO SOMEONE.
EVEN YOU.
ZZAACTTT
SHE THINKS US STUPID.
JESSICA, WE KNOW YOUR POWER SET AND WE ACTED ACCORDINGLY.
WHO SENT YOU?
WHAT DO YOU KNOW OF THE SPACEKNIGHT?
THE WHAT?

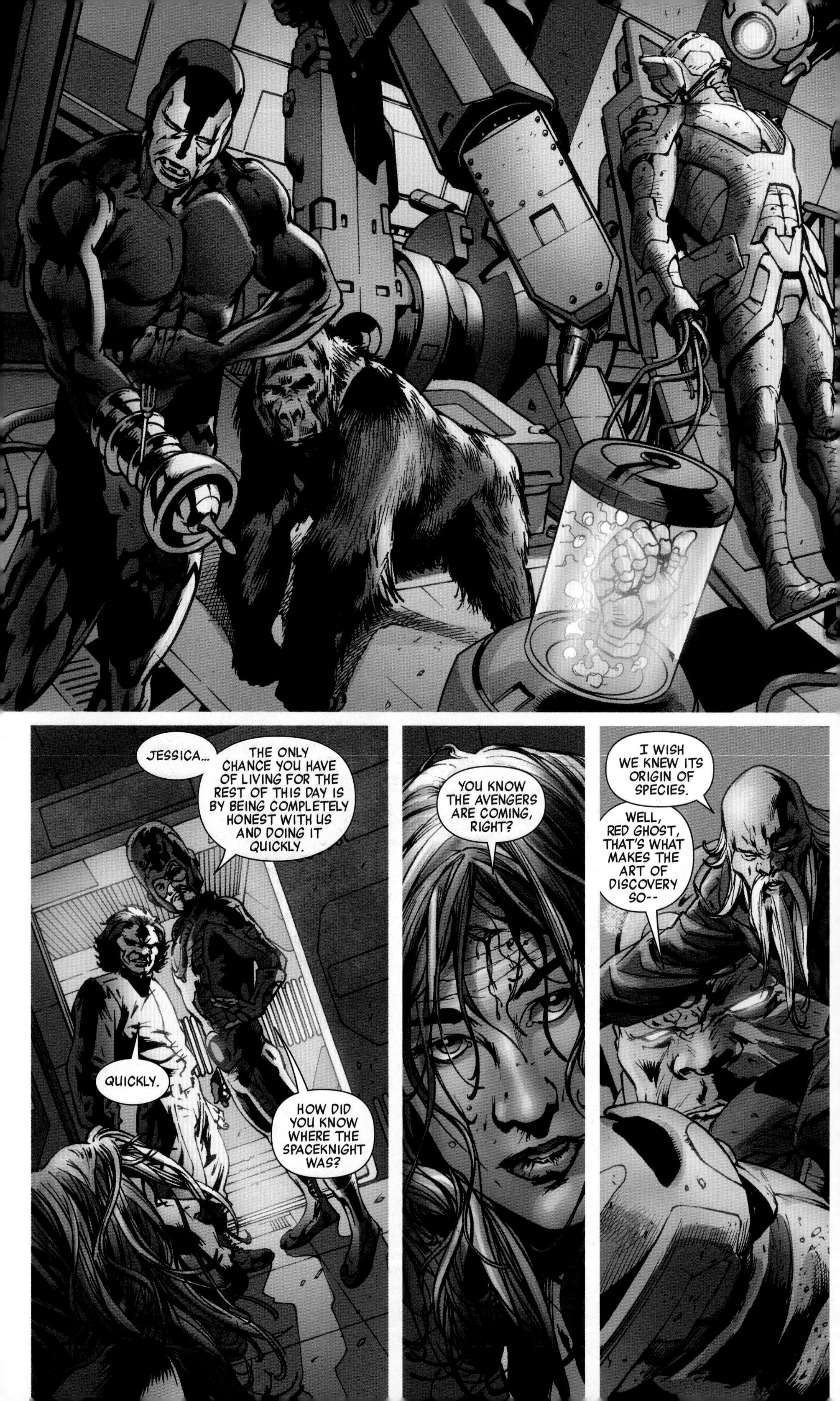
JESSICA...
THE ONLY CHANCE YOU HAVE OF LIVING FOR THE REST OF THIS DAY IS BY BEING COMPLETELY HONEST WITH US AND DOING IT QUICKLY.
QUICKLY.
HOW DID YOU KNOW WHERE THE SPACEKNIGHT WAS?
YOU KNOW THE AVENGERS ARE COMING, RIGHT?
I WISH WE KNEW ITS ORIGIN OF SPECIES.
WELL, RED GHOST, THAT'S WHAT MAKES THE ART OF DISCOVERY SO--

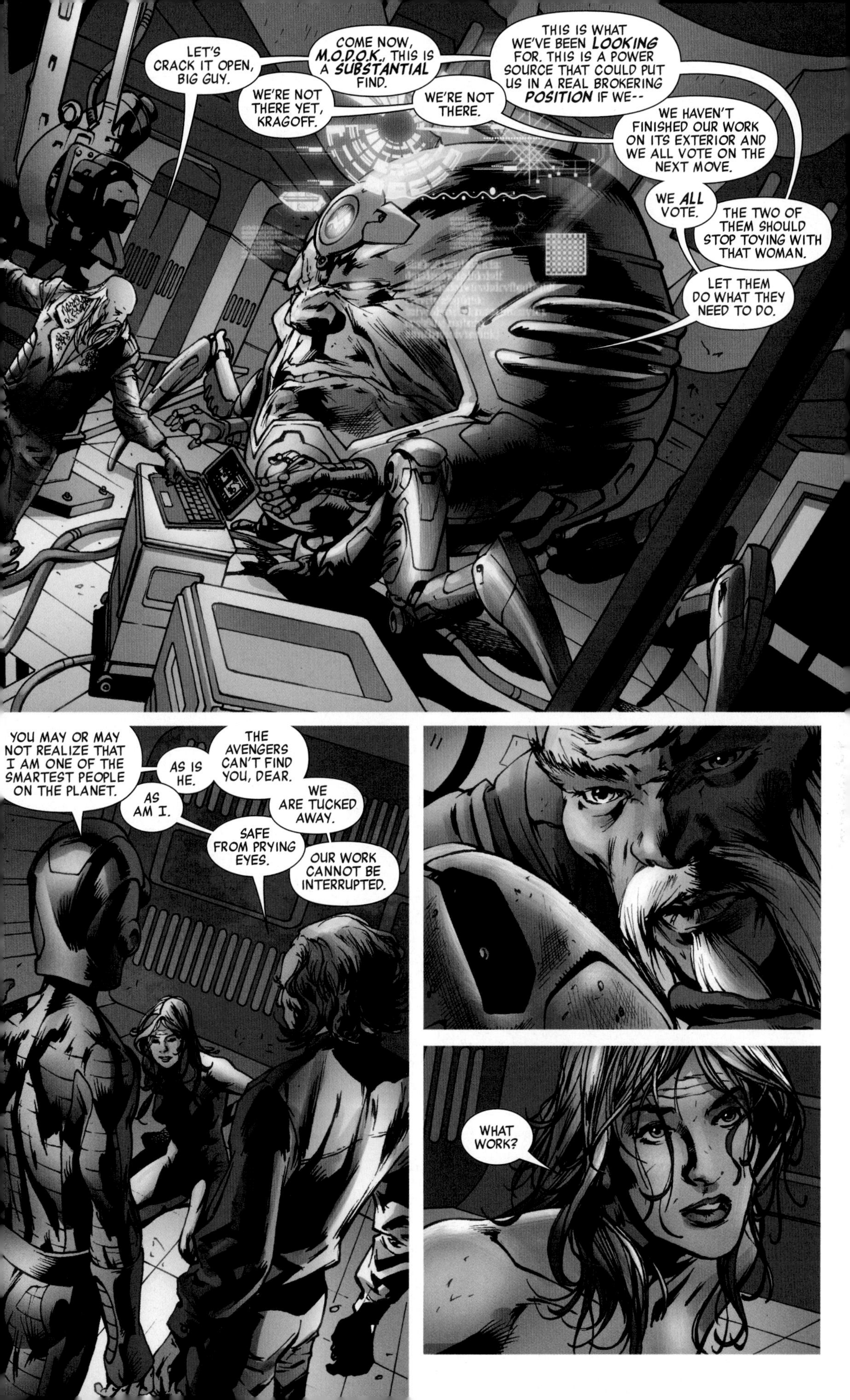
LET'S CRACK IT OPEN, BIG GUY.
COME NOW, M.O.D.O.K., THIS IS A SUBSTANTIAL FIND.
THIS IS WHAT WE'VE BEEN LOOKING FOR. THIS IS A POWER SOURCE THAT COULD PUT US IN A REAL BROKERING POSITION IF WE--
WE'RE NOT THERE YET, KRAGOFF.
WE'RE NOT THERE.
WE HAVEN'T FINISHED OUR WORK ON ITS EXTERIOR AND WE ALL VOTE ON THE NEXT MOVE.
WE ALL VOTE.
THE TWO OF THEM SHOULD STOP TOYING WITH THAT WOMAN.
LET THEM DO WHAT THEY NEED TO DO.
YOU MAY OR MAY NOT REALIZE THAT I AM ONE OF THE SMARTEST PEOPLE ON THE PLANET.
AS IS HE.
AS AM I.
THE AVENGERS CAN'T FIND YOU, DEAR.
WE ARE TUCKED AWAY.
SAFE FROM PRYING EYES.
OUR WORK CANNOT BE INTERRUPTED.
WHAT WORK?

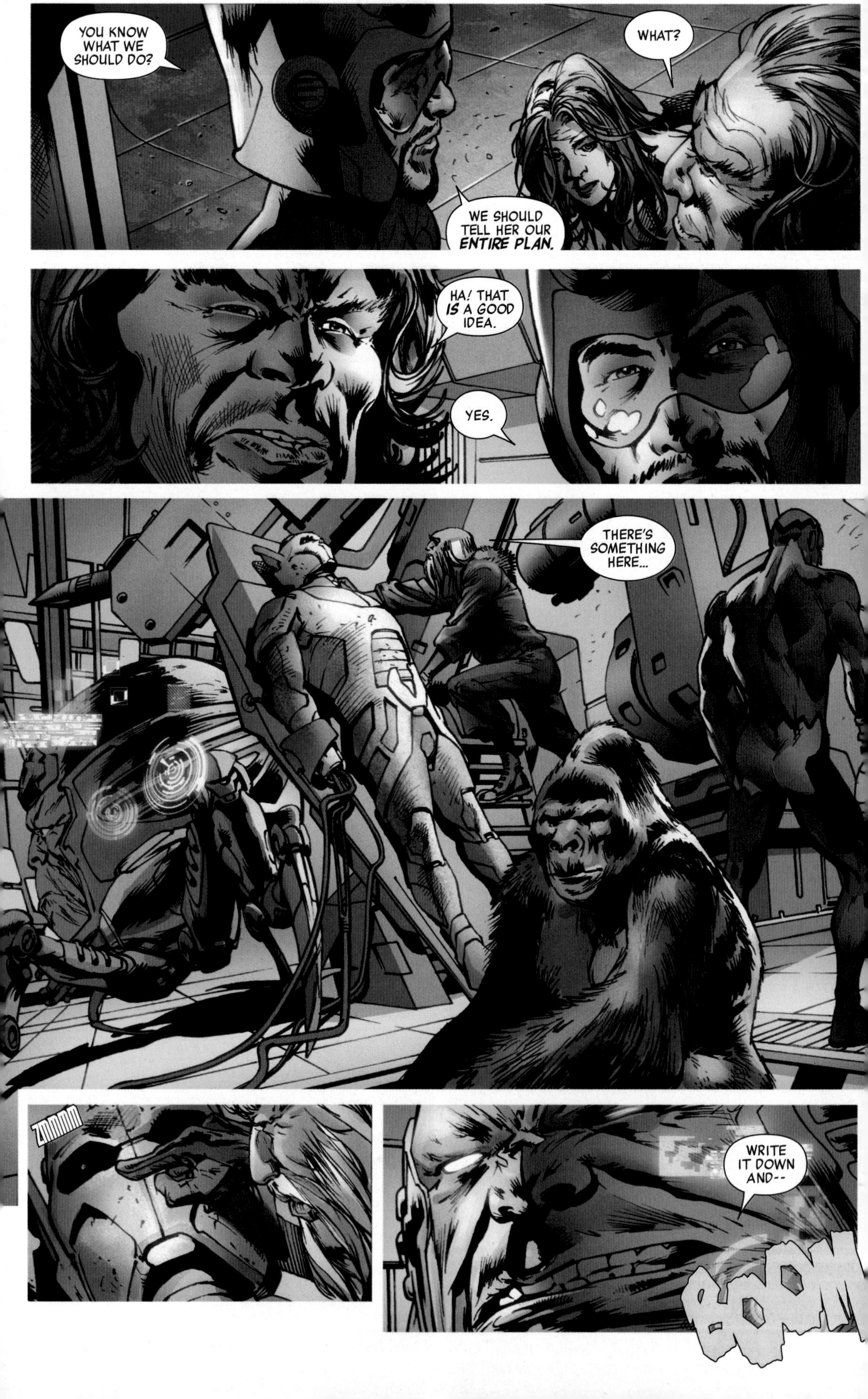
YOU KNOW WHAT WE SHOULD DO?
WHAT?
WE SHOULD TELL HER OUR ENTIRE PLAN.
HA! THAT IS A GOOD IDEA.
YES.
THERE'S SOMETHING HERE...
ZMMMM
WRITE IT DOWN AND--
BOOM

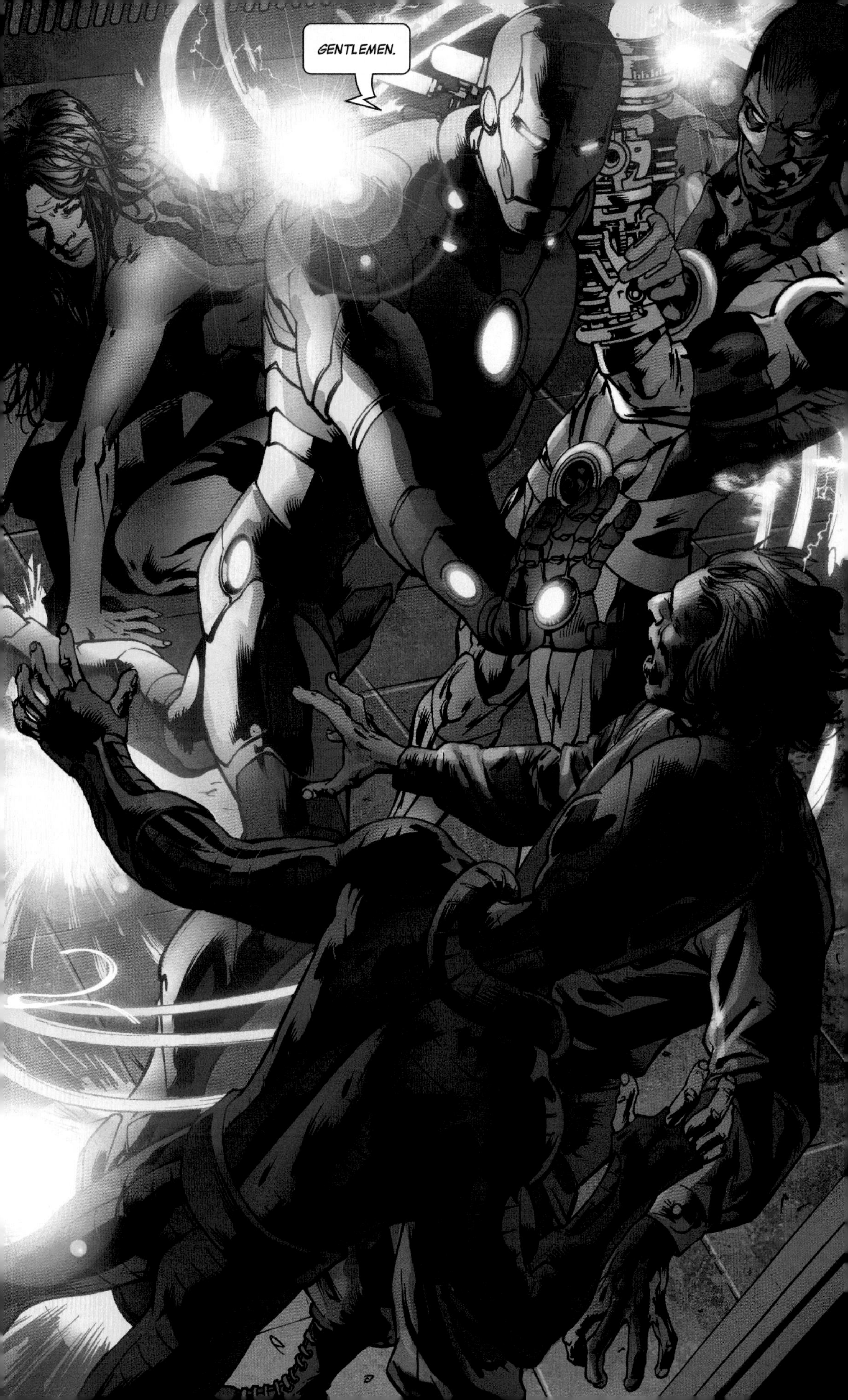
GENTLEMEN.

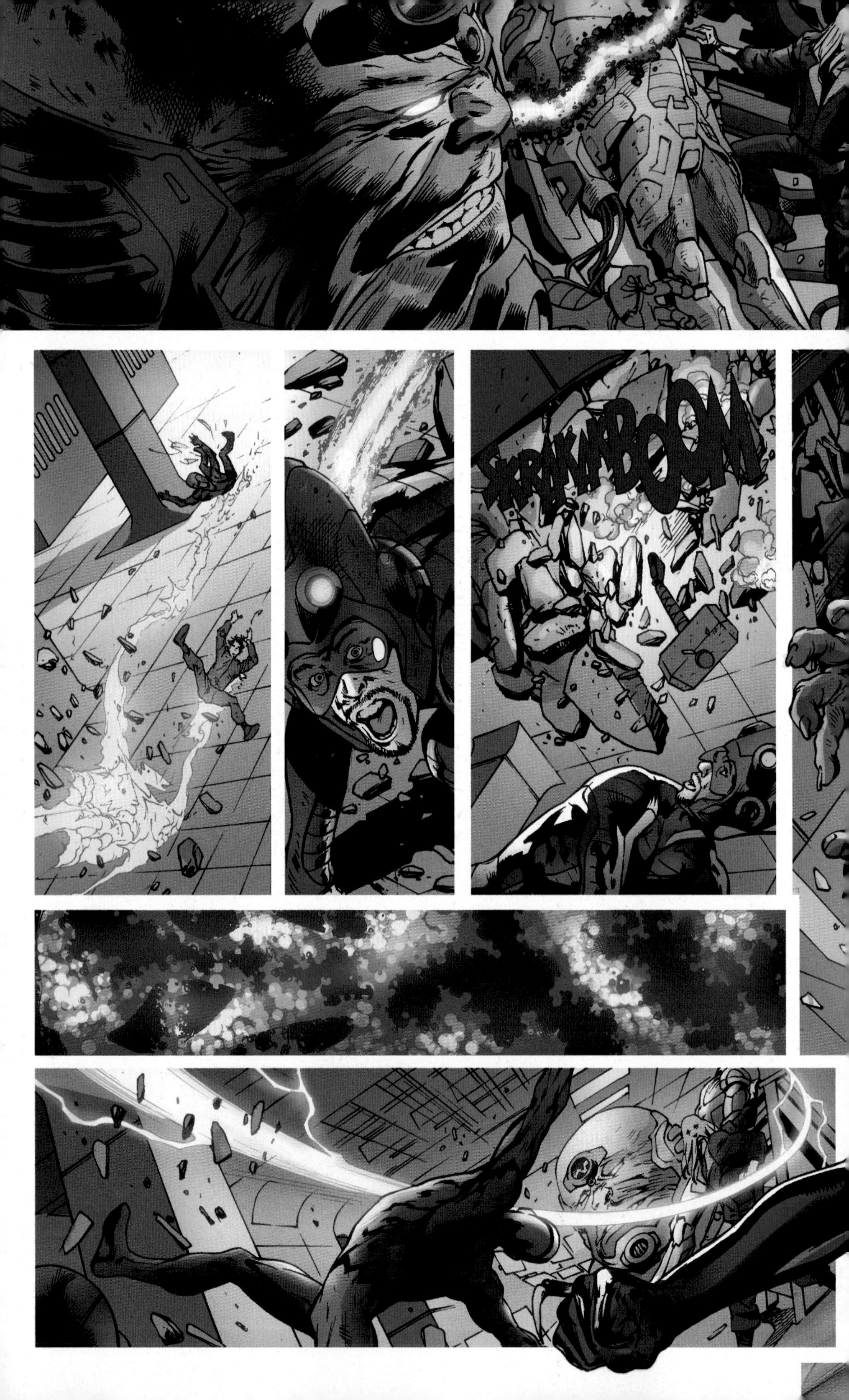
SKRAKAKABOOM

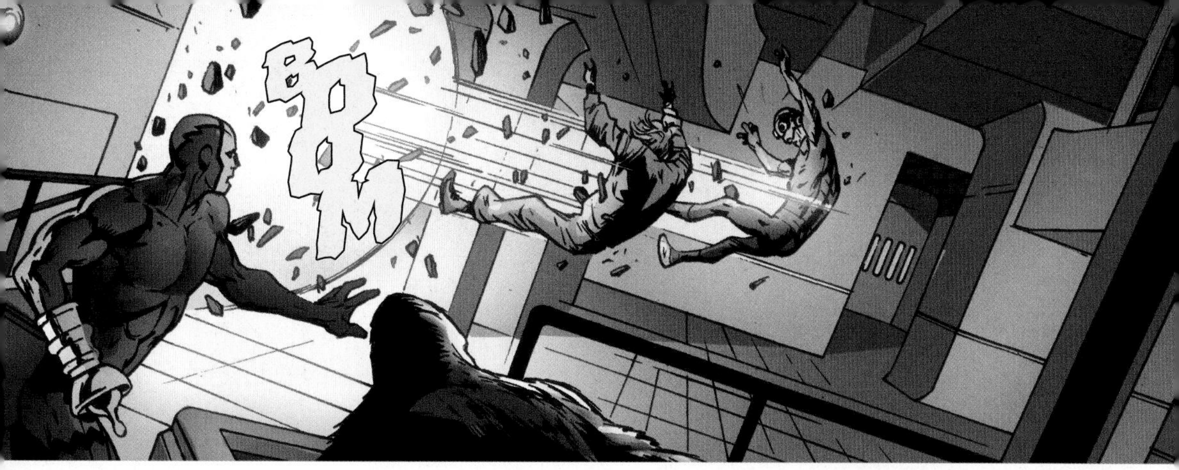
BOOM

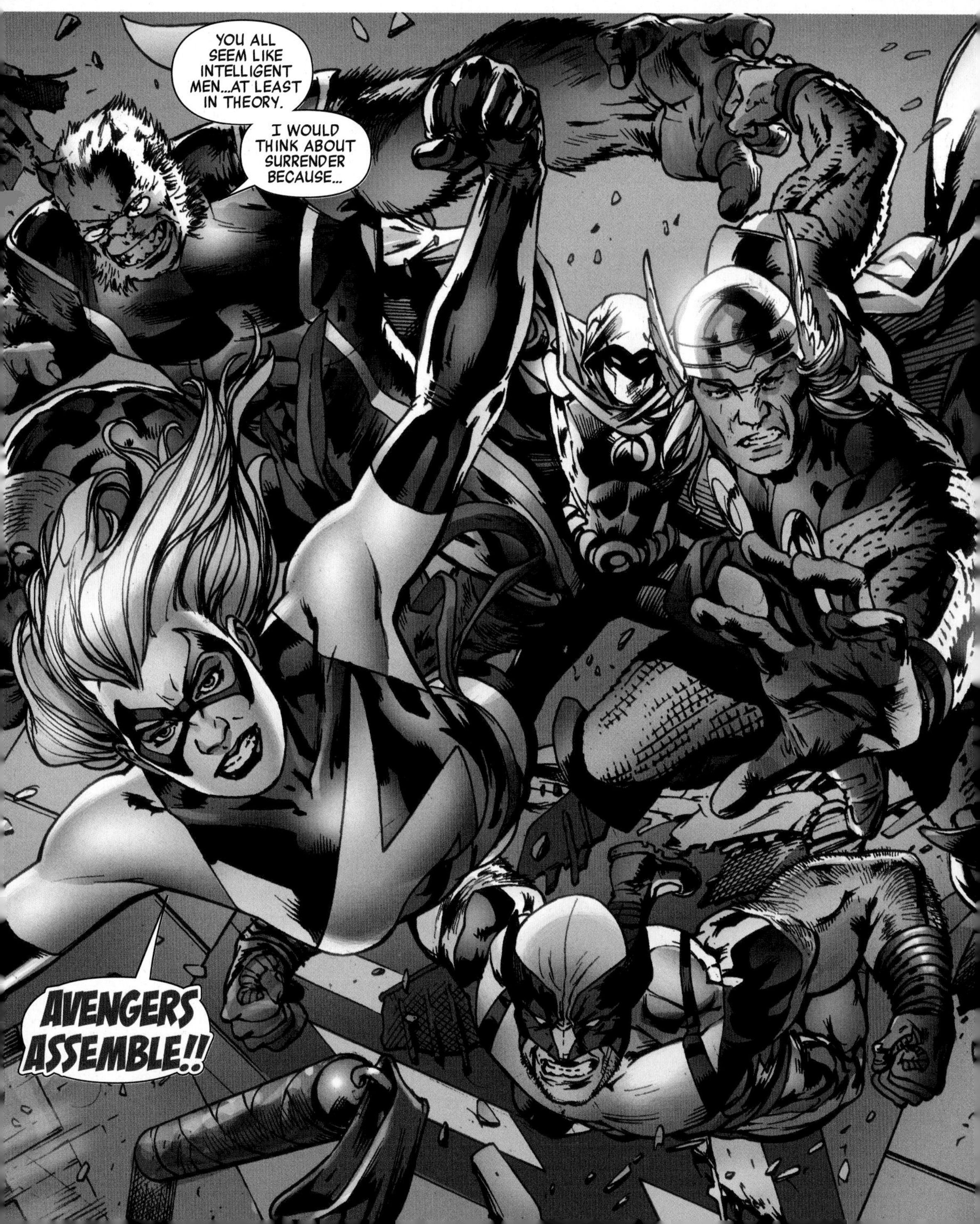
YOU ALL SEEM LIKE INTELLIGENT MEN...AT LEAST IN THEORY.
I WOULD THINK ABOUT SURRENDER BECAUSE...
AVENGERS ASSEMBLE!!

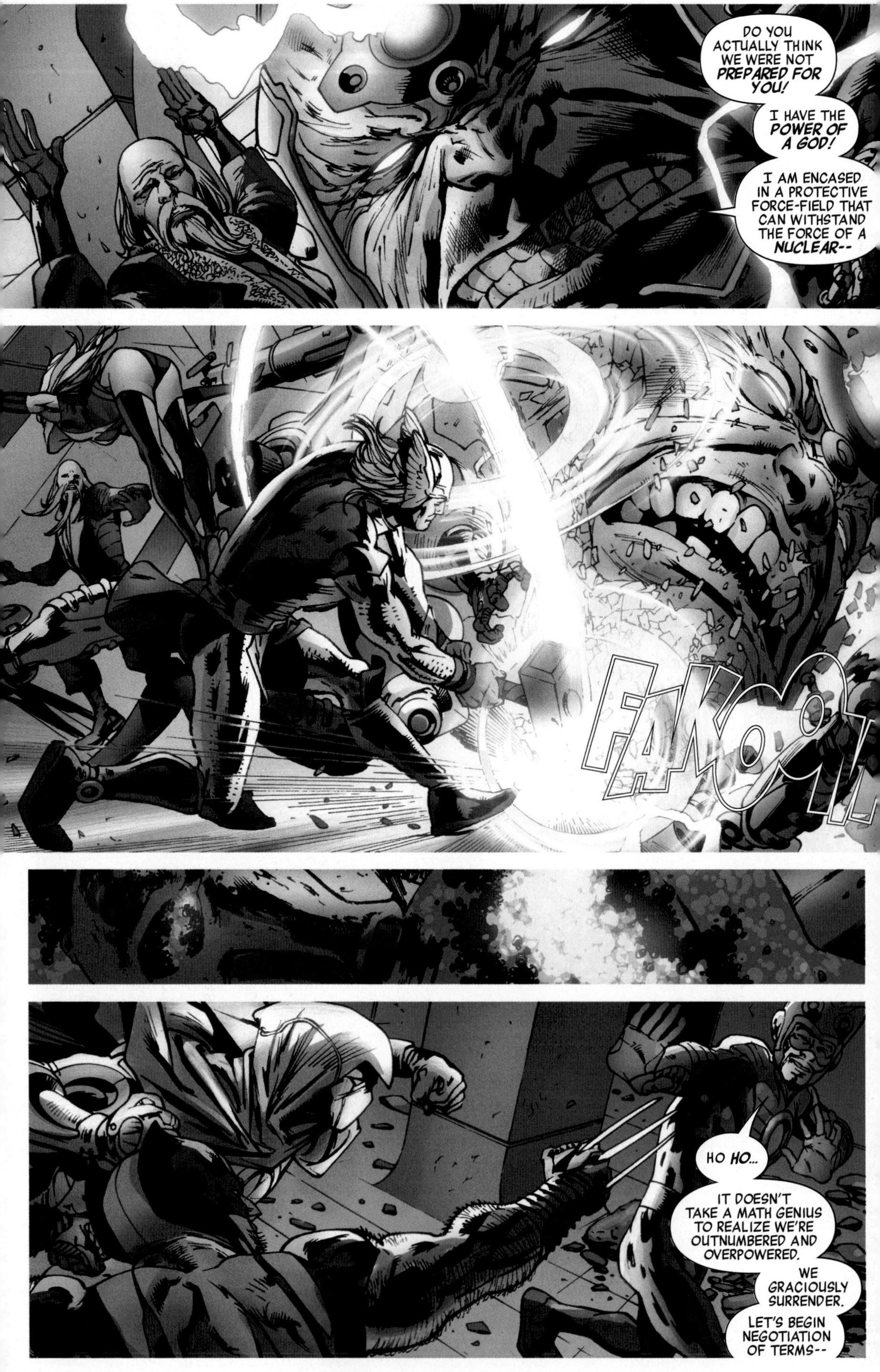
DO YOU ACTUALLY THINK WE WERE NOT PREPARED FOR YOU!
I HAVE THE POWER OF A GOD!
I AM ENCASED IN A PROTECTIVE FORCE-FIELD THAT CAN WITHSTAND THE FORCE OF A NUCLEAR--
FAKOOM
HO HO...
IT DOESN'T TAKE A MATH GENIUS TO REALIZE WE'RE OUTNUMBERED AND OVERPOWERED.
WE GRACIOUSLY SURRENDER.
LET'S BEGIN NEGOTIATION OF TERMS--

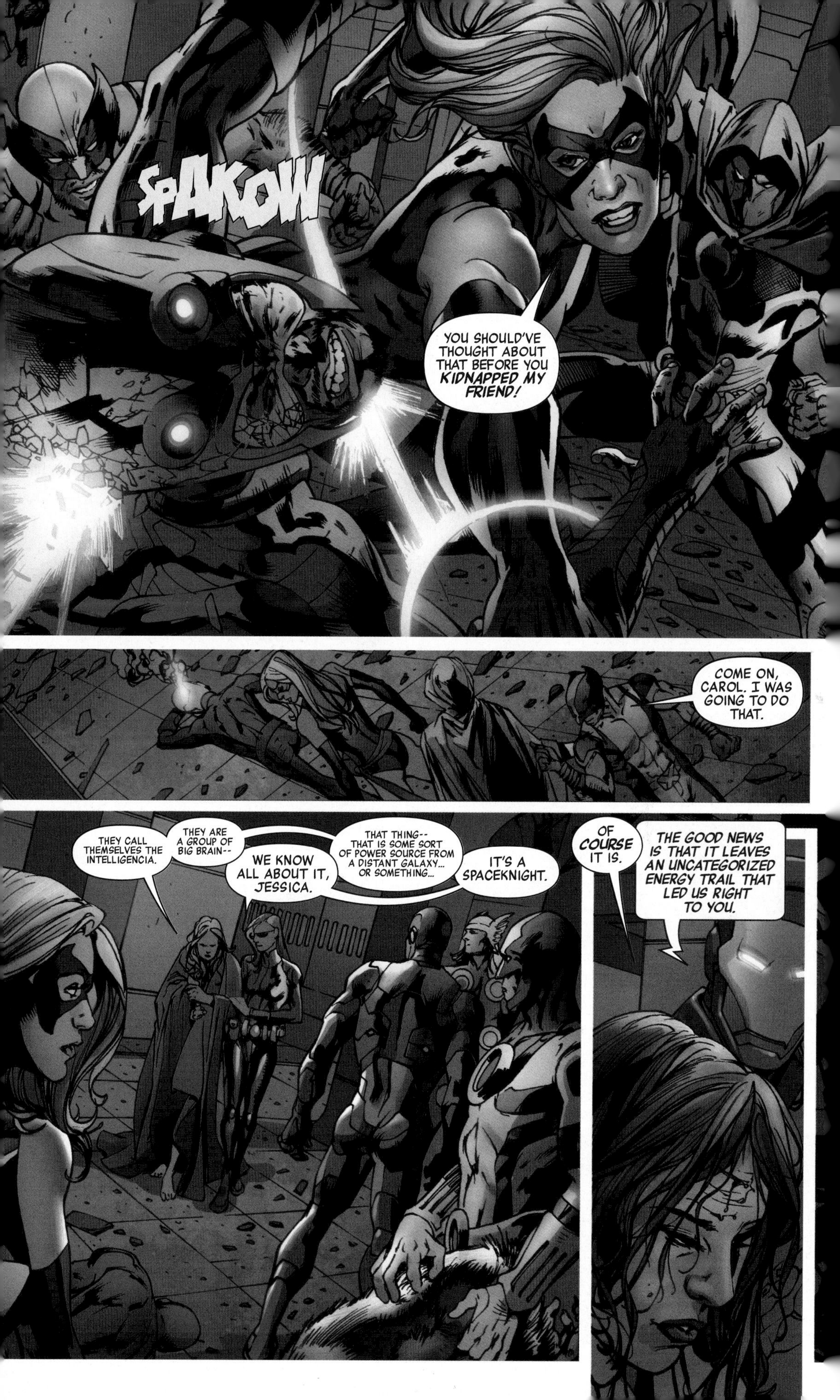
SPAKOW
YOU SHOULD'VE THOUGHT ABOUT THAT BEFORE YOU KIDNAPPED MY FRIEND!
COME ON, CAROL. I WAS GOING TO DO THAT.
THEY CALL THEMSELVES THE INTELLIGENCIA.
THEY ARE A GROUP OF BIG BRAIN--
WE KNOW ALL ABOUT IT, JESSICA.
THAT THING-- THAT IS SOME SORT OF POWER SOURCE FROM A DISTANT GALAXY... OR SOMETHING...
IT'S A SPACEKNIGHT.
OF COURSE IT IS.
THE GOOD NEWS IS THAT IT LEAVES AN UNCATEGORIZED ENERGY TRAIL THAT LED US RIGHT TO YOU.

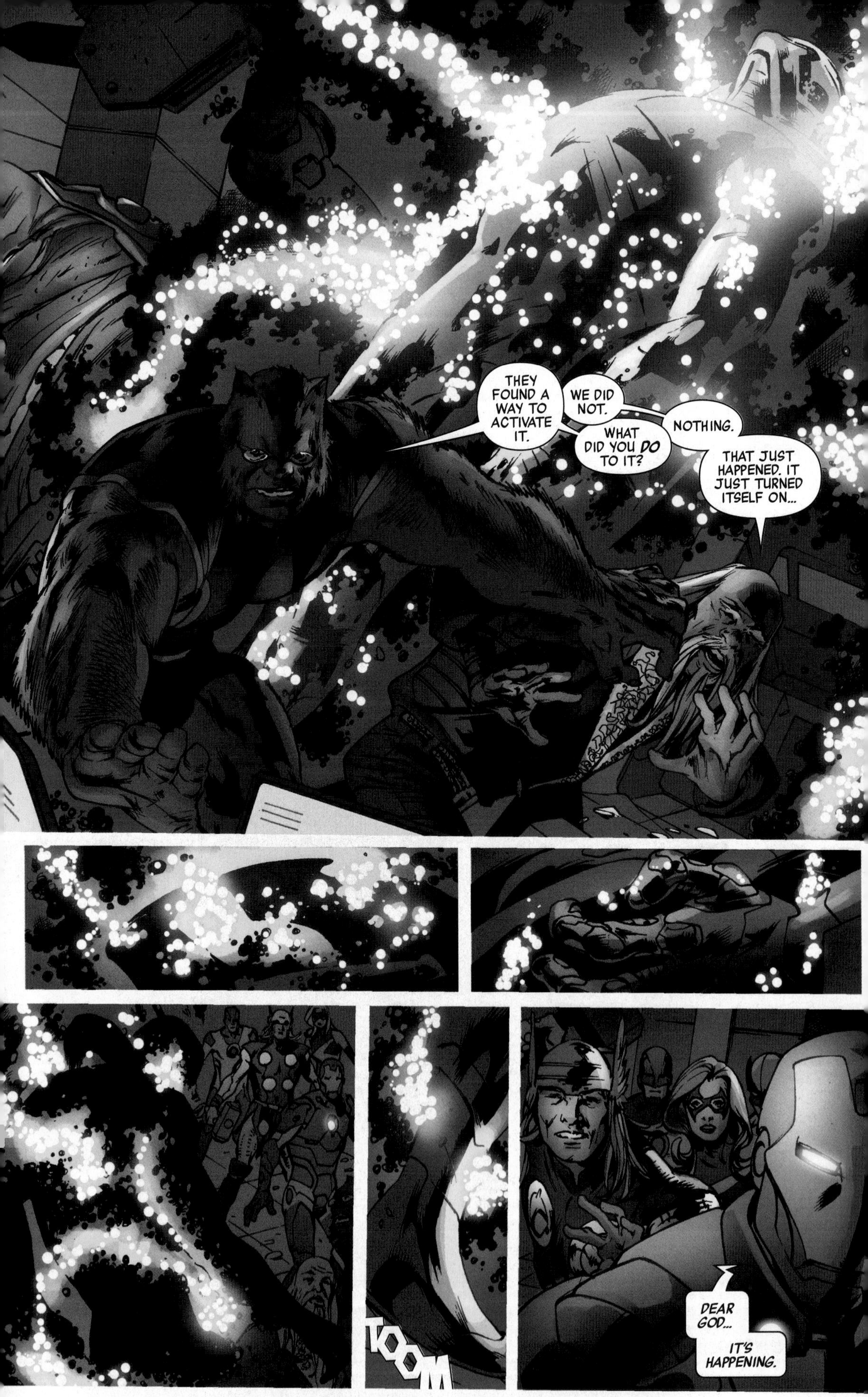
THEY FOUND A WAY TO ACTIVATE IT.
WE DID NOT.
WHAT DID YOU DO TO IT?
NOTHING.
THAT JUST HAPPENED. IT JUST TURNED ITSELF ON...
TOOM
DEAR GOD...
IT'S HAPPENING.

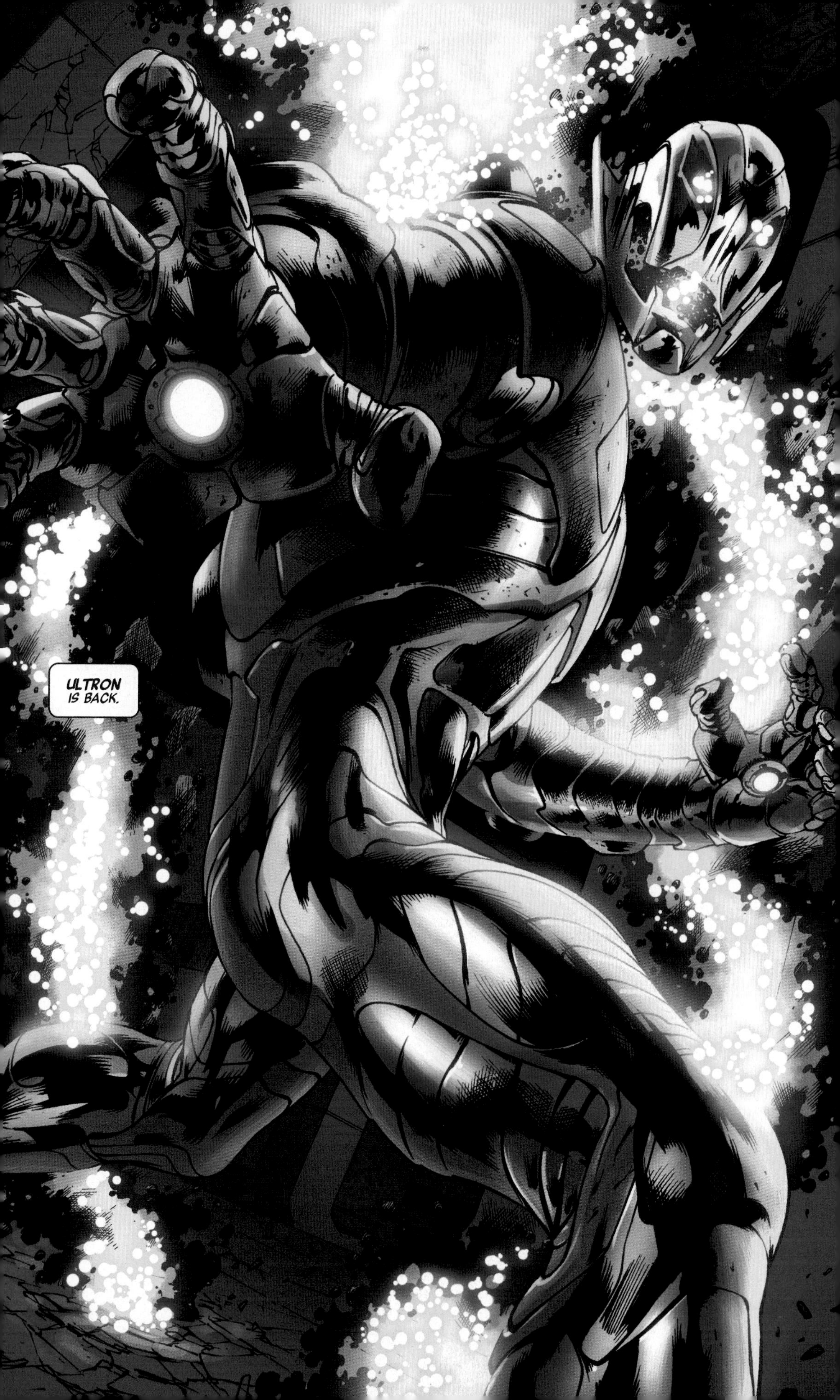
ULTRON IS BACK.

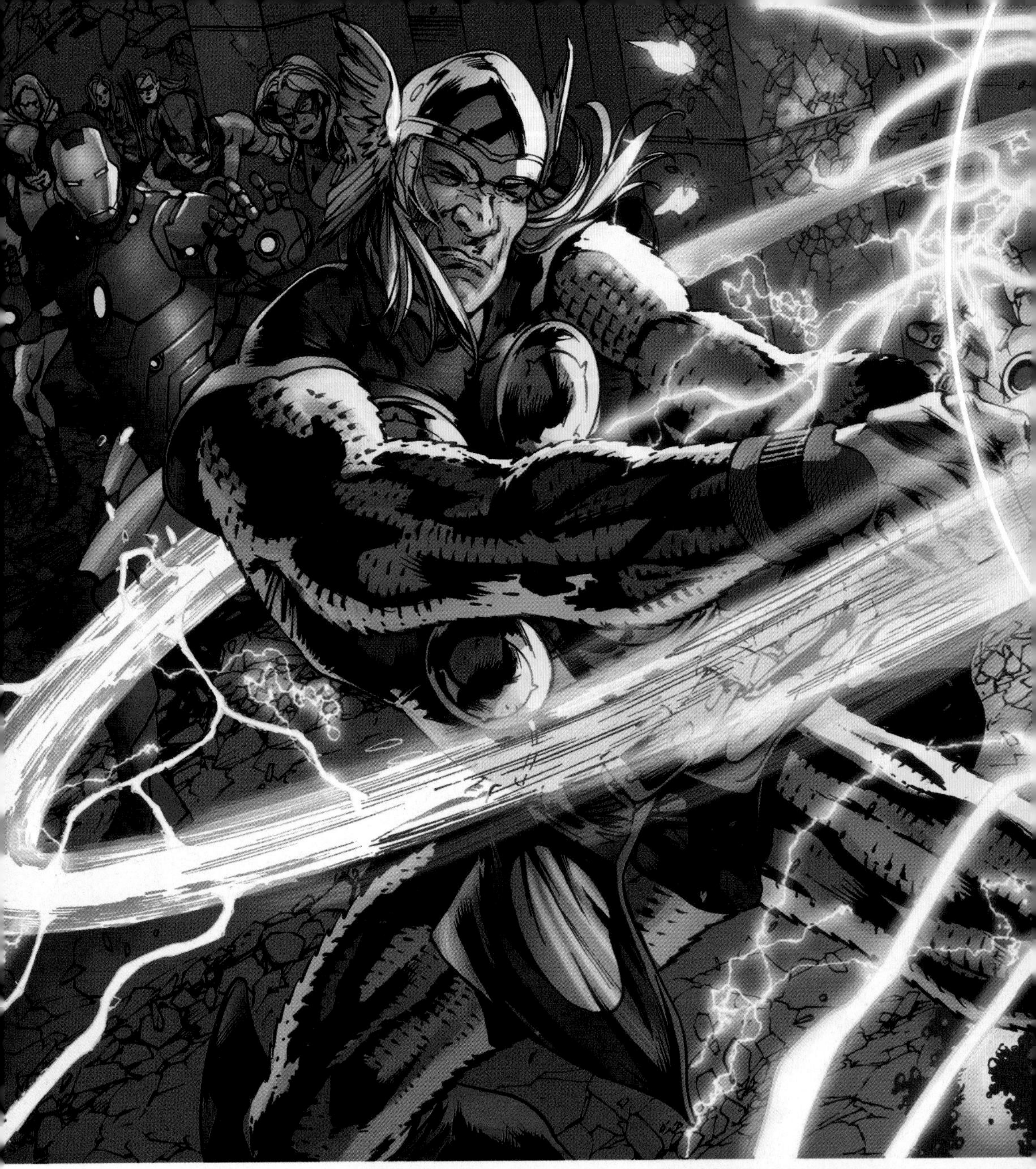

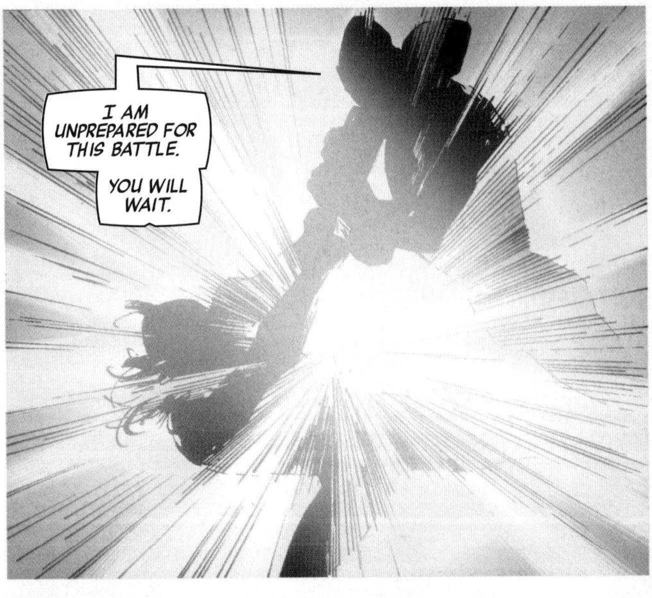
I AM UNPREPARED FOR THIS BATTLE.
YOU WILL WAIT.

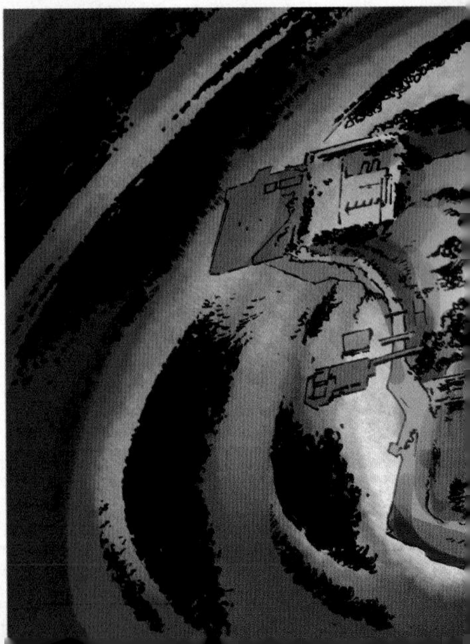

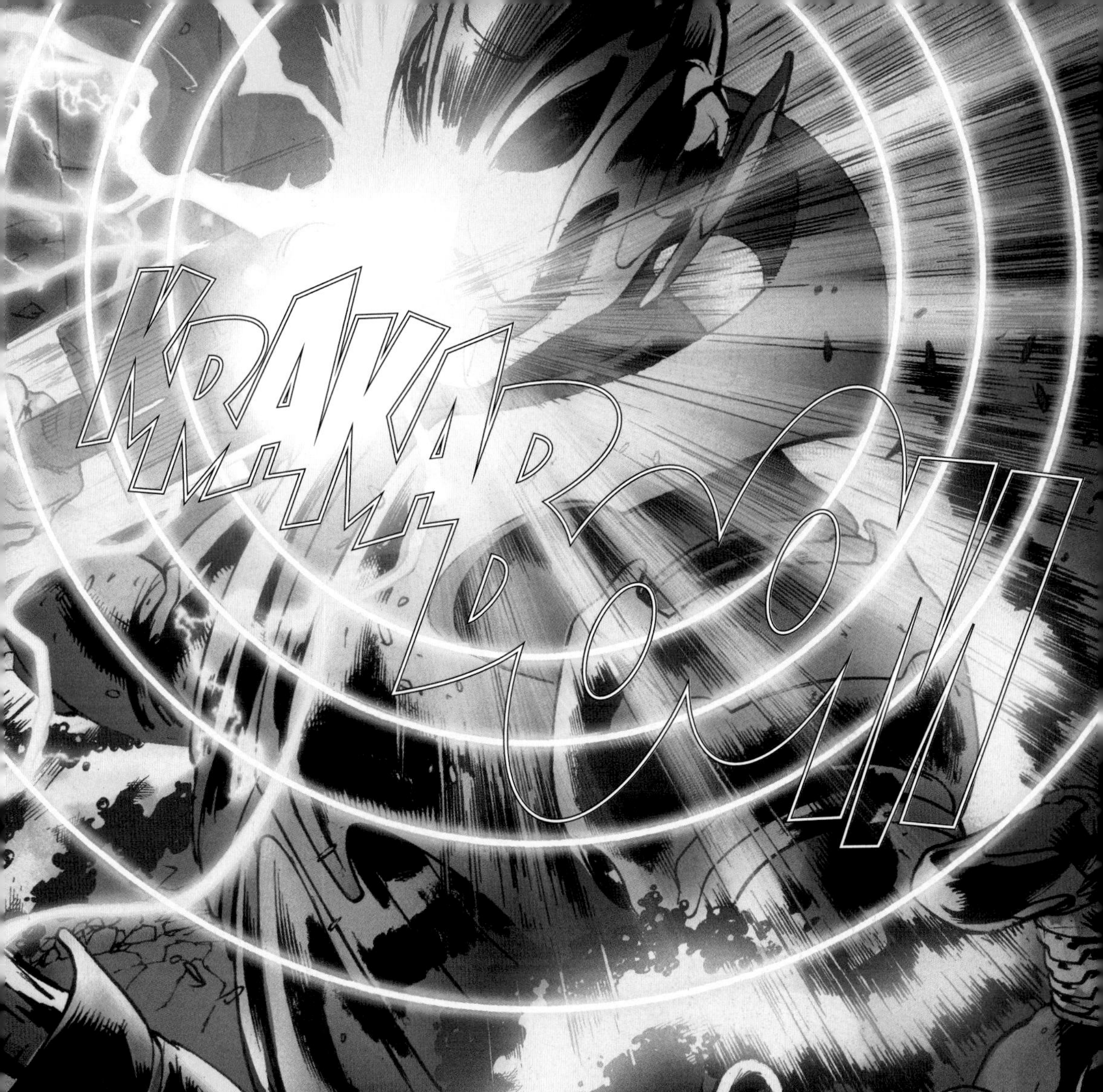
KRAKADOOM!!

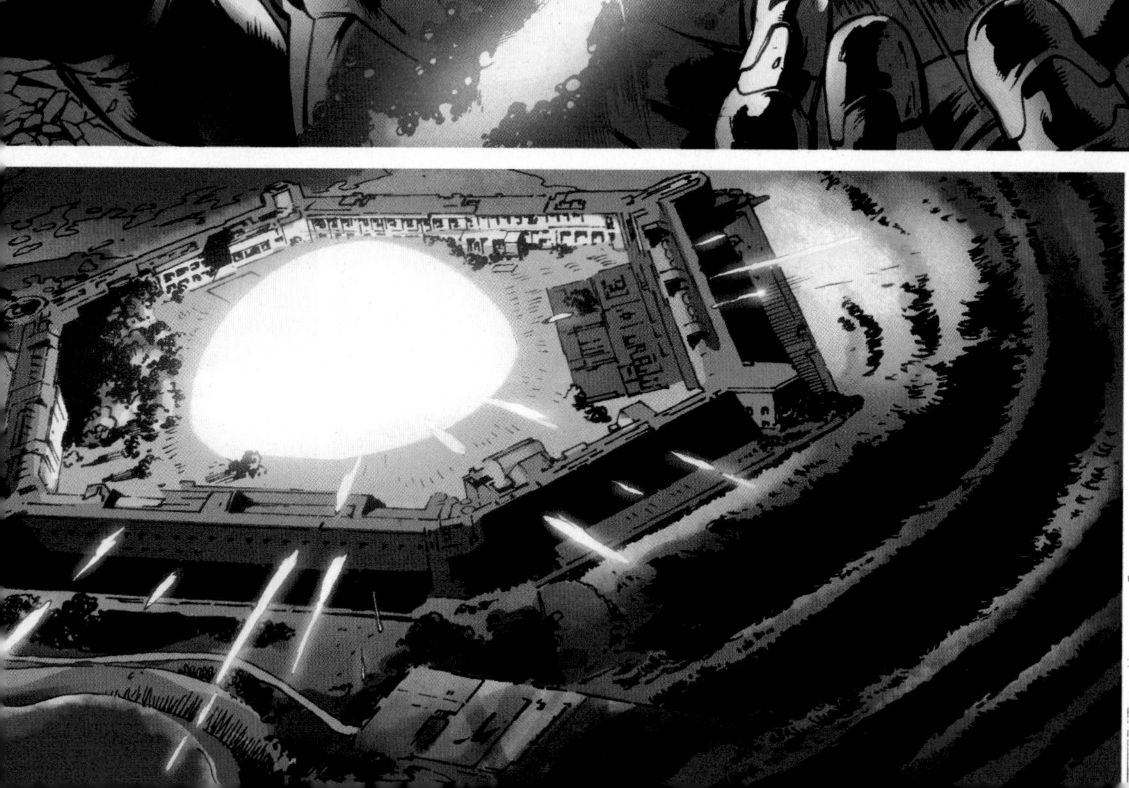

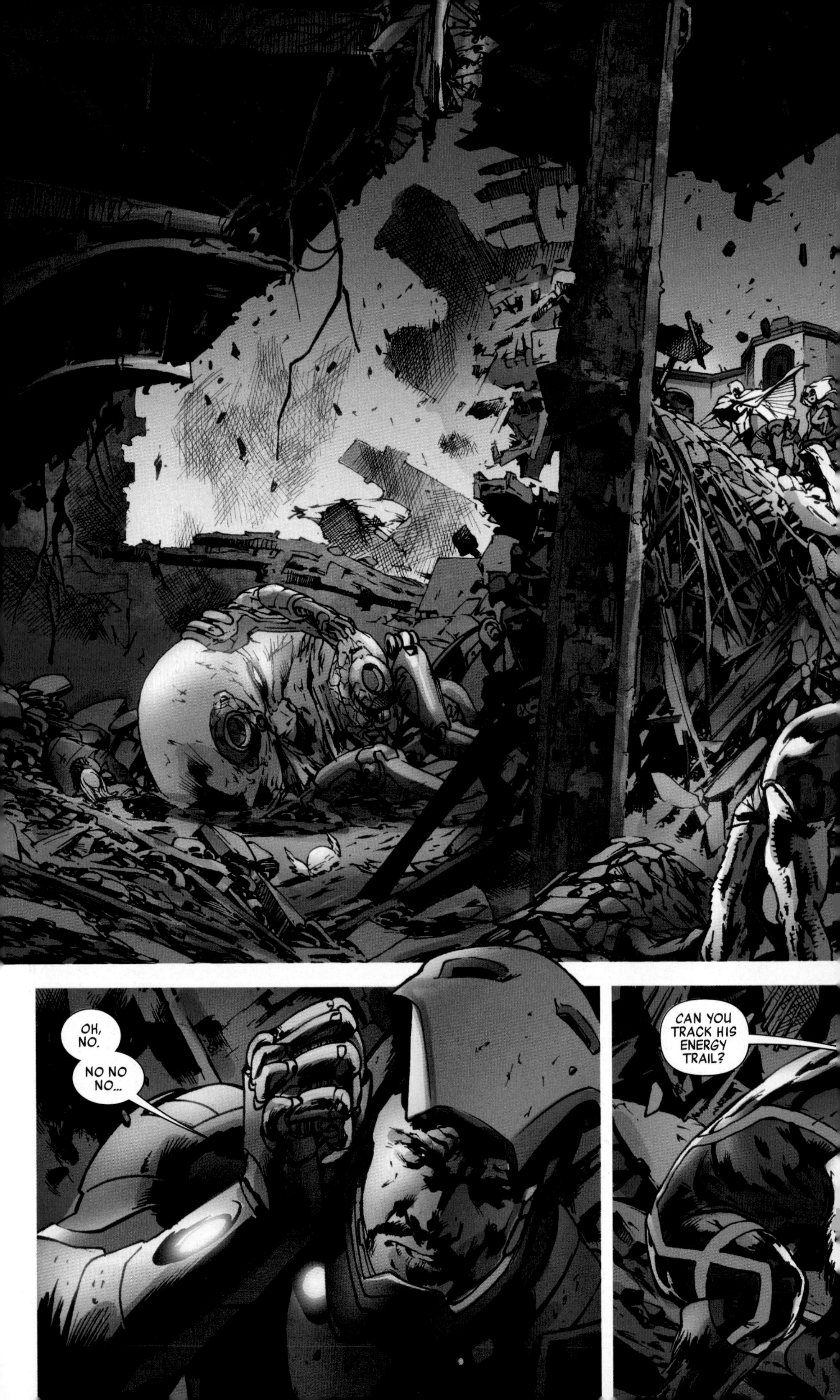
OH, NO.
NO NO NO...
CAN YOU TRACK HIS ENERGY TRAIL?

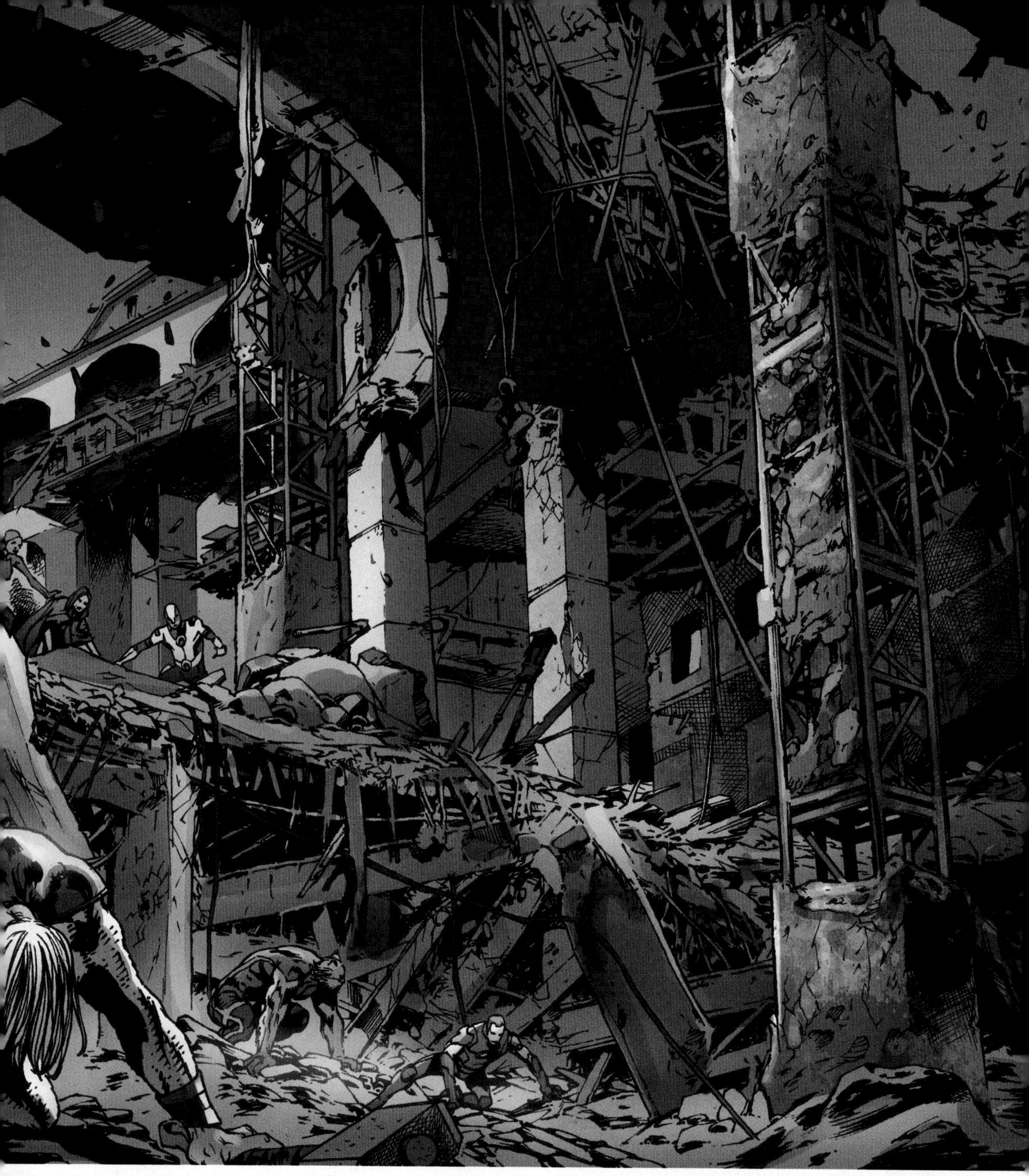

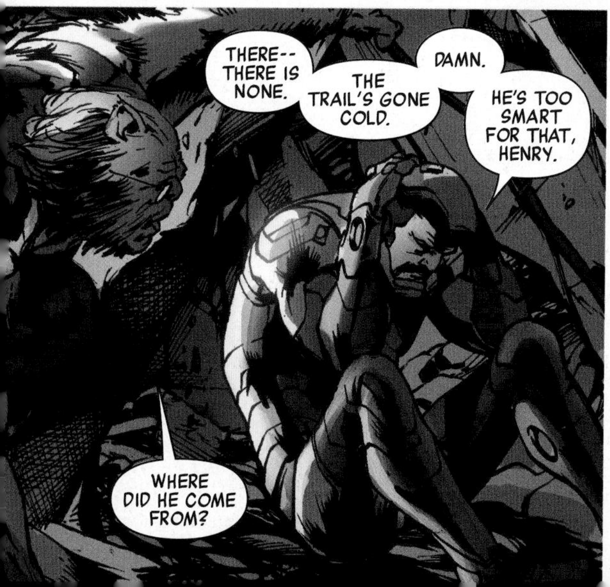
THERE--
THERE IS
NONE.
THE
TRAIL'S GONE
COLD.
DAMN.
HE'S TOO
SMART
FOR THAT,
HENRY.
WHERE
DID HE COME
FROM?

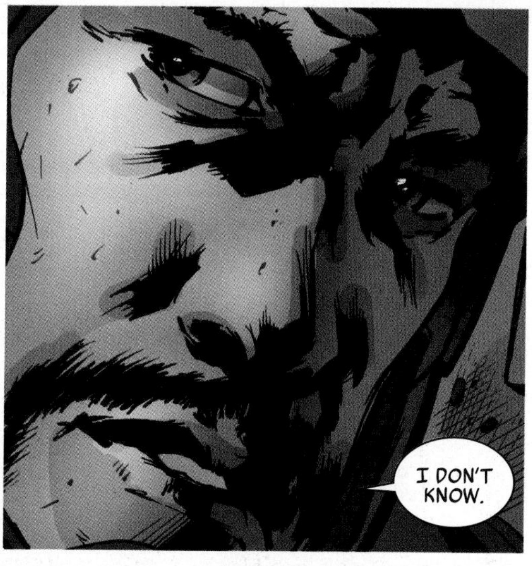
I DON'T
KNOW.

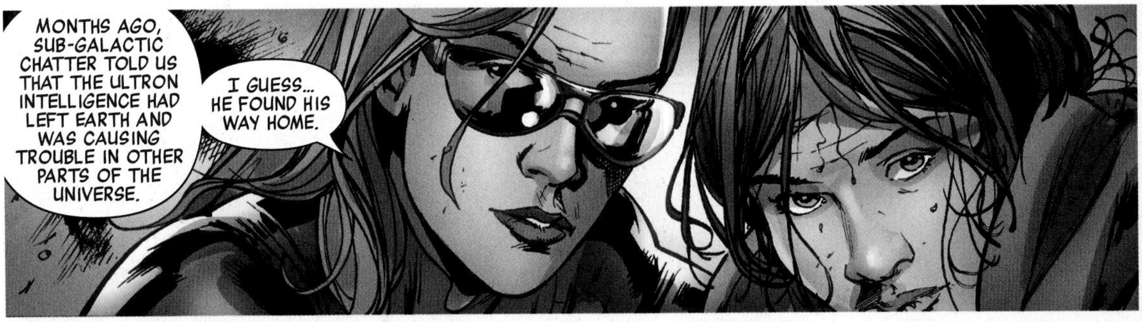
MONTHS AGO, SUB-GALACTIC CHATTER TOLD US THAT THE ULTRON INTELLIGENCE HAD LEFT EARTH AND WAS CAUSING TROUBLE IN OTHER PARTS OF THE UNIVERSE.
I GUESS... HE FOUND HIS WAY HOME.

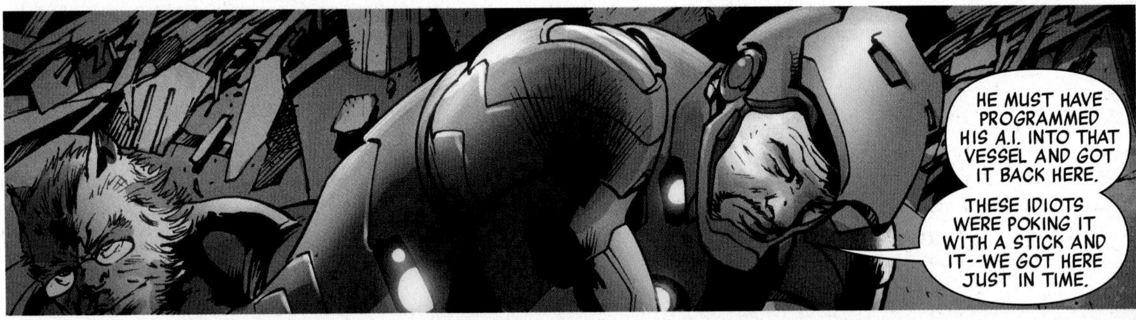
HE MUST HAVE PROGRAMMED HIS A.I. INTO THAT VESSEL AND GOT IT BACK HERE.
THESE IDIOTS WERE POKING IT WITH A STICK AND IT--WE GOT HERE JUST IN TIME.

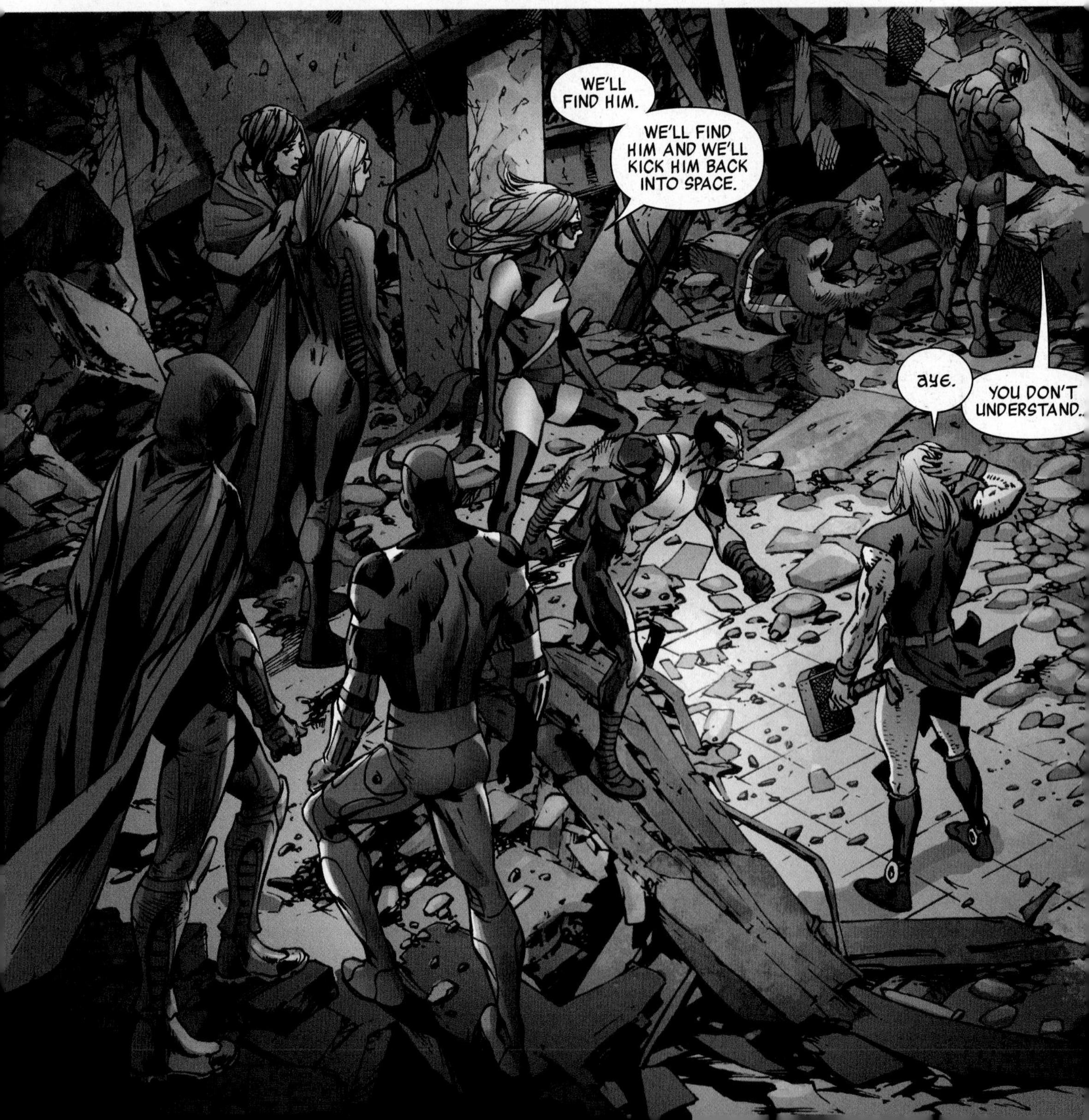
WE'LL FIND HIM.
WE'LL FIND HIM AND WE'LL KICK HIM BACK INTO SPACE.
aye.
YOU DON'T UNDERSTAND.

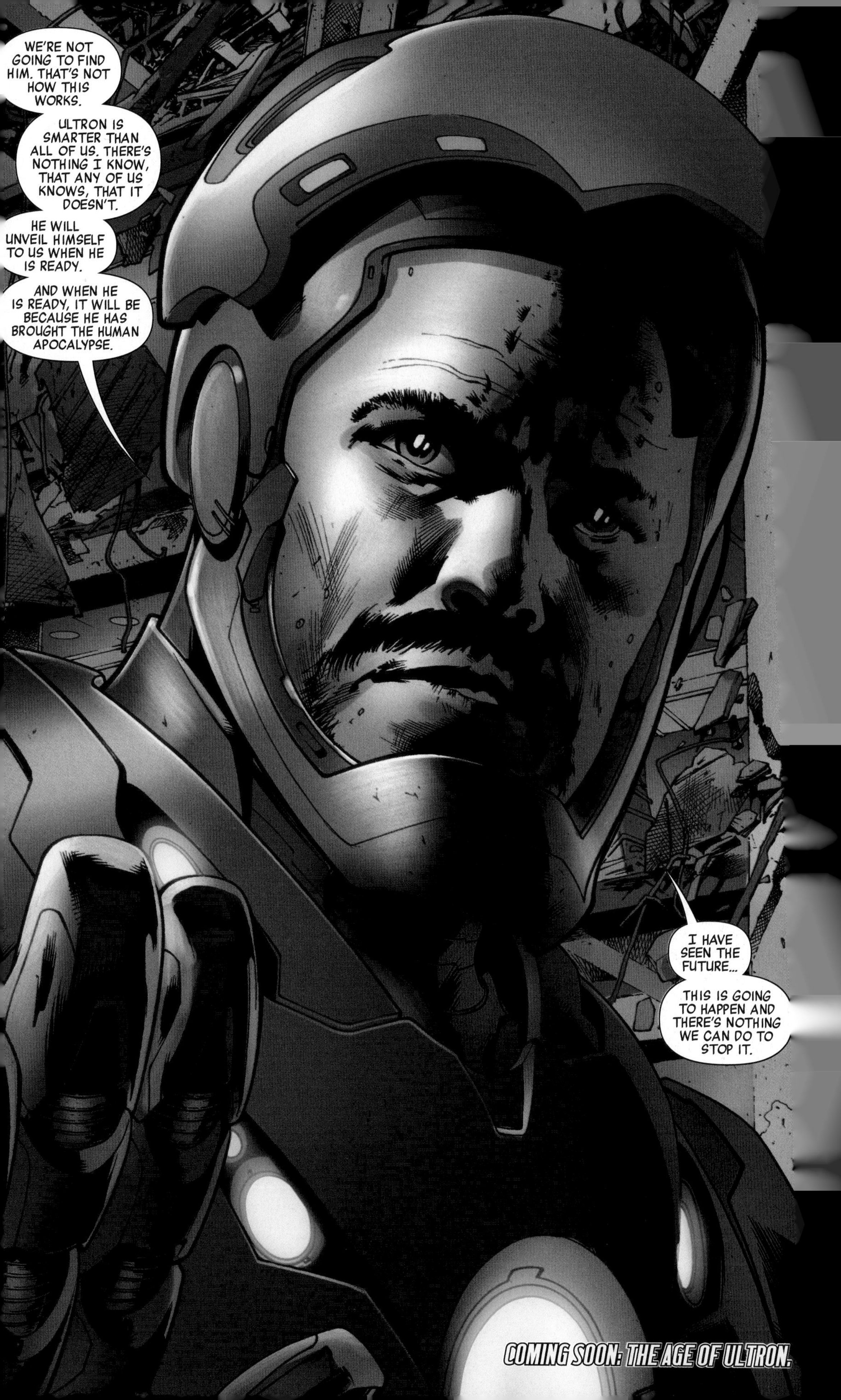
WE'RE NOT GOING TO FIND HIM. THAT'S NOT HOW THIS WORKS.
ULTRON IS SMARTER THAN ALL OF US. THERE'S NOTHING I KNOW, THAT ANY OF US KNOWS, THAT IT DOESN'T.
HE WILL UNVEIL HIMSELF TO US WHEN HE IS READY.
AND WHEN HE IS READY, IT WILL BE BECAUSE HE HAS BROUGHT THE HUMAN APOCALYPSE.
I HAVE SEEN THE FUTURE...
THIS IS GOING TO HAPPEN AND THERE'S NOTHING WE CAN DO TO STOP IT.
COMING SOON: THE AGE OF ULTRON.

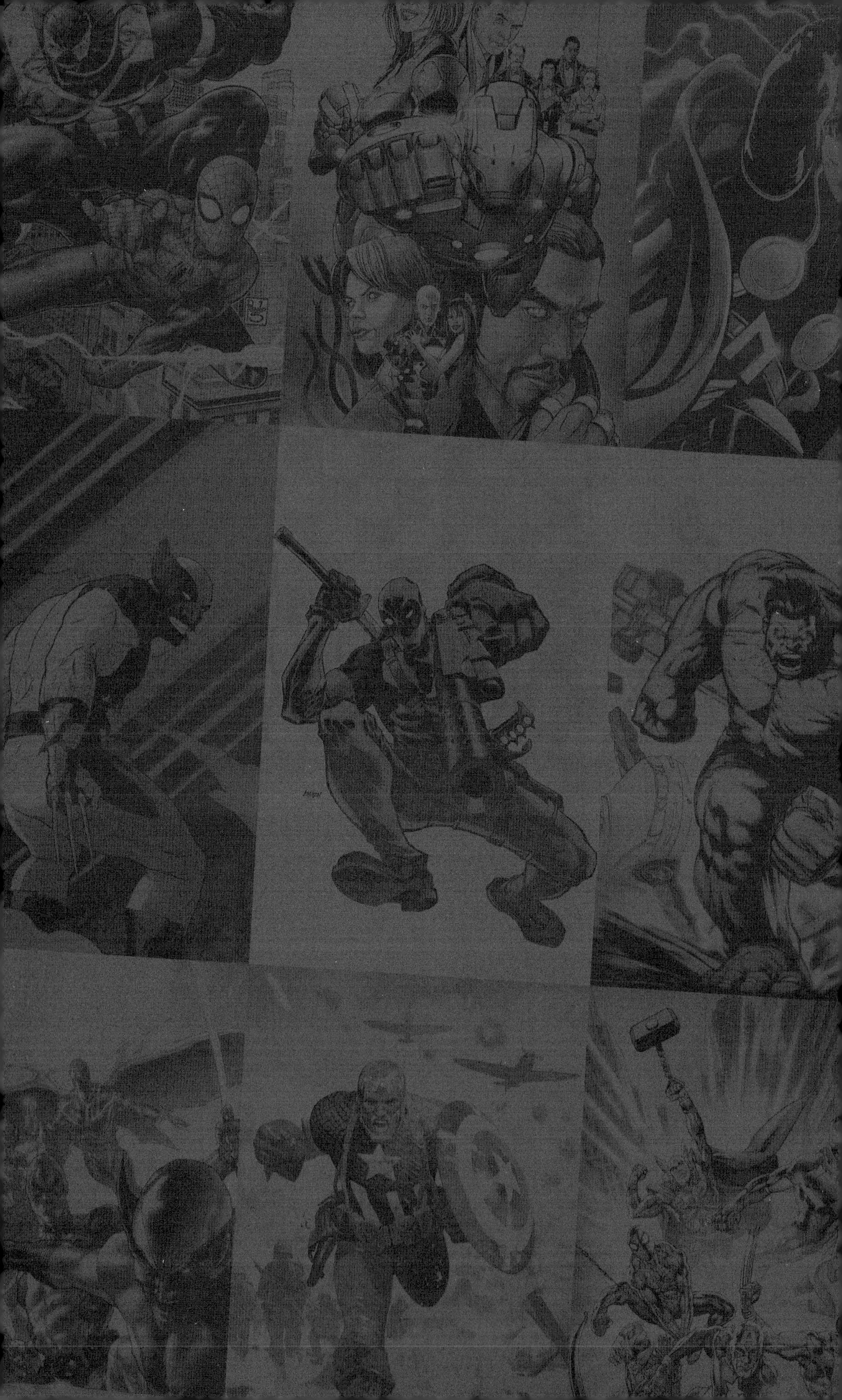

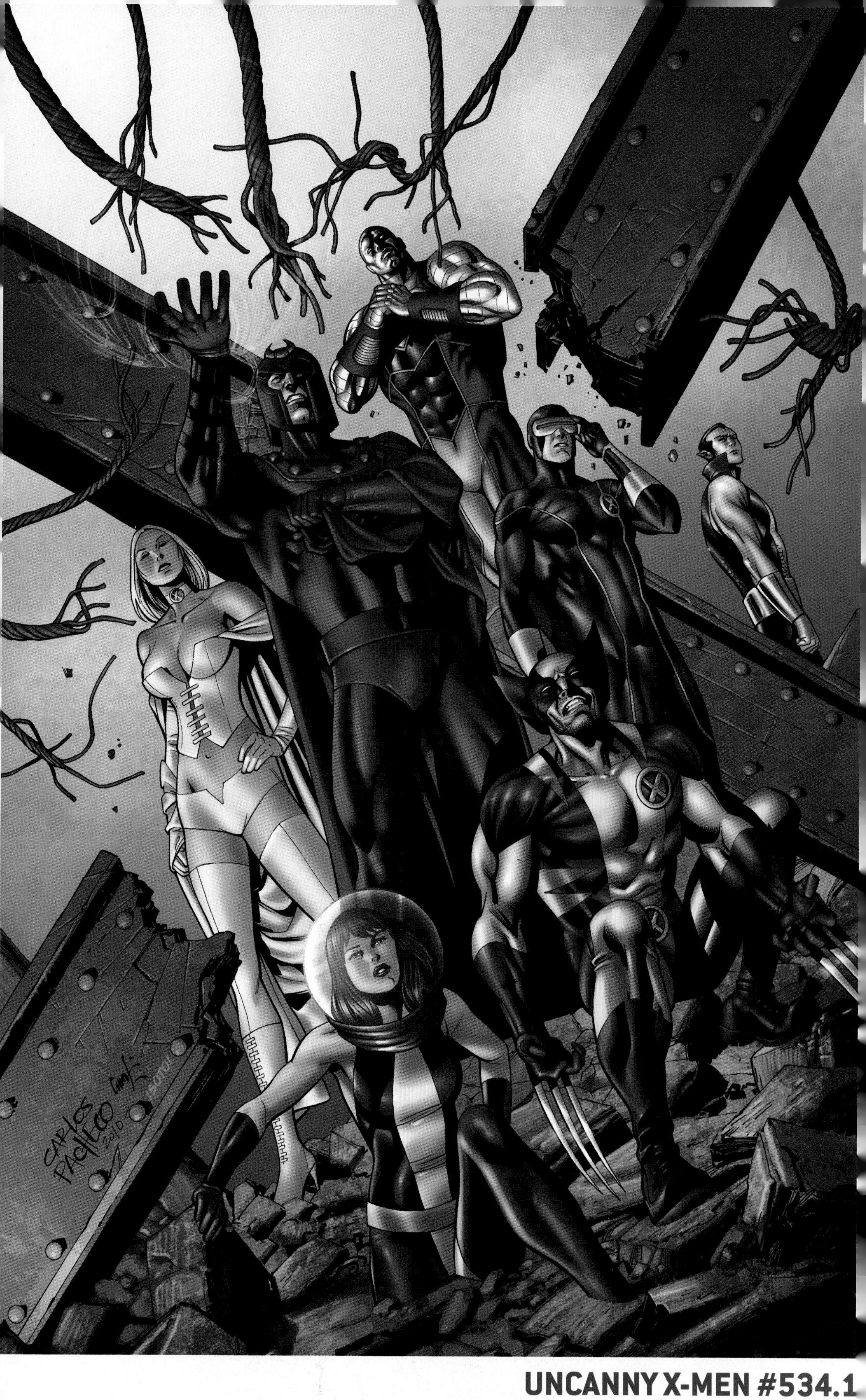
CARLOS PACHECO 2010

UNCANNY X-MEN #534.1

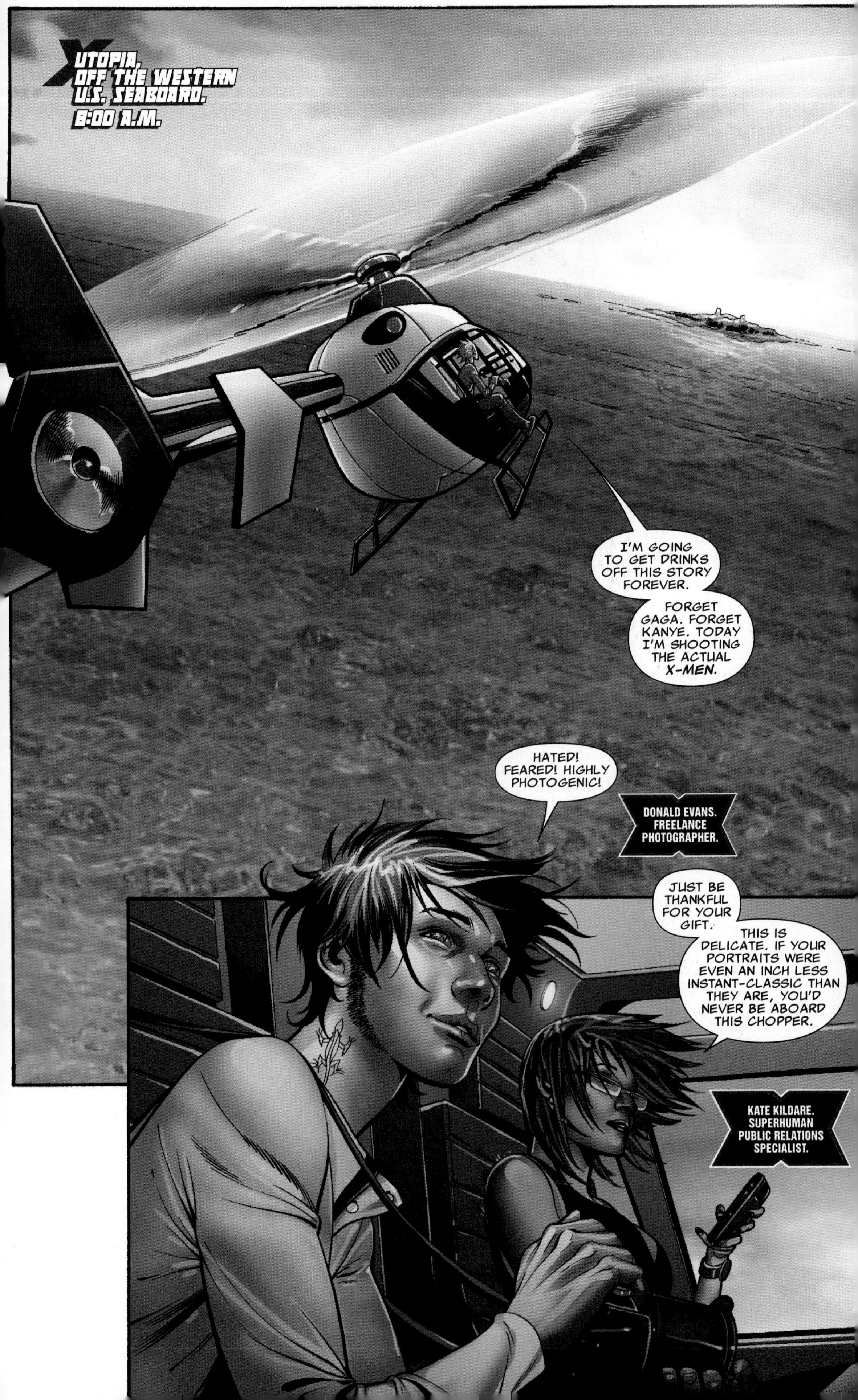
UTOPIA, OFF THE WESTERN U.S. SEABOARD. 8:00 A.M.
I'M GOING TO GET DRINKS OFF THIS STORY FOREVER.
FORGET GAGA. FORGET KANYE. TODAY I'M SHOOTING THE ACTUAL X-MEN.
HATED! FEARED! HIGHLY PHOTOGENIC!
DONALD EVANS. FREELANCE PHOTOGRAPHER.
JUST BE THANKFUL FOR YOUR GIFT.
THIS IS DELICATE. IF YOUR PORTRAITS WERE EVEN AN INCH LESS INSTANT-CLASSIC THAN THEY ARE, YOU'D NEVER BE ABOARD THIS CHOPPER.
KATE KILDARE. SUPERHUMAN PUBLIC RELATIONS SPECIALIST.

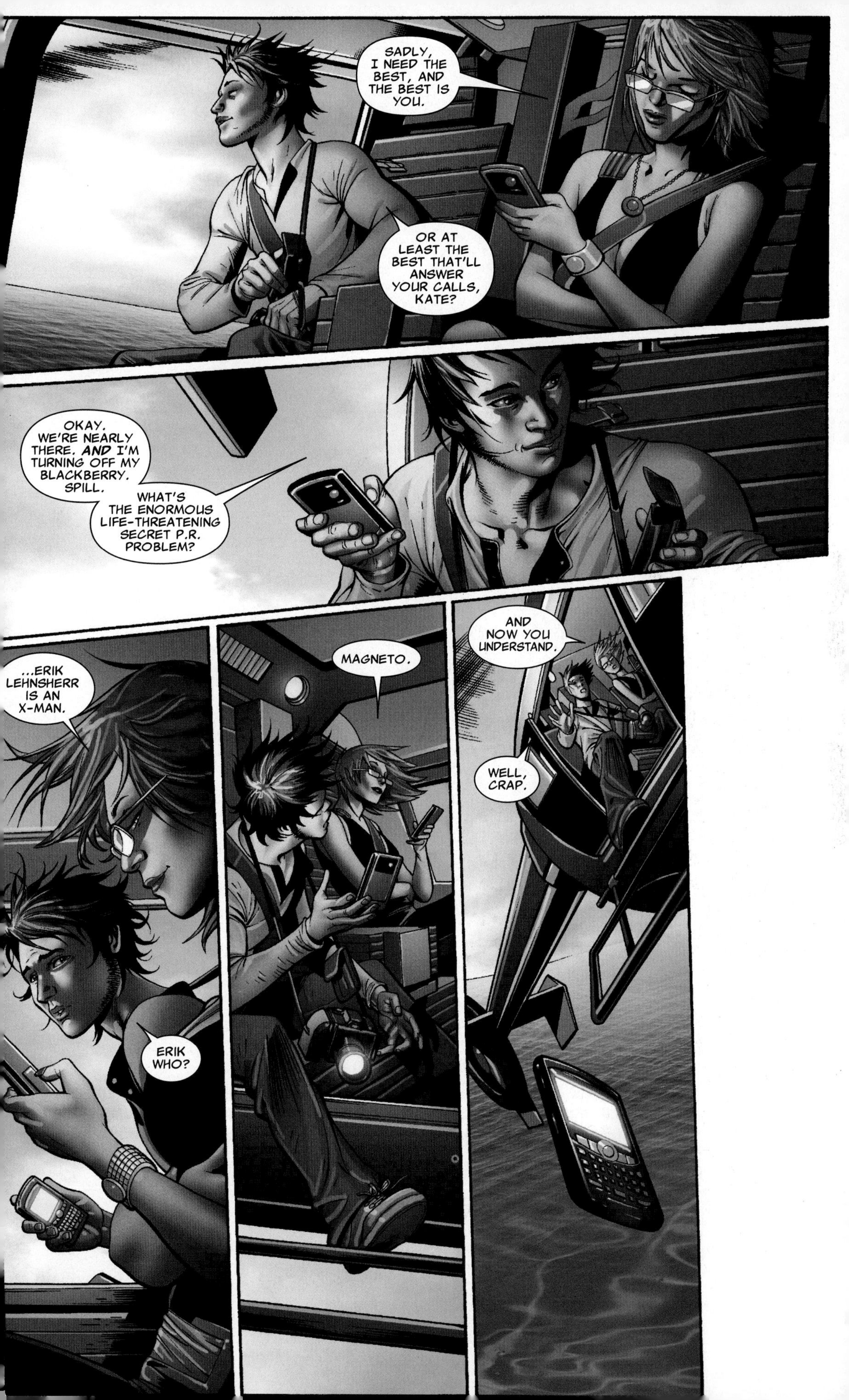
SADLY, I NEED THE BEST, AND THE BEST IS YOU.
OR AT LEAST THE BEST THAT'LL ANSWER YOUR CALLS, KATE?
OKAY. WE'RE NEARLY THERE. AND I'M TURNING OFF MY BLACKBERRY. SPILL.
WHAT'S THE ENORMOUS LIFE-THREATENING SECRET P.R. PROBLEM?
...ERIK LEHNSHERR IS AN X-MAN.
ERIK WHO?
MAGNETO.
AND NOW YOU UNDERSTAND.
WELL, CRAP.

BORN DIFFERENT WITH AMAZING SUPER-POWERS, THESE MUTANTS CAME TOGETHER TO PROTECT THOSE THAT HATE AND FEAR THEM. NOW, THEY HAVE DRAWN TOGETHER, LIVING ON THE ISLAND OF UTOPIA OFF THE COAST OF SAN FRANCISCO. THEY ARE...THE UNCANNY X-MEN.

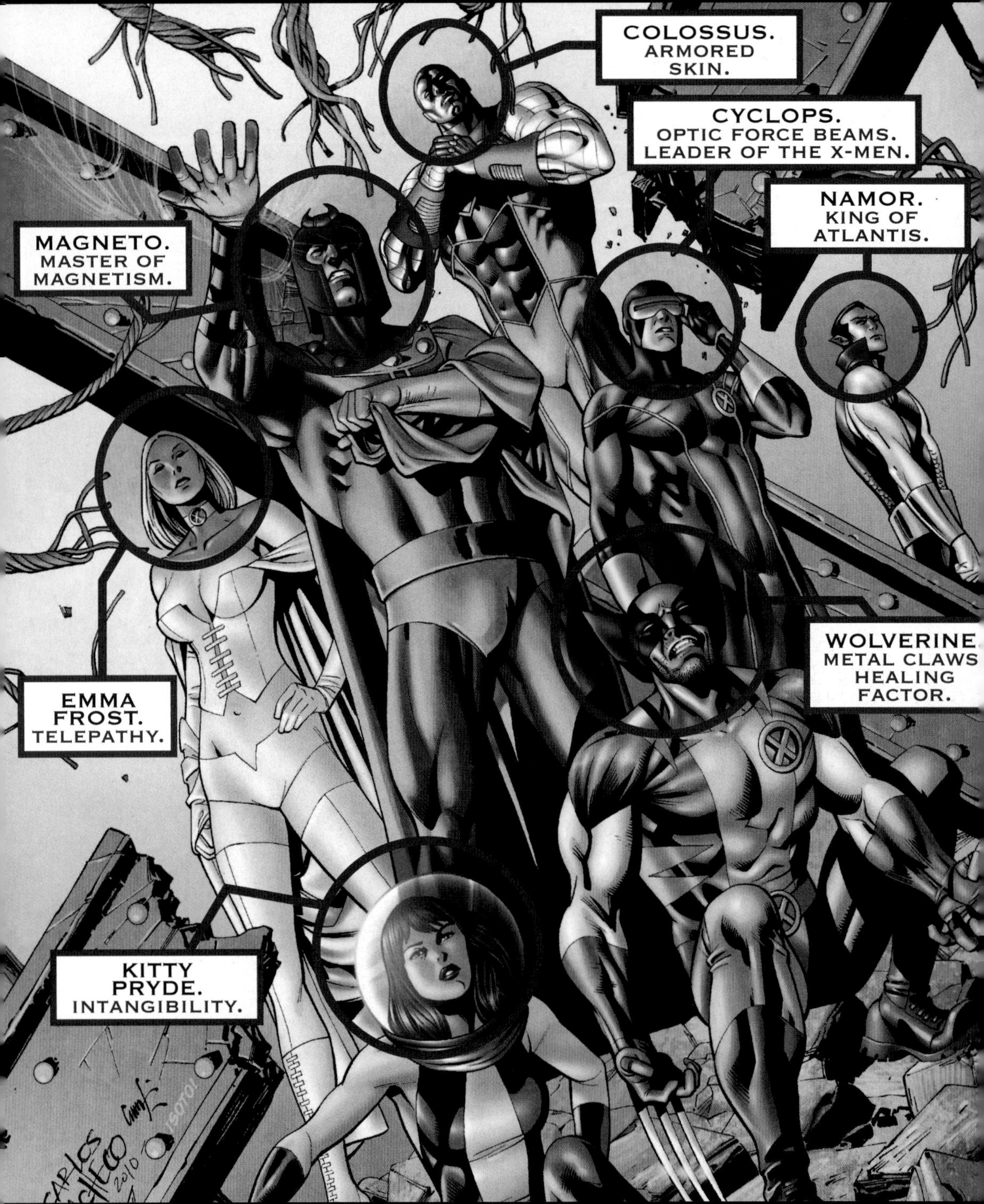
COLOSSUS. ARMORED SKIN.
CYCLOPS. OPTIC FORCE BEAMS. LEADER OF THE X-MEN.
NAMOR. KING OF ATLANTIS.
MAGNETO. MASTER OF MAGNETISM.
WOLVERINE METAL CLAWS HEALING FACTOR.
EMMA FROST. TELEPATHY.
KITTY PRYDE. INTANGIBILITY.
CARLOS PACHECO 2010

KIERON GILLEN – WRITER CARLOS PACHECO – PENCILS
CAM SMITH W/ DAN GREEN & NORMAN LEE – INKS FRANK D'ARMATA – COLORS
VC's JOE CARAMAGNA – LETTERS PACHECO, SMITH & SOTOCOLOR – COVER ART
JORDAN D. WHITE – ASSISTANT EDITOR DANIEL KETCHUM – ASSOCIATE EDITOR NICK LOWE – EDITOR
AXEL ALONSO – EDITOR IN CHIEF JOE QUESADA – CHIEF CREATIVE OFFICER
DAN BUCKLEY – PUBLISHER ALAN FINE – EXECUTIVE PRODUCER

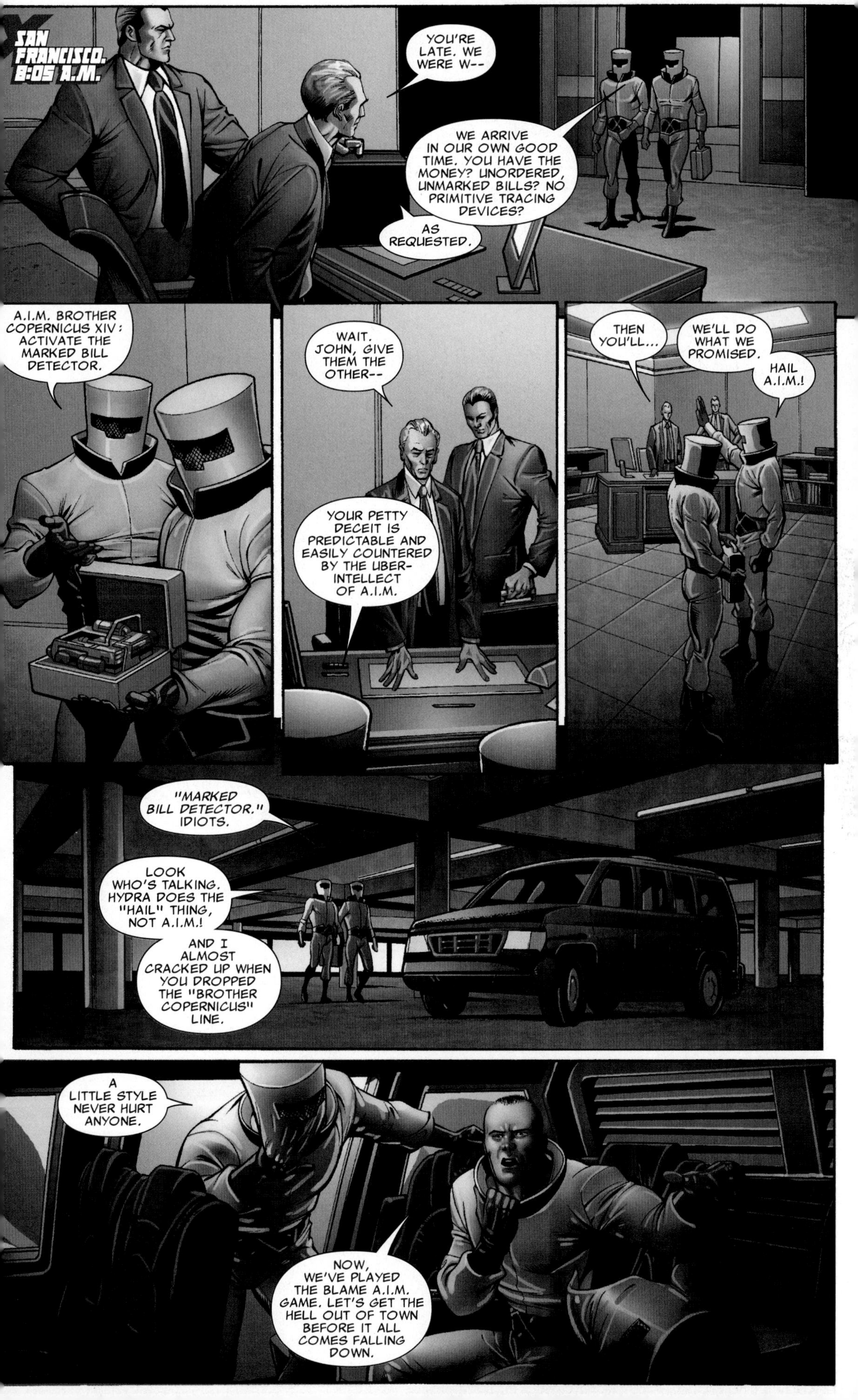
SAN FRANCISCO. 8:05 A.M.
YOU'RE LATE. WE WERE W--
WE ARRIVE IN OUR OWN GOOD TIME. YOU HAVE THE MONEY? UNORDERED, UNMARKED BILLS? NO PRIMITIVE TRACING DEVICES?
AS REQUESTED.
A.I.M. BROTHER COPERNICUS XIV: ACTIVATE THE MARKED BILL DETECTOR.
WAIT. JOHN, GIVE THEM THE OTHER--
YOUR PETTY DECEIT IS PREDICTABLE AND EASILY COUNTERED BY THE UBER-INTELLECT OF A.I.M.
THEN YOU'LL...
WE'LL DO WHAT WE PROMISED.
HAIL A.I.M.!
"MARKED BILL DETECTOR." IDIOTS.
LOOK WHO'S TALKING. HYDRA DOES THE "HAIL" THING, NOT A.I.M.!
AND I ALMOST CRACKED UP WHEN YOU DROPPED THE "BROTHER COPERNICUS" LINE.
A LITTLE STYLE NEVER HURT ANYONE.
NOW, WE'VE PLAYED THE BLAME A.I.M. GAME. LET'S GET THE HELL OUT OF TOWN BEFORE IT ALL COMES FALLING DOWN.

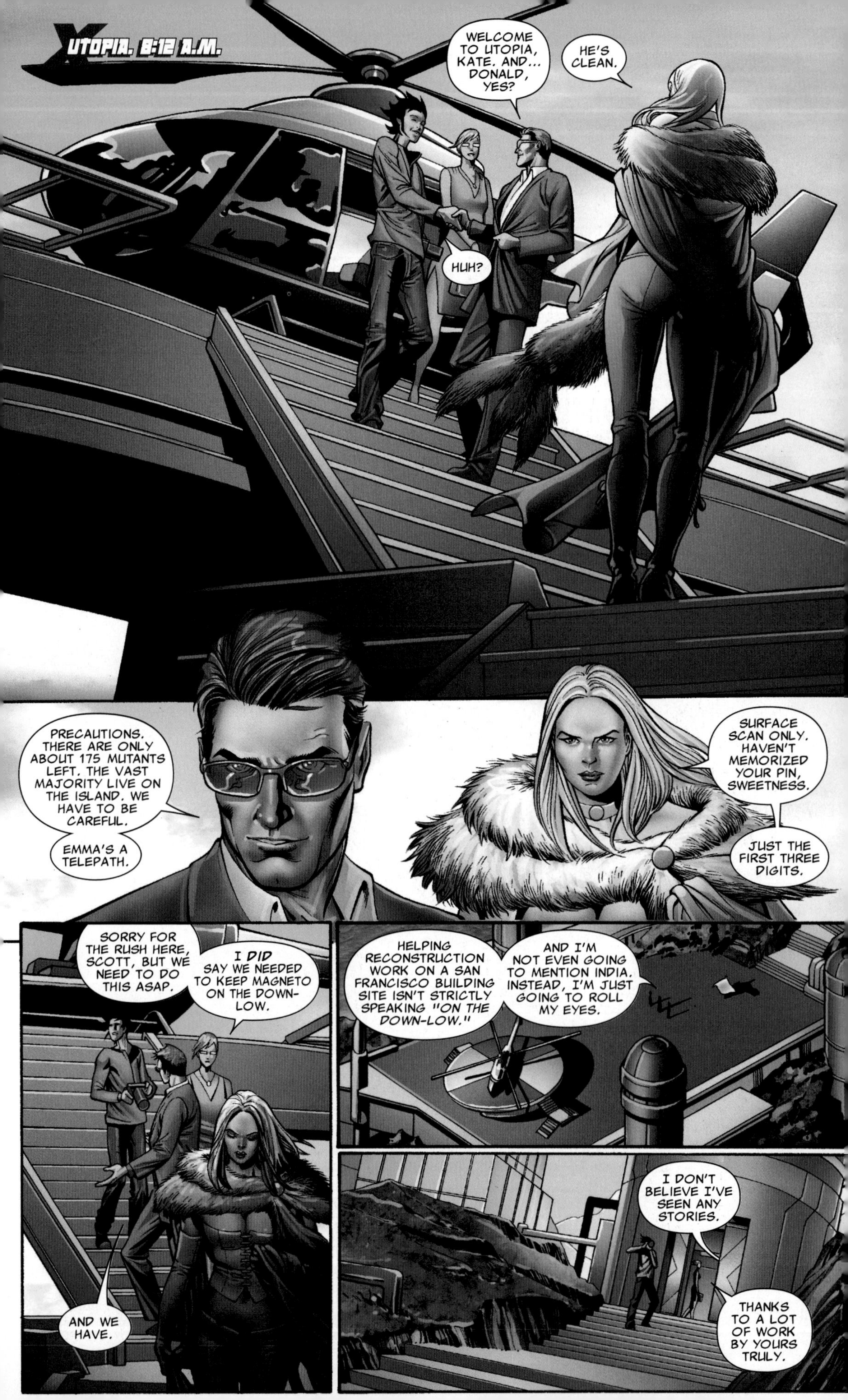
UTOPIA. 8:12 A.M.
WELCOME TO UTOPIA, KATE. AND... DONALD, YES?
HE'S CLEAN.
HUH?
PRECAUTIONS. THERE ARE ONLY ABOUT 175 MUTANTS LEFT. THE VAST MAJORITY LIVE ON THE ISLAND. WE HAVE TO BE CAREFUL.
EMMA'S A TELEPATH.
SURFACE SCAN ONLY. HAVEN'T MEMORIZED YOUR PIN, SWEETNESS.
JUST THE FIRST THREE DIGITS.
SORRY FOR THE RUSH HERE, SCOTT, BUT WE NEED TO DO THIS ASAP.
I *DID* SAY WE NEEDED TO KEEP MAGNETO ON THE DOWN-LOW.
AND WE HAVE.
HELPING RECONSTRUCTION WORK ON A SAN FRANCISCO BUILDING SITE ISN'T STRICTLY SPEAKING "ON THE DOWN-LOW."
AND I'M NOT EVEN GOING TO MENTION INDIA. INSTEAD, I'M JUST GOING TO ROLL MY EYES.
I DON'T BELIEVE I'VE SEEN ANY STORIES.
THANKS TO A LOT OF WORK BY YOURS TRULY.

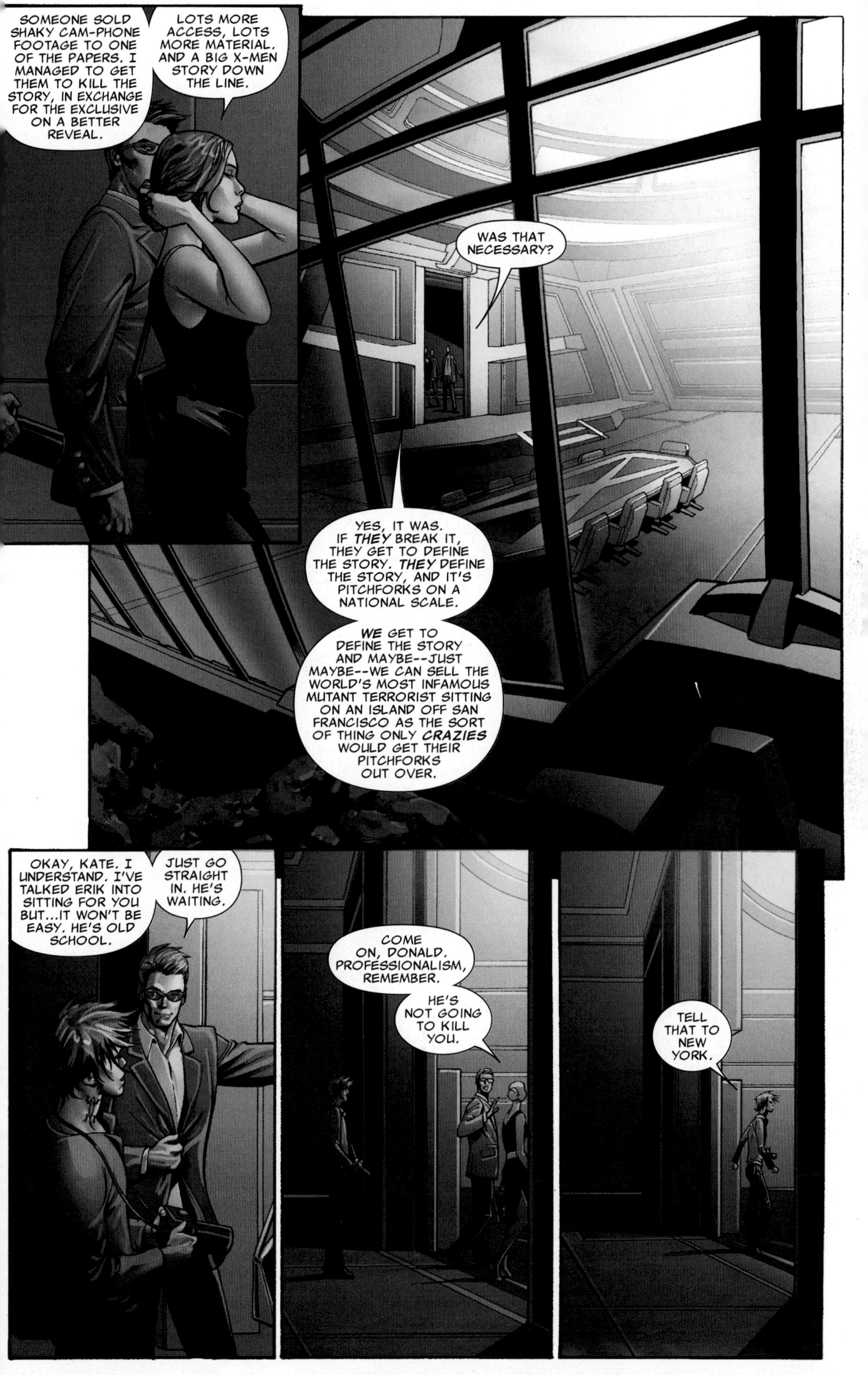
SOMEONE SOLD SHAKY CAM-PHONE FOOTAGE TO ONE OF THE PAPERS. I MANAGED TO GET THEM TO KILL THE STORY, IN EXCHANGE FOR THE EXCLUSIVE ON A BETTER REVEAL.
LOTS MORE ACCESS, LOTS MORE MATERIAL. AND A BIG X-MEN STORY DOWN THE LINE.
WAS THAT NECESSARY?
YES, IT WAS. IF *THEY* BREAK IT, THEY GET TO DEFINE THE STORY. *THEY* DEFINE THE STORY, AND IT'S PITCHFORKS ON A NATIONAL SCALE.
WE GET TO DEFINE THE STORY AND MAYBE--JUST MAYBE--WE CAN SELL THE WORLD'S MOST INFAMOUS MUTANT TERRORIST SITTING ON AN ISLAND OFF SAN FRANCISCO AS THE SORT OF THING ONLY *CRAZIES* WOULD GET THEIR PITCHFORKS OUT OVER.
OKAY, KATE. I UNDERSTAND. I'VE TALKED ERIK INTO SITTING FOR YOU BUT...IT WON'T BE EASY. HE'S OLD SCHOOL.
JUST GO STRAIGHT IN. HE'S WAITING.
COME ON, DONALD. PROFESSIONALISM, REMEMBER.
HE'S NOT GOING TO KILL YOU.
TELL THAT TO NEW YORK.

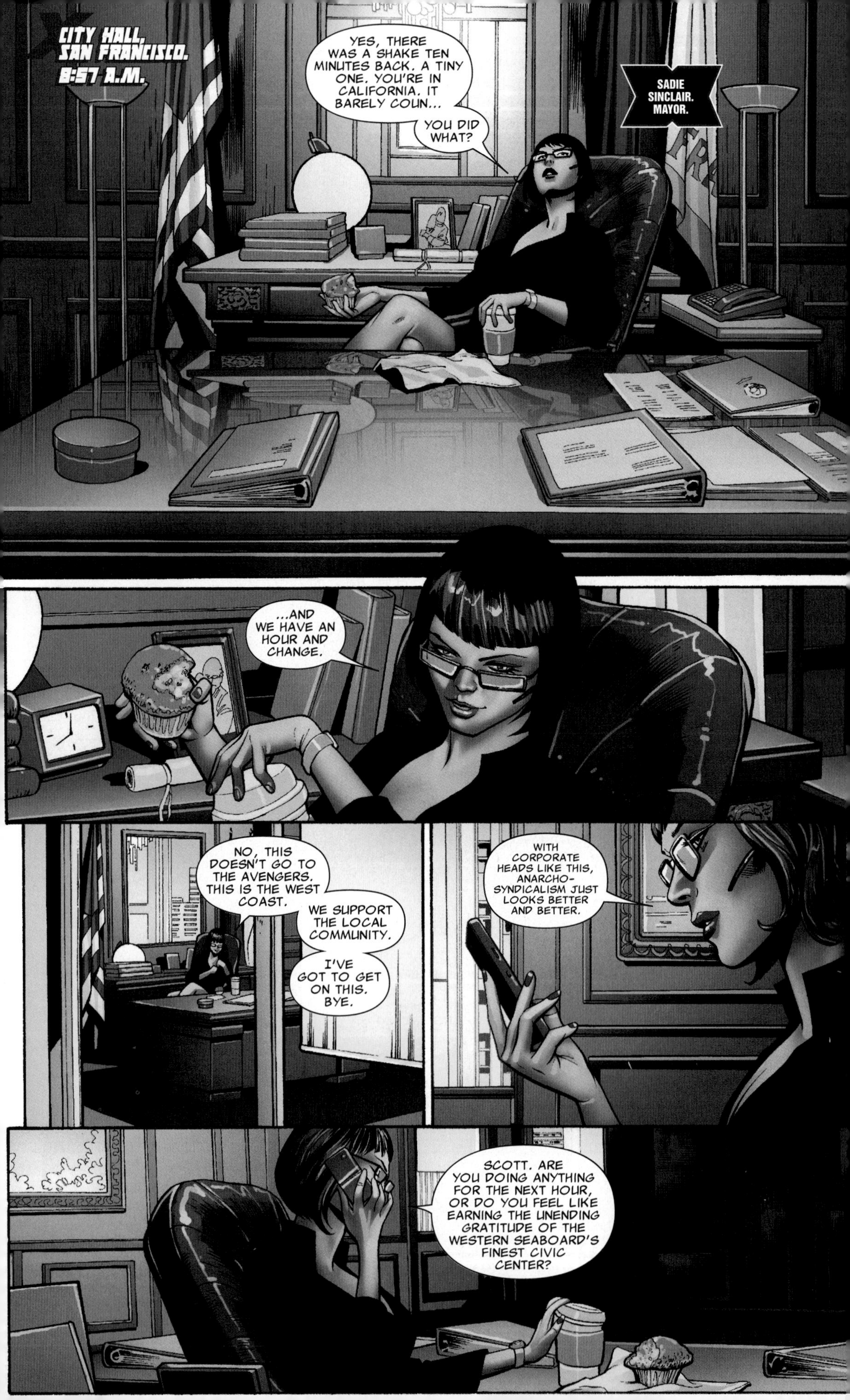

CITY HALL, SAN FRANCISCO.
8:57 A.M.
YES, THERE WAS A SHAKE TEN MINUTES BACK. A TINY ONE. YOU'RE IN CALIFORNIA. IT BARELY COUN...
YOU DID WHAT?
SADIE SINCLAIR. MAYOR.
...AND WE HAVE AN HOUR AND CHANGE.
NO, THIS DOESN'T GO TO THE AVENGERS. THIS IS THE WEST COAST.
WE SUPPORT THE LOCAL COMMUNITY.
I'VE GOT TO GET ON THIS. BYE.
WITH CORPORATE HEADS LIKE THIS, ANARCHO-SYNDICALISM JUST LOOKS BETTER AND BETTER.
SCOTT. ARE YOU DOING ANYTHING FOR THE NEXT HOUR, OR DO YOU FEEL LIKE EARNING THE UNENDING GRATITUDE OF THE WESTERN SEABOARD'S FINEST CIVIC CENTER?

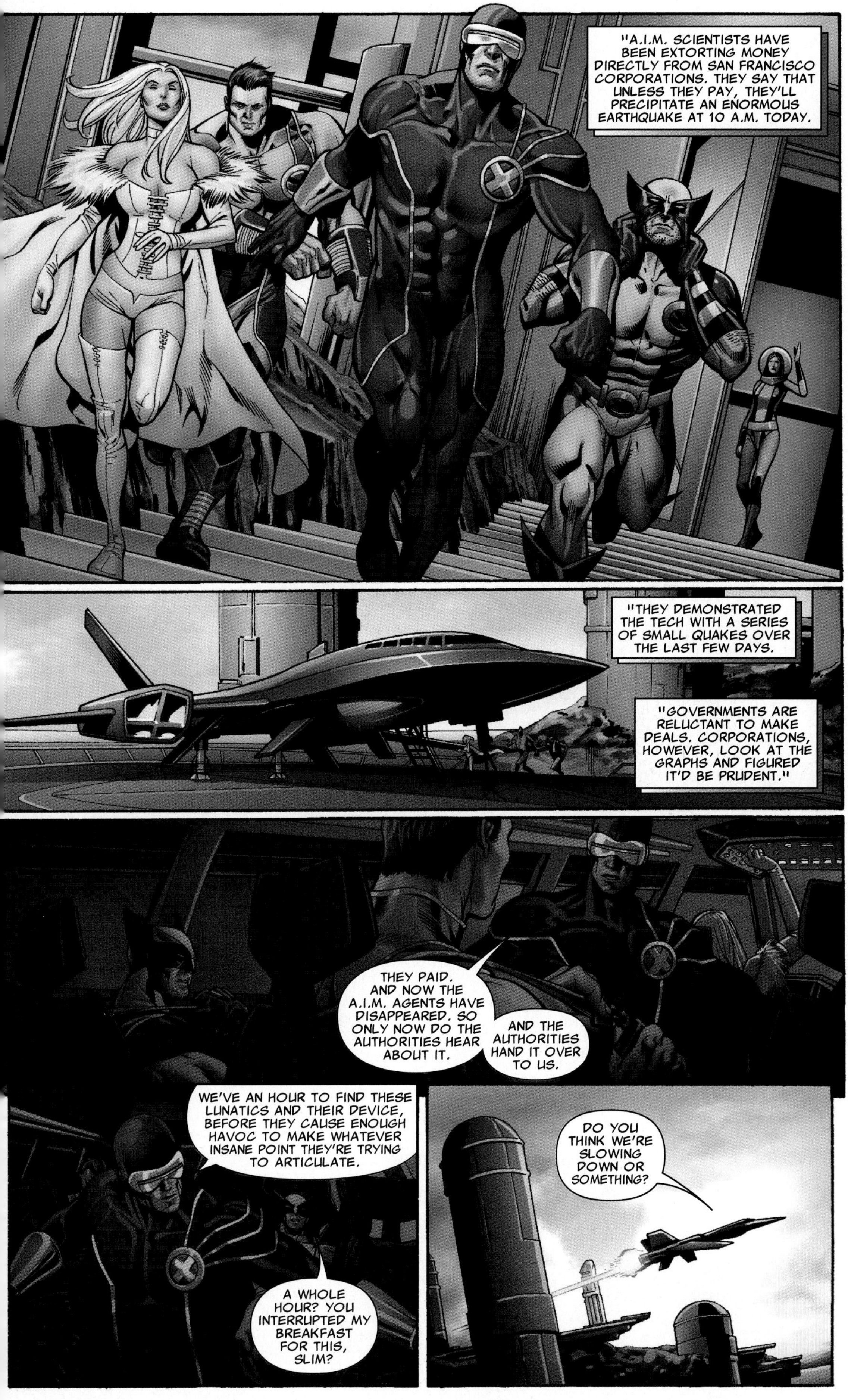
"A.I.M. SCIENTISTS HAVE BEEN EXTORTING MONEY DIRECTLY FROM SAN FRANCISCO CORPORATIONS. THEY SAY THAT UNLESS THEY PAY, THEY'LL PRECIPITATE AN ENORMOUS EARTHQUAKE AT 10 A.M. TODAY.
"THEY DEMONSTRATED THE TECH WITH A SERIES OF SMALL QUAKES OVER THE LAST FEW DAYS.
"GOVERNMENTS ARE RELUCTANT TO MAKE DEALS. CORPORATIONS, HOWEVER, LOOK AT THE GRAPHS AND FIGURED IT'D BE PRUDENT."
THEY PAID. AND NOW THE A.I.M. AGENTS HAVE DISAPPEARED. SO ONLY NOW DO THE AUTHORITIES HEAR ABOUT IT.
AND THE AUTHORITIES HAND IT OVER TO US.
WE'VE AN HOUR TO FIND THESE LUNATICS AND THEIR DEVICE, BEFORE THEY CAUSE ENOUGH HAVOC TO MAKE WHATEVER INSANE POINT THEY'RE TRYING TO ARTICULATE.
A WHOLE HOUR? YOU INTERRUPTED MY BREAKFAST FOR THIS, SLIM?
DO YOU THINK WE'RE SLOWING DOWN OR SOMETHING?

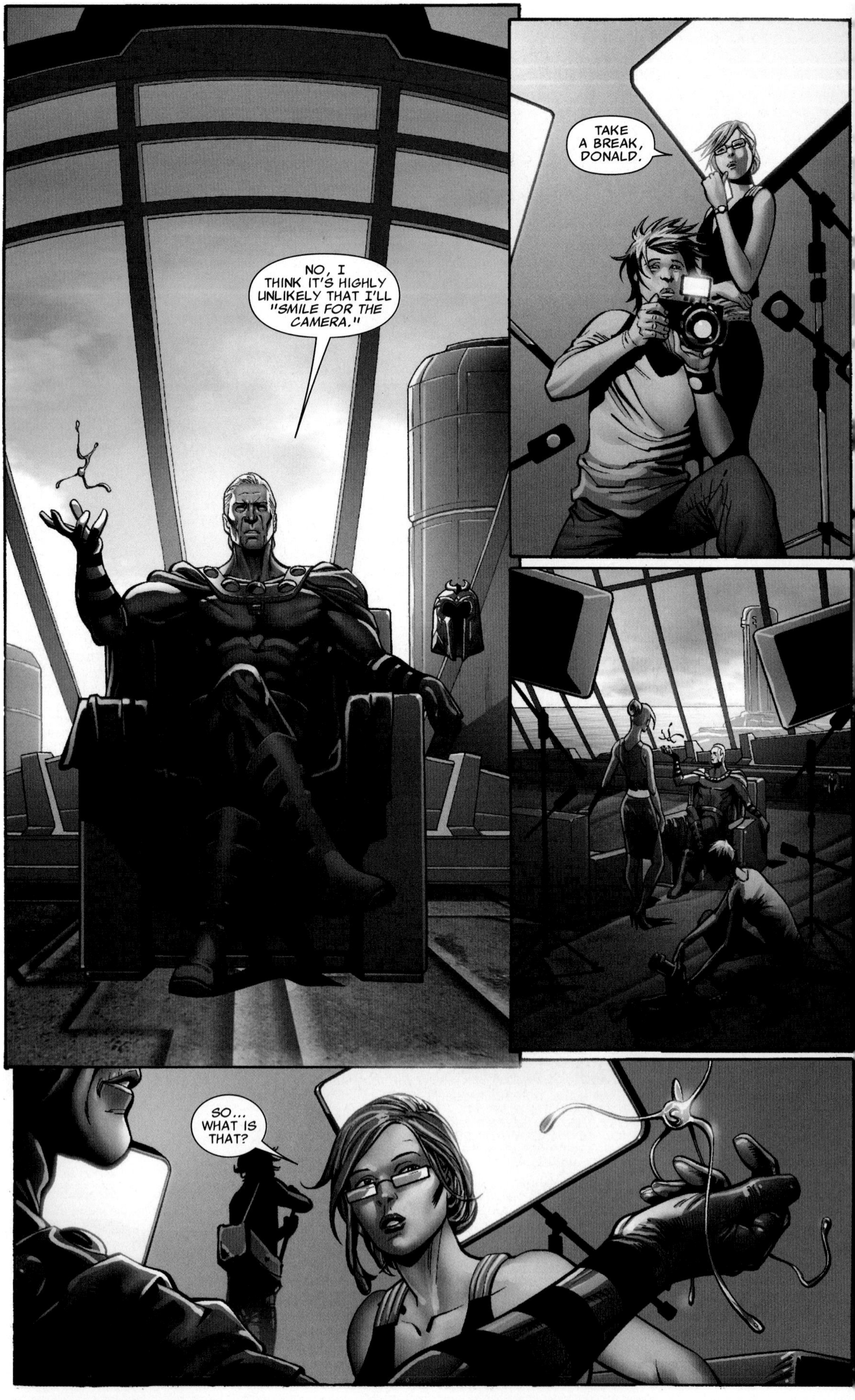
NO, I THINK IT'S HIGHLY UNLIKELY THAT I'LL "SMILE FOR THE CAMERA."
TAKE A BREAK, DONALD.
SO... WHAT IS THAT?

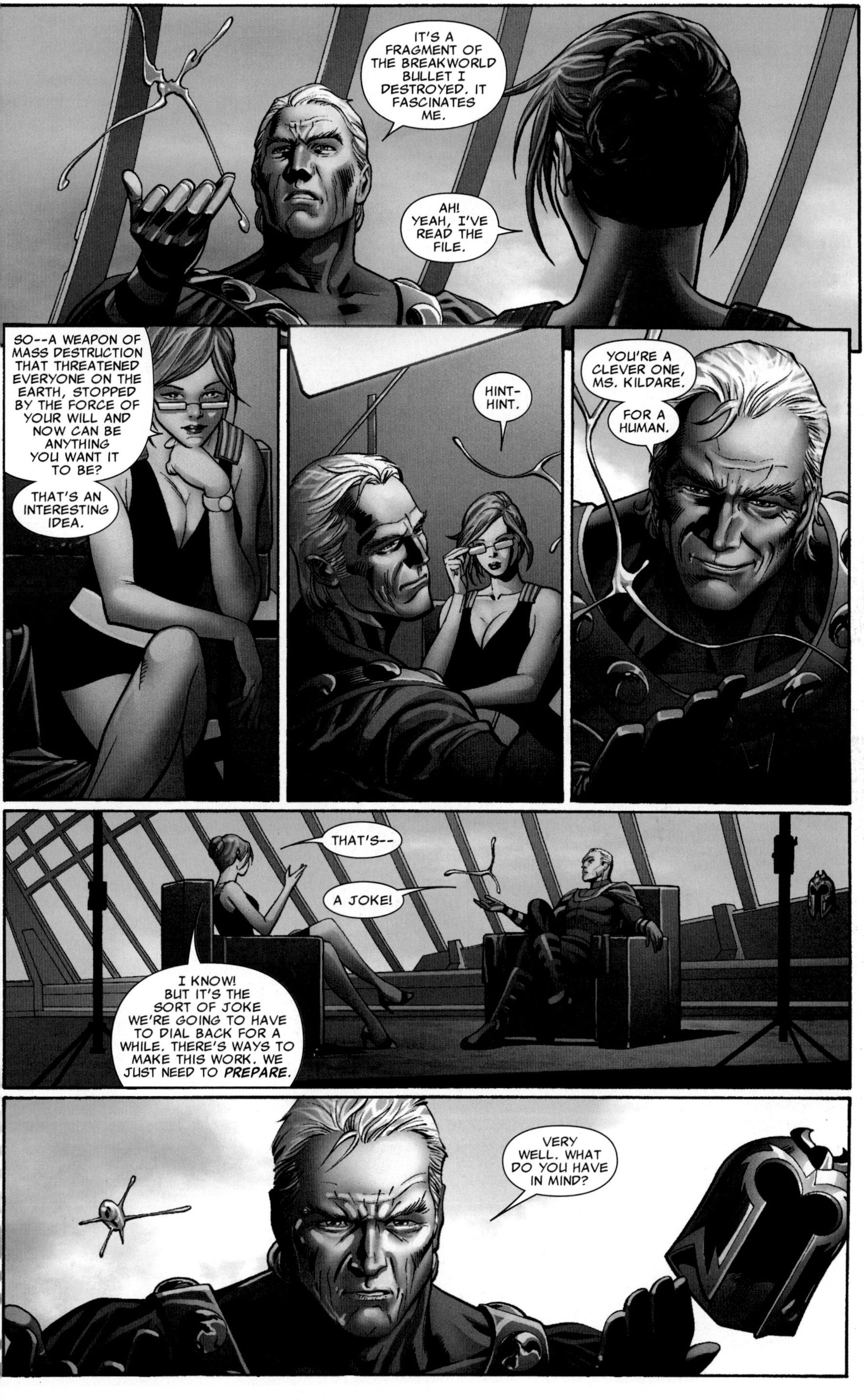
IT'S A FRAGMENT OF THE BREAKWORLD BULLET I DESTROYED. IT FASCINATES ME.
AH! YEAH, I'VE READ THE FILE.
SO--A WEAPON OF MASS DESTRUCTION THAT THREATENED EVERYONE ON THE EARTH, STOPPED BY THE FORCE OF YOUR WILL AND NOW CAN BE ANYTHING YOU WANT IT TO BE?
THAT'S AN INTERESTING IDEA.
HINT-HINT.
YOU'RE A CLEVER ONE, MS. KILDARE.
FOR A HUMAN.
THAT'S--
A JOKE!
I KNOW! BUT IT'S THE SORT OF JOKE WE'RE GOING TO HAVE TO DIAL BACK FOR A WHILE. THERE'S WAYS TO MAKE THIS WORK. WE JUST NEED TO *PREPARE*.
VERY WELL. WHAT DO YOU HAVE IN MIND?

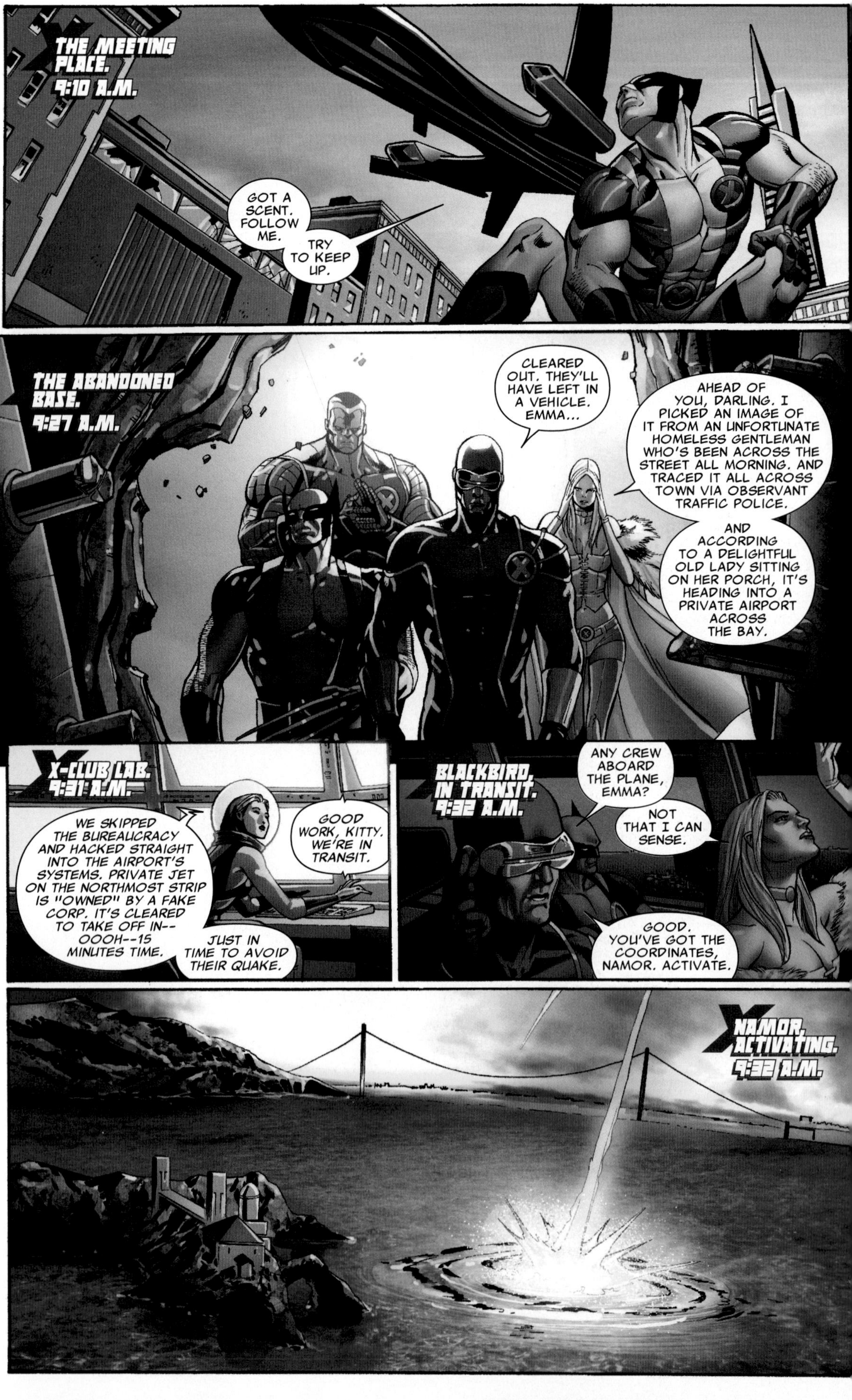
THE MEETING PLACE. 9:10 A.M.
GOT A SCENT. FOLLOW ME.
TRY TO KEEP UP.
THE ABANDONED BASE. 9:27 A.M.
CLEARED OUT. THEY'LL HAVE LEFT IN A VEHICLE. EMMA...
AHEAD OF YOU, DARLING. I PICKED AN IMAGE OF IT FROM AN UNFORTUNATE HOMELESS GENTLEMAN WHO'S BEEN ACROSS THE STREET ALL MORNING. AND TRACED IT ALL ACROSS TOWN VIA OBSERVANT TRAFFIC POLICE.
AND ACCORDING TO A DELIGHTFUL OLD LADY SITTING ON HER PORCH, IT'S HEADING INTO A PRIVATE AIRPORT ACROSS THE BAY.
X-CLUB LAB. 9:31 A.M.
WE SKIPPED THE BUREAUCRACY AND HACKED STRAIGHT INTO THE AIRPORT'S SYSTEMS. PRIVATE JET ON THE NORTHMOST STRIP IS "OWNED" BY A FAKE CORP. IT'S CLEARED TO TAKE OFF IN-- OOOH--15 MINUTES TIME.
GOOD WORK, KITTY. WE'RE IN TRANSIT.
JUST IN TIME TO AVOID THEIR QUAKE.
BLACKBIRD, IN TRANSIT. 9:32 A.M.
ANY CREW ABOARD THE PLANE, EMMA?
NOT THAT I CAN SENSE.
GOOD. YOU'VE GOT THE COORDINATES, NAMOR. ACTIVATE.
NAMOR, ACTIVATING. 9:32 A.M.

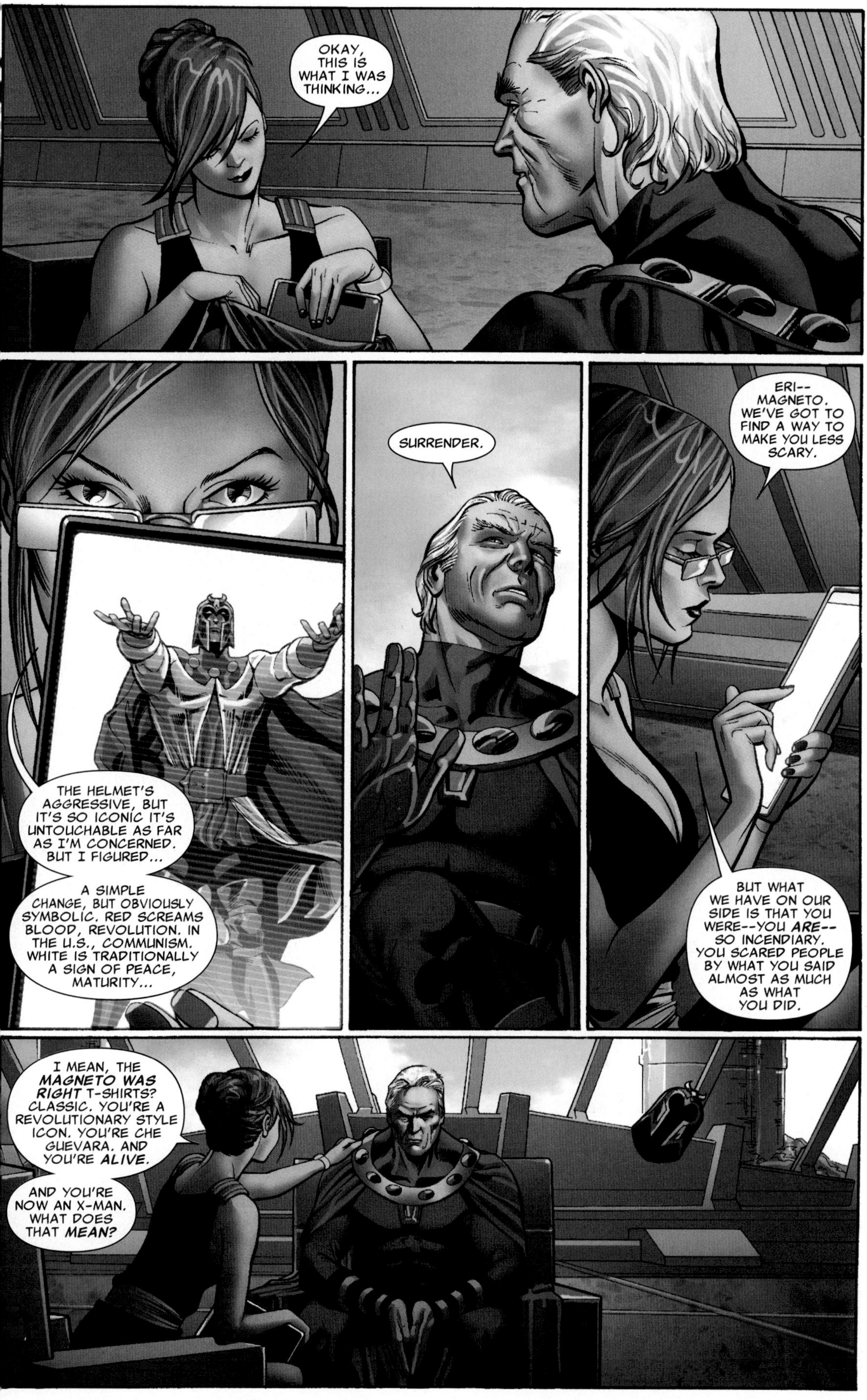
OKAY, THIS IS WHAT I WAS THINKING...
THE HELMET'S AGGRESSIVE, BUT IT'S SO ICONIC IT'S UNTOUCHABLE AS FAR AS I'M CONCERNED. BUT I FIGURED...
A SIMPLE CHANGE, BUT OBVIOUSLY SYMBOLIC. RED SCREAMS BLOOD, REVOLUTION. IN THE U.S., COMMUNISM. WHITE IS TRADITIONALLY A SIGN OF PEACE, MATURITY...
SURRENDER.
ERI--MAGNETO. WE'VE GOT TO FIND A WAY TO MAKE YOU LESS SCARY.
BUT WHAT WE HAVE ON OUR SIDE IS THAT YOU WERE--YOU *ARE*--SO INCENDIARY. YOU SCARED PEOPLE BY WHAT YOU SAID ALMOST AS MUCH AS WHAT YOU DID.
I MEAN, THE *MAGNETO WAS RIGHT* T-SHIRTS? CLASSIC. YOU'RE A REVOLUTIONARY STYLE ICON. YOU'RE CHE GUEVARA. AND YOU'RE *ALIVE*.
AND YOU'RE NOW AN X-MAN. WHAT DOES THAT *MEAN?*

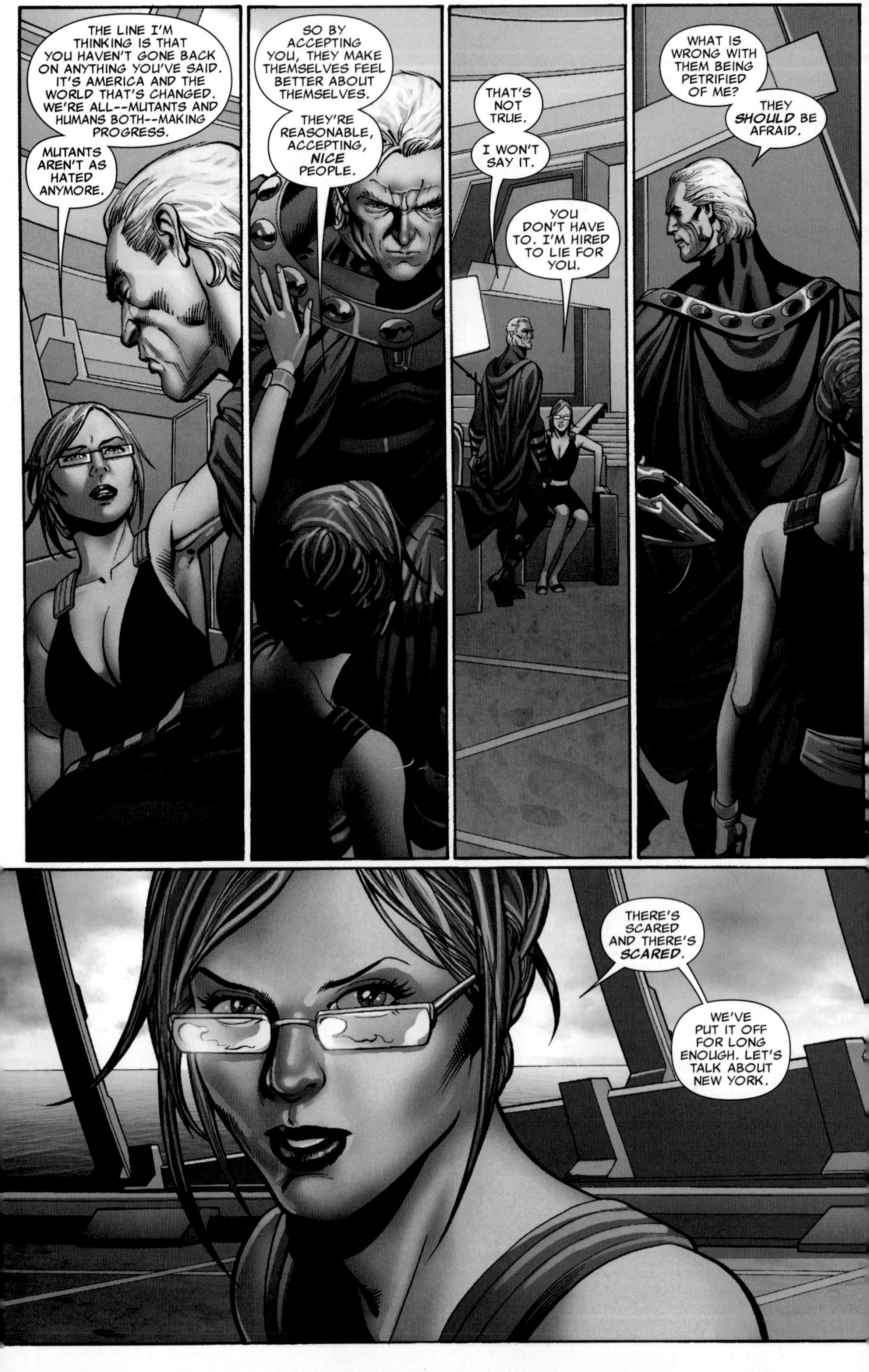
THE LINE I'M THINKING IS THAT YOU HAVEN'T GONE BACK ON ANYTHING YOU'VE SAID. IT'S AMERICA AND THE WORLD THAT'S CHANGED. WE'RE ALL--MUTANTS AND HUMANS BOTH--MAKING PROGRESS.
MUTANTS AREN'T AS HATED ANYMORE.
SO BY ACCEPTING YOU, THEY MAKE THEMSELVES FEEL BETTER ABOUT THEMSELVES.
THEY'RE REASONABLE, ACCEPTING, **NICE** PEOPLE.
THAT'S NOT TRUE.
I WON'T SAY IT.
YOU DON'T HAVE TO. I'M HIRED TO LIE FOR YOU.
WHAT IS WRONG WITH THEM BEING PETRIFIED OF ME?
THEY **SHOULD** BE AFRAID.
THERE'S SCARED AND THERE'S **SCARED**.
WE'VE PUT IT OFF FOR LONG ENOUGH. LET'S TALK ABOUT NEW YORK.

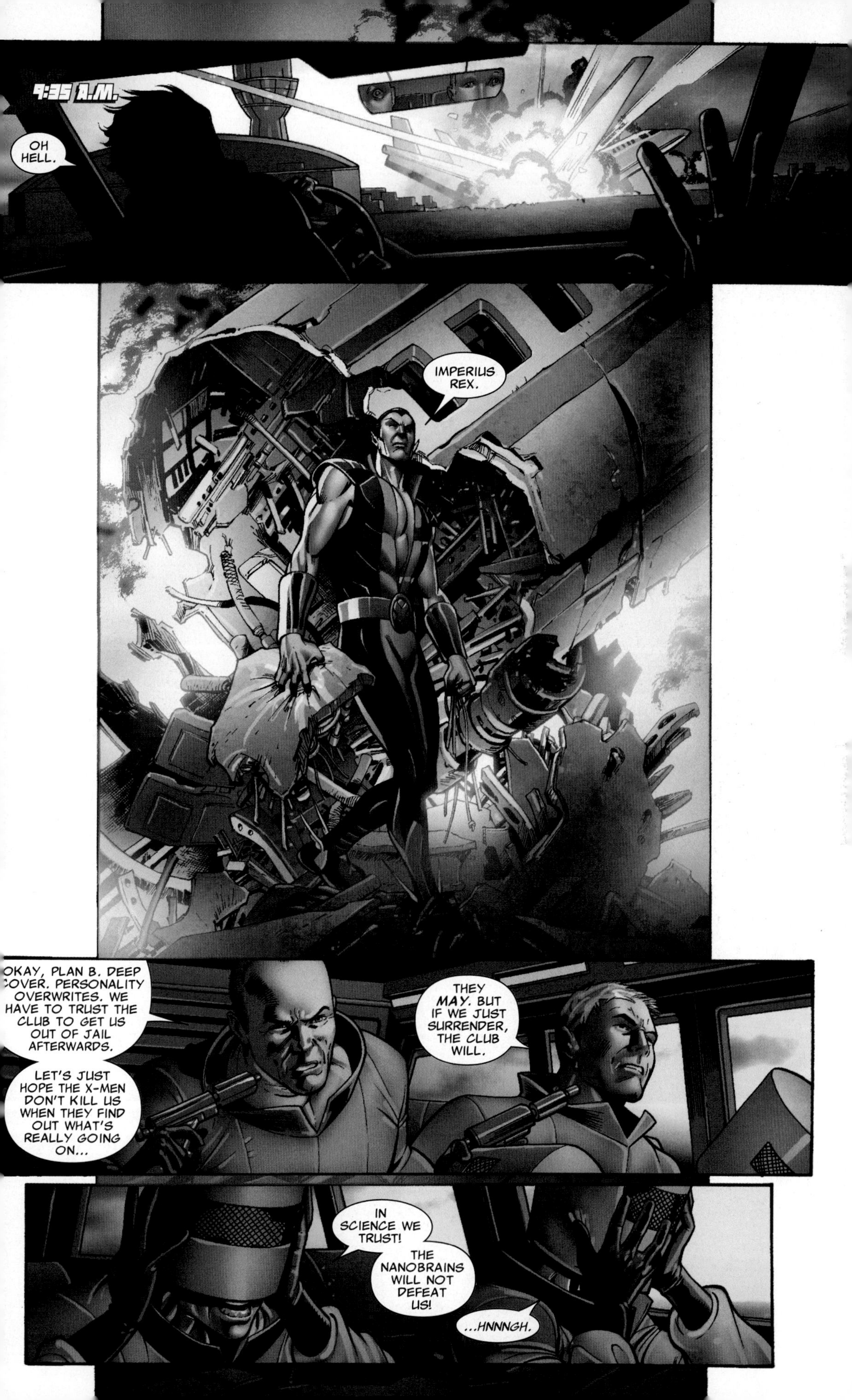
9:35 A.M.
OH HELL.
IMPERIUS REX.
OKAY, PLAN B. DEEP COVER. PERSONALITY OVERWRITES. WE HAVE TO TRUST THE CLUB TO GET US OUT OF JAIL AFTERWARDS.
LET'S JUST HOPE THE X-MEN DON'T KILL US WHEN THEY FIND OUT WHAT'S REALLY GOING ON...
THEY MAY. BUT IF WE JUST SURRENDER, THE CLUB WILL.
IN SCIENCE WE TRUST!
THE NANOBRAINS WILL NOT DEFEAT US!
...HNNNGH.

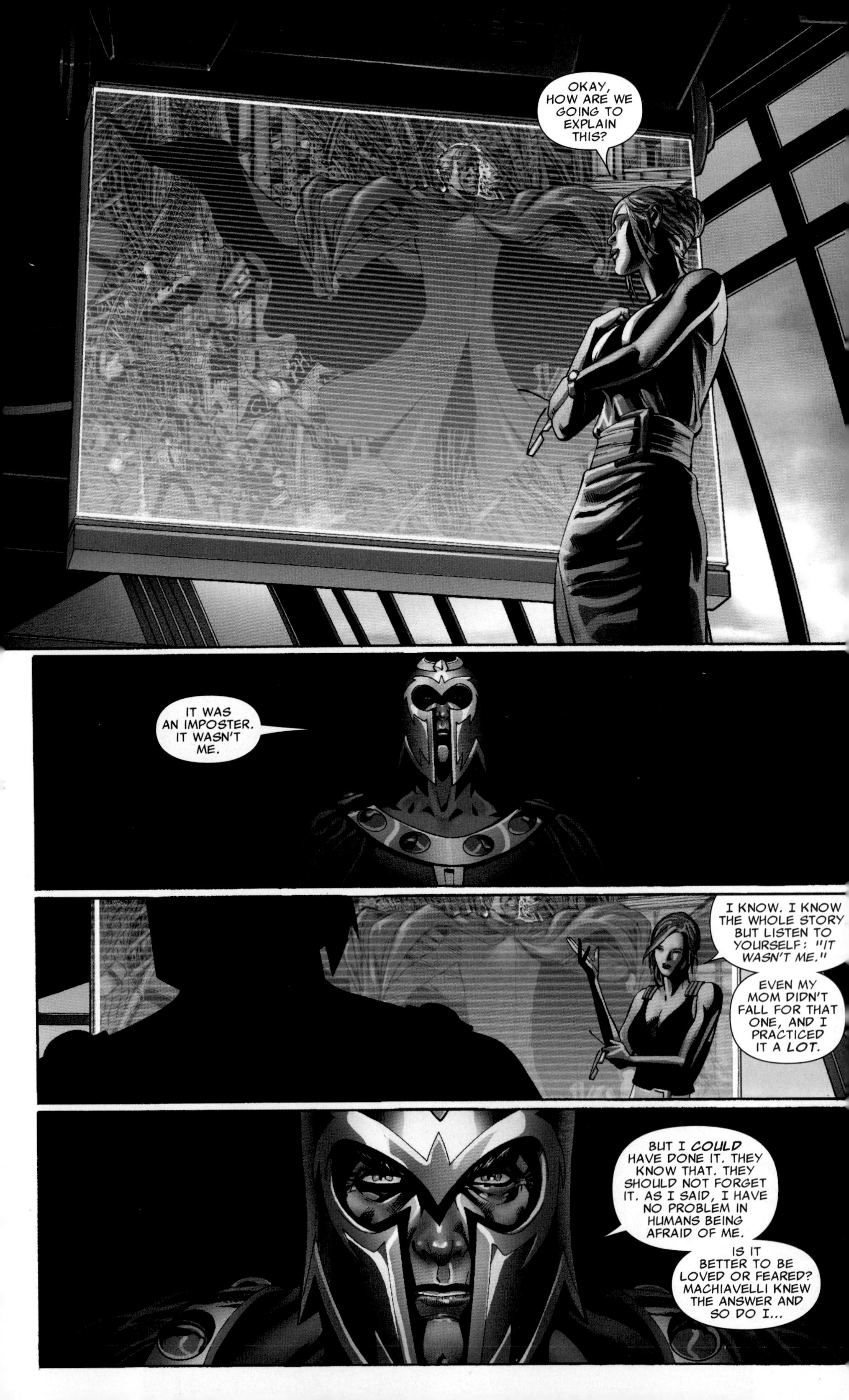
OKAY, HOW ARE WE GOING TO EXPLAIN THIS?
IT WAS AN IMPOSTER. IT WASN'T ME.
I KNOW. I KNOW THE WHOLE STORY BUT LISTEN TO YOURSELF: "IT WASN'T ME."
EVEN MY MOM DIDN'T FALL FOR THAT ONE, AND I PRACTICED IT A LOT.
BUT I COULD HAVE DONE IT. THEY KNOW THAT. THEY SHOULD NOT FORGET IT. AS I SAID, I HAVE NO PROBLEM IN HUMANS BEING AFRAID OF ME.
IS IT BETTER TO BE LOVED OR FEARED? MACHIAVELLI KNEW THE ANSWER AND SO DO I...

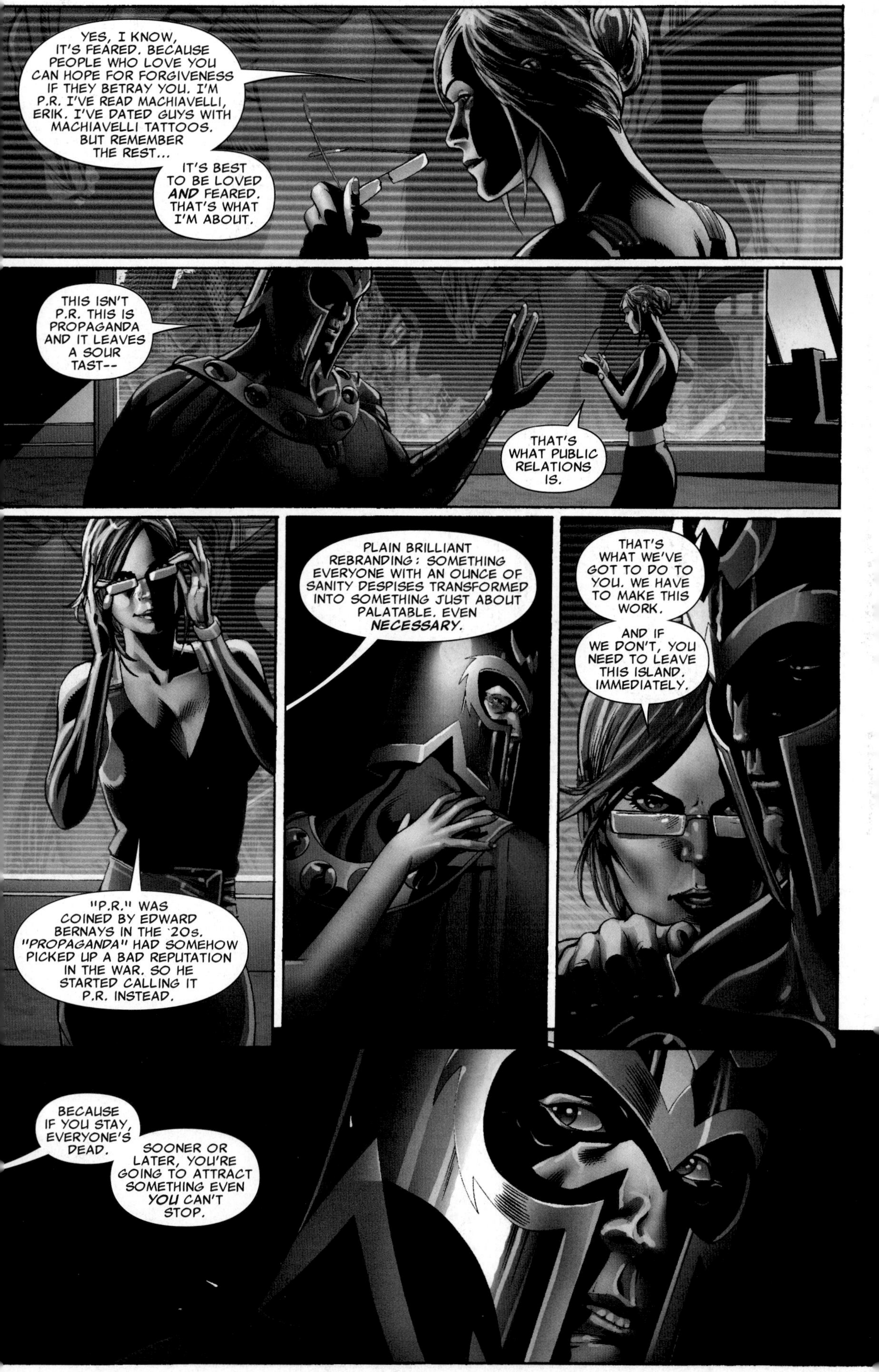
YES, I KNOW, IT'S FEARED. BECAUSE PEOPLE WHO LOVE YOU CAN HOPE FOR FORGIVENESS IF THEY BETRAY YOU. I'M P.R. I'VE READ MACHIAVELLI, ERIK. I'VE DATED GUYS WITH MACHIAVELLI TATTOOS. BUT REMEMBER THE REST...
IT'S BEST TO BE LOVED AND FEARED. THAT'S WHAT I'M ABOUT.
THIS ISN'T P.R. THIS IS PROPAGANDA AND IT LEAVES A SOUR TAST--
THAT'S WHAT PUBLIC RELATIONS IS.
"P.R." WAS COINED BY EDWARD BERNAYS IN THE '20s. "PROPAGANDA" HAD SOMEHOW PICKED UP A BAD REPUTATION IN THE WAR. SO HE STARTED CALLING IT P.R. INSTEAD.
PLAIN BRILLIANT REBRANDING: SOMETHING EVERYONE WITH AN OUNCE OF SANITY DESPISES TRANSFORMED INTO SOMETHING JUST ABOUT PALATABLE. EVEN NECESSARY.
THAT'S WHAT WE'VE GOT TO DO TO YOU. WE HAVE TO MAKE THIS WORK.
AND IF WE DON'T, YOU NEED TO LEAVE THIS ISLAND. IMMEDIATELY.
BECAUSE IF YOU STAY, EVERYONE'S DEAD.
SOONER OR LATER, YOU'RE GOING TO ATTRACT SOMETHING EVEN YOU CAN'T STOP.

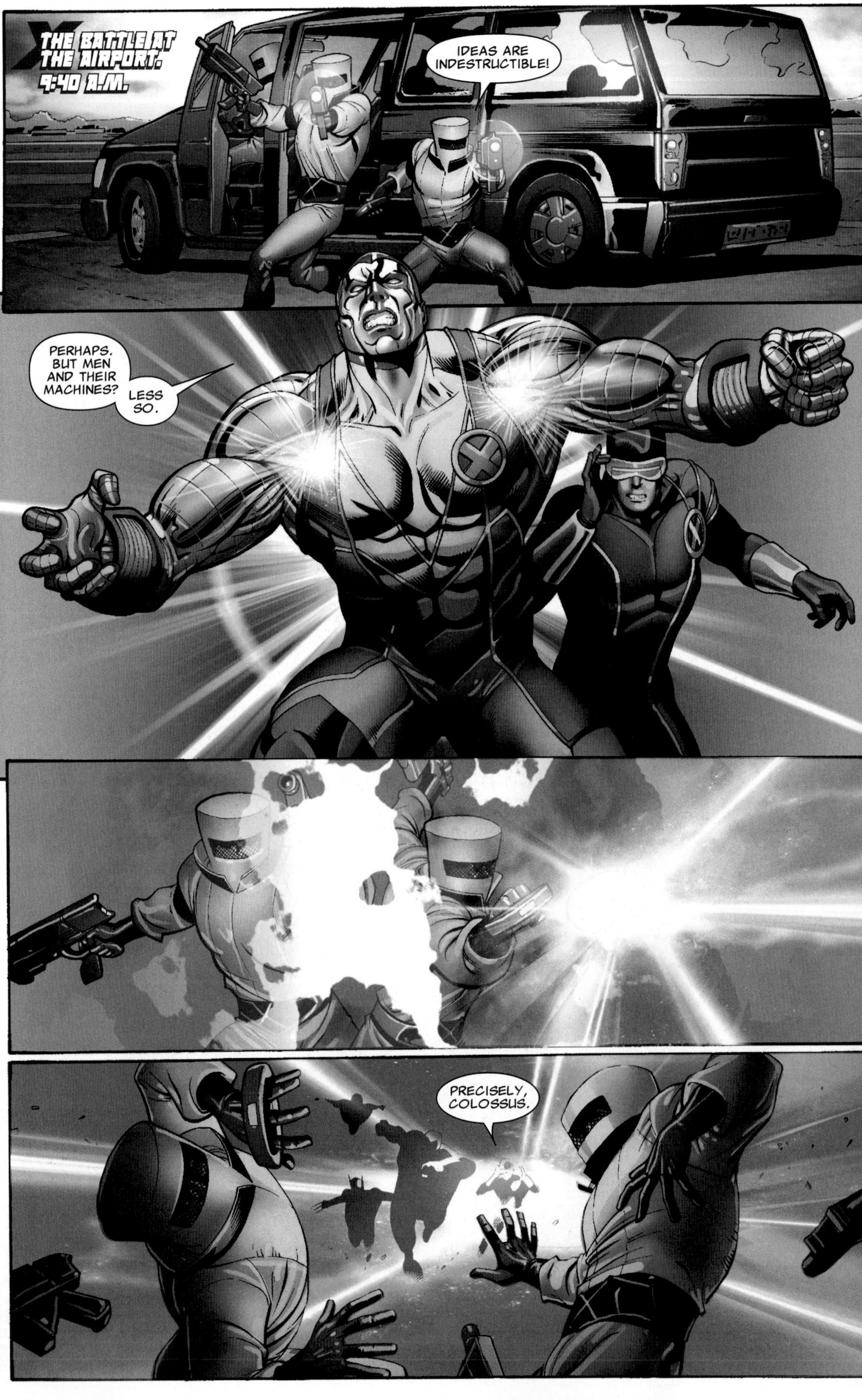
THE BATTLE AT THE AIRPORT. 9:40 A.M.
IDEAS ARE INDESTRUCTIBLE!
PERHAPS. BUT MEN AND THEIR MACHINES?
LESS SO.
PRECISELY, COLOSSUS.

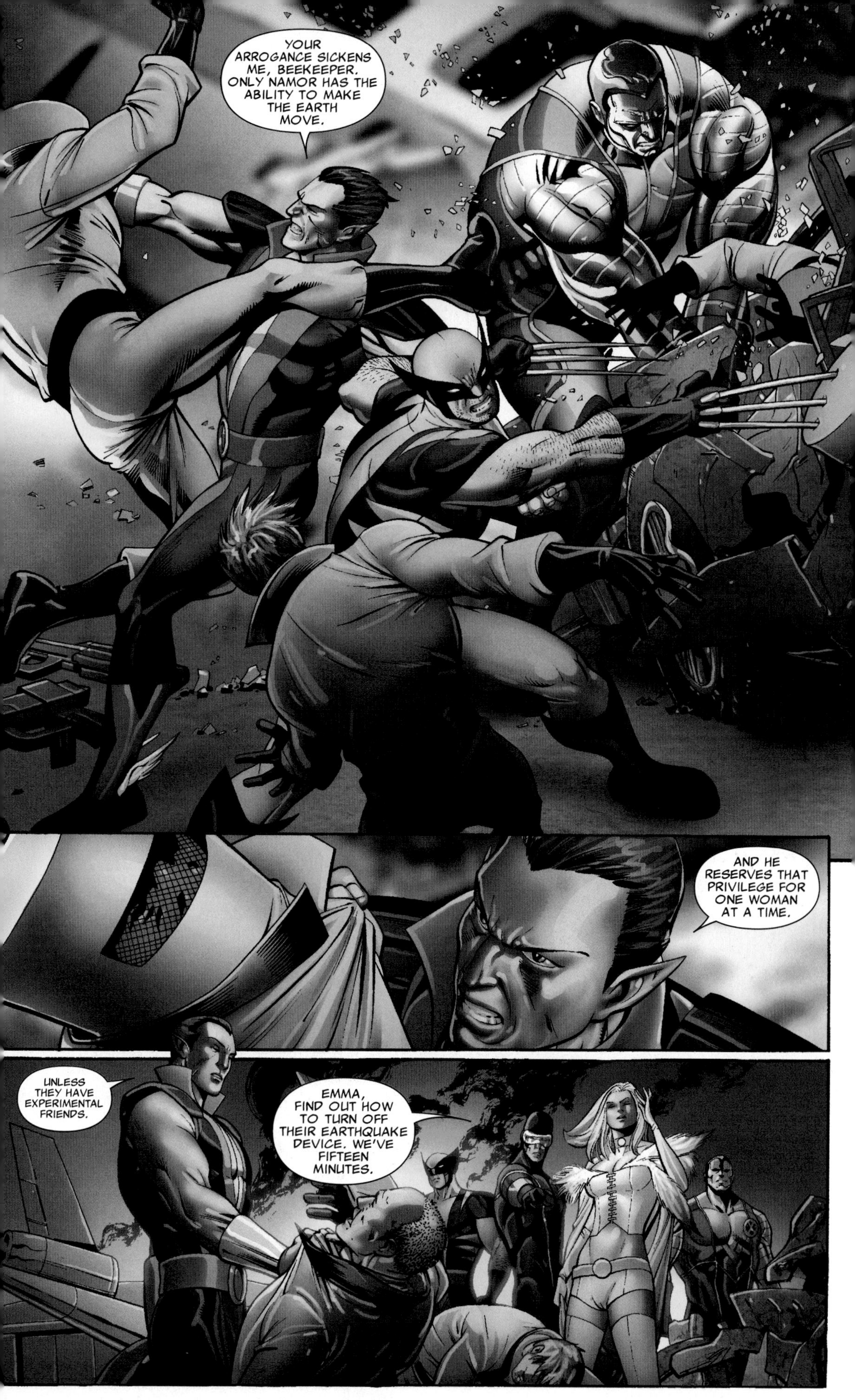
YOUR ARROGANCE SICKENS ME, BEEKEEPER. ONLY NAMOR HAS THE ABILITY TO MAKE THE EARTH MOVE.
AND HE RESERVES THAT PRIVILEGE FOR ONE WOMAN AT A TIME.
UNLESS THEY HAVE EXPERIMENTAL FRIENDS.
EMMA, FIND OUT HOW TO TURN OFF THEIR EARTHQUAKE DEVICE. WE'VE FIFTEEN MINUTES.

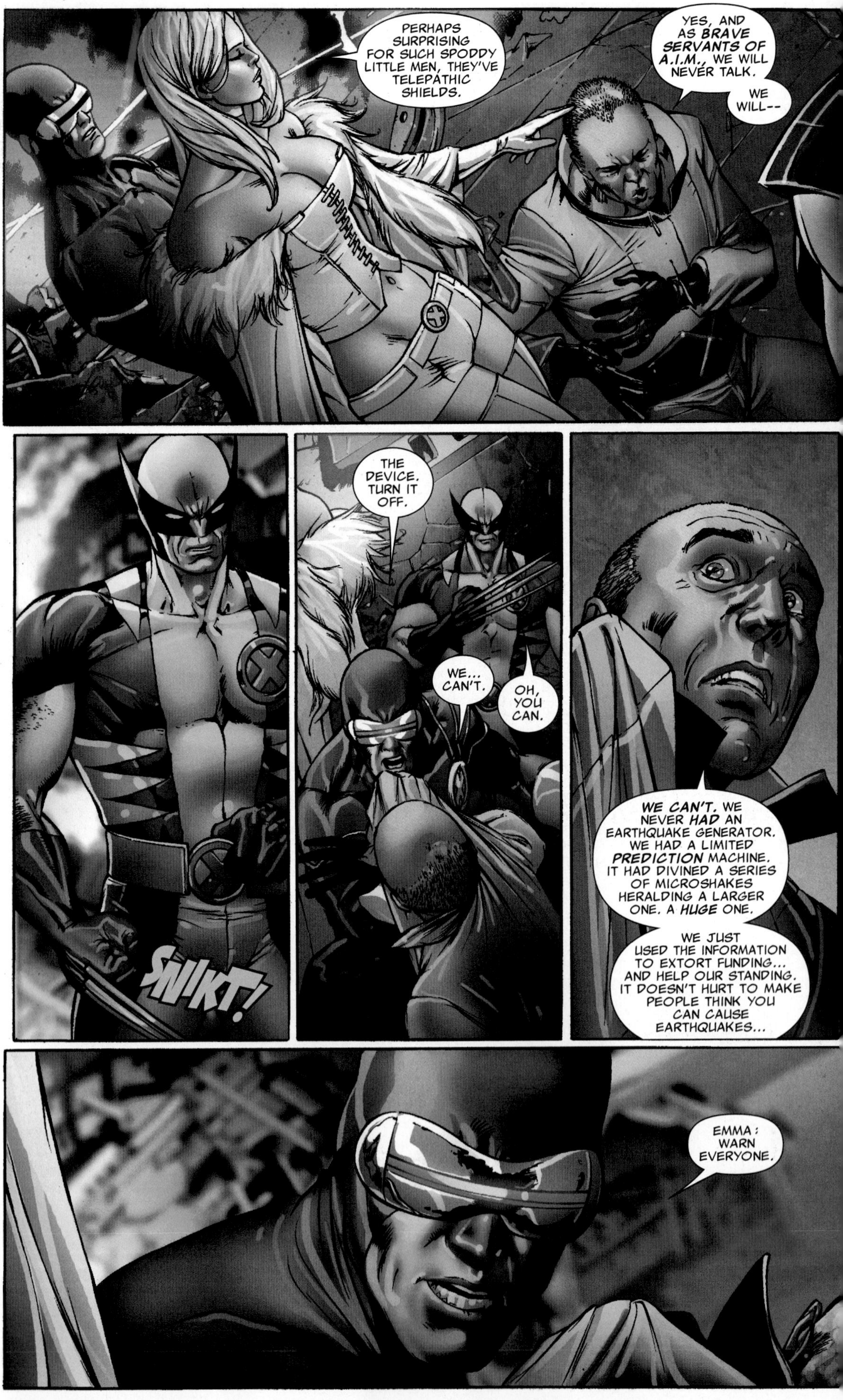
PERHAPS SURPRISING FOR SUCH SPODDY LITTLE MEN, THEY'VE TELEPATHIC SHIELDS.
YES, AND AS BRAVE SERVANTS OF A.I.M., WE WILL NEVER TALK.
WE WILL--
SNIKT!
THE DEVICE. TURN IT OFF.
WE... CAN'T.
OH, YOU CAN.
WE CAN'T. WE NEVER HAD AN EARTHQUAKE GENERATOR. WE HAD A LIMITED PREDICTION MACHINE. IT HAD DIVINED A SERIES OF MICROSHAKES HERALDING A LARGER ONE. A HUGE ONE.
WE JUST USED THE INFORMATION TO EXTORT FUNDING... AND HELP OUR STANDING. IT DOESN'T HURT TO MAKE PEOPLE THINK YOU CAN CAUSE EARTHQUAKES...
EMMA: WARN EVERYONE.

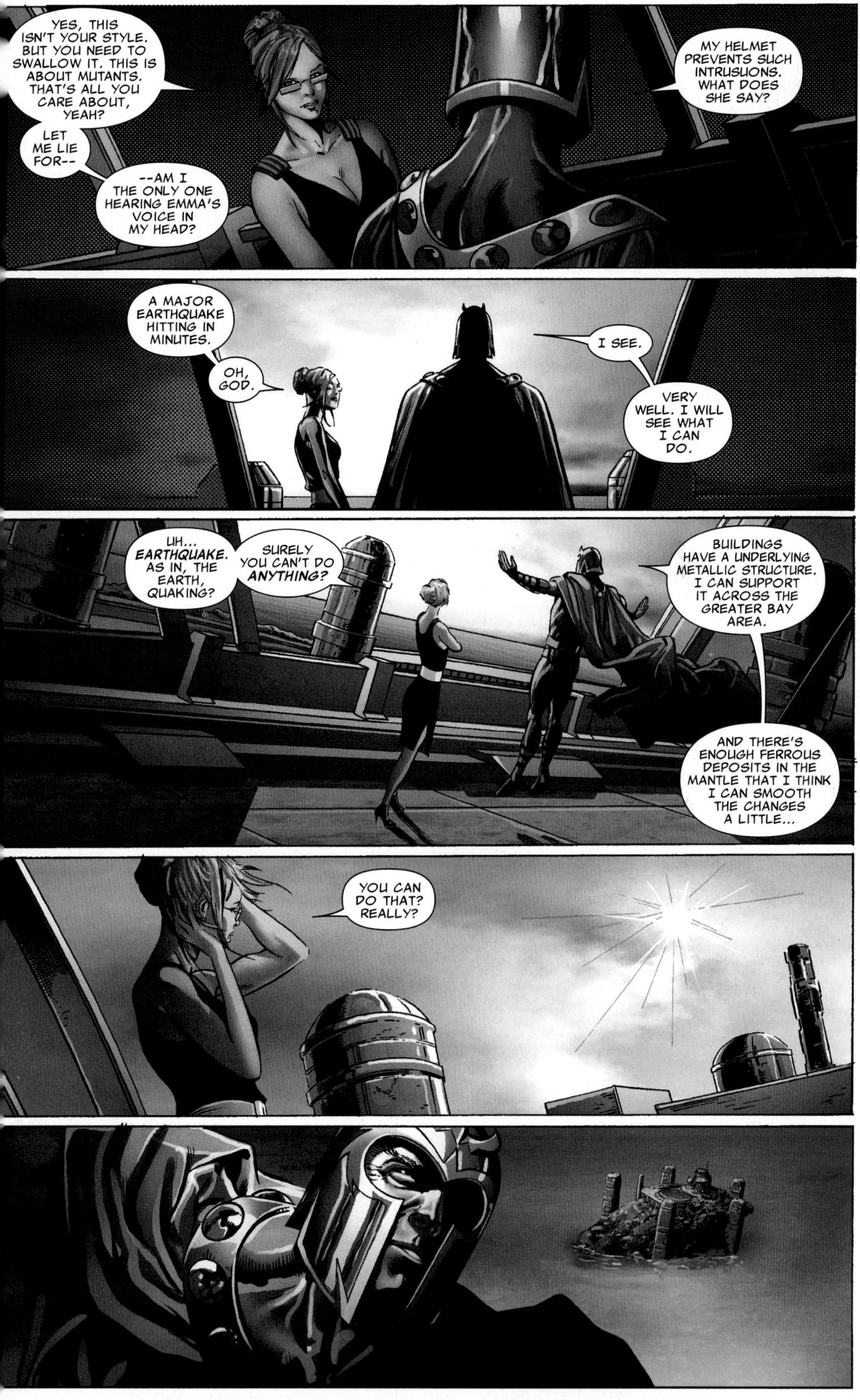
YES, THIS ISN'T YOUR STYLE. BUT YOU NEED TO SWALLOW IT. THIS IS ABOUT MUTANTS. THAT'S ALL YOU CARE ABOUT, YEAH?
LET ME LIE FOR--
--AM I THE ONLY ONE HEARING EMMA'S VOICE IN MY HEAD?
MY HELMET PREVENTS SUCH INTRUSIONS. WHAT DOES SHE SAY?
A MAJOR EARTHQUAKE HITTING IN MINUTES.
OH, GOD.
I SEE.
VERY WELL. I WILL SEE WHAT I CAN DO.
UH... EARTHQUAKE. AS IN, THE EARTH, QUAKING?
SURELY YOU CAN'T DO ANYTHING?
BUILDINGS HAVE A UNDERLYING METALLIC STRUCTURE. I CAN SUPPORT IT ACROSS THE GREATER BAY AREA.
AND THERE'S ENOUGH FERROUS DEPOSITS IN THE MANTLE THAT I THINK I CAN SMOOTH THE CHANGES A LITTLE...
YOU CAN DO THAT? REALLY?

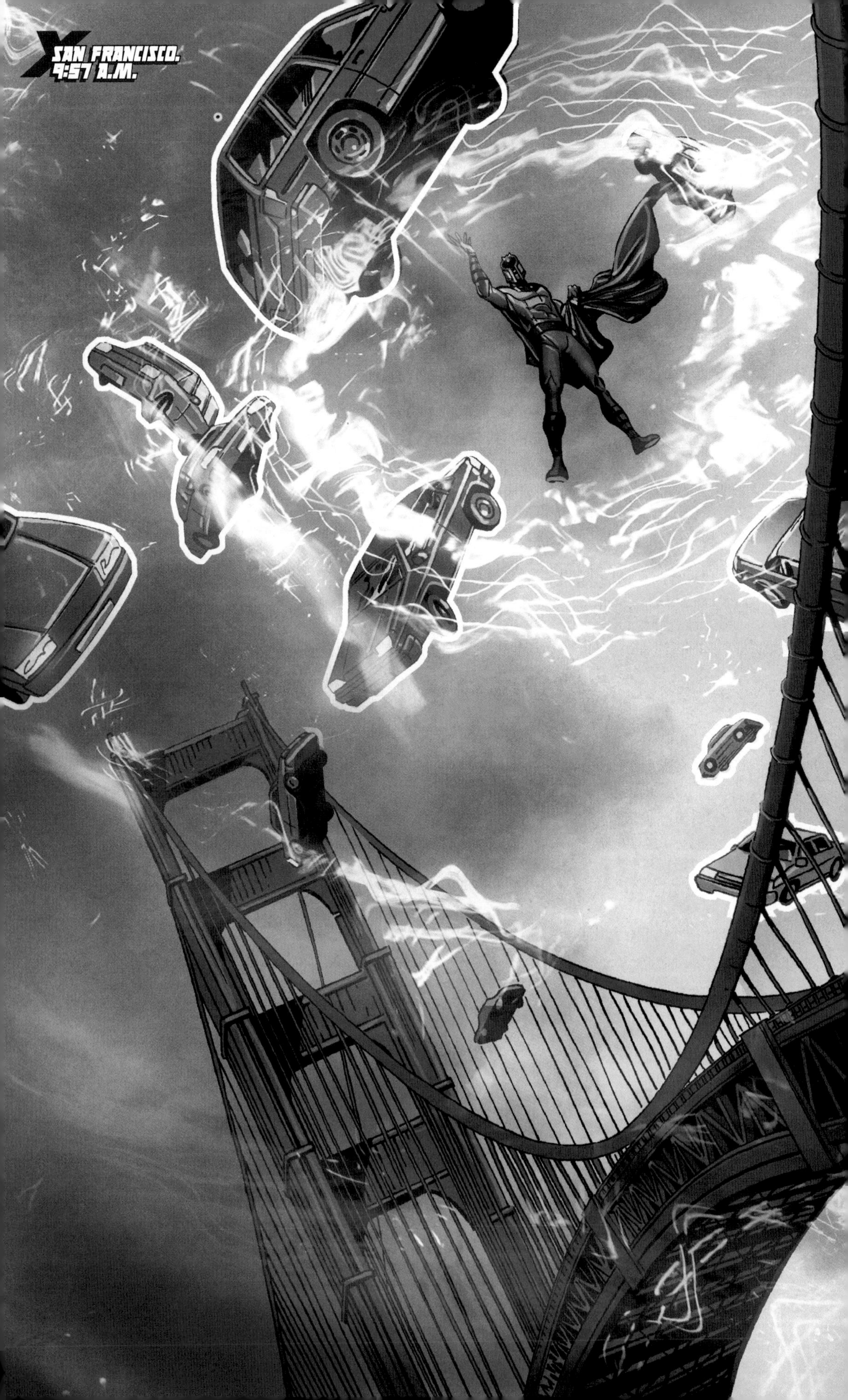
SAN FRANCISCO.
9:57 A.M.

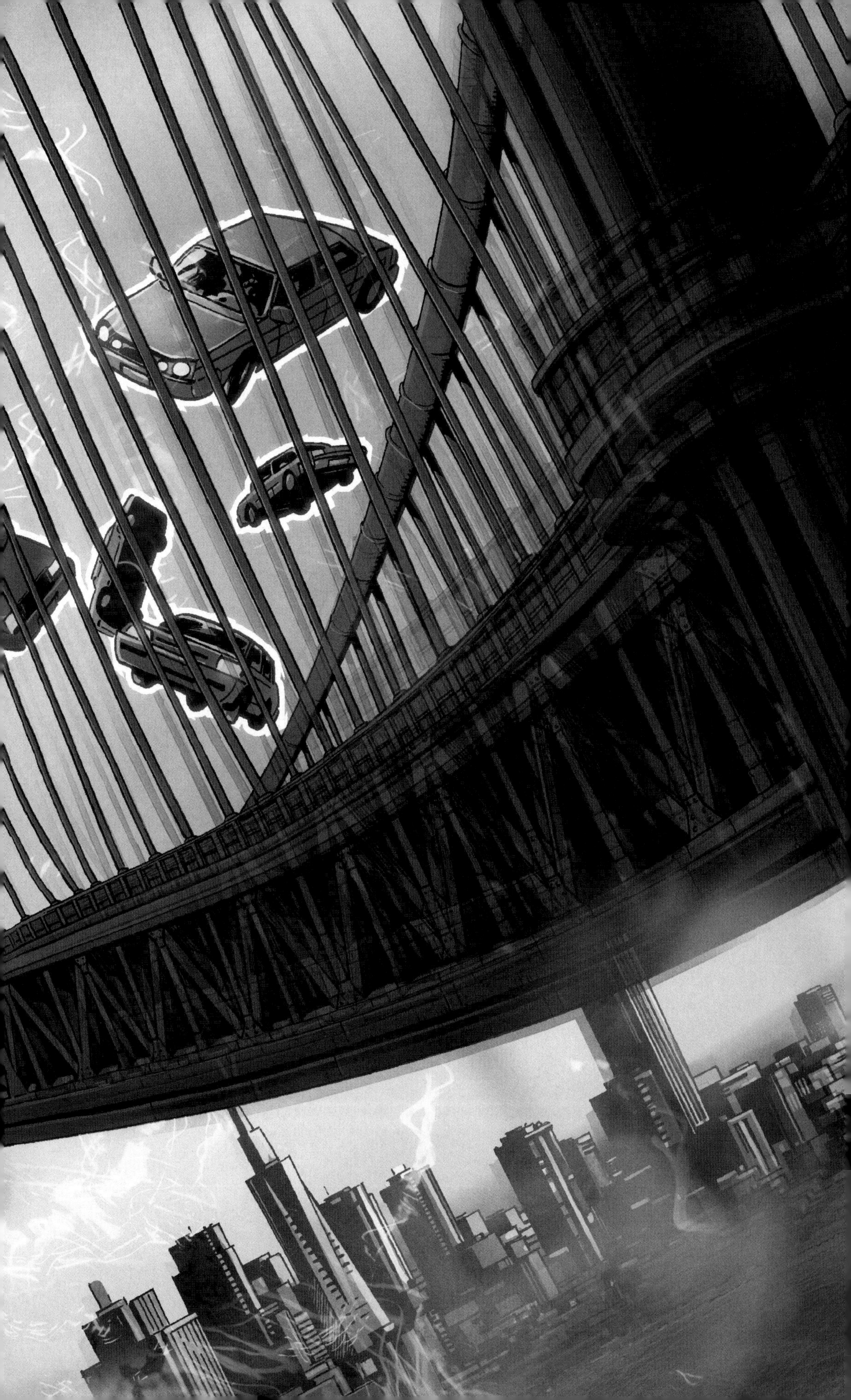

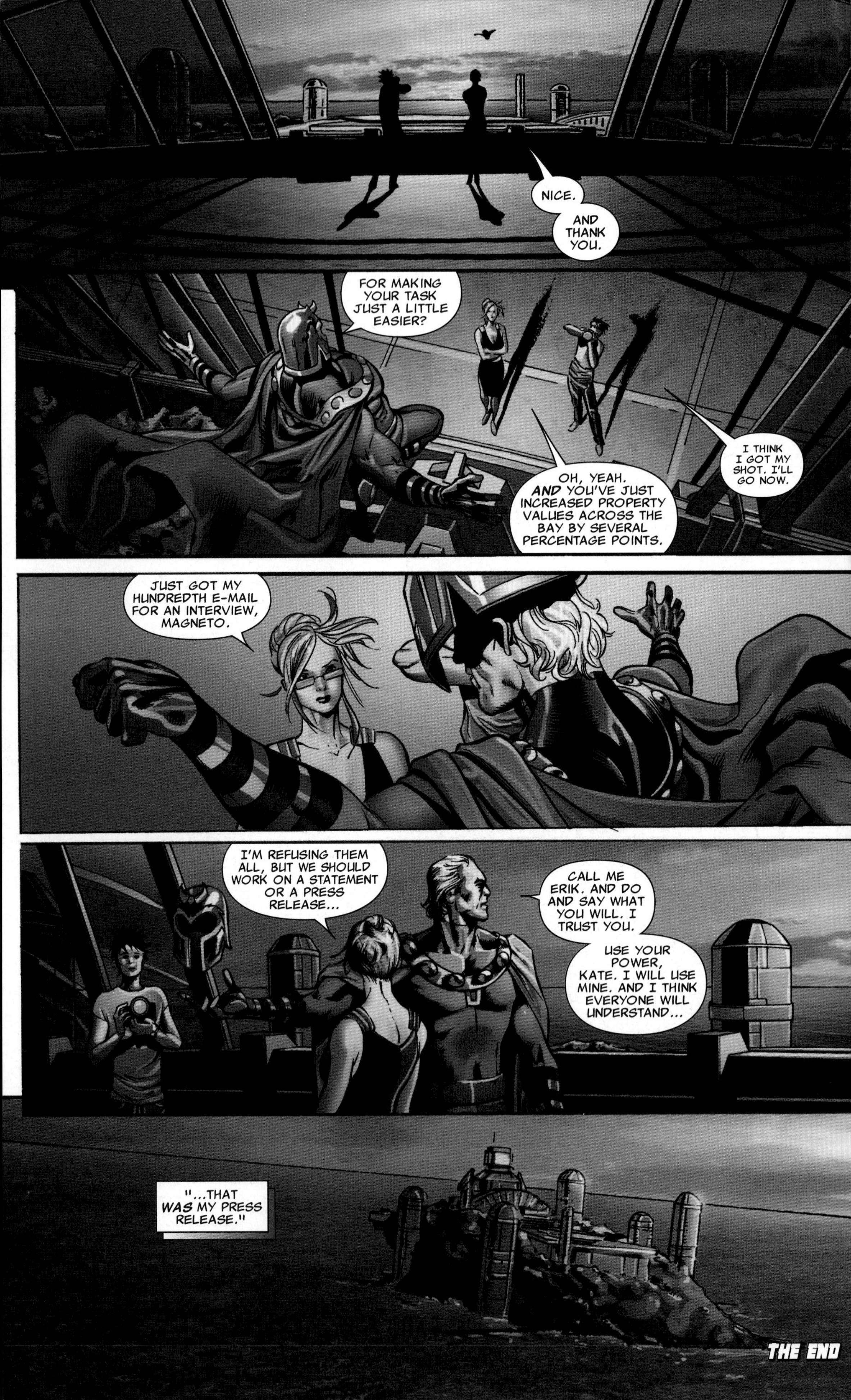
NICE.
AND THANK YOU.
FOR MAKING YOUR TASK JUST A LITTLE EASIER?
OH, YEAH. **AND** YOU'VE JUST INCREASED PROPERTY VALUES ACROSS THE BAY BY SEVERAL PERCENTAGE POINTS.
I THINK I GOT MY SHOT. I'LL GO NOW.
JUST GOT MY HUNDREDTH E-MAIL FOR AN INTERVIEW, MAGNETO.
I'M REFUSING THEM ALL, BUT WE SHOULD WORK ON A STATEMENT OR A PRESS RELEASE...
CALL ME ERIK. AND DO AND SAY WHAT YOU WILL. I TRUST YOU.
USE YOUR POWER, KATE. I WILL USE MINE. AND I THINK EVERYONE WILL UNDERSTAND...
"...THAT **WAS** MY PRESS RELEASE."
THE END

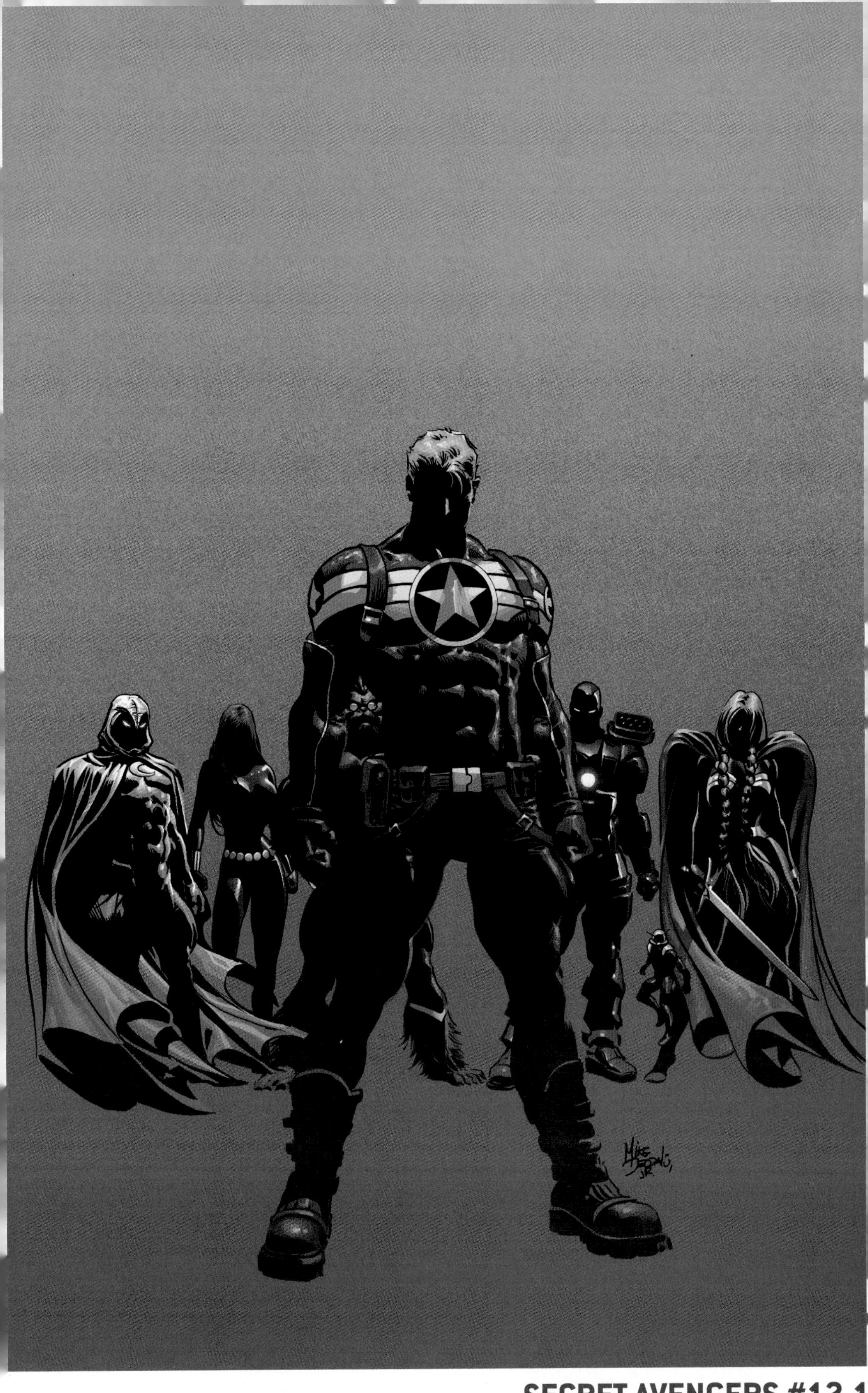

SECRET AVENGERS #12.1

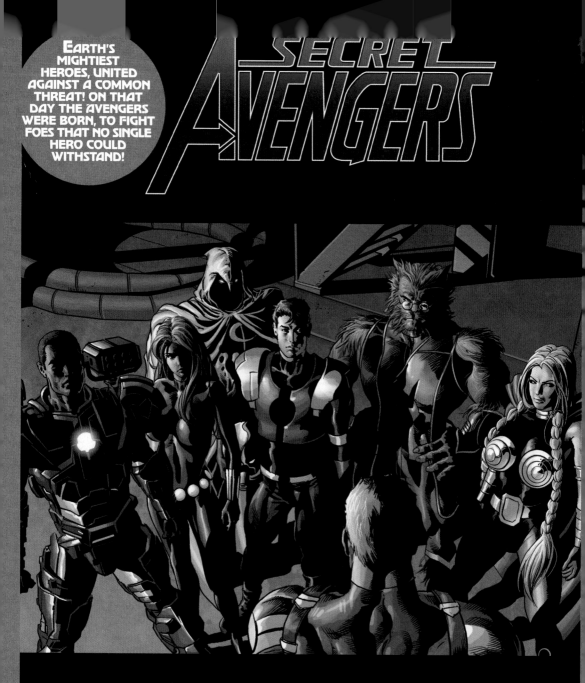

EARTH'S MIGHTIEST HEROES, UNITED AGAINST A COMMON THREAT! ON THAT DAY THE AVENGERS WERE BORN, TO FIGHT FOES THAT NO SINGLE HERO COULD WITHSTAND!

SECRET AVENGERS

BROUGHT TOGETHER AS A BLACK OPS UNIT BY FORMER CAPTAIN AMERICA STEVE ROGERS TO TAKE ON THE WORLD'S BIGGEST THREATS, WAR MACHINE, MOON KNIGHT, BEAST, ANT-MAN, BLACK WIDOW, VALKYRIE AND SHARON CARTER ARE THE SECRET AVENGERS.

NICK **SPENCER**
WRITER

SCOT **EATON**
PENCILER

JAIME **MENDOZA**
INKER

FRANK **D'ARMATA**
COLORIST

DAVE **LANPHEAR**
LETTERER

MIKE **DEODATO** & RAIN **BEREDO**
COVER ART

MAYELA **GUTIERREZ**
PRODUCTION

LAUREN **SANKOVITCH**
ASSOCIATE EDITOR

TOM **BREVOORT**
EDITOR

AXEL **ALONSO**
EDITOR IN CHIEF

JOE **QUESADA**
CHIEF CREATIVE OFFICER

DAN **BUCKLEY**
PUBLISHER

ALAN **FINE**
EXEC. PRODUCER

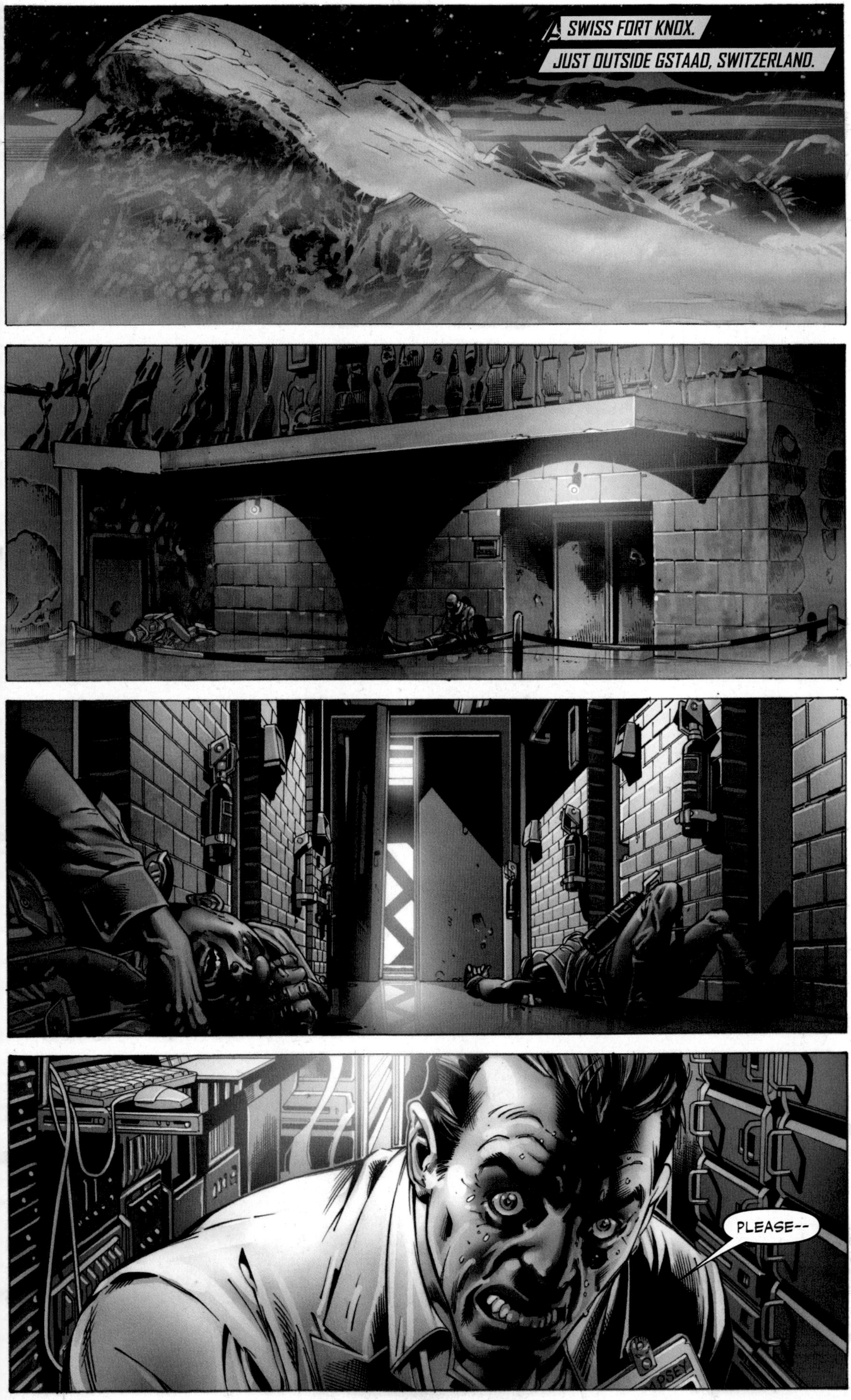
SWISS FORT KNOX.
JUST OUTSIDE GSTAAD, SWITZERLAND.
PLEASE--

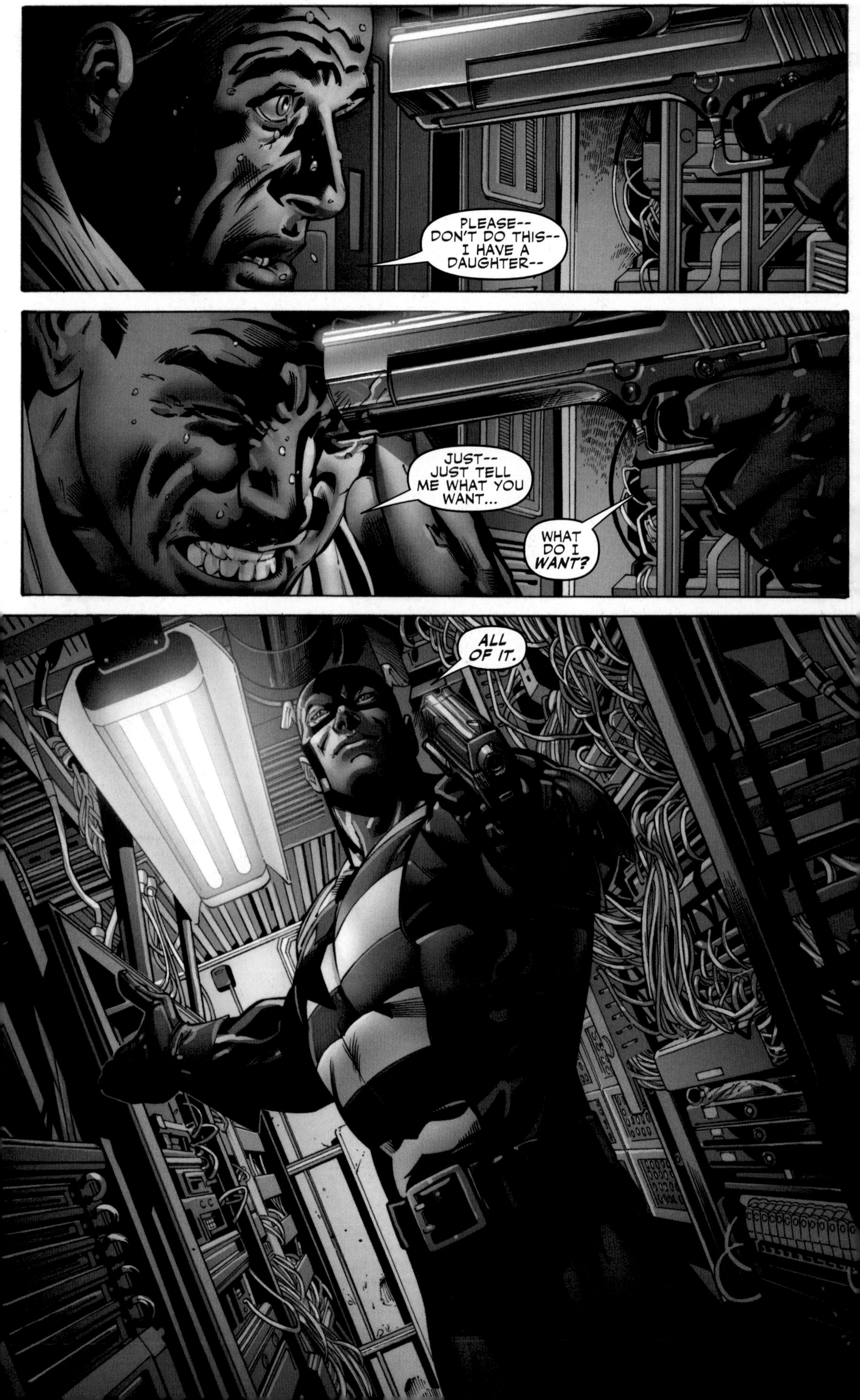
PLEASE-- DON'T DO THIS-- I HAVE A DAUGHTER--
JUST-- JUST TELL ME WHAT YOU WANT...
WHAT DO I *WANT?*
ALL OF IT.

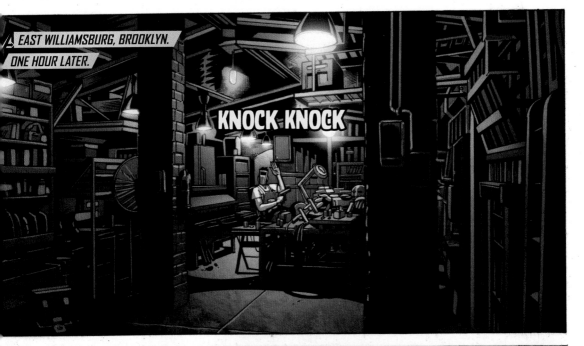

EAST WILLIAMSBURG, BROOKLYN. ONE HOUR LATER.

KNOCK KNOCK

KNOCK KNOCK KNOCK

HOLD ON A DAMN SECOND! WHAT THE HELL DO YOU--

MISTER NEGATIVE!

HELLO, FRANKLIN. I HOPE THIS ISN'T A BAD TIME.

HUH? OH, NO, NOT AT ALL--

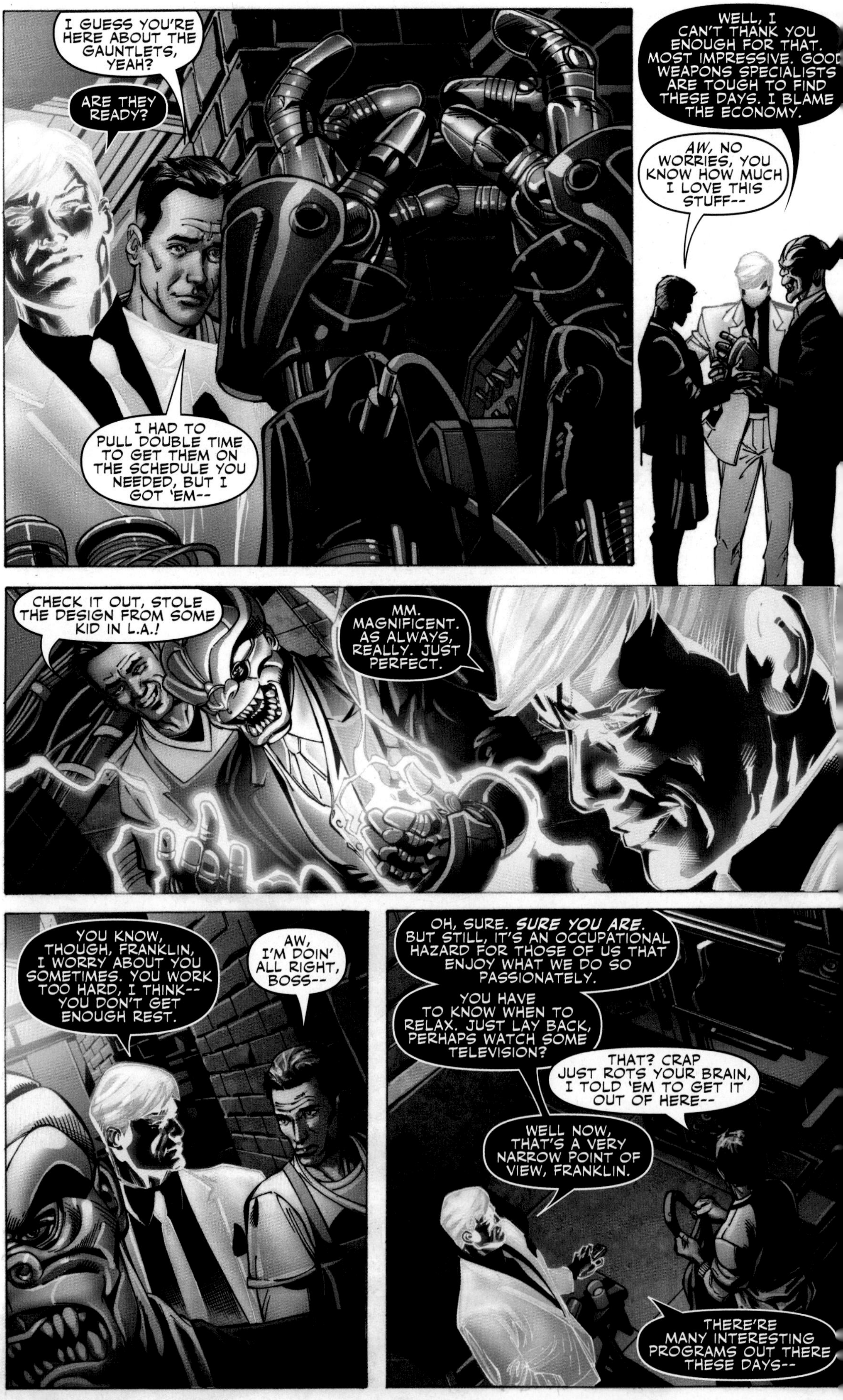
I GUESS YOU'RE HERE ABOUT THE GAUNTLETS, YEAH?
ARE THEY READY?
I HAD TO PULL DOUBLE TIME TO GET THEM ON THE SCHEDULE YOU NEEDED, BUT I GOT 'EM--
WELL, I CAN'T THANK YOU ENOUGH FOR THAT. MOST IMPRESSIVE. GOOD WEAPONS SPECIALISTS ARE TOUGH TO FIND THESE DAYS. I BLAME THE ECONOMY.
AW, NO WORRIES, YOU KNOW HOW MUCH I LOVE THIS STUFF--
CHECK IT OUT, STOLE THE DESIGN FROM SOME KID IN L.A.!
MM. MAGNIFICENT. AS ALWAYS, REALLY. JUST PERFECT.
YOU KNOW, THOUGH, FRANKLIN, I WORRY ABOUT YOU SOMETIMES. YOU WORK TOO HARD, I THINK-- YOU DON'T GET ENOUGH REST.
AW, I'M DOIN' ALL RIGHT, BOSS--
OH, SURE. ***SURE YOU ARE.*** BUT STILL, IT'S AN OCCUPATIONAL HAZARD FOR THOSE OF US THAT ENJOY WHAT WE DO SO PASSIONATELY.
YOU HAVE TO KNOW WHEN TO RELAX. JUST LAY BACK, PERHAPS WATCH SOME TELEVISION?
THAT? CRAP JUST ROTS YOUR BRAIN, I TOLD 'EM TO GET IT OUT OF HERE--
WELL NOW, THAT'S A VERY NARROW POINT OF VIEW, FRANKLIN.
THERE'RE MANY INTERESTING PROGRAMS OUT THERE THESE DAYS--

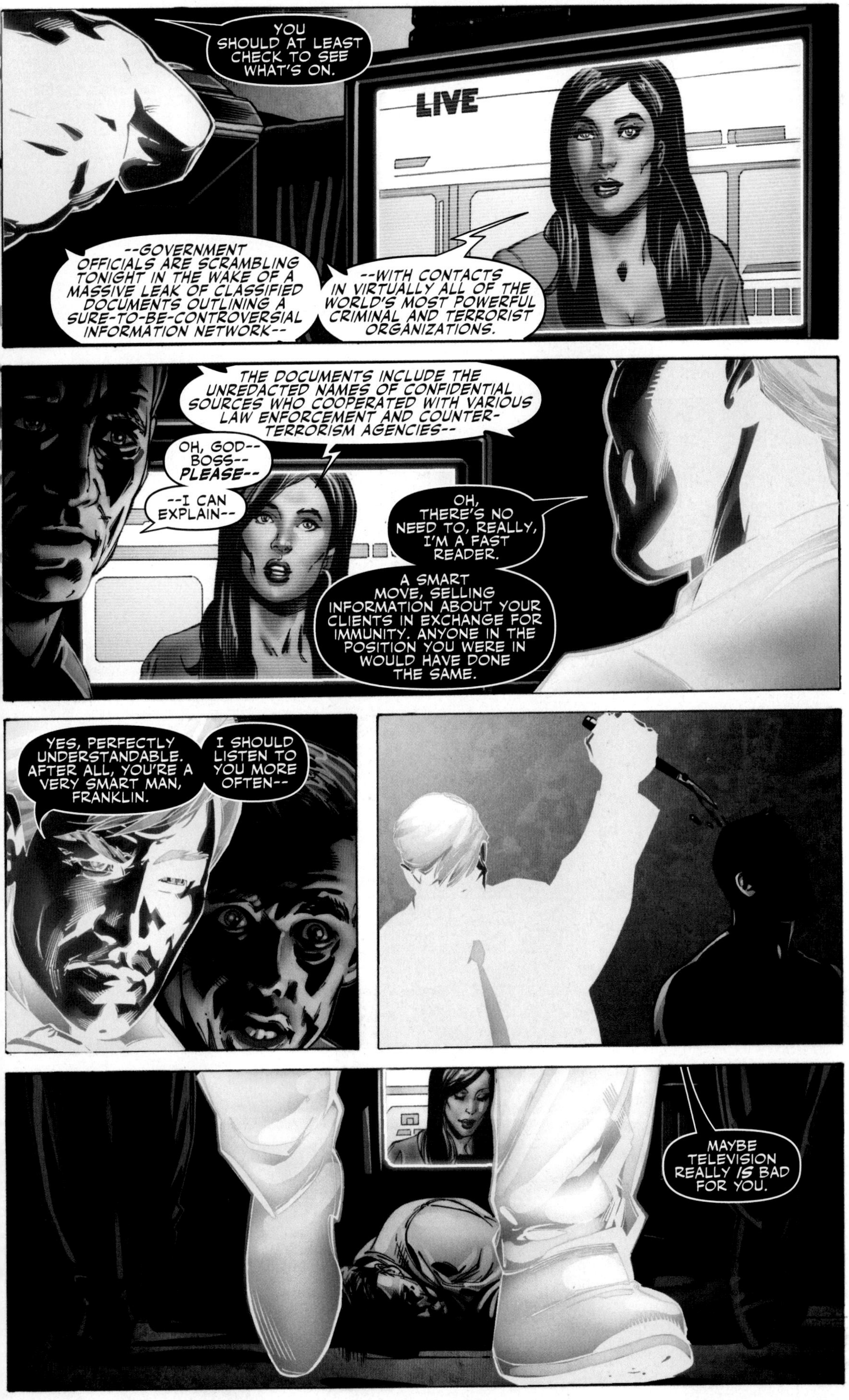
YOU SHOULD AT LEAST CHECK TO SEE WHAT'S ON.
LIVE
--GOVERNMENT OFFICIALS ARE SCRAMBLING TONIGHT IN THE WAKE OF A MASSIVE LEAK OF CLASSIFIED DOCUMENTS OUTLINING A SURE-TO-BE-CONTROVERSIAL INFORMATION NETWORK--
--WITH CONTACTS IN VIRTUALLY ALL OF THE WORLD'S MOST POWERFUL CRIMINAL AND TERRORIST ORGANIZATIONS.
THE DOCUMENTS INCLUDE THE UNREDACTED NAMES OF CONFIDENTIAL SOURCES WHO COOPERATED WITH VARIOUS LAW ENFORCEMENT AND COUNTER-TERRORISM AGENCIES--
OH, GOD-- BOSS-- PLEASE--
--I CAN EXPLAIN--
OH, THERE'S NO NEED TO, REALLY, I'M A FAST READER.
A SMART MOVE, SELLING INFORMATION ABOUT YOUR CLIENTS IN EXCHANGE FOR IMMUNITY. ANYONE IN THE POSITION YOU WERE IN WOULD HAVE DONE THE SAME.
YES, PERFECTLY UNDERSTANDABLE. AFTER ALL, YOU'RE A VERY SMART MAN, FRANKLIN.
I SHOULD LISTEN TO YOU MORE OFTEN--
MAYBE TELEVISION REALLY IS BAD FOR YOU.

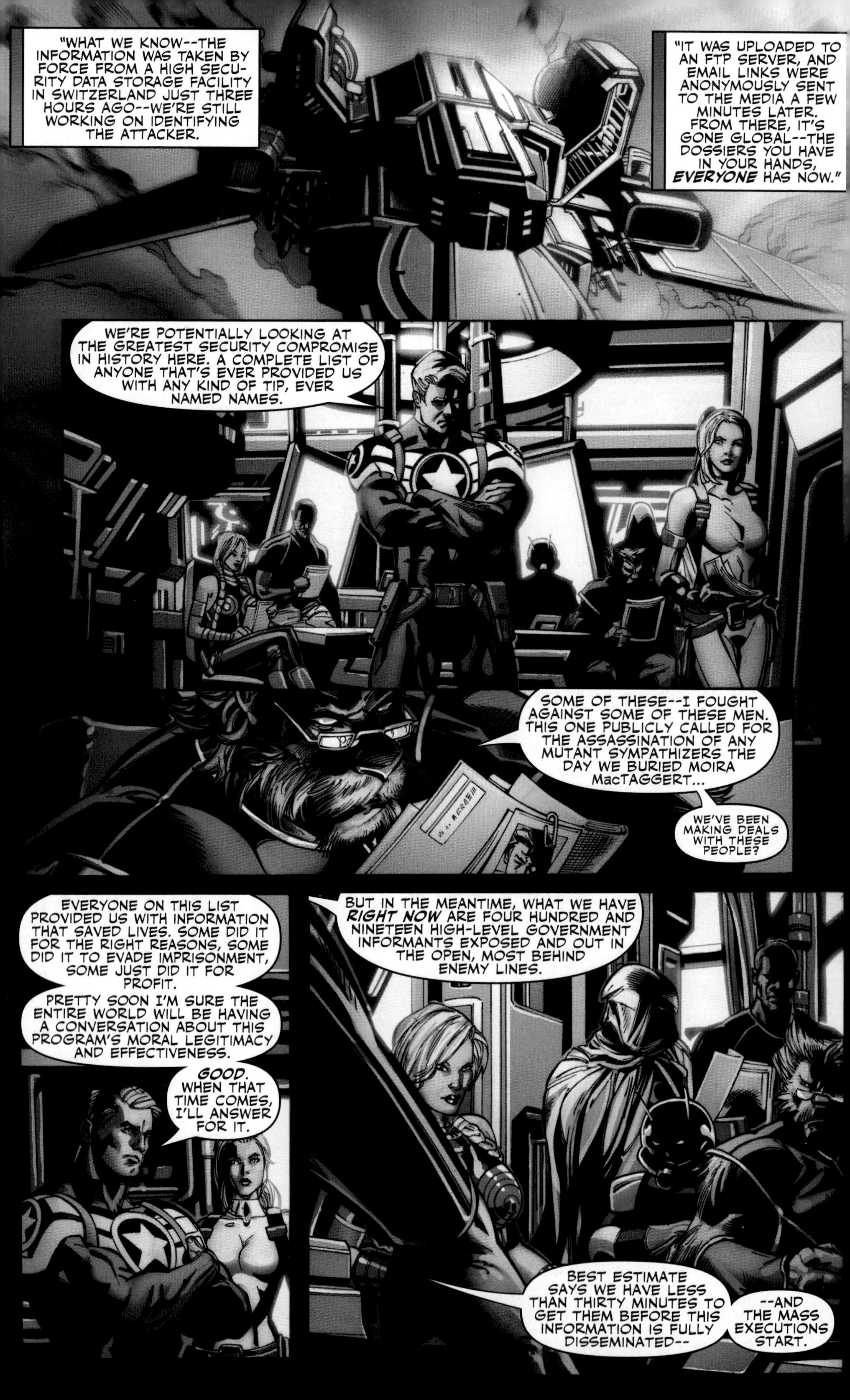
"WHAT WE KNOW--THE INFORMATION WAS TAKEN BY FORCE FROM A HIGH SECURITY DATA STORAGE FACILITY IN SWITZERLAND JUST THREE HOURS AGO--WE'RE STILL WORKING ON IDENTIFYING THE ATTACKER.
"IT WAS UPLOADED TO AN FTP SERVER, AND EMAIL LINKS WERE ANONYMOUSLY SENT TO THE MEDIA A FEW MINUTES LATER. FROM THERE, IT'S GONE GLOBAL--THE DOSSIERS YOU HAVE IN YOUR HANDS, EVERYONE HAS NOW."
WE'RE POTENTIALLY LOOKING AT THE GREATEST SECURITY COMPROMISE IN HISTORY HERE. A COMPLETE LIST OF ANYONE THAT'S EVER PROVIDED US WITH ANY KIND OF TIP, EVER NAMED NAMES.
SOME OF THESE--I FOUGHT AGAINST SOME OF THESE MEN. THIS ONE PUBLICLY CALLED FOR THE ASSASSINATION OF ANY MUTANT SYMPATHIZERS THE DAY WE BURIED MOIRA MacTAGGERT...
WE'VE BEEN MAKING DEALS WITH THESE PEOPLE?
EVERYONE ON THIS LIST PROVIDED US WITH INFORMATION THAT SAVED LIVES. SOME DID IT FOR THE RIGHT REASONS, SOME DID IT TO EVADE IMPRISONMENT, SOME JUST DID IT FOR PROFIT.
PRETTY SOON I'M SURE THE ENTIRE WORLD WILL BE HAVING A CONVERSATION ABOUT THIS PROGRAM'S MORAL LEGITIMACY AND EFFECTIVENESS.
GOOD. WHEN THAT TIME COMES, I'LL ANSWER FOR IT.
BUT IN THE MEANTIME, WHAT WE HAVE RIGHT NOW ARE FOUR HUNDRED AND NINETEEN HIGH-LEVEL GOVERNMENT INFORMANTS EXPOSED AND OUT IN THE OPEN, MOST BEHIND ENEMY LINES.
BEST ESTIMATE SAYS WE HAVE LESS THAN THIRTY MINUTES TO GET THEM BEFORE THIS INFORMATION IS FULLY DISSEMINATED--
--AND THE MASS EXECUTIONS START.

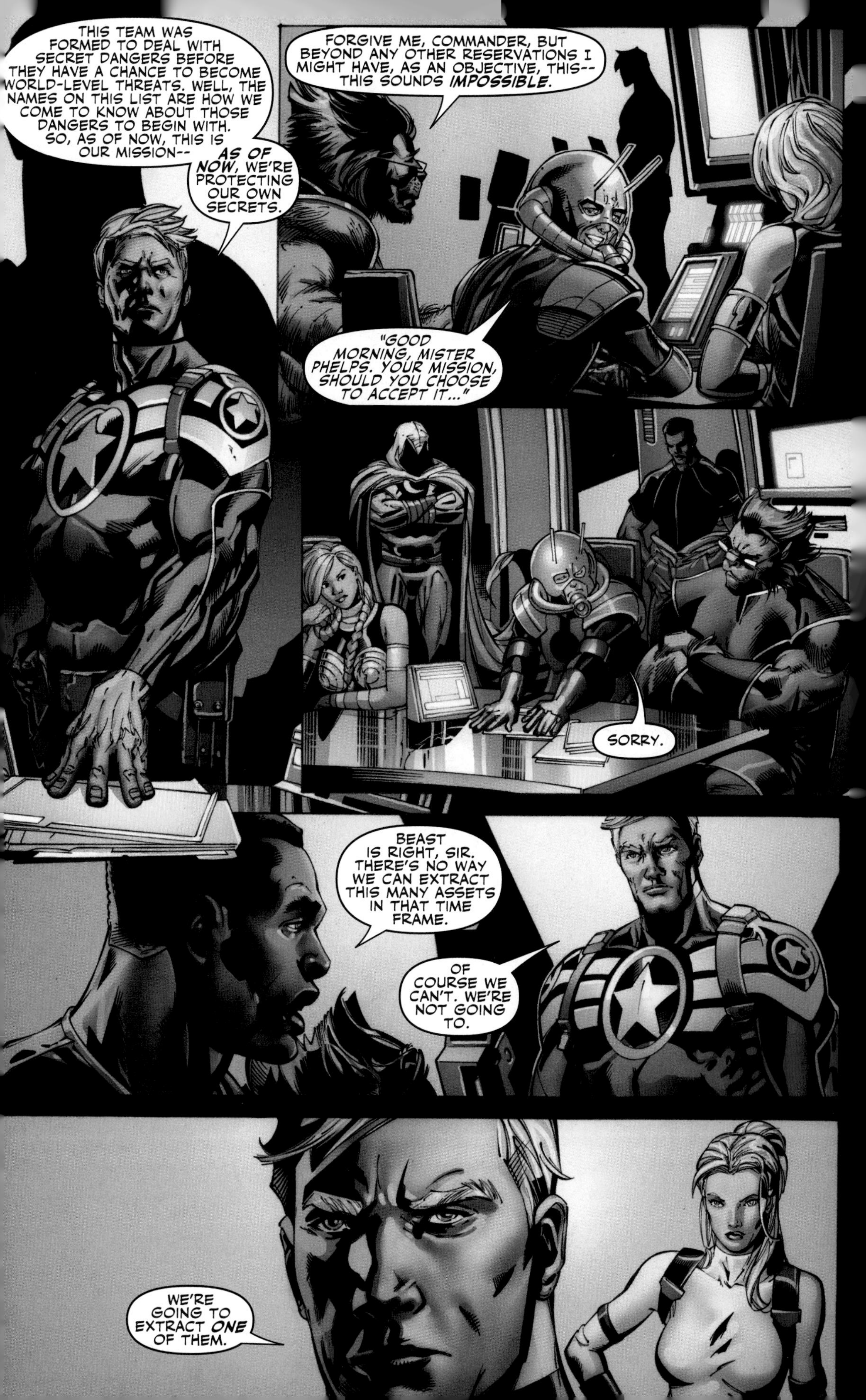
THIS TEAM WAS FORMED TO DEAL WITH SECRET DANGERS BEFORE THEY HAVE A CHANCE TO BECOME WORLD-LEVEL THREATS. WELL, THE NAMES ON THIS LIST ARE HOW WE COME TO KNOW ABOUT THOSE DANGERS TO BEGIN WITH. SO, AS OF NOW, THIS IS OUR MISSION--
AS OF NOW, WE'RE PROTECTING OUR OWN SECRETS.
FORGIVE ME, COMMANDER, BUT BEYOND ANY OTHER RESERVATIONS I MIGHT HAVE, AS AN OBJECTIVE, THIS-- THIS SOUNDS *IMPOSSIBLE*.
"GOOD MORNING, MISTER PHELPS. YOUR MISSION, SHOULD YOU CHOOSE TO ACCEPT IT..."
SORRY.
BEAST IS RIGHT, SIR. THERE'S NO WAY WE CAN EXTRACT THIS MANY ASSETS IN THAT TIME FRAME.
OF COURSE WE CAN'T. WE'RE NOT GOING TO.
WE'RE GOING TO EXTRACT *ONE* OF THEM.

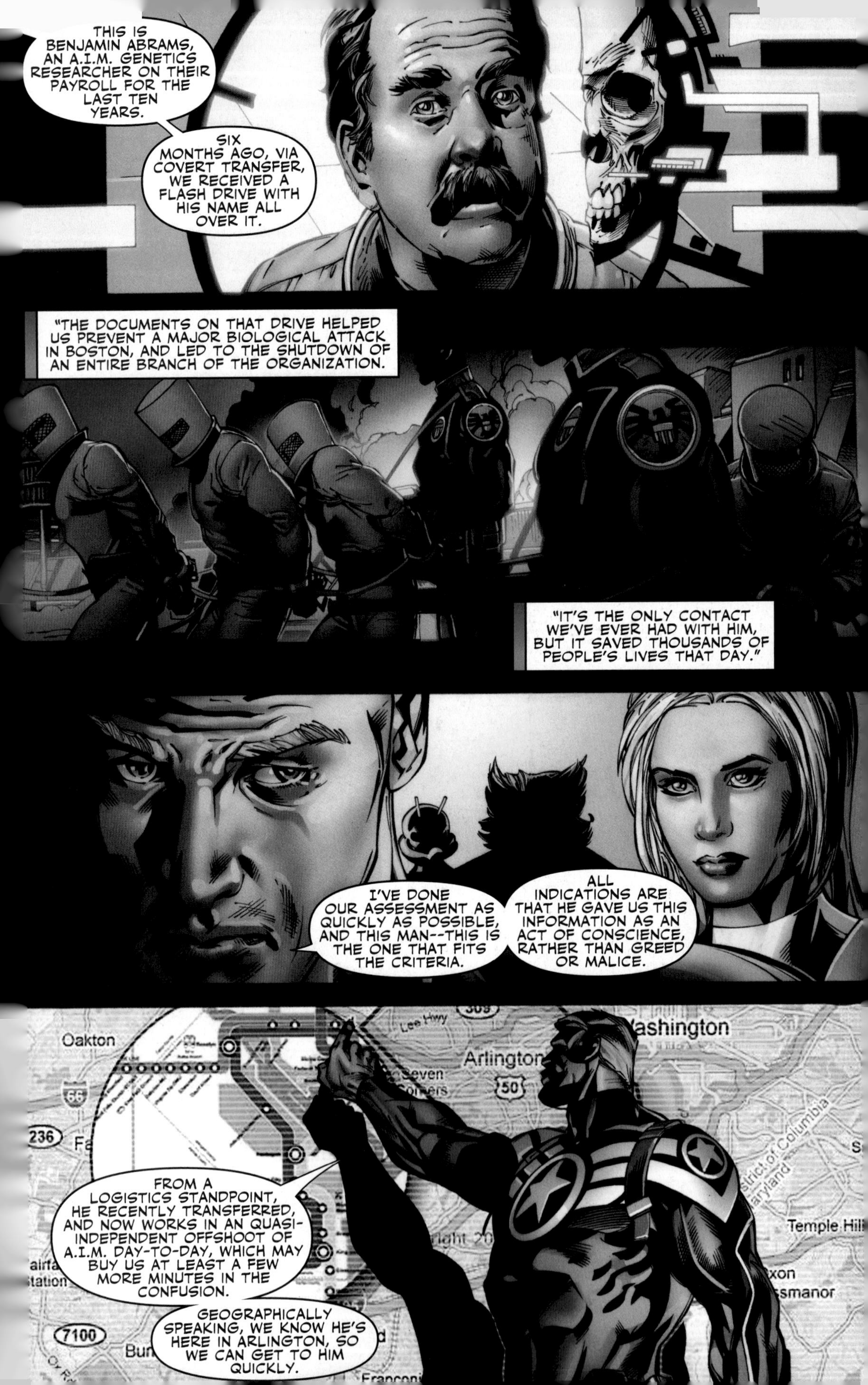
THIS IS BENJAMIN ABRAMS, AN A.I.M. GENETICS RESEARCHER ON THEIR PAYROLL FOR THE LAST TEN YEARS.
SIX MONTHS AGO, VIA COVERT TRANSFER, WE RECEIVED A FLASH DRIVE WITH HIS NAME ALL OVER IT.
"THE DOCUMENTS ON THAT DRIVE HELPED US PREVENT A MAJOR BIOLOGICAL ATTACK IN BOSTON, AND LED TO THE SHUTDOWN OF AN ENTIRE BRANCH OF THE ORGANIZATION.
"IT'S THE ONLY CONTACT WE'VE EVER HAD WITH HIM, BUT IT SAVED THOUSANDS OF PEOPLE'S LIVES THAT DAY."
I'VE DONE OUR ASSESSMENT AS QUICKLY AS POSSIBLE, AND THIS MAN--THIS IS THE ONE THAT FITS THE CRITERIA.
ALL INDICATIONS ARE THAT HE GAVE US THIS INFORMATION AS AN ACT OF CONSCIENCE, RATHER THAN GREED OR MALICE.
Oakton
Washington
Arlington
Lee Hwy
Seven Corners
66
50
236
Temple Hill
District of Columbia
Maryland
7100
FROM A LOGISTICS STANDPOINT, HE RECENTLY TRANSFERRED, AND NOW WORKS IN AN QUASI-INDEPENDENT OFFSHOOT OF A.I.M. DAY-TO-DAY, WHICH MAY BUY US AT LEAST A FEW MORE MINUTES IN THE CONFUSION.
GEOGRAPHICALLY SPEAKING, WE KNOW HE'S HERE IN ARLINGTON, SO WE CAN GET TO HIM QUICKLY.

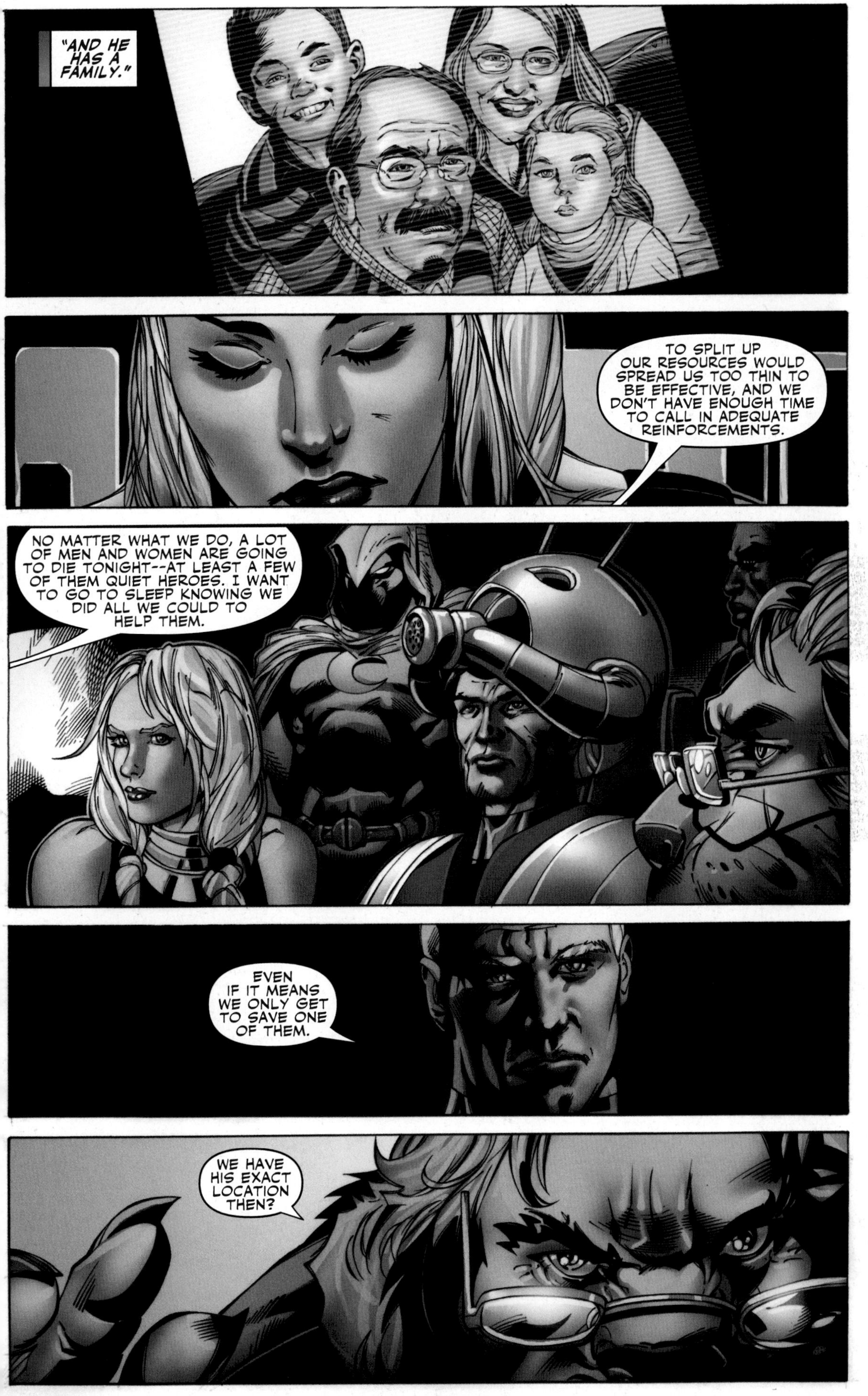
"AND HE HAS A FAMILY."
TO SPLIT UP OUR RESOURCES WOULD SPREAD US TOO THIN TO BE EFFECTIVE, AND WE DON'T HAVE ENOUGH TIME TO CALL IN ADEQUATE REINFORCEMENTS.
NO MATTER WHAT WE DO, A LOT OF MEN AND WOMEN ARE GOING TO DIE TONIGHT--AT LEAST A FEW OF THEM QUIET HEROES. I WANT TO GO TO SLEEP KNOWING WE DID ALL WE COULD TO HELP THEM.
EVEN IF IT MEANS WE ONLY GET TO SAVE ONE OF THEM.
WE HAVE HIS EXACT LOCATION THEN?

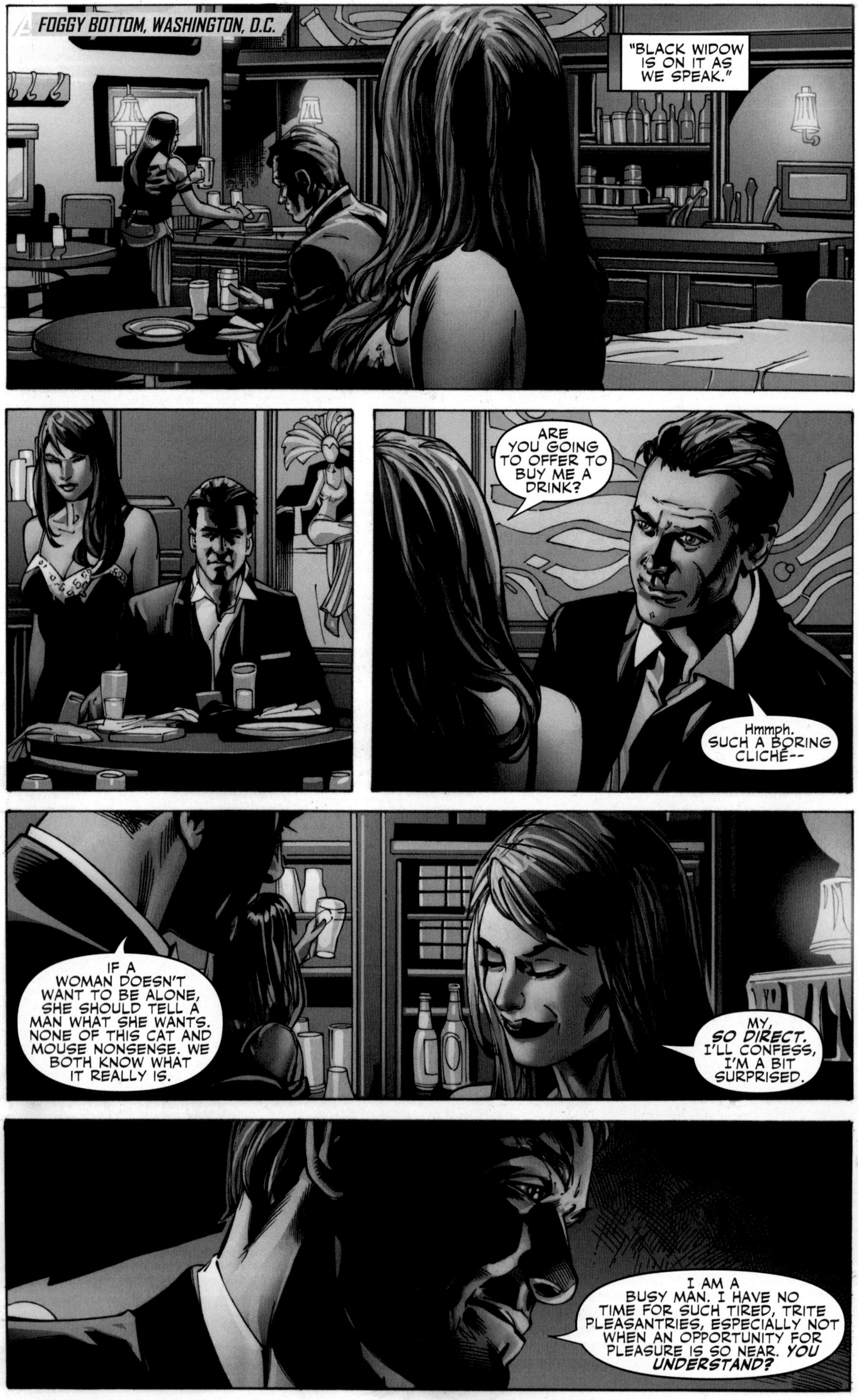
FOGGY BOTTOM, WASHINGTON, D.C.
"BLACK WIDOW IS ON IT AS WE SPEAK."
ARE YOU GOING TO OFFER TO BUY ME A DRINK?
Hmmph. SUCH A BORING CLICHÉ--
IF A WOMAN DOESN'T WANT TO BE ALONE, SHE SHOULD TELL A MAN WHAT SHE WANTS. NONE OF THIS CAT AND MOUSE NONSENSE. WE BOTH KNOW WHAT IT REALLY IS.
MY, SO DIRECT. I'LL CONFESS, I'M A BIT SURPRISED.
I AM A BUSY MAN. I HAVE NO TIME FOR SUCH TIRED, TRITE PLEASANTRIES, ESPECIALLY NOT WHEN AN OPPORTUNITY FOR PLEASURE IS SO NEAR. YOU UNDERSTAND?

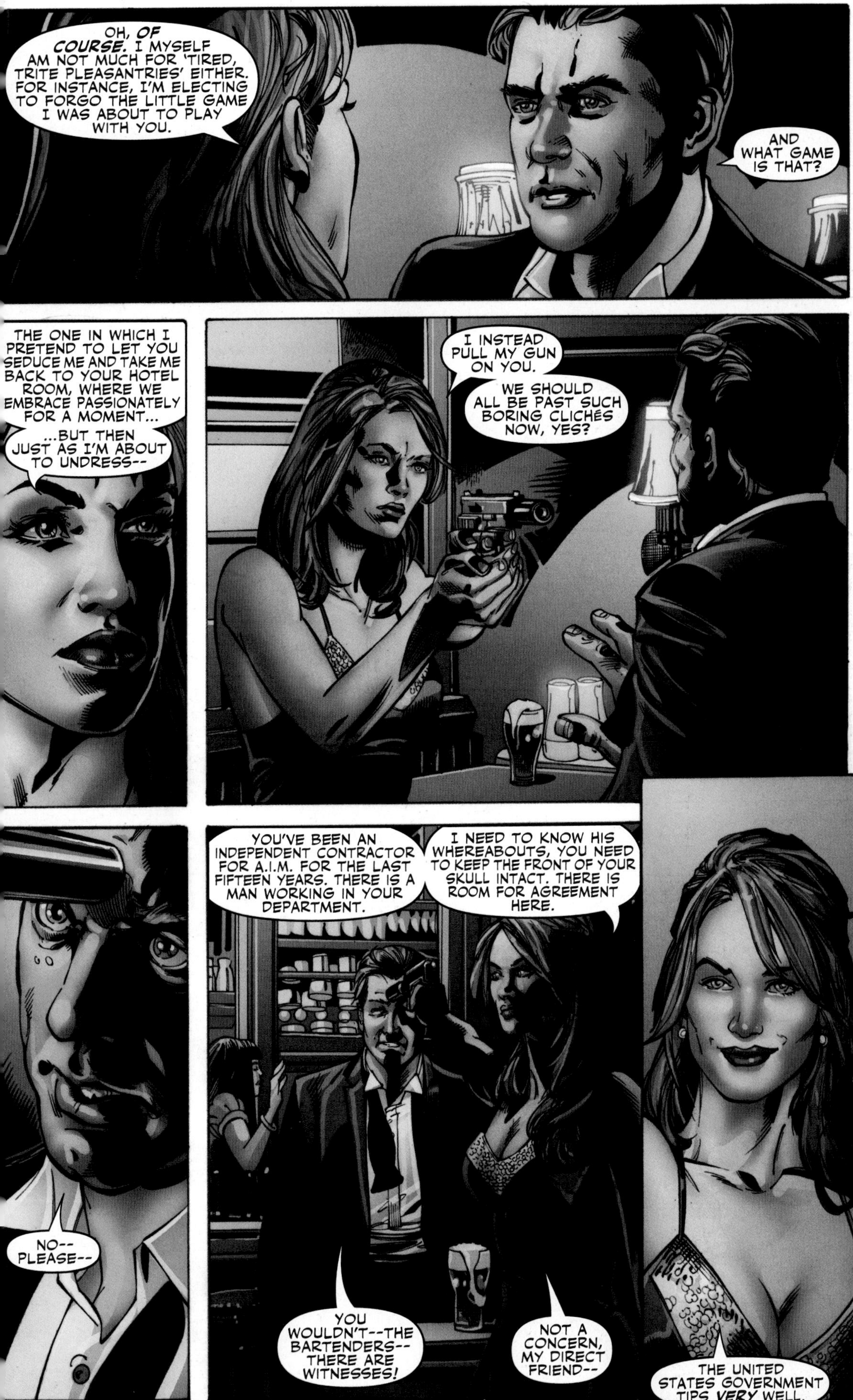

OH, *OF COURSE.* I MYSELF AM NOT MUCH FOR 'TIRED, TRITE PLEASANTRIES' EITHER. FOR INSTANCE, I'M ELECTING TO FORGO THE LITTLE GAME I WAS ABOUT TO PLAY WITH YOU.
AND WHAT GAME IS THAT?
THE ONE IN WHICH I PRETEND TO LET YOU SEDUCE ME AND TAKE ME BACK TO YOUR HOTEL ROOM, WHERE WE EMBRACE PASSIONATELY FOR A MOMENT...
...BUT THEN JUST AS I'M ABOUT TO UNDRESS--
I INSTEAD PULL MY GUN ON YOU.
WE SHOULD ALL BE PAST SUCH BORING CLICHÉS NOW, YES?
NO-- PLEASE--
YOU'VE BEEN AN INDEPENDENT CONTRACTOR FOR A.I.M. FOR THE LAST FIFTEEN YEARS. THERE IS A MAN WORKING IN YOUR DEPARTMENT.
I NEED TO KNOW HIS WHEREABOUTS, YOU NEED TO KEEP THE FRONT OF YOUR SKULL INTACT. THERE IS ROOM FOR AGREEMENT HERE.
YOU WOULDN'T--THE BARTENDERS-- THERE ARE WITNESSES!
NOT A CONCERN, MY DIRECT FRIEND--
THE UNITED STATES GOVERNMENT TIPS *VERY* WELL.

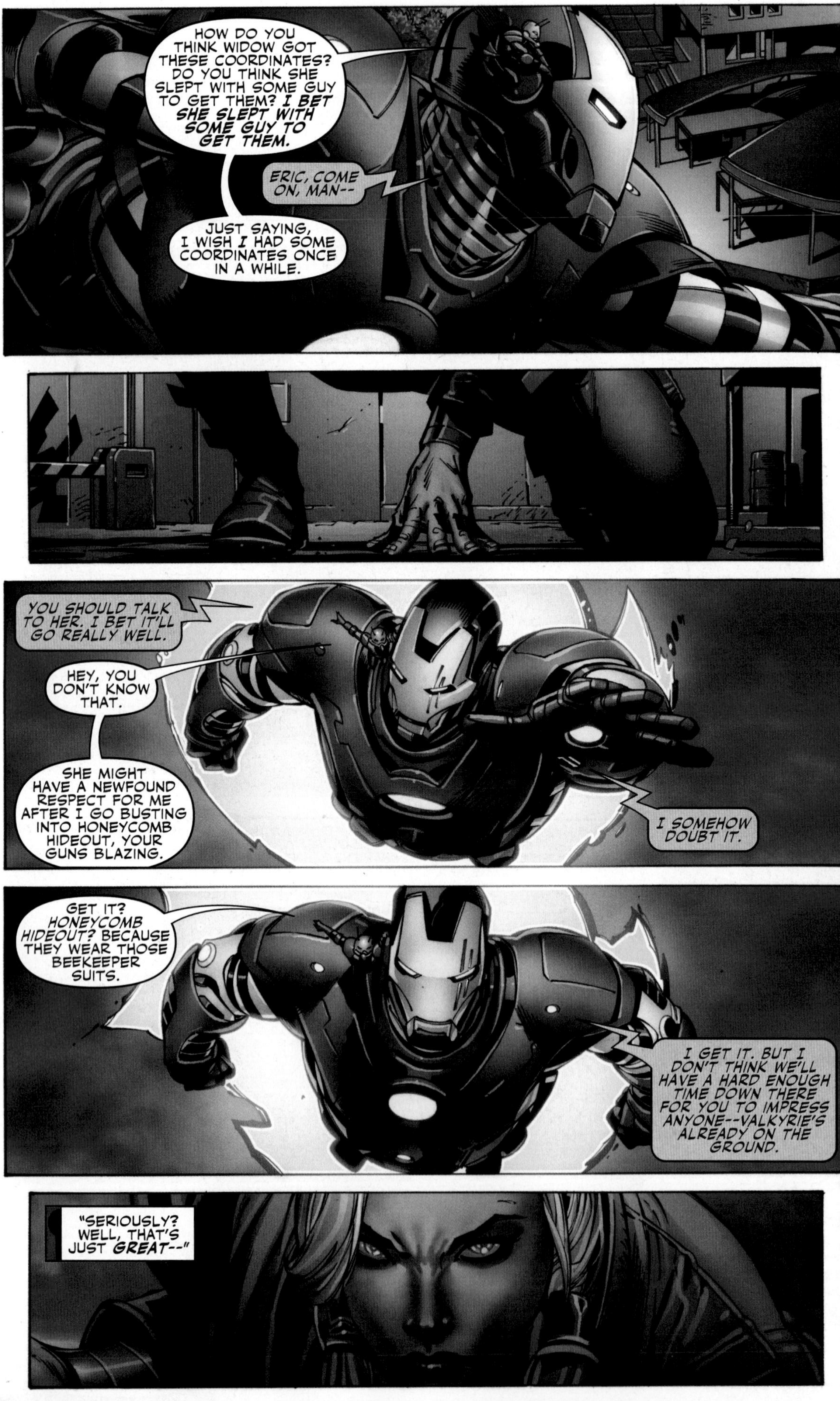
HOW DO YOU THINK WIDOW GOT THESE COORDINATES? DO YOU THINK SHE SLEPT WITH SOME GUY TO GET THEM? ***I BET SHE SLEPT WITH SOME GUY TO GET THEM.***
ERIC, COME ON, MAN--
JUST SAYING, I WISH ***I*** HAD SOME COORDINATES ONCE IN A WHILE.
YOU SHOULD TALK TO HER. I BET IT'LL GO REALLY WELL.
HEY, YOU DON'T KNOW THAT.
SHE MIGHT HAVE A NEWFOUND RESPECT FOR ME AFTER I GO BUSTING INTO HONEYCOMB HIDEOUT, YOUR GUNS BLAZING.
I SOMEHOW DOUBT IT.
GET IT? ***HONEYCOMB HIDEOUT?*** BECAUSE THEY WEAR THOSE BEEKEEPER SUITS.
I GET IT. BUT I DON'T THINK WE'LL HAVE A HARD ENOUGH TIME DOWN THERE FOR YOU TO IMPRESS ANYONE--VALKYRIE'S ALREADY ON THE GROUND.
"SERIOUSLY? WELL, THAT'S JUST ***GREAT***--"

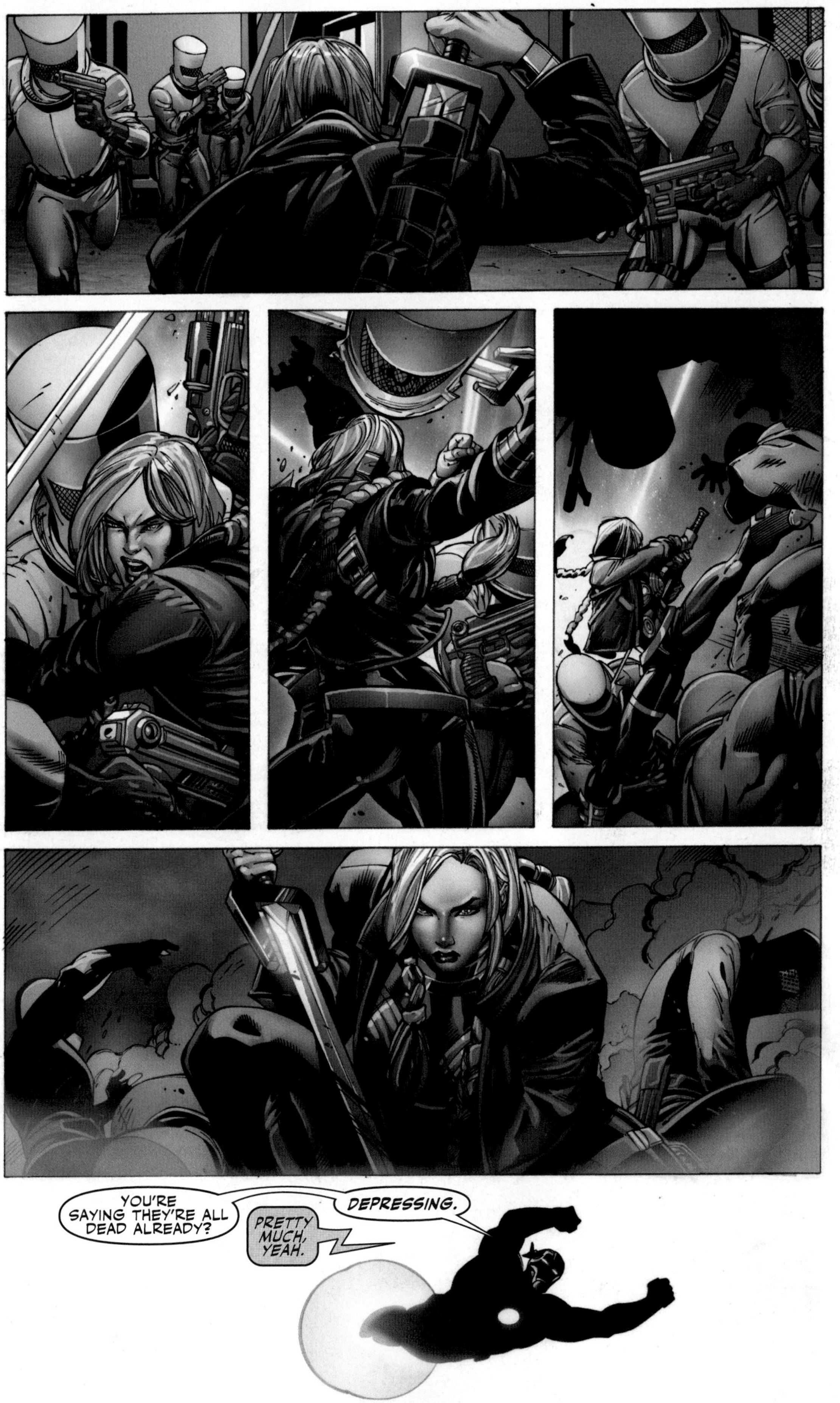

YOU'RE SAYING THEY'RE ALL DEAD ALREADY?
DEPRESSING.
PRETTY MUCH, YEAH.

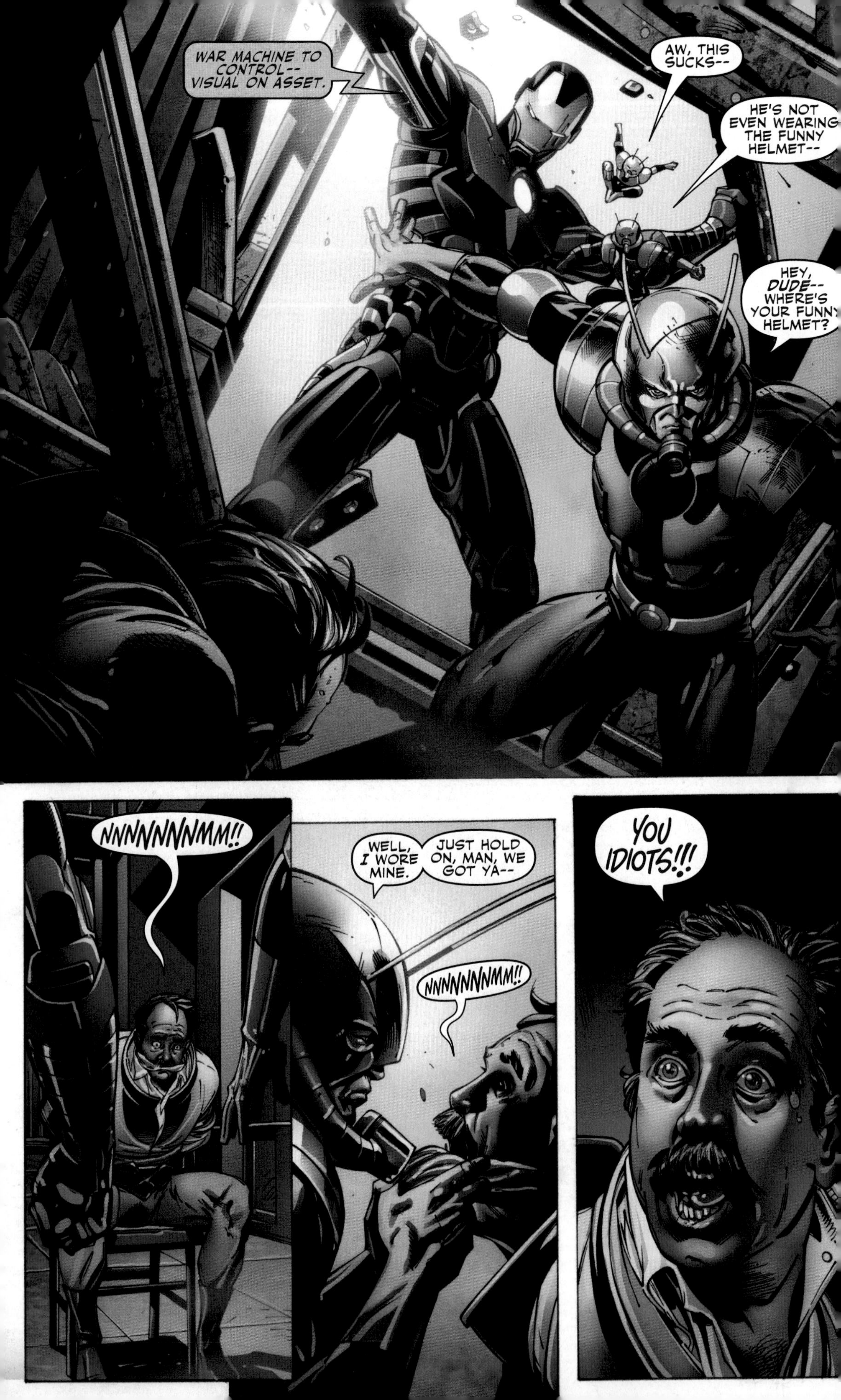

WAR MACHINE TO CONTROL-- VISUAL ON ASSET.
AW, THIS SUCKS--
HE'S NOT EVEN WEARING THE FUNNY HELMET--
HEY, DUDE-- WHERE'S YOUR FUNNY HELMET?
NNNNNNNMM!!
WELL, I WORE MINE.
JUST HOLD ON, MAN, WE GOT YA--
NNNNNNNMM!!
YOU IDIOTS!!!

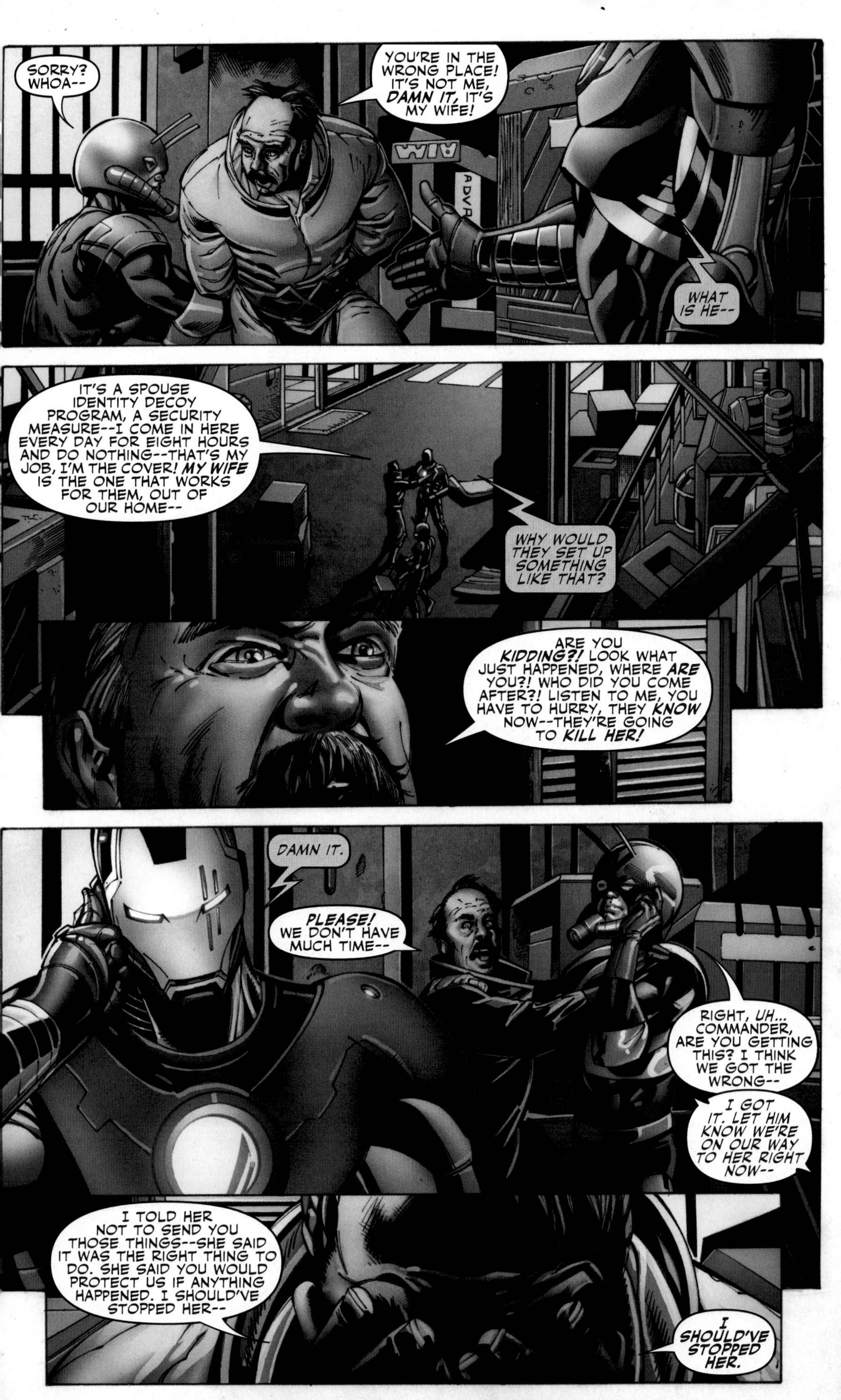
SORRY? WHOA--
YOU'RE IN THE WRONG PLACE! IT'S NOT ME, DAMN IT, IT'S MY WIFE!
WHAT IS HE--
IT'S A SPOUSE IDENTITY DECOY PROGRAM, A SECURITY MEASURE--I COME IN HERE EVERY DAY FOR EIGHT HOURS AND DO NOTHING--THAT'S MY JOB, I'M THE COVER! MY WIFE IS THE ONE THAT WORKS FOR THEM, OUT OF OUR HOME--
WHY WOULD THEY SET UP SOMETHING LIKE THAT?
ARE YOU KIDDING?! LOOK WHAT JUST HAPPENED, WHERE ARE YOU?! WHO DID YOU COME AFTER?! LISTEN TO ME, YOU HAVE TO HURRY, THEY KNOW NOW--THEY'RE GOING TO KILL HER!
DAMN IT.
PLEASE! WE DON'T HAVE MUCH TIME--
RIGHT, UH... COMMANDER, ARE YOU GETTING THIS? I THINK WE GOT THE WRONG--
I GOT IT. LET HIM KNOW WE'RE ON OUR WAY TO HER RIGHT NOW--
I TOLD HER NOT TO SEND YOU THOSE THINGS--SHE SAID IT WAS THE RIGHT THING TO DO. SHE SAID YOU WOULD PROTECT US IF ANYTHING HAPPENED. I SHOULD'VE STOPPED HER--
I SHOULD'VE STOPPED HER.

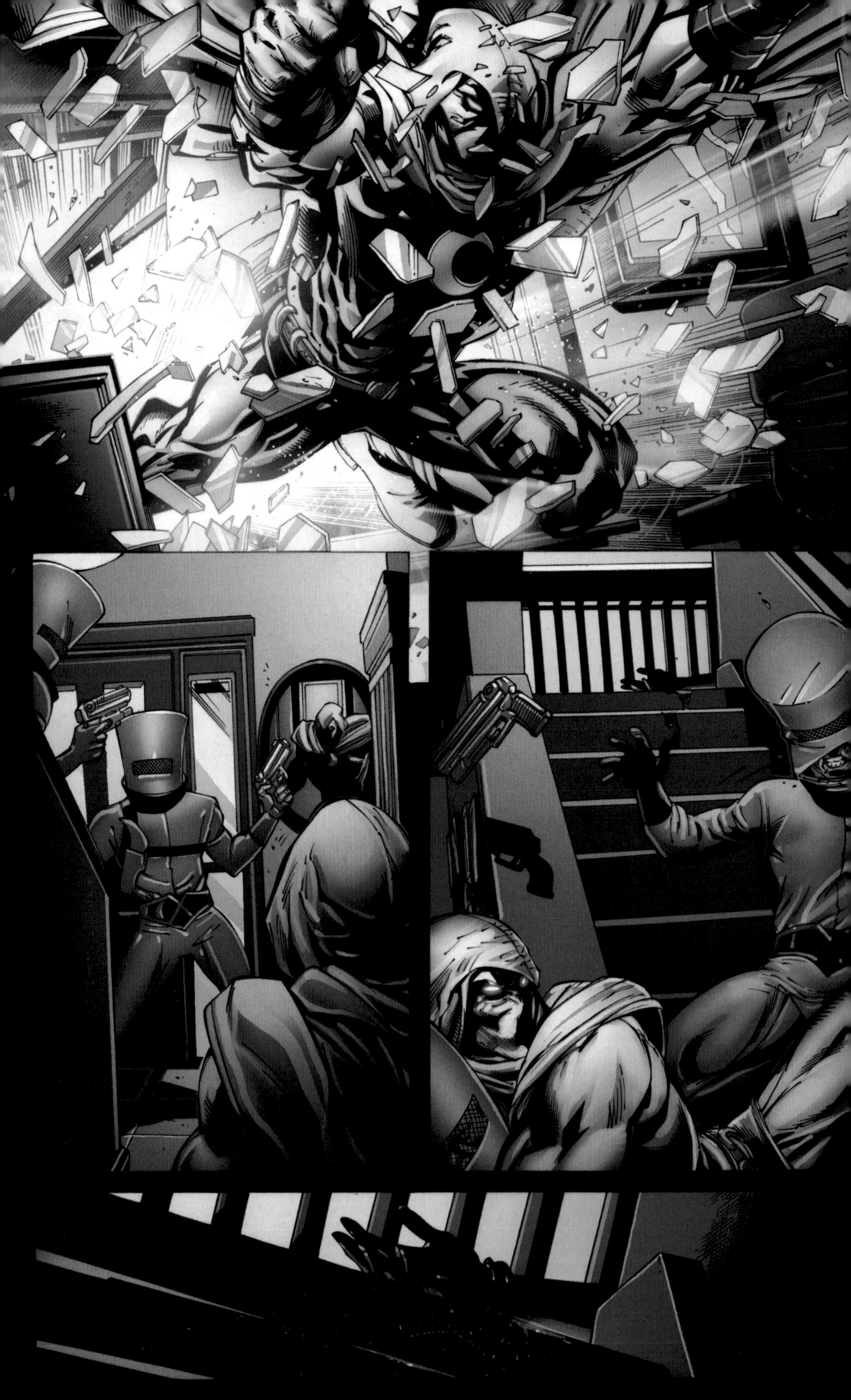

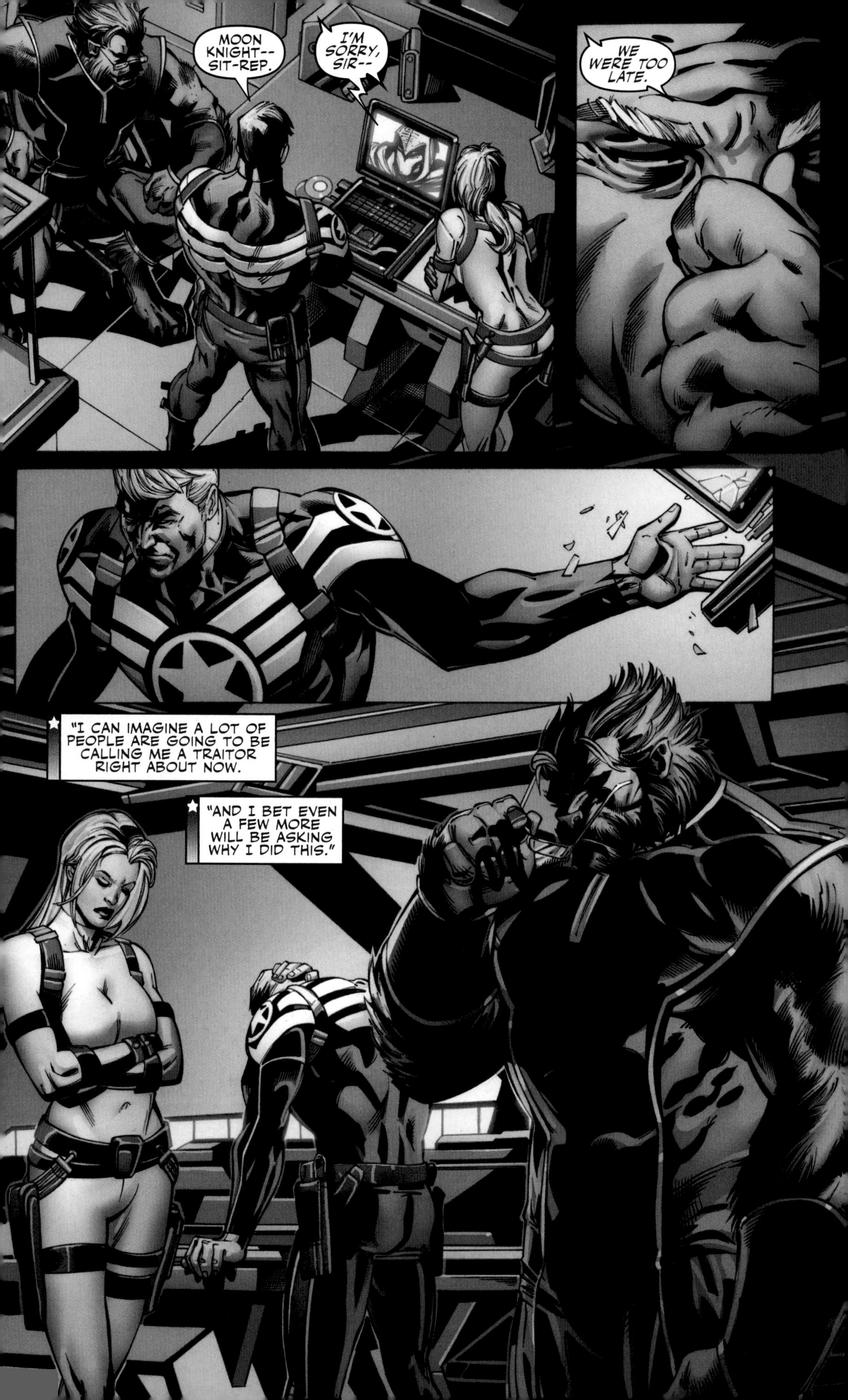

MOON KNIGHT-- SIT-REP.
I'M SORRY, SIR--
WE WERE TOO LATE.
"I CAN IMAGINE A LOT OF PEOPLE ARE GOING TO BE CALLING ME A TRAITOR RIGHT ABOUT NOW.
"AND I BET EVEN A FEW MORE WILL BE ASKING WHY I DID THIS."

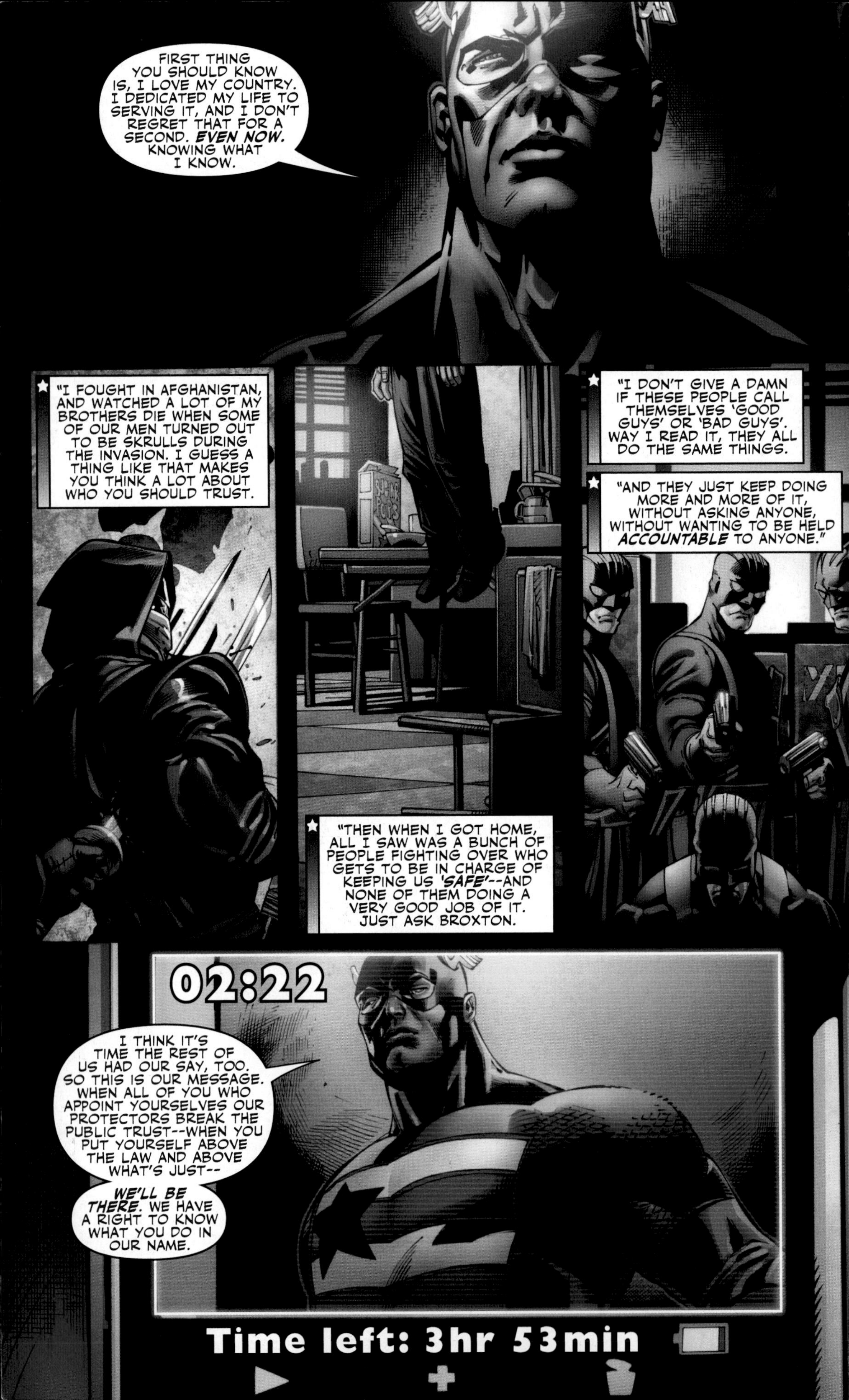
FIRST THING YOU SHOULD KNOW IS, I LOVE MY COUNTRY. I DEDICATED MY LIFE TO SERVING IT, AND I DON'T REGRET THAT FOR A SECOND. EVEN NOW. KNOWING WHAT I KNOW.
"I FOUGHT IN AFGHANISTAN, AND WATCHED A LOT OF MY BROTHERS DIE WHEN SOME OF OUR MEN TURNED OUT TO BE SKRULLS DURING THE INVASION. I GUESS A THING LIKE THAT MAKES YOU THINK A LOT ABOUT WHO YOU SHOULD TRUST.
"THEN WHEN I GOT HOME, ALL I SAW WAS A BUNCH OF PEOPLE FIGHTING OVER WHO GETS TO BE IN CHARGE OF KEEPING US 'SAFE'--AND NONE OF THEM DOING A VERY GOOD JOB OF IT. JUST ASK BROXTON.
"I DON'T GIVE A DAMN IF THESE PEOPLE CALL THEMSELVES 'GOOD GUYS' OR 'BAD GUYS'. WAY I READ IT, THEY ALL DO THE SAME THINGS.
"AND THEY JUST KEEP DOING MORE AND MORE OF IT, WITHOUT ASKING ANYONE, WITHOUT WANTING TO BE HELD ACCOUNTABLE TO ANYONE."
02:22
I THINK IT'S TIME THE REST OF US HAD OUR SAY, TOO. SO THIS IS OUR MESSAGE. WHEN ALL OF YOU WHO APPOINT YOURSELVES OUR PROTECTORS BREAK THE PUBLIC TRUST--WHEN YOU PUT YOURSELF ABOVE THE LAW AND ABOVE WHAT'S JUST--
WE'LL BE THERE. WE HAVE A RIGHT TO KNOW WHAT YOU DO IN OUR NAME.
Time left: 3hr 53min

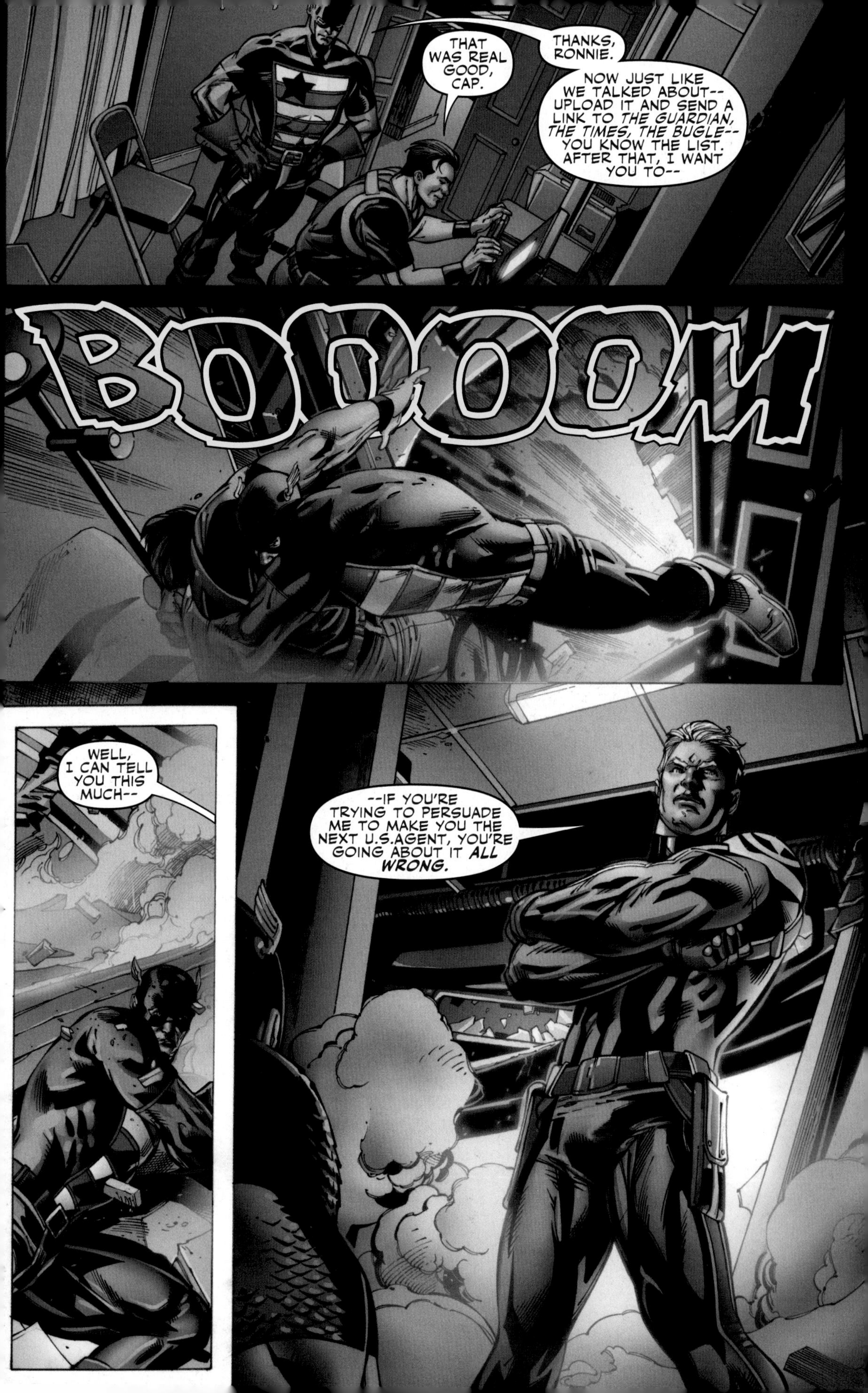
THAT WAS REAL GOOD, CAP.
THANKS, RONNIE.
NOW JUST LIKE WE TALKED ABOUT-- UPLOAD IT AND SEND A LINK TO *THE GUARDIAN, THE TIMES, THE BUGLE*-- YOU KNOW THE LIST. AFTER THAT, I WANT YOU TO--
BOOOOM
WELL, I CAN TELL YOU THIS MUCH--
--IF YOU'RE TRYING TO PERSUADE ME TO MAKE YOU THE NEXT U.S.AGENT, YOU'RE GOING ABOUT IT ***ALL WRONG.***

FUNNY, BUT NOT QUITE. MY MEMORY'S A BIT LONGER THAN THAT. YOU REMEMBER WHEN *YOU* WORE THIS UNIFORM, DON'T YOU?

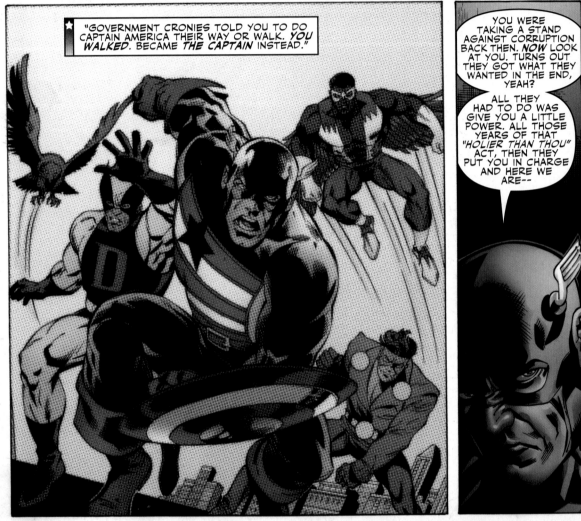

"GOVERNMENT CRONIES TOLD YOU TO DO CAPTAIN AMERICA THEIR WAY OR WALK. *YOU WALKED*. BECAME *THE CAPTAIN* INSTEAD."

YOU WERE TAKING A STAND AGAINST CORRUPTION BACK THEN. *NOW* LOOK AT YOU. TURNS OUT THEY GOT WHAT THEY WANTED IN THE END, YEAH?

ALL THEY HAD TO DO WAS GIVE YOU A LITTLE POWER. ALL THOSE YEARS OF THAT *"HOLIER THAN THOU"* ACT, THEN THEY PUT YOU IN CHARGE AND HERE WE ARE--

OUR GOVERNMENT IN BED WITH A BUNCH OF TERRORISTS, MURDERERS, AND DESPOTS, MOST OF 'EM SELLING EACH OTHER OUT TO GET AHEAD. SECRET AVENGERS TEAMS THAT DON'T ANSWER TO ANYONE BUT YOU--

YOU SOLD US OUT! WE DESERVE TO KNOW WHAT'S GOING ON--THE PEOPLE HAVE A RIGHT TO--

CRACK

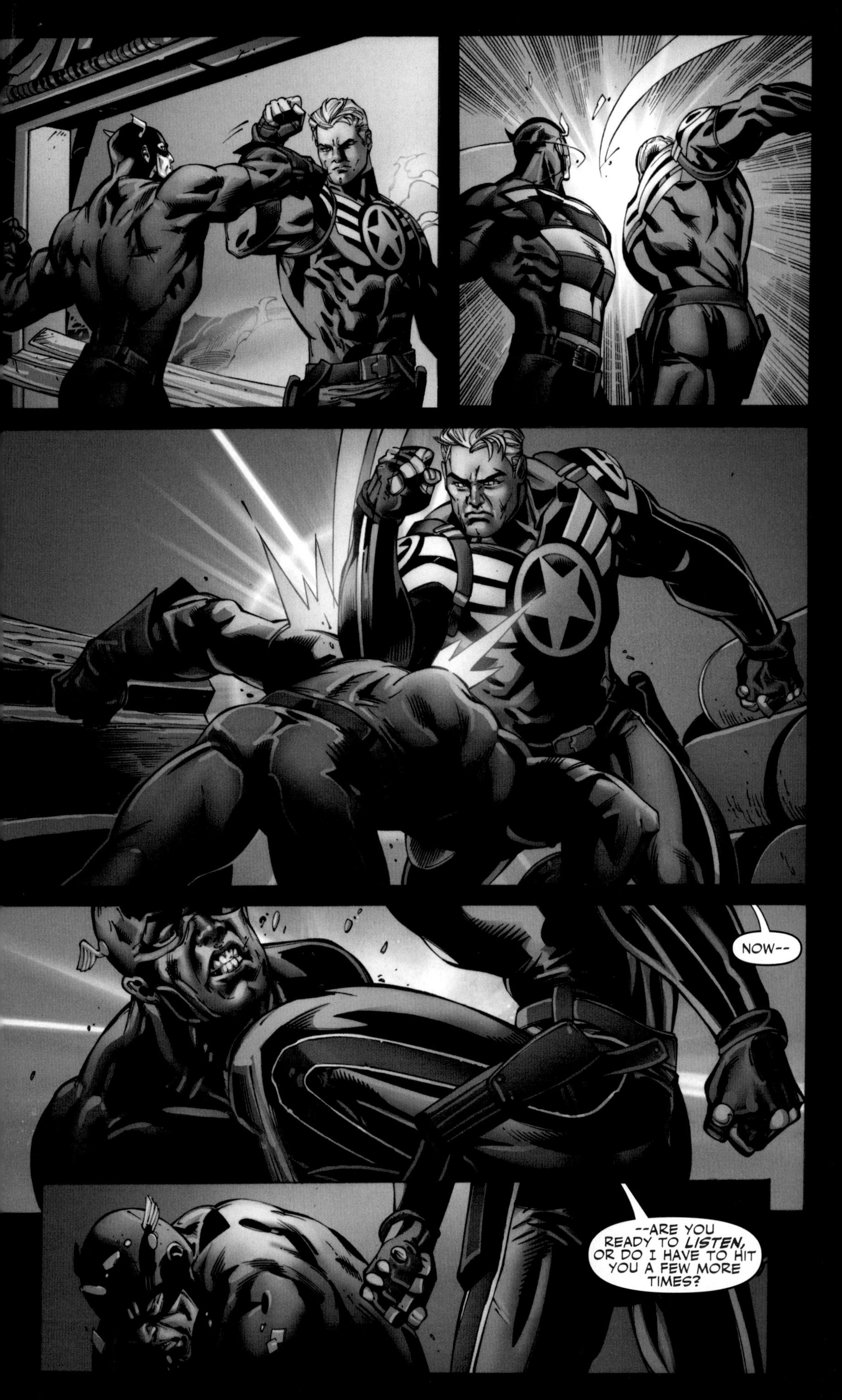
NOW--
--ARE YOU READY TO LISTEN, OR DO I HAVE TO HIT YOU A FEW MORE TIMES?

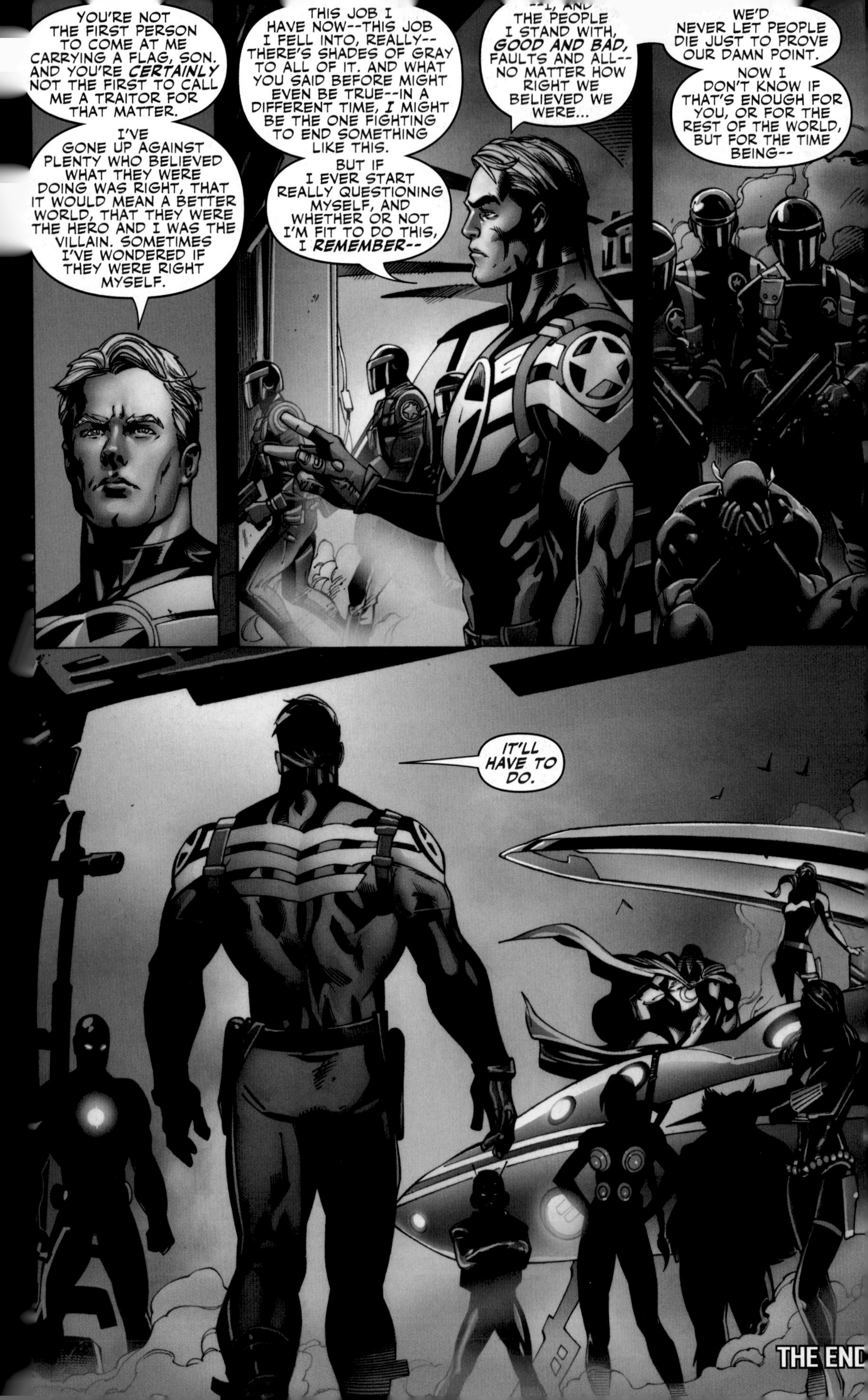
YOU'RE NOT THE FIRST PERSON TO COME AT ME CARRYING A FLAG, SON. AND YOU'RE *CERTAINLY* NOT THE FIRST TO CALL ME A TRAITOR FOR THAT MATTER.
I'VE GONE UP AGAINST PLENTY WHO BELIEVED WHAT THEY WERE DOING WAS RIGHT, THAT IT WOULD MEAN A BETTER WORLD, THAT THEY WERE THE HERO AND I WAS THE VILLAIN. SOMETIMES I'VE WONDERED IF THEY WERE RIGHT MYSELF.
THIS JOB I HAVE NOW--THIS JOB I FELL INTO, REALLY--THERE'S SHADES OF GRAY TO ALL OF IT. AND WHAT YOU SAID BEFORE MIGHT EVEN BE TRUE--IN A DIFFERENT TIME, *I* MIGHT BE THE ONE FIGHTING TO END SOMETHING LIKE THIS.
BUT IF I EVER START REALLY QUESTIONING MYSELF, AND WHETHER OR NOT I'M FIT TO DO THIS, I *REMEMBER*--
THE PEOPLE I STAND WITH, *GOOD AND BAD,* FAULTS AND ALL--NO MATTER HOW RIGHT WE BELIEVED WE WERE...
WE'D NEVER LET PEOPLE DIE JUST TO PROVE OUR DAMN POINT.
NOW I DON'T KNOW IF THAT'S ENOUGH FOR YOU, OR FOR THE REST OF THE WORLD, BUT FOR THE TIME BEING--
IT'LL HAVE TO DO.
THE END